Statistics for the Behavioral Sciences

A First Course for Students of
Psychology and Education

Statistics for the Behavioral Sciences

A First Course for Students of Psychology and Education

Frederick J. Gravetter
State University of New York, College at Brockport

Larry B. Wallnau
State University of New York, College at Brockport

West Publishing Company
St. Paul   New York   Los Angeles   San Francisco

Cover and interior design   Design Office/Peter E. Martin
Copyediting   James Hartman
Composition and artwork   Graphic Typesetting Service
Art editing   Hal Lockwood/Bookman Productions
Indexing   Janet Greenblat
Cover art   "Men working" by Leonardo da Vinci.
                Copyright reserved. Reproduced by gracious permission of
                Her Majesty Queen Elizabeth II.

Library of Congress Cataloging in Publication Data

Gravetter, Frederick J.
   Statistics for the behavioral sciences.

   Includes index.
   1. Psychometrics.   2. Educational statistics.
I. Wallnau, Larry B.   II. Title.
BF39.G72   1985   519.5   84–17210
IBSN 0–314–85241–7
2nd Reprint—1987

In loving memory of Ida Levine Brownstein.
"Next year in Jerusalem, Bubbie."

Contents

CHAPTER 7

Probability and Samples: The Distribution of Sample Means

CHAPTER 8

Introduction to Hypothesis Testing

CHAPTER 9

Estimation, Directional Tests, and Power

CHAPTER 20

Nonparametric Tests for Ordinal Data: Mann-Whitney and Wilcoxon Tests

Preface

Statistics often are described as "tools" for science. Like most tools, statistical techniques, both individually and collectively, have been developed to serve a purpose. Our goal in this book is to introduce these valuable tools and, more importantly, to help students gain an understanding of their general use and purpose. Throughout the book we have taken time to explain and discuss each statistical technique. If you are familiar with other statistics textbooks, you probably will notice immediately that this book has a lot of text relative to the number of formulas. We haven't skimped on the formulas; we simply have expanded the discussion.

For many students this book will be the first hands-on experience with the scientific approach to problem solving. With statistics, students will quickly learn the value of organization, precision, and goal-directed thinking. Statistics are used to find answers to questions and to demonstrate that the answers are correct. You cannot get by with creative speculation, personal values, or persuasive argument. In statistics a mistake is a mistake; an answer can be checked and proved right or wrong. In this sense, statistics introduce a general problem-solving skill that is invaluable in any job or profession.

This textbook has developed from years of teaching introductory statistics. Initially we were content to discuss small details of lecture material and student response to that material. However, these discussions eventually became more global, dealing with our approach in the statistics course as a whole and with the idea of writing a text. Our students have been most helpful in this regard. Their feedback assisted in both the evolution of the course and the development of the book. We have kept them in mind in every phase of writing this book. In many respects they have been our teachers.

We thank the people at West Publishing. Their enthusiasm for this project was rivaled only by that of our parents. We are especially grateful to Pam Rost for her outstanding work on the production of the book and to our editor Pat Fitzgerald for direction and encouragement throughout this project. Many of our colleagues reviewed all or portions of the manuscript. Their comments and advice were invaluable in preparing the final manuscript. We thank the following people for their diligent and helpful reviews:

> Nancy S. Anderson, University of Maryland
>
> Mark Bearse, Northeastern University
>
> Robert Grissom, San Francisco State University
>
> Frederick L. Kitterle, University of Toledo
>
> Willard Larkin, University of Maryland
>
> Scott E. Maxwell, University of Notre Dame
>
> Lawrence Melamed, Kent State University
>
> Jill Wallace, University of Northern Iowa

The authors are also grateful to the literary executor of the late Sir Ronald A. Fisher, F.R.S., to Dr. Frank Yates, F.R.S., and to Longman Group Ltd. (London) for permission to adapt Table III from their book *Statistical Tables for Biological, Agricultural and Medical Research* (6th edition, 1974).

Finally, we are indebted to the following friends and family for their assistance, encouragement, and patience: Carol and Justin Gravetter, Sandy Rose, Naomi Wallnau, and Henry Williams.

A Note to the Instructor: The Organization of this Book and the Organization of Your Course

We have arranged the chapters in this book in a sequence that we find logical and that has proved to be effective through years of teaching. However, we recognize that there is no absolute order for presenting the various topics that comprise an introductory statistics course. Therefore, we have tried to structure the book so that individual instructors have some flexibility in reordering topics without compromising the integrity of the material. Some specific examples follow.

Correlation and Regression. Many instructors prefer to introduce correlation as a descriptive statistic immediately following central tendency, variability, and z-scores. To accommodate this preference, we have separated the topics of correlation and regression into two chapters (Chapters 16 and 17). The correlation chapter focuses on the descriptive aspects of correlation and could be covered much earlier in the course without any confusion to students. The first four sections of the regression chapter also could be presented with correlation as a descriptive topic. However, analysis of regression (Section 17.5) should follow the introduction to inferential techniques in Chapter 8 and, ideally, should follow the introduction to analysis of variance in Chapter 13. Analysis of regression is presented as a separate section at the end of the regression chapter so that it could be omitted entirely.

We have placed correlation and regression very late in the book because our experience indicates that inserting these topics earlier tends to interrupt a very natural flow. Beginning with means and variances, we move directly to z-scores and then to probability using z-scores; then we introduce hypothesis testing using z-scores to test hypotheses about means. The result is an integrated and coherent series in which each new topic builds directly on the preceding material.

Binomial Distribution. The binomial distribution often is used to introduce the logic of hypothesis testing. In this book we have elected to place this topic much later in the sequence (Chapter 18) along with other nonparametric techniques. However, this chapter could be presented immediately after Chapter 6 (on probability) provided the instructor prepares students by discussing some of the basic terminology of hypothesis testing.

Analysis of Variance. We have used three separate chapters to cover ANOVA: Chapter 13 introduces the topic, Chapter 14 presents the single-factor repeated measures analysis, and Chapter 15 introduces two-factor designs. Chapter 13 is a prerequisite for either of the other two chapters in this series. However, Chapters 14 and 15 are structured so that either one or both could be omitted, or they could be presented in reverse order.

CHAPTER 1

Introduction to Statistics

1.1
Statistics, Science, and Observations

Definitions of Statistics

"Why study statistics?" is a question countless students ask. One simple answer is that statistics have become a common part of everyday life and therefore deserve some attention. A quick glance at the newspaper yields statistics that deal with crime rates, birth rates, average income, average snowfall, and so on. By a common definition, therefore, statistics consist of facts and figures.

DEFINITION

Statistics are facts and figures.

These statistics generally are informative and time saving because they condense large quantities of information into a few simple figures or statements. For example, the average snowfall in Chicago during the month of January is based on many observations made over many years. Few people would be interested in seeing a complete list of day-by-day snowfall amounts for the past 50 years. Even fewer people would be able to make much sense of all those numbers at a quick glance. But nearly everyone can understand and appreciate the meaning of an average. You should note that although statistics can be informative, they also can be a source of misinformation and misinterpretation if used improperly (see Box 1.1).

There is another definition of statistics which applies to many of the topics in this book. When statisticians use the word statistics, they are referring to a set of methods and procedures that help present, characterize, analyze, and interpret observations.

Statistics consist of a set of methods and rules for organizing and interpreting observations.

These statistical procedures help ensure that the data (or observations) are presented and interpreted in an accurate and informative way. Although facts and figures can be interesting and important, this book will focus on methods and procedures of statistics.

BOX 1.1 | **Misuse of Statistical Information**

Sometimes statistical information can be a source of misinformation, rather than being helpful in understanding the observations that we make. Hooke (1983) provides an example of misinterpretation based on a commonly quoted statistic:

"More accidents happen around the home than anywhere else." This is a statistic. It doesn't quote any numbers, but numbers can probably be unearthed to support it. With or without numbers, it is not a very informative statistic. The only conclusion it can possibly lead to is that home is the most dangerous place to be, which is obviously false. "Most car accidents happen within x miles of home," we're often told, x being some small number. Does that mean that we would be wiser to garage the car x miles from home and walk back and forth to it? Undoubtedly not, except for the possible benefits of the exercise and saving of gasoline.

A little-known fact about the subject of statistics is that it has mostly to do with probability, or chances. The accident statistics just quoted are not useful because they don't tell us anything about our chances. People have more accidents at home than anywhere else because home is where many of them are. More car accidents occur within x miles of home because most of the driving occurs there. If you really care about your chances of having an accident within x miles of home, you have to find statistics that take into account the amount of time spent or the number of miles driven within x miles of home. Such refinements may be very hard to obtain, but don't give anyone part credit for quoting useless, unrefined statistics just because meaningful statistics are hard to obtain. If a space program fails to put a man on the

Statistics and Science

It is frequently said that science is *empirical*. That is, scientific investigation is based on making observations. Statistical methods enable researchers to describe and analyze the observations they have made. Thus, statistical methods are tools for science. We might think of science as consisting of methods for making observations and of statistics as consisting of methods for analyzing them.

These observations should be public, in the sense that others are able to repeat the observations using the same methods to see if the same findings will be obtained.

On a recent mission by the space shuttle Columbia, so much scientific data were relayed to computers on earth that scientists were hard pressed to convey, in terms the public could grasp, how much information had been gathered. One individual made a few quick computations on a pocket calculator and determined that if all the data from the mission were printed on pages, they would pile up as high as the Washington Monument. Such an enormous amount of scientific observation is unmanageable in this crude form. To interpret the data, many months of work will have to be done by many people to statistically analyze them. Statistical methods serve scientific investigation by organizing and interpreting data.

1.2
Populations and Samples

What Are They?

A *population* is the entire group of individuals that a researcher wishes to study. By entire group, we literally mean every single individual.

DEFINITION

A *population* consists of every member of a group that a researcher would like to study.

As you can well imagine, a population can be quite large—for example, the number of women on the planet earth. A researcher might be more specific, limiting the population for study to women who are registered voters in the United States. Perhaps the investigator would like to study the population consisting of women who are heads of state. Populations can obviously vary in size from extremely large to very small, depending on how the investigator defines the population. The population being studied should always be identified by the researcher. In addition, the population need not consist of people—it could be a population of rats, corporations, parts produced in a factory, or anything else an investigator wants to study. In practice, populations are typically very large, such as the population of fourth-grade children in the United States or the population of small businesses.

A *sample* is a subset of a population. It is a part of the population that is selected for study. A sample should always be identified in terms of the population from which it was selected.

DEFINITION

A *sample* is a portion of the population that is selected for observation.

Also, just as we saw with populations, samples can vary greatly in size. Imagine that you are about to conduct an opinion poll in a large city. You are going to ask people if they believe the mayor is doing a good job. Since the poll will be conducted by telephone, you define your population as people who live in the city and are listed in the telephone directory. Realizing that it would take more time than you can spend to call everyone in the phone book (the entire population), you call 100 people. Notice that it is often necessary to study a sample because the population is so large that it would be impractical to study every member of the population. If you are more ambitious, you could use a larger sample—for example, 1000 people. Later in this book we will examine the benefits of using large samples.

Parameters and Statistics

When describing data, it is necessary to distinguish whether the data come from a population or a sample. Any characteristic of a population, for example, its average, is called a population *parameter*. On the other hand, a characteristic of a sample is called a *statistic*. The average of the scores for a sample is a statistic. The range of scores for a sample is another type of statistic. As we shall see later, statisticians frequently use different symbols for a parameter and a statistic. By using different symbols, we can readily tell if a characteristic, such as an average, is describing a population or a sample.

A *parameter* is a measurement that describes a characteristic of a population, such as a population average.

A *statistic* describes a characteristic of a sample.

Descriptive and Inferential Statistical Methods

There are two major types of statistical methods. The first type, *descriptive statistics*, is used to simplify and summarize data. Data typically consist of a set of scores called a *distribution*. These scores result from measurements taken during the course of making observations. For example, they may be IQ scores, ages, blood-alcohol levels, or number of correct responses. The original measurements or values in a distribution are called *raw scores*.

Descriptive statistical methods summarize, organize and simplify data.

A *distribution* is a set of scores.

A *raw score* is an original measurement or value in a distribution.

It should be noted that when we have a distribution of scores, it is necessary to identify whether it is a population or a sample. Descriptive statistics are techniques that take the raw scores from a distribution and summarize them in a form that is more manageable. There are many descriptive procedures, but a common technique is to compute an average. Note that even if the distribution has hundreds of scores, the average of those scores provides a single descriptive value for the entire distribution. Other descriptive techniques, including tables and graphs, will be covered in the next several chapters.

Inferential statistics are techniques that use sample data to make general statements about a population.

Inferential statistics consist of techniques that allow us to study samples and then make generalizations about the population from which they were selected.

As we saw with the telephone survey, it is usually not practical to make observations of every member of the population of interest. Suppose we wish to study the prevalence of drug use on American college campuses. Students are asked to fill out a questionnaire which asks about the type and frequency of drug use. We define the population as students enrolled on a full time basis in American colleges and universities. The population is much too large to have every individual fill out a questionnaire. Therefore, a sample of students is selected, and they respond to the questionnaire. By analyzing the results for the sample, we hope to make general statements about the population. Sample data are being used to *infer* something about the population; in this case it is drug use patterns.

Inferential statistics are a very crucial part of conducting experiments in that these techniques are used to assess whether or not a treatment effect has occurred. Suppose a researcher would like to test the effectiveness of a new therapy program for depression. It would be too costly and time-consuming to test the program on all depressed individuals. Therefore, the treatment is tested on a sample of depressed patients. Of course, the researcher would like to see these people overcome their misery, but keep in mind that one is not just interested in this sample of individuals. The investigator would like to generalize the findings to the entire population. If the treatment program is effective for the sample of depressed people, it would be great to be able to state with confidence that it will also work for others. It is important to note that inferential statistical methods will allow meaningful generalizations only if the individuals in the sample are representative of the population. One way to ensure that the sample is representative is to use *random selection*. In random sampling, every individual in the population has the same chance of being selected. There will be much more to say about this topic in later chapters.

DEFINITION

In *random selection*, every person has the same chance of being selected for the sample.

LEARNING CHECK

1. Science is empirical. This means that science is based on

_____ .

2. Science consists of methods for making observations, and statistics are methods for _____ them.
3. A descriptive characteristic of a population is a _____ . A characteristic of a sample is called a _____ .
4. What is the purpose of descriptive statistics?
5. Inferential statistics attempt to use _____ to make general statements about _____ .
6. One way to ensure that a sample is representative of a population is to use _____ selection of the sample.

ANSWERS

1. observation
2. analyzing
3. parameter, statistic
4. to simplify and summarize data
5. sample data, a population
6. random

1.3

The Scientific Method and the Design of Experiments

Objectivity

As noted earlier, science is empirical in that knowledge is acquired by observation. Another important aspect of scientific inquiry is that it should be *objective*. That is, theoretical biases of the researcher should not be allowed to influence the findings. Usually when a study is conducted, the investigator has a hunch about how it will turn out. This hunch, actually a prediction about the outcome of the study, is typically based on a theory that the researcher has. It is important that scientists conduct their studies in a way that will prevent these hunches or biases from influencing the outcome of the research. Experimenter bias can operate very subtly. Rosenthal and Fode (1963) had student volunteers act as experimenters in a learning study. The students were given rats to train in a maze. Half of the students were led to believe that their rats were "maze-bright," while the remainder were told their rats were "maze-dull." In reality they all received the same kind of rat. Nevertheless, the data showed real differences in the rats' performance for the two groups of experimenters. Somehow the students' expectations influenced the outcome of the experiment. Apparently there were differences between the groups in how the students handled the rats, and these differences accounted for the effect. For a detailed look at experimenter bias, you might read the review by Rosenthal (1964).

Relationships Between Variables

Science attempts to discover orderly relationships. Even people of ancient civilizations noted regularity in the world around them—the change of seasons, changes in the moon's phases, changes in the tides—and they were able to make many observations to document these orderly changes. A relationship exists when changes occur interdependently: Whenever X changes, Y also changes in a predictable way. Something that can change or have different values is called a *variable*.

DEFINITION

A *variable* is something that can change and have different values.

Science involves a search for relationships between variables. For example, there is a relationship between the amount of rainfall and crop growth. Rainfall is one of the variables. It varies from year to year and season to season. Crop growth is the other variable. Some years the corn stalks seem short and stunted; other years they are tall and full. When there is very little rainfall, the crops are short and shriveled. When rain is ample, the crops show vigorous growth. Note that in order to document the relationship, one must make observations—that is, measurements of the amount of rainfall and size of the crops.

The simplest way to look for relationships between variables is to make observations of changes in two variables. This is frequently called an *observational* or *correlational method*.

DEFINITION

In a *correlational method*, changes are observed in two variables to see if there is a relationship.

Suppose a researcher wants to examine whether or not a relationship exists between length of time in an executive position and assertiveness. A large sample of executives takes a personality test designed to measure assertiveness. Also, the investigator determines how long each person has served in an executive-level job. Suppose the investigator found that there is a relationship between the two variables—that the longer a person had an executive position, the more assertive that person tended to be. Naturally, one might jump to the conclusion that being an executive for a long time makes a person more assertive. The problem with the correlational method is that it provides no information about cause-and-effect relationships. An equally plausible explanation for the relationship is that assertive people choose to stay or survive longer in executive positions than less assertive individuals. To determine the cause and the effect in a relationship, it is necessary to manipulate and control one of the variables being studied. This is accomplished by the experimental method.

The Experimental Method

A distinguishing characteristic of the *experimental method* is that the researcher manipulates and controls one of the variables under study. One then looks for the effect of this manipulation on the other variable.

DEFINITION

In the *experimental method*, one variable is controlled and manipulated while changes are observed in another variable.

By intentionally altering one variable while at the same time monitoring the other, a cause-and-effect relationship can be established. For example, suppose a psychologist would like to examine the effect of different methods of practice on learning performance. He solicits volunteers (often called *subjects*) to participate. One group of subjects memorizes a list of words by practicing for 30 minutes. This group is called the massed-practice condition. A second group of people practice for the same total amount of time but in three 10-minute sessions, with a 15-minute rest period between the practice sessions. This group is the distributed-practice condition. Shortly after practice is completed, both groups are tested for how many words were learned. The experiment is diagrammed in Figure 1.1. The experimenter is manipulating the type of practice the people have to use. The amount of learning is measured by the number of words they can jot down after practicing. If method of practice has an effect, these two groups should perform differently on the test. To determine if an effect did occur, the data from the experiment would have to be statistically analyzed.

The Independent and Dependent Variables

Specific names are used for the two variables that are studied by the experimental method. The variable that is manipulated by the experimenter is called the *independent variable*. It can be identified as the treatment conditions to which subjects are assigned. For the example in Figure 1.1, the method of practice (massed or distributed) is the independent variable. The variable that is observed to assess a possible effect of the manipulation is the *dependent variable*.

Figure 1.1

Volunteers are randomly assigned to one of two treatment groups: massed practice or distributed practice. After memorizing a list of words using one of these methods, subjects are tested by having them write down as many words as possible from the list. A difference between the groups in performance is attributed to the treatment—the type of practice.

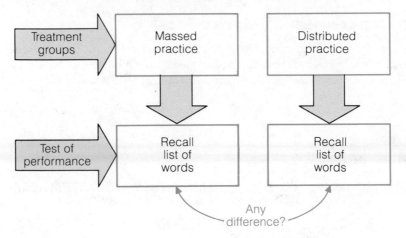

DEFINITIONS

The *independent variable* consists of the treatment conditions to which subjects are exposed. It is the variable that is controlled and manipulated by the researcher.

The *dependent variable* is the one that is observed for changes in order to assess the effect of the treatment.

In psychological research, the dependent variable is typically a measure of some form of behavior. For the practice experiment (Figure 1.1), the dependent variable is the number of words recalled on the learning test. Differences between groups in performance on the dependent variable suggest that the manipulation had an effect. That is, changes in the dependent variable *depend on* the independent variable.

Often we can identify one condition of the independent variable that receives no treatment. It is used for comparison purposes and is called the *control group*. The group that does receive the treatment is the *experimental group*.

A *control group* is a condition of the independent variable that receives no treatment. It is used for the purpose of making comparisons.

An *experimental group* does receive a treatment.

For example, a researcher performs an experiment to assess the effect of alcohol on motor performance. Volunteers in one group are required to drink three bottles of beer in a 12-minute period. Subjects of the other group drink the same amount of a nonalcoholic beer-type beverage. Thirty minutes later, all people from both groups try to balance a broomstick on the index finger of their right hand. To make the task more difficult, they must perform the task while seated. Performance is measured by the number of attempts it takes for a subject to balance the stick for 30 seconds. This type of measure is sometimes called a trials-to-criterion task. The structure of the experiment is depicted in Figure 1.2. For this study, the independent variable is the type of beverage consumed (alcoholic or nonalcoholic). The experimental group is treated with the alcoholic beverage. In contrast, the control group does not consume alcohol, and it is used for comparison with the experimental group in terms of their performance. The dependent variable is the number of trials required to reach the criterion (30 seconds of balancing). If alcohol impairs performance for this task, then people in the beer-drinking group should require more attempts at balancing the stick than subjects in the control group. A statistical analysis would have to be performed to determine if an effect occurred.

A trials-to-criterion measure is commonly used in studies of skill acquisition.

Remember, the independent variable consists of treatments, and the dependent variable is the method of assessment.

Problems That Can Arise in Experiments

Researchers must use great care in planning and designing an experiment because a seemingly small flaw in a study can make the result uninterpretable. This situation is always unfortunate because time and resources are wasted. There are more ways that an experiment can be flawed than can be enumerated here, but a few examples will alert you to common problems that may occur.

One way an experiment can be flawed is by the presence of *confounding variables*. This problem occurs when a researcher allows the experimental conditions to differ with respect to some characteristic other than the independent variable.

Figure 1.2

Volunteers are randomly assigned to one of two treatment groups: nonalcoholic beverage or alcoholic beverage. Type of beverage is the independent variable. The effects of this manipulation are assessed for motor performance. Specifically, the motor task consists of balancing a stick, and the dependent variable is the number of trials required to reach a criterion (30 seconds of balancing).

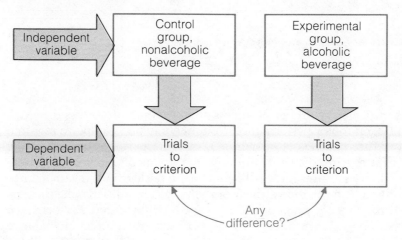

A *confounding variable* is an uncontrolled variable that is unintentionally allowed to vary with the independent variable.

For example, an instructor would like to assess the effectiveness of computer laboratory exercises in assisting students to grasp the fundamentals of statistics. There are two treatment conditions. One section of statistics is taught three times a week as a lecture course. A second section of students also meets three times a week, but one of these meetings is devoted to computer exercises in statistics. Professor Smith teaches the lecture, and Professor Jones teaches the second group of students. At the end of the semester, both groups receive the same final exam, and their performances are compared. The experiment is summarized in Figure 1.3.

Let's assume that a statistical analysis determined that the lecture/lab students performed better on the final exam. Can the instructors conclude that the method of instruction had an effect on learning? The answer is emphatically *no*. The independent variable, method of instruction, is not the only way the groups differ in terms of how they are treated. The instructor was allowed to vary along with the method of instruction. It is possible that the lecture/lab group performed better because Professor Jones is a better instructor, one who motivates students and can explain concepts in understandable terms. Perhaps

Figure 1.3

In this experiment, the effect of instructional method (the independent variable) on test performance (the dependent variable) is examined. However, any difference between groups in performance cannot be attributed to the method of instruction. In this experiment, there is a confounding variable. The instructor teaching the course varies with the independent variable, so that the treatment of the groups differs in more ways than one (instructional method and instructor vary).

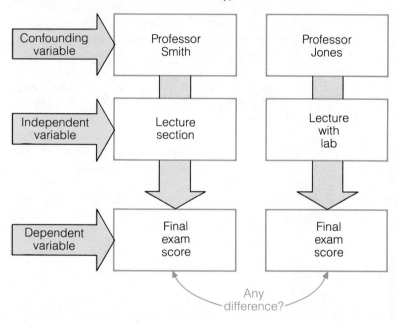

Professor Smith has less experience. That is, the difference between groups in performance might be due to the different instructors rather than the different treatments. One cannot be sure which interpretation is correct. When a study is confounded, it is impossible to make meaningful conclusions about the results.

Another problem that can occur is that the groups may differ *even before* they receive the treatments. Then the difference in performance between groups at the end of the experiment is incorrectly attributed to the effect of the independent variable. For example, an experiment was done to determine if stress associated with decision making would lead to the development of ulcers (Brady et al., 1958). Four monkeys in the "executive" (decision-making) group were paired with four control monkeys. The monkeys in each pair were restrained in chairs next to each other. The executive had to press a lever often enough to avoid electric shock. If the subject stopped pressing the lever for a short time, *both* monkeys in the pair would get shocked. Thus, the executive and control monkeys received the same number of shocks, but only the executive had to make decisions. After several weeks, it was noted that the executive monkeys, but not the controls, had many stomach ulcers.

This type of pairing of control and experimental subjects is sometimes called a yoked control.

This result would seem to support the hypothesis that the stress of responsibility promotes the development of ulcers. However, the outcome of the study may be difficult to interpret because the monkeys were not randomly assigned to treatment groups. The first four monkeys who learned to press the lever to avoid shock were assigned to the executive group, and the remaining animals served as controls. It is possible that the earlier learners were the most sensitive or emotionally reactive of all the animals. On this basis alone, one would expect the early learners to develop more ulcers when shocked. Therefore, the findings of the executive monkey experiment may be due to a bias in group assignments rather than to a treatment (decision-making) effect. The groups may have been different all along.

When we interpret the outcome of an experiment, we assume that the groups were initially the same. If this assumption is violated, then the differences observed following treatment may have nothing to do with the independent variable. Random assignment of subjects to treatments helps avoid this problem, but just to be sure, a researcher may also give the subjects a pretest before the study. That is, one might take measurements of the dependent variable prior to the treatment, as well as after it, to be certain that the groups are initially equivalent. Box 1.2 deals with a similar problem in an applied research setting.

Theories and Hypotheses

A theory is especially helpful if it generates many testable *hypotheses. By* testable *we mean the hypothesis can be confirmed or disconfirmed by making* observations *(conducting studies).*

Theories are a very important part of psychological research. A psychological theory typically consists of a number of statements about the underlying mechanisms of behavior. Theories are important in that they help organize and unify many observations. They may try to account for very large areas of psychology, such as a general theory of learning. However, they may be more specific, such as a theory of the mechanisms involved in just avoidance learning. A theory is especially useful if it directs and promotes future research and provides specific predictions for the outcomes of that research.

When an investigator designs an experiment, there almost always is a specific hypothesis which is addressed. A *hypothesis* is a hunch about the result that will be obtained from the experiment.

DEFINITION

A *hypothesis* is a prediction about the outcome of an experiment.

Hypotheses are often derived from the theory that the researcher is developing. An experimenter can state the hypothesis as a prediction—specifically, as a relationship between the independent and dependent variables. Simply stated, a hypothesis is a prediction about

BOX 1.2 Other Things Being Equal

When assessing the effect of a treatment, we assume that groups differ only with respect to the treatment condition, and that other conditions are the same or equal for the groups in the study. In the following example, Hooke (1983) illustrates the problems of interpretation that arise in research when other things are *not* equal.

> *Ceteris paribus* means "other things being equal," and I drag in this bit of Latin to suggest the antiquity of the phrase. Often we assume that other things are equal without saying so, and then we may forget that the assumption was made. Data pushers like to profit from our habit of making this tacit assumption.
>
> During the 1970s a report was issued describing data for crude cancer mortality rates in two groups of ten American cities, one group that had added fluoride to the drinking water and one that had not. Between 1950 and 1970 the cancer mortality rate rose in both groups of cities, but it rose considerably faster in the fluoridated group. Some data pushers were more than willing to attribute the difference to the fluoride, without pointing out that they were assuming "other things being equal."
>
> The National Cancer Institute asserted that indeed other things were not equal and that the difference between the two groups of cities was explained by differences in the age, race, and sex distributions of the two groups of cities; these three demographic characteristics all have known effects on cancer mortality rates. In Great Britain the Royal College of Physicians asked for comment from the Royal Statistical Society. Two statisticians were chosen to analyze the data, and here is what they found.
>
> The cities that were to be fluoridated already had, before fluoridation, an excess of cancer deaths over the "control," cities that went unfluoridated. Between 1950 and 1970 the demographic differences between the two groups became even greater. Taking into account the known effects of age, race, and sex on cancer death rate, they found that the remaining unaccounted-for part of the cancer mortality rate was actually somewhat smaller in the fluoridated cities than in the others.
>
> Which all goes to show that *ceteris* are not necessarily *paribus*, and that the reason things are often not what they seem is that we may be assuming things about them that are not true.

Excerpt reprinted from R. Hooke, *How to Tell the Liars from the Statisticians*, 1983, pp. 21–22, by courtesy of Marcel Dekker, Inc.

the effect of the treatments. Therefore, we can think of an experiment as a test of a hypothesis. A very important part of inferential statistics consists of the statistical analysis of hypothesis tests. Much of the book will focus on this topic.

When an experiment is performed, the researcher is trying to determine if the evidence confirms or refutes a specific hypothesis. Confirming these predictions strengthens the theory, suggesting it is correct and useful for guiding future research. In a sense, an experiment poses a problem of detection. The investigator attempts to detect a treatment effect to support a hypothesis. It is possible to have "false alarms" in an experiment—for the investigator to conclude there is evidence for an effect in the experiment when in reality no such treatment effect exists. The goal of the statistical techniques for testing hypotheses is to detect treatment effects but at the same time reduce the chances of false alarms. As Box 1.3 points out, anytime we have a detection situation, there is always a risk of false alarms.

Constructs and Operational Definitions

Theories contain hypothetical concepts which help describe the mechanisms that underlie behavioral phenomena. These concepts are called *constructs*, and they cannot be observed because they are hypothetical. For example, intelligence, personality types, and motives are hypothetical constructs. They are used in theories to organize observations in terms of underlying mechanisms. If constructs are hypothetical and cannot be observed, then how can they possibly be studied? The answer is that we have to *define* the construct so that it can be studied. An *operational definition* defines a construct in terms of an observable and measurable response. This definition should include the process and operations involved in making the observations. For example, an operational definition for emotionality might be stated as "the amount of increase in heart rate after a person is insulted." An operational definition of intelligence might be "the score on the Wechsler Adult Intelligence Scale."

DEFINITIONS

Constructs are hypothetical concepts that are used in theories to organize observations in terms of underlying mechanisms.

An *operational definition* defines a construct in terms of a measurable response.

LEARNING CHECK

1. It is possible for a study to be objective even if the researcher's hypotheses or beliefs are allowed to influence the results. (True or false?)

BOX 1.3 | The Plague of False Alarms

The headline in a Rochester, New York newspaper stated, "City May Charge for False Alarms." The article noted the following:

> The city of Rochester hopes to cut the number of false alarms plaguing its police and fire departments by making negligent alarm owners pay for their mistakes.
>
> Officials estimate that false alarms cost the city about $500,000 a year in such things as police time lost answering the calls. Of the 21,320 alarms automatically called into the city police last year, 96.5 percent were false, according to Police Department statistics. The year before 97 percent of the alarms were false.
>
> A proposed city ordinance will include a $5 annual permit fee for all burglar and fire alarms in the city. . . . At permit renewal time, the owner would pay $50 for each false alarm over three the city responded to during the year.

According to the article, the "$50 charge would provide an incentive for owners to repair faulty burglar alarms and to make sure that they are properly maintained."

Anytime we attempt to detect something, be it a treatment effect or a burglary, there is always the chance that we will make a mistake. A scientist tries to avoid false alarms—that is, concluding there is a treatment effect when there really is no effect. He or she structures and conducts the statistical test in a way that minimizes the likelihood that a false alarm will occur. Faced with a similar and very costly dilemma, the city of Rochester is trying to structure and implement its laws to minimize false alarms in the detection of burglars and fires. As the proposed ordinance suggests, the city officials are willing to risk a maximum of three false alarms per business each year. Like the scientist trying to detect a treatment effect, they are reducing the chances of a certain type of error that can occur in detection situations.

Article excerpts are reprinted courtesy of the *Democrat and Chronicle*, Rochester, New York.

2. Cause-and-effect relationships cannot be determined by a correlational method. (True or false?)
3. In a memory experiment, subjects memorize a list of words and then must recall as many words as possible after a 6-hour retention interval. One group sleeps during the retention interval, while people in the other group remain awake and go about their daily routine. The number of words recalled is measured for each subject. The experimenter wants to determine if type of activity during the retention interval has an effect on the num-

ber of words recalled. For this study, what is the independent variable? What is the dependent variable?

4. A confounding variable will assist the experimenter in making a meaningful interpretation of the data. (True or false?)

5. A hypothesis can be stated as a prediction about the effect of _____ on _____ .

6. An operational definition defines a construct in terms of _____ .

ANSWERS

1. false
2. true
3. type of activity during the retention interval; the number of words recalled
4. false
5. an independent variable (or treatment); a dependent variable
6. a measurable response

1.4

Scales of Measurement

What Is a Measurement?

It should be obvious by now that data collection requires that we make measurements of our observations. Measurement involves either categorizing events (qualitative measurements) or using numbers to characterize the size of the event (quantitative measurement). There are several types of scales that are associated with measurements. The distinctions among the scales are important because they underscore the limitations of certain types of measurements and because certain statistical procedures are appropriate for data collected on some scales but not on others.

The Nominal Scale

A *nominal scale* of measurement labels observations so that they fall into different categories.

DEFINITION

In a *nominal scale* of measurement, observations are labeled and categorized.

The word *nominal* means "having to do with names." Measurements that are made on this scale involve naming things. For example, if we wish to know the sex of a person responding to a questionnaire, it would be measured on a nominal scale consisting of two categories. A product warranty card might have you check the box that best describes your occupation, and it lists "sales," "professional," "skilled trade," "other (please specify)." Occupations are being measured in terms of categories; therefore a nominal scale is being used. A researcher observing the behavior of a group of infant monkeys might categorize responses as playing, grooming, feeding, acting aggressive, or showing submissiveness. Again, this instance typifies a nominal scale of measurement. The nominal scale consists of qualitative distinctions. No attempt is made to measure the size of the event or response. The scales that follow do reflect an attempt to make quantitative distinctions.

The Ordinal Scale

In an *ordinal scale* of measurement, observations are ranked in terms of size or magnitude. As the word ordinal implies, the investigator simply places the observation in order from biggest to smallest.

DEFINITION

An *ordinal scale* of measurement consists of ranking observations in terms of size or magnitude.

For example, a job supervisor is asked to rank employees in terms of how well they perform their work. The resulting data (Table 1.1) will tell us who the supervisor considers the best worker, the second best, and so on. However, the data provide no information about the amount that the workers differ in job performance. The data may reveal that Jan is viewed as doing better work than Joe but *not how much* better. This is a limitation of measurements on an ordinal scale.

Table 1.1
Rank Order of Workers' Performance According to Supervisor

Rank	Worker
1	Sandy
2	Jan
3	Joe
4	Hoyt
5	Ellen
6	Bill

The Interval Scale

In an *interval scale* of measurement, intervals between numbers reflect differences in magnitude. That is, it allows you to measure differences in the size or amount of events.

DEFINITION

In an *interval scale*, the difference (or interval) between numbers on the scale reflects a difference in magnitude. However, ratios of magnitudes are not meaningful.

For example, if on June 1 the temperature is 80°F and on November 1 it is 40°, then we can say that the temperature on June 1 was 40° higher than on November 1. If Jim scored 160 on an IQ test and Sam scored 80, then Jim's score is 80 points higher. Note that with an interval scale we can determine which observation is of greater magnitude and by *how much* it is greater.

However, we *cannot* say that it was *twice* as hot on June 1 as on November 1 or that Jim is twice as smart as Sam. These statements require that you form a ratio of the two observations. A ratio will only be meaningful when the scale of measurement has a true zero point. For example, zero on the Fahrenheit scale does not mean there is "no temperature." It certainly can get colder than 0°F. Likewise, there is no meaningful zero point that would indicate that a person has absolutely "no intelligence." These scales start at arbitrary zero points, making ratio comparisons meaningless.

The Ratio Scale

Most dependent variables we will encounter can be measured on either an interval or a ratio scale.

A *ratio scale* of measurement has a meaningful zero point, and thus ratios of numbers on this scale do reflect ratios of magnitudes.

DEFINITION

In a *ratio scale*, ratios of numbers do reflect ratios of magnitudes. This scale has a meaningful zero point.

For example, two warehouse workers have a contest to see who can lift the heaviest carton. Bill lifts a 200-pound carton and John lifts a 100-pound box. It can be said that Bill is able to lift twice as much as John. Note that a ratio scale of measurement allows one to draw the same conclusions as with ordinal and interval scales, plus it allows one to form ratios to compare the magnitude of measurements. In a psychology laboratory, a researcher might measure people's reaction times to stimuli. For example, it takes Joan 500 milliseconds to respond to a stimulus, and Mary takes only 250 milliseconds. Therefore, Mary responds in half as much time as Joan.

1.5

Discrete and Continuous Variables

What Are They and How Do They Differ?

The variables in a study can be characterized by the type of values that can be assigned to them. A *discrete variable* is one that can have only a finite number of values between any two values. In fact, between neighboring values, no other values can be found. Consider the values displayed when dice are rolled. Between neighboring values, for example, seven dots and eight dots, no other values can ever be observed. Therefore, a discrete variable is typically restricted to whole *countable* numbers.

DEFINITION

In a *discrete variable*, there is a finite number of values between any two values. No values can be found between neighboring values.

For example, if you observe class attendance from day to day, you will note that this variable can vary only in countable steps. That is, the number of students attending class will be a whole number value, and between any two possible values a finite number of values will exist. One day the attendance may be 18 people, and another day 23 students may show for class. There are a finite number of possible values between these two observations (namely, 19, 20, 21, and 22 people). Values such as 18.5 or 20.17 are not possible because there is no continuum of values between 18 and 23 students, just discrete countable steps. A discrete variable may also consist of observations that differ qualitatively. For example, a psychologist examines patients and then makes diagnostic distinctions between them. Some patients are classified as having panic disorders, others as having dissociative disorders, and some as having psychotic disorders. The type of disorder is a discrete variable in that there are distinct and finite "values" (actually categories) that can be observed.

On the other hand, it is possible for a *continuous variable* to take on an infinite number of values. Specifically, between any two values of a continuous variable, you can always find a third value.

A *continuous variable* can take on an infinite number of values.

For example, subjects are given problems to solve, and the researcher measures their problem-solving skill by the amount of time it takes them to find the solutions. Problem-solving skill is a continuous variable. Its measurement, time to solution, lies on a continuum. That is, one person may take 31 seconds to solve the problem, while another may take 32 seconds. Between these two values it is possible to find any fractional amount—$31\frac{1}{2}$, $31\frac{1}{4}$, 31.12—provided the measurement instrument is accurate enough.

Intervals and Continuous Variables

A continuous variable can be pictured on a number line that is continuous. That is, there are an infinite number of points on this line. However, when a continuous variable is measured, we typically do not assign our observation to a single point value on the line. In practice we assign the observation to an *interval* on the number line. For example, body weight is a continuous variable because there are an infinite number of possible weights between any two weights. Suppose we measure body weight to the nearest pound. Two people actually weigh 150.3 and 149.6 pounds. Their weights are located on the segment of the number line in Figure 1.4. What weights will we assign to these people? In the first case, 150.3 is rounded down to 150, and for the second person 149.6 is rounded up to 150. Even though their actual weights differ slightly, they are assigned the same value in whole numbers. In fact, any person whose actual weight is somewhere in the interval between 149.5 and 150.5 will be assigned the weight of 150 pounds. Therefore, when we measure weight to the nearest pound, we are actually assigning observations to intervals on the continuum. When body weight is reported, it typically is reported in whole numbers. This practice does not mean that body weight is a discrete variable. Body weight is a continuous variable, but the observations are being assigned to intervals on the number line rather than points. Sometimes limitations in the precision of a measurement tool (your bathroom scale, for example) necessitates this type of assignment.

A Word of Caution About Continuous Variables

As can be seen in the previous example, a variable that is really continuous may give the appearance of being discrete because of the measurement scale that is used. In these instances, one must consider the theoretical or conceptual basis for the measurements to determine if the variable is discrete or continuous. Specifically, the type of con-

Figure 1.4

When measuring weight to the nearest whole pound, 149.6 and 150.3 are assigned the value of 150 (top). Any value in the interval between 149.5 and 150.5 will be given the value of 150.

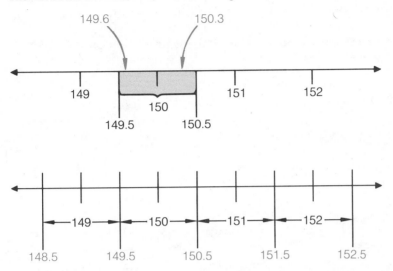

structs involved should give the researcher some clues. Scores on intelligence tests, for example, are reported as whole numbers, and there is a maximum and minimum score that can be obtained. While this gives the superficial appearance of a discrete variable, it is really a result of restrictions imposed by the measurement instrument (the test). Theoretically, intelligence could come in any amount and therefore is a continuous variable.

Consider the example in which the effect of alcohol on motor performance was assessed (page 11). Motor performance was measured by the number of trials required to reach a criterion. The data, therefore, will consist of whole countable numbers. These data give the appearance that motor performance is a discrete variable. However, motor performance (in this case, how well a person balances a stick) should be able to vary continuously. In fact, if the researcher measured performance in terms of the amount of time (in seconds) the stick is balanced, it would be more obvious that the variable is continuous. If it is possible to measure a variable with numbers that lie on a continuum, then the variable is continuous—no matter what type of measurement was actually used.

LEARNING CHECK

1. An instructor records the order in which students complete their tests—that is, the first to finish, the second to finish, etc. A(n) _____ scale of measurement is used in this instance.
2. The Scholastic Aptitude Test (SAT) most likely measures aptitude on a(n) _____ scale.
3. In a study on perception of facial expressions, subjects must

classify the emotions displayed in photographs of people as either anger, sadness, joy, disgust, fear, or surprise. Emotional expression is measured on a(n) _____ scale.

4. A researcher studies the factors that determine how many children couples decide to have. The variable, number of children, is a _____ (discrete/continuous) variable.

5. An investigator studies how concept-formation ability changes with age. Age is a _____ (discrete/continuous) variable.

ANSWERS

1. ordinal
2. interval
3. nominal
4. discrete
5. continuous

1.6
Statistical Notation

Measurements of behavior will provide data composed of numerical values. These numbers form the basis of the computations that are done for statistical analyses. There is a standardized notation system for statistical procedures, and it is used to identify terms in equations and mathematical operations. Some general mathematical operations, notation, and basic algebra are outlined in the review section of Appendix A. There is also a skills assessment exam (page A-1) to help you determine if you need the basic mathematics review. Here we will introduce some statistical notation that is used throughout this book. In subsequent chapters, additional notation will be introduced as it is needed.

Scores

Making observations of a dependent variable in a study will typically yield values or scores for each subject. Raw scores are the original, unchanged set of scores obtained in the study. Scores for a particular variable are represented by the letter X. For example, if performance in your statistics course is measured by tests and you obtain a 35 on the first test, then we could state that $X = 35$. A set of scores can be presented in a column that is headed by X. For example, a list of quiz scores from your class might be presented as follows:

X
37
35
35
30
25
17
16

When observations are made for two variables, there will be two scores for each subject. The data can be presented as two lists labeled X and Y for the two variables. For example, observations for people's height in inches (variable X) and weight in pounds (variable Y) can be presented in the following manner.

X	Y
72	165
68	151
67	160
68	146
70	160
66	133

It is also useful to determine how many scores are in a set. This information is obtained by simply counting the number of scores, and it is represented by the letter N. (As we shall see later, in some situations the lowercase letter n is used.) For the height and weight data, $N = 6$ for both of the variables.

Summation Notation

Many of the computations required in statistics will involve adding up a set of scores. Because this procedure is used so frequently, there is a special notation used to refer to the sum of a set of scores. The Greek letter sigma, or Σ, is used to stand for summation. The expression ΣX means to add all the scores for variable X. The summation sign Σ can be read as "the sum of." Thus ΣX is read "the sum of the scores." For the following set of quiz scores,

10, 6, 7, 4

$\Sigma X = 27$ and $N = 4$. There are a number of rules of summation that help identify which scores are added together and which mathematical operation is performed first when several are required. These rules are summarized as follows.

1. When there are two variables X and Y, ΣX indicates the sum of the Xs, and ΣY refers to the sum of the Ys. For the following data, $\Sigma X = 16$, and $\Sigma Y = 34$:

X	Y
3	10
1	4
7	6
3	5
2	9

2. When two variables (X and Y) are multiplied together, the product is represented by the symbols XY. Note that the multiplication sign is not written between the symbols ($X \times Y$ can cause confusion). The expression XY is understood to mean "X times Y." Following are three pairs of scores, each pair representing a score for variable X and one for variable Y for a particular person:

X	Y	XY
2	4	8
3	1	3
4	3	12

The column for XY represents the product of X and Y scores for each person. The total for the X values, ΣX, is obtained by adding the scores in that column, and the sum of Y is obtained by adding the Y column:

$$\Sigma X = 2 + 3 + 4 = 9$$
$$\Sigma Y = 4 + 1 + 3 = 8$$

The expression ΣXY means "sum the products of X and Y." The first step is to compute the product for each pair of X and Y scores. These products are displayed in the column headed by "XY." In the second step, the products are added together. For this example, the sum of the products is $\Sigma XY = 23$:

$$\Sigma XY = 8 + 3 + 12 = 23$$

It is very important to note that ΣXY *does not equal* $\Sigma X \Sigma Y$. The latter expression means "the sum of X times the sum of Y." For these data, it is easy to demonstrate that the two expressions are not the same:

$$\Sigma XY \neq \Sigma X \Sigma Y$$
$$23 \neq 9(8)$$
$$23 \neq 72$$

Note that for the expression $\Sigma X \Sigma Y$ the order of operations is the reverse of ΣXY. First we sum the Xs and sum the Ys, and then we take the product of the totals. Therefore, $\Sigma X \Sigma Y$ is the "product of the totals," while ΣXY is the "total of the products."

3. When a constant amount C is added to each score, the expression for the resulting scores is $X + C$. In the following example, the constant equals 4. If this value is added to every score, a column headed by "$X + 4$" can be made.

X	X + 4
1	5
4	8
6	10

When a constant value is added to every score, it is necessary to use parentheses to represent the sum of these new scores, $\Sigma(X + 4)$. The calculations within the parentheses are always done first. Because the summation symbol is outside the parentheses, finding the sum is performed last. Therefore, to compute $\Sigma(X + 4)$, the constant 4 is first added to every score, creating the new "$X + 4$" column of numbers. Then these new numbers are added together. For this example,

$$\Sigma(X + 4) = 5 + 8 + 10 = 23$$

A word of caution is necessary. If parentheses are not used, then the meaning of the expression is changed. That is, $\Sigma X + 4$ means the total for X is added to the constant of 4:

$$\Sigma X + 4 = 11 + 4 = 15$$

Note that $\Sigma(X + C)$ *does not equal* $\Sigma X + C$.

4. The squared value of a score is represented by the symbol X^2. If every score in the group is squared, then a new column of squared values can be listed:

X	X^2
3	9
1	1
4	16
2	4

Remember, when a number is squared, it is multiplied by itself. A common mistake is to multiply a number by 2 instead of squaring it. The expression ΣX^2 means the "sum of the squared scores." Each score is first squared, and then the sum is found for the squared values. In this example, adding the "X^2" column reveals that

$$\Sigma X^2 = 9 + 1 + 16 + 4 = 30$$

Be careful! The symbol $(\Sigma X)^2$ represents a different order of operations, and the resulting value is not the same as that of ΣX^2. The operations inside the parentheses are performed first. Therefore, the sum of the Xs is determined first. The exponent is outside the parentheses, so the squaring is done last. The expression $(\Sigma X)^2$ means the "squared total." In the example, this value is

$$(\Sigma X)^2 = (10)^2 = 100$$

Therefore, $(\Sigma X)^2$ is *not the same* expression as ΣX^2. It is very important to remember the order of operations for these two expressions. Later we will have to use statistical formulas that contain both of these expressions. It is imperative that you do not confuse them for each other.

For the following data, find the values for the listed expressions.

X	Y
3	1
3	2
1	1
2	3
4	5

1. ΣX 5. $(\Sigma Y)^2$
2. ΣX^2 6. $\Sigma X \Sigma Y$
3. $(\Sigma X)^2$ 7. ΣXY
4. ΣY^2 8. N for the X scores

ANSWERS

1.	13	5.	144
2.	39	6.	156
3.	169	7.	36
4.	40	8.	5

Summary

1. By common usage, the word *statistics* means facts and figures. In this book, the general use of the word is in reference to techniques and procedures for analyzing data.

2. Science is empirical in that it provides methods for making observations. Statistics consist of methods for organizing and interpreting them.

3. A population is composed of every individual from the group one wishes to study. A sample is a subset of the population. Samples are drawn from the population for study because the population in question is usually so large that it is not feasible to study every individual in it.

4. Descriptive statistics simplify and summarize data, so that the data are more manageable. Inferential statistics are techniques that allow one to use sample data to make general statements about a population. Meaningful generalizations are possible only if the sample is representative of the population from which it was drawn. Random sampling helps ensure that it is representative.

5. A correlational method looks for interrelationships between variables but cannot determine the cause-and-effect nature of the relationship. The experimental method is able to establish causes and effects in a relationship.

6. In the experimental method, one variable (the independent variable) is intentionally manipulated and controlled by the experimenter. Then changes are noted in another variable (the dependent variable) as a result of the manipulation. The results of an experiment will be uninterpretable when a confounding variable is present. A confounding variable unintentionally varies along with the independent variable, so that groups differ in terms of how they are treated in more than one way.

7. A hypothesis is a prediction about the effect of an independent variable on a dependent variable. Hypotheses are usually derived from theories. Experiments basically involve the test of a hypothesis.

8. Constructs are hypothetical concepts used in theories to describe the mechanisms of behavior. Because they are hypothetical, they cannot be observed. Constructs are studied by

providing operational definitions for them. An operational definition defines a construct in terms of an observable and measurable response or event.

9. A nominal scale labels observations so that they fall into different categories. A nominal scale involves making qualitative distinctions. No attempt is made to measure the magnitude of the event.

10. An ordinal scale involves ranking observations in terms of size or magnitude. Although this scale will tell us which observation is larger, it will not tell us how much larger it is.

11. In an interval scale, intervals between numbers reflect differences in magnitude of observations. It is possible to determine which event is of greater magnitude and how much larger it is.

12. A ratio scale has all of the characteristics of an interval scale, and ratios of measurements on this scale reflect ratios of magnitudes. Unlike the interval scale, a ratio scale has a meaningful zero point.

13. A discrete variable is one that can have only a finite number of values between any two values. It typically consists of whole numbers that vary in countable steps. A continuous variable can have an infinite number of values between any two values. When a continuous variable is measured, we typically assign the observation to an interval on the number line rather than a single point.

14. The letter X is used to represent scores for a variable. If a second variable is used, Y represents its scores. The letter N is used as the symbol for the number of scores in a set. The Greek letter sigma Σ is used to stand for summation. Therefore, the expression ΣX is read "the sum of the scores."

Key Terms

statistics
population
sample
population parameter
sample statistic
descriptive statistics
distribution
raw scores
inferential statistics
random selection
variable
correlational method
experimental method
independent variable

dependent variable
control group
experimental group
confounding variable
hypothesis
construct
operational definition
nominal scale
ordinal scale
interval scale
ratio scale
discrete variable
continuous variable

Problems for Chapter 1:
Introduction to Statistics

*1. Scientific study is empirical and objective. What is meant by this statement?

2. Describe the purposes of descriptive and inferential statistical techniques.

*3. What is the shortcoming of the correlational method of study?

4. Describe how the experimental method is conducted. What is the distinction between the two types of variables that are used?

*5. What type of problems can occur in the experimental method that may lead to an incorrect interpretation of the findings?

6. A researcher would like to examine the effect of the amount of sleep on performance of a vigilance task. One group of subjects is allowed to sleep all night without interruptions. A second group of subjects is awakened six times during the night. In the morning, all of the subjects are tested on a vigilance task. They are required to observe a radar screen display and respond anytime a small spot of light briefly flashes somewhere on the screen. The experimenter records the number of errors subjects make. For this experiment, what is the independent variable? What is the dependent variable?

*7. Contrast the nominal scale of measurement to the ordinal scale. What type of scale is used in a list of the order of finish in a horse race? What type of scale is used when describing the sex of the jockeys?

8. Describe the difference between an ordinal scale of measurement and an interval scale.

*9. What is the difference between the interval scale and ratio scale of measurement?

10. What is the distinction between a construct and an operational definition?

*11. For the following set of scores, calculate the value for each of the expressions listed:

*Solutions for problems marked with an asterisk are given in Appendix C.

X
5
9
6
7
13

a. ΣX
b. $\Sigma X + 5$
c. $\Sigma (X + 5)$
d. $\Sigma (X - 3)$
e. $\Sigma X - 3$
f. N

12. For the following set of scores, find the value for the expressions listed:

X	Y
1	3
3	2
2	1
1	5
4	2

a. ΣX
b. ΣY
c. $\Sigma X + \Sigma Y$
d. $\Sigma (X + Y)$
e. ΣXY
f. $\Sigma X \Sigma Y$

*13. For the following set of scores, calculate the value for the expressions:

X
3
5
2
1
4

a. ΣX
b. ΣX^2
c. $(\Sigma X)^2$

14. Using the following data, calculate each requested value:

X	Y
1	4
7	8
6	11
12	16
8	9
5	13

a. ΣX
b. ΣX^2
c. ΣY
d. ΣY^2
e. $\Sigma X \Sigma Y$
f. ΣXY

*15. For the following data, find each requested value:

X	Y
2.3	3.1
4.0	11.5
6.7	2.0
4.5	9.4
5.6	7.2
8.0	1.0
3.3	6.7

a. ΣX^2
b. ΣY
c. ΣY^2
d. $\Sigma X \Sigma Y$
e. ΣXY
f. $(\Sigma X)^2$
g. $(\Sigma Y)^2$

16. For both samples, calculate the values for the expressions:

Sample 1		Sample 2	
X	Y	X	Y
1	5	1	13
2	7	2	11
3	9	3	9
4	11	4	7
5	13	5	5

a. ΣX f. $(\Sigma Y)^2$

b. ΣY g. ΣXY

c. ΣX^2 h. $\Sigma X \Sigma Y$

d. ΣY^2 i. Explain why the value for ΣXY is different for the two

e. $(\Sigma X)^2$ samples, while all of the other sums are identical.

*17. For the following data, find the value for each of the expressions:

X	
10.1	a. ΣX
9.3	b. ΣX^2
21.5	c. $(\Sigma X)^2$
7.0	d. N
8.7	
17.4	
10.6	
8.9	
11.6	
14.0	
12.7	
10.2	
19.3	
9.6	
12.5	

18. For the following set of scores, find the value of each expression:

X	
3	a. ΣX
5	b. $\Sigma(X - 3)$
10	c. $\Sigma(X - 3)^2$
8	d. $(\Sigma X)^2 - \Sigma X^2$
7	e. $(\Sigma X + 2)^2 - \Sigma(X + 2)^2$

*19. For the following set of scores, find the value of each expression:

X
-2
5
-4
0
7
-1

a. ΣX

b. $\Sigma(X + 2)$

c. ΣX^2

20. For the following set of scores, find the value of each expression:

X	Y
-3	2
4	3
-6	-1
5	-2
-5	4

a. ΣX

b. ΣY

c. ΣXY

d. $\Sigma X \Sigma Y$

Frequency Distributions

TOOLS
YOU WILL
NEED

The following items are considered essential background material for this chapter. If you doubt your knowledge of any of these items, you should review the appropriate chapter or section before proceeding.

1. Proportions (math review, Appendix A)
   a. Fractions
   b. Decimals
   c. Percentages
2. Scales of measurement (Chapter 1)
   a. Continuous and discrete
   b. Nominal, ordinal, interval, and ratio

Reading a textbook is much different from reading a novel or a newspaper. With a textbook, your goal is to study and to learn the material, not simply to entertain yourself. As a result you must work to identify and understand the important points. You must take time to digest the material, and it helps to stop and question yourself regularly to be sure that you fully comprehend what you are reading. All this may sound like the same old "how to study" lecture that you probably have heard a hundred times by now. But it is true, and it works.

Experiments have demonstrated that reading strategy can significantly affect comprehension and test performance. In 1974, John Boker presented college students with long passages (2500 words) selected from college-level texts (Boker, 1974). One group of students served as a control group and simply read straight through the material from beginning to end. For the experimental group, the passage was divided into 10 sections, each about 250 words, and the students were presented with questions at the end of each section. A week later, both groups were given a 40-question multiple-choice test covering the passage they had read. Hypothetical data similar to those obtained by Boker are shown in Table 2.1.

Table 2.1

Hypothetical Data from an Experiment Comparing Two Strategies for Studying College Textbook Material.[a]

Control Group		Experimental Group	
25	32	28	29
27	20	25	31
28	23	31	19
17	21	29	35
24	34	30	28
22	29	24	30
24	25	33	27
21	18	34	26
19	22	29	29
30	24	27	32
26	27	30	36
24	23	22	23
23	25	32	33

[a]The experimental group had questions interspersed through the material as they were reading. The control group read through the material without seeing any questions. One week later both groups were given a 40-item multiple-choice test on the material they had read. The data given are the scores on this test.

From looking at the data in Table 2.1, does it appear that one group did better than the other? Because these data are not organized in any systematic way, you probably find it difficult to discern any differences. This is a basic problem confronting any researcher after data are collected. To make sense of the experiment, you must organize the mass of numbers into a simpler form so that it is possible to "see" what happened. One solution is to present the scores in an organized table or a graph. Figure 2.1 shows the same data that are in Table 2.1, but now they are simplified and organized in a graph. Looking at the figure, does it appear that one group did better than the other?

It should be clear that graphing these data makes it easy to see the difference between the two groups. The students who read the passage with interspersed questions performed much better on the test—about five points better, which is quite a bit on a 40-question test.

There are two important points to be learned from this discussion. First, you should appreciate the value of simplifying and organizing a set of data. By structuring the data properly, it becomes possible to see at a glance what happened in an experiment. This helps researchers to decide exactly how the data should be analyzed and interpreted, and it helps others to understand the significance of the experiment. In this chapter we will examine several statistical techniques for organizing data. The second point concerns the implications of Boker's experiment. The way you study can have a tremendous influence on what you learn. As you read through this book, you will find lots of sample problems in the examples and learning checks that appear in each chapter. Take time to work through these problems, answer the questions, and test yourself. A little extra time and effort can increase your understanding of the material, and it can improve your grade.

Figure 2.1

The two graphs show the same data that were listed in Table 2.1. In these graphs each student is represented by a block that is placed directly above his/ her exam score. Notice that the experimental group generally performed better than the control group. For students in the experimental group, the exam scores pile up around $X = 29$. For the control group, the scores pile up around $X = 24$.

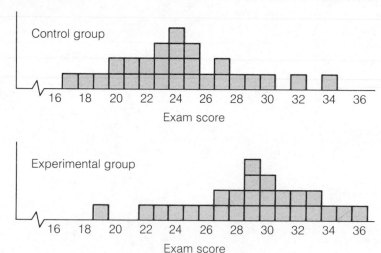

2.1
Introduction

When a researcher finishes the data collection phase of an experiment, the results usually consist of pages of numbers. The immediate problem for the researcher is to organize the scores into some comprehensible form so that any trends in the data can be seen easily and communicated to others. This is the job of descriptive statistics: to simplify the organization and presentation of data. One of the most common procedures for organizing a set of data is to place the scores in a frequency distribution.

DEFINITION

A *frequency distribution* is a record of the number of individuals located in each category on the scale of measurement.

A frequency distribution allows the researcher to see "at a glance" the entire set of scores. It shows whether the scores are generally high or low and whether they are concentrated in one area or spread out across the entire scale and generally provides an organized picture of the data. Frequency distributions can be structured either as tables or graphs, but both show the original measurement scale and the frequencies associated with each category. Thus, they present a picture of how the individual scores are distributed on the measurement scale—hence the name *frequency distribution*.

2.2
Frequency Distribution Tables

The simplest frequency distribution table presents the measurement scale by listing the individual scores in a column from highest to lowest. Beside each score, we indicate the frequency or number of times the score occurred in the data. It is customary to use an X as the column heading for the scores and an f as the column heading for the frequencies. An example of a frequency distribution table follows.

EXAMPLE 2.1
The following set of $N = 20$ scores were obtained from a 10-point statistics quiz. We will organize these scores by constructing a frequency distribution table. Scores:

8, 9, 8, 7, 10, 9, 6, 4, 9, 8
7, 8, 10, 9, 8, 6, 9, 7, 8, 8

1. The highest score is $X = 10$, and the lowest score is $X = 4$. Therefore, the first column of the table will list scores (X values) from 10 down to 4.

Notice that all of the possible values are listed in the table. For example, no one had a score of $X = 5$, but this value is included.

2. The frequency associated with each score is recorded in the second column. For example, two people had scores of $X = 6$, so there is a 2 in the f column beside $X = 6$.

X	f
10	2
9	5
8	7
7	3
6	2
5	0
4	1

Because the table organizes the scores, it is possible to see very quickly the general quiz results. For example, there were only two perfect scores, but most of the class had high grades (8s and 9s). With one exception (the score of $X = 4$) it appears that the class has learned the material fairly well.

You also should notice that the frequencies can be used to find the total number of scores in the distribution. By adding up the frequencies, you will obtain the total number of individuals:

$$\Sigma f = N$$

Proportions and Percentages

In addition to the two basic columns of a frequency distribution, there are other measures that describe the distribution of scores and which can be incorporated into the table. The two most common are proportion and percentage.

Proportion measures the fraction of the total group that is associated with each score. In Example 2.1, there were two individuals with $X = 6$. Thus, 2 out of 20 people had $X = 6$, so the proportion would be $2/20 = 0.10$. In general, the proportion associated with each score is

$$\text{proportion} = p = \frac{f}{N}$$

Because proportions describe the frequency (f) in relation to the total number (N), they often are called relative frequencies. Although proportions can be expressed as fractions (for example, 2/20), they more commonly appear as decimals. A column of proportions, headed with a p, can be added to the basic frequency distribution table (see Example 2.2).

In addition to using frequencies (f) and proportions (p), researchers often describe a distribution of scores with percentages. For example, an instructor might describe the results of an exam by saying that 15% of the class earned As, 23% Bs, etc. To compute the percentage associated with each score, you first find the proportion *(p)* and then multiply by 100:

$$\text{percentage} = p(100) = \frac{f}{N}(100)$$

Percentages can be included in a frequency distribution table by adding a column headed with % (see Example 2.2).

> EXAMPLE 2.2
> The frequency distribution table from Example 2.1 is repeated here. This time we have added columns showing the proportion *(p)* and the percentage (%) associated with each score.

X	f	p = f/N	% = p(100%)
10	2	2/20 = 0.10	10%
9	5	5/20 = 0.25	25%
8	7	7/20 = 0.35	35%
7	3	3/20 = 0.15	15%
6	2	2/20 = 0.10	10%
5	0	0/20 = 0	0%
4	1	1/20 = 0.05	5%

Grouped Frequency Distribution Tables

When a set of data covers a wide range of values, it is unreasonable to list all of the individual scores in a frequency distribution table. For example, a set of exam scores ranges from a low of $X = 41$ to a high of $X = 96$. These scores cover a range of over 50 points. The precise range is determined by

$$\text{range} = \text{high} - \text{low} + 1$$

For these exam scores the range would be

$$\text{range} = 96 - 41 + 1$$
$$= 56$$

If we were to list all of the individual scores, it would take 56 rows to complete the frequency distribution table. This would contradict the goal of a frequency distribution table, which is to simplify the presentation of the data. The solution to this problem is to divide the range of scores into intervals and then list these intervals in the frequency distribution table. For example, we could construct a table showing the number of students who had scores in the 90s, the number with scores in the 80s, etc. The result is called a *grouped frequency distribution table* because we are presenting groups of scores rather than individual values. The groups, or intervals, are called *class intervals*.

There are several rules that help guide you in the construction of a grouped frequency distribution table. These rules should be consid-

In the formula for the range, the +1 is included because both extremes (high and low) are counted along with the other scores in determining the range. For example, scores from 1 to 5 cover a range of five points.

ered as guidelines, rather than as absolute requirements, but they do help produce a simple, well-organized, and easily understood table.

RULE 1 The grouped frequency distribution table should have about 10 class intervals. If a table has many more than 10 intervals, it becomes cumbersome and defeats the purpose of a frequency distribution table. On the other hand, if you have too few intervals, you begin to lose information about the distribution of the scores. At the extreme, with only one interval, the table would not tell you anything about how the scores are distributed. Remember, the purpose for a frequency distribution is to help a researcher see the data. With too few or too many intervals, the table will not provide a clear picture. You should note that 10 intervals is a general guide. If you were constructing a table on a blackboard, for example, you probably would want only 5 or 6 intervals. If the table were to be printed in a scientific report, you may want 12 or 15 intervals. In each case your goal is to present a table that is relatively easy to see and understand.

RULE 2 The width of each interval should be a relatively simple number. For example, 2, 5, 10, or 20 would be good choices for the interval width. Notice that it is easy to count by 5s or 10s. These numbers are easy to understand and make it possible for someone to see quickly how you have divided the range.

RULE 3 The bottom score in each class interval should be a multiple of the width. If you are using a width of 10, for example, the intervals should start with 10, 20, 30, 40, etc. Again, this makes it easier for someone to understand how the table has been constructed.

RULE 4 All intervals should be the same width, and they should cover the range of scores completely with no gaps.

The application of these rules is demonstrated in Example 2.3.

EXAMPLE 2.3
An instructor has obtained the set of $N = 25$ exam scores shown here. To help organize these scores, we will place them in a frequency distribution table. Scores:

82, 75, 88, 93, 53, 84, 87, 58, 72
94, 69, 84, 61, 91, 64, 87, 84, 70
76, 89, 75, 80, 73, 78, 60

The first step is to determine the range of scores. For these data, the smallest score is $X = 53$, and the largest score is $X = 94$, so the range is

$$\text{range} = \text{high} - \text{low} + 1$$
$$= 94 - 53 + 1$$
$$= 42$$

Because it would require 42 rows to list each individual score in a frequency distribution table, we will have to group the scores into class intervals.

The best method for determining the appropriate interval width is to use Rules 1 and 2 simultaneously. According to Rule 1, we want about 10 intervals; according to Rule 2, we want the width to be a simple number. If we try a width of 2, how many intervals would it take to cover the range of scores? With each interval only 2 points wide, we would need 21 intervals to cover a range of 42 points. This is too many. What about an interval width of 5? What about a width of 10? The following table shows how many intervals would be needed for each possible width:

Width	Number of Intervals Needed to Cover a Range of 42 Points	
2	21	(too many)
5	9	(OK)
10	5	(too few)

Notice that an interval width of 5 will result in "about 10" intervals, which is exactly what we want.

The next step is to actually identify the intervals. The lowest score for these data is $X = 53$, so the lowest interval should contain this value. Because the interval should have a multiple of 5 as its bottom score, the interval would be 50 to 54. Notice that this interval contains five values (50, 51, 52, 53, 54), so it does have a width of 5. The next interval would start at 55 and go to 59. The complete frequency distribution table showing all of the class intervals is presented in Table 2.2.

Table 2.2

A Grouped Frequency Distribution Table Showing the Data from Example 2.3[a]

X	f
90–94	3
85–89	4
80–84	5
75–79	4
70–74	3
65–69	1
60–64	3
55–59	1
50–54	1

[a]The original scores range from a high of $X = 94$ to a low of $X = 53$. This range has been divided into nine intervals with each interval exactly five points wide. The frequency column (f) lists the number of individuals with scores in each of the class intervals.

Once the class intervals are listed, you complete the table by adding a column of frequencies or proportions or percentages. The values in the frequency column indicate the number of individuals whose scores are located in that class interval. For this example, there were four students with scores in the 60–64 interval, so the frequency for this class interval is $f = 4$ (see Table 2.2).

Continuous Variables and Real Limits

You should recall that a continuous variable has an infinite number of possible values. When measuring individuals on a continuous variable, a researcher must select a unit of measurement and then round off the actual measurements so that the scores correspond to the units selected. For example, if you are measuring time to the nearest second, measurements of 2.34 seconds and 1.98 seconds both would be rounded to scores of $X = 2$ seconds. Thus, a score of $X = 2$ is not a specific point on the scale but rather an interval on the scale. In this example, a score of $X = 2$ seconds actually corresponds to an interval from 1.5 seconds to 2.5 seconds. Any measurement within this interval will be assigned a score of $X = 2$. The boundaries that separate the intervals are called the real limits of the interval.

DEFINITION

For a continuous variable, each score actually corresponds to an interval on the scale. The boundaries that separate these intervals are called *real limits*. The real limit separating two adjacent scores is located exactly halfway between the scores. Each score has two real limits, one at the top of its interval called the *upper real limit* and one at the bottom of its interval called the *lower real limit*. Note that the upper real limit of one interval is also the lower real limit of the next higher interval.

The concept of real limits may be easier to understand if you picture a continuous variable as a line with the scores corresponding to locations on the line (see Figure 2.2).

When data are grouped into class intervals, the concept of real limits applies to the intervals. For example, an interval of 40–49 contains scores from $X = 40$ to $X = 49$. These values are called the *apparent limits* of the interval because it appears that they form the upper and lower boundaries for the class interval. But $X = 40$ is actually an interval from 39.5 to 40.5. Similarly, $X = 49$ is an interval from 48.5 to 49.5. Therefore, the real limits of the interval are 39.5 (the lower real limit) and 49.5 (the upper real limit). Notice that the next higher class interval would be 50–59, which has a lower real limit of 49.5.

Figure 2.2
The relationship between real limits and scores for a continuous variable. Notice that the score $X = 2$ actually corresponds to an interval on the scale bounded by a lower real limit of 1.5 and an upper real limit of 2.5. Any measurement within this interval will be assigned a score of $X = 2$.

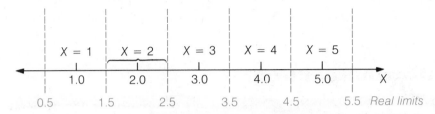

Thus, the two intervals meet at the real limit 49.5, so there are no gaps in the scale. You also should notice that the interval width becomes easier to understand when you consider the real limits of an interval. For example, the interval 50–54 has real limits of 49.5 and 54.5. The distance between these two real limits (five points) is the width of the interval.

The concept of real limits will be used later for constructing graphs and for various calculations with continuous scales. For now, however, you should realize that real limits are a necessity whenever measurements are made of a continuous variable.

LEARNING
CHECK

1. Place the following scores in a frequency distribution table showing proportion and percentage as well as the frequency for each score. Scores: 2, 3, 1, 2, 5, 4, 5, 5, 1, 4, 2, 2, 5, 5, 4, 2, 3, 1, 5, 4.

2. A set of scores ranges from a high of $X = 142$ to a low of $X = 65$. If these scores are to be placed in a grouped frequency distribution table, then
   a. What interval width should be used?
   b. What are the apparent limits of the bottom interval?
   c. What are the real limits of the bottom interval?

ANSWERS

1.

X	f	p	%
5	6	0.30	30%
4	4	0.20	20%
3	2	0.10	10%
2	5	0.25	25%
1	3	0.15	15%

2. a. The scores cover a range of 78 points. With an interval width of 5 points, you would need 16 intervals to cover the range.

With an interval width of 10, you would need 8 intervals. For most purposes, a width of 10 points probably is best.

b. With a width of 10, the bottom interval would have apparent limits of 60–69.

c. The real limits of the bottom interval would be 59.5 and 69.5.

2.3
Frequency Distribution Graphs

A frequency distribution graph is basically a picture of the information available in a frequency distribution table. We will consider several different types of graphs, but all start with two perpendicular lines called axes. The horizontal line is called the X-axis or the abscissa. The vertical line is called the Y-axis or the ordinate. The scores are listed along the X-axis in increasing value from left to right. The frequencies are listed on the Y-axis in increasing value from bottom to top. As a general rule, the point where the two axes intersect should have a value of zero for both the scores and the frequencies. A final general rule is that the graph should be constructed so that its height (Y-axis) is approximately three-quarters of its length (X-axis). Violating these guidelines can result in graphs that give a misleading picture of the data (see Box 2.1).

Histograms and Bar Graphs

The first type of graph we will consider is called either a histogram or a bar graph. For this type of graph, you simply draw a bar above each score so that the height of the bar corresponds to the frequency of the score. As you will see, the distinction between histograms and bar graphs is determined by the scale of measurement.

When a frequency distribution graph is showing data from a continuous variable, the bars are drawn so that adjacent bars touch each other. The touching bars produce a continuous figure which emphasizes the continuity of the variable. This type of frequency distribution graph is called a histogram.

DEFINITION

For a *histogram*, vertical bars are drawn above each score so that

1. The height of the bar corresponds to the frequency
2. The width of the bar extends to the real limits of the score

---

Figure 2.3

An example of a frequency distribution histogram. The same set of data is presented in a frequency distribution table and in a histogram.

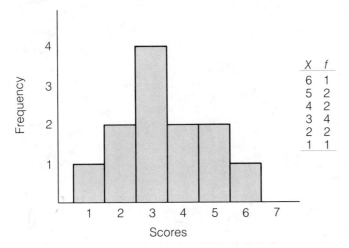

X	f
6	1
5	2
4	2
3	4
2	2
1	1

Although histograms are most appropriate for continuous variables, they are traditionally used whenever the data are measured on an interval scale or a ratio scale even when the variable is not continuous. An example of a histogram is presented in Figure 2.3.

When data have been grouped into class intervals, you can construct a frequency distribution histogram by drawing a bar above each interval so that the width of the bar extends to the real limits of the interval. This process is demonstrated in Figure 2.4.

When you are presenting the frequency distribution for a discrete variable, the graph is constructed so that there is some space between the bars. In this case the separate bars emphasize that the variable consists of separate, distinct categories. The resulting graph is called a bar graph. It is customary to use a bar graph whenever data are measured on a nominal scale or an ordinal scale. An example of a frequency distribution bar graph is given in Figure 2.5.

DEFINITION

For a *bar graph,* a vertical bar is drawn above each score (or category) so that

1. The height of the bar corresponds to the frequency
2. There is a space separating each bar from the next

Figure 2.4

An example of a frequency distribution histogram for grouped data. The same set of data is presented in a grouped frequency distribution table and in a histogram.

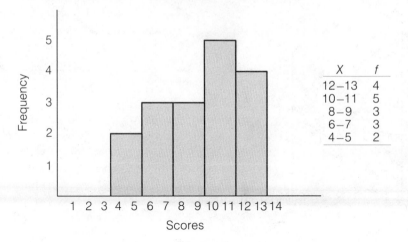

X	f
12–13	4
10–11	5
8–9	3
6–7	3
4–5	2

Figure 2.5

A bar graph showing the distribution of personality types in a sample of college students. Because personality type is a discrete variable measured on a nominal scale, the graph is drawn with space between the bars.

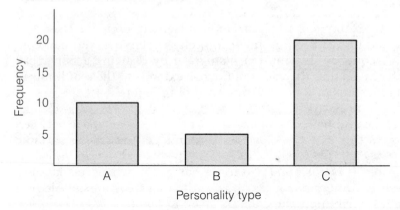

Frequency Distribution Polygons

Instead of a histogram, many researchers prefer to display a frequency distribution using a polygon.

DEFINITION

In a *frequency distribution polygon,* a single dot is drawn above each score so that:

1. The dot is centered above the score
2. The height of the dot corresponds to the frequency

A continuous line is then drawn connecting these dots. The graph is completed by drawing a line down to the *X*-axis (zero frequency) at each end of the range of scores.

As with a histogram, the frequency distribution polygon is intended for use with continuous variables. An example of a polygon is shown in Figure 2.6. A polygon also can be used with data that have been grouped into class intervals. In this case, you position the dots directly above the midpoint of each class interval. The midpoint can be found by averaging the apparent limits of the interval or by averaging the real limits of the interval. For example, a class interval of 40–49 would have a midpoint of 44.5.

$$\text{Apparent limits:} \quad \frac{40 + 49}{2} = \frac{89}{2} = 44.5$$

$$\text{Real limits:} \quad \frac{39.5 + 49.5}{2} = \frac{89}{2} = 44.5$$

An example of a frequency distribution polygon with grouped data is shown in Figure 2.7.

Relative Frequencies and Smooth Curves

Often it is impossible to construct a frequency distribution for a population because there are simply too many individuals for a researcher to obtain measurements and frequencies for the entire group. In this

Figure 2.6

An example of a frequency distribution polygon. The same set of data is presented in a frequency distribution table and in a polygon. Note that these data are shown in a histogram in Figure 2.3.

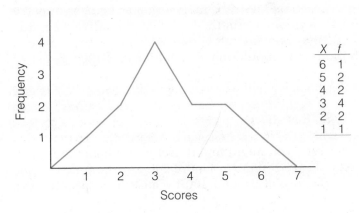

X	f
6	1
5	2
4	2
3	4
2	2
1	1

Figure 2.7

An example of a frequency distribution polygon for grouped data. The same set of data is presented in a grouped frequency distribution table and in a polygon. Note that these data are shown in a histogram in Figure 2.4.

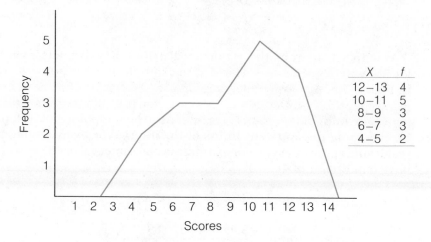

case, it is customary to draw a frequency distribution graph showing relative frequencies (or proportions) on the vertical axis. For example, a researcher may know that a particular species of animal has three times as many females as males in the population. This fact could be displayed in a bar graph by simply making the bar above "female" three times as tall as the bar above "male." Notice that the actual frequencies are unknown but that the relative frequency of males and females can still be presented in a graph.

It also is possible to use a polygon to show relative frequencies for scores in a population. In this case, it is customary to draw a smooth curve instead of the series of straight lines that normally appears in a polygon. The smooth curve indicates that you are not connecting a series of dots (real frequencies) but rather are showing a distribution that is not limited to one specific set of data. One commonly occurring population distribution is the normal curve. The word *normal* refers to a specific shape that can be precisely defined by an equation. Less precisely, we can describe a normal distribution as being symmetrical, with the greatest frequency in the middle and relatively smaller frequencies as you move toward either extreme. A good example of a normal distribution is the population distribution for IQ scores shown in Figure 2.8.

Throughout this book we will be referring to *distributions of scores*. Whenever the term *distribution* appears, you should conjure up an image of a frequency distribution graph. The graph provides a picture showing exactly where the individual scores are located. To make this concept more concrete, you might find it useful to think of the graph as showing a pile of individuals. In Figure 2.8, for example, the pile is highest at an IQ score of around 100 because most people have

Figure 2.8

The population distribution of IQ scores: an example of a normal distribution.

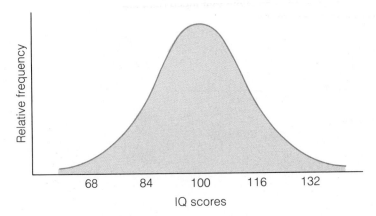

"average" IQs. There are only few individuals piled up at an IQ score of 130; it must be lonely at the top.

2.4
The Shape of a Frequency Distribution

Rather than drawing a complete frequency distribution graph, researchers often simply describe a distribution by listing its characteristics. There are three characteristics that completely describe any distribution: shape, central tendency, and variability. In simple terms, central tendency measures where the center of the distribution is located. Variability tells whether the scores are spread over a wide range or are clustered together. Central tendency and variability will be covered in detail in Chapters 3 and 4. Technically, the shape of a distribution is defined by an equation that prescribes the exact relation between each X and Y value on the graph. However, we will rely on a few less precise terms that will serve to describe the shape of most distributions.

Nearly all distributions can be classified as being either symmetrical or skewed.

DEFINITIONS

In a *symmetrical distribution* it is possible to draw a vertical line through the middle so that one side of the distribution is an exact mirror image of the other (see Figure 2.9).

In a *skewed distribution* the scores tend to pile up toward one end of the scale and taper off gradually at the other end (see Figure 2.9).

Figure 2.9

Examples of different shapes for distributions.

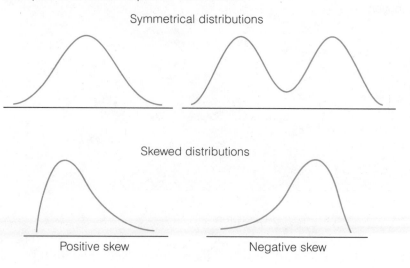

Symmetrical distributions

Skewed distributions

Positive skew   Negative skew

The section where the scores taper off toward one end of a distribution is called the *tail* of the distribution.

A skewed distribution with the tail to the right-hand side is said to be *positively skewed* because the tail points toward the positive (above-zero) end of the *X*-axis. If the tail points to the left, the distribution is said to be *negatively skewed* (see Figure 2.9).

For a very difficult exam, most scores will tend to be low, with only a few individuals earning high scores. This will produce a positively skewed distribution. Similarly, a very easy exam will tend to produce a negatively skewed distribution, with most of the students earning high scores and only a few with low values.

One specific shape is sufficiently common to deserve special notice. This is the normal distribution. We described the normal distribution earlier using IQ scores as an example (see Figure 2.8). Because normal shaped distributions occur commonly and because this shape is mathematically guaranteed in certain situations, it will receive extensive attention throughout this book.

LEARNING
CHECK

1. Sketch a frequency distribution histogram and a frequency distribution polygon for the data in the following table:

X	f
5	4
4	6
3	3
2	1
1	1

2. Describe the shape of the distribution in exercise 1.
3. Sketch a histogram and a polygon showing the distribution of scores in the following table:

X	f
10–11	2
8–9	4
6–7	5
4–5	3
2–3	1

4. What shape would you expect for the distribution of salaries for all employees of a major industry?

ANSWERS

1. The graphs are shown in Figure 2.10.
2. The distribution is negatively skewed.
3. The graphs are shown in Figure 2.10.
4. The distribution probably would be positively skewed, with most employees earning an average salary and a relatively small number of top executives with very large salaries

2.5
Other Types of Graphs

In addition to displaying frequency distributions, graphs can be used to show relationships between variables. Perhaps the most common use is to show the results of an experiment by graphing the relation between the independent variable and the dependent variable. You should recall that the dependent variable is the score obtained for each subject and that the independent variable distinguishes the different treatment conditions or groups used in the experiment. For example, a researcher testing a new diet drug might compare several different dosages by measuring the amount of food that animals consume at each dose level. Figure 2.11 shows hypothetical data from this experiment. Notice that the four dose levels (the independent variable) are on the X-axis and that food consumption (the dependent variable) is shown on the Y-axis. The points in the graph represent the average food consumption for the group at each dose level. In this graph the points are connected with a line because the X-axis variable (drug dose) is continuous.

Figure 2.10
Answers to Learning Check Exercises 1 and 3.

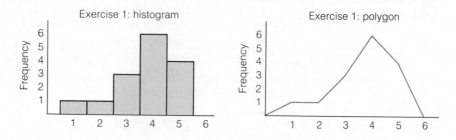

Exercise 1: histogram

Exercise 1: polygon

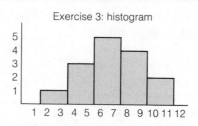

Exercise 3: histogram

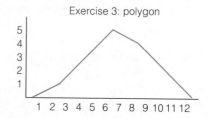

Exercise 3: polygon

Figure 2.11
The relationship between an independent variable (drug dose) and a dependent variable (food consumption). Because drug dose is a continuous variable, a continuous line is used to connect the different dose levels.

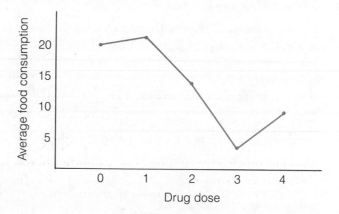

Figure 2.12 shows results from another experiment where the independent variable is discrete. In this graph, we have used separate bars for each position on the *X*-axis to indicate that we are comparing separate (discrete) categories.

Figure 2.12

The relationship between a discrete independent variable (brand of pain reliever) and a dependent variable (pain tolerance). Because the brand of pain reliever is a discrete variable, the graph uses separate bars.

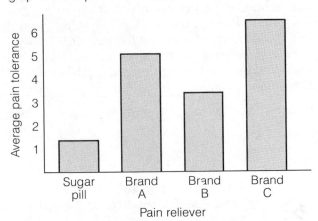

When constructing graphs of any type, you should recall the basic rules we mentioned earlier:

1. The height of a graph should be approximately three-quarters of its length.
2. Normally, you start numbering both the X-axis and the Y-axis with zero at the point where the two axes intersect.

More importantly, you should remember that the purpose of a graph is to give an accurate representation of the information in a set of data. Box 2.1 demonstrates what can happen when these basic principles are ignored.

2.6
Percentiles and Percentile Ranks

Although the primary purpose of a frequency distribution is to provide a description of an entire set of scores, it also can be used to describe the position of an individual within the set. Individual scores, or X values, are called raw scores. By themselves, raw scores do not provide much information. For example, if you are told that your score on an exam is $X = 43$, you cannot tell how well you did. To evaluate your score, you need more information such as the average score or the number of people who had scores above and below you. With this additional information you would be able to determine your relative position in the class. Because raw scores do not provide much information, it is desirable to transform them into a more meaningful form. One transformation that we will consider changes raw scores into percentiles.

Although graphs are intended to provide an accurate picture of a set of data, they can be used to exaggerate or misrepresent a set of scores. These misrepresentations generally result from failing to follow the basic rules for graph construction. The following example demonstrates how the same set of data can be presented in two entirely different ways by manipulating the structure of a graph.

For the past several years, the city has kept records of the number of major felonies. The data are summarized as follows:

Year	Number of Major Felonies
1982	218
1983	225
1984	229

These same data are shown in two different graphs in Figure 2.13. In the first graph we have exaggerated the height, and we started numbering the Y-axis at 210 rather than at zero. As a result, the graph seems to indicate a rapid rise in the crime rate over the 3-year period. In the second graph, we have stretched out the X-axis and used zero as the starting point for the Y-axis. The result is a graph that shows no change in the crime rate over the 3-year period.

Figure 2.13

Two graphs showing the number of major felonies in a city over a 3-year period. Both graphs are showing exactly the same data. However, the first graph gives the appearance that the crime rate is high and rising rapidly. The second graph gives the impression that the crime rate is low and has not changed over the 3-year period.

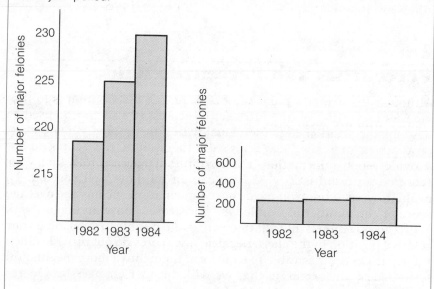

continued

Which graph is correct? The answer is that neither one is very good. Remember that the purpose of a graph is to provide an accurate display of the data. The first graph in Figure 2.13 exaggerates the differences between years, and the second graph conceals the differences. Some compromise is needed. You also should note that in some cases a graph may not be the best way to display information. For these data, for example, showing the numbers in a table would be better than either graph.

DEFINITIONS

The *rank* or *percentile rank* of a particular score is defined as the percentage of individuals in the distribution with scores at or below the particular value.

When a score is identified by its percentile rank, the score is called a *percentile*.

Suppose, for example, that you have a score of $X = 43$ on an exam and that you know that exactly 60% of the class had scores of 43 or lower. Then your score $X = 43$ has a percentile rank of 60%, and your score would be called the 60th percentile. Notice that *percentile rank* refers to a percentage and that *percentile* refers to a score. Also notice that your rank or percentile describes your exact position within the distribution.

Cumulative Frequency and Cumulative Percentage

The first step in determining percentiles is to find the number of individuals who are located at or below each point in the distribution. This can be done most easily with a frequency distribution table by simply counting the number who are in or below each category on the scale. The resulting values are called *cumulative frequencies* because they represent the accumulation of individuals as you move up the scale.

> EXAMPLE 2.4
> In the following frequency distribution table we have included a cumulative frequency column headed by *cf*. For each row the cumulative frequency value is obtained by adding up the frequencies in that category or lower. For

example, the score $X = 3$ has a cumulative frequency of 14 because exactly 14 individuals had scores in this category or in a lower category.

X	f	cf
5	1	20
4	5	19
3	8	14
2	4	6
1	2	2

The cumulative frequencies show the number of individuals located at or below each score. To find percentiles, we must convert these frequencies into percentages. The resulting values are called cumulative percentages because they show the percent of individuals who are accumulated as you move up the scale.

EXAMPLE 2.5

This time we have added a cumulative percentage column (c%) to the frequency distribution table from Example 2.4. The values in this column represent the percent of the individuals who are located in each category or lower. For example, 70% of the individuals (14 out of 20) had scores of $X = 3$ or lower. Cumulative percentages can be computed by

$$c\% = \frac{cf}{N}(100\%)$$

X	f	cf	c%
5	1	20	100%
4	5	19	95%
3	8	14	70%
2	4	6	30%
1	2	2	10%

The cumulative percentages in a frequency distribution table give the percent of individuals with scores at or below each X value. However, you must remember that the X values in the table are not points on the scale but rather intervals. A score of $X = 2$, for example, means that the measurement was somewhere between the real limits of 1.5 and 2.5. Thus, when a table shows that a score of $X = 2$ has a cumulative percentage of 30%, you should interpret this as meaning that 30% of the individuals have been accumulated by the time you reach the top of the interval for $X = 2$. Notice that each cumulative percentage value is associated with the upper real limit of its interval. This point is demonstrated in Figure 2.14, which shows the same data that were used in Example 2.5. Figure 2.14 shows that two people, or 10%, had scores of $X = 1$; that is, two people had scores between 0.5 and 1.5. You cannot be sure that all such individuals have been accumulated until you reach 1.5, the upper real limit of the interval. Similarly, a cumulative percentage of 30% is reached at 2.5 on the scale, a percentage of 70% is reached at 3.5, etc.

Interpolation

It is possible to determine some percentiles and percentile ranks directly from a frequency distribution table provided that the percentiles are upper real limits and that the ranks are percentages that appear in the table. Using the table in Example 2.5, for example, you should be able to answer the following questions:

1. What is the 95th percentile? (Answer: $X = 4.5$.)
2. What is the percentile rank for $X = 3.5$? (Answer: 70%.)

However, there are many values that do not appear directly in the table, and it is impossible to determine these values precisely. Referring to the table in Example 2.5 again,

1. What is the 50th percentile?
2. What is the percentile rank for $X = 4$?

Because these values are not specifically reported in the table, you cannot answer the questions. However, it is possible to obtain estimates of these intermediate values by using a standard procedure known as interpolation.

Before we apply the process of interpolation to percentiles and percentile ranks, we will use a simple, commonsense example to intro-

---

Figure 2.14

The relationship between cumulative frequencies (*cf* values) and upper real limits. Notice that two people had scores of $X = 1$. These two individuals are located between the real limits of 0.5 and 1.5. Although their exact locations are not known, you can be certain that both had scores below the upper real limit of 1.5.

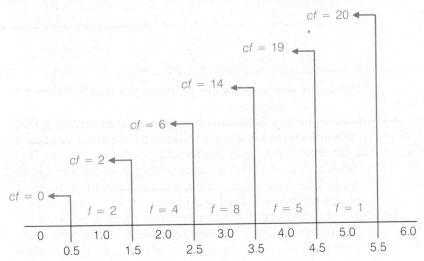

duce this concept. Suppose you hear the weather report at 8 a.m. and again at noon. At 8:00 the temperature was 60°, and at noon it was 64°. What is your estimate of the temperature at 9:00? To make your task a bit easier, we shall sketch a table showing the time and temperature relations:

Time	Temperature
8:00	60
12:00	64

If you estimated the temperature to be 61° at 9:00, you have done interpolation. You probably went through the following logical steps:

1. The total time from 8:00 to 12:00 is 4 hours.
2. During this time, the temperature changed 4°.
3. 9:00 represents 1 hour, or one-fourth of the total time.
4. Assuming that the temperature went up at a constant rate, it should have increased by 1° during the hour because 1° equals one-fourth of the temperature change.

Now try answering the following questions about other times and temperatures:

1. At what time did the temperature reach 62°?
2. What was the temperature at 11:00?

If you got answers of 10:00 and 63°, you have mastered the process of interpolation.

Notice that interpolation provides a method for finding intermediate values, that is, values that are located between two specified numbers. This is exactly the problem we faced with percentiles and percentile ranks. Some values are given in the table, but others are not. Also notice that interpolation only *estimates* the intermediate values. In the time and temperature example we do not know what the temperature was at 10:00. It may have soared to 80° between 8:00 and noon. The basic assumption underlying interpolation is that the change from one end of the interval to the other is a regular, linear change. We assumed, for example, that the temperature changed in a regular, linear manner throughout the time period. Because interpolation is based on this assumption, the values we calculate are only estimates. The general process of interpolation can be summarized as follows:

1. A single interval is measured on two separate scales (for example, time and temperature). The endpoints of the interval are known for each scale.
2. You are given an intermediate value on one of the scales. The problem is to find the corresponding intermediate value on the other scale.
3. The interpolation process requires four steps:
   a. Find the width of the interval on both scales.
   b. Locate the position of the intermediate value in the

interval. This position corresponds to a fraction of the whole interval:

$$\text{fraction} = \frac{\text{distance from the top of the interval}}{\text{interval width}}$$

c. Use this fraction to determine the distance from the top of the interval on the other scale:

distance = fraction(width)

d. Use the distance from the top to determine the position on the other scale.

The following examples demonstrate the process of interpolation as it is applied to percentiles and percentile ranks. The key to successfully working these problems is that each cumulative percentage in the table should be associated with the upper real limits of its score interval.

You may notice that in each of these problems we use interpolation working from the *top* of the interval. However, this choice is arbitrary, and you should realize that interpolation can be done just as easily working from the bottom of the interval.

EXAMPLE 2.6

Using the following distribution of scores, we will find the percentile rank corresponding to $X = 7.0$:

X	f	cf	c%
10	2	25	100%
9	8	23	92%
8	4	15	60%
7	6	11	44%
6	4	5	20%
5	1	1	4%

Note that $X = 7.0$ is located in the interval bounded by real limits of 6.5 and 7.5. The cumulative percentages corresponding to these real limits are 20% and 44%, respectively. These values are shown in the following table:

Scores (X)	Percentages
7.5	44%
7.0	?
6.5	20%

For interpolation problems, it is always helpful to sketch a table showing the range on both scales.

STEP 1. For the scores, the width of the interval is 1 point. For the percentages, the width is 24 points.

STEP 2. Our particular score is located 0.5 point from the top of the interval. This is exactly halfway down in the interval.

STEP 3.   Halfway down on the percentage scale would be

$$\tfrac{1}{2}(24 \text{ points}) = 12 \text{ points}$$

STEP 4.   For the percentages, the top of the interval is 44%, so 12 points down would be

$$44\% - 12\% = 32\%$$

This is the answer. A score of $X = 7.0$ corresponds to a percentile rank of 32%.

EXAMPLE 2.7

Using the same distribution of scores that was given in Example 2.6, we will find the 50th percentile.

First, you should notice that 50% is not given in the table. It is located between the table values of 60% and 44%. These two percentages correspond to real limits of $X = 8.5$ and $X = 7.5$, respectively. These values are shown in the following table:

Scores (X)	Percentages
8.5	60%
?	50%
7.5	44%

STEP 1.   For the scores, the width of the interval is 1 point. For the percentages, the width is 16 points.

STEP 2.   The value of 50% is located 10 points down from the top of the interval. This gives a fraction of the total interval equal to

$$\text{fraction} = \frac{10}{16} = 0.625$$

STEP 3.   Using this same fraction on the scores produces a distance of

$$\text{distance} = 0.625(1) = 0.625$$

The position we want is 0.625 point down from the top of the interval.

STEP 4.   For the scores, the top of the interval is 8.5, so 0.625 points down would be

$$8.5 - 0.625 = 7.875$$

This is the answer. The 50th percentile is $X = 7.875$.

This same interpolation procedure can be used with data that have been grouped into class intervals. Once again, you must remember that the cumulative percentage values are associated with the upper real limits of each interval. The following two examples demonstrate the calculation of percentiles and percentile ranks using data in a grouped frequency distribution.

EXAMPLE 2.8
Using the following distribution of scores, we will use interpolation to find the 50th percentile:

X	f	cf	c%
20–24	2	20	100%
15–19	3	18	90%
10–14	3	15	75%
5–9	10	12	60%
0–4	2	2	10%

A percentage value of 50% is not given in the table; however, it is located between 60% and 10%, which are given. These two percentage values correspond to scores of 9.5 and 4.5, respectively. These values are the upper and lower real limits of the 5–9 interval. These values are shown in the following table:

Scores	Percentages
9.5	60%
?	50%
4.5	10%

STEP 1.   For the scores, the width of the interval is 5 points. For the percentages, the width is 50 points.

STEP 2.   The value of 50% is located 10 points from the top of the percentage interval. As a fraction of the whole interval, this is 10 out of 50 or $\frac{1}{5}$ of the total interval.

STEP 3.   Using this same fraction for the scores, we obtain a distance of

$$\text{distance} = \tfrac{1}{5}(5 \text{ points}) = 1 \text{ point}$$

The location we want is 1 point down from the top of the score interval.

STEP 4.   Because the top of the interval is 9.5, the position we want is

$$9.5 - 1 = 8.5$$

This is the answer. The 50th percentile is $X = 8.5$.

EXAMPLE 2.9
Using the same grouped frequency distribution that was given in Example 2.8, we will find the percentile rank corresponding to $X = 21$.

The score $X = 21$ is located in the class interval 20–24. The real limits of this interval are 19.5 and 24.5. The cumulative percentages corresponding to these limits are 90% and 100%, respectively. These values are shown in the following table:

Scores	Percentages
24.5	100%
21	?
19.5	90%

STEP 1. For the scores, the width of the interval is 5 points. For the percentages, the width is 10 points.

STEP 2. The value $X = 21$ is located 3.5 points from the top of the score interval. This distance corresponds to a fraction of the total interval equal to

$$\text{fraction} = \frac{3.5}{5} = 0.70$$

STEP 3. Using this same fraction for the percentages, we obtain a distance equal to

0.70(10 points) = 7 points

The value we want is located 7 points down from the top of the interval.

STEP 4. The top of the percentage interval is 100%, so the position we want is

100% − 7% = 93%

This is the answer. The score $X = 21$ has a percentile rank of 93%.

1. For the distribution of scores presented in the following table,
   a. Find the 60th percentile.
   b. Find the percentile rank for $X = 39.5$.
   c. Find the 40th percentile.
   d. Find the percentile rank for $X = 32$.

X	f	cf	c%
40–49	4	25	100%
30–39	6	21	84%
20–29	10	15	60%
10–19	3	5	20%
0–9	2	2	8%

ANSWERS

1. a. $X = 29.5$ is the 60th percentile.
    b. $X = 39.5$ has a rank of 84%.
    c. Because 40% is between the values of 20% and 60% in the table, you must use interpolation. The score corresponding to a rank of 40% is $X = 24.5$.
    d. Because $X = 32$ is between the real limits of 29.5 and 39.5, you must use interpolation. The percentile rank for $X = 32$ is 66%.

2.7
Stem and Leaf Displays

In 1977 J. W. Tukey presented a technique for organizing data that provides a simple alternative to a frequency distribution table or graph (Tukey, 1977). This technique, called a *stem and leaf display*, requires that each score be separated into two parts: the first digit (or digits) is called the *stem*, and the last digit (or digits) is called the *leaf*. For example, $X = 85$ would be separated into a stem of 8 and a leaf of 5. Similarly, $X = 42$ would have a stem of 4 and a leaf of 2. To construct a stem and leaf display for a set of data, the first step is to list all the stems in a column. For the data in Table 2.3, for example, the lowest scores are in the 30s and the highest scores are in the 90s, so the list of stems would be

The general term display is used because a stem and leaf display combines the elements of a table and a graph.

Stems

3
4
5
6
7
8
9

The next step is to go through the data, one score at a time, and write the leaf for each score beside its stem. For the data in Table 2.3, the first score is $X = 83$, so you would write 3 (the leaf) beside the 8 in the column of stems. This process is continued for the entire set of scores. The complete stem and leaf display is shown with the original data in Table 2.3.

Table 2.3

A Set of $N = 24$ Scores Presented as Raw Data and Organized in a Stem and Leaf Display

Data			Stem and Leaf Display	
83	82	63	3	23
62	93	78	4	26
71	68	33	5	6279
76	52	97	6	283
85	42	46	7	1643846
32	57	59	8	3521
56	73	74	9	37
74	81	76		

Comparing Stem and Leaf Displays with Frequency Distributions

You should notice that the stem and leaf display is very similar to a grouped frequency distribution. Each of the stem values corresponds to a class interval. For example, the stem 3 represents all scores in the 30s, that is, all scores in the interval 30–39. The number of leaves in the display show the frequency associated with each stem. It also should be clear that the stem and leaf display has several advantages over a traditional frequency distribution:

1. The stem and leaf display is very easy to construct. By going through the data only one time, you can construct a complete display.

2. The stem and leaf display allows you to identify every individual score in the data. In the display shown in Table 2.3, for example, you know that there were three scores in the 60s, and you know that the specific values were 62, 68, and 63. A frequency distribution would tell you only the frequency, not the specific values.

3. The stem and leaf display provides both a listing of the scores and a picture of the distribution. If a stem and leaf display is placed on its side, it is essentially the same as a frequency distribution histogram (see Figure 2.15).

4. Because the stem and leaf display presents the actual value for each score, it is easy to modify a display if you want a more detailed picture of a distribution. The modification simply requires that each stem be split into two (or more) parts. For example, Table 2.4 shows the same data that were presented in Table 2.3, but now we have split each stem in half. Notice that each stem value is now listed twice in the display. The first half of each stem is associated with the lower leaves (values 0–4), and the second half is associated with the upper leaves (values 5–9). In essence, we have regrouped the distribu-

tion using an interval width of 5 points instead of a width of 10 points in the original display.

Although stem and leaf displays are quite useful, you should be warned that they are considered to be a preliminary means for organizing data. Typically, a researcher would use a stem and leaf display to get a first look at experimental data. The final, published report normally would present the distribution of scores in a traditional frequency distribution table or graph.

Figure 2.15
A grouped frequency distribution histogram and a stem and leaf display showing the distribution of scores from Table 2.3. The stem and leaf display is placed on its side to demonstrate that the display gives the same information that is provided in the histogram.

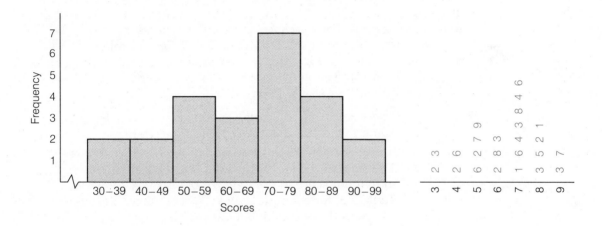

Table 2.4
A Stem and Leaf Display with Each Stem Split into Two Parts[a]

Stem	Leaf
3	23
3	
4	2
4	6
5	2
5	679
6	23
6	8
7	1434
7	686
8	321
8	5
9	3
9	7

[a]Note that each stem value is listed twice: The first occurrence is associated with the lower leaf values (0–4), and the second occurrence is associated with the upper leaf values (5–9). The data shown in this display are taken from Table 2.3.

Comparing Two Distributions with Stem and Leaf Displays

An additional advantage of stem and leaf displays is that two separate sets of data can be presented in a single display. As before, the stems are listed in a column, and the leaves for one set of data are presented on the right-hand side of this column. The leaf values for the second set of data can be placed on the left-hand side of the stem column. For example, in the preview section of this chapter we presented data from an experiment comparing two different study strategies (see Table 2.1). These same data are reproduced in a stem and leaf display in Table 2.5, with the scores for the experimental group shown on the right-hand side of the stems and the control group scores on the left. This single display makes it very easy to see that the experimental group generally had higher scores than the control group.

Table 2.5

A Stem and Leaf Display Showing Two Separate Sets of Data.[a]

```
                    | 1 |
              897   | 1 | 9
    342130341424    | 2 | 432
       57596875     | 2 | 8599798769
            420     | 3 | 103402102
                    | 3 | 56
```

[a]The data are taken from Table 2.1. The scores for the experimental group are shown on the right-hand side of the stems, and the control group scores are on the left-hand side. Note that each stem has been split in half to provide a more detailed picture of the two distributions.

LEARNING
CHECK

1. Use a stem and leaf display to organize the following set of scores: 86, 114, 94, 107, 96, 100, 98, 118, 107, 132, 106, 127, 124, 108, 112, 119, 125, 115
2. Modify the following stem and leaf display by splitting each stem in half so that you obtain a more detailed picture of the distribution:

```
6 | 286
7 | 0619378
8 | 35272949
9 | 2510
```

ANSWERS

1. The stem and leaf display for these data would be

```
 8 | 6
 9 | 468
10 | 70768
11 | 48295
12 | 745
13 | 2
```

2. The modified stem and leaf display would be

```
6 | 2
6 | 86
7 | 013
7 | 6978
8 | 3224
8 | 5799
9 | 210
9 | 5
```

Summary

1. The goal of descriptive statistics is to simplify the organization and presentation of data. One descriptive technique is to place data in a frequency distribution table or graph that shows how the scores are distributed across the measurement scale.

2. A frequency distribution table lists scores (from highest down to lowest) in one column and the frequency of occurrence for each score in a second column. The table may include a proportion column showing the relative frequency for each score:

$$\text{proportion} = p = \frac{f}{N}$$

And the table may include a percentage column showing the percentage associated with each score:

$$\text{percentage} = \% = \frac{f}{N}(100)$$

3. When the scores cover a range that is too broad to list each individual value, it is customary to divide the range into sections called class intervals. These intervals are then listed in the frequency distribution table along with the frequency or number of individuals with scores in each interval. The result is called a grouped frequency distribution. The guidelines for constructing a grouped frequency distribution table are as follows:
   a. There should be about 10 intervals.
   b. The width of each interval should be a simple number (e.g., 2, 5, 10, etc.)
   c. The bottom score in each interval should be a multiple of the width.
   d. All intervals should be the same width, and they should cover the range of scores with no gaps.

4. For a continuous variable, each score corresponds to an interval on the scale. The boundaries that separate intervals are called real limits. The real limits are located exactly halfway between adjacent scores.

5. A frequency distribution graph lists scores on the horizontal axis and frequencies on the vertical axis. There are two types of frequency distribution graphs: histograms or bar graphs and polygons. For a histogram or bar graph, a bar is drawn above each score so that the height of the bar corresponds to the frequency. In histograms the bars extend to the real limits of each score so that adjacent bars touch. Histograms are used with interval and ratio scales. Bar graphs are used with nominal and ordinal scales and are drawn with gaps between the bars. For a polygon, a dot is placed above the midpoint of each score or class interval so that the height of the dot corresponds to the frequency. Then lines are drawn to connect the dots.

6. Shape is one of the basic characteristics used to describe a distribution of scores. Most distributions can be classified as either symmetrical or skewed. A skewed distribution that tails off to the right is said to be positively skewed. If it tails off to the left, it is negatively skewed.

7. Cumulative percentage is the percentage of individuals with scores at or below a particular point in the distribution. The cumulative percentage values are associated with the upper real limits of the corresponding score or interval.

8. Percentiles and percentile ranks are used to describe the position of individual scores within a distribution. Percentile rank gives a cumulative percentage associated with a particular score. A score that is identified by its rank is called a percentile.

9. When a desired percentile or percentile rank is located between two known values, it is possible to estimate the desired value using the process of interpolation. Interpolation assumes a regular linear change between the two known values.

10. A stem and leaf display is an alternative procedure for organizing data. Each score is separated into a stem (the first digit or digits) and a leaf (the last digit or digits). The display consists of the stems listed in a column, with the leaf for each score written beside its stem. A stem and leaf display combines the characteristics of a table and a graph and produces a concise, well-organized picture of the data.

Key Terms

frequency distribution
grouped frequency distribution
range
class interval
upper real limit

symmetrical distribution
positively skewed distribution
negatively skewed distribution
tail(s) of a distribution
percentile

lower real limit
apparent limits
histogram
bar graph
polygon

percentile rank
cumulative frequency *(cf)*
cumulative percentage *(c%)*
interpolation
stem and leaf display

Problems for Chapter 2:
Frequency Distributions

*1. Place the following set of scores in a frequency distribution table, and draw a polygon showing the distribution of scores. Scores: 6, 1, 3, 5, 5, 4, 5, 6, 3, 4, 2, 5, 4.

2. For the set of scores shown in the following frequency distribution table,

   a. How many scores are in the distribution? (N = ?)

   b. Find ΣX for this set of scores.

X	f
4	6
3	1
2	3
1	2

*3. For the following set of scores,

   a. Construct a frequency distribution table to organize the quiz scores.

   b. Draw a frequency distribution histogram for these data.

$$3, \ 5, \ 4, \ 6, \ 2, \ 3, \ 4, \ 1, \ 4, \ 3$$
$$7, \ 7, \ 3, \ 4, \ 5, \ 8, \ 2, \ 4, \ 7, \ 3$$
$$10, \ 2, \ 3, \ 3, \ 6, \ 2, \ 5, \ 4$$

4. Use a frequency distribution table to organize the following set of scores:

$$206, \ 350, \ 590, \ 473, \ 450, \ 483$$
$$112, \ 380, \ 584, \ 620, \ 743, \ 816$$
$$685, \ 592, \ 712, \ 727, \ 686, \ 592$$
$$542, \ 490, \ 684, \ 491, \ 520, \ 380$$

*5. Place the following 35 scores in a grouped frequency distribution table using

   a. An interval width of 2

   b. An interval width of 5

$$23, \quad 12, \quad 16, \quad 16, \quad 17, \quad 19, \quad 28$$
$$20, \quad 14, \quad 21, \quad 18, \quad 24, \quad 29, \quad 24$$
$$18, \quad 21, \quad 22, \quad 27, \quad 21, \quad 25, \quad 19$$
$$22, \quad 23, \quad 21, \quad 30, \quad 27, \quad 23, \quad 18$$
$$25, \quad 22, \quad 31, \quad 27, \quad 16, \quad 15, \quad 23$$

6. Five sets of data are described. For each set the range of scores (lowest to highest) is given. Describe how each set should be presented in a grouped frequency distribution. That is, give the interval width that you would suggest and the number of intervals needed.

   a. 3–24   d. 132–207

   b. 41–93   e. 161–786

   c. 11–18

*7. Complete the cumulative frequency column and the cumulative percentage column for the following table:

X	f	cf	c%
5	1		
4	2		
3	4		
2	1		
1	2		

8. Using the following frequency distribution, find each of the percentiles and percentile ranks requested:

X	f	cf	c%
6	2	20	100%
5	2	18	90%
4	4	16	80%
3	6	12	60%
2	4	6	30%
1	2	2	10%

   a. What is the 30th percentile?

   b. What is the percentile rank for X = 4.5?

   c. What is the 70th percentile?

   d. What is the percentile rank for X = 3?

   e. What is the minimum score needed to be in the top 25% of this distribution? That is, find the 75th percentile.

*9. Find each value requested for the frequency distribution presented in the following table:

X	f	cf	c%
20–24	10	50	100%
15–19	10	40	80%
10–14	15	30	60%
5–9	10	15	30%
0–5	5	5	10%

a. Find the percentile rank for $X = 17$.

b. What is the 84th percentile?

c. Find the percentile rank for $X = 10$.

d. If this were a distribution of quiz scores and the instructor decided to fail the bottom 33% of the class, what score would separate passing from failing?

10. The following two sets of scores are from two different sections of an introductory statistics class:

		Section I							Section II			
70	83	60	68	58	85		93	57	83	70	86	76
73	76	70	67	83	65		85	67	72	82	77	87
77	75	93	89	76	75		69	87	89	91	77	94
92	63	62	79	86	80		97	92	62	85	72	87
74	81	69	78	80	71		65	81	75	90	82	79
82	85	72	80	66	78		92	85	95	74	89	80
73	86	75	91	79	83		91	86	93	97		

a. Organize the scores from each section into a grouped frequency distribution polygon using an interval width of 5 for each graph.

b. Describe the similarities and differences between the two sections.

*11. A psychologist would like to examine the effects of diet on intelligence. Two groups of rats are selected with 12 rats in each group. One group is fed the regular diet of Rat Chow, while the second group has special vitamins and minerals added to their food. After 6 months each rat is tested on a discrimination problem. The psychologist records the number of errors each animal makes before it solves the problem. The data from this experiment are as follows:

Regular diet scores: 13, 11, 12, 13, 11, 9
12, 10, 12, 14, 10, 12

Special diet scores: 9, 8, 7, 8, 9, 10
7, 8, 9, 6, 8, 10

a. Identify the independent variable and the dependent variable for this experiment.

b. Sketch a frequency distribution polygon for the group of rats with the regular diet. On the same graph (in a different color), sketch the distribution for the rats with the special diet.

c. From looking at your graphs, would you say that the special diet had any effect on intelligence? Explain your answer.

12. College officials recently conducted a survey to determine students' attitudes toward extending the library hours. Four different groups of students were surveyed, representing the four major subdivisions of the college. The average score for each group was as follows:

Humanities: 7.25

Sciences: 5.69

Professions: 6.85

Fine arts: 5.90

Use a graph to present the results of this survey.

*13. A recent study reports the effect of alcohol on simple reaction time. The relation between reaction time and blood alcohol level is shown in the following table:

Blood Alcohol Level	Reaction Time
0.06	205
0.08	214
0.10	232
0.12	230
0.14	241

Construct a graph showing these data.

14. Use a stem and leaf display to organize the following scores:

43, 56, 35, 47, 48, 52, 66, 57, 46

39, 43, 47, 61, 55, 50, 49, 39, 40

*15. Place both sets of data from Problem 10 in a single stem and leaf display. (Put the Section I scores on one side of the stems and the Section II scores on the other side.)

16. Place the following set of scores in a frequency distribution table:

1, 3, 1, 1, 4, 1, 4, 5, 6, 2, 1, 1, 5

1, 3, 2, 1, 6, 2, 4, 5, 2, 3, 2, 3

Compute the proportion and the percentage of individuals with each score. From your frequency distribution table, you should be able to identify the shape of this distribution.

*17. The same set of scores is presented in a regular frequency distribution table and in a grouped frequency distribution table as follows:

X	f	cf	c%
7	2	40	100%
6	4	38	95%
5	4	34	85%
4	11	30	75%
3	9	19	47.5%
2	6	10	25%
1	4	4	10%

X	f	cf	c%
6–7	6	40	100%
4–5	15	34	85%
2–3	15	19	47.5%
0–1	4	4	10%

Notice that when the scores are grouped into class intervals you lose information about the distribution.

a. Find the 25th percentile for each frequency distribution table. Note that this value is determined precisely in one table but must be estimated in the other.

b. Find the percentile rank for $X = 4$ for each table. Which value would you consider more accurate?

18. The same final exam is given to two different sections of a general psychology course. The scores for each section are as follows:

Section A					Section B			
69	52	74	46		70	86	75	50
37	43	52	58		62	73	72	85
48	59	90	56		95	48	53	79
82	76	35	64		65	47	39	82
81	60	53	39		71	91	88	90
41	45	71	65		83	58	61	77
55					61			

a. Construct a grouped frequency distribution histogram using an interval width of 10 points for each of the two sections.

b. Describe the differences between the two distributions.

c. If Tom had a score of $X = 65$ on the exam, find his percentile rank if he were in section A.

d. Find Tom's percentile rank if he were in section B. (Note that percentile rank measures position in a distribution relative to the other scores.)

*19. For the past several weeks a bored statistician has kept records of the post position of the winning horse for each race at a local track. The following data represent all races with exactly eight horses:

Post Position of the Winning Horse

1	3	3	7	4	5	1
3	2	8	5	3	6	1
4	7	1	2	5	8	5
3	4	8	1	8	3	2
6	7	3	4	2	6	5
4	8	2	6	4	7	2

a. Construct a frequency distribution graph showing the number of winners for each of the eight post positions.

b. Describe the shape of this frequency distribution.

c. On the basis of these data, if you were betting on a race where you knew nothing about the horses or the jockeys, which post position would you choose? Explain your answer.

 20. The following data are attitude scores for a sample of 40 students. A high score indicates a positive attitude, and a low score indicates a negative attitude.

Attitude Scores

68	22	9	73	62	52	14	46
27	60	31	26	74	61	13	5
18	53	79	58	16	62	7	55
61	12	77	43	30	68	23	11
54	70	42	78	10	66	32	25

a. Construct a stem and leaf display to organize these data.

b. Using your stem and leaf display, construct a grouped frequency distribution table for these scores.

c. Looking at the distribution of scores, which of the following descriptions best fit these data?

  1. This group has a generally positive attitude.
  2. This group has a generally negative attitude.
  3. This group is sharply split with attitudes at both extremes.

CHAPTER 3

Central Tendency

TOOLS
YOU WILL
NEED

The following items are considered essential background material for this chapter. If you doubt your knowledge of any of these items, you should review the appropriate chapter or section before proceeding.

1. Summation notation (Chapter 1)
2. Frequency distributions (Chapter 2)
3. Cumulative frequency (Chapter 2)
4. Interpolation (Chapter 2)

In a classic study examining the relation between heredity and intelligence, Tryon (1940) used a selective breeding program to develop separate strains of "smart" and "dumb" rats. Starting with a large sample of rats, Tryon tested each animal on a maze-learning problem. Based on their error scores for the maze, the brightest rats and the dullest rats were selected from this sample. The brightest males were mated with the brightest females. Similarly, the dullest rats were interbred. This process of testing and selectively breeding was continued for several generations until Tryon had established a line of maze-bright rats and a separate line of maze-dull rats. The results obtained by Tryon are shown in Figure 3.1.

Notice that after seven generations there is an obvious difference between the two groups. As a rule, the maze-bright animals outperform the maze-dull animals. It is tempting to describe the results of this experiment by saying that the maze-bright rats are better learners than the maze-dull rats. However, you should notice that there is some overlap between the two groups; not all of the bright rats are really bright, and not all of the dull animals are really dull. In fact, some of the animals bred for brightness are actually poorer learners than

some of the animals bred for dullness. What is needed is a simple way of describing the general difference between these two groups while still acknowledging the fact that some individuals may contradict the general trend.

The solution to this problem is to avoid comparisons between specific individuals. Instead, we will identify the typical or average rat as the representative for each group. Then the experimental results can be described by saying that the typical maze-bright rat is a faster learner than the typical maze-dull rat. On the average, the bright rats really are brighter.

In this chapter we will introduce the statistical techniques used to identify the typical or average score for a distribution. Although there are several reasons for defining the average score, the primary advantage of an average is that it provides a single number that describes an entire distribution and can be used for comparison with other distributions.

As a footnote, you should know that later research with Tryon's rats revealed that the maze-bright rats were not really more intelligent than the maze-dull rats. Although the bright rats had developed specific abilities that are useful in mazes, the dull rats proved to be just as smart when tested on a variety of other tasks.

Figure 3.1

Distribution of error scores for the original sample of rats (Parents, top figure) and for the two separate lines that were selectively bred for either good or poor maze performance (Maze-Bright and Maze-Dull, bottom figure).

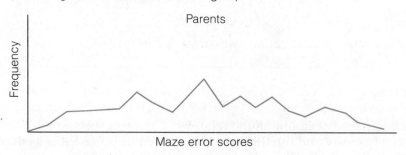

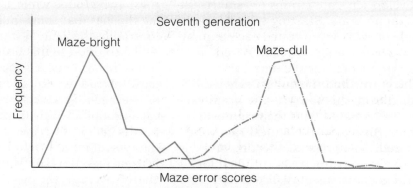

Tyron, R. C. (1940). "Genetic differences in maze-learning ability in rats." *The Thirty-ninth Yearbook of the National Society for the Study of Education*, 111–119. Adapted and reprinted with permission of the National Society for the Study of Education.

3.1
Introduction

The goal in measuring central tendency is to describe a group of individuals (more accurately, their scores) with a single measurement. Ideally, the value we use to describe the group will be the single value that is most representative of all the individuals.

DEFINITION

Central tendency is a statistical measure that identifies the single most representative score for an entire distribution.

Usually, we want to choose a value in the middle of the distribution because central scores are often the most representative. In everyday language, the goal of central tendency is to find the "average" or "typical" individual. For example, recent archeological discoveries indicate that the average height for men in the ancient Roman city of Pompeii was 5 feet, 7 inches. Obviously, not all of the men were exactly 5 feet, 7 inches, but this average value provides a general description of the population. Measures of central tendency also are useful for making comparisons between groups of individuals or between sets of figures. For example, weather data indicate that during the month of December, Seattle averages only 2 hours of sunshine per day, while Miami averages over 6 hours. The point of these examples is to demonstrate the great advantage of being able to describe a large set of data with a single, representative number. Central tendency characterizes what is typical for a large population and in doing so makes large amounts of data more digestible. Statisticians sometimes use the expression "number crunching" to illustrate this aspect of data description. That is, we take a distribution consisting of many scores and "crunch" them down to a single value that describes them all.

There are three standard ways to measure central tendency: the mode, the median, and the mean. They are computed differently and have different characteristics. To decide which of the three measures is best for any particular distribution, you should keep in mind that the general purpose of central tendency is to find the single most representative score. Each of the three measures we shall present has been developed to work best in a specific situation. We will examine this issue in more detail after we define the three measures.

3.2
The Mode

In its common usage, the word *mode* means "the customary fashion" or "a popular style." The statistical definition is similar in that the mode is the most common observation among a group of scores.

DEFINITION

In a frequency distribution, the *mode* is the score that has the greatest frequency.

The mode can be used to describe what is typical for any scale of measurement (see Chapter 1). Suppose, for example, you ask a sample of 100 students on campus to name their favorite restaurant in town. Your data might look like the results shown in Table 3.1. These are nominal data because the scale of measurement involves separate,

Table 3.1

Favorite Restaurants Named by a Sample of $N = 100$ Students

Restaurant	f
College Grill	5
George & Harry's	16
Luigi's	42
Oasis Diner	18
Roxbury Inn	7
Sutter's Mill	12

unordered categories (restaurants). For these data, the modal response is Luigi's. This restaurant was named most frequently as a favorite place.

In a graph, the mode is identified by the tallest part of the figure. Figure 3.2 shows the age at which children take their first steps (hypothetical data). The tallest bar in the histogram represents the greatest frequency. For this distribution, the mode is 14 months.

It is possible for a distribution to have more than one mode. Figure 3.3 shows the number of fish caught at various times during the day. There are two distinct peaks in this distribution, one at 6 a.m. and one at 6 p.m. Each of these values is a mode in the distribution. Note that the two modes do not have identical frequencies. Twelve fish were caught at 6 a.m., and 11 were caught at 6 p.m. Nonetheless, both of these points are called modes because they correspond to distinct peaks in the distribution. The taller peak is called the *major mode,* and the shorter one is the *minor mode.* Of course, it also is possible to have a distribution with two (or more) separate peaks that are exactly the same height. A distribution with two modes is said to be *bimodal.*

Figure 3.2

Frequency distribution for the age at which children take their first steps.

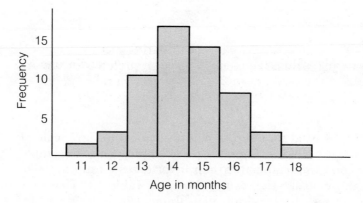

When a distribution has more than two modes, it is called *multimodal*. It also is common for a distribution with several equally high points to be described as having no mode.

Figure 3.3

The effect of time of day on the number of fish caught.

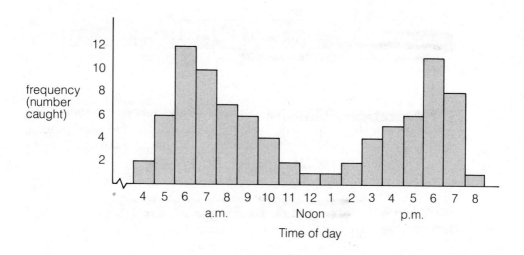

LEARNING CHECK

1. Find the mode for the set of scores shown in the following frequency distribution table:

X	f
5	2
4	6
3	4
2	2
1	1

2. In a recent survey comparing picture quality for three brands of color televisions, 63 people preferred brand A, 29 people preferred brand B, and 58 people preferred brand C. What is the mode for this distribution?

ANSWERS

1. The mode is X = 4.
2. The mode is brand A.

3.3
The Median

The median is the score that divides a distribution exactly in half. Exactly one-half of the scores are less than or equal to the median, and exactly one-half are greater than or equal to the median. Because exactly 50% of the scores fall at or below the median, this value is equivalent to the 50th percentile (see Chapter 2).

DEFINITION

The *median* is the 50th percentile. Exactly 50% of the individuals in a distribution have scores at or below the median.

The goal of the median is to determine the precise midpoint of a distribution. This commonsense goal is demonstrated in the following three examples. The three examples are intended to cover all of the different types of data you are likely to encounter.

Method 1: When N Is an Odd Number

Consider the following set of $N = 5$ scores:

8, 5, 3, 11, 10

By midpoint of the distribution we mean that the area in the graph is divided into two equal parts. We are not locating the midpoint of the range of scores.

To find the median, first rearrange the scores in ascending order, that is, from lowest to highest:

3, 5, 8, 10, 11

The middle score is $X = 8$, so the median is equal to 8.0. In a graph, the median divides the space or area of the graph in half (Figure 3.4). The amount of area above the median consists of $2\frac{1}{2}$ "boxes," the same as the area below the median (shaded portion).

Figure 3.4

The median divides the area in the graph exactly in half.

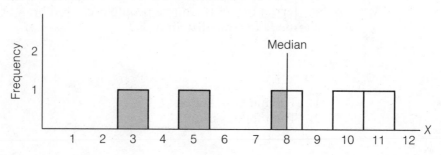

Method 2: When N Is an Even Number

With an even number of scores in the distribution, the method for finding the median is somewhat different. Consider the following population:

   8, 3, 4, 5, 3, 7

Again, it is helpful to arrange the scores in ascending order:

   3, 3, 4, 5, 7, 8

Now we select the middle pair of scores (4 and 5), add them together, and divide by 2:

$$\text{median} = \frac{4+5}{2} = \frac{9}{2} = 4.5$$

In terms of a graph, we see again that the median divides the area of the distribution exactly in half (Figure 3.5). There are three scores (or boxes) above the median and three below the median.

Method 3: When There Are Several Scores with the Same Value in the Middle of the Distribution

In nearly all cases, one of the two methods already outlined will provide you with a reasonable value for the median. However, when you have more than one individual at the median, these simple procedures may oversimplify the computations. Consider the following set of scores:

   1, 2, 2, 3, 4, 4, 4, 4, 4, 5

There are 10 scores (an even number), so you normally would use method 2 and average the middle pair to determine the median. By this method, the median would be 4.

Figure 3.5
The median divides the area of the graph exactly in half.

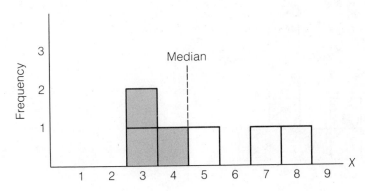

In many ways this is a perfectly legitimate value for the median. However, when you look closely at the distribution of scores (see Figure 3.6), you probably get the clear impression that $X = 4$ is not in the middle. The problem comes from the tendency to interpret the value of 4 as meaning exactly 4.00 instead of meaning an interval from 3.5 to 4.5. The simple method for computing the median has determined that the value we want is located in this interval. To locate the median with greater precision, it is necessary to use the process of interpolation (see Chapter 2, page 57). The following example demonstrates how interpolation is used to find the median.

EXAMPLE 3.1

For this example we will use the data shown in Figure 3.6. The data are reproduced in the following frequency distribution table:

X	f	cf
5	1	10
4	5	9
3	1	4
2	2	3
1	1	1

Note that we have included a cumulative frequency column in this table. Because the median divides the distribution exactly in half, we want 5 of the 10 scores above the median and 5 below. Thus, we are looking for the score that corresponds to a cumulative frequency of 5.

A cumulative frequency of 5 does not appear in the table. It is located between the *cf* values of 4 and 9, so we must interpolate. The cumulative frequency of 4 is reached at a score of $X = 3.5$ (the upper real limit of the 3s). The cumula-

---

Figure 3.6

A distribution with several scores clustered at the median.

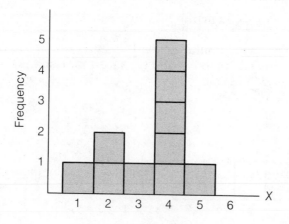

tive frequency of 9 is reached at $X = 4.5$. These cumulative frequencies and their associated scores are as follows:

Score (X)	Cumulative Frequency
4.5	9
$X = ?$ ------------------------- $cf = 5$	
3.5	4

The cumulative frequencies cover a range from 9 to 4. The value we have, $cf = 5$, is located four-fifths of the way down from the top of this interval.

The scores cover a range of one point, so four-fifths of this interval would be $\frac{4}{5}(1) = 0.80$. Starting at the top and moving down 0.80 gives a score of

$$X = 4.5 - 0.80 = 3.70$$

The median for this set of scores is 3.70. This is the point that has exactly 5 scores at or below it ($cf = 5$).

3.4
The Mean

The mean, commonly known as the arithmetic average, is computed by adding up all the scores in the distribution and dividing by the number of scores. The mean for a population will be identified by the Greek letter mu, μ (pronounced "myoo"), and the mean for a sample will be identified by $\overline{X}$ (read "x-bar").

DEFINITION

The *mean* for a distribution is the sum of the scores divided by the number of scores.

The formula for the population mean is

$$(3.1) \quad \mu = \frac{\Sigma X}{N}$$

First, sum all the scores in the population and then divide by N. For a sample, the computation is done the same way, but the formula uses symbols that signify sample values:

$$(3.2) \quad \text{sample mean} = \overline{X} = \frac{\Sigma X}{n}$$

In general, we will use Greek letters to identify characteristics of a population and letters of our own alphabet to stand for sample values. If a mean is identified with the symbol $\overline{X}$, you should realize that we are dealing with a sample. Also note that n is used as the symbol for the number of scores in the sample.

EXAMPLE 3.2

For a population of $N = 4$ scores,

$$3, \quad 3, \quad 4, \quad 6$$

the mean would be

$$\mu = \frac{\Sigma X}{N} = \frac{16}{4} = 4$$

An alternative way to think of the mean is to consider it as the amount each individual would get if the total (ΣX) were divided equally among all the individuals (N) in the population. This somewhat socialistic viewpoint is particularly useful in problems where you know the mean and must find the total. Consider the following example.

EXAMPLE 3.3

A group of six students decided to earn some extra money one weekend picking vegetables at a local farm. The average earnings for this group was $30. If they decide to pool all their money together for a party, how much will they have?

You don't know how much money each student earned. But you do know that the average is $30. This is the amount that each student would have if the total were divided equally. For each of the six students to have $30, you must start with 6 × $30 = $180. The total, ΣX, is $180. To check this answer, use the formula for the mean:

$$\mu = \frac{\Sigma X}{N} = \frac{\$180}{6} = \$30$$

The Weighted Mean

Often it is necessary to combine two sets of scores and then find the overall mean for the combined group. For example, an instructor teaching two sections of introductory psychology obtains an average quiz score of $\overline{X} = 6$ for the 12 students in one section and an average of $\overline{X} = 7$ for the 8 students in the other section. If the two sections are combined, what is the mean for the total group?

The solution to this problem is straightforward if you remember the definition of the mean:

$$\overline{X} = \frac{\Sigma X}{n}$$

To find the overall mean, we must first find the total number of students (n) and we must find the overall sum of scores for the combined group (ΣX). Finding the number of students is easy. If there are $n = 12$ in one group and $n = 8$ in the other, then there must be $n = 20$ (12 + 8) in the combined group. To find the sum of scores for the combined group, we will use this same method: First find the sum for one group, then find the sum for the other, and then add the two sums together.

We know that the first section has $n = 12$ and $\overline{X} = 6$. Using these values in the equation for the mean gives

$$\overline{X} = \frac{\Sigma X}{n}$$

$$6 = \frac{\Sigma X}{12}$$

$$12(6) = \Sigma X$$

$$72 = \Sigma X$$

The second section has $n = 8$ and $\overline{X} = 7$, so ΣX must be equal to 56. When these two groups are combined, the sum of all 20 scores will be

$$128 = 72 + 56$$

Finally, the mean for the combined group is

$$\overline{X} = \frac{\Sigma X}{n} = \frac{128}{20} = 6.4$$

Notice that this value is not obtained by simply averaging the two means. (If we had simply averaged $\overline{X} = 6$ and $\overline{X} = 7$, we would obtain a mean of 6.5.) Because the samples are not the same size, one will make a larger contribution to the total group and, therefore, will carry more weight in determining the overall mean. For this reason, the overall mean we have calculated is called the weighted mean. In this example, the overall mean of $\overline{X} = 6.4$ is closer to the value of $\overline{X} = 6$ (the larger sample) than it is to $\overline{X} = 7$ (the smaller sample).

Computing the Mean from a Frequency Distribution Table

Table 3.2 shows the scores on a quiz for a section of statistics students. Instead of listing all of the individual scores, these data are organized into a frequency distribution table. To compute the mean for this sample, you must use all the information in the table, the f values as well as the X values.

Table 3.2

Statistics Quiz Scores for a Section of $n = 8$ Students

Quiz Score (X)	f	fX
10	1	10
9	2	18
8	4	32
7	0	0
6	1	6

It is very common for people to make mistakes when determining ΣX from a frequency distribution table. Often the column labeled X is summed, while the frequency column is ignored. Be sure to use the information in the f column when determining ΣX.

To find the mean for this sample, we will need the sum of the scores (ΣX) and the number of scores (n). The number n can be found by summing the frequencies:

$$n = \Sigma f = 8$$

Note that there is one 10, two 9s, four 8s, and one 6 for a total of $n = 8$ scores. To find ΣX, you must be careful to add up all eight scores:

$$\Sigma X = 10 + 9 + 9 + 8 + 8 + 8 + 8 + 6 = 66$$

This sum also can be found by multiplying each score by its frequency and then adding up the results. This is done in the third column (fX) in Table 3.2. Note, for example, that the two 9s contribute 18 to the total.

Once you have found ΣX and n, you compute the mean as usual:

$$\bar{X} = \frac{\Sigma X}{n} = \frac{\Sigma fX}{\Sigma f} = \frac{66}{8} = 8.25$$

LEARNING CHECK

1. Compute the mean for the sample of scores shown in the following frequency distribution table:

X	f
4	2
3	4
2	3
1	1

2. If the following two samples are combined, what is the value of the mean for the total group:

Sample 1: $n = 4$, $\overline{X} = 30$
Sample 2: $n = 16$, $\overline{X} = 50$

ANSWERS

1. $\overline{X} = \frac{27}{10} = 2.7$

2. $\overline{X} = \frac{920}{20} = 46$

Characteristics of the Mean

The mean has many characteristics that will be important in future discussions. In general, these characteristics result from the fact that every score in the distribution contributes to the value of the mean. Specifically, every score must be added into the total in order to compute the mean. Four of the more important characteristics will now be discussed.

1. *Changing a Score or Introducing a New Score.* Changing the value of any score, or adding a new score to the distribution, will change the mean. For example, the quiz scores for a psychology lab section consist of

9, 8, 7, 5, and 1

The mean for this sample is

$$\overline{X} = \frac{\Sigma X}{n} = \frac{30}{5} = 6.00$$

Suppose that the student who received the score of $X = 1$ returned a few days later and explained that she was ill on the day of the quiz. In fact, she went straight to the infirmary after class and was admitted for two days with the flu. Out of the goodness of the instructor's heart, the student was given a makeup quiz, and she received an 8. By having changed her score from 1 to 8, the distribution now consists of

9, 8, 7, 5, and 8

The new mean is

$$\overline{X} = \frac{\Sigma X}{n} = \frac{37}{5} = 7.40$$

Changing a single score in this sample has given us a different mean.

2. *Adding or Subtracting a Constant from Each Score.* If a constant value is added to every score in a distribution, the same constant will be added to the mean. Similarly, if you subtract a constant from every score, the same constant will be subtracted from the mean.

Consider the feeding scores for a sample of $n = 6$ rats. See Table 3.3. These scores are the amounts of food (in grams) they ate during a 24-hour testing session. The $\Sigma X = 26$ for $n = 6$ rats, so $\overline{X} = 4.33$.

On the following day, each rat is given an experimental drug that reduces appetite. Suppose that this drug has the effect of reducing the meal size by 2 grams for each rat. Note that the effect of the drug is to subtract a constant (two points) from each rat's feeding score. The new distribution is shown in Table 3.4. Now $\Sigma X = 14$ and n is still 6, so the mean amount of food consumed is $\overline{X} = 2.33$. Subtracting two points from each score has changed the mean by the same constant, from $\overline{X} = 4.33$ to $\overline{X} = 2.33$. (It is important to note that experimental effects are practically never so simple as the adding or subtracting of a constant. Nonetheless, the principle of this characteristic of the mean is important and will be addressed in later chapters when we are using statistics to evaluate the effects of experimental manipulations.)

Table 3.3
Amount of Food (in Grams) Consumed During Baseline Session

Rat's Identification	Amount (X)
A	6
B	3
C	5
D	3
E	4
F	5

Table 3.4
Amount of Food (in Grams) Consumed After Drug Injections

Rat	Baseline Score Minus Constant	Drug Score
A	6 − 2	4
B	3 − 2	1
C	5 − 2	3
D	3 − 2	1
E	4 − 2	2
F	5 − 2	3

Similar to subtraction, adding a constant value to every score in the distribution will increase the mean by that constant. Suppose the drug increased appetite and caused every animal to eat 5 more grams of food. Adding five points to each of the original scores would give us a new mean of $4.33 + 5 = 9.33$; the new mean equals the original mean plus five points. This situation is shown graphically in Figure 3.7. Notice that adding five points to each score simply moves that score five points up the scale. As a result, the entire distribution is shifted to a new location, and the mean also is moved to a new position five points higher than the original mean.

Figure 3.7

The original distribution of feeding scores for our sample of
$n = 6$ rats and the distribution that is obtained after adding five
points to each rat's score.

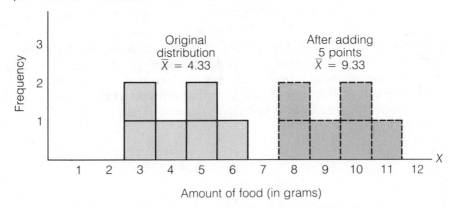

3. *Multiplying or Dividing Each Score by a Constant.* If every score in a distribution is multiplied by (or divided by) a constant value, the mean will be changed in the same way.

Suppose that a sample of $n = 5$ people give estimates of line length in a perception study. Table 3.5 shows the estimates given by the subjects when the stimulus was a 12-inch line. Although the people were asked to estimate length in inches (for their convenience), the metric system of measure usually is used in scientific reports. Therefore, to prepare the data for a report, every person's judgment must be changed to centimeters (cm). There are 2.54 cm in each inch, so each person's estimate must be multiplied by 2.54. As you can see in Table 3.5, multiplying each score by 2.54 causes the mean to be multiplied by exactly the same value. You should note that multiplying by 2.54 did not change any of the lengths. It simply changed the unit of measurement. The average of $\overline{X} = 10$ inches is identical in length to the average of $\overline{X} = 25.4$ cm.

Table 3.5
Length Estimates for a 12-Inch Line

Person	Length Estimate (in.)	Conversion to Centimeters
1	10	25.40
2	9	22.86
3	12	30.48
4	8	20.32
5	11	27.94
	$\Sigma X = 50$	$\Sigma X = 127.00$
	$\overline{X} = 10$ in.	$\overline{X} = 25.4$ cm

4. *The Mean Is a Balance Point for the Distribution.* In addition to its mathematical definition, the mean can be considered as a balancing point for a distribution of scores. Consider a population consisting of $N = 4$ scores (2, 2, 6, 10) and its frequency distribution histogram shown in Figure 3.8. For this population, $\Sigma X = 20$ and $N = 4$, so $\mu = \frac{20}{4} = 5$.

Now imagine that this frequency distribution histogram is a seesaw. The X-axis, or number line, is the plank of wood that can swing up and down, and the scores are boxes of equal weight that are piled on the seesaw. If the plank is placed so that it pivots at the value equal to the mean, the seesaw will be balanced and will rest level (see Figure 3.9).

Figure 3.8

The frequency distribution for a population consisting of $N = 4$ scores. The mean for this population is $\mu = 5$.

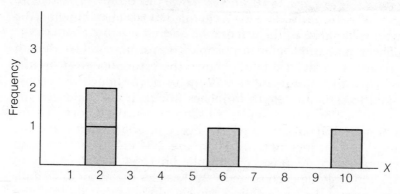

Figure 3.9

The frequency distribution shown as a seesaw balanced at the mean.

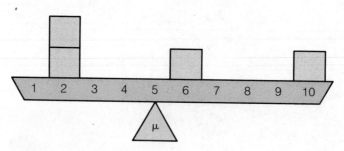

Adapted from *Statistics: An Intuitive Approach,* 4th ed. by G. Weinberg, J. Schumaker, and D. Oltman. Copyright © 1981, 1974, 1969, 1962 by Wadsworth Inc. Reprinted by permission of Brooks/Cole Publishing Co. Monterey, CA 93940.

The reason the plank is balanced over the mean becomes clear when we measure the distance of each box (score) from the mean:

Score	Distance from the Mean
$X = 2$	3 points below the mean
$X = 2$	3 points below the mean
$X = 6$	1 point above the mean
$X = 10$	5 points above the mean

Notice that the mean balances the distances. That is, the total distance below the mean is the same as the total distance above the mean:

$$3 \text{ points below} + 3 \text{ points below} = 6 \text{ points below}$$
$$1 \text{ point above} + 5 \text{ points above} = 6 \text{ points above}$$

What happens if we add one more score to the distribution? For instance, another score of $X = 10$ is added so that the distribution now is comprised of 2, 2, 6, 10, and 10. If we place another box at the position of $X = 10$, the seesaw no longer is balanced (see Figure 3.10). Remember, changing a single score, or adding a score, changes the mean. There is a new balance point. Now we have $\Sigma X = 30$ and $N = 5$, so the new mean is $\mu = \frac{30}{5} = 6$. If we slide the plank over so it swings at $\mu = 6$, the seesaw will balance (Figure 3.11). As before, the distances above and below the mean are balanced:

Figure 3.10

When a new score ($X = 10$) is added to the distribution, it no longer balances at $X = 5$.

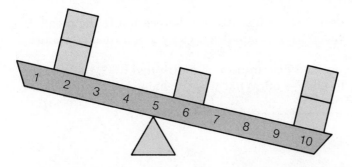

Adapted from *Statistics: An Intuitive Approach*, 4th ed. by G. Weinberg, J. Schumaker, and D. Oltman. Copyright © 1981, 1974, 1969, 1962 by Wadsworth Inc. Reprinted by permission of Brooks/Cole Publishing Co. Monterey, CA 93940.

Score	Distance from the Mean
$X = 2$	4 points below the mean
$X = 2$	4 points below the mean
$X = 6$	0 point from the mean
$X = 10$	4 points above the mean
$X = 10$	4 points above the mean

This balancing characteristic of the mean will play an important role in our discussion of variability in Chapter 4.

Figure 3.11

Adding a new score ($X = 10$) to the distribution causes the balance point (the mean) to change.

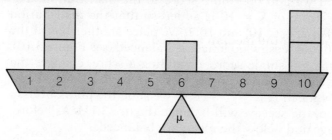

Adapted from *Statistics: An Intuitive Approach,* 4th ed. by G. Weinberg, J. Schumaker, and D. Oltman. Copyright © 1981, 1974, 1969, 1962 by Wadsworth Inc. Reprinted by permission of Brooks/Cole Publishing Co. Monterey, CA 93940.

LEARNING CHECK

1. a. Compute the mean for the following sample of scores:

    6, 1, 8, 0, 5

    b. Add four points to each score and then compute the mean.
    c. Multiply each of the original scores by 5 and then compute the mean.
2. After every score in a distribution is multiplied by 3, the mean is calculated to be $\overline{X} = 60$. What was the mean for the original distribution?

ANSWERS

1. a. $\overline{X} = \frac{20}{5} = 4$
    b. $\overline{X} = \frac{40}{5} = 8$
    c. $\overline{X} = \frac{100}{5} = 20$
2. The original mean was $\overline{X} = 20$.

3.5

Comparing the Mean, Median, and Mode

How do you decide which measure of central tendency to use? The answer to this question depends on several factors that we will now discuss. Before we begin, however, it should be noted that the mean is most often the preferred measure of central tendency. Because the mean uses every score in the distribution, it almost always is a good representative value. Remember, the goal of central tendency is to find the single value that best represents the entire distribution. Besides being a good representative, the mean has the added advantage of being a good measure for purposes of inferential statistics. Specifically, whenever you take a sample from a population, the sample mean will give a good indication of the value of the population mean. For these reasons, and others, the mean generally is considered to be the best of the three measures of central tendency. But there are specific situations where it either is impossible to compute a mean or where the mean is not particularly representative. It is in these situations that the mode and the median are used.

When to Use the Mode

The mode has two distinct advantages over the mean. First, it is easy to compute. Second, it can be used with any scale of measurement (nominal, ordinal, interval, ratio; see Chapter 1).

It is a bit misleading to say that the mode is easy to calculate because actually no calculation is required. When the scores are arranged in a frequency distribution, you identify the mode simply by finding the score with the greatest frequency. Because the value of the mode can be determined "at a glance," it is often included as a supplementary measure along with the mean or median as a no-cost extra. The value of the mode (or modes) in this situation is to give an indication of the shape of the distribution as well as a measure of central tendency. For example, if you are told that a set of exam scores has a mean of 72 and a mode of 80, you should have a better picture of the distribution than would be available from the mean alone. Specifically, it is lopsided, with scores piled up on the right-hand side of the mean (see Section 3.6).

The fact that the mode can be used with any scale of measurement makes it a very flexible value. When scores are measured on a nominal scale, it is impossible to calculate either a mean or a median, so the mode is the only way to describe central tendency (see Box 3.1). Consider the frequency distribution shown in Figure 3.12. These data were obtained by recording the academic major for each student in a psychology lab section. Notice that "academic major" forms a nominal scale that simply classifies individuals into discrete categories.

Figure 3.12

Major field of study for *n* = 9 students enrolled in an experimental psychology laboratory section.

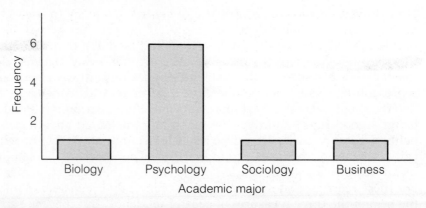

BOX 3.1	**Nominal Scales and Central Tendency**

It is possible to code nominal categories with numbers. This occurs frequently, for example, on computerized questionnaires where one might designate his/her sex by darkening circle 1 for male or 2 for female (Figure 3.13). Other demographic data, such as occupation, might be coded similarly on a questionnaire. The computer scans the pencil marks and tallies the numbers for each category.

Even though the numbers 1 and 2 can be used to code sex for the computer scanning, we still are dealing with data from a nominal scale of measurement. It would be absurd, I hope for obvious reasons, to say that the mean sex of students in the class is μ = 1.63. You should note, however, that when nominal data are coded as numbers, a mean value can be calculated (computers don't know any better) and these "means" can be informative. For example, a class with a mean sex of μ = 1.30 would have more males (*M* = 1) than a class with a mean sex of μ = 1.80. But the information provided by the mean is basically the same information provided by the mode; that is, which is greater, males or females.

You cannot compute a mean for these data because it is impossible to determine ΣX. (How much is one biologist plus six psychologists?) Also note that there is no natural ordering for the four categories in this distribution. It is a purely arbitrary decision to place biology on the scale before psychology. Because it is impossible to specify any order for the scores, you cannot determine a median. (Should sociology come before or after the middle?) The mode, on the other hand, provides a very good measure of central tendency. The mode for this

Figure 3.13

Several items from a questionnaire given to psychology majors.
Note that item 1 is a categorical variable coded with numbers.

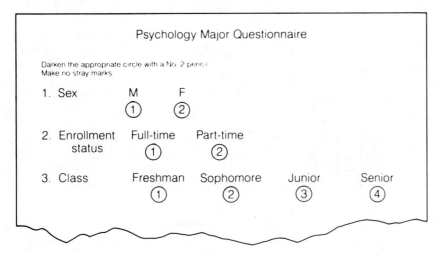

sample is psychology. This category describes the typical, or most representative, academic major for the sample.

Because the mode identifies the most typical case, it often produces a more sensible measure of central tendency. The mean, for example, will generate conclusions such as "the average family has 2.4 children and a house with 5.33 rooms." Many people would feel more comfortable saying "the typical, or modal, family has 2 children and a house with 5 rooms" (see Box 3.2).

When to Use the Median

There are two specific situations where the median serves as a valuable alternative to the mean. These occur when (1) there are a few extreme scores in the distribution and (2) some scores have undetermined values.

Extreme Scores When a distribution has a few extreme scores, scores that are very different in value from most of the others, then the mean will not be a good representative of the majority of the distribution. The problem comes from the fact that one or two extreme values can have a large influence and cause the mean to be displaced. In this situation, the fact that the mean uses all of the scores equally can be a disadvantage. For example, suppose a sample of $n = 10$ rats is tested in a T-maze for food reward. The animals must choose the correct arm of the T (right or left) to find the food in the goal box. The experimenter records the number of errors each rat makes before it solves the maze. Hypothetical data are presented in Figure 3.14.

Figure 3.14

Frequency distribution of errors committed before reaching learning criterion.

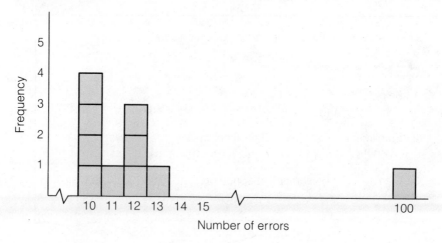

Number of errors

The mean for this sample is

$$\overline{X} = \frac{\Sigma X}{n} = \frac{200}{10} = 20$$

Notice that the mean is not very representative of any score in this distribution. Most of the scores are clustered at 10 and 12. The extreme score of $X = 100$ (a slow learner) inflates the value of ΣX and distorts the mean.

The median, on the other hand, is not easily affected by extreme scores. For this sample, $n = 10$, so there should be five scores on either side of the median. The median is 11.50. Notice that this is a very representative value. Also note that the median would be unchanged even if the slow learner made 1000 errors instead of only 100.

The median commonly is used when income figures are reported. This is done because there is a small segment of the population with income that is astronomical by any standard (some high-priced professional athletes are paid more than $20,000 a week). These extreme incomes distort the mean so that it is not very representative of the salaries that most of us earn. As in the previous example, the median is the preferred measure of central tendency when extreme scores exist.

Undetermined Values Occasionally, you will encounter a situation where an individual has an unknown or undetermined score. In psychology, this often occurs in learning experiments where you are measuring the number of errors (or amount of time) required for an individual to solve a particular problem. For example, suppose a sample of $n = 6$ people were asked to assemble a wooden puzzle as quickly as possible. The experimenter records how long (in minutes) it takes each individual to arrange all the pieces to complete the puzzle. Table 3.6 presents the outcome of this experiment.

BOX 3.2 | What Is the "Average"?

The word *average* is used in everyday speech to describe what is typical and commonplace. Statistically, averages are measured by the mean, median, or mode. U.S. Government agencies frequently characterize demographic data, such as average income or average age, with the median. Winners of elections are determined by the mode, the most frequent choice. Scholastic Aptitude Test (SAT) scores for large groups of students usually are described with the mean. The important thing to remember about these measures of central tendency (or the "average") is that they describe and summarize a group of individuals rather than any single person. In fact, the "average person" may not actually exist. Figure 3.15 shows data which were gathered from a sample of $n = 9$ infants. The age at which each infant said his/her first word was recorded by the parents. Note that the mean for this group is $\overline{X} = 11$ months and that there are three infants who uttered their first intelligible words at this age.

Figure 3.15
Frequency distribution showing the age at which each infant in a sample of $n = 9$ uttered his/her first word.

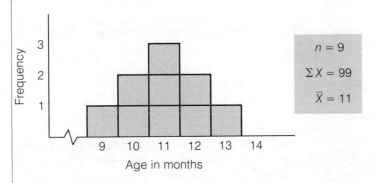

$n = 9$
$\Sigma X = 99$
$\overline{X} = 11$

Now look at the results of a different study using a sample of $n = 6$ infants (Figure 3.16). Note that the mean for this group is also $\overline{X} = 11$ months but that the "average infant" does not exist in this sample.

continued

BOX 3.2   *continued*

Figure 3.16

Frequency distribution showing the age at which each infant in a
sample of *n* = 6 uttered his/her first word.

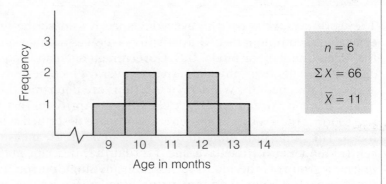

The mean describes the group, not a single individual. It is for
this reason that we find humor in statements like "the average
American family has 2.4 children," fully knowing that we never
will encounter this family.

Table 3.6
Amount of Time to Complete Puzzle

Person	Time (min.)
1	8
2	11
3	12
4	13
5	17
6	Never finished

Notice that person 6 never completed the puzzle. After an hour, he
still showed no sign of solving the puzzle, so the experimenter stopped
him. This person has an undetermined score. (There are two important points to be noted. First, the experimenter should not throw out
this individual's score. The whole purpose for using a sample is to
gain a picture of the population, and this individual tells us that part
of the population cannot solve the puzzle. Second, this person should
not be given a score of $X = 60$ minutes. Even though the experimenter
stopped the individual after 1 hour, the person did not finish the puzzle. The score that is recorded is the amount of time needed to finish.
For this individual, we do not know how long this would be.)

It is impossible to compute the mean for these data because of the undetermined value. We cannot calculate the ΣX part of the formula for the mean. However, it is possible to compute the median. For these data the median is 12.5. Three scores are below the median, and three scores (including the undetermined value) are above the median.

3.6

Central Tendency and the Shape of the Distribution

Symmetrical Distributions

For a symmetrical distribution, the right-hand side of the graph will be a mirror image of the left-hand side. By definition, the median will be exactly at the center of a symmetrical distribution because exactly half of the area in the graph will be on either side of the center. The mean also will be exactly at the center of a symmetrical distribution, because each individual score in the distribution has a corresponding score on the other side (the mirror image), so that the average of these two values is exactly in the middle. Because all the scores can be paired in this way, the overall average will be exactly at the middle. For any symmetrical distribution, the mean and the median will be the same (Figure 3.17).

If a symmetrical distribution has only one mode, then it must be exactly at the center so that all three measures of central tendency will have the same value (see Figure 3.17). On the other hand, a bimodal distribution that is symmetrical [Figure 3.17(b)] will have the mean and median together in the center with the modes on each side. A rectangular distribution [Figure 3.17(c)] has no mode because all X values occur with the same frequency. Still, the mean and the median will be in the center of the distribution and equivalent in value.

Figure 3.17

Measures of central tendency for three symmetrical distributions: normal, bimodal, and rectangular.

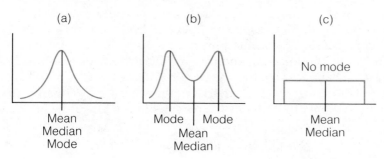

Skewed Distributions

Distributions are not always symmetrical. In fact, quite often they are lopsided, or skewed. If an experimenter is measuring reaction times, for example, skewed distributions are very common. Figure 3.18 shows that most subjects can respond very quickly, usually between 250 and 500 milliseconds ($\frac{1}{4}$-$\frac{1}{2}$ second). However, the curve is not symmetrical because there are a few people with relatively long reaction times. Perhaps they were not paying attention to the task, or maybe some subjects were unusually tired that day. This distribution has positive skew; that is, the tail of extreme scores points in the positive direction on the X-axis. Where will the mode, median, and mean be located in skewed distributions?

For a positively skewed distribution, the peak (highest frequency) is on the left-hand side. This is the position of the mode. The median will be located to the right of the mode. The position of the median can be understood if you consider the tail of the skewed distribution. Suppose you chopped off this tail and made the distribution symmetrical. If this were done, the median would be located at the same spot as the mode. Putting the tail back on the right-hand side causes the median to be moved to the right. Because the mean is influenced most by extreme scores, it will be displaced farthest to the right by the scores in the tail. Therefore, in a positively skewed distribution, the mean will have the largest value, followed by the median and then the mode (see Figure 3.19).

Negatively skewed distributions are lopsided in the opposite direction, with the scores piling up on the right-hand side and the tail tapering off to the left. The grades on an easy exam, for example, will tend to form a negatively skewed distribution (see Figure 3.20). For a distribution with negative skew, the mode is on the right-hand side (with the peak), while the mean is displaced on the left by the extreme

---

Figure 3.18

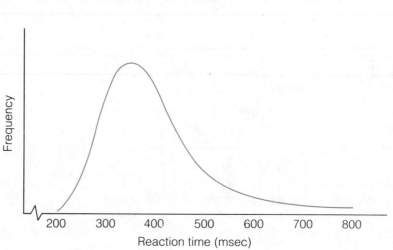

scores in the tail. As before, the median is located between the mean and the mode. In order from highest value to lowest value, the three measures of central tendency will be the mode, the median, and the mean.

Figure 3.19
Measures of central tendency in a positively skewed distribution.

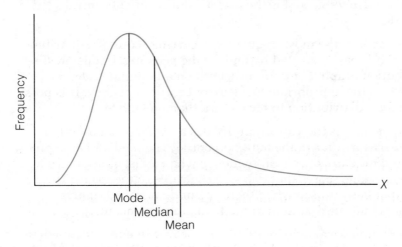

Figure 3.20
Measures of central tendency in a negatively skewed distribution.

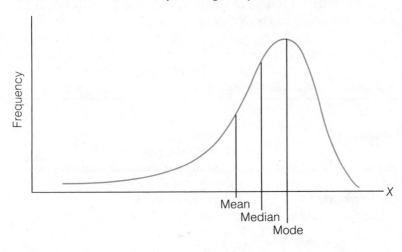

Summary

1. The purpose of central tendency is to determine the single value that best represents the entire distribution of scores. The three standard measures of central tendency are the mode, the median, and the mean.

2. The mean is the arithmetic average. It is computed by adding up all the scores and then dividing by the number of scores. Changing any score in the distribution will cause the mean to be changed. When a constant value is added to (or subtracted from) every score in a distribution, the same constant value is added to (subtracted from) the mean. If every score is multiplied by a constant, the mean will be multiplied by the same constant. In nearly all circumstances, the mean is the best representative value and is the preferred measure of central tendency.

3. The mode is the most frequently occurring score in a distribution. It is easily located by finding the peak in a frequency distribution graph. For data measured on a nominal scale, the mode is the appropriate measure of central tendency. It is possible for a distribution to have more than one mode.

4. The median is the value that divides a distribution exactly in half. The median is the 50th percentile. The median is the preferred measure of central tendency when a distribution has a few extreme scores that displace the value of the mean. The median also is used when there are undetermined (infinite) scores that make it impossible to compute a mean.

5. For symmetrical distributions, the mean will equal the median. If there is only one mode, then it will have the same value too.

6. For skewed distributions, the mode will be located toward the side where the scores pile up, and the mean will be pulled toward the extreme scores in the tail. The median will be located between these two values.

Key Terms

central tendency

mode

major mode

minor mode

bimodal distribution

multimodal distribution

median

mean

weighted mean

symmetrical distribution

skewed distribution

positive skew

negative skew

Problems for Chapter 3:
Central Tendency

*1. Find the mean, median, and mode for the following set of scores: 2, 4, 3, 4, 1, 5, 4, 2.

2. Find the mean, median, and mode for the set of scores in the following frequency distribution table:

X	f
6	1
5	2
4	1
3	1
2	2
1	3

*3. a. Find the mean, median, and mode for the scores in the following frequency distribution table. Note that you must use interpolation to find the median.

b. Looking at the values you obtained for the mean, median, and mode, is this distribution positively or negatively skewed?

X	f
8	1
7	1
6	1
5	2
4	2
3	4
2	1

4. A population of $N = 10$ scores has a mean of $\mu = 50$. If one of the scores is changed from $X = 60$ to $X = 80$, what will happen to the mean? Find the value for the new mean.

*5. A psychologist has measured how much time is required to solve a problem for each person in a sample of $n = 30$. The average time was $\overline{X} = 330$ seconds. If the psychologist converted all of the scores from seconds to minutes, what value would be obtained for the mean?

6. A distribution has a mean of 50 and a median of 43. Is it more likely that this distribution is positively skewed or negatively skewed? Explain your answer.

*7. Two sets of data follow:

Data set I: 3, 4, 1, 5, 4, 5, 2, 6, 4, 7, 3, 4
Data set II: 3, 1, 4, 3, 2, 1, 7, 1, 2, 5, 1, 6

a. Sketch a frequency distribution histogram for each set of scores.

b. Without doing any calculations, estimate the mean for each set of scores. You should be able to estimate fairly accurately by simply looking at your graphs.

c. Calculate the mean for each set, and compare the results with your estimates.

8. A psychologist would like to determine how many errors are made, on the average, before rats can learn a particular maze. A sample of $n = 10$ rats is obtained, and each rat is tested on the maze. The scores for the first 9 rats are as follows: 6, 2, 4, 5, 3, 7, 6, 2, 1.

   a. Calculate the mean and the median for these data. On the average, how many errors does each rat make?

   b. The tenth rat in the sample committed 100 errors before mastering the maze. When this rat is included in the sample, what happens to the mean? What happens to the median? What general conclusion can be drawn from this result?

*9. In a problem-solving experiment with $n = 100$ children, five of the children failed to complete the problem within 10 minutes and were simply marked as "failed." If the experimenter wanted to find a measure of central tendency to describe the "average" amount of time needed to complete the problem, what measure should be used? Explain your answer.

10. Four students have part-time jobs in the same store. The mean weekly pay for these students is $30, and the median weekly pay is $25.

    a. If one of the students gets a $10 raise, what is the new mean?

    b. If one of the students gets a $10 raise, what is the new median? (Be careful and explain your answer.)

    c. If one student gets a $10 raise and another gets a $20 raise, what is the new mean?

    d. If the student with the highest salary gets a $10 raise, what is the new median?

*11. The final exam grades for two sections of the same course are reported as follows:

$$\text{Section I:} \quad n = 30, \quad \overline{X} = 63$$
$$\text{Section II:} \quad n = 70, \quad \overline{X} = 78$$

If both sections are combined, what is the average grade for the entire set of students?

12. A 20-point quiz is given to each of two sections of an introductory statistics class. The scores for each section are as follows:

Section I: 6, 5, 5, 7, 17,
           5, 6, 5
Section II: 9, 8, 10, 7, 8,
           9, 1, 0, 9, 9

a. Sketch a histogram showing the distribution of scores for section I.

b. Sketch a histogram showing the distribution for section II.

c. Looking at your graphs, which section would you say had better scores?

d. Calculate the mean and the median for each section. Which measure of central tendency best describes the difference between these two distributions?

*13. To evaluate his teaching effectiveness, a professor measures each student's attitude toward psychology at the beginning of the course and again at the end. For each person, the change in atttitude is computed. A positive score means that the person's opinion of psychology went up; a negative score means that the person's opinion went down. The scores are as follows:

$$-12, \quad 31, \quad 20, \quad 1, \quad 4, \quad 12, \quad 13,$$
$$-6, \quad 7, \quad -9 \quad 11, \quad -4, \quad 10, \quad 0,$$
$$3, \quad 6, \quad 2, \quad -18, \quad -2, \quad 21, \quad 9$$

a. Compute the mean change for this sample of $n = 21$ students.

b. Because the professor does not like to work with negative numbers, 20 points are added to each score and then the mean is calculated. How should this mean compare with the value you obtained in part a? Exactly what value should be obtained?

14. A school psychologist has computed the average IQ for a sample of $n = 99$ children and obtained a mean of $\overline{X} = 104$. If one additional student with an IQ of 133 is included in this sample, what will the average IQ be for the entire group of 100 students?

*15. A professor teaches a morning class of $n = 61$ students and an afternoon class of $n = 34$. The same test is given to both classes. The mean for the morning group is $\overline{X} = 44.1$, and the mean for the afternoon group is $\overline{X} = 50.3$. If the two classes are combined, what is the mean for the entire group of students?

*16. A social psychologist is interested in the effect of failure on a person's mood. A sample of $n = 9$ students is obtained and each student is given a mood inventory questionnaire. After completing the questionnaire, each student is given a word problem to solve. Although the problem is impossible to solve, the psychologist says that an average student can finish it in about 10 minutes. After working on the problem for 15 minutes, each student is stopped and once again completes the mood questionnaire. The data from this experiment are as follows:

Mood Scores

Before	After
17	12
25	18
16	19
20	11
30	27
19	14
23	21
26	19
29	18

a. Calculate the mean for the initial mood scores and for the scores after failing to solve the problem. What is the difference between these two means?

b. Find the change in mood for each individual subject (before versus after). Calculate the mean for these difference scores (remember, some differences may be positive, and some may be negative). You should find that the mean difference is identical to the difference between the means.

17. A psychologist is collecting attitude scores for high school students as part of an experiment. Because the testing room will hold only 15 people, the students are tested in three separate groups. The data for these three groups are as follows:

$$\text{Group 1:} \quad n = 15, \quad \overline{X} = 46.5$$
$$\text{Group 2:} \quad n = 14, \quad \overline{X} = 43.2$$
$$\text{Group 3:} \quad n = 11, \quad \overline{X} = 50.9$$

Find the overall mean for the entire group of high school students.

18. The monthly telephone costs for the Department of Psychology last year are as follows:

Monthly Phone Bills

Jan.	$121.83	Jul.	$ 83.15
Feb.	$173.21	Aug.	$121.33
Mar.	$165.12	Sep.	$215.50
Apr.	$182.86	Oct.	$201.45
May	$142.67	Nov.	$172.80
Jun.	$104.28	Dec.	$162.25

Find the mean monthly bill.

*19. Reaction time data for a sample of $n = 15$ subjects are as follows:

$$1.0, \quad 0.9, \quad 1.2, \quad 1.3, \quad 0.9, \quad 0.8, \quad 1.0,$$
$$0.7, \quad 0.9, \quad 1.1, \quad 0.7, \quad 1.2, \quad 1.0, \quad 1.1, \quad 0.8$$

Find the mean and the median for these scores. (*Hint:* If you first multiply each score by 10, you will get rid of the decimals.)

20. The Jones & Jones Corporation is currently involved in negotiations with the employees' labor union. The hourly wages for the 20 employees at Jones & Jones are as follows:

Hourly Wages

8.50	7.40	7.25	12.00
7.50	8.00	8.55	7.30
7.00	11.00	9.50	7.25
8.20	7.10	10.50	9.00
9.50	7.10	7.25	8.50

The union and the company both have access to these figures. The statewide average hourly wage for this type of industry is $8.25.

a. Calculate the mean and the median hourly wage for the Jones & Jones employees.

b. If you were a company official arguing that the present salaries are reasonable, which measure of central tendency would you prefer? Using this measure, how does the "average" wage at Jones & Jones compare with the statewide average?

c. If you were a union official arguing for a salary increase, which measure of central tendency would you prefer? How does this "average" compare with the statewide average?

*21. On a standardized reading achievement test, the nationwide average for seventh grade children is $\mu = 7.00$. A seventh grade teacher is interested in comparing his class reading scores with the national average. The scores for his 24 students are as follows:

$$6.5, \quad 7.2, \quad 7.8, \quad 7.2, \quad 7.9, \quad 6.1$$
$$6.8, \quad 7.1, \quad 8.3, \quad 6.9, \quad 7.2, \quad 7.5$$
$$8.2, \quad 7.4, \quad 6.2, \quad 6.8, \quad 7.6, \quad 7.1$$
$$7.3, \quad 6.2, \quad 8.1, \quad 7.0, \quad 7.1, \quad 6.8$$

Calculate the mean for this class. On the average, how does this class compare with the national norm?

22. In the preview section of Chapter 2 we presented test scores for students using two different strategies for studying. One group read straight through the material, and the second group had their reading divided into sections with questions at the end of each section. The data from this experiment are as follows:

Read Straight Through				Interspersed Questions			
25	32	27	20	28	29	25	31
28	23	17	21	31	19	29	35
24	34	22	29	30	28	24	30
24	25	21	18	33	27	34	26
19	22	30	24	29	29	27	32
26	27	24	23	30	36	22	23
23	25			32	33		

Calculate the mean for each group. On the average, how much difference is there between these two study techniques?

CHAPTER 4

Variability

TOOLS
YOU WILL
NEED

The following items are considered essential background material for this chapter. If you doubt your knowledge of any of these items, you should review the appropriate chapter or section before proceeding.

1. Summation notation (Chapter 1)
2. Percentiles (Chapter 2)
3. Central tendency (Chapter 3)
   a. Mean
   b. Median

It's 10 a.m., and Mary L. is washing her hands for the tenth time today. Before she goes to sleep tonight, she will have washed her hands over 60 times. Is this normal?

To differentiate between normal and abnormal behavior, some psychologists have resorted to using a *statistical model*. For example, we could survey a large sample of individuals and record the number of times each person washes his/her hands during a typical day. Because people are different, the scores should be variable, and the data from this survey should produce a distribution similar to the one shown in Figure 4.1. Notice that most people will have average or moderate scores located in the central part of the distribution. Others, such as Mary L., will deviate from average. According to the statistical model, those who show substantial deviation are abnormal. Note that this model simply defines abnormal as being unusual or different from normal. The model does not imply that abnormal is necessarily negative or undesirable. Mary L. may have a compulsive personality disorder, or she may be a dentist washing her hands between patients.

The statistical model for abnormality requires two statistical concepts: a measure of the average and a measure of deviation from average. In Chapter 3 we examined the standard techniques for defining the average score for a distribution. In this chapter we will examine methods for measuring deviations. The

Figure 4.1
The statistical model for defining abnormal behavior. The distribution of behavior scores for the entire population is divided into three sections. Those individuals with average scores are defined as normal, and individuals who show extreme deviation from average are defined as abnormal.

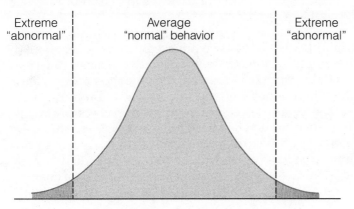

Extreme "abnormal" | Average "normal" behavior | Extreme "abnormal"

fact that scores deviate from average means that they are variable. Variability is one of the most basic statistical concepts. As an introduction to the concept, this chapter will concentrate on defining and measuring variability. In later chapters we will explore sources of variability and examine how variability affects the interpretation of other statistical measurements.

One additional point should be made before we proceed. You probably have noticed that central tendency and variability are closely related. Whenever one appears, the other usually is close at hand. You should watch for this association throughout the book. The better you understand the relations between central tendency and variability, the better you will understand statistics.

4.1
Introduction

The term *variability* has much the same meaning in statistics as it has in everyday language; to say that things are variable means that they are not all the same. In statistics our goal is to measure the amount of variability for a particular set of scores, a distribution. In simple terms, if the scores in a distribution are all the same, then there is no variability. If there are small differences between scores, then the variability is small, and if there are big differences between scores, then the variability is large.

DEFINITION

Variability provides a quantitative measure of the degree to which scores in a distribution are spread out or clustered together.

The purpose of measuring variability is to obtain an indication of how spread out a distribution of scores is. Are the scores all clustered close together, or are they scattered over a wide range of values? A good measure of variability should provide an accurate picture of the spread of the distribution. Variability, along with central tendency and shape, is one of the three basic descriptive indices that are used to describe distributions of scores.

In addition to providing a description of the distribution, a good measure of variability also serves two other valuable purposes. First, variability gives an indication of how accurately the mean describes the distribution. If the variability is small, then the scores are all close together, and each individual score is close to the mean. In this situation, the mean is a good representative of all the scores in the distribution. On the other hand, when variability is large, the scores are all spread out, and they are not necessarily close to the mean. In this case, the mean may be less representative of the whole distribution. To make this point more concrete, consider the two "games of chance" described in Box 4.1.

BOX 4.1 An Example of Variability

To examine the role of variability, we will consider two "games of chance."

For the first game you pay $1 to play, and you get back 90 cents every time. That's right, you pay me $1, and I give you back 90 cents. Notice that this game has no variability; exactly the same thing happens every time. On the average, you lose 10 cents each time you play, and, in this case, the average gives a perfect description of the outcome of the game.

For the second game the rules are a little different. It still costs $1 to play, but this time you have a 1-out-of-10 chance of winning $9. The rest of the time you win nothing. For this second game we have added variability; the outcomes are not all the same. Notice, however, that in the long run you still lose 10 cents each time you play. In 10 games, for example, you would expect to win once ($9), but you would have paid $10 to play. You expect to lose $1 during 10 games for an average loss of 10 cents per game.

On the average these two games are identical. But in one case the average perfectly describes every single outcome, and in the other case the average is not at all representative of what actually happens on any single trial. The difference between these two games is the variability.

You also should notice the number of times you would need to watch each game in order to understand it. For the first game, any individual outcome (pay $1 and get back 90 cents) gives a complete description of the game. After only one observation, you know the entire game. For the second game, however, you would need to watch a long time before the nature of the game became clear. In this case it would take a large sample to provide a good description of the game.

The second valuable purpose served by a good measure of variability is to give an indication of how well an individual score (or group of scores) represents the entire distribution. Although we usually will use the mean as the best representative score for a population, there are occasions where the mean is unknown. In these situations, a sample is selected from the population, and the sample is then used to represent the entire distribution. This is particularly important in the area of inferential statistics where relatively small samples are used to answer general questions about large populations. If the scores in a distribution are all clustered together (small variability), then any individual score will be a reasonably accurate representative of the entire distribution. But if the scores are all spread out, then a single value selected from the distribution often will not be representative of the rest of the group. This point also is illustrated in Box 4.1.

In this chapter we will consider three different measures of variability: the range, the interquartile range, and the standard deviation. Of these three, the standard deviation (and the related measure of variance) is by far the most important.

4.2
The Range

DEFINITION

The *range* is the distance between the largest score and the smallest score in a distribution. Once you have identified the highest and lowest scores, the range is determined by

range = high − low + 1

Remember, the +1 is included in this formula because both the high score and the low score are counted in determining the range. The range extends from the extreme lower real limit to the extreme upper real limit.

The range is perhaps the most obvious way of describing how spread out the scores are; simply subtract to find the difference between the biggest score and the smallest score. The problem with using the range as a measure of variability is that it is completely determined by the two extreme values and ignores the other scores in the distribution. For example, the following two distributions have exactly the same range, 10 points in each case. However, the scores in the first distribution are clustered together at one end of the range, while the scores in the second distribution are spread out over the entire range.

Distribution 1: 1, 8, 9, 9, 10, 10
Distribution 2: 1, 2, 4, 6, 8, 10

If, for example, these were scores on a 10-point quiz for two different class sections, there are clear differences between the two sections. Nearly all the students in the first section have mastered the material, but there is a wide range of different abilities for students in the second section. A good measure of variability should show this difference.

Because the range does not consider all of the scores in the distribution, it often does not give an accurate description of the variability for the entire distribution. For this reason, the range is considered to be a crude and unreliable measure of variability.

4.3
The Interquartile Range and Semi-interquartile Range

In Chapter 3 we defined the median as the score that divides a distribution exactly in half. In a similar way, a distribution can be divided into four equal parts using quartiles. By definition, the first quartile ($Q1$) is the score that separates the lower 25% of the distribution from the rest. The second quartile ($Q2$) is the score that has exactly two quarters, or 50%, of the distribution below it. Notice that the second quartile and the median are the same. Finally, the third quartile ($Q3$) is the score that divides the bottom three-fourths of the distribution from the top quarter. The interquartile range is defined as the distance between the first and third quartiles.

DEFINITION

The *interquartile range* is the distance between the first quartile and the third quartile:

$$\text{interquartile range} = Q3 - Q1$$

When the interquartile range is used to describe variability, it commonly is transformed into the *semi-interquartile range.* As the name implies, the semi-interquartile range is simply one-half of the interquartile range.

Because the semi-interquartile range focuses on the middle 50% of a distribution, it is less likely to be influenced by extreme scores and, therefore, gives a better and more stable measure of variability than the range. Nevertheless, the semi-interquartile range does not take into account the actual distances between individual scores, so it does not give a complete picture of how scattered or clustered the scores are. Like the range, the semi-interquartile range is considered to be a somewhat crude measure of variability.

4.4
Standard Deviation and Variance for a Population

The standard deviation is the most commonly used and the most important measure of variability. Standard deviation uses the mean of the distribution as a reference point and measures variability by considering the distance between each score and the mean. It determines whether the scores are generally near or far from the mean. That is, are the scores clustered together or scattered? In simple terms, the standard deviation approximates the average distance from the mean.

Although the concept of standard deviation is straightforward, the actual equations will appear complex. Therefore, we will begin by looking at the logic that leads to these equations. If you remember that our goal is to measure the average distance from the mean, then this logic and the equations that follow should be easier to remember.

Step 1. The first step in finding the average distance from the mean is to determine the deviation, or distance from the mean, for each individual score. By definition, the deviation for each score is the difference between the score and the mean. This deviation score often is identified by the lowercase letter x.

Deviation is distance from the mean:

deviation score = $x = X - \mu$

For a distribution of scores with $\mu = 50$, if your score is $X = 53$, then your deviation score is

$X - \mu = 53 - 50 = 3$

If your score were $X = 45$, then your deviation score would be

$X - \mu = 45 - 50 = -5$

Notice that there are two parts to a deviation score: the sign (+ or −) and the number. The sign tells the direction from the mean, that is, whether the score is located above (+) or below (−) the mean. The number gives the actual distance from the mean. For example, a deviation score of −6 corresponds to score that is below the mean by six points.

Step 2. The Mean of the Deviation Scores. Because our goal is to compute a measure of the average distance from the mean, the obvious next step is to calculate the mean of the deviation scores. To compute this mean, you first add up the deviation scores and then divide by N. This process is demonstrated in the following example.

EXAMPLE 4.1

We start with the following set of $N = 4$ scores. These scores add up to $\Sigma X = 12$, so the mean is $\mu = \frac{12}{4} = 3$. For each score we have computed the deviation.

X	$X - \mu$
8	+5
1	−2
3	0
0	−3
$\Sigma(X - \mu) = 0$	

Remember, the mean is the balancing point for the distribution.

Notice that the deviation scores add up to zero. This should not be surprising if you remember that the mean serves as a balance point for the distribution. The distances above the mean are equal to the distances below the mean (see page 92). Logically, the deviation scores must always add up to zero. Consider what it would mean if this did not happen. Suppose, for example, the deviation scores added up to some positive number. If the sum of the deviations is positive, then the average deviation score also would be positive. But a positive deviation indicates a value above the mean. If the average of the deviation scores were positive, this would imply that on average the scores are above the mean; that is, the average score is above average. Clearly this cannot be true. By a similar argument, the mean of the deviation scores cannot be negative. This leaves the conclusion that the mean deviation must be zero.

The fact that the mean deviation is always zero means that it is of no value as a measure of variability. It is zero whether the scores are grouped together or are all scattered out. The mean deviation score provides no information about variability. (You should note, however, that the constant value of zero can be useful in other ways. Whenever you are working with deviation scores, you can check your calculations by making sure that the deviation scores add up to zero.)

Step 3. The reason that the average of the deviation scores will not work as a measure of variability is that it is always zero. Clearly, this problem results from the positive and negative values canceling each other out. The solution is to get rid of the signs (+ and −). The standard procedure for accomplishing this is to square each deviation score. Before we look at this process, however, we will briefly consider what appears to be a more direct solution; that is, just ignore the signs and use the absolute values of the deviation scores. This procedure will give us what is literally the average distance from the mean or what is called the average deviation.

DEFINITION

Average deviation is the average of the absolute values of the deviation scores.

To find the absolute value of a number, remove the sign (+ or −) and consider only the magnitude. The absolute value of −3 is 3.

But there is a serious problem with this measure of variability. You should recall that one of the basic principles of statistics is that samples should be representative of the populations they come from. The average deviation violates this principle. The average deviation computed from a sample bears no consistent relationship to the average deviation for its population. Therefore, the sample value will not be representative of the population. For this reason, the average deviation is said to be *unstable under sampling* and is of little value as a measure of variability.

As noted earlier, the standard procedure of getting rid of the plus and minus signs is to square each deviation score. Using these squared values, you then compute the average squared deviation, which is called variance.

DEFINITION

Population variance = average squared deviation.

We should note that the process of squaring deviation scores does much more than simply get rid of plus and minus signs. In fact, there is a sophisticated system of mathematical techniques that has been developed for use with squared values. By defining variance in terms of squared deviations, it because possible to take advantage of these techniques whenever variance is used as the measure of variability. As a result, variance fits into a mathematical system that can be used to develop other statistical procedures. This makes variance an extremely valuable measure of variability.

Step 4. Remember that our goal is to compute a measure of the average distance from the mean. Although variance is not exactly what we want, it is a step in the right direction. Variance is the average squared deviation, or the average squared distance from the mean. The final step simply makes a correction for having squared all the distances. Standard deviation is the square root of the variance.

DEFINITION

Standard deviation $= \sqrt{\text{variance}}$.

Technically, standard deviation is the square root of the average squared deviation. But, in simple terms, standard deviation provides a value that is roughly equivalent to the average distance from the mean. As the name implies, standard deviation measures the standard, or typical, deviation score.

Formulas for Standard Deviation and Variance

Keeping in mind the logic that leads to standard deviation and variance, we now will begin to look at some equations and calculations. Variance, you should recall, is defined as the average squared deviation. This average is computed exactly the same way you compute any average: First get the sum, and then divide by the number of scores:

$$\text{variance} = \text{average squared deviation} = \frac{\text{sum of squared deviations}}{\text{number of scores}}$$

The value in the numerator of this equation, the sum of the squared deviations, is a basic component of variability, and we will focus on it. To simplify things, it is identified by the notation *SS* (for sum of squared deviations), and it generally is referred to as the *sum of squares*.

DEFINITION

SS, or *sum of squares*, is the sum of the squared deviation scores.

There are two formulas you will need to know in order to compute *SS*. These formulas are algebraically equivalent (they always produce the same answer), but they look different and are used in different situations.

The first of these formulas is called the **definitional formula** because the terms in the formula literally define the process of adding up the squared deviations:

(4.1) Definitional formula: $SS = \Sigma(X - \mu)^2$

Note that the formula directs you to square each deviation score $(X - \mu)^2$ and then add them up. The result is the sum of the squared deviations or *SS*. Following is an example using this formula.

EXAMPLE 4.2
We will compute *SS* for the following set of $N = 4$ scores. These scores add up to $\Sigma X = 8$, so the mean is $\mu = \frac{8}{4} = 2$. For each score, we have computed the deviation and the squared deviation. The squared deviations add up to $SS = 22$.

X	$X - \mu$	$(X - \mu)^2$	
1	-1	1	$\Sigma X = 8$
0	-2	4	$\mu = 2$
6	$+4$	16	
1	-1	1	
		22 $= \Sigma(X - \mu)^2$	

Caution: *The definitional formula requires that you first square the deviations and then add them.*

The second formula for *SS* is called the **computational formula** (or the **machine formula**) because it works directly with the scores (X values) and, therefore, is generally easier to use for calculations, especially with an electronic calculator:

(4.2) Computational formula: $SS = \Sigma X^2 - \dfrac{(\Sigma X)^2}{N}$

The first part of this formula directs you to square each score and then add them up (ΣX^2). The second part requires you to add up the scores (ΣX) and then square this total and divide the result by N. The use of this formula is shown in Example 4.3 with the same set of scores we used for the definitional formula.

EXAMPLE 4.3
The computational formula is used to calculate *SS* for the same set of $N = 4$ scores we used in Example 4.2. First, compute ΣX. Then square each score and compute ΣX^2. These two values are used in the formula.

X	X^2	
1	1	$\Sigma X = 8$
0	0	
6	36	$\Sigma X^2 = 38$
1	1	

$$SS = \Sigma X^2 - \frac{(\Sigma X)^2}{N}$$

$$= 38 - \frac{(8)^2}{4}$$

$$= 38 - \frac{64}{4}$$

$$= 38 - 16$$

$$= 22$$

Notice that the two formulas produce exactly the same value for SS. Although the formulas look different, they are in fact equivalent. The definitional formula should be very easy to learn if you simply remember that SS stands for the sum of the squared deviations. If you use notation to write out "the sum of" (Σ) "squared deviations" $(X - \mu)^2$, then you have the definitional formula. Unfortunately, the terms in the computational formula do not translate directly into "sum of squared deviations," so you simply need to memorize this formula.

The definitional formula for SS is the most direct way of calculating sum of squares, but it can be very awkward to use for most sets of data. In particular, if the mean is not a whole number, then the deviation scores will all be fractions or decimals, and the calculations become difficult. In addition, calculations with decimals or fractions introduce the opportunity for rounding error, which makes the results less accurate. For these reasons, the computational formula is used most of the time. If you have a small group of scores and the mean is a whole number, then the definitional formula is fine; otherwise, use the computational formula.

With the definition and calculation of SS behind you, the equations for variance and standard deviation become simple. Remember, variance is defined as the average squared deviation. The average is the sum divided by N, so the equation for variance is

$$\text{variance} = \frac{SS}{N}$$

Standard deviation is the square root of variance, so the equation for standard deviation is

$$\text{standard deviation} = \sqrt{\frac{SS}{N}}$$

There is one final bit of notation before we work completely through an example computing SS, variance, and standard deviation. Like the mean (μ), variance and standard deviation are parameters of a population and will be identified by Greek letters. To identify the standard deviation, we use the Greek letter sigma (the Greek letter "s," standing for standard deviation). The capital letter sigma (Σ) has been used already, so we now use the lowercase sigma, σ:

$$(4.3) \quad \text{population standard deviation} = \sigma = \sqrt{\frac{SS}{N}}$$

The symbol for population variance should help you remember the relation between standard deviation and variance. If you square the standard deviation, you will get the variance. The symbol for variance is sigma squared, σ^2:

$$(4.4) \quad \text{population variance} = \sigma^2 = \frac{SS}{N}$$

EXAMPLE 4.4
The following population of scores will be used to demonstrate the calculation of SS, variance, and standard deviation:

$$1, \quad 9, \quad 5, \quad 8, \quad 7$$

These five scores add up to $\Sigma X = 30$, so the mean is $\frac{30}{5} = 6$. Before we do any other calculations, remember that the purpose of variability is to determine how spread out the scores are. Standard deviation accomplishes this by providing a measurement of the standard distance from the mean. The scores we are working with have been placed in a frequency distribution histogram in Figure 4.2 so you can see the variability more easily. Note that the score closest to the mean

Figure 4.2
A frequency distribution histogram for a population of $N = 5$ scores. The mean for this population is $\mu = 6$. The smallest distance from the mean is one point, and the largest distance is five points. The standard distance (or standard deviation) should be between one and five points.

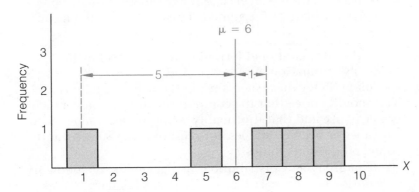

is $X = 5$ or $X = 7$, both of which are only one point away. The score farthest from the mean is $X = 1$, and it is five points away. For this distribution, the biggest distance from the mean is five points, and the smallest distance is one point. The average, or standard, distance should be somewhere between 1 and 5. By looking quickly at a distribution in this way, you should be able to make a rough estimate of the standard deviation. In this case, the standard deviation should be between 1 and 5, probably around three points. Making a preliminary judgment of standard deviation can help you avoid errors in calculation. If, for example, you worked through the formulas and ended up with a value of $\sigma = 12$, you should realize immediately that you have made an error. (If the biggest deviation is only five points, then it is impossible for the standard deviation to be 12.)

Now we will start the calculations. The first step is to find SS for this set of scores.

Because the mean is a whole number ($\mu = 6$), we can use the definitional formula for SS:

X	$X - \mu$	$(X - \mu)^2$	
1	-5	25	$\Sigma X = 30$
9	$+3$	9	$\mu = 6$
5	-1	1	
8	$+2$	4	
7	$+1$	1	
		$\overline{40}$	$= \Sigma(X - \mu)^2 = SS$

$$\sigma^2 = \frac{SS}{N}$$

$$= \frac{40}{5} = 8$$

$$\sigma = \sqrt{8} = 2.83$$

For this set of scores, the variance is $\sigma^2 = 8$, and the standard deviation is $\sigma = \sqrt{8} = 2.83$. Note that the value for the standard deviation is in excellent agreement with our preliminary estimate of the standard distance from the mean.

LEARNING CHECK

1. a. Using the computational formula, calculate SS for the following population of scores: 0, 1, 9.
   b. Calculate SS for these scores using the definitional formula. You should notice that the computational formula is much easier to use and that it probably will produce a more accurate answer because it does not require that you constantly round off decimal values.
2. a. Sketch a frequency distribution histogram for the following population of scores: 1, 3, 3, 9. Using this histogram, make

an estimate of the standard deviation (i.e., the standard distance from the mean.)

b. Calculate *SS*, variance, the standard deviation for these scores. How well does your estimate from part a compare with the real standard deviation?

ANSWERS

1. For this population, $SS = 48.67$.
2. a. Your sketch should show a mean of $\mu = 4$. The score closest to the mean is $X = 3$, and the farthest score is $X = 9$. The standard deviation should be somewhere between one point and five points.
   b. For this population, $SS = 36$; the variance is $\frac{36}{4} = 9$; the standard deviation is $\sqrt{9} = 3$.

Graphic Representation of the Mean and Standard Deviation

In frequency distribution graphs we will identify the position of the mean by drawing a vertical line and labeling it with μ or $\overline{X}$ (see Figure 4.3). Because the standard deviation measures distance from the mean, it will be represented by a line drawn from the mean outward for a distance equal to the standard deviation (see Figure 4.3). For rough sketches, you can identify the mean with a vertical line in the middle of the distribution. The standard deviation line should extend approximately halfway from the mean to the most extreme score.

Figure 4.3

The graphic representation of a population with a mean of $\mu = 40$ and a standard deviation of $\sigma = 4$.

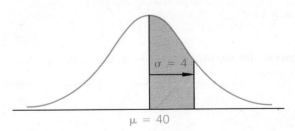

$\mu = 40$

4.5
Standard Deviation and Variance for Samples

The goal of inferential statistics is to use the limited information from samples to draw general conclusions about populations. The basic assumption of this process is that samples should be representative of the populations from which they come. This assumption poses a special problem for variability because samples consistently tend to be less variable than their populations. An example of this general tendency is shown in Figure 4.4. The fact that a sample tends to be less variable than its population means that sample variability gives a *biased* estimate of population variability. This bias is in the direction of underestimating the population value rather than being right on the mark. To correct for this bias, it is necessary to make an adjustment in the calculation of variability when you are working with sample data. The intent of the adjustment is to make the resulting value for sample variability a more accurate estimate of the population variability.

To compute sample variability, we begin by defining the deviation for each score in the sample. As before, deviation measures the distance from the mean, but now we are using the sample mean in place of the population mean:

(4.5) sample deviation score $= X - \overline{X}$

The deviation scores will have a sign and a magnitude. The sign tells the direction from the mean ($+$ for above, $-$ for below), and the magnitude tells the distance from the mean. The deviation scores always add up to zero.

Variance and standard deviation for sample data have the same basic definitions as they do for populations: Variance measures the average squared distance from the mean, and standard deviation is the square root of variance. To compute the values, we first will need to find SS, the sum of squared deviations. The formulas we use to

---

Figure 4.4

The population of adult heights forms a normal distribution. If you select a sample from this population, you are most likely to obtain individuals who are near average in height. As a result, the scores in the sample will be less variable (spread out) than the scores in the population.

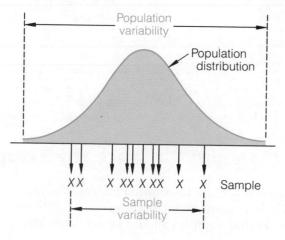

compute sample SS are essentially identical to the formulas used for populations:

(4.6) Definitional formula: $SS = \Sigma(X - \overline{X})^2$

(4.7) Computational formula: $SS = \Sigma X^2 - \dfrac{(\Sigma X)^2}{n}$

Note that the only difference between these formulas and the population formulas is a minor change in notation. We have substituted $\overline{X}$ in place of μ and n in place of N. For all practical purposes the population and sample formulas for SS are interchangeable. The difference in notation will have no effect on the calculations.

After you compute SS, however, it becomes critical to differentiate between samples and populations. To correct for the bias in sample variability, it is necessary to make an adjustment in the formulas for sample variance and standard deviation. With this in mind, sample variance (identified by the symbol s^2) is defined as

(4.8) sample variance $= s^2 = \dfrac{SS}{n - 1}$

Sample standard deviation (identified by the symbol s) is simply the square root of the variance:

(4.9) sample standard deviation $= s = \sqrt{\dfrac{SS}{n - 1}}$

Notice that these sample formulas use $n - 1$ instead of n. This is the adjustment that is necessary to correct for the bias in sample variability. The effect of the adjustment is to increase the value you will obtain. Dividing by a smaller number ($n - 1$ instead of n) produces a larger result and makes sample variability an accurate, or unbiased, estimator of population variability. (See Box 4.2.)

Remember, sample variability tends to underestimate population variability unless some correction is made.

A complete example showing the calculation of sample variance and standard deviation will now be worked out.

EXAMPLE 4.5
We have selected sample of $n = 7$ scores from a population. The scores are 1, 6, 4, 3, 8, 7, 6. The frequency distribution histogram for this sample is shown in Figure 4.5. Before we begin any calculations, you should be able to look at the sample distribution and make a preliminary estimate of the outcome. Remember that standard deviation measures the standard distance from the mean. For this sample the mean is $\overline{X} = 5$ ($\frac{35}{7} = 5$). The scores closest to the mean are $X = 4$ and $X = 6$, both of which are exactly one point away. The score farthest from the mean is $X = 1$, which is four points away. With the smallest distance from the mean equal to 1 and the largest distance equal to 4, we should obtain a standard distance somewhere around 2.5 (between 1 and 4).

BOX 4.2 Using $n - 1$ to Compute Sample Variance

The purpose of this example is to demonstrate that using $n - 1$ to compute sample variance produces an unbiased estimate of the population variance. We begin with a very simple population consisting of only four scores: 1, 1, 3, 3. The mean for this population is $\mu = 2$ (halfway between the 1s and the 3s). Note that all the scores in the population are exactly one point away from the mean. Because all the deviations are equal to 1, the standard deviation will be $\sigma = 1$. Therefore, the variance for this population is $\sigma^2 = 1$. (Try computing the variance directly to check this reasoning.)

If you select a sample of $n = 2$ scores from this population, there are only four possible samples that could be obtained. These four samples are listed in Table 4.1.

The next column in the table shows SS for each sample. Note that two of the samples have no variability, so $SS = 0$. For the other two samples, both scores are exactly one point from the mean, so SS (the sum of squared deviations) would be $1 + 1 = 2$.

Next we compute variance for each sample using the $SS/(n - 1)$ formula. And we have computed the variance values that would be obtained using n instead of $n - 1$. These values are shown in the last two columns of the table.

Finally, we compute the average of the four sample variances. Using $n - 1$ to compute sample variance, the four values add up to 4 $(0 + 2 + 2 + 0)$, so the average is 1. Note that the average of these sample variances is exactly the same as the population variance. This is what is meant when we say that sample variance (using $n - 1$) is an unbiased estimator of population variance. On the average, this sample variance will give a precise estimate of the population variance. Now consider what happens if you were to use n in the formula for sample variance. In this case the four values add up to 2 $(0 + 1 + 1 + 0)$, so the average is $\frac{1}{2}$. Notice that on average this measure of sample variance underestimates the population variance. Using n, instead of $n - 1$, results in a biased measure of sample variance.

Table 4.1

All the Possible Random Samples of Size $n = 2$ Selected from a Population Consisting of Four Scores (1, 1, 3, 3)[a]

Sample	First Score	Second Score	Sample SS	Sample Variance Using $n - 1$	Sample Variance Using n
1	1	1	0	0	0
2	1	3	2	2	1
3	3	1	2	2	1
4	3	3	0	0	0

[a]The final two columns show the unbiased variance (using $n - 1$) for each sample and the biased variance (using n).

Figure 4.5

The frequency distribution histogram for a sample of $n = 7$ scores. The sample mean is $\overline{X} = 5$. The smallest distance from the mean is one point, and the largest distance from the mean is four points. The standard distance (standard deviation) should be between one and four points.

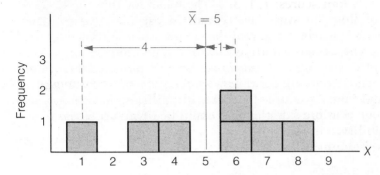

Now let's begin the calculations. First, we will find SS for this sample. Because there are only a few scores and the mean is a whole number, the definitional formula will be easy to use. You should try this formula for practice. Meanwhile, we will work with the computational formula.

X	X^2	
1	1	$\Sigma X = 35$
6	36	$\Sigma X^2 = 211$
4	16	
3	9	
8	64	
7	49	
6	36	

$$SS = \Sigma X^2 - \frac{(\Sigma X)^2}{n}$$

$$= 211 - \frac{(35)^2}{7}$$

$$= 211 - \frac{1225}{7}$$

$$= 211 - 175$$

$$= 36$$

Caution: *For sample variance, you use* n − 1 *after calculating* SS. *Do not use* n − 1 *in the formula for* SS.

SS for this sample is 36. You should obtain exactly the same answer using the definitional formula. Continuing the calculations,

$$\text{sample variance} = s^2 = \frac{SS}{n - 1} = \frac{36}{7 - 1} = 6$$

Finally, the standard deviation is

$$s = \sqrt{s^2} = \sqrt{6} = 2.45$$

Note that the value we obtained is in excellent agreement with our preliminary prediction.

Remember that the formulas for sample variance and standard deviation were constructed so that the sample variability would provide a good estimate of population variability. For this reason, sample variance is often called *estimated population variance*, and the sample standard deviation is called *estimated population standard deviation*. When you have only a sample to work with, the sample variance and standard deviation provide the best possible estimates of the population variability.

LEARNING CHECK

1. a. Sketch a frequency distribution histogram for the following sample of scores: 1, 1, 9, 1. Using your histogram, make an estimate of the standard deviation for this sample.
   b. Calculate SS, variance, and standard deviation for this sample. How well does your estimate from part a compare with the real standard deviation?

ANSWERS

1. a. Your graph should show a sample mean of $\overline{X} = 3$. The score farthest from the mean is $X = 9$, and the closest score is $X = 1$. You should estimate the standard deviation to be between two points and six points.
   b. For this sample, $SS = 48$; the sample variance is $\frac{48}{3} = 16$; the sample standard deviation is $\sqrt{16} = 4$.

Sample Variability and Degrees of Freedom

Although the concept of a deviation score and the calculation of SS are almost exactly the same for samples and populations, the minor differences in notation are really very important. When you have only a sample to work with, you must use the sample mean as the reference point for measuring deviations. Using $\overline{X}$ in place of μ places a restriction on the amount of variability in the sample. The restriction on variability comes from the fact that you must know the value of $\overline{X}$ before you can begin to compute deviations or SS. Notice that if you know the value of $\overline{X}$, then you also must know the value of ΣX. For example, if you have a sample of $n = 3$ scores and you know that $\overline{X} = 10$, then you also know that ΣX must be equal to 30 ($\overline{X} = \Sigma X/n$).

The fact that you must know $\overline{X}$ and ΣX before you can compute variability implies that not all of the scores in the sample are free to vary. Suppose, for example, that you are taking a sample of $n = 3$

scores and you know that $\Sigma X = 30$ $(\overline{X} = 10)$. Once you have identified the first two scores in the sample, the value of the third score is restricted. If the first scores were $X = 0$ and $X = 5$, then the last score would have to be $X = 25$ in order for the total to be $\Sigma X = 30$. Note that the first scores in this sample could have any values but that the last score is restricted. As a result, the sample is said to have $n - 1$ degrees of freedom; that is, only $n - 1$ of the scores are free to vary.

DEFINITION

Degrees of freedom, or *df*, for a sample are defined as

$$df = n - 1$$

where n is the number of scores in the sample.

The $n - 1$ degrees of freedom for a sample is the same $n - 1$ that is used in the formulas for sample variance and standard deviation. Remember that variance is defined as the average squared deviation. As always, this average is computed by finding the sum and dividing by the number of scores:

$$\text{average} = \frac{\text{sum}}{\text{number}}$$

To calculate sample variance (average squared deviation), we find the sum of the squared deviations (SS) and divide by the number of scores that are free to vary. This number is $n - 1 = df$.

$$s^2 = \frac{\text{sum of squared deviations}}{\text{number of scores free to vary}} = \frac{SS}{df} = \frac{SS}{n - 1}$$

Later in this book we will use the concept of degrees of freedom in several different situations. For now, you should remember that knowing the sample mean places a restriction on sample variability. Only $n - 1$ of the scores are free to vary; $df = n - 1$.

4.6
Properties of the Standard Deviation

Occasionally it is convenient to transform a set of scores by adding a constant to each score or by multiplying each score by a constant value. This is done, for example, when you want to "curve" a set of exam scores by adding a fixed amount to each individual's grade or when you want to convert measurements from minutes to seconds (multiply by 60). What happens to the standard deviation when the scores are transformed in this manner?

The easiest way to determine the effect of a transformation is to remember that the standard deviation is a measure of distance. If you select any two scores and see what happens to the distance between them, you also will find out what happens to the standard deviation.

1. *Adding a constant to each score will not change the standard deviation*. If you begin with a distribution that has $\mu = 40$ and $\sigma = 10$, what happens to σ if you add five points to every score? Consider any two scores in this distribution: Suppose, for example, that these are exam scores and that you had $X = 41$ and your friend had $X = 43$. The distance between these two scores is $43 - 41 = 2$ points. After adding the constant, five points, to each score, your score would be $X = 46$, and your friend would have $X = 48$. The distance between scores is still two points. Adding a constant to every score will not affect any of the distances and, therefore, will not change the standard deviation.

This fact can be seen clearly if you look at the graph for a frequency distribution. If you added 10 points to each score shown in Figure 4.5, what would happen? Each score would be moved 10 points to the right. The result is that the entire distribution is shifted to a new position 10 points up the scale. Note that the mean moves along with the scores and is increased by 10 points. However, the variability does not change because each of the deviation scores $(X - \mu)$ does not change.

2. *Multiplying each score by a constant causes the standard deviation to be multiplied by the same constant*. Consider the same distribution of exam scores we looked at earlier. If $\mu = 40$ and $\sigma = 10$, what would happen to σ if each score were multiplied by 2? Again we will look at two scores, $X = 41$ and $X = 43$, with a distance between them equal to two points. After all the scores have been multiplied by 2, these scores would become $X = 82$ and $X = 86$. Now the distance between scores is four points, twice the original distance. Multiplying each score causes each distance to be multiplied, and so the standard deviation also is multiplied by the same amount.

The effect of multiplying each score by a constant is demonstrated in the following example.

EXAMPLE 4.6
We begin with a sample of $n = 5$ scores. These scores add up to $\Sigma X = 15$, so the mean is $\overline{X} = 3$. The deviations and squared deviations are computed for each score, and then the squared deviations are added up to find SS. Finally, the variance and standard deviation are computed, and we find that $s = 2$ points.

X	$X - \overline{X}$	$(X - \overline{X})^2$
0	-3	9
4	$+1$	1
5	$+2$	4
2	-1	1
4	$+1$	1
		$16 = \Sigma(X - \overline{X})^2$

$$s^2 = \frac{SS}{n-1} = \frac{16}{4} = 4$$

$$s = \sqrt{s^2} = \sqrt{4} = 2$$

Now each score is multiplied by 3, and we repeat the calculations. Note that the scores now add up to $\Sigma X = 45$, so the new mean is $\overline{X} = 9$ (three times the original mean).

X	$X - \overline{X}$	$(X - \overline{X})^2$
0	-9	81
12	$+3$	9
15	$+6$	36
6	-3	9
12	$+3$	9
		$144 = \Sigma(X - \overline{X})^2$

$$s^2 = \frac{SS}{n-1} = \frac{144}{4} = 36$$
$$s = \sqrt{s^2} = \sqrt{36} = 6$$

Notice that multiplying the scores by 3 causes each deviation and the standard deviation also to be multiplied by 3.

Multiplying each score by a constant value is a commonly used method for changing the unit of measurement. If the original scores in this example were measurements in yards, then the mean is $\overline{X} = 3$ yards, and the standard deviation is $s = 2$ yards. Multiplying by 3 would convert the measurements from yards to feet. After this conversion, we find a mean of $\overline{X} = 9$ feet and a standard deviation of $s = 6$ feet. Because we simply converted the scores to new units (yards to feet), the two standard deviation values should be equivalent measurements. In fact, they are: $s = 2$ yards and $s = 6$ feet are the same.

4.7

Comparing Measures of Variability

By far the most commonly used measure of variability is standard deviation (together with the related measure of variance). Nonetheless, there are situations where the range or the semi-interquartile range may be preferred. The advantages and disadvantages of each of these three measures will be discussed.

In simple terms, there are two considerations that determine the value of any statistical measurement:

1. The measure should provide a stable and reliable description of the scores. Specifically, it should not be greatly affected by minor details in the set of data.
2. The measure should have a consistent and predictable relationship with other statistical measurements.

We will examine each of these considerations separately.

Factors that Affect Variability

1. *Extreme Scores.* Of the three measures of variability, the range is most affected by extreme scores. A single

extreme value will have a large influence on the range. In fact, the range is determined exclusively by the two extremes of the distribution. Standard deviation and variance also are influenced by extreme scores. Because these measures are based on squared deviations, a single extreme value can have a disproportionate effect. For example, a score that is 10 points away from the mean will contribute $10^2 = 100$ points to the SS. For this reason, standard deviation and variance should be interpreted carefully in distributions with one or two extreme values. Because the semi-interquartile range focuses on the middle of the distribution, it is least affected by extreme values. For this reason, the semi-interquartile range often provides the best measure of variability for distributions that are very skewed or that have a few extreme scores.

2. *Sample Size.* As you increase the number of scores in a sample, you also tend to increase the range because each additional score has the potential to replace the current highest or lowest value in the set. Thus, the range is directly related to sample size. This relationship between sample size and variability is unacceptable. A researcher should not be able to influence variability by manipulating sample size. Standard deviation, variance, and the semi-interquartile range are relatively unaffected by sample size and, therefore, provide better measures.

3. *Stability Under Sampling.* If you take several different samples from the same population, you should expect the samples to be similar. Specifically, if you compute variability for each of the separate samples, you should expect to obtain similar values. Because all of the samples come from the same source, it is reasonable that there should be some "family resemblance." When standard deviation and variance are used to measure variability, the samples will tend to have similar variability. For this reason, standard deviation and variance are said to be stable under sampling. The semi-interquartile range also provides a reasonably stable measure of variability. The range, however, will change unpredictably from sample to sample and is said to be unstable under sampling.

4. *Open-Ended Distributions.* When a distribution does not have any specific boundary for the highest score or the lowest score, it is open-ended. This can occur when you have infinite or undetermined scores. For example, a subject who cannot solve a problem has taken an undetermined or infinite amount of time to reach the solution. In an open-ended distribution, you cannot compute the range, or the standard deviation, or the variance. In

this situation, the only available measure of variability is the semi-interquartile range.

Relationship with Other Statistical Measures

As noted earlier, variance and standard deviation are computed from squared deviation scores. Because they are based on squared distances, these measures fit into a coherent system of mathematical relationships that underlies many of the statistical techniques we will examine in this book. Although we generally will not present the underlying mathematics, you will notice that variance and standard deviation appear repeatedly. For this reason, they are valuable measures of variability. Also, you should notice that variance and standard deviation have a direct relation to the mean (they are based on deviations from the mean). Therefore, the mean and standard deviation tend to be reported together. Because the mean is the most common measure of central tendency, the standard deviation will be the most common measure of variability.

Because the median and the semi-interquartile range are both based on percentiles, they share a common foundation and tend to be associated. When the median is used to report central tendency, the semi-interquartile range is commonly used to report variability.

The range has no direct relationship to any other statistical measure. For this reason, it is rarely used in conjunction with other statistical techniques.

Summary

1. The purpose of variability is to determine how spread out the scores are in a distribution. There are four basic measures of variability: the range, the semi-interquartile range, the variance, and the standard deviation.

    The range is the distance between the biggest and the smallest scores in the distribution. The semi-interquartile range is one-half the distance between the first quartile (25th percentile) and the third quartile (75th percentile). Variance is defined as the average squared deviation. Standard deviation is the square root of the variance.

    Standard deviation and variance are by far the most commonly used measures of variability.

2. The logical steps leading to the formulas for variance and standard deviation are summarized as follows. Remember that the purpose of standard deviation is to provide a measure of the standard distance from the mean.
    a. A deviation score is defined as $X - \mu$ and measures the direction and distance from the mean for each score.
    b. Because of the plus and minus signs, the sum of the deviation scores and the average of the deviation scores will always be zero.

c. To get rid of the signs, we square each deviation and then compute the average squared deviation, or the variance.

d. Finally, we correct for having squared all the deviations by taking the square root of the variance. The result is the standard deviation, and it gives a measure of the standard distance from the mean.

3. To calculate either variance or standard deviation, you first need to find the sum of the squared deviations, SS. There are two formulas for SS:

$$\text{Definitional formula: } SS = \Sigma(X - \mu)^2$$

$$\text{Computational formula: } SS = \Sigma X^2 - \frac{(\Sigma X)^2}{N}$$

4. Variance is the average squared deviation and is obtained by finding the sum of squared deviations and then dividing by the number. For a population, variance is

$$\sigma^2 = \frac{SS}{N}$$

For a sample, only $n - 1$ of the scores are free to vary (degrees of freedom or $df = n - 1$), so sample variance is

$$s^2 = \frac{SS}{n - 1}$$

5. Standard deviation is the square root of the variance. For a population this is

$$\sigma = \sqrt{\frac{SS}{N}}$$

Sample standard deviation is

$$s = \sqrt{\frac{SS}{n - 1}}$$

Using $n - 1$ in the sample formulas makes sample variance and sample standard deviation accurate and unbiased estimates of the corresponding population parameters.

6. Adding a constant value to every score in a distribution will not change the standard deviation. Multiplying every score by a constant, however, will cause the standard deviation to be multiplied by the same constant.

Key Terms

variability	variance
range	standard deviation
semi-interquartile range	sum of squares (SS)

deviation score   degrees of freedom (*df*)
average deviation

Problems for Chapter 4:
Variability

 1. Briefly define or explain each of the following:

    a. *SS*

    b. Variance

    c. Standard deviation

2. For the following population of scores, calculate the mean and then compute the deviation score for each individual. Show that the sum of the deviation scores is zero. Scores: 4, 3, 7, 0, 1, 9.

*3. Compute *SS* for the following set of scores using the definitional formula and then using the computational formula. (You should get the same result from both formulas.) Scores: 1, 3, 2, 7, 1, 0, 3, 2, 1, 0.

4. The quiz scores for a class of $N = 6$ students are as follows: 1, 3, 8, 5, 0, 1.

    a. Using the definitional formula, compute *SS* and variance for these scores (assume that the set of scores is a population).

    b. The instructor would like to "curve" this distribution by adding two points to each score so that the mean becomes $\mu = 5$. Add two points to each score and then recalculate *SS* and variance.

       (You should find that adding a constant does not change any of the deviation scores.)

*5. Two sets of data are presented here. Each set is a population.

    Data set A: 3, 5, 7, 3, 5, 6, 4, 7, 4, 6

    Data set B: 6, 4, 5, 3, 7

    a. Sketch a frequency distribution histogram for each population.

    b. Looking at your graphs, does it appear that one population is more variable than the other?

    c. Compute *SS* for each population. You should get different values. Does this mean that one population is more variable than the other?

    d. Compute variance for each population. The two values should be the same.

e. Explain why variance is a better measure of variability than SS.

6. If a population of scores has $\mu = 0$, then $SS = \Sigma X^2$.
   a. Make up a set of $N = 4$ scores so that $\mu = 0$.
   b. Using the definitional formula, compute SS for your scores.
   c. Explain why $SS = \Sigma X^2$ whenever $\mu = 0$.

*7. A population has $\mu = 100$ and $\sigma = 20$. If you select a single score from this population, on the average, how close would it be to the population mean? Explain your answer.

8. The following scores are brain weights in grams for a sample of $n = 5$ fish. Calculate the mean and variance for these data. (*Hint:* Multiply each score by 100 to get rid of the decimal places. Remember to correct for this multiplication before you report your answer.) Scores: 0.08, 0.09, 0.08, 0.11, 0.09.

*9. Calculate SS, variance, and standard deviation for the following sample of scores. (*Hint:* The calculations will be easier if you first subtract 430 from each score. For example, $431 - 430 = 1$, and $436 - 430 = 6$. (Remember, subtracting a constant will not affect these measures of variability.) Scores: 431, 432, 435, 432, 436, 431, 434.

10. A population of scores has $\mu = 50$ and $\sigma = 0$.
   a. What value would be obtained for SS for this population?
   b. What value would be obtained for the population variance?
   c. Describe the scores in the population. (What are the scores?)

*11. Can SS ever have a value less than zero? Explain your answer.

*12. A set of $n = 20$ quiz scores has a mean of $\overline{X} = 20$. One person is selected from the class to be the "mystery person." If the deviation scores for the other 19 students in the class add up to $+6$, what score did the mystery person have?

13. Two sets of scores are presented here:

    Set A: 4, 1, 3, 2
    Set B: 9, 6, 8, 9

   a. Calculate the mean for each set.
   b. If you had to calculate SS for each set of scores, which formula would you prefer to use for set A? Which formula would you prefer for set B?
   (Try both formulas on both sets of data until you are sure

which is easier to use. In general, when should you use the definitional formula and when should you use the computational formula for *SS*?)

*14. Find the range, the semi-interquartile range, and the standard deviation for the following population of scores: 1, 3, 5, 4, 2, 8, 4, 5.

15. Two populations are presented here:

$$\text{Population A:} \quad 53, \quad 58, \quad 52, \quad 55, \quad 57$$
$$\text{Population B:} \quad 31, \quad 47, \quad 53, \quad 71, \quad 79$$

a. Just looking at these data, which population will have the larger standard deviation? Explain your answer.

b. Without precisely calculating the mean, *SS*, etc., make an estimate of the standard deviation for each population. (First make a rough estimate of the mean. Then judge the average distance from the mean to the rest of the scores.)

c. Compute the standard deviation for each population.

*16. When a population consists of only two scores, it is very easy to calculate the standard deviation.

a. Use the definitional formula to compute *SS*, variance, and standard deviation for the population that consists of $X = 1$ and $X = 5$. You should find that the mean is halfway between these two scores at $\mu = 3$. Each score has the same deviation, two points from the mean. If every score has a deviation of two points, then the standard deviation must be $\sigma = 2$ points.

   Use this general rule to find the standard deviation for each of the following populations

b. $X = 20$ and $X = 30$

c. $X = 0$ and $X = 1$

d. $X = 57$ and $X = 73$

17. Use the following procedure to obtain a sample of $n = 4$ scores: First, close your book. Then, without looking, open to any page and write down the last digit of the left-hand page number. Repeat this procedure until you have four numbers. (*Note:* It is OK if the same digit appears more than once in your sample.)

a. Calculate the mean and variance for your sample.

b. You probably noticed that the left-hand pages all have even numbers. If you consider only the last digit of these numbers, the whole set of possible values is 0, 2, 4, 6, 8. This is the population that your sample came from. Calculate the mean and variance for this population.

c. How well did your sample statistics (mean and variance) approximate the population parameters? Note that you do not expect the sample values to be identical to the population, but they should be close.

*18. People are most accurate at remembering and describing other individuals when they share some characteristics with the person being described. This fact can be very important in eye-witness testimony. A typical experiment examining this phenomenon is presented here.

Two groups of subjects are used: The first group consists of college students, all 18–20 years old. The second group consists of businessmen aged 38–40. Each group views a short film of a bank robbery. The criminal in the film is a 40-year-old man wearing a suit and tie. After viewing the film, each subject is asked to describe the bank robber. This description includes an estimate of the robber's age. The data, showing each witness's estimate of age, are as follows:

College students: 35, 30, 55, 40, 40, 50, 45, 28, 33, 50

Businessmen: 40, 45, 40, 42, 40, 40, 35, 40, 41, 38

a. Calculate the mean for each sample. Based on the two means, does it appear that one group is more accurate than the other?

b. Calculate the standard deviation for each sample. Based on these values, does it appear that one group is more accurate than the other? Explain your answer.

19. For the following population,

$$19, \quad 23, \quad 17, \quad 27, \quad 21, \quad 20, \quad 18$$
$$22, \quad 19, \quad 18, \quad 25, \quad 21, \quad 29, \quad 24$$

a. Calculate the mean.

b. By just looking at the scores, estimate the standard deviation for this population. Remember, standard deviation measures the standard distance from the mean.

c. Calculate, SS, variance, and standard deviation for these scores. Compare the actual standard deviation with your estimate.

20. The following data are from two separate experiments:

Experiment I		Experiment II	
A	B	C	D
4	7	6	12
5	9	0	2
4	8	4	8
3	8	13	14
5	7	1	3
4	9	4	12
3	8	0	5

Experiment I compares the scores for subjects given treatment A versus subjects given treatment B. In experiment II, we are comparing scores for subjects given treatment C versus scores for subjects given treatment D.

a. For experiment I, sketch a histogram showing the distribution of scores for the two treatment conditions. Show both treaments in the same histogram, using different colors to differentiate the two treatment conditions.

b. Looking at your graph, does it appear that there is a difference between the two treatments? Are the scores in treatment A noticeably different from the scores in treatment B?

c. Calculate the mean and standard deviation for each treatment condition. Is there a mean difference between the treatments?

d. Now sketch a histogram showing the distributions for experiment II. Again, use different colors to differentiate the two treatments.

e. Looking at the graph for experiment II, does it appear that treatment C is different from treatment D?

f. Compute the mean and the standard deviation for each treatment in experiment II. Is there a mean difference between these two treatments?

Note: You should find a four-point difference between the treatment means in each experiment. However, in experiment I this difference is easy to see because the variability is low. In experiment II, the four-point difference gets lost in the overall variability.

*21. The following data represent the daily high temperatures for the month of February and for the month of April:

February				April		
27	24	29		31	38	32
25	19	21		48	32	51
22	31	24		65	46	31
17	23	28		63	73	59
29	32	25		46	29	35
35	28	23		48	64	78
27	21	16		74	52	61
28	25	24		42	48	60
23	32	31		66	73	84
29				81	73	79

a. Compute the mean temperature and the standard deviation for each month. Assume each set of data is a sample.

b. How well does the mean describe a "typical" day in February? How well does the mean describe a "typical" day in April? In general, how does the standard deviation affect the interpretation of the mean?

22. For the scores in the following sample,

19, 22, 25, 60, 16, 21, 22, 27
26, 22, 20, 15, 17, 21, 23, 29

a. Sketch a histogram showing the distribution of scores.

b. Calculate the mean and standard deviation for this sample.

c. Calculate the median and the semi-interquartile range for this sample.

d. Which measures of central tendency and variability seem to provide the better description of the sample? Why?

*23. A psychologist is interested in the relation between personality types and occupation. A sample of $n = 15$ adult males is obtained to represent the general population. Then a sample of $n = 15$ successful salesmen is obtained. Each individual is given a personality questionnaire measuring introversion/extroversion on a scale from 0 (extreme introvert) to 100 (extreme extrovert). The data for the two samples are as follows:

General Population		Salesmen	
23	49	76	85
61	38	62	77
82	53	71	85
34	58	90	82
79	47	80	74
37	81	84	88
53	86	82	79
41		72	

a. Calculate the mean and standard deviation for each sample.

b. Based on the sample means, how would you describe the personalities of salesmen relative to personalities in the general population?

c. Based on the sample standard deviations, how would you describe the personalities of salesmen relative to personalities in the general population?

z-Scores: Location of Scores and Standardized Distributions

TOOLS YOU WILL NEED

The following items are considered essential background material for this chapter. If you doubt your knowledge of any of these items, you should review the appropriate chapter or section before proceeding.

1. The mean (Chapter 3)
2. The standard deviation (Chapter 4)
3. Basic algebra (math review, Appendix A)

In the previous chapters we have looked at many ways of describing a set of scores. For instance, we can summarize and organize the data in frequency distribution tables and graphs. A measure of central tendency may be used to describe the typical value of the distribution. Variability measurements will tell us how clustered or scattered the scores are, and the shape of the distribution indicates in which region most of the scores lie. These methods summarize and describe groups of scores. However, it is often necessary to describe an individual score or, specifically, where the score is located in the distribution.

Suppose you are told that your exam score in statistics is $X = 22$. How well did you do on the test? Obviously, raw scores by themselves do not give you much information. To answer this question, you need to know something about the entire distribution of the class. It would help if you knew the mean of the test scores and how variable they are. This information will allow you to evaluate the location of your score in the distribution.

Let us assume that your instructor tells you that the mean for the class is $\mu = 20$. This bit of information should come as a relief because you now know that your score is above average. Specifically, your score is two points above the mean. But do you really know how good your score is? Two points above the mean might give you one of the highest scores in the class, or it may be a very "average"

score. More information is needed to locate your score in the distribution.

Your instructor now tells you that the standard deviation for the class is $\sigma = 2$. Consider this new information along with a sketch of the class distribution (Figure 5.1, distribution A). With a mean of 20 and a standard deviation of 2, your score ($X = 22$) is one of the highest in the class. There is so little variability in the distribution that even a score that is a few points above the mean is nearly the top score.

Consider a different outcome. Suppose the distribution for the class is much more variable, with $\sigma = 6$. As you can see, the hypothetical data in Figure 5.1, distribution B, are more scattered. In this distribution, a score of 22 seems to occupy a more central position compared to the rest of the scores. Notice that the score in question is two points above the mean in both distributions. Yet when there is little variability (distribution A), the score is near the top of the distribution. In contrast, when the standard deviation is larger (distribution B), the score of 22 is near the center of the distribution. Therefore, when locating a score in a distribution, we need to know more than simply the number of points between the score and the mean. We must also consider how much variability there is in the distribution. In this chapter, we will look at z-scores, which measure the distance of raw scores from the mean in terms of standard deviation units.

Figure 5.1

Two hypothetical distributions of test scores for a statistics class. For both distributions, $N = 16$ and $\mu = 20$. In distribution A, where there is little variability, a score of 22 is nearly the top score. In distribution B there is more variability, and the same score occupies a more central position in the distribution.

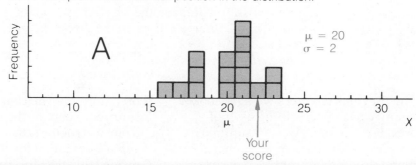

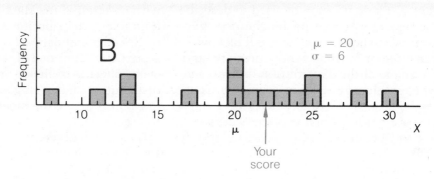

5.1

z-Scores and Location in a Distribution

What Is a *z*-Score?

The preview example demonstrates that a raw score by itself does not provide much information about its position in the distribution. To find the location of the score, you must also know the mean and standard deviation of the distribution. The purpose of *z*-scores is to take all of this information and combine it into a single value that specifies the exact location of a score in the distribution (see Box 5.1). Every raw score in a distribution has a corresponding *z*-score that specifies how many standard deviations away from the mean the raw score is.

DEFINITION

A *z-score* indicates the distance between a raw score and the mean, using standard deviation units to measure that distance.

BOX 5.1 | **Why Is Location in the Distribution Important?**

In the preview section, we noted the type of information that is needed to determine the location of a score in a distribution. Why is position in a distribution important to know? As we shall see in this chapter, anytime we wish to compare the standing of two or more scores, we must determine their positions in the distribution. Also, whenever we measure the relationship between two variables, it is helpful to determine the positions of the scores in their distribution (Chapter 16). In chapters on inferential statistics, we will need to locate the position of sample data in a distribution in order to make a general statement and conclusion about the population (for example, Chapters 8 and 9). Thus, the z-score has many uses, both in descriptive and inferential statistics.

A z-score has two parts: the sign (positive or negative) and the numerical value. The sign specifies whether the score is above the mean (positive) or below the mean (negative). The numerical value of the z-score specifies the distance from the mean by counting the number of standard deviations between X and μ.

EXAMPLE 5.1
A distribution of exam scores has a mean (μ) of 50 and a standard deviation (σ) of 8.

1. For this distribution, what is the z-score corresponding to $X = 58$? Because 58 is *above* the mean, the z-score has a positive sign. The score is eight points greater than the mean. This distance is exactly one standard deviation (because $\sigma = 8$), so the z-score is

$$z = +1$$

This z-score indicates that the raw score is one standard deviation above the mean.

2. What is the z-score corresponding to $X = 46$? The z-score will be negative because 46 is *below* the mean. The X value is four points away from the mean. This distance is exactly one-half of the standard deviation; therefore the z-score is

$$z = -\frac{1}{2}$$

This z-score tells us that the X value is one-half of a standard deviation below the mean.

3. For this distribution, what raw score corresponds to a z-score of $+2$? This z-score indicates that the X value is two standard deviations

above the mean. One standard deviation is 8 points, so two standard deviations would be 16 points. Therefore, the score we are looking for is 16 points above the mean. The mean for the distribution is 50, so the X value is

$$X = 50 + 16 = 66$$

The z-Score Formula

The relation between X values and z-scores can be expressed symbolically in a formula. The formula for transforming raw scores into z-scores is

(5.1) $z = \dfrac{X - \mu}{\sigma}$

The numerator of the equation, $X - \mu$, is a deviation score (Chapter 4, page 118) and measures the distance in points between X and μ. We divide this difference by σ because we want the z-score to measure distance in terms of standard deviation units. Remember, the purpose of a z-score is to specify an exact location in a distribution. The z-score formula provides a standard procedure for determining a score's location by calculating the direction and distance from the mean.

Remember, σ is always positive because it is based on squared deviation scores (Chapter 4).

1. *Direction.* If a raw score is less than the mean, then the z-score will have a negative sign. If X is greater in value than μ, z will be positive . These points should become obvious when you look at the numerator of the z-score formula, $X - \mu$. If $X = 48$ and $\mu = 51$, then $X - \mu = -3$. When this value is divided by the standard deviation, the result is a z-score that is negative. This indicates that the raw score is below the mean. By similar reasoning, if $X = 56$ and $\mu = 51$, then $X - \mu = +5$. This value in turn will result in a positive z-score. Therefore, the direction (above or below) of score from the mean is indicated by the sign ($+$ and $-$) of the z-score.

2. *Distance.* The distance of a score from the mean is indicated by the number value of the z-score. The greater the magnitude of this value, the farther X is from μ. A raw score with a z of -3 is farther from the mean than a score with a z of -1. The first score would be three standard deviations below the mean, while the second is only one standard deviation below μ.

EXAMPLE 5.2
A distribution of general psychology test scores has a mean of $\mu = 60$ and a standard deviation of $\sigma = 4$. What is the z-score for a student who received a 66?

Figure 5.2

For the population of general psychology test scores, $\mu = 60$ and $\sigma = 4$. A student whose score is 66 is 1.5σ above the mean or has a z-score of $+1.5$.

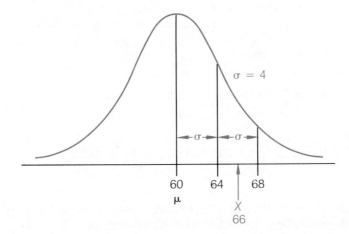

Looking at a sketch of the distribution (Figure 5.2), we see that the raw score is above the mean by at least one standard deviation but not quite by two. Judging from the graph, 66 appears to be approximately $1\frac{1}{2}$ standard deviations from the mean. The computation of the z-score with the formula confirms our guess:

$$z = \frac{X - \mu}{\sigma} = \frac{66 - 60}{4} = \frac{+6}{4} = +1.5$$

Figure 5.3

The population of verbal SAT scores has $\mu = 500$ and $\sigma = 100$. What is the z-score that corresponds to the raw score of 450?

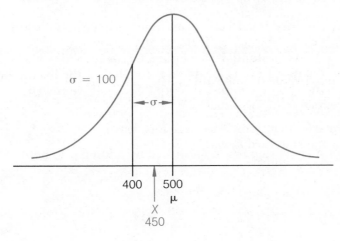

EXAMPLE 5.3

The distribution of SAT verbal scores for high school seniors has a mean of $\mu = 500$ and a standard deviation of $\sigma = 100$. Joe took the SAT and scored 450 on the verbal subtest. Locate his score in the distribution by using a z-score.

According to Figure 5.3, Joe's score is less than one standard deviation below the mean. The z-score should be negative and have a magnitude that is less than 1. Using the formula, his z-score is

$$z = \frac{X - \mu}{\sigma} = \frac{450 - 500}{100} = \frac{-50}{100} = -0.5$$

Determining a Raw Score from a *z*-Score

There may be situations in which you have an individual's z-score and would like to determine the corresponding raw score. When you start with a z-score, it is easier to compute the X value by using a different version of the z-score formula. By multiplying each side of the original equation by σ, we obtain

$$z\sigma = \left(\frac{X - \mu}{\sigma}\right)\sigma$$

$$z\sigma = X - \mu$$

Because $X - \mu$ is a deviation score, we can rewrite the equation as

(5.2) deviation score $= z\sigma$

For example, if a population has $\mu = 80$ and $\sigma = 12$, what is the X value corresponding to a z-score of $-\frac{1}{2}$. Using Formula (5.2), we obtain

deviation score $= z\sigma = -0.5(12) = -6$

A deviation score of -6 means that the raw score is six points *below* the mean. Since the mean has a value of 80, the X value must be 74. You can check this answer by computing the z-score for 74. You should get $z = -0.5$.

The raw score we obtained is perfectly consistent with the definition of a z-score. The value of $z = -0.5$ indicates that the raw score is below the mean by one-half of a standard deviation. One standard deviation is 12 points, so the raw score is located 6 points below the mean, or $X = 74$. The X value can be computed more directly if we rewrite the deviation score formula [Formula (5.2)] as

$$X - \mu = z\sigma$$

and now solve it for X. This step is accomplished by adding μ to both sides of the equation:

(5.3) $\mu + (X - \mu) = \mu + z\sigma$

$$\mu + X - \mu = \mu + z\sigma$$

$$X = \mu + z\sigma$$

Note that we can rewrite the equation as

raw score = mean + deviation score

The sign (+ or −) of the deviation score will be determined by the sign of the z-score. If a score is below the mean of the distribution, then z will be negative, and you will subtract the deviation score from the mean. In contrast, scores that are above the mean will have positive z-scores, so that the deviation score will be added to the mean.

The Characteristics of a z-Score Distribution

It is possible to describe the location of every raw score in the distribution by assigning z-scores to all of them. The result would be a transformation of the distribution of raw scores into a distribution of z-scores. That is, for each and every X value in the distribution of raw scores, there would be a corresponding z-score in the new distribution. This new distribution has specific characteristics—characteristics which make a z-score transformation a very useful tool in statistics. If every X value is transformed into a z-score, then the distribution of z-scores will have the following properties:

1. *Shape.* The shape of the z-score distribution will be the same as the original distribution or raw scores. If the original distribution is negatively skewed, for example, then the z-score distribution will also be negatively skewed. It does not matter what shape the original distribution has. The z-score distribution will look just like it. Transforming raw scores into z-scores does not change the shape of the distribution.

2. *The Mean.* When raw scores are transformed into z-scores, the resulting z-score distribution will *always* have a mean of zero. This is the case regardless of what the value of μ is for the raw score distribution. Suppose a population of scores has $\mu = 75$ and $\sigma = 15$. What is the z-score for the value $X = 75$? Notice that the X value equals the mean of the distribution, so its z-score will also be the z-score for the mean.

[handwritten margin note: z-score corresponding to mean is 0]

$$z = \frac{X - \mu}{\sigma} = \frac{75 - 75}{15} = \frac{0}{15} = 0$$

The mean of the distribution has a z-score of zero. This fact makes the mean a convenient reference point. You will remember that raw scores that fall below the mean have negative z-scores (that is, z-scores *less than zero*) and that X values above the mean have positive z-scores *(greater than zero)*.

3. *The Standard Deviation.* When a distribution of X values is transformed into a distribution of z-scores, the new distribution will have a standard deviation of 1. For example, a distribution of raw scores has $\mu = 100$ and σ

Figure 5.4

Following a z-score transformation, the X-axis is relabeled in z-score units. The distance that is equivalent to one standard deviation on the X-axis (σ = 10 points in this example) corresponds to 1 point on the z-score scale.

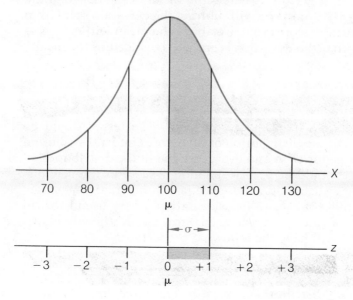

= 10. In this distribution a raw score of 110 will have a z-score of $+1$ (one standard deviation above the mean). When X is 90, the z will be -1 (or one standard deviation below the mean). When X is 120, z is $+2$, and so on. The distribution in Figure 5.4 is labeled in terms of both X values and their corresponding z-scores. Note that 10 points on the X scale is the equivalent of one standard deviation. Furthermore, the distance of one standard deviation on the X scale corresponds to 1 point on the z-score scale. That is, the X scale has merely been relabeled following a z transformation, so that 1 point on the z scale corresponds to one standard deviation unit on the X scale. This relabeling will give the z-score distribution a standard deviation of 1 point.

Demonstrating the Properties of a z-Score Transformation

By using a small population of raw scores, it is easy to demonstrate the characteristics of a distribution following a z-score transformation. A population of $N = 6$ scores consists of the following values:

0, 6, 5, 2, 3, 2

The population mean is

$$\mu = \frac{\Sigma X}{N} = \frac{18}{6} = 3$$

The population standard deviation is

$$\sigma = \sqrt{\frac{SS}{N}} = \sqrt{\frac{24}{6}} = \sqrt{4} = 2$$

To demonstrate the characteristics of a z-score distribution, we must transform every raw score into a z-score using Formula (5.1):

$$z = \frac{X - \mu}{\sigma}$$

Therefore, for $X = 0$,

$$z = \frac{0 - 3}{2} = -1.5$$

For $X = 6$,

$$z = \frac{6 - 3}{2} = +1.5$$

For $X = 5$,

$$z = \frac{5 - 3}{2} = +1.0$$

For $X = 2$,

$$z = \frac{2 - 3}{2} = -0.5$$

For $X = 3$,

$$z = \frac{3 - 3}{2} = 0$$

For $X = 2$,

$$z = -0.5 \quad \text{(already computed)}$$

The distribution now consists of $N = 6$ z-scores:

$$-1.5, \quad +1.5, \quad +1.0, \quad -0.5, \quad 0, \quad -0.5$$

Notice that the shape of the distribution has not been changed by the z-score transformation (Figure 5.5). This observation will be true regardless of the shape of the original raw score distribution. The X-axis is simply relabeled in z-score units after the transformation. For the mean of the z distribution, we add all the z-scores and divide by N:

$$\mu_z = \frac{\Sigma z}{N} = \frac{-1.5 + 1.5 + 1 + -0.5 + 0 + (-0.5)}{6}$$

$$= \frac{-2.5 + 2.5}{6} = \frac{0}{6} = 0$$

Figure 5.5

Transforming a distribution of raw scores (top) into z-scores (bottom) will not change the shape of the distribution.

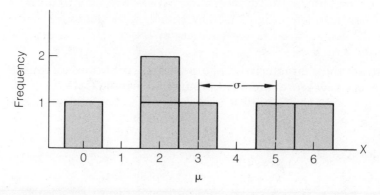

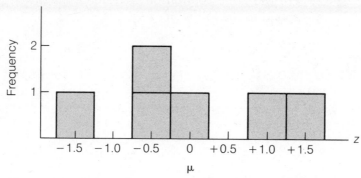

The mean of the distribution of z-scores (μ_z) will always equal zero, regardless of the value of the mean for the raw scores.

To determine the standard deviation of the z-scores, we use the standard deviation formula but plug in z-scores in place of X values. Therefore, the sum of squares for a z-score distribution is

$$SS_z = \Sigma(z - \mu_z)^2$$

Table 5.1 summarizes the steps for the computation of SS_z. For the standard deviation of the z-score distribution (σ_z), we obtain

Table 5.1

For a distribution of z-scores, $\mu_z = 0$. Therefore, z = z − μ_z.

z	z − μ_z	$(z - \mu_z)^2$
−1.5	−1.5	2.25
+1.5	+1.5	2.25
+1.0	+1.0	1.00
−0.5	−0.5	0.25
0	0	0
−0.5	−0.5	0.25

$$SS_z = \Sigma(z - \mu_z)^2 = 6.00$$

$$\sigma_z = \sqrt{\frac{SS_z}{N}} = \sqrt{\frac{6}{6}} = \sqrt{1} = 1$$

In summary, transforming raw scores to z-scores will give us a new distribution with the same shape as the original, a mean of zero, and a standard deviation equal to 1 regardless of the parameters of the distribution of raw scores.

1. A population of scores has $\mu = 45$ and $\sigma = 5$. Find the z-scores for the following raw scores:
   a. $X = 47$ e. $X = 52$
   b. $X = 48$ f. $X = 39$
   c. $X = 40$ g. $X = 45$
   d. $X = 44$ h. $X = 56$

2. For the same population, determine the raw scores that correspond to the following z-scores:
   a. $z = +1.3$ d. $z = -1.5$
   b. $z = -0.4$ e. $z = +2.8$
   c. $z = -3.0$ f. $z = 0$

ANSWERS

1. a. +0.4   2. a. 51.5
   b. +0.6   b. 43
   c. −1.0   c. 30
   d. −0.2   d. 37.5
   e. +1.4   e. 59
   f. −1.2   f. 45
   g.   0
   h. +2.2

5.2
Using z-Scores for Making Comparisons

Standard Scores

The transformation of raw scores into z-scores is very useful when we want to compare scores from two different distributions. For example, Bob received a 60 on a psychology exam. For this class, the mean was 50 and $\sigma = 10$. In biology, Bob's test score was 56, and for this class $\mu = 48$ with $\sigma = 4$. In which course does Bob have a higher standing? First, you should notice that Bob's psychology score is higher than his score in biology ($X = 60$ versus $X = 56$). Also, if you look at deviation scores, Bob is 10 points above the mean in psychology and only 8 points above the mean in biology. Does this mean that he performed better in psychology than in biology? Not necessarily! The problem is that we cannot simply compare his psychology score to his biology score because these scores come from *different distributions*. For the psychology class, $\mu = 50$ and $\sigma = 10$, and for biology, $\mu = 48$ and $\sigma = 4$. A score of 60 in psychology means something different from a score of 56 in biology. Any comparisons between these two test scores would be like the proverbial comparison of "apples to oranges."

To determine the class in which Bob did better, we must *standardize* the distribution of both classes to make them similar so that meaningful comparisons can be made. Remember, a z-score transformation will always produce a distribution that has $\mu = 0$ and $\sigma = 1$. Therefore, if every raw score in the psychology and biology classes is transformed into a z-score, the resulting distributions for both classes would have $\mu = 0$ and $\sigma = 1$. All we need to do is compare Bob's z-score for psychology with his z-score for biology to determine which exam score is better. When data transformations are used to make distributions comparable, we are using *standardized distributions*. The z-scores in this instance are often called *standard scores*.

DEFINITIONS

A *standardized distribution* is composed of transformed scores that result in set values for μ and σ, regardless of their values for the raw score distribution. Standardized distributions are used to make dissimilar distributions comparable.

A *standard score* is a transformed score that provides information of its location in a distribution. A z-score is an example of a standard score.

Making Comparisons with z-Scores

In practice it is not necessary to transform every score in a distribution to make comparisons between two scores. We need to transform only the two scores in question. In Bob's case, we must find the z-scores for his psychology and biology scores. For psychology, Bob's z-score is

Be sure to use the μ and σ values for the distribution to which X belongs.

$$z = \frac{X - \mu}{\sigma} = \frac{60 - 50}{10} = \frac{10}{10} = +1.0$$

For biology, Bob's z-score is

$$z = \frac{56 - 48}{4} = \frac{8}{4} = +2.0$$

Note that Bob's z-score for biology is $+2.0$, which means that his test score is two standard deviations above the class mean. On the other hand, his z-score is $+1.0$ for psychology, or one standard deviation above the mean. In terms of relative class standing, Bob is doing much better in the biology class. Unlike the absolute size of the raw scores, the z-scores describe *relative* positions within a distribution.

EXAMPLE 5.4

Suppose that in Caribou, Maine the average snowfall per year is $\mu = 110$ inches with $\sigma = 30$. In Boston, however, let us assume the yearly average of snowfall is only 24 inches with $\sigma = 5$. Last winter Caribou received 125 inches of snow, and Boston had 39 inches. In which city was the winter much worse than average for its residents?

To answer this question, we must standardize the distributions to make them comparable. Specifically, z-scores should be computed so that we can compare the two cities in terms of how out of the ordinary the snowfall amounts are. For Caribou, the z-score for last winter's snowfall is

$$z = \frac{X - \mu}{\sigma} = \frac{125 - 110}{30} = \frac{15}{30} = +0.5$$

For Boston, the z-score is

$$z = \frac{X - \mu}{\sigma} = \frac{39 - 24}{5} = \frac{15}{5} = +3.0$$

Boston's snowfall was much worse than average for that area—three standard deviations above the mean. In contrast, it was a fairly typical winter for Caribou residents. Their snowfall was only one-half of a standard deviation above the average for that region. In an absolute sense, Caribou had much more snow than Boston (125 versus 39 inches), but as far as Caribou winters go, it was another typical season for its residents. Just imagine if one winter Boston receives 125 inches of snow when its residents are accustomed to 24-inch seasons!

LEARNING
CHECK

1. Why is it possible to compare scores from different distributions after each distribution is transformed into z-scores?
2. For distribution A, $\mu = 20$ and $\sigma = 7$. Distribution B has $\mu = 23$ and $\sigma = 2$. In which distribution will a raw score of 27 have a higher standing?

ANSWERS

1. Comparisons are possible because both distributions will have the same μ and σ ($\mu = 0$, $\sigma = 1$) following a z-score transformation.
2. For distribution A, a raw score of 27 has a z-score of $+1.0$. For distribution B, a score of 27 corresponds to a z-score of $+2.0$. Therefore, a raw score of 27 has a higher relative standing in distribution B.

5.3

Other Standardized Distributions Based on z-Scores

Transforming z-Scores to a Predetermined μ and σ

Although z-score distributions have distinct advantages, many people find them cumbersome because they contain negative values and decimals. For these reasons, it is common to standardize a distribution by transforming z-scores to a distribution with a predetermined mean and standard deviation that are whole round numbers. Standardized scores of this type are frequently used in psychological testing. For example, raw scores of the Scholastic Aptitude Test (SAT) are transformed to a standardized distribution that has μ = 500 and σ = 100. For intelligence tests, raw scores are frequently converted to standard scores that have a mean of 100 and a standard deviation of 15. If the same standardized scale is used for several types of intelligence tests, then the exam scores on different tests can be more readily compared because the distributions will have the same mean and standard deviation. Basically, two steps are involved in standardizing distributions so that they have the same μ and σ: (1) All of the raw scores from both distributions are transformed to z-scores, and (2) all z-scores are then converted back into X values so that a particular μ and σ will be achieved.

EXAMPLE 5.5

An instructor gives different versions of an exam to his two psychology classes. For class 1, the mean is μ = 57 with σ = 14. Joe and Harry are two of the students in this class, and they have scores of 64 and 43 respectively. For the second class, μ = 31 and σ = 6. In this class, Mary had a score of 34, and Bill received a 28. These data are summarized in Table 5.2. The instructor would like to make the scores of both classes comparable by transforming all raw scores so that each class distribution will be standardized with μ = 50 and σ = 5. What will the standardized scores be for Joe, Harry, Mary, and Bill?

Step 1. Transform all of the raw scores into z-scores. For Joe, X = 64, so his z-score is

$$z = \frac{X - \mu}{\sigma} = \frac{64 - 57}{14} = +0.5$$

For Harry, X = 43, and his z-score is

$$z = \frac{X - \mu}{\sigma} = \frac{43 - 57}{14} = -1.0$$

Remember, the values of μ and σ are for the distribution from which X was taken.

For Mary, $X = 34$, and her z-score is

$$z = \frac{X - \mu}{\sigma} = \frac{34 - 31}{6} = +0.5$$

And for Bill, who scored a 28, the z-score is

$$z = \frac{X - \mu}{\sigma} = \frac{28 - 31}{6} = -0.5$$

Step 2. Change the z-scores to the new standardized scores. The instructor wants to have a standardized distribution with $\mu = 50$ and $\sigma = 5$. Joe's z-score is $+0.5$. What X value in the new standardized distribution will correspond to $z = +0.5$? Joe's z-score indicates that he is one-half of a standard deviation above the mean. Since the mean of the standardized distribution will be set at 50 and its $\sigma = 5$, Joe is 2.5 points above 50. That is, he will have a standardized score of 52.5. Mary's z-score is the same as Joe's, $z = +0.5$, so she too will have a score of 52.5 in the new standardized distribution. Harry is one standard deviation below the mean ($z = -1.0$), so his score will be 5 points below the mean in the standardized distribution, or $X = 45$. Bill is one-half of a standard deviation below the mean ($z = -0.5$). His standardized score, therefore, is 2.5 points below 50, or $X = 47.5$. These results are summarized in Table 5.2. To complete the construction of the standardized distribution, the instructor must repeat steps 1 and 2 for each raw score in the original distributions for both classes.

A Formula for Finding the Standardized Score

Earlier in the chapter, we derived a formula [Formula (5.3)] to find the raw score that corresponds to a particular z-score:

$$X = \mu + z\sigma$$

Table 5.2

| | Class 1: $\mu = 57, \sigma = 14$ | | Class 2: $\mu = 31, \sigma = 6$ | |
	Joe	Harry	Mary	Bill
Raw score	$X = 64$	43	34	28
Step 1: compute z-score	$z = +0.5$	-1.0	$+0.5$	-0.5
Step 2: standard score	52.5	45	52.5	47.5

For purposes of computing the new standardized score, we can rewrite the equation:

(5.4) standard score = $\mu_{new} + z\sigma_{new}$

The standard score equals the mean of the new standardized distribution plus its z-score times the standard deviation of the new standardized distribution. The z-score in the formula is the one computed for the original raw score (step 1). Notice that $z\sigma$ is the deviation score of the standard score. If the raw score is below the mean, then its z-score and $z\sigma$ will be negative. For scores above the mean, $z\sigma$ is positive.

EXAMPLE 5.6

A psychologist has developed a new intelligence test. For years he has given the test to a large number of people and finds that for this population $\mu = 65$ and $\sigma = 10$. He would like to make the scores of his subjects comparable to scores on other IQ tests, which have $\mu = 100$ and $\sigma = 15$. If he standardized his test so that it is comparable (has the same μ and σ) to other tests, what would be the standardized scores for the following individuals?

Person	X
1	70
2	75
3	60
4	50
5	80

Table 5.3

	Computations	
	Step 1: $z = \dfrac{X - \mu}{\sigma}$	Step 2: $X = \mu + z\sigma$
Person 1	$z = \dfrac{70 - 65}{10} = +0.5$	$X = 100 + 0.5(15)$ $= 100 + 7.5 = 107.5$
Person 2	$z = \dfrac{75 - 65}{10} = +1.0$	$X = 100 + 1(15)$ $= 100 + 15 = 115$
Person 3	$z = \dfrac{60 - 65}{10} = -0.5$	$X = 100 + -0.5(15)$ $= 100 - 7.5 = 92.5$
Person 4	$z = \dfrac{50 - 65}{10} = -1.5$	$X = 100 + -1.5(15)$ $= 100 - 22.5 = 77.5$
Person 5	$z = \dfrac{80 - 65}{10} = +1.5$	$X = 100 + 1.5(15)$ $= 100 + 22.5 = 122.5$

Step 1. Compute the z-score for each individual. Remember, the original distribution has $\mu = 65$ and $\sigma = 10$.

Step 2. Compute the standardized score for each person. Remember that the standardized distribution will have $\mu = 100$ and $\sigma = 15$. Table 5.3 summarizes the computations for these steps and the results.

Summary

Person	X	z	Standardized Scores
1	70	+0.5	107.5
2	75	+1.0	115
3	60	−0.5	92.5
4	50	−1.5	77.5
5	80	+1.5	122.5

LEARNING CHECK

1. Distribution A from Figure 5.1 has $\mu = 20$ and $\sigma = 2$. The raw scores from this distribution are as follows:

16, 17, 18, 18, 18, 20, 20, 20

21, 21, 21, 21, 21, 22, 23, 23

a. Transform this distribution so that it has $\mu = 50$ and $\sigma = 10$.

b. Compute the values for μ and σ for the new distribution. They should equal 50 and 10, respectively.

ANSWERS

a.

X	z	Standard Score
16	−2	30
17	−1.5	35
18	−1	40
18	−1	40
18	−1	40
20	0	50
20	0	50
20	0	50
21	+0.5	55
21	+0.5	55
21	+0.5	55
21	+0.5	55
21	+0.5	55
22	+1	60
23	+1.5	65
23	+1.5	65

b. For standard scores,

$N = 16$

$\Sigma X = 800$

$\mu = 50$

$SS = 1600$

$\sigma = 10$

Summary

1. A z-score measures the location of a score in a distribution. It measures how far a raw score is from the mean in standard deviation units.

2. The sign of the z-score is determined by the deviation score in the numerator of the z-score formula:

$$z = \frac{X - \mu}{\sigma}$$

3. Positive signs indicate the raw scores are above the mean, and negative signs indicate the scores are below it.

4. The numerical value of the z-score tells us how many standard deviations a score is from the mean.

5. It is possible to determine the value of a raw score when its z-score is provided. This is accomplished by solving the z-score formula for X:

$$X = \mu + z\sigma$$

6. This formula may be rewritten as

raw score = mean + deviation score

7. When a z-score is computed for every X-score, the transformation will produce a distribution of z-scores that will have the same shape as the distribution of raw scores.

8. The mean of the z-score distribution will be zero and the standard deviation will equal 1 regardless of the values of μ and σ for the raw score distribution.

9. When comparing raw scores from different distributions, it is necessary to standardize the distributions with a z-score transformation. The distributions will then be comparable because they will have the same parameters ($\mu = 0, \sigma = 1$). In practice, it is necessary to transform only those raw scores that are being compared.

10. In certain situations, such as in psychological testing, the z-scores are converted into standardized distributions that have a particular mean and standard deviation.

Key Terms

z-score
deviation score
raw score

z-score transformation
standard score
standardized distribution

Problems for Chapter 5:
z-Scores: Location of Scores and Standardized Distributions

*1. For a population of scores with $\mu = 100$ and $\sigma = 16$,

   a. Find the z-score that corresponds to each of the following X values:

$X = 108$	$X = 104$
$X = 132$	$X = 92$
$X = 100$	$X = 120$
$X = 124$	$X = 84$

   b. Find the raw scores for each of the following z-scores:

$z = -1.00$	$z = +\frac{1}{2}$
$z = +1.50$	$z = -1.25$
$z = 0$	$z = +0.25$
$z = +2.00$	$z = -2.00$

*2. Describe exactly what information is provided by a z-score.

3. Describe the characteristics of a distribution following a z transformation.

4. A population of scores has $\mu = 80$ and $\sigma = 20$. Find the z-score corresponding to each of the following X values:

   85, 90, 110, 75, 60, 45

   130, 82, 68, 80, 95, 30

*5. A population has $\mu = 50$ and $\sigma = 6$. Find the raw score for each of the following z-scores:

   2.50, 1, -3, -1.33, -1.5, $+\frac{1}{2}$, -2, 0, $-\frac{1}{2}$

6. For a population with $\mu = 50$, a raw score of 43 corresponds to a z-score of -1.00. What is the standard deviation of this population?

*7. For a population with $\sigma = 40$, a score of $X = 320$ corresponds to a z-score of $+2.00$. What is the mean for this population?

8. The grades from a physics exam were reported in X values and in corresponding z-scores. For this exam, a raw score of 65 corresponds to a z-score of $+2.00$. Also, when $X = 50$, $z = -1.00$. Find the mean and standard deviation for the distribution of exam scores. (*Hint:* Sketch the distribution, and locate the positions for the two scores. How many standard deviations fall between the two X values?)

*9. On a statistics quiz you obtain a score of 7. Would you rather be in section A where $\sigma = 2$ or in section B where $\sigma = 1$? Assume that $\mu = 6$ for both sections.

10. Answer the same question in Problem 9, but assume that $\mu = 8$ for both sections. Explain your answer.

*11. In psychology, you received an exam score of 37, while the mean for the class is $\mu = 28$ with $\sigma = 6$. In another general psychology section, your friend received a 46. The distribution for this class has $\mu = 35$ and $\sigma = 10$. Who has a higher standing in the class?

12. The mean of a distribution after a z-score transformation is always zero because $\Sigma z = 0$. Explain why Σz must always equal zero. (*Hint:* Examine the z-score formula.)

*13. The Wechsler Adult Intelligence Scale is composed of a number of subtests. Each subtest has been standardized so that $\mu = 10$ and $\sigma = 3$. A psychologist is updating some of the subtests. In particular, he has developed a new vocabulary subtest to replace the old one. For the new subtest, the psychologist finds $\mu = 35$ and $\sigma = 6$. Following are the raw scores for some of the subjects who took the new vocabulary subtest:

$$41, \quad 32, \quad 39, \quad 44, \quad 45, \quad 24, \quad 37, \quad 27$$

What will their scores be when standardized?

14. A population of $N = 5$ scores consists of

$$1, \quad 3, \quad 5, \quad 6, \quad 7$$

a. Computer μ and σ for this population.

b. Find the z-score for each raw score in the distribution.

c. Compute the mean and stardard deviation for the set of z-scores (round off all calculations to two decimal places). What is demonstrated about z-score transformations?

d. Explain the advantages of the characteristics of z transformations.

*15. For the following population of raw scores, perform a z-score transformation:

71	84	61	70	57	81
72	77	69	67	80	61
75	76	88	93	74	76
79	86	80	62	64	91
71	80	79	68	82	73
78	66	81	71	86	82
83	78	92	74	87	73

16. Two groups are given a different form of a reading comprehen-

sion test. The distribution of raw scores for each group is as follows:

Form A		Form B	
26	34	39	41
40	31	35	47
38	30	34	30
21	26	49	28
31	38	51	25
28	23	42	53
29	27	39	47
31	43	43	37

a. Compute μ and σ for both distributions.

b. Standardize the distributions so that $\mu = 500$ and $\sigma = 100$ for both sets of data.

c. Compute μ and σ for each distribution of standard scores. For each distribution, μ should be 500, and σ should be 100.

d. Which raw score is better: $X = 40$ on form A or $X = 47$ on form B?

e. Which raw score is worse: $X = 21$ on form A or $X = 30$ on form B?

*17. For the following population of raw scores,

$$
\begin{array}{ccccc}
23 & 26 & 23 & 25 & 28 \\
22 & 19 & 15 & 21 & 11 \\
15 & 15 & 19 & 14 & 18 \\
16 & 21 & 21 & 22 & 33 \\
24 & 23 & 22 & 10 & 17 \\
11 & 24 & 28 & 21 & 23 \\
27 & 28 & 22 & 31 & 32
\end{array}
$$

a. Compute μ and σ.

b. Transform the distribution to z-scores.

c. Compute the μ and σ for the distribution of z-scores.

18. For the following population of raw scores,

$$
\begin{array}{ccccc}
18.0 & 15.6 & 11.8 & 11.5 & 10.9 \\
10.6 & 7.7 & 12.1 & 11.3 & 8.1 \\
9.0 & 14.8 & 11.2 & 11.4 & 12.5 \\
10.5 & 9.3 & 12.0 & 17.2 & 13.3 \\
9.9 & 10.4 & 11.7 & 11.4 & 9.8 \\
11.4 & 9.8 & 8.7 & 10.8 & 14.2
\end{array}
$$

a. Compute μ and σ.

b. Transform the distribution into z-scores.

c. Check the z-score distribution to see if $\mu = 0$.

*19. For the following population of raw scores,

10	47	37	74	56	91	34	64	73	49
9	33	74	60	83	24	34	46	66	51
57	61	27	42	77	81	49	55	90	38
39	58	63	52	71	67	60	26	40	53

    a. Compute μ and σ.

    b. Transform the distribution into z-scores.

    c. Check the z-score distribution to see if $\mu = 0$.

20. Standardize the distribution in Problem 18 so that $\mu = 50$ and $\sigma = 5$.

*21. Standardize the distribution in Problem 19 so that $\mu = 100$ and $\sigma = 10$. Compute μ and σ for the standardized distribution to check your work.

Probability

The following items are considered essential background material for this chapter. If you doubt your knowledge of any of these items, you should review the appropriate chapter or section before proceeding.

1. Proportions (math review, Appendix A)
   a. Fractions
   b. Decimals
   c. Percentages
2. Basic algebra (math review, Appendix A)
3. Percentiles and percentile ranks (Chapter 2)
4. z-Scores (Chapter 5)

As you read through this textbook (or a novel, or a newspaper, etc.), which of the following are you more likely to encounter.

1. A word beginning with the letter K?
2. A word with a K as its third letter?

If you think about this question and answer honestly, you probably will decide that words beginning with a K are more probable.

A similar question was asked of a group of subjects in an experiment reported by Tversky and Kahneman (1973). Their subjects estimated that words beginning with K are twice as likely as words with K in the third position. In truth, the relation is just the opposite: There are more than twice as many words with a K in the third position as there are words beginning with a K. How can people be so wrong? Do they completely misunderstand probability?

When you were deciding which type of K words are more likely, you probably tried to estimate which words are more common in the English language. How many words can you think of that start with the letter K? How many words can you think of that have a K as the third letter? Because you have years of practice alphabetizing words according to their first letter, you find it much easier to search through your memory for words beginning with a K than to search for words with a K in third position. Consequently, you conclude that first-letter K words are more common.

Notice that when you use the strategy of counting words, you are not actually estimating probabilities; rather, you are estimating frequencies or proportions in the population. Most people seem to think of probability in terms of proportion. As you will see later in the chapter, this is a perfectly reasonable concept. Your error in judging the relative probabilities was not due to a misunderstanding of probability; instead, you simply were misled by the availability of the two types of words in your mind. If you had searched through a passage of text (instead of your mind), you probably would have found more third-letter K words, and you would have concluded (correctly) that these words are more probable.

In this chapter we will examine the statistical concept of probability. Although some of the mathematics and definitions may be new to you, there is a good chance that much of the material will be consistent with your present understanding of probability.

6.1

Introduction

Until this point, we have been concerned primarily with descriptive statistics, that is, finding ways to simplify the description and organization of a set of scores. Now we will begin to lay the foundations for inferential statistics. The goal of inferential statistics is to use the limited information from samples to draw general conclusions about populations. Remember, most experiments start with a general question concerning a population: for example,

Does vitamin E affect the life span of rats?

Will increased homework assignments improve reading scores for sixth graders?

Will overcrowding increase hostility among monkeys?

In each case the population is much too large to be examined directly. Instead, we must be content to work with a sample and hope that the information from the specific sample will help to answer our general question. The problem for inferential statistics is to define precisely the relationship between the sample and the population. However, when the values in a population are variable (not all the same), it is impossible to specify exactly which scores will be selected for any particular sample. Thus, there is not a perfect, one-to-one relationship between samples and populations. For this reason, relations between samples and populations most often are described in terms of probability. Suppose, for example, you are selecting a sample of 1 marble from a jar that contains 50 black and 50 white marbles. Although you cannot guarantee the exact outcome of your sample, it is possible to talk about the potential outcomes in terms of probabilities. In this case, you have a fifty-fifty chance of getting either color. Now consider another jar (population) that has 90 black and only 10 white marbles. Again, you cannot specify the exact outcome of a sample, but now you know that the sample probably will be a black marble. By knowing the makeup of a population, we can determine the probability of obtaining specific samples. In this way, probability gives us a connection between populations and samples.

You may have noticed that the preceding examples all begin with a population and then use probability to describe the samples that could be obtained. This is exactly backwards from what we want to do with inferential statistics. Remember, our goal is to begin with a sample and then answer general questions about the population. We will reach this goal in a two-stage process. In the first stage, we develop probability as a bridge from population to samples. This stage involves identifying the types of samples that probably would be obtained from a specific population. Once this bridge is established, we simply reverse the probability rules to allow us to move from samples to populations (see Figure 6.1). The process of reversing the probability relation can be demonstrated by considering again the two jars of marbles we looked at earlier. (One jar has 50 black and 50 white marbles; the other jar has 90 black and only 10 white marbles.) This time, suppose that you are blindfolded when the sample is selected and that your task is to use the sample to help you to decide which jar was used. If you select a sample of $n = 4$ marbles and all are black, where did the sample come from? It should be clear that it would be relatively unlikely (low probability) to obtain this sample from jar 1; in four draws, you almost certainly would get at least 1 white marble. On the other hand, this sample would have a high probability from jar 2 where nearly all the marbles are black. Your decision, therefore, is that the sample probably came from jar 2. Notice that you now are using the sample to make a decision about the population.

6.2
Probability Definition

Probability is a huge topic that extends far beyond the limits of introductory statistics, and we will not attempt to examine all of it here.

Figure 6.1

The role of probability in inferential statistics. The goal of inferential statistics is to use the limited information from samples to draw general conclusions about populations. The relationship between samples and populations usually is defined in terms of probability. Probability allows you to start with a population and predict what kind of sample is likely to be obtained. This forms a bridge between populations and samples. Inferential statistics uses the *probability bridge* as a basis for moving from samples to populations.

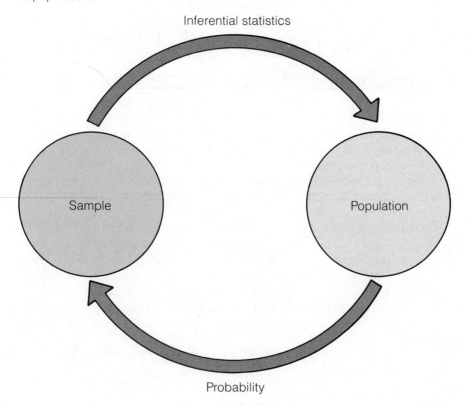

Inferential statistics

Sample

Population

Probability

Instead, we will concentrate on the few concepts and definitions that are needed for an introduction to inferential statistics. We begin with a relatively simple definition of probability.

In a situation where several different outcomes are possible, we define the *probability* for any particular outcome as a fraction or proportion. If the possible outcomes are identified as A, B, C, D, etc., then

$$\text{probability of } A = \frac{\text{number of outcomes classified as } A}{\text{total number of possible outcomes}}$$

For example, when you toss a balanced coin, the outcome will be either heads or tails. Because heads is one of two possible outcomes, the probability of heads is $P = \frac{1}{2}$.

If you are selecting 1 card from a complete deck, there are 52 possible outcomes. The probability of selecting the king of hearts would be $P = \frac{1}{52}$. The probability of selecting an ace would be $P = \frac{4}{52}$ because there are four aces in the deck.

To simplify the discussion of probability, we will use a notation system that eliminates a lot of the words. The probability of a specific outcome will be expressed with a capital P (for probability) followed by the specific outcome in parentheses. For example, the probability of selecting a king from a deck of cards would be written as $P(\text{king})$. The probability of obtaining heads for a coin toss would be written as $P(\text{heads})$.

You should note that probability is defined as a proportion. This definition makes it possible to restate any probability problem as a proportion problem. For example, the probability problem "What is the probability of obtaining a king from a deck of cards?" can be restated as "Out of the whole deck, what proportion are kings?" In each case, the answer is $\frac{4}{52}$ or "four out of fifty-two." This translation from probability to proportion may seem trivial now, but it will be a great aid when the probability problems become more complex. In most situations we are concerned with the probability of obtaining a particular sample from a population. The terminology of *sample* and *population* will not change the basic definition of probability. For example, the whole deck of cards can be considered as a population, and the single card we select is the sample.

The definition we are using identifies probability as fraction or a proportion. If you work directly from this definition, the probability values you obtain will be expressed as fractions. For example, if you are selecting a card,

$$P(\text{spade}) = \frac{13}{52} = \frac{1}{4}$$

Or if you are tossing a coin,

$$P(\text{heads}) = \frac{1}{2}$$

You should be aware that these fractions can be expressed equally well as either decimals or percentages:

$$P = \frac{1}{4} = 0.25 = 25\%$$

$$P = \frac{1}{2} = 0.50 = 50\%$$

By convention, probability values most often are expressed as decimal values. But you should realize that any of these three forms is acceptable.

You also should note that all the possible probability values are contained in a limited range. At one extreme, when an event never occurs, the probability is zero or 0% (see Box 6.1). At the other extreme, when an event always occurs, the probability is 1 or 100%. For example, suppose you have a jar containing 10 white marbles. The probability of randomly selecting a black marble would be

$$P(\text{black}) = \frac{0}{10} = 0$$

The probability of selecting a white marble would be

$$P(\text{white}) = \frac{10}{10} = 1$$

If you are unsure how to convert from fractions to decimals or percentages, you should review the section on proportions in the math review, Appendix A.

| BOX 6.1 | Zero Probability |

An event that never occurs has a probability of zero. However, the opposite of this statement is not always true: A probability of zero does not mean that the event is guaranteed never to occur.

Whenever there is an extremely large number of possible events, the probability of any specific event is assigned the value zero. This is done because the probability value tends toward zero as the number of possible events gets large. Consider, for example, the series

$$\frac{1}{10} \quad \frac{1}{100} \quad \frac{1}{1000} \quad \frac{1}{10000} \quad \frac{1}{100000}$$

Note that the value of the fraction is getting smaller and smaller, headed toward zero. At the far extreme, when the number of possible events is so large that it cannot be specified, the probability of a single, specific event is said to be zero.

$$\frac{1}{\text{infinite number}} = 0$$

continued

BOX 6.1 *continued*

Consider, for example, the fish in the ocean. If there were only 10 fish, then the probability of selecting any particular one would be $P = \frac{1}{10}$. Note that if you add up the probabilities for all 10 fish, you get a total of 1.00. Of course, there really are billions of fish in the ocean, and the probability of catching any specific one would be 1 out of billions; for all practical purposes, $P = 0$. However, this does not mean that you are doomed to fail whenever you go fishing. The zero probability simply means that you cannot predict in advance which fish you will catch. Note that each individual fish has a probability of zero, but there are so many fish that when you add up all the zeros you still get a total of 1.00. In probability, a value of zero doesn't mean never. But, practically speaking, it does mean very, very close to never.

Random Sampling

For the preceding definition of probability to be accurate, it is necessary that the outcomes be obtained by a process called random sampling.

DEFINITION

A *random sample* must satisfy two requirements:

1. Each individual in the population has an *equal chance* of being selected.
2. If more than one individual is to be selected for the sample, there must be *constant probability* for each and every selection.

Each of the two requirements for random sampling has some interesting consequences. The first assures that there is no bias in the selection process. For a population with N individuals, each individual must have the same probability, $P = 1/N$, of being selected. This means, for example, that selecting names from the telephone book would not give a random sample of people in your city. (People without phones are excluded; for them, $P = 0$.) Similarly, you would not get a random sample of college students by selecting individuals from your psychology classes. You also should note that the first requirement of random sampling prohibits you from applying the definition of probability to situations where the possible outcomes are not equally likely. Consider, for example, the question of whether or not there is life on Mars. There are only two possible alternatives:

1. There is life on Mars.
2. There is not life on Mars.

However, you cannot conclude that the probability of life on Mars is $P = \frac{1}{2}$.

The second requirement also is more interesting than may be apparent at first glance. Consider, for example, the selection of $n = 2$ cards from a complete deck. For the first draw, what is the probability of obtaining the jack of diamonds?

$$P(\text{jack of diamonds}) = \frac{1}{52}$$

Now, for the second draw, what is the probability of obtaining the jack of diamonds? Assuming you still are holding the first card, there are two possibilities:

$P(\text{jack of diamonds}) = \frac{1}{51}$ if the first card was not the jack of diamonds

or

$P(\text{jack of diamonds}) = 0$ if the first card was the jack of diamonds

In either case, the probability is different from its value for the first draw. This contradicts the requirement for random sampling which says that the probability must stay constant. To keep the probabilities from changing from one selection to the next, it is necessary to replace each sample before you make the next selection. This is called *sampling with replacement*. The second requirement for random samples (constant probability) demands that you sample with replacement.

(*Note:* It should be noted that we have taken a very conservative and narrow point of view in our definition of a random sample. Specifically, we have defined what is often called a *simple random sample* or an *independent random sample;* other types of random sampling are possible. You also should note that the requirement for replacement becomes unimportant with very large populations. With large populations the probability values stay essentially constant whether or not you use replacement. For example, a probability of 1 out of 100,000 is not noticeably different from a probability of 1 out of 99,999.)

6.3
Probability Rules

There are two general rules that are used commonly in working with probabilities. They are known as the addition rule and the multiplication rule.

The *addition rule* concerns the probability that either one of two possible events will occur. If A and B are two events, then this rule states that

6.1 $P(A \text{ or } B) = P(A) + P(B) - P(A \text{ and } B \text{ together})$

EXAMPLE 6.1

If you are tossing a single die (one-half of a pair of dice), what is the probability of rolling either a 2 or a 6? According to the rule,

$$P(2 \text{ or } 6) = P(2) + P(6) - P(2 \text{ and } 6 \text{ together})$$

$$= \frac{1}{6} + \frac{1}{6} - 0$$

$$= \frac{2}{6} = \frac{1}{3}$$

Because it is impossible to get a 2 and a 6 together on one toss, this part of the equation is zero.

To check the rule, we will use the definition of probability. When you toss a die, there are six possible outcomes (1, 2, 3, 4, 5, 6). Two out of these six are either a 2 or a 6. Therefore, according to the definition of probability,

$$P(2 \text{ or } 6) = \frac{2}{6} = \frac{1}{3}$$

For Example 6.1, the final part of the rule, $P(A \text{ and } B \text{ together})$, did not play any role. When two events cannot occur simultaneously, they are said to be *mutually exclusive:* The existence of either one excludes the other. In this case, $P(A \text{ and } B \text{ together}) = 0$ and does not contribute to the probability value. The next example shows how this part of Formula (6.1) can be important.

EXAMPLE 6.2

If you are selecting a card from a complete deck, what is the probability that you will obtain either a king or a diamond? According to the rule,

$$P(\text{king or diamond}) = P(\text{king}) + P(\text{diamond}) -$$

$$P(\text{king and diamond together})$$

$$= \frac{4}{52} + \frac{13}{52} - \frac{1}{52}$$

$$= \frac{16}{52}$$

This time it is possible to have a king and a diamond together in the same card: the king of diamonds.

Once again, we will use the definition of probability to check the answer. When you select a card from a complete deck, there are 52 possible outcomes. Of the 52 cards, 13 are diamonds (including the king of diamonds), and there are 3 other kings. This gives a total of 16 cards that are either kings or diamonds. Therefore, according to the definition of probability,

$$P(\text{king or diamond}) = \frac{16}{52}$$

The *multiplication rule* concerns the probability associated with a sequence of events, or the simultaneous occurrence of two events. If A and B are two possible outcomes, then the probability of A and B occurring in sequence or simultaneously is

6.2 $P(A \text{ and } B) = P(A) \times P(B)$

This rule is valid only if A and B are *independent events*; that is, the probability of A is not affected by the occurrence of B, and the probability of B is not affected by the occurrence of A. Successive coin tosses, for example, are independent. The probability of heads for any particular toss does not depend on the outcome of previous tosses. (The coin does not remember whether it came up heads or tails on earlier tosses.) On the other hand, if you are selecting cards from a deck, the successive outcomes will be independent only if you sample with replacement. Otherwise, the probabilities will change from one draw to the next depending on which cards you selected on previous draws.

EXAMPLE 6.3
If you toss a balanced coin two times, what is the probability that you will get heads both times? According to the rule,

$$P(\text{heads then heads}) = P(\text{heads}) \times P(\text{heads})$$

$$= \frac{1}{2} \times \frac{1}{2}$$

$$= \frac{1}{4}$$

Again, we will check this answer using the definition of probability. When you toss a coin twice, there are four possible outcomes:

Outcome	First Toss	Second Toss
1	Heads	Heads
2	Heads	Tails
3	Tails	Heads
4	Tails	Tails

Out of these four possible outcomes, only one has two heads. Therefore, according to the definition of probability,

$$P(\text{heads then heads}) = \frac{1}{4}$$

1. The animal colony in the psychology department contains 20
    male rats and 30 female rats. Of the 20 males, 15 are white and
    5 are spotted. Of the 30 females, 15 are white and 15 are
    spotted. If you randomly select 1 rat from this colony,
    a. What is the probability of obtaining a female?
    b. What is the probability of obtaining a white male?
    c. What is the probability of obtaining a rat that is spotted or
        female?
    d. If you take a random sample of 2 rats from this colony and
        the first is a white male, what is the probability that the
        second will be a white female?

Caution:
*Remember the
definition of ran-
dom sampling.*

ANSWERS

1. a. $P = \frac{30}{50} = 0.60$
    b. $P = \frac{15}{50} = 0.30$
    c. $P = \frac{20}{50} + \frac{30}{50} - \frac{15}{50} = \frac{35}{50} = 0.70$
    d. $P = \frac{15}{50}$

6.4
Probability and Frequency Distributions

The situations where we are concerned with probability generally
involve a population of scores that can be displayed in a frequency
distribution and a sample that consists of individual scores. There are
two important considerations that differentiate this situation from
selecting a card or tossing a coin. First, it now is possible to represent
the whole population in a frequency distribution graph. Second, we
now are using scores that are measures of a continuous variable. Tossing a coin allows only two discrete outcomes, heads and tails. With a
continuous variable, there are an infinite number of possible outcomes. To examine the effects of these two factors, we begin with a
very simple population that contains only $N = 10$ scores with values
1, 1, 2, 3, 3, 4, 4, 4, 5, 6. This population is shown in the frequency
distribution graph in Figure 6.2. If you are taking a random sample
of $n = 1$ score from this population, what is the probability that you
will obtain a score greater than 4? In probability notation,

$$P(X > 4) = ?$$

Using the definition of probability, there are 2 scores that meet this
criterion out of the total group of $N = 10$ scores, so the answer would
be $P = \frac{2}{10}$. This answer can be obtained directly from the frequency
distribution graph if you recall that probability and proportion measure the same thing. Looking at the graph (Figure 6.2), what proportion of the population consists of scores greater than 4? The answer
is the shaded part of the distribution, that is, 2 squares out of the
total of 10 squares in the distribution. Notice that we now are defining probability as proportion of *area* in the frequency distribution

graph. This provides a very concrete and graphic way of representing probability.

Using the same population once again, what is the probability of selecting a score less than 5? In symbols,

$$P(X < 5) = ?$$

Going directly to the distribution in Figure 6.2, we now want to know what part of the graph is not shaded. The unshaded portion consists of 8 out of the 10 blocks ($\frac{8}{10}$ of the area of the graph), so the answer is $P = \frac{8}{10}$.

Figure 6.2

A frequency distribution histogram for a population that consists of $N = 10$ scores. The shaded part of the figure indicates the portion of the whole population that corresponds to scores greater than $X = 4$. The shaded portion is two-tenths ($P = \frac{2}{10}$) of the whole distribution.

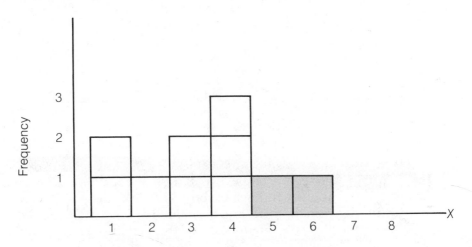

6.5
Probability and the Normal Distribution

The normal distribution was first introduced in Chapter 2 as an example of a commonly occurring shape for population distributions. An example of a normal distribution is shown in Figure 6.3. Although the exact shape for the normal distribution is precisely defined by an equation (see Figure 6.3), we can easily describe its general characteristics: It is a symmetrical distribution, with the highest frequency in the middle (mode = mean = median) and the frequencies tapering off gradually as the scores get farther and farther from the mean. In simple terms, in a normal distribution most individuals are around average, and extreme scores are relatively rare. This shape describes many common variables such as adult heights, intelligence scores, personality scores, etc.

Figure 6.3

The normal distribution. The exact shape of the normal distribution is specified by an equation relating each X value (score) with each Y value (frequency). The equation is

$$Y = \frac{1}{\sqrt{2\pi\sigma^2}}\, e^{-(X-\mu)^2/2\sigma^2}$$

(π and e are mathematical constants.) In simpler terms, the normal distribution is symmetrical with a single mode in the middle. The frequency tapers off as you move farther from the middle in either direction.

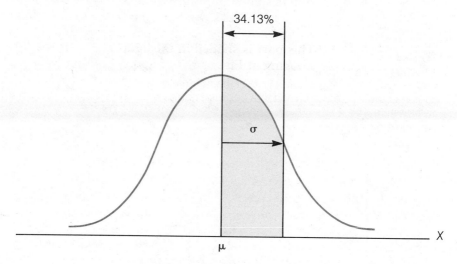

The normal shape also can be defined by the proportions of area contained in each section of the distribution. For instance, all normal shaped distributions will have exactly 34.13% of their total area in the section between the mean and the point that is one standard deviation above the mean (see Figure 6.3). By this definition, a distribution is normal if and only if it has all the right proportions.

Because the normal distribution is a good model for many naturally occurring distributions and because this shape is guaranteed in some circumstances (as you will see in Chapter 7), we will devote considerable attention to this particular distribution.

The process of answering probability questions about a normal distribution is introduced in the following example.

EXAMPLE 6.4

Adult heights form a normal shaped distribution with a mean of 68 inches and a standard deviation of 6 inches. Given this information about the population, our goal is to determine the probability associated with specific samples. For example, what is the probability of randomly selecting an individual who is taller than 6 feet (6 feet = 72 inches)? Restating this question in probability notation, we get

$$P(X > 72) = ?$$

We will follow a step-by-step process to find the answer to this question.

1. First, the probability question is translated to a proportion question: Out of all the possible adult heights, what proportion is greater than 72 inches?
2. You know that "all the possible adult heights" is simply the population distribution. This population is shown in Figure 6.4(a).
3. We want to find what portion of the distribution (what area) consists of values greater than 72. This part is shaded in the figure.
4. Looking at Figure 6.4(a), it appears that we have shaded in approximately 0.25 (or 25%) of the distribution. This is the answer we wanted.

The Unit Normal Table

Obviously, the probability answer we obtained for the preceding example was just a rough approximation. To make the answer more precise, we need a way to accurately measure the area in the normal distribution. Conceivably, you could do this by very carefully drawing the distribution on graph paper and then precisely measuring the amount of area in each section. Fortunately, this work already has been done, and the results are available in a table. The table, called the unit normal table, lists areas, or proportions, for all the possible sections of the normal distribution.

To use the unit normal table, you first need to transform the distribution of adult heights into a distribution of z-scores. Remember, changing from X values to z-scores will not change the shape of the distribution (it still will be normal), but it will transform the mean from $\mu = 68$ to $z = 0$ and will transform the standard deviation to 1. This is called *standardizing* the distribution. You should note that standardizing any normal distribution will produce the same result. No matter what mean or standard deviation you begin with, the standardized distribution (of z-scores) will be normal, with $\mu = 0$ and $\sigma = 1$. Because all normal distributions transform to this single standardized normal distribution, it is possible to have a single table that serves for every normal distribution.

Our distribution of adult heights is redrawn and standardized in Figure 6.4(b). Note that we have simply converted X values to z-scores. The value of $X = 72$ corresponds to a z-score of $z = \frac{4}{6}$ or 0.67. Our problem now is to determine what proportion of the normal distribution corresponds to z-scores greater than $+0.67$. Now the answer can be found in the unit normal table. This table lists the proportion of area corresponding to every possible z-score for the normal distribution.

Figure 6.4
(a) The distribution of adult heights. This is a normal distribution with $\mu = 68$ and $\sigma = 6$. The portion of the distribution corresponding to scores greater than 72 has been shaded.
(b) The distribution of adult heights after being transformed into z-scores. The mean is changed to $z = 0$, and the value of $X = 72$ is transformed to $z = +0.67$. The portion of the distribution corresponding to z-scores greater than $+0.67$ has been shaded.

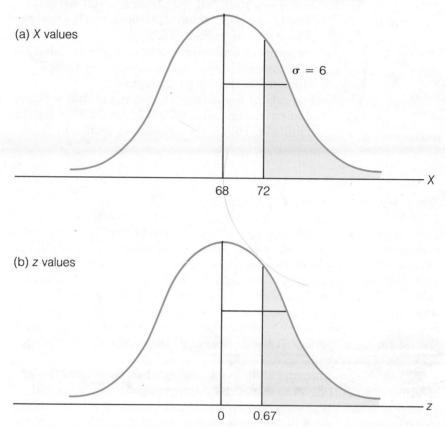

(a) X values

$\sigma = 6$

68   72   X

(b) z values

0   0.67   z

Using the Unit Normal Table

A complete unit normal table is provided in Appendix B on page A-24, and a portion of the table is reproduced in Figure 6.5. The unit normal table can be structured in many different ways (see Box 6.2), but the specific table we will use lists two proportions associated with each z-score. The z-scores are listed in column A of the table. Column B lists the proportion of the distribution that is located between the mean and each z-score. Column C lists the proportion of the distribution that lies in the tail beyond each z-score.

For a z-score of $z = 0.25$, for example, the table lists 0.0987 in column B and 0.4013 in column C. Of the entire normal distribution, 0.0987 (9.87%) is located between the mean and a z-score of $+0.25$

Figure 6.5

A portion of the unit normal table. This table lists proportions of the normal distribution corresponding to each z-score value. Column A of the table lists z-scores. Column B lists the proportion of the normal distribution that is located between the mean and the z-score value. Column C lists the proportion of the normal distribution that is located in the tail of the distribution beyond the z-score value.

(A) z	(B) Area Between Mean and z	(C) Area Beyond z
0.00	.0000	.5000
0.01	.0040	.4960
0.02	.0080	.4920
0.03	.0120	.4880
0.20	.0793	.4207
0.21	.0832	.4168
0.22	.0871	.4129
0.23	.0910	.4090
0.24	.0948	.4052
0.25	.0987	.4013
0.26	.1026	.3974
0.27	.1064	.3936
0.28	.1103	.3897
0.29	.1141	.3859
0.30	.1179	.3821
0.31	.1217	.3783
0.32	.1255	.3745
0.33	.1293	.3707
0.34	.1331	.3669

(see Figure 6.6). Similarly, the tail of the distribution beyond $z = +0.25$ contains 0.4013 (40.13%) of the distribution (see Figure 6.6). Notice that these two values account for exactly one-half or 50% of the distribution:

$$0.0987 + 0.4013 = 0.5000$$

To use the table for a variety of different types of problems, you need to remember two facts about the normal distribution and z-scores:

1. The distribution is symmetrical, so the mean equals the median. This means that exactly $\frac{1}{2}$ (0.5000 or 50%) of the distribution is on each side of $z = 0$.

To change from a decimal value to a percentage, you multiply by 100 or simply move the decimal point two places to the right.

Figure 6.6

The relationship between the values in the unit normal table and the area in a normal distribution. Column A of the table lists z-score values. Column B gives the proportion of a normal distribution that is located between the mean and the z-score. Column C gives the proportion of the distribution located in the tail beyond the z-score. For this example, $z = +0.25$ (column A), the portion of the distribution identified by B is 0.0987 of the distribution, and the portion identified by C is 0.4013.

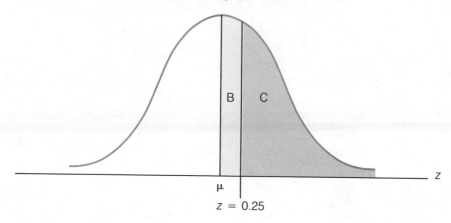

2. The z-score values also are symmetrical, with 0 in the middle, positive values to the right, and negative values to the left.

The following examples demonstrate several different ways the table can be used to find proportions or probabilities.

EXAMPLE 6.5a

Find the proportion of the normal distribution corresponding to z-scores greater than $+0.25$. The portion we want has been shaded in the normal distribution shown in Figure 6.7(a).

First, find the z-score value in the table. Because we want the portion of the distribution beyond $z = +0.25$, use column C. The answer is 0.4013 (40.13%).

EXAMPLE 6.5b

Find the proportion of the normal distribution corresponding to z-scores less than $+0.25$. This portion has been shaded in Figure 6.7(b).

Look up $z = +0.25$ in the table, and you find proportions of 0.0987 and 0.4013. Neither of these values corresponds to the portion we want. However, either of these two values can be used to obtain an answer.

Because 0.0987 is the area between the mean and the z-score, it is only part of the total value we want. To get the

Figure 6.7

Proportions of the normal distribution.
(a) The portion consisting of z-values greater than +0.25.
(b) The portion consisting of z-values less than +0.25.
(c) The portion consisting of z-values less than −0.25.
(d) The portion consisting of z-values greater than −0.25.

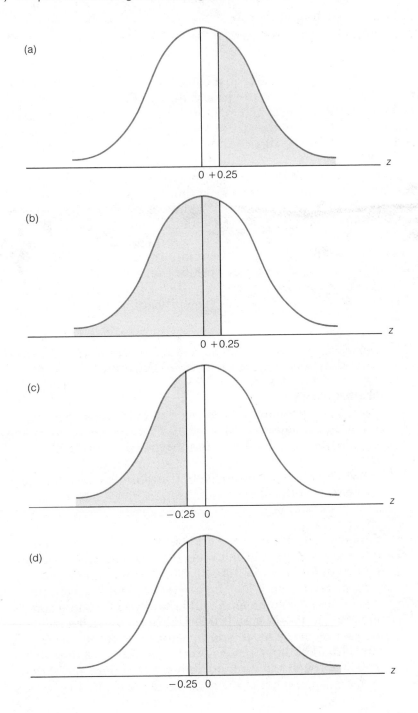

(a)

0 +0.25

z

(b)

0 +0.25

z

(c)

−0.25 0

z

(d)

−0.25 0

z

total, you add the 0.5000 to the left of the mean and the 0.0987 to the right to get an answer of

$$0.5000 + 0.0987 = 0.5987$$

The other value listed in the table, 0.4013, is the area in the tail of the distribution. This is precisely the portion of the distribution that we don't want. To find the rest of the distribution, you simply subtract from 1:

$$1.0000 - 0.4013 = 0.5987$$

Remember, probability equals proportion.

The two examples we have just completed can be used to demonstrate another characteristic of probability as it applies to continuous distributions. What proportion of the normal distribution corresponds to a z-score equal to 0.25? We already have determined that 40.13% (0.4013) of the distribution corresponds to z-scores greater than 0.25. And we have determined that 59.87% (0.5987) corresponds to z-scores less than 0.25. This accounts for 100% of the distribution. Therefore, the proportion corresponding to $z = 0.25$ must be zero. This is a general characteristic of continuous distributions: The proportion (or probability) associated with a specific value is zero. If you recall the definition of *continuous*, this result should be expected. A continuous variable contains an infinite number of points, so the probability associated with any specific value would be one out of infinity, or zero. For this example, $z = 0.25$ is one point in an infinite number of possible z-score values. The probability associated with $z = 0.25$ is zero.

EXAMPLE 6.5c
Find the proportion of the normal distribution corresponding to z-scores less than -0.25. This portion has been shaded in Figure 6.7(c).

Because there are no negative values in the unit normal table, you cannot look up $z = -0.25$. But the distribution is symmetrical, so the proportion beyond $z = -0.25$ is the same as the proportion beyond $z = +0.25$. Looking up $z = +0.25$, you find a value of 0.4013 in column C. This is the value we want.

EXAMPLE 6.5d
Find the proportion of the normal distribution corresponding to z-scores greater than -0.25. This portion has been shaded in Figure 6.7(d).

Again, you cannot look up $z = -0.25$, but you can use $+0.25$. Using column B, we find that the proportion corresponding to this z-score is 0.0987. This is the proportion of area between the mean and $z = -0.25$. Because this is only part of the total portion we want, you must add the other 0.5000 of the distribution to obtain a final answer:

$$0.5000 + 0.0987 = 0.5987$$

BOX 6.2 Alternative Formats for the Unit Normal Table

It is possible for the unit normal table to be structured in a variety of different ways. In this book, the table lists the proportion of the normal distribution that is located between the mean and each z-score as well as the proportion located beyond the z-score. There are two other formats for a z-score table that are very common and likely to be encountered in other books. We will examine each of these:

1. Often a unit normal table lists only the proportion between the mean and each z-score value. For example, a z-score of 0.25 would have a corresponding proportion of 0.0987. By listing only one proportion for each z-score, it is possible to condense the entire unit normal table to a single page. You should notice that this single proportion can be used to find the area in the tail of the distribution by simply subtracting from 0.5000.

2. Another common value found in a unit normal table is the cumulative proportion corresponding to each z-score value, that is, how much of the distribution has been accumulated by the time you get up to the z-score. In a table like this, for example, a z-score of $z = +0.25$ would have a corresponding proportion of 0.5987 (see Example 6.5b). You should be able to construct a cumulative table by starting with the unit normal table in this book.

The important point to remember is that there are lots of different ways of presenting the same information. Whenever you are using a unit normal table (or any other table), be sure you understand exactly how it is organized before you start any calculations.

LEARNING CHECK

1. Find the proportion of a normal distribution that is located in the tail beyond each z-score listed:
   a. $z = +1.00$
   b. $z = +0.80$
   c. $z = -2.00$
   d. $z = -0.33$

To help avoid mistakes, always sketch a normal distribution and shade in the portion you want.

2. Find the proportion of a normal distribution that is located between the mean and each z-score listed:
   a. $z = -0.50$
   b. $z = -1.50$
   c. $z = +0.67$
   d. $z = +2.00$

3. Find the proportion of a normal distribution that is located between the z-score boundaries listed:
   a. Between $z = -0.50$ and $z = +0.50$
   b. Between $z = -1.00$ and $z = +1.00$
   c. Between $z = -1.96$ and $z = +1.96$

ANSWERS

1. a. 0.1587 (15.87%)
   b. 0.2119 (21.19%)
   c. 0.0228 (2.28%)
   d. 0.3707 (37.07%)
2. a. 0.1915 (19.15%)
   b. 0.4332 (43.32%)
   c. 0.2486 (24.86%)
   d. 0.4772 (47.72%)
3. a. 0.3830 (38.30%)
   b. 0.6826 (68.26%)
   c. 0.9500 (95.00%)

6.6
Answering Probability Questions with the Unit Normal Table

The unit normal table provides a listing of proportions or probability values corresponding to every possible z-score in a normal distribution. To use this table to answer probability questions, it is necessary that you first transform the X values into z-scores (standardize the distribution) and then use the table to look up the probability value. This process is illustrated graphically with the map in Figure 6.8. Notice that you cannot go directly from a score to a probability value; you always must go by way of z-scores.

EXAMPLE 6.6
We now can use the unit normal table to get a precise answer to the probability problem we started earlier in the chapter (see Example 6.4). The goal is to find the probability or randomly selecting an individual who is taller than 6 feet (72 inches). We know that the distribution of adult heights is normal with $\mu = 68$ and $\sigma = 6$. In symbols, we want

$$P(X > 72) = ?$$

Restated as a proportion question, we want to find the proportion of the whole distribution that corresponds to values greater than 72. The whole distribution is drawn in Figure 6.4, and the part we want has been shaded.

The first step is to change the X values to z-scores. Specifically, the score of $X = 72$ is changed to

Figure 6.8

This map shows how to find a probability value that corresponds to any specific score, or how to find the score that corresponds to any specific probability value. Note that you cannot move directly between scores (*X* values) and probabilities (*P* values). You always must go by way of *z*-score. The horizontal leg of the map (changing *X* to *z* or changing *z* to *Z*) uses the *z*-score formula. The vertical leg (moving from *z*-scores to probability or back) uses the unit normal table.

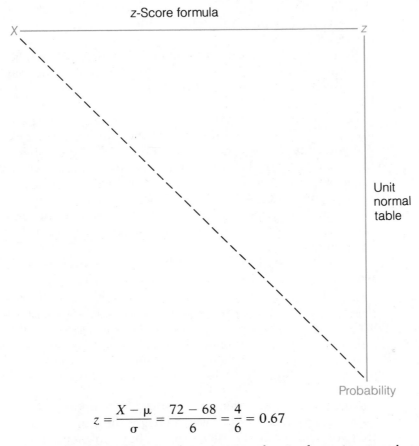

z-Score formula

Unit normal table

Probability

$$z = \frac{X - \mu}{\sigma} = \frac{72 - 68}{6} = \frac{4}{6} = 0.67$$

Next, you look up this *z*-score value in the unit normal table. Because we want the proportion of the distribution that is located beyond $z = 0.67$, the answer will be found in column C. A *z*-score of 0.67 corresponds to a proportion of 0.2514.

The probability of randomly selecting someone taller than 72 inches is 0.2514 or about 1 out of 4:

$$P(X > 72) = 0.2514 \qquad (25.14\%)$$

In Example 6.6 we started with an *X* value and used the table to find the corresponding probability value. Looking at the map in Figure 6.8, we started at *X* and moved to *P*. Like most maps, this one can be used to guide travel in either direction; that is, it is possible to start at *P* and move to *X*. To move in this direction means that you start with a specific probability value and then find the corresponding score. The following example demonstrates a problem of this type.

EXAMPLE 6.7

A mathematics aptitude test is constructed so that the scores for the general population will form a normal distribution with $\mu = 100$ and $\sigma = 16$. For this distribution, what score is necessary to place you in the top 60% of the population? In other words, what score separates the top 60% from the rest of the population? This problem is shown graphically in Figure 6.9.

Notice that we now start with a proportion (60% = 0.60) and must find the corresponding score. Looking at the map (Figure 6.8), you cannot go directly from P to X; you must go by way of z-scores.

The first step is to move from $P = 0.60$ to the corresponding z-score. This step requires using the unit normal table. But you cannot look up $P = 0.60$ in the table. Remember, the proportions in the table correspond to the area between the mean and the z-score (column B) or the area beyond the z-score (column C). All of these proportions have a value of 0.5 or smaller. Before you can use the table, the proportion stated in the problem must be transformed into one of the listed areas.

Looking again at Figure 6.9, you should see that the 60% which is shaded can be divided into 50% on the right of the mean and 10% to the left of the mean. You also should note that the 10% on the left is located between the mean and the z-score value. Similarly, you should see that 40% of the distribution (the unshaded portion) is located in the tail beyond the z-score we want. Thus, you can use either 10% (0.1000) in column B or 40% (0.4000) in column C to find the z-score.

Now that we have identified 0.1000 as the appropriate P value to find in column B, we can begin the search. Note that you will not find 0.1000 exactly, but you should find the closest value possible. The best value is $P = 0.0987$. This value corresponds to a z-score of $z = 0.25$.

Again you must be careful. Remember, the table lists only positive z-values. For this problem, the value we want is below the mean, so the z-score would be $z = -0.25$. To be sure that you have the correct sign ($+$ or $-$), it is best to sketch the problem like we did in Figure 6.9.

Now that you have found that $z = -0.25$, you are ready to complete the last leg of the trip, that is, change the z-score into an X value. Using the z-score formula and the known values of μ, σ, and z, we obtain

$$z = \frac{X - \mu}{\sigma}$$

Figure 6.9

The distribution of mathematics aptitude scores. The problem is to locate the score that separates the top 60% from the rest of the distribution. A line is drawn to divide the distribution roughly into 60% and 40% sections. Because 60% is slightly more than half, the line is placed slightly to the left of the mean.

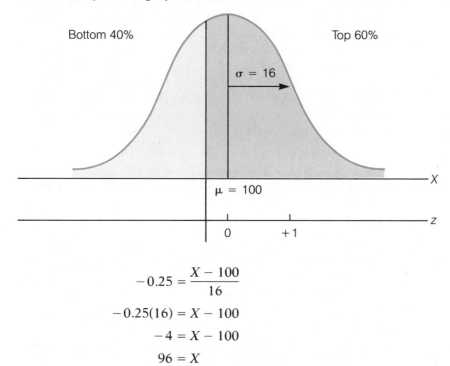

$$-0.25 = \frac{X - 100}{16}$$

$$-0.25(16) = X - 100$$

$$-4 = X - 100$$

$$96 = X$$

Notice that we could have obtained this final answer by using the definition of a z-score. The z-score of -0.25 indicates that the X value we want is located below the mean (negative value) by 0.25 standard deviation. A whole standard deviation is 16 points, so a quarter of a standard deviation would be 4 points. The score we want is below the mean by 4 points. Because the mean is $\mu = 100$, the score must be $X = 96$.

The conclusion for this example is that you must have a mathematics aptitude score of at least 96 in order to be in the top 60% of the population.

EXAMPLE 6.8
Scores on the Scholastic Appitude Test (the SAT) form a normal distribution with $\mu = 500$ and $\sigma = 100$. What value separates the top 15% of the SAT scores from the rest of the distribution? This problem is shown graphically in Figure 6.10. Notice that this problem is asking you to find the 85th percentile.

Again, we are starting with a proportion (15% = 0.15) and looking for a score. According to the map in Figure 6.8, we can move from P (proportion) to X (score) by going via z-scores.

The score we want separates the top 15% of the distribution from the rest. This means that we want to locate the z-score that has 15%, or 0.1500, of the distribution located beyond it (column C). The closest value listed in the table is 0.1492, and z-score that corresponds to this value $z = 1.04$.

Looking at the graph of the problem in Figure 6.10, you should realize that the score we want is above the mean, so the z-score is positive, $z = +1.04$. This z-score indicates a location that is above the mean by 1.04 standard deviations. The standard deviation is $\sigma = 100$, so 1.04 standard deviations would be

$$1.04(100) = 104 \text{ points}$$

The score we want is above the mean by 104 points. This score is $X = 500 + 104 = 604$. To be in the top 15% of the distribution on the SAT, you must have a score of at least 604.

EXAMPLE 6.9

This example demonstrates the process of determining a probability associated with a specified range of scores in a normal distribution. Once again, we will use the distribution of SAT scores which is normal with $\mu = 500$ and $\sigma = 100$. For this distribution, what is the probability of randomly selecting an individual with a score between $X = 600$ and $X = 650$? In probability notation, the problem is to find

$$P(600 < X < 650) = ?$$

Figure 6.10

The distribution of SAT scores. The problem is to locate the score that separates the top 15% from the rest of the distribution. A line is drawn to divide the distribution roughly into 15% and 85% sections.

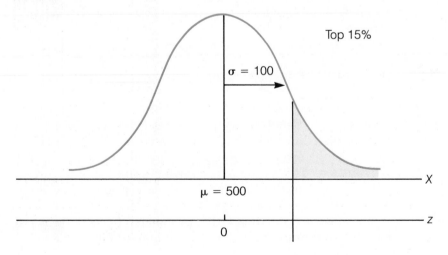

Figure 6.11 shows the distribution of SAT scores with the relevant portion shaded. Remember, finding the probability is the same as finding the proportion of the distribution located between 600 and 650.

The first step is to transform each of the X values into a z-score:

$$\text{For } X = 600: \quad z = \frac{X - \mu}{\sigma} = \frac{600 - 500}{100} = \frac{100}{100} = 1.00$$

$$\text{For } X = 650: \quad z = \frac{X - \mu}{\sigma} = \frac{650 - 500}{100} = \frac{150}{100} = 1.50$$

The problem now is to find the proportion of the distribution that is located between $z = +1.00$ and $z = +1.50$. There are several different ways this problem can be solved using the information in the unit normal table. One technique is described here.

Using column C of the table, we find that the area beyond $z = 1.00$ is 0.1587. This includes the portion we want, but it also includes an extra portion in the tail. This extra portion is the area beyond $z = 1.50$, and according to the table (column C), it is 0.0668 of the total distribution. Subtracting out the extra portion, we obtain a final answer of

$$P(600 < X < 650) = 0.1587 - 0.0668$$

$$= 0.0919$$

Figure 6.11

The distribution of SAT scores. The problem is to find the proportion of this distribution located between the values $X = 600$ and $X = 650$. This portion is shaded in the figure.

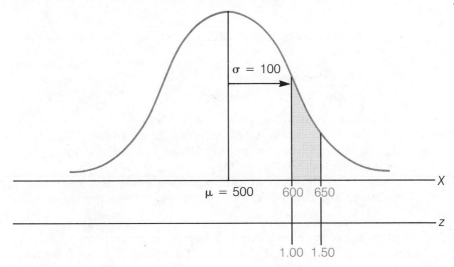

Thus, the probability of randomly selecting an individual with a SAT score between 600 and 650 is $P = 0.0919$ (9.19%).

LEARNING CHECK

1. For a normal distribution with a mean of 80 and a standard deviation of 10, find each probability value requested.
   a. $P(X > 85) = ?$
   b. $P(X < 95) = ?$
   c. $P(X > 70) = ?$
   d. $P(75 < X < 100) = ?$
2. For a normal distribution with a mean of 100 and a standard deviation of 20, find each value requested.
   a. What is the 60th percentile?
   b. What is the minimum score needed to be in the top 5% of this distribution?
   c. What scores form the boundaries for the middle 60% of this distribution?

ANSWERS

1. a. $P = 0.3085$ (30.85%)
   b. $P = 0.9332$ (93.32%)
   c. $P = 0.8413$ (84.13%)
   d. $P = 0.6687$ (66.87%)
2. a. $z = +0.25; X = 105$
   b. $z = +1.64; X = 132.8$
   c. $z = \pm0.84$; boundaries are 83.2 and 116.8

Summary

1. The probability of a particular event A is defined as a fraction or proportion:

$$P(A) = \frac{\text{number of outcomes classified as } A}{\text{total number of possible outcomes}}$$

2. This definition is accurate only for a random sample. There are two requirements that must be satisfied for a random sample:
   a. Every individual in the population has an equal chance of being selected.
   b. When more than one individual is being selected, the probabilities must stay constant. This means there must be sampling with replacement.

3. All probability problems can be restated as proportion problems. The "probability of selecting a king from a deck of cards"

is equivalent to the "proportion of the deck that consists of kings." For frequency distributions, probability questions can be answered by determining proportions of area. The "probability of selecting an individual with an IQ greater than 108" is equivalent to the "proportion of the whole population that consists of IQs above 108."

4. For normal distributions, these probabilities (proportions) can be found in the unit normal table. This table provides a listing of the proportions of a normal distribution that correspond to each z-score value. With this table it is possible to move between X values and probabilities using a two-step procedure:
    a. The z-score formula (Chapter 5) allows you to transform X to z or to change z back to X.
    b. The unit normal table allows you to look up the probability (proportion) corresponding to each z-score or the z-score corresponding to each probability.

Key Terms

probability
random sample
sampling with replacement
the addition rule

the multiplication rule
mutually exclusive events
independent events
unit normal table

Problems for Chapter 6:
Probability

*1. In a psychology class of 60 students there are 15 males and 45 females. Of the 15 men, only 5 are freshmen. Of the 45 women, 20 are freshmen. If you randomly sample an individual from this class,
    a. What is the probability of obtaining a female?
    b. What is the probability of obtaining a freshman?
    c. What is the probability of obtaining a female or a freshman?
    d. What is the probability of obtaining a male freshman?

2. A jar contains 10 black marbles and 20 white marbles. If you are taking a random sample of three marbles from this jar and the first two marbles are both white, what is the probability that the third marble will be black?

*3. Find the proportion of the normal distribution that lies in the tail beyond each of the following z-scores:
    a. $z = 0.50$ c. $z = -1.50$
    b. $z = 1.75$ d. $z = -0.25$

4. Find the proportion of the normal distribution that is located between the following z-score boundaries:
   a. Between $z = 0.25$ and $z = 0.75$
   b. Between $z = -1.00$ and $z = +1.00$
   c. Between $z = 0$ and $z = 1.50$
   d. Between $z = -0.75$ and $z = 2.00$

*5. Find the z-score that separates a normal distribution into the following two portions:
   a. Lowest 10% versus highest 90%
   b. Lowest 25% versus highest 75%
   c. Lowest 60% versus highest 40%
   d. Lowest 80% versus highest 20%

6. For a normal distribution with a mean of $\mu = 80$ and $\sigma = 12$,
   a. What is the probability of randomly selecting a score greater than 83?
   b. What is the probability of randomly selecting a score greater than 74?
   c. What is the probability of randomly selecting a score less than 92?
   d. What is the probability of randomly selecting a score less than 62?

*7. A normal distribution has a mean of 120 and a standard deviation of 20. For this distribution,
   a. What score separates the top 40% (highest scores) from the rest?
   b. What score would you need to be in the top 10% of the distribution?
   c. What range of scores would form the middle 60% of this distribution?

8. It takes Tom an average of $\mu = 30$ minutes to drive to work. The distribution of driving times is nearly normal with $\sigma = 10$ minutes. If Tom leaves home at 9:05, what is the probability that he will be late for a 9:30 meeting at work?

*9. A normal distribution has a mean of 80 and a standard deviation of 10. For this distribution, find each of the following probability values:
   a. $P(X > 75) = ?$ c. $P(X < 100) = ?$
   b. $P(X < 65) = ?$ d. $P(65 < X < 95) = ?$

10. IQ scores form a normal distribution with $\mu = 100$ and $\sigma = 15$.

   a. An IQ below 70 is designated as "mentally retarded." What proportion of the population is in this category?

   b. IQ scores between 90 and 110 are designated "average." What proportion of the population is average?

   c. IQ scores between 120 and 130 are designated "superior." What proportion of the population is superior?

*11. The scores on a psychology exam form a normal distribution with $\mu = 80$ and $\sigma = 8$. On this exam, Tom has a score of $X = 84$. Mary's score is located at the 60th percentile. John's score corresponds to a z-score of $z = +0.75$. If these three students are listed from highest score to lowest score, what is the correct ordering?

12. Scores on the college entrance exam are normally distributed with $\mu = 500$ and $\sigma = 100$.

   a. What is the minimum score needed to be in the top 2% on this exam?

   b. What is the 70th percentile on this exam?

   c. John has an exam score of $X = 630$. What is his percentile rank?

   d. What scores (X values) form the boundaries for the middle 95% of this distribution?

*13. A positively skewed distribution has a mean of 100 and a standard deviation of 12. What is the probability of randomly selecting a score greater than 106 from this distribution? (Be careful; this is a trick problem.)

14. If you are tossing a balanced coin,

   a. What is the probability of getting two heads in a row?

   b. What is the probability of getting three heads in a row?

   c. If you toss the coin four times, which of the following sequences would you predict is more probable:

      Sequence 1: heads—heads—heads—heads
      Sequence 2: heads—tails—heads—tails

   d. Calculate the exact probability for each sequence in part c. (You should find that these two sequences are equally probable.)

   e. If you toss the coin three times, what is the probability that you will obtain at least one tail? (*Hint:* Before you try to calculate this directly, check your answer to part b.)

*15. Three archers A, B, and C each shoot one arrow at a target. The probabilities of hitting the target are

$$P(A \text{ hits}) = 0.5$$
$$P(B \text{ hits}) = 0.25$$
$$P(C \text{ hits}) = 0.75$$

Determine the probability for each of the following outcomes:

a. A and B both hit the target.

b. A and B both miss the target.

c. A or B will hit the target.

d. All three will miss the target.

e. A or B or C will hit the target.

16. A normal distribution has a mean of 60 and a standard deviation of 10.

a. Find the semi-interquartile range for this distribution.

b. If the standard deviation were 20, what would be the value for the semi-interquartile range?

c. In general, what is the relation between the standard deviation and the semi-interquartile range for a normal distribution?

*17. A mathematics instructor teaches the same algebra course to a section of humanities students and to a section of pre-engineering students. The results of the final exam for each section are summarized as follows. Assume that both distributions are normal.

Humanities	Engineering
$\mu = 63$	$\mu = 72$
$\sigma = 12$	$\sigma = 8$

a. Bill is in the humanities section and earned a grade of $X = 74$ on the final. What is his percentile rank in this section? What would his rank be if he were in the pre-engineering section?

b. Tom is in the pre-engineering section. His grade on the final exam corresponds to a percentile rank of 40%. What rank would he have if he were in the humanities section?

c. Mary scored at the 60th percentile in the humanities section, and Jane scored at the 31st percentile in the pre-engineering section. Who had the better exam score (X value)?

18. All entering freshmen are required to take an English proficiency placement exam (EPPE). Based on these exam scores, the college assigns students to different sections of introductory English. The top 25% of the class goes into the advanced

course, the middle 50% goes into the regular English course, and students in the bottom 25% are assigned to a remedial English course. For this year's class the distribution of EPPE scores was approximately normal with $\mu = 68$ and $\sigma = 7.5$. What scores should be used as the cutoff values for assigning students to the three English courses?

*19. The scores on a civil service exam form a normal distribution with $\mu = 100$ and $\sigma = 20$. Only those individuals scoring in the top 20% on this exam are interviewed for jobs.

a. What is the minimum score needed to qualify for an interview?

b. Because there was an unusually high demand for new employees this year, the civil service board offered job interviews to everyone scoring above $X = 108$. What percentage of the individuals taking the exam were offered interviews?

20. A social psychologist has developed a new test designed to measure social aggressiveness. The scores on this test form a normal distribution with $\mu = 60$ and $\sigma = 9$. Based on these test scores, the psychologist wants to classify the population into five categories of aggressiveness:

> I: The meek (the lowest 5%)
> II: The mild (the next 20%)
> III: The average (the middle 50%)
> IV: The aggressive (the next 20%)
> V: The dangerous (the top 5%)

What scores should be used to form the boundaries for these categories?

*21. The college admissions office reports that applicants for last year's freshman class had an average SAT score of $\mu = 480$ with $\sigma = 90$. The minimum SAT required for admission last year was $X = 450$. The distribution of SAT scores for this year's applicants has $\mu = 500$ with $\sigma = 80$. This year's cutoff for admission is $X = 470$. Assume that both distributions are normal.

a. What proportion of last year's applicants were offered admission?

b. What proportion of this year's applicants were offered admission?

c. Of the students who were admitted last year, what proportion would have been rejected if the college had been using this year's cutoff?

d. Of the students who were rejected this year, what proportion would have been accepted if the college were still using last year's standards?

Caution: *For parts c and d of Problem 21 you are asked for a proportion of a proportion.*

CHAPTER 7

Probability and Samples: The Distribution of Sample Means

TOOLS
YOU WILL
NEED

The following items are considered essential background material for this chapter. If you doubt your knowledge of any of these items, you should review the appropriate chapter or section before proceeding.

1. Random sampling (Chapter 6)
2. Probability and the normal distribution (Chapter 6)
3. z-Scores (Chapter 5)

Now that you have some understanding of probability, consider the following problem:

> Imagine an urn filled with balls. Two-thirds of the balls are one color, and the remaining one-third is a second color. One individual selects 5 balls from the urn and finds that 4 are red and 1 is white. Another individual selects 20 balls and finds that 12 are red and 8 are white. Which of these two individuals should feel more confident that the urn contains two-thirds red balls and one-third white balls, rather than the opposite?*

When Tversky and Kahneman (1974) presented this problem to a group of experimental subjects, they found that most people felt that the first sample (4 out of 5) provided much stronger evidence and therefore should give more confidence. At first glance, it may appear that this is the correct decision. After all, the first sample contained $\frac{4}{5}$ = 80% red balls, and the second sample contained only $\frac{12}{20}$ = 60% red balls. However, you should also notice that the two samples differ in another important respect: the sample size. One sample contains only $n = 5$, and the other sample contains $n = 20$.

The correct answer to the problem is that the larger sample (12 out of 20) gives a much stronger justification for concluding that the balls in the urn are predominately red. It appears that most people tend to focus on the sample proportion and pay very little attention to the sample size.

The importance of sample size may be easier to appreciate if you approach the urn problem from a different perspective. Suppose that you are the individual assigned responsibility for selecting a sample and then deciding which color is in the majority. Before you select your sample, you are offered a choice of selecting either a sample of 5 balls or a sample of 20 balls. Which would you prefer? It should be clear that the larger sample would be better. With a small number, you risk obtaining an unrepresentative sample. By chance, you could end up with 3 white balls and 2 red balls even though the reds outnumber the whites by two to one. The larger sample is much more likely to provide an accurate representation of the population. This is an example of the *law of large numbers*, which states that large samples will be representative of the population from which they are selected. One final example should help demonstrate this law. If you were tossing a coin, you probably would not be greatly surprised to obtain 3 heads in a row. However, if you obtained a series of 20 heads in a row, you almost certainly would suspect a trick coin. The large sample has more authority.

---

*Adapted from Tversky, A., and Kahneman, D. (1974). Judgments under uncertainty: Heuristics and biases. *Science*, 185, 1124–1131. Copyright 1974 by the AAAS.

In this chapter we will examine the relation between samples and populations. More specifically, we will consider the relation between sample means and the population mean. As you will see, sample size is one of the primary considerations in determining how well a sample mean represents the population mean. In its more formal statement, the law of large numbers says the following:

> The larger the sample size, the more probable it is that the sample mean will be close to the population mean.

7.1
Samples and Sampling Error

The purpose of this chapter is to establish the set of rules that relate samples to populations. These rules primarily will be based on probabilities. For example, what kind of sample will probably be obtained from a particular population or, conversely, what kind of population probably produced a particular sample? Although the general topic of probability has already been discussed (Chapter 6), in this chapter we will be looking at samples that consist of more than a single score, for example, a sample of $n = 20$ rats in a learning experiment or a sample of personality scores for a group of $n = 100$ college freshmen.

In most situations, researchers must depend on the limited data from samples to answer general questions about populations. For example, a researcher might be interested in whether or not a special vitamin-enriched diet has any effect on intellectual development. To examine this question, the researcher could do the following experiment. First, a sample of rats is obtained, and the sample is randomly divided into two groups. The rats in one group are raised on a regular diet, and the animals in the other group are fed the special diet. After 6 months, all of the rats are tested on a learning problem. The researcher now has two sets of data: the performance scores for the regular diet group and the scores for the special diet group. The structure of this experiment is shown in Figure 7.1.

The researcher wants to know whether or not the treatment (the special diet) has any effect on the population; is the population of scores with the treatment any different from the population of scores without the treatment? The researcher must rely on the two samples to provide accurate information about these two populations. It is reasonable to assume that each sample would give a pretty good picture of its own population. After all, the sample was randomly selected from the population, and therefore it should be a representative group. On the other hand, the rats in each sample are only a small part of the whole population, and generally a sample will not be identical to its population. In particular, the data the researcher gets will depend on the individual rats selected for each sample. If a different group of individuals had been selected, they would have different scores, and the researcher would end up with a different set of data. How can you tell that a particular sample is really representative of the population? Maybe a different sample would have been better.

Figure 7.1

A diagram of the structure of the experimental design. The purpose of the experiment is to determine whether the special diet has any effect on intelligence. The reseacher would like to compare the mean intelligence for rats on the special diet versus rats on the regular diet. Because the populations are too large to work with, the researcher must use samples as the basis for comparing the two populations.

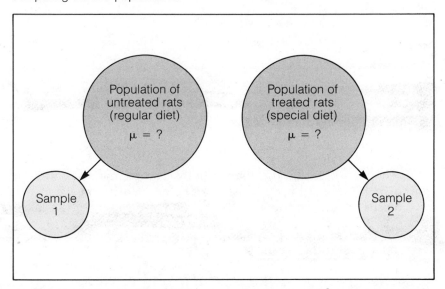

This is the general difficulty that is part of working with samples: Samples generally are not identical to the populations from which they come. The difference, or *error*, between a sample and its population is referred to as *sampling error*. Furthermore, samples are variable; they are not all the same. If you take two separate samples from the same population, the samples will be different. They will contain different individuals, they will have different scores, and they will have different sample means. How can you tell which sample is giving the best description of the population? Can you even predict how well a sample will describe its population? These are the kinds of questions we will be answering in this chapter.

7.2
The Distribution of Sample Means

As noted, two separate samples probably will be different even if they are taken from exactly the same population. The samples will have different individuals, different scores, different means, etc. In most cases, it is possible to obtain thousands of different samples from one population. Consider the population of college students. Suppose you took a sample of $n = 20$ students and measured their IQ scores. Now take a second sample. What would your chances be of getting exactly the same set of 20 scores for both samples? It should be clear that it would be very unlikely to exactly duplicate your first sample, even if you continued taking samples for the rest of your life. With all these different samples coming from the same population, it may seem hopeless to try to establish some simple rules for the relations between samples and populations. But fortunately the huge set of possible samples does fall into a relatively simple, orderly, and predictable pattern that makes it possible to accurately predict the characteristics of a sample if you know about the population it is coming from. These general characteristics are specified by the distribution of sample means.

DEFINITION

The distribution of sample means is the collection of sample means for all the possible random samples of a particular size (n) that can be obtained from a population.

You should notice that the distribution of sample means is different from distributions we have considered before. Until now we always have discussed distributions of scores; now the values in the distribution are not scores, they are statistics (sample means). Because statistics are obtained from samples, a distribution of statistics is referred to as a sampling distribution.

DEFINITION

A *sampling distribution* is a distribution of statistics obtained by selecting all the possible samples of a specific size from a population.

Thus, the distribution of sample means is an example of sampling distribution. In fact, it often is called the sampling distribution of $\overline{X}$.

Before we consider the general rules concerning this distribution, we will look at a simple example that provides an opportunity to examine the distribution in detail.

EXAMPLE 7.1
Consider a population that consists of only four scores: 2, 4, 6, 8. This population is pictured in the frequency distribution histogram in Figure 7.2.

Remember, random sampling requires sampling with replacement.

We are going to use this population as the basis for constructing the distribution of sample means for $n = 2$. Remember, this distribution is the collection of all the possible sample means for random samples of $n = 2$ from this population. We begin by looking at all the possible samples and computing the mean for each sample. Each of the 16 different samples is listed in Table 7.1.

Figure 7.2

Frequency distribution histogram for a population of four scores: 2, 4, 6, 8.

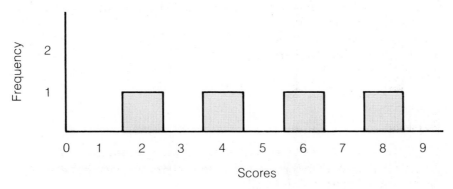

Now we have all of the 16 possible samples, with $n = 2$, that can be obtained from this population, and we have the mean for each sample. The 16 sample means form the distribution of sample means. These 16 values are organized in a frequency distribution histogram in Figure 7.3.

Table 7.1

All the Possible Samples of $n = 2$ Scores that Can Be Obtained from the Population Presented in Figure 7.2[a]

Sample	Scores First	Second	Sample Mean, $\overline{X}$
1	2	2	2
2	2	4	3
3	2	6	4
4	2	8	5
5	4	2	3
6	4	4	4
7	4	6	5
8	4	8	6
9	6	2	4
10	6	4	5
11	6	6	6
12	6	8	7
13	8	2	5
14	8	4	6
15	8	6	7
16	8	8	8

[a]Notice that the table lists *random samples*. This requires sampling with replacement, so it is possible to select the same score twice. Also note that samples are listed systematically: The first four samples are all the possible samples that have $X = 2$ as the first score; the next four samples all have $X = 4$ as the first score; etc. This way we are sure to have all the possible samples listed, although the samples probably would not be selected in this order.

Figure 7.3

The distribution of sample means for $n = 2$. This distribution shows the 16 sample means from Table 7.1.

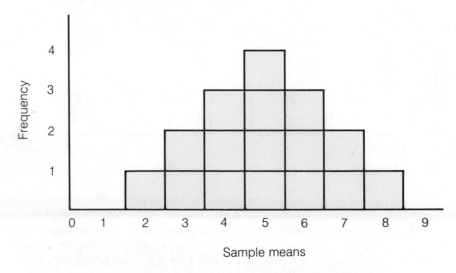

Notice that the distribution of sample means has some predictable and some very useful characteristics:

1. The sample means tend to pile up around the population mean. For this example, the population mean was $\mu = 5$, and the sample means are clustered around a value of 5. It should not surprise you that the sample means tend to approximate the population mean. After all, samples are supposed to be representative of the population.

2. The distribution of sample means is approximately normal in shape. This is a characteristic that will be discussed in detail later and will be extremely useful because we already know a great deal about probabilities and the normal distribution (Chapter 6).

3. Finally, you should notice that we can use this distribution to answer questions about probabilities and sample means. Probability has been defined as a proportion, and we can translate any probability problem into a proportion problem. For example, what is the probability of taking a random sample of $n = 2$ scores from this population and obtaining a sample mean $(\overline{X})$ that is greater than 7? In symbols, $P(\overline{X} > 7) = ?$. Restated as a proportion problem, this becomes the following: Of all the possible sample means,

what proportion has values greater than 7? In this form, the question is easily answered by looking at the distribution of sample means. All 16 of the possible sample means are pictured (Figure 7.3), and only 1 out of 16 has a value greater than 7. The answer, therefore, is 1 out of 16, or $P = \frac{1}{16}$.

The Central Limit Theorem

Example 7.1 demonstrates the construction of the distribution of sample means for a relatively simple, specific situation. In most cases, however, it will not be possible to list all the samples and compute all the possible sample means. Therefore, it is necessary to develop the general characteristics of the distribution of sample means that can be applied in any situation. Fortunately, these characteristics are specified in a mathematical proposition known as the *central limit theorem*. This important and useful theorem serves as a cornerstone for much of inferential statistics. Following is the essence of the theorem:

DEFINITION

Central Limit Theorem: For any population with mean μ and standard deviation σ, the distribution of sample means for sample size n will approach a normal distribution with a mean of μ and a standard deviation of $\sigma/\sqrt{n}$ as n approaches infinity.

The value of this theorem comes from two simple facts. First, it describes the distribution of sample means for *any population*, no matter what shape, or mean, or standard deviation. Second, the distribution of sample means "approaches" a normal distribution very rapidly. By the time the sample size reaches $n = 30$ or more, the distribution is almost perfectly normal.

Notice that the central limit theorem describes the distribution of sample means by identifying the three basic characteristics (parameters) that describe any distribution: shape, central tendency, and variability. Each of these will be examined.

The Shape of the Distribution of Sample Means

It has been observed that the distribution of sample means tends to be a normal distribution. In fact, this distribution will be almost perfectly normal if either one of the following two conditions is satisfied.

1. The population from which the samples are selected is a normal distribution.

2. The number of scores (n) in each sample is relatively large, around 30 or more. (As n gets larger, the distribution of sample means will closely approximate a normal distribution. With $n > 30$ the distribution is almost perfectly normal.)

The fact that the distribution of sample means tends to be normal should not be surprising. Whenever you take a sample from a population, you expect the sample mean to be near to the population mean. When you take lots of different samples, you expect the sample means to "pile up" around μ, resulting in a normal shaped distribution. This fact is demonstrated in the following example.

EXAMPLE 7.2

Consider a population that consists of only two scores: $X = 0$ and $X = 4$. This population is shown in the frequency distribution graph in Figure 7.4.

Using this population, we first will look at the distribution of sample means based on $n = 2$, that is, the set of all the possible sample means for samples with $n = 2$ in each sample. For this population, there are only four possible random samples, and they are presented in Figure 7.5. The mean for each sample has been computed, and the set of means is presented in the frequency distribution graph. This graph shows the distribution of sample means for $n = 2$. Notice that the distribution has some of the characteristics of the original population (the values at 0 and at 4), plus it has some characteristics of the normal distribution (the sample means are beginning to pile up in the middle of the distribution).

Next, we will look at the distribution of sample means based on $n = 4$. This time there are 16 possible random samples, and they are presented in Figure 7.6. The mean for each of these samples has been computed, and the set of means is presented in the frequency distribution graph. This graph shows the distribution of sample means for $n = 4$.

Figure 7.4

Original population consisting of only two scores.

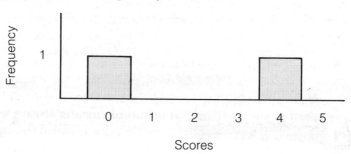

Figure 7.5

All of the possible samples with $n = 2$ scores and the distribution of sample means for $n = 2$. Samples were selected from the population shown in Figure 7.4.

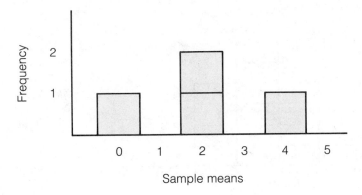

| | Scores | | Sample mean, |
Sample	First	Second	$\overline{X}$
1	0	0	0
2	0	4	2
3	4	0	2
4	4	4	4

Notice that the distribution of sample means for $n = 4$ is much more normal shaped than the distribution for $n = 2$. This general trend continues, so that when $n = 30$ or more, the distribution of sample means is essentially a perfect normal distribution.

The Mean of the Distribution of Sample Means: The Expected Value of $\overline{X}$

You probably have noticed in all of the examples so far that the distribution of sample means is centered around the mean of the population from which the samples were obtained. In each case, the average value of all the sample means is exactly equal to the value of the population mean. This fact should be intuitively reasonable; the sample means are expected to be close to the population mean, and they do tend to pile up around μ. The formal statement of this phenomenon is that the mean of the distribution of sample means always will be identical to the population mean. This mean value is called the *expected value of $\overline{X}$*.

Figure 7.6

All of the possible samples with $n = 4$ scores and the distribution of sample means for $n = 4$. Samples were selected from the population shown in Figure 7.4.

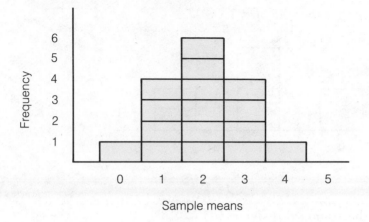

Frequency

Sample means

	Scores				Sample mean, $\overline{X}$
Sample	First	Second	Third	Fourth	
1	0	0	0	0	0
2	0	0	0	4	1
3	0	0	4	0	1
4	0	0	4	4	2
5	0	4	0	0	1
6	0	4	0	4	2
7	0	4	4	0	2
8	0	4	4	4	3
9	4	0	0	0	1
10	4	0	0	4	2
11	4	0	4	0	2
12	4	0	4	4	3
13	4	4	0	0	2
14	4	4	0	4	3
15	4	4	4	0	3
16	4	4	4	4	4

DEFINITION

The mean of the distribution of sample means will be equal to μ (the population mean) and is called the *expected value of $\overline{X}$*.

In commonsense terms, a sample mean is "expected" to be near its population mean. When all of the possible sample means are obtained, the average value will be identical to μ.

The Standard Error of $\overline{X}$

So far we have considered the shape and the central tendency of the distribution of sample means. To completely describe this distribution, we need one more characteristic, variability. The value we will be working with is the standard deviation for the distribution of sample means, and it is called the *standard error of* $\overline{X}$.

DEFINITION

The standard deviation of the distribution of sample means is called the *standard error of* $\overline{X}$.

Like any measure of standard deviation, the standard error defines the standard, or typical, distance from the mean. In this case, we are measuring the standard distance between a single sample mean $\overline{X}$ and the population mean μ.

The notation that is used to identify the standard error is $\sigma_{\bar{x}}$. The σ indicates that we are measuring a standard deviation or a standard distance from the mean. The lowercase $\bar{x}$ indicates that we are measuring standard deviation for sample means.

$$\text{standard error} = \sigma_{\bar{x}} = \text{standard distance between } \overline{X} \text{ and } \mu$$

The standard error is an extremely valuable measure because it specifies precisely how well a sample mean estimates its population mean, that is, how much error you should expect, on the average, between $\overline{X}$ and μ. Remember, one basic reason for taking samples is to use the sample data to answer questions about the population. Specifically, we can use the sample mean as an estimate of the population mean. Although we do not expect a sample mean to be exactly the same as the population mean, it should provide a good estimate. The standard error tells how good the estimate will be.

The numerical value of the standard error is determined by two characteristics: (1) the variability of the population from which the sample is selected and (2) the size of the sample. We will examine each of these separately.

1. *Variability of the Population.* If each individual score in a sample is close to the population mean, then the sample mean ($\overline{X}$) certainly will be close to the population mean. This will happen when the population standard deviation is small, that is, when all the scores in the population are generally close to the mean. On the other hand, when σ is large, the individual scores are not near to the population mean. In this case, the sample is likely to contain a few extreme scores that will draw the sample mean away from μ. The general conclusion from this argument is that a sample mean is

Remember the law of large numbers.

more likely to be a good estimate of the population mean if all the scores in the population are clustered together, i.e., if the population has a small standard deviation.

2. *The Sample Size.* As a general rule, the larger the sample, the more accurately the sample represents its population. If you were assigned the job of estimating the average IQ for freshmen at your college, you would expect to get a more accurate measure from a group of n = 100 than from a sample of n = 2. The larger the sample, the smaller the standard error.

Combining these two characteristics results in the following formula for the standard error:

7.1 $$\text{standard error} = \sigma_{\bar{x}} = \frac{\sigma}{\sqrt{n}}$$

Notice that when the population standard deviation (σ) is small, the standard error will be small. Also, if the sample size (n) is increased, the standard error will get smaller (see Box 7.1).

BOX 7.1 The Components of Standard Error

Because it often is impossible to work with entire populations, researchers usually rely on samples to provide information. The sample data are used to estimate the characteristics of the population. Standard error gives the researcher an idea of how accurate this estimation will be.

The formula for standard error may seem difficult to understand, but it uses the same commonsense factors that you would expect to influence any estimation. For example, suppose you are asked to estimate the age and the yearly income for a "mystery person." If you are not given any information about the person, how accurately would you expect to estimate his/her age? How accurately would you expect to estimate income?

The person's age could be any value from 1 to 100 years, but your best guess would be an average value around 40. You would not expect to guess the person's age precisely, but it is reasonable to expect this estimate to be within 20 or 30 years of the actual value. On the other hand, the mystery person's income could be any value from 0 to $100,000. Your best bet would be to estimate an average value of about $20,000 because this is around the mean value for the population of American families. Again, you don't expect your estimate to be exactly correct. This time you probably would be satisfied if you guessed within $5000 or $10,000 of the correct figure.

Notice that you would expect to estimate age much more accurately than you would expect to estimate salary (an error of 20 or 30 for age versus an error of 5000 or 10,000 for salary). The differ-

---

BOX 7.1 continued

ence between these two estimates is due to the variability of the scores in the population. Ages are much less variable (less spread out) than salaries. The smaller the variability, the more accurate the estimate.

Now suppose that you are given some information about the mystery person. Suppose you are told that the person is a man who has been working as a marketing executive for a major computer company for 15 years. Once again, try to estimate the person's age and income. Would you expect your estimates now to be more accurate than the ones you made before? It should be clear that the more information you have, the more accurately you can make estimates.

In general, the accuracy of an estimate, or its standard error, is determined by two things: first, by how much variability there is in the item you are trying to estimate and secondly how much information you have when you make your estimate. These two things are the basis for the standard error formula:

$$\text{standard error} = \sigma_{\bar{x}} = \frac{\sigma}{\sqrt{n}}$$

The σ measures the variability of the scores, and the n gives the size of the sample (how much "information" you have taken from the population).

The exact derivation of the standard error formula is a bit complex, but we can use a simple example to show that the formula does work.

EXAMPLE 7.3
Earlier we considered a population that consisted of only two scores: $X = 0$ and $X = 4$ (see Figure 7.4). The standard deviation for this population is $\sigma = 2$ (check it for yourself). We also looked at the distribution of sample means based on $n = 4$ for this population (see Figure 7.6). With $n = 4$ there are 16 possible samples, and each of the 16 sample means will be listed again (Table 7.2). Note that the 16 sample means are not all the same; they are variable, and we can compute SS and standard deviation for these values.

First, notice that the average value for these 16 sample means is 2. This is the same as the population mean. Remember, the expected value of $\bar{X}$ is equal to μ.

Second, for each sample we can compute a deviation score. The deviation simply is the distance from the mean ($\mu = 2$) and indicates how close the sample mean comes to the population mean.

Table 7.2

All of the Possible Sample Means for Samples of $n = 4$ Scores Taken from a Population that Consists of Only Two Scores: $X = 0$ and $X = 4$[a]

Sample	Sample Mean, $\overline{X}$	Deviation (Distance from μ)	Squared Deviation
1	0	−2	4
2	1	−1	1
3	1	−1	1
4	2	0	0
5	1	−1	1
6	2	0	0
7	2	0	0
8	3	+1	1
9	1	−1	1
10	2	0	0
11	2	0	0
12	3	+1	1
13	2	0	0
14	3	+1	1
15	3	+1	1
16	4	+2	4

[a]The 16 different samples are shown in Figure 7.6.

Third, we square each deviation score and compute the sum of squared deviations for the sample means, $SS = 16$.

Next, calculate the average squared deviation, the variance:

$$\text{variance of sample means} = \frac{SS}{N} = \frac{16}{16} = 1$$

Because the distribution of sample means contains all the possible sample means, it is a population. Therefore, we are using the formula for population variance.

Finally, calculate the standard deviation for this set of sample means:

$$\text{standard deviation of sample means} = \sqrt{\frac{SS}{N}} = \sqrt{1} = 1$$

This is the standard error. It is the standard deviation of the distribution of sample means, and it measures the standard distance between a sample mean and the population mean. Notice that we could have computed this value directly by using the formula for standard error:

$$\text{standard error} = \sigma_{\overline{x}} = \frac{\sigma}{\sqrt{n}} = \frac{2}{\sqrt{4}} = \frac{2}{2} = 1$$

The formula provides a much more direct way of computing standard error. Again, standard error measures the standard distance between $\overline{X}$ and μ. It tells how much error to expect, on the average, if you are using a sample mean to estimate a population mean.

1. A population of scores is normal with $\mu = 50$ and $\sigma = 12$. Describe the distribution of sample means for samples of size $n = 16$ selected from this population. (Describe shape, central tendency, and variability for the distribution.)
2. A population of scores is normal with $\mu = 100$ and $\sigma = 16$.
    a. If you randomly select one score from this population, then, on the average, how close should the score be to the population mean?
    b. If you selected a random sample of $n = 4$ scores, how much error would you expect, on the average, between the sample mean and the population mean?
    c. If you selected a random sample of $n = 64$ scores, how much error, on the average, should there be between the sample mean and the population mean?

ANSWERS

1. The distribution of sample means will be normal because the population is normal. It will have an expected value of $\mu = 50$ and a standard error of $\sigma_{\bar{x}} = 12/\sqrt{16} = 3$.
2. a. Standard deviation, $\sigma = 16$, measures standard distance from the mean.
    b. For a sample of $n = 4$ the standard error would be $16/\sqrt{4} = 8$ points.
    c. For a sample of $n = 64$ the standard error would be $16/\sqrt{64} = 2$ points.

7.3
Applications of the Distribution of Sample Means

The reason for developing the distribution of sample means is to help establish the relationship between populations and samples. Specifically, the distribution helps us to predict exactly what kinds of samples we are likely to obtain from any given population. For example, you know what value to expect for the sample mean; the expected value of $\bar{X}$ is μ. Also, you know that samples generally will not be identical to the population they come from. The sample mean should be a close approximation to μ, but there will be some difference between $\bar{X}$ and μ. The standard error defines the standard distance between a sample mean and its population mean.

In addition to these general relationships, the distribution of sample means makes it possible for us to describe the relation between a specific sample and its population. Because we know about the entire set of all the possible $\bar{X}$s, we can find the location of any specific sample in this distribution. Consider the following example.

EXAMPLE 7.4
Suppose we have a population that is normal and has $\mu = 100$ and $\sigma = 16$. What value should be expected for $\bar{X}$ if you

take a random sample of $n = 4$ scores from this population? First, we can look at all the possible $\overline{X}$s that could be obtained for n = 4. This is the distribution of sample means. It will be normal because the population is normal. It will have a mean of $\mu = 100$ because the population mean is 100. Finally, it will have a standard error of $\sigma_{\overline{x}} = 8$; using Formula (7.1), we obtain

$$\sigma_{\overline{x}} = \frac{\sigma}{\sqrt{n}} = \frac{16}{\sqrt{4}} = \frac{16}{2} = 8$$

This distribution is shown in Figure 7.7.

Any specific sample can be located in this distribution. A sample mean of $\overline{X} = 108$, for example, is located exactly eight points or one standard error above the mean (see Figure 7.7). The exact location of this sample mean can be specified by a z-score. As before, the sign of the z-score indicates whether the value is above ($+$) or below ($-$) the mean. The distance from the mean is specified by the number of standard deviation units (in this case, the number of standard error units). For this example, our sample mean of $\overline{X} = 108$ is above the mean by exactly one standard error, so it has a z-score of $z = +1.00$.

Remember, z-scores are used to specify an exact location within a distribution.

As demonstrated in Example 7.4, it is possible to use a z-score to describe the position of any specific sample within the distribution of sample means. The z-score tells exactly where a specific sample is located in relation to all the other possible samples that could have been obtained. A z-score of $z = +2.00$, for example, indicates that the sample mean is much larger than usually would be expected: It is greater than the expected value of $\overline{X}$ by twice the standard distance. The z-score for each sample mean can be computed by using the standard z-score formula with a few minor changes. First, the value we

---

Figure 7.7

The distribution of sample means for $n = 4$. Samples were selected from a normal population with $\mu = 100$ and $\sigma = 16$.

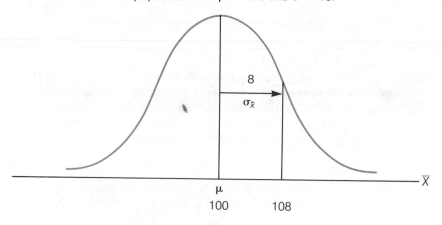

are locating is a sample mean rather than a score, so the formula uses $\overline{X}$ in place of X. Second, the standard deviation for this distribution is measured by the standard error, so the formula uses $\sigma_{\overline{x}}$ in place of σ (see Box 7.2). The resulting formula, giving the z-score value corresponding to any sample mean, is

7.2
$$z = \frac{\overline{X} - \mu}{\sigma_{\overline{x}}}$$

Every sample mean has a z-score that describes its position in the distribution of sample means.

An additional advantage of computing a z-score for each sample is the fact that we often can use z-scores to find probabilities. This is especially true when the distribution is normal, and you should recall that the distribution of sample means tends to be normal. In this case, we can use the unit normal table to look up probabilities for each z-score value. Using the z-scores and the probabilities, it is possible to make precise predictions about the kinds of samples that should be obtained from any population. The following examples outline the kinds of questions that can be answered using this procedure.

EXAMPLE 7.5

The population of scores on the SAT forms a normal distribution with $\mu = 500$ and $\sigma = 100$. If you take a random sample of $n = 25$ students, what is the probability that you would obtain a sample mean greater than $\overline{X} = 540$?

First, you can restate this probability question as a proportion question: Out of all the possible sample means, what proportion has values greater than 540? You know about "all the possible sample means"; this is simply the distribution of sample means. The problem is to find a specific portion of this distribution. The parameters of this distribution are the following:

Caution: Whenever you have a probability question about a sample mean, you must use the distribution of sample means.

a. The distribution is normal because the population is normal.
b. The distribution has a mean of 500 because the population mean is $\mu = 500$.
c. The distribution has a standard error of $\sigma_{\overline{x}} = 20$:

$$\sigma_{\overline{x}} = \frac{\sigma}{\sqrt{n}} = \frac{100}{\sqrt{25}} = \frac{100}{5} = 20$$

This distribution of sample means is shown in Figure 7.8.

We are interested in sample means greater than 540 (the shaded area in Figure 7.8), so the next step is to locate the exact position of $\overline{X} = 540$ in the distribution. The z-score for this value is

$$z = \frac{\overline{X} - \mu}{\sigma_{\overline{x}}} = \frac{540 - 500}{20} = \frac{40}{20} = 2.00$$

Figure 7.8
The distribution of sample means for $n = 25$. Samples were
selected from a normal population with $\mu = 500$ and $\sigma = 100$.

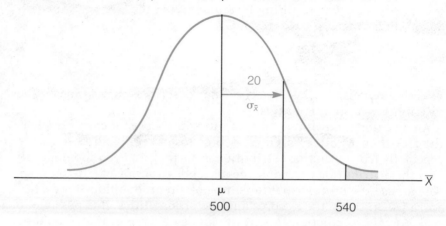

Because this distribution of sample means is normal, you
can use the unit normal table to find the probability associated with $z = +2.00$. The table indicates that 0.0228 of the
distribution is located in the tail of the distribution beyond
$z = +2.00$. Our conclusion is that it is very unlikely, $P =$
0.0228 (2.28%), to obtain a random sample of $n = 25$ students with an average SAT score greater than 540.

EXAMPLE 7.6
Suppose you simply wanted to predict the kind of value that
would be expected for the mean SAT score for a random
sample of $n = 25$ students. For example, what range of
values would be expected for the sample mean 80% of the
time? The simplest way of answering this question is to look
at the distribution of sample means. Remember, this distribution is the collection of all the possible sample means,
and it will show which samples are likely to be obtained
and which are not.

As demonstrated in Example 7.5, the distribution of sample means for $n = 25$ will be normal, will have an expected
value of $\mu = 500$, and will have a standard error of $\sigma_{\bar{x}} = 20$.
Looking at this distribution, shown again in Figure 7.9, it is
clear that the most likely value to expect for a sample mean
is around 500. To be more precise, we can identify the range
of values that would be expected 80% of the time by locating the middle 80% of the distribution. The distribution is
normal, so we can look up the percentage in the unit normal
table. To find the middle 80%, we need exactly 40% (or 0.40)
between the mean and the z-score on each side. Looking up
a proportion of 0.40 in the unit normal table (column B)
gives a z-score of $z = 1.28$. By definition, a z-score of 1.28
indicates that the score is 1.28 standard error units from

*Remember, when
answering proba-
bility questions,
it always is help-
ful to sketch a
distribution and
shade in the por-
tion you are
trying to find.*

Figure 7.9

The middle 80% of the distribution of sample means for $n = 25$. Samples were selected from a normal population with $\mu = 500$ and $\sigma = 100$.

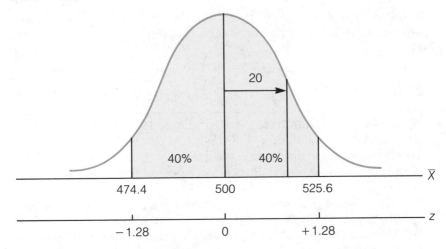

this mean. This distance is $1.28 \times 20 = 25.6$ points. The mean is 500, so 25.6 points either direction would give a range from 474.4 to 525.6. This is the middle 80% of all the possible sample means, so you can expect any particular sample mean to be in this range 80% of the time.

| BOX 7.2 | **The Difference Between Standard Deviation and Standard Error** |

A constant source of confusion for many students is the difference between standard deviation and standard error. You should remember that standard deviation measures the standard distance between a *score* and the population mean. As the name implies, it is the "standard" deviation $(X - \mu)$. Whenever you are working with a distribution of scores, the standard deviation is the appropriate measure of variability. Standard error, on the other hand, measures the standard distance between a *sample mean* and the population mean: the standard $(\overline{X} - \mu)$. Whenever you have a question concerning a sample, the standard error is the appropriate measure of variability.

If you still find the distinction confusing, there is a simple solution. Namely, if you always use standard error, you always will be right. Consider the formula for standard error:

$$\text{standard error} = \sigma_{\overline{x}} = \frac{\sigma}{\sqrt{n}}$$

If you are working with a single score, then $n = 1$, and the standard error becomes

continued

BOX 7.2   *continued*

$$\text{standard error} = \sigma_{\bar{x}} = \frac{\sigma}{\sqrt{n}} = \frac{\sigma}{\sqrt{1}} = \sigma = \text{standard deviation}$$

Thus, standard error always measures the standard distance from the population mean, whether you have a sample of $n = 1$ or $n = 100$.

1. A normal population has $\mu = 80$ and $\sigma = 10$. A sample of $n = 25$ scores has a mean of $\bar{X} = 83$. What is the z-score corresponding to this sample mean?

2. A random sample of $n = 9$ scores is selected from a normal population with $\mu = 40$ and $\sigma = 6$.
   a. What is the probability of obtaining a sample mean greater than 41?
   b. What is the probability of obtaining a sample mean less than 46?

3. A skewed distribution has $\mu = 60$ and $\sigma = 8$.
   a. What is the probability of obtaining a sample mean greater than $\bar{X} = 62$ for a sample of $n = 4$? (Be careful.)
   b. What is the probability of obtaining a sample mean greater than $\bar{X} = 62$ for a sample of $n = 64$?

ANSWERS

1. The standard error is 2. $z = \frac{3}{2} = 1.5$.
2. a. $\bar{X} = 41$ corresponds to $z = +0.50$. The probability is 0.3085 (30.85%).
   b. $\bar{X} = 46$ corresponds to $z = +3.0$. The probability is 0.9987 (99.87%).
3. a. Cannot answer because the distribution of sample means is not normal.
   b. With $n = 64$ the distribution of sample means will be normal. $\bar{X} = 62$ corresponds to $z = +2.0$. The probability is 0.0228 (2.28%).

Summary

1. The distribution of sample means is defined as the set of all the possible $\bar{X}$s for a specific sample size (n) that can be obtained from a given population. The parameters of the distribution of sample means are as follows:
   a. *Shape.* The distribution of sample means will be normal if either one of the following two conditions is satisfied:
      (1) The population from which the samples are selected is normal.

(2) The size of the samples is relatively large (around $n = 30$ or more).

  b. *Central Tendency.* The mean of the distribution of sample means will be identical to the mean of the population from which the samples are selected. The mean of the distribution of sample means is called the expected value of $\overline{X}$.

  c. *Variability.* The standard deviation of the distribution of sample means is called the standard error of $\overline{X}$ and is defined by the formula

$$\sigma_{\overline{x}} = \frac{\sigma}{\sqrt{n}}$$

  Standard error measures the standard distance between a sample mean $\overline{X}$ and the population mean μ.

2. One of the most important concepts in this chapter is the standard error. The standard error is the standard deviation of the distribution of sample means. It measures the standard distance between a sample mean $(\overline{X})$ and the population mean (μ). The standard error tells how much error to expect if you are using a sample mean to estimate a population mean.

3. The location of each $\overline{X}$ in the distribution of sample means can be specified by a z score:

$$z = \frac{\overline{X} - \mu}{\sigma_{\overline{x}}}$$

  Because the distribution of sample means tends to be normal, we can use these z-scores and the unit normal table to find probabilities for specific sample means. In particular, we can identify which sample means are likely and which are very unlikely to be obtained from any given population. This ability to find probabilities for samples is the basis for the inferential statistics in the chapters ahead.

Key Terms

law of large numbers
sampling error
distribution of sample means
sampling distribution

central limit theorem
expected value of $\overline{X}$
standard error of $\overline{X}$

Problems for Chapter 7:
Probability and Samples: The Distribution of Sample Means

1. Briefly define each of the following:

   a. The distribution of sample means

b. Expected value of $\overline{X}$

c. Standard error of $\overline{X}$

2. You have a population with $\mu = 100$ and $\sigma = 30$.

 a. If you randomly select a single score from this population, then, on the average, how close would you expect the score to be to the population mean?

 b. If you randomly select a sample of $n = 100$ scores, then, on the average, how close would you expect the sample mean to be to the population mean?

*3. The distribution of SAT scores is normal with $\mu = 500$ and $\sigma = 100$.

 a. If you selected a random sample of $n = 4$ scores from this population, how much error would you expect between the sample mean and the population mean?

 b. If you selected a random sample of $n = 25$ scores, how much error would you expect between the sample mean and the population mean?

 c. How much error would be expected for a sample of $n = 100$ scores?

4. On an immediate memory test, 10-year-old children can correctly recall an average of $\mu = 7$ digits. The distribution of recall scores is normal with $\sigma = 2$.

 a. What is the probability of randomly selecting a child with a recall score less than 6?

 b. What is the probability of randomly selecting a sample of $n = 4$ children whose average recall score is less than 6?

*5. Simple reaction times for college students form a normal distribution with $\mu = 200$ milliseconds and $\sigma = 20$.

 a. What is the probability of randomly selecting a student whose reaction time is less than 190?

 b. What is the probability of randomly selecting a sample of $n = 4$ students with an average reaction time less than 190?

 c. What is the probability of randomly selecting a sample of $n = 25$ students with an average reaction time less than 190?

6. If you are taking a random sample from a normal population with $\mu = 100$ and $\sigma = 12$, which of the following outcomes is more likely?

 a. A sample mean greater than 106 for a sample of $n = 4$ scores

b. A sample mean greater than 103 for a sample of $n = 36$ scores

*7. IQ scores form a normal distribution with $\mu = 100$ and $\sigma = 15$.

    a. What is the probability of randomly selecting a sample of $n = 9$ students so that their average IQ is different by more than one point from the population mean? (What is the probability of obtaining a sample mean greater than 101 or less than 99?)

    b. What is the probability of randomly selecting a sample of $n = 100$ individuals so that their average IQ is more than one point away from the population mean?

8. Standard error measures the standard distance between a sample mean and the population mean. For a population with $\sigma = 20$,

    a. How large a sample would be needed to obtain a standard error of less than 10 points?

    b. How large a sample would be needed to have a standard error smaller than 5 points?

    c. If you wanted your sample mean to be within 1 point of the population mean (on the average), how large a sample should you use?

*9. The light bulbs used in the U.S. space shuttle have an average life expectancy of $\mu = 100$ hours. The distribution of life expectancies is normal with $\sigma = 10$ hours. For a trip that is expected to last 380 hours, the crew take along four new bulbs (one in place and three spares). Assuming that each bulb is replaced immediately when it burns out, what is the probability that the four bulbs will be sufficient for the entire 380-hour trip? *Note:* For the four bulbs to total 380 hours, they must average 95 hours per bulb.

10. Scores on a personality questionnaire form a normal distribution with $\mu = 80$ and $\sigma = 12$. If a random sample of $n = 16$ people is selected and the average personality score is computed for this sample, then

    a. Sketch the distribution of all the possible sample means that could be obtained.

    b. Of all the possible sample means, what proportion will be greater than 86?

    c. Of all the possible sample means, what proportion will be within three points of the population mean?

*11. A population is normally distributed with $\mu = 100$ and $\sigma = 20$.

a. Find the z-score corresponding to each of the following samples:

$$\text{Sample 1:} \quad n = 4; \quad \overline{X} = 110$$
$$\text{Sample 2:} \quad n = 25; \quad \overline{X} = 105$$
$$\text{Sample 3:} \quad n = 100; \quad \overline{X} = 104$$

b. Which of the samples in part a is least likely to be obtained by random sampling?

12. A random sample of $n = 36$ scores is obtained from a population with $\sigma = 12$. The sample mean is $\overline{X} = 43$.

a. If you had to estimate the mean for the population, what value would you use? Explain the reasoning behind your answer.

b. If you use the sample mean to estimate the population mean, then how accurate would you expect this estimate to be?

*13. a. Calculate the mean and standard deviation for the population of digits 0 through 9.

b. If you took a random sample of $n = 8$ digits from this population, what is the probability that the digits in your sample would total 50 or more? (*Note:* For 8 digits to total 50, they must average 6.25 each.) Assume the distribution of sample means is normal even though $n = 8$.

c. If you took a random sample of 12 digits, what is the probability that they would total 50 or more? Assume the distribution of sample means is normal even though $n = 12$.

14. The 27 freshmen in Tower Dormatory finished their first semester with a mean grade point average of 2.61. They consider this to be a remarkable achievement because the mean GPA for the entire freshman class was only $\mu = 2.35$. If GPAs are normally distributed with $\sigma = 0.27$, what is the probability that a random sample of $n = 27$ would have an average GPA of 2.61 or higher? Are the freshmen in Tower Dorm justified in being proud?

*15 The local hardware store sells screws in 1-pound bags. Because the screws are not identical, the number of screws per bag varies with $\mu = 115$ and $\sigma = 6$. A carpenter needs a total of 600 screws for a particular project. What is the probability that he will have enough screws if he buys five bags? (Assume the distribution is normal.)

16. The average age for registered voters in the county is $\mu = 39.7$ years with $\sigma = 11.8$. The distribution of ages is approxi-

mately normal. During a recent jury trial in the county court-house, a statistician noted that the average age for the 12 jurors was $\overline{X}$ = 51.4 years.

a. How likely is it to obtain a jury this old or older by chance?

b. Is it reasonable to conclude that this jury is not a random sample of registered voters?

*17. At the beginning of this chapter we noted that the law of large numbers says that the larger the sample, the more likely that the sample mean will be close to the population mean. This law can be demonstrated using IQ scores which form a normal distribution with μ = 100 and σ = 16.

a. What is the probability of randomly selecting one individual whose IQ is within five points of the population mean?

b. If you select a sample of five people, how likely is it that their average IQ will be within five points of the population mean?

c. How likely is it for a sample of 10 people to have an average IQ within five points of the population mean?

18. A manufacturer of flashlight batteries claims that its batteries will last an average of μ = 34 hours of continuous use. Of course, there is some variability in life expectancy with σ = 1 hour. During consumer testing, a sample of 30 batteries lasted an average of only $\overline{X}$ = 31.5 hours. How likely is it to obtain a sample that performs this badly if the manufacturer's claim is true?

*19. Error scores for laboratory rats on a standardized discrimination problem form a normal distribution with μ = 85 and σ = 15.

a. Sketch the distribution of sample means for samples of size n = 10.

b. Find the range of values corresponds to the middle 95% of this distribution. Note that 95% of all the possible samples will have a mean in this range.

c. What is the range of sample means that would contain 99% of all the possible samples of n = 10 rats?

20. A large grocery store chain in New York has received a shipment of 1000 cases of oranges. The shipper claims that the cases average μ = 40 oranges with a standard deviation of σ = 2. To check this claim, the store manager randomly selects 4 cases and counts the number of oranges in each case. For these 4 cases, the average number of oranges is $\overline{X}$ = 38.

a. Assuming that the shipper's claim is true, what is the probability of obtaining a sample mean this small?

b. Based on your answer for part a, does the grocery store manager have reason to suspect that he has been cheated? Explain your answer.

CHAPTER 8

Introduction to Hypothesis Testing

The following items are considered essential background material for this chapter. If you doubt your knowledge of any of these items, you should review the appropriate chapter or section before proceeding.

1. *z*-Scores (Chapter 5)
2. Distribution of sample means (Chapter 7)
   a. Expected value
   b. Standard error
   c. Probability of sample means

The goal of inferential statistics is to draw general conclusions about a population using only the limited data from a sample. Hypothesis testing is one of the basic methods of inferential statistics. A researcher states a hypothesis about a population and then uses the data from a sample either to support or to refute the hypothesis.

DEFINITION

Hypothesis testing uses sample data to evaluate the tenability and credibility of a hypothesis about the population.

For example, psychologists have noted that stimulation during infancy can have profound effects on development. For infant rats, it has been noted that stimulation (for example, increased handling) and even stress (mild electric shock) result in eyes opening sooner, more rapid brain maturation, decreases is emotionality, faster growth, and larger body weight (see Levine, 1960). In fact, one might argue that increased stimulation and possibly occasional mild stress early in life can be beneficial. Suppose a researcher would like to assess the effect of increased handling during infancy on growth and body weight in humans, rather than rats. The hypothesis might state the following: For the population of infants, extra handling early in life has an effect on growth in weight. Notice that the hypothesis makes a prediction about the relationship between the independent (handling) and dependent (weight) variables. Also note that the hypothesis makes a prediction for the population.

Of course, it would be impossible to test the entire population of infants for the effects of handling on their growth in weight. It is reasonable, however, to test the effects of handling for a relatively small sample of infants. Thus, a random sample is selected, and the researcher instructs the parents in providing additional handling of the infants. The body weights of the infants are measured when they reach 2 years of age. The researcher then uses these data from the sample to evaluate the original hypothesis. Specifically, if the treatment really does have an effect, it should show up in the sample data. For this example, the investigator would determine whether or not the infants receiving extra handling weighed substantially more than is normally expected at 2 years of age.

This example provides just a glimpse of the hypothesis testing procedure. The actual mechanics of hypothesis tests are a little more involved because the researcher would like to make conclusions about the treatment effect with confidence that he/she is not in error. In this chapter we will elaborate on the step-by-step methods involved in hypothesis testing and look at the types of errors that can be made.

The Logic of Hypothesis Testing

The First Step: Stating the Hypotheses

The goal of inferential statistics is to make general statements about the population by using sample data. Therefore, when testing hypotheses, we make our predictions about the population parameters.

In the preview example, the psychologist is investigating the effect of increased handling during infancy on the body weight attained at the age of 2 years. The researcher knows, based on years of gathering health statistics, that the average weight for 2-year-olds who are *not receiving* any special treatment is $\mu = 26$ pounds. By using this information, hypotheses about the effect of extra handling can be stated. There are two hypotheses that are made, and both are always stated in terms of population parameters.

The first is the *null hypothesis*, or H_0. This hypothesis states that the treatment will have no effect (no change, no difference, nothing, null). In this example, the null hypothesis states that additional handling during infancy will have *no effect* on body weight for the population of infants. In symbols, this hypothesis would be

H_0: $\mu_{\text{infants handled}} = 26$ pounds   (Even with extra handling, the mean weight at 2 years is still 26 pounds.)

DEFINITION

The *null hypothesis* (H_0) predicts that the independent variable (treatment) has no effect on the dependent variable for the population.

The second hypothesis is simply the opposite of the null hypothesis, and it is called the *scientific* or *alternative hypothesis* (H_1). This hypothesis states that the treatment will have an effect on the dependent variable. For this example, it predicts that handling does alter growth for the population. In symbols, it is represented as

H_1: $\mu_{\text{infants handled}} \neq 26$ (With handling, the mean will be different from 26 pounds.)

Notice that in this case the alternative hypothesis simply states that there will be some type of change. It does not specify whether the effect will be increased or decreased growth. However, there are instances in which H_1 specifies the direction of the effect, and these will be examined in detail later (Chapter 9). For this example, we are examining whether handling in infancy does alter growth in some way (H_1) or has no effect (H_0). You should also note that both hypotheses refer to a population whose mean is unknown—namely, the population of infants who receive extra handling early in life. The two hypotheses are depicted in terms of population distributions in Figure 8.1.

The *alternative hypothesis* (H_1) predicts that the independent variable (treatment) will have an effect on the dependent variable for the population.

Figure 8.1

The effect of extra handling during infancy on body weight is assessed. Specifically we ask, What is the mean weight for the population after treatment? This question is answered by sample data. The top figure shows the situation if the null hypothesis (H_0) is correct and the treatment has no effect. The figure on the bottom shows the situation if the alternative hypothesis (H_1) is correct and the treatment has changed the population mean.

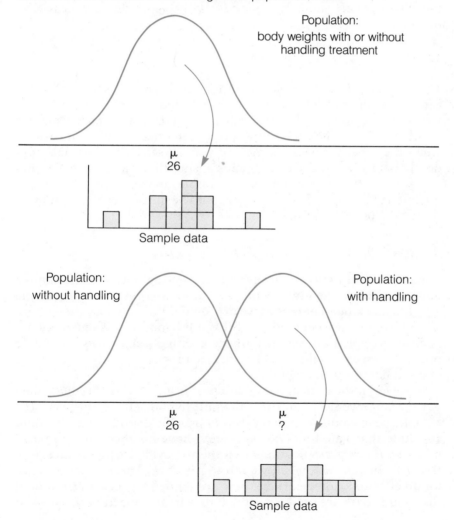

Determining What Data Are Unlikely to Be Obtained

The hypothesis testing procedure is designed to test the credibility of the null hypothesis. To do this, we use the null hypothesis to make a prediction about the population and use sample data to test that prediction. What kind of sample data would be expected if the null hypothesis were true? On the other hand, what kind of data would be very *unlikely* if the null hypothesis were true? For the example, if the null hypothesis were true (handling has no effect), then we would expect the average weight for our sample of 2-year-olds to be around 26 pounds, close to that of the untreated population. It would be very unlikely to obtain an average weight for the sample that is much different from 26 pounds if H_0 were true. Such a difference, if large enough, would cause us to conclude that H_0 is false and that an effect of handling did in fact occur. Thus, the second step of hypothesis testing is determining how unlikely the sample data must be before we conclude that an effect has occurred. There are guidelines for defining what data are unlikely, and these will be considered later in Section 8.2.

Collecting Sample Data

The next step in hypothesis testing is to obtain the sample data. A random sample of infants would be selected and parents would be trained to provide additional daily handling during the first few months of infancy. Then the body weight of the infants would be measured when they reach 2 years of age. Of course, selecting a sample randomly is important because it helps ensure that the sample is representative of the population. For example, it would help avoid the selection of a group of infants that would be unusually small or large, regardless of the treatment.

Evaluating the Null Hypothesis

The fourth and final step in hypothesis testing is to use the sample data to evaluate the null hypothesis. Do the scores from our sample look like the kind of data that we expected if the null hypothesis were true? If so, then we conclude that the null hypothesis is tenable. That is, if the sample data reveal that the average weight was around 26 pounds, then we would conclude that there is no evidence for an effect of extra handling during infancy.

However, if the data are very different from what H_0 predicts, then our decision would be to *reject* the null hypothesis. In this case, the sample mean would be much different from 26 pounds, and we would conclude that handling does appear to have an effect. Note that in rejecting H_0 we are concluding that there is evidence for an effect (see Box 8.1). In contrast, when we fail to reject H_0, there is no evidence for an effect. As noted earlier, there are guidelines for determining if the sample data are unlikely enough to warrant rejecting H_0. We will turn our attention to these rules and examine their role in evaluating hypotheses later. But first we must consider the types of errors that can occur in hypothesis testing.

BOX 8.1 | **Rejecting the Null Hypothesis Versus Proving the Alternative Hypothesis**

It may seem awkward to pay so much attention to the null hypothesis. After all, the purpose of most experiments is to show that a treatment does have an effect, and the null hypothesis states that there is no effect. The reason for focusing on the null hypothesis rather than the alternative hypothesis comes from the limitations of inferential logic. Remember, we want to use the sample data to draw conclusions, or inferences, about a population. Logically, it is much easier to demonstrate that a universal (population) hypothesis is false than to demonstrate that it is true. This principle is shown more clearly in a simple example. Suppose you make the universal statement "all dogs have four legs" and you intend to test this hypothesis by using a sample of one dog. If the dog in your sample does have four legs, have you proved the statement? It should be clear that one four-legged dog does not prove the general statement to be true. On the other hand, suppose the dog in your sample has only three legs. In this case, you have proved the statement to be false. Again, it is much easier to show that something is false than to prove that it is true.

Hypothesis testing uses this logical principle to achieve its goals. It would be difficult to state "the treatment has an effect" as the hypothesis and then try to prove that this is true. Therefore, we state the null hypothesis, "the treatment has no effect," and try to show that it is false. The end result still is to demonstrate that the treatment does have an effect. That is, we find support for the alternative hypothesis by disproving (rejecting) the null hypothesis.

Errors in Hypothesis Testing

The problem in hypothesis testing is deciding whether or not the sample data are consistent with the null hypothesis. In the second step of the hypothesis testing procedure, we identify the kind of data that are expected if the null hypothesis is true. If the outcome of the experiment is consistent with this prediction, then there is no need to be suspicious about the truthfulness or credibility of the null hypothesis. If on the other hand the outcome of the experiment is very different from this prediction, then we would reject the null hypothesis because the evidence is overwhelmingly against it. In either case, it is possible that the decision we make about the tenability of H_0 is an incorrect decision. The two possibilities are presented here (and in Box 8.2).

Type I Errors It is possible to reject the null hypothesis when in reality the treatment has no effect. The outcome of the experiment could be different from what H_0 predicted just by chance. After all, unusual events do occur. For example, it is possible, although unlikely, to toss a balanced coin five times and have it turn up heads every time. In the experiment we have been considering, it is possible just by chance to select a sample of exceptional infants who display unusual (much less or much greater than normal) growth patterns even though the handling treatment has no effect. In this situation the data would lead us to reject the null hypothesis even though it is correct. This kind of mistake is called a *type I error* (see Table 8.1), and in psychology it is very serious mistake. A type I error results in the investigator making a false report of a treatment effect. In the handling experiment, the researcher would claim that handling during infancy alters growth when in fact no such effect exists.

DEFINITION

A *type I error* consists of rejecting the null hypothesis when H_0 is actually true.

Type II Errors It also is possible for the data to be consistent with the null hypothesis even when H_0 is false. Suppose that handling has a small effect on growth so that even with early handling our sample averages slightly above 26 pounds at 2 years of age. However, the difference between the sample and the predicted (H_0) data is too small to confidently reject H_0. Another possibility is that the sample of infants was exceptionally small at the start. Handling increases their growth but only to the extent that they reach the expected weight of 26 pounds at 2 years. In these cases, we would decide to retain a null hypothesis when in reality it is false, a *type II error* (Table 8.1). That is, we conclude that the treatment has no effect when in fact it does.

DEFINITION

In a *type II error*, the investigator fails to reject a null hypothesis that is really false.

Most experiments in psychology are done with the hope of rejecting the null hypothesis. Remember, the null hypothesis states that the treatment has no effect on the dependent variable. However, we face a dilemma in reaching a decision about H_0. On one hand, we would like to establish that there is a treatment effect (reject H_0). But we also would like to avoid a type I error (rejecting H_0 when it really is true).

Table 8.1

Possible Outcomes of a Statistical Decision

		Actual Situation	
		No Effect, H_0 True	Effect Exists, H_0 False
Experimenter's Decision	Reject H_0	Type I error	Decision correct
	Retain H_0	Decision correct	Type II error

A similar dilemma occurs in the "hypothesis testing" that is done in the courtroom. Just as we assume H_0 is true before we collect our data, the jury is instructed to assume that the accused person is innocent of a crime—innocent until proven guilty. A type I error would occur if the jury decides a person is guilty when in reality that person did not commit the crime (see Table 8.2). A type I error is serious: An innocent person would be sent to prison. Just as in scientific research, it is desirable to avoid making a type I error. This may mean that the jury will let a guilty person off the hook, a type II error (Table 8.2). To deal with the dilemma of testing a person's innocence while avoiding a type I error, the judge instructs the jury that the accused individual should be found guilty only if the evidence is "beyond a reasonable shadow of a doubt." This guideline will reduce the chance that the jury will commit a type I error and punish an innocent person.

Likewise, it is important for scientists to minimize the likelihood of making a type I error in their investigations. It is highly desirable to avoid making a false report that a treatment effect exists. To be

Table 8.2

Possible Outcomes of a Jury's Decision

		Actual Situation	
		Did Not Commit Crime	Committed Crime
Jury's Verdict	Guilty	Type I error	Verdict correct
	Innocent	Verdict correct	Type II error

Adapted from *Essence of Statistics*, by G. R. Loftus and E. F. Loftus. Copyright © 1982 by Wadsworth Inc. Reprinted by permission of Brooks/Cole Publishing Company, Monterey, Calif.

sure a type I error is avoided, the H_0 is rejected only when the sample data are very extreme and unlikely for H_0 to be true. That is, the evidence must be so overwhelming against H_0 that the researcher can reject the null hypothesis with the confidence that the "verdict" is correct "beyond a reasonable shadow of a doubt." How unlikely or overwhelming must the sample data be before the researcher can confidently reject H_0 and conclude there is an effect? The guideline is provided by the level of significance that the investigator uses in testing the hypothesis. We will examine this guideline in Section 8.2.

BOX 8.2 A Summary of Statistical Errors

Definitions:

> A type I error is rejecting a true null hypothesis.
>
> A type II error is failing to reject a false null hypothesis.

Interpretation:

Type I error: The researcher concludes that the treatment does have an effect when, in fact, there is no treatment effect.

Type II error: The researcher concludes that there is no evidence for a treatment effect when, in fact, the treatment does have an effect.

How Does it Happen?:

Type I error: By chance, the sample consists of individuals with extreme scores. As a result, the sample looks different from what we would have expected according to H_0. Note that the treatment has not actually affected the individuals in the sample—they were different from average from the start of the experiment.

Type II error: Although there are several explanations for a type II error, the simplest is that the treatment effect was too small to have a noticeable effect on the sample. As a result, the sample does not appear to have been affected by the treatment. It is also possible that, just by chance, the sample was extreme to start with and in the opposite direction of the treatment effect. The treatment effect, in turn, restores the sample to the average that is expected by H_0. A treatment effect does not appear to have occurred even though it did.

Consequences:

Type I error: Because the sample data appear to demonstrate a treatment effect, the researcher may claim in a published report that the treatment has an effect. This is a false report and can have serious consequences. For one, other researchers may spend precious time and resources trying to replicate the findings to no avail. In addition, the false report creates a false data base upon which other workers develop theories and plan new experiments. In real-

BOX 8.2 *continued*

ity, they may be taking a journey down an experimental and theoretical dead end.

Type II error: In this case, the sample data do not provide sufficient evidence to say that the treatment has any effect. The researcher can interpret this finding in two different ways:

> First, the researcher can conclude that the treatment probably does have an effect but the experiment was not good enough to find it. Perhaps an improved experiment (larger sample, better measurement, more potent treatment, etc.) would be able to demonstrate the treatment effect. The consequence is that refined experiments may be capable of detecting the effect.

> Second, the researcher may believe that the statistical decision is correct. Either the treatment has no effect, or the effect is too small to be important. In this case, the experiment is abandoned. Note that this interpretation can have serious consequences in the event a type II error has occurred. It means that the researcher is giving up a line of research that could have otherwise provided important findings.

LEARNING CHECK

1. What does the null hypothesis predict about a population?
2. Why do we evaluate (decide to reject or not reject) the null hypothesis instead of evaluating the alternative hypothesis?
3. What is a type I error? A type II error?
4. Is it possible to commit a type II error when H_0 is rejected? Explain your answer.
5. Why do we state hypotheses in terms of population parameters?

ANSWERS

1. The null hypothesis predicts that the treatment will have no effect on the dependent variable for the population.
2. It is much easier to disprove a universal (population) statement than to prove one. Therefore, to find support for a treatment effect in the population, we must obtain sample data that suggest we should reject H_0. That is, we support the presence of a treatment effect when we disprove the null hypothesis.
3. A type I error occurs when the experimenter rejects a null hypothesis that is actually true. An effect is reported when none exists. A type II error occurs when the decision is "fail to reject H_0" but the null hypothesis is really false. One fails to report an effect that does exist.

4. No. A type II error results from *failing to reject* a false H_0. Therefore, it cannot result from rejecting the null hypothesis.
5. We make predictions about the population because the goal of inferential statistics is to make general statements about the *population* based on the sample data.

Evaluating Hypotheses

As previously noted, there is always the possibility for error in making an inference. As a result, we can never be absolutely positive that a hypothesis test has produced the correct decision. Although we cannot know for certain if our decision is right or wrong, we can know the probabilities for being right or wrong. Specifically, the hypothesis testing procedure is structured so that a researcher can specify and control the probability of making a type I error. By keeping this probability small, a researcher can be confident that the risk of error is very low whenever the null hypothesis is rejected.

Alpha Level: Minimizing the Risk of a Type I Error

To make a decision about a null hypothesis, it is necessary to determine what data are expected if H_0 is true and what data are very unlikely. The *level of significance*, also called the *alpha level*, simply defines the very unlikely data. It marks off the part of the distribution from which it is highly unlikely to obtain sample data if H_0 is true. Obtaining sample data from this part of the distribution would lead us to reject the null hypothesis. To minimize the risk of committing a type I error, we mark off regions of the distribution that are extreme and improbable. For example, if we use an alpha (α) level of 5%, then the sample data would have to be from the most extreme 5% of the distribution in order to reject H_0. The probability that we would commit a type I error in that case would equal alpha, or $\alpha = 5\%$.

DEFINITION

Alpha (α) is the risk of committing a type I error. The selected alpha determines the *level of significance* of a hypothesis test, the level at which we reject H_0 and conclude there is evidence for a treatment effect.

Traditionally, alpha levels are set at 5% (.05), 1% (.01), or 0.1% (.001). We will examine the role that alpha plays in the hypothesis testing procedures by returning to the example of the effects of increased handling during infancy.

Procedure and Steps

Recall that the study examines the effect of extra handling during infancy on growth. We will begin with the simplest possible experiment for now, using a sample of only one infant ($n = 1$). The parents are instructed in how to provide additional handling during the first few months of their infant's life, and then the child's weight is measured at 2 years of age. Let us assume that weights are normally distributed with $\mu = 26$ pounds and $\sigma = 4$ for the population of untreated (did not receive additional handling) children. There are four steps to hypothesis testing: (1) stating the hypotheses and selecting an alpha level, (2) using the alpha level to define what kind of sample data would warrant rejection of H_0, (3) analyzing the sample data, and (4) making a decision about H_0. We will use these steps to assess the effect of additional handling during infancy on growth.

STEP 1. We must state the hypotheses and select an alpha level. The null hypothesis predicts that no effect will occur. That is, even with additional handling during infancy, the population mean weight for 2-year-olds will still be 26 pounds. In symbols, this hypothesis is stated as follows:

$$H_0: \quad \mu_{\text{handling in infancy}} = 26 \text{ pounds}$$

The alternative hypothesis states that early handling will change the mean weight for the population. In symbols, this hypothesis would state the following:

$$H_1: \quad \mu_{\text{handling}} \neq 26 \text{ pounds}$$

We will select an alpha level of 5%, or in terms of a proportion, $\alpha = .05$. This means that in order to reject the null hypothesis, the sample data must be extremely convincing—the data must be in the most extreme 5% of the distribution. By setting α to this level, we are limiting the probability of a type I error to only 5%.

STEP 2. We must define what kind of sample data would warrant rejection of the null hypothesis. We begin by looking at all the possible data that could be obtained if the null hypothesis were true. If H_0 is true, then the distribution of handled infants would be the same as the original distribution of untreated infants. That is, it would be a normal distribution with $\mu = 26$ and $\sigma = 4$ (Figure 8.2).

If H_0 is true we expect to obtain a score near the population mean, $\mu = 26$. Extreme values in the tails of the distribution would be extremely unlikely.

We have selected the value of $\alpha = .05$ for the level of significance. This proportion is divided evenly between the two tails of the distribution (see Figure 8.2). It is very unlikely that we would sample a score from this area of the distribution if H_0 is true. The area between the tails is the middle 95% of the distribution. This area contains the most likely

Figure 8.2

The distribution of all the possible scores that could be obtained if H_0 is true. The boundaries separate the middle 95% from the most extreme 5% ($\alpha = .05$).

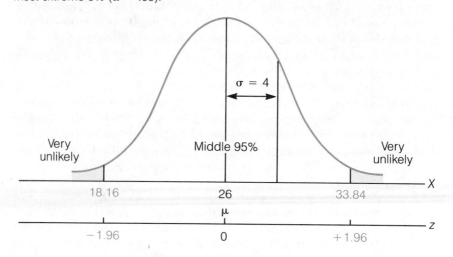

scores (weights) in the population, and it is very likely that we would obtain a sample score from this region if H_0 is true. Notice that the boundaries that separate the middle 95% from the extreme 5% (2.5% in each tail) are located at the z-score values of $+1.96$ and -1.96 (from the unit normal table in Appendix B). A z-score of 1.96 indicates that the corresponding score is 1.96 standard deviations away from the mean. For this example, 1.96 standard deviations is equal to 7.84 points. For the population weight distribution, the score that corresponds to $z = +1.96$ is $X = 33.84$, and the score that corresponds to $z = -1.96$ is $X = 18.16$. These values mark off the boundaries between the middle 95% and the extreme tails of the distribution (see Figure 8.2).

If we randomly select one subject from the population, then we would expect to observe a weight near 26 pounds. Most of the time (95% to be exact) we would expect the score to be in the middle section of the distribution. It is very improbable that we would randomly sample a score that is out in the extreme tails of the distribution if H_0 is true. These extreme tails, the shaded areas in Figure 8.2, are called the *critical region* of the distribution. If H_0 were true, then it would be extremely unlikely to obtain a score in the critical region. Notice that we have defined "extremely unlikely" as meaning "having a probability less than alpha." For this example, the H_0 is rejected only when the sample data are really extreme—when the probability of our sample observation is less than the alpha level ($p < .05$). In other words, H_0 is rejected when the sample data fall in the critical region.

Remember, X = μ + zσ (Chapter 5).

When an alpha level is reported as a probability, a lowercase p is traditionally used.

The *critical region* is composed of extreme sample values that are very unlikely to be obtained if the null hypothesis is true. The size of the critical region is determined by the alpha level. Sample data that fall in the critical region will warrant the rejection of the null hypothesis.

STEP 3. We now turn our attention to the sample data. In this particular example, the sample size is $n = 1$. Suppose the infant that received extra handling early in life weighed 34 pounds at 2 years of age. What can we conclude about the relationship between handling in infancy and growth?

STEP 4. We must make a decision about the null hypothesis. The result we obtained from the sample, $X = 34$, lies in the critical region (Figure 8.2). The sample is not what we expected if the null hypothesis is true. It is an extremely unlikely outcome ($p < .05$) if H_0 is true. Therefore, we decide to reject the null hypothesis and conclude that extra handling during infancy did have a statistically significant effect on growth. With this statistical decision, we are risking a type I error. That is, we could be rejecting a true null hypothesis. It is possible that the handling had no effect on growth and that the infant we sampled would have reached 34 pounds anyway. However, this is very unlikely. If H_0 is true, the probability of obtaining any score in the critical region is less than 5%, the alpha level we selected. The maximum probability of committing a type I error is equal to alpha.

z-Scores and Hypothesis Testing

In the handling example, our decision to reject H_0 was based on the obtained score of $X = 34$, which falls within the critical region. We could have based this decision entirely on z-scores. For this example, the critical region consists of any z value greater than $+1.96$ or less than -1.96 (Figure 8.2). We can simply convert the obtained X value into a z-score to determine its location. That is, we determine whether or not it is in the critical region. For the score obtained,

$$z = \frac{X - \mu}{\sigma} = \frac{34 - 26}{4} = 2.00$$

The obtained z-score is greater than $+1.96$ and thus lies in the critical region. The statistical decision would be the same, H_0 is rejected. Notice that the z-score is being used to test a hypothesis. In this use, the z-score is often called a *test statistic*. We will examine other types of test statistics which are used in hypothesis testing in later chapters.

Failures to Reject the Null Hypothesis

Using the handling example again, let us suppose that we obtained a sample infant that attained a weight of 31 pounds at 2 years. Steps 1 and 2 (stating the hypotheses and locating the critical region) remain the same. For step 3, we can analyze the sample finding by computing a z-score. If $X = 31$, then

$$z = \frac{X - \mu}{\sigma} = \frac{31 - 26}{4} = \frac{5}{4} = 1.25$$

Limitations in the logic of inference make it easier to disprove a hypothesis about the population (Box 8.1).

In the final step, the statistical decision is made. The z-score for the obtained sample score is not in the critical region. This is the kind of outcome we would expect if H_0 were true. It is important to note that we have not proved that the null hypothesis is true. The sample provides only limited information about the entire population, and, in this case, we did not obtain sufficient evidence to confidently claim that additional handling early in life does or does not have an effect on growth. For this reason, researchers avoid using the phrase "accepting the null hypothesis," opting instead for "failing to reject the null hypothesis." The latter phrase is more consistent with the logic of hypothesis testing. When the data are not overwhelmingly contrary to H_0, at best all we can say is that the data do not provide sufficient evidence to reject the null hypothesis.

Our decision to "fail to reject" H_0 means that we are risking a type II error. For this example, a type II error would mean that the extra handling actually did have some effect and yet we failed to discover it. A type II error generally is not as serious a mistake as a type I error. The consequences of a type II error would be that a real effect is not reported. If a researcher suspects that a type II error has occurred, there is always the option of repeating the experiment, usually with some refinements or modifications. There are lots of reasons why any particular experiment may fail. When a researcher is personally convinced that a treatment should have an effect, he/she has every right to try to demonstrate it with another experiment (see Box 8.3). However, you should realize that it is not reasonable to continue doing the same experiment over and over until it eventually produces the results you want.

Unlike type I errors where the exact amount of risk is specified by the alpha level (α), there is no simple way to determine the probability of a type II error. In fact, this probability is not a single value but rather depends on the size of the treatment effect. For example, if the treatment has a very large effect, then it almost certainly would be evident in the experiment, and the chances of missing it (a type II error) would be very small. On the other hand, if the treatment effect is minimal, then the scores following the treatment will look very much like they did before the treatment, and we are likely to conclude that there is no treatment effect. In this case, a type II error, failing to find a treatment effect when one does exist, is highly likely. Although the exact probability of committing a type II error is not easily calculated, it is identified by the Greek letter beta, β. We will examine β again in Chapter 9 when statistical power is considered.

α is for type I, and β is for type II.

BOX 8.3 | Problems in Replication

What does it really mean when we fail to find a treatment effect? What happens when a researcher repeatedly fails to replicate an earlier finding in his or her own laboratory? This problem occurred in the laboratory of Dr. Neal E. Miller, a very prominent psychologist who for years did outstanding research at Yale University and later Rockefeller University. He wanted to see if rats could learn to control their involuntary vital responses by operant conditioning and do so without the aid of voluntary movements. For example, if a rat is given a reward (pleasurable brain stimulation) for slowing down its heart rate, would it learn to control its heart and make it beat slower to get the reward? There was a "catch" to the experiment. The rats had to learn to control heart rate without voluntary movements (like becoming very relaxed) that could slow the heart. So rats were temporarily paralyzed with a drug called curare. Sure enough, even though their muscles were paralyzed, the rats could still learn to control how fast their hearts would beat. Miller and the scientific community in general were excited by the findings and the possible applications for treating psychosomatic disorders. However, after reporting the results of the first few experiments, Miller and his co-workers found that they could no longer get the same effects. He could not replicate the conditioning of involuntary responses by the use of reward. What went wrong? Perhaps the new batch of rats was somehow different from the previous animals. Miller tried a different kind of rat to no avail. Perhaps the paralyzing drug had gone bad and interfered with the conditioning of heart rates. He tried a new sample of curare, but nothing changed. Perhaps the reward was no longer as effective as before, or perhaps changes in the laboratory diet caused general physiological changes in the animals that prevented the effect. The list of possible reasons why the conditioning effect could not be replicated seems endless. As Miller and Dworkin (1974) pointed out,

> The problem is that, whereas there often are millions of ways of doing something wrong, there may be only one or two ways of doing it right. Thus, one positive result can yield vastly more information than many negative ones (p. 315).

Thus, there may be "millions" of ways of doing an experiment incorrectly, each producing no evidence for an effect, each retaining a null hypothesis. Yet we cannot make a general conclusion when we fail to reject H_0. Had we used the right combination of treatment conditions in the experiment, had we done the experiment in the "one or two ways of doing it right," an effect may have emerged. Therefore, retaining the null hypothesis in many experiments will not advance our knowledge as much as finding an effect in a single experiment.

1. Define alpha.
2. If H_0 is rejected when alpha is .05, will it necessarily be rejected when alpha has been set at .01?
3. What is the critical region? How is it used?
4. Experimenter 1 typically sets alpha to .10, while experimenter 2 always uses an alpha level of .05. In the long run, which experimenter will make more type I errors?

ANSWERS

1. Alpha is the risk an investigator takes in committing a type I error. The alpha level determines the level of significance of a statistical test.
2. Not necessarily. The data may be extreme enough to warrant rejecting H_0 at the 5% level of significance but not extreme enough for the same decision at the 1% level.
3. The critical region consists of extreme sample values that are very unlikely to be obtained (probability less than α) if the null hypothesis is true. If sample data fall in the critical region, we reject H_0.
4. Experimenter 1 is taking a greater risk (10%) of committing a type I error.

8.3
Hypothesis Testing with Samples of More than One Score

Up to this point we have examined the hypothesis testing procedure with samples consisting of only one subject ($n = 1$). In practice, however, many subjects are selected for the sample. In such a case, our hypothesis no longer hinges on a single X value but on the mean of the sample, $\overline{X}$. The general procedure for hypothesis testing is the same whether you have a sample of $n = 1$ or $n = 100$. In step 1, you state the hypotheses (H_0 and H_1) and specify an alpha level. In step 2, you locate the critical region—that is, you look at all the possible results that could be obtained if H_0 were true and then identify the most extreme, most unlikely outcomes. In step 3, the sample data are collected and analyzed, and in step 4, a decision is made about the null hypothesis. The size of the sample (n) becomes important in the second and third steps. Instead of looking at all the possible scores that could be obtained (that is, when $n = 1$), we now must look at all the possible sample means that could be obtained. You should recall from the previous chapter that "all the possible sample means" is, by definition, the distribution of sample means. The following example demonstrates how this distribution is used in hypothesis tests with samples of more than $n = 1$.

EXAMPLE 8.1

Once again we will look at the effect of handling early in life on growth. This time, however, a sample of $n = 25$ infants is selected. The parents are instructed in providing additional handling during the first few months. The body weight of all subjects is measured at 2 years of age. As before, body weight is normally distributed with $\mu = 26$ and $\sigma = 4$. Suppose that the sample of $n = 25$ children had a mean body weight of $\overline{X} = 30$.

Steps and Procedures

STEP 1. The null hypothesis states that the extra handling will have no effect on growth (mean body weight). In symbols, H_0 states that

$$H_0: \quad \mu_{\text{handling}} = 26 \text{ pounds}$$

That is, even with additional handling during infancy, the population mean would still be 26 pounds. The alternative hypothesis states that the handling treatment will produce a change in growth. In symbols, it is represented as

$$H_1: \quad \mu_{\text{handling}} \neq 26 \text{ pounds}$$

If the alternative hypothesis is correct, the population mean for children that receive extra handling during infancy will be different from the mean of the regular population of untreated children. We select an alpha level of $\alpha = .05$ (5%). This means that we are willing to take a 5% risk of committing a type I error.

STEP 2. If the null hypothesis is true, it is possible to examine the distribution of all the possible sample means that could be obtained from this experiment. This distribution is the distribution of sample means based on samples of $n = 25$. It will have an expected value of $\mu = 26$ when H_0 is true. Furthermore, this distribution will have a standard error of $\sigma_{\overline{x}} = 0.8$ according to the following formula:

Remember, a property of the distribution of sample means is that the expected value equals μ.

$$\sigma_{\overline{x}} = \frac{\sigma}{\sqrt{n}} = \frac{4}{\sqrt{25}} = \frac{4}{5} = 0.8$$

The distribution of sample means is shown in Figure 8.3. It is this distribution for which we locate the critical region. We have set alpha to .05, so the critical region consists of the most extreme 5% of all the possible sample means. Because this distri-

The distribution of sample means is normal when the population is normal.

bution is normal, the most extreme 5% consists of values with z-scores greater than $+1.96$ or less than -1.96 (2.5% in each tail, the shaded area in Figure 8.3).

Notice that the middle 95% of the distribution consists of samples wih means within 1.96 standard errors of 26 pounds. We would expect to obtain a sample mean in this neighborhood if H_0 were true and handling had no effect. If our data fall in this middle section, we will conclude that the results are consistent with the null hypothesis, and we will retain (fail to reject) H_0. Also note that all of the values in this distribution are possible if H_0 is true. Specifically, it is possible to randomly select a sample whose mean falls in the critical region. However, this is a very unlikely possibility if H_0 is true because of how the critical region was determined. By definition, the critical region consists of the most extreme 5% of all the possible sample means. That is, it is only 5% likely that the sample data will be in the critical region if H_0 were true—which means that there is only a 5% chance of committing a type I error if H_0 is rejected.

STEP 3. At this stage, the sample data are collected and analyzed. As noted earlier, the obtained sample mean is $\overline{X} = 30$. Where is this sample located within the distribution of sample means shown in Figure 8.3? The most direct way of answering this

---

Figure 8.3

The distribution of sample means for $n = 25$ if H_0 is true. This is the set of all the possible experimental outcomes that could be obtained if handling has no effect on weight gain.

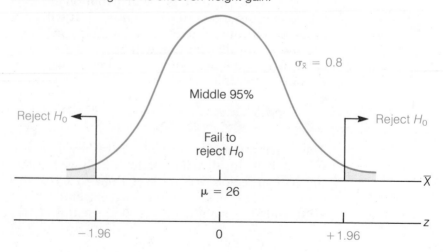

question is to compute a z-score. The test statistic for these data is

$$z = \frac{\overline{X} - \mu}{\sigma_{\overline{x}}} = \frac{30 - 26}{0.8} = \frac{4}{0.8} = 5.0$$

Careful! Be sure to use $\sigma_{\overline{x}}$.

Remember, this test statistic finds the location of a sample mean within the distribution of sample means.

STEP 4. It now is possible to make a statistical decision. The result of the study was a sample with a mean weight of $\overline{X} = 30$ pounds. This value corresponds to a z-score of $z = +5.0$. Note that the obtained z-score falls in the critical region on the right-hand side of the distribution (Figure 8.3). This means that the observed sample data are very unlikely to have occurred if H_0 is true. Because the results are overwhelmingly inconsistent with H_0, we reject the null hypothesis. We conclude that additional handling during infancy does have an effect on weight. Of course in making this decision, it is possible that we have made a type I error—that these extreme data were obtained by chance alone and that handling has no effect. However, this error is not very likely because a level of significance of 5% was used. The probability that we have committed a type I error, rejecting a true H_0, is $p < .05$. (See Box 8.4.)

BOX 8.4 **Reporting the Results of the Statistical Test**

There is a special jargon and notational system that is used in published reports of hypothesis tests. When you are reading a scientific journal, for example, you will not be told explicitly that the researcher evaluated the data using a z-score as a test statistic with an alpha level of .05. Instead, you will see a statement like

"The treatment effect was significant, $z = 3.85$, $p < .05$."

Let us examine this statement part by part.

First, what is meant by the term *significant*? In statistical tests, this word indicates that the result is different from what would be expected by chance. A significant result means that the null hypothesis has been rejected. That is, the data are in the critical region and not what we would have expected to obtain if H_0 were true. In simple terms, a significant result means that either the treatment worked or that a very improbable event has occurred.

Next, what is the meaning of "$z = 3.85$?" The z indicates that the data were used to compute a z-score for a test statistic and that

continued

BOX 8.4 *continued*

its value was 3.85. Finally, what is meant by "$p < .05$?" This part of the statement is the conventional way of specifying the alpha level that was used for the hypothesis test. More specifically, we are being told that the result of the experiment would occur by chance with a probability (p) that is less than .05.

In circumstances where the statistical decision is to fail to reject H_0, the report might state that

"There was no evidence for an effect, $z = 1.30, p > .10$."

In this case, we are saying that the obtained result, $z = 1.30$, is not unusual (not in the critical region) and is relatively likely to occur by chance (the probability is greater than .10).

The Structure of the *z*-Score Formula

It is useful to define the *z*-score formula

$$z = \frac{\overline{X} - \mu}{\sigma_{\overline{x}}}$$

in terms of the important steps and elements of hypothesis testing. Specifically, we test the null hypothesis (that is, we try to disprove it) in order to show a treatment effect. The null hypothesis is represented in the formula by μ. The value of μ that we use in the formula is the value predicted by H_0. We test H_0 by collecting sample data, which are represented by the sample mean ($\overline{X}$) in the formula. Thus the numerator of the *z* formula can be rewritten as

$$\overline{X} - \mu = \text{sample data} - \text{population hypothesis}$$

You should recall that the standard error ($\sigma_{\overline{x}}$) measures the standard distance between a sample mean and the population mean. Thus, standard error measures the expected difference (due to chance) between $\overline{X}$ and μ. Now we can restate the entire *z*-score test statistic as

$$z = \frac{\text{sample data} - \text{population hypothesis}}{\text{standard error between } \overline{X} \text{ and } \mu}$$

Notice that the difference between the sample data and the null hypothesis must be substantially larger than would be expected by chance in order to obtain a *z*-score that is large enough to fall in the critical region. The structure of this *z*-score formula will form the basis for some of the test statistics to follow in later chapters.

Assumptions for Hypothesis Tests with z-Scores

It will become evident in later chapters that certain conditions must be present for each type of hypothesis test to be an appropriate and accurate procedure. These conditions are assumed to be satisfied when the results of a hypothesis test are interpreted. However, the decisions based on the test statistic (that is, rejecting or not rejecting H_0) may be compromised if these assumptions are not satisfied. In practice, researchers are not overly concerned with the conditions of a statistical test unless they have strong suspicions that the assumptions have been violated. Nevertheless, it is crucial to keep in mind the fundamental conditions that are associated with each type of statistical test to ensure that it is being used appropriately. The assumptions for hypothesis tests with z-scores which involve one sample are summarized below.

Random Sampling It is assumed that the subjects used to obtain the sample data were selected randomly. Remember, we wish to generalize our findings from the sample to the population. This task is accomplished when we use sample data to test a hypothesis about the population. Therefore, the sample must be representative of the population from which it has been drawn. Random sampling helps to ensure that it is representative.

The Value of σ is Unchanged by the Treatment The general purpose of hypothesis testing is to determine whether or not a treatment (independent variable) produces a change in the population mean. The null hypothesis, the critical region, and the z-score statistic all are concerned with the treated population. In the z-score formula we use $\overline{X}$ from the treated sample, a hypothesized value of μ for the treated population and a standard error that indicates how close $\overline{X}$ should be to μ. However, you may have noticed that when we compute the standard error, we use the standard deviation from the untreated population. Thus, the z-score appears to be using values from two different populations: $\overline{X}$ and μ for the treated population and σ from the untreated population. To justify this apparent contradiction we must make an assumption. Specifically, we must assume that the value of σ is the same after treatment as it was before treatment.

Actually, this assumption is the consequence of a more general assumption that is part of many statistical procedures. This general assumption states that the effect of the treatment is to add (or subtract) a constant amount to every score in the population. You should recall that adding (or subtracting) a constant will change the mean but will have no effect on the standard deviation. This point is depicted in the bottom of Figure 8.1 which shows a treatment that increases the population mean but leaves the variability unaffected. You also should note that this assumption is a theoretical ideal. In actual experiments a treatment generally will not show a perfect and consistent additive effect.

Normal Sampling Distribution   To evaluate hypotheses with z-scores, we have used the unit normal table to identify the critical region. This table can be used only if the distribution of sample means is normal.

LEARNING
CHECK

1. An instructor has been teaching large sections of general psychology for the past 10 semesters. As a group, final exam scores are normally distributed with $\mu = 42$ and $\sigma = 9$. With the current class of $n = 100$ students, the instructor tries a different teaching format. Once a week the class breaks down into smaller groups that meet with the instructor for discussion of recent lecture and reading material. At the end of the semester, the instructor notes that the mean for this section on the final exam was $\overline{X} = 46.5$. Did the teaching format have a significant effect on performance on the final exam? Test with alpha set at .05.
   a. State the hypotheses.
   b. Locate the critical region.
   c. Compute the test statistic.
   d. Make a decision regarding H_0.
   e. For this example, identify the independent and dependent variables.

ANSWERS

1. a. H_0: $\mu_{\text{discussion groups}} = 42$; H_1: $\mu_{\text{discussion groups}} \neq 42$.
   b. The critical region consists of z-score values greater than $+1.96$ or less than -1.96.
   c. $\sigma_{\overline{x}} = 0.9$; $z = +5.0$.
   d. Reject H_0.
   e. The independent variable is teaching format. The dependent variable is the score on the final exam.

Summary

1. Hypothesis testing is an inferential procedure for using the limited data from a sample to draw a general conclusion about a population. It begins with hypothesizing values for the mean of an unknown population, generally a population that has received a treatment (Figure 8.1).

2. The null hypothesis (H_0) states that the treatment has not changed the mean. That is, it is the same as the mean for a known and untreated population. At this stage we also select an alpha level, usually $\alpha = .05$ or $.01$, which sets the risk of committing a type I error. Alpha determines the level of significance of a statistical test.

3. The second step involves locating the critical region. We examine all of the possible experimental outcomes if the null hypothesis is true and then identify the most unlikely values. We define "unlikely according to H_0" as the outcomes with a probability less than alpha. Thus, the selected alpha level determines the critical z-scores that are associated with the critical region. Sample data that produce a z-score that falls within the critical region would imply that H_0 is not tenable.

4. The sample data are collected. Specifically, the sample mean $\overline{X}$ is used to test a hypothesis about μ. To determine how unlikely the obtained sample mean is, we must locate it within the distribution of sample means. This is accomplished by computing a z-score for $\overline{X}$:

$$z = \frac{\overline{X} - \mu}{\sigma_{\overline{x}}}$$

When a z-score is used in the test of a hypothesis, it is called a test statistic.

5. The z-score equation can be expressed as

$$z = \frac{\text{sample mean} - \text{hypothesized population mean}}{\text{standard error between } \overline{X} \text{ and } \mu}$$

That is, the difference between the sample mean and the hypothesized population mean (according to H_0) is compared to (divided by) the amount of error we would expect between $\overline{X}$ and μ.

6. In the fourth step, we compare the obtained data to the set of possible results that were outlined in the second step. That is, if the obtained z-score falls in the critical region, we reject H_0 because it is very unlikely that these data would be obtained if H_0 were true. We would conclude that a treatment effect occurred. If the data are not in the critical region, then there is not sufficient evidence to reject H_0. The statistical decision is "fail to reject H_0." We conclude that we failed to find sufficient evidence for an effect.

7. Whatever decision is reached in a hypothesis test, there is always a risk of making the incorrect decision. There are two types of errors that can be committed.
    A type I error is defined as rejecting a true H_0. This is a serious error because it results in falsely reporting a treatment effect. The risk of a type I error is determined by the alpha level and, therefore, is under the experimenter's control.
    A type II error is defined as failing to reject a false H_0. In this case, the experiment fails to report an effect that actually occurred. The probability of a type II error cannot be specified as a single value and depends in part on the size of the treatment effect. It is identified by the symbol β (beta).

Key Terms

hypothesis testing   level of significance
null hypothesis   alpha level
alternative hypothesis   critical region
type I error   test statistic
type II error   beta

Problems for Chapter 8:
Introduction to Hypothesis Testing

*1. After several years of studying human performance in flight simulators, a psychologist knows that reaction times to an overhead emergency indicator form a normal distribution with $\mu = 200$ milliseconds and $\sigma = 20$. The psychologist would like to determine if placing the indicator in front of the person at eye level has any effect on reaction time. A random sample of $n = 25$ people is selected, they are tested in a simulator with the indicator light at eye level, and their reaction times are recorded.

     a. Identify the dependent variable and the independent variable.

     b. State the null hypothesis using a sentence that includes the dependent and independent variables.

     c. Using symbols, state the hypotheses (H_0 and H_1) that the psychologist is testing.

     d. Sketch the appropriate distribution and locate the critical region for the .05 level of significance.

     e. If the psychologist obtained an average reaction time of $\overline{X} = 195$ milliseconds for this sample, then what decision would be made about the null hypothesis?

     f. If the psychologist had used a sample of $n = 100$ subjects and obtained an average reaction time of $\overline{X} = 195$, then what decision would be made about the effects of the position of the indicator? Explain why this conclusion is different from the one in part e.

2. Suppose that scores on the Scholastic Aptitude Test form a normal distribution with $\mu = 500$ and $\sigma = 100$. A high school counselor has developed a special course designed to boost SAT scores. A random sample of $n = 16$ students is selected to take the course and then the SAT. The sample had an average score of $\overline{X} = 554$. Does the course have an effect on SAT scores?

     a. What are the dependent and independent variables for this experiment?

b. Using symbols, state the hypotheses.

c. For $\alpha = .05$, sketch the distribution of sample means and locate the critical region.

d. Compute the test statistic.

e. What decision should be made regarding H_0?

f. If $\alpha = .01$ were used instead, what z-score values would be associated with the critical region?

g. For part f, what decision should be made regarding H_0? Compare to part e and explain the difference?

*3. Explain the structure of the z-score formula as it is used for hypothesis testing.

a. What does $\overline{X} - \mu$ tell us in a hypothesis testing situation?

b. What does the standard error indicate?

4. Discuss the errors that can be made in hypothesis testing.

a. What is a type I error? Why might it occur?

b. What is a type II error? How does it happen?

*5. Why do we test H_0 to establish an effect instead of H_1?

6. A developmental psychologist has prepared a training program that, according to a psychological theory, should improve problem-solving ability. For the population of 6-year-olds, the average score on a standardized problem-solving test is known to be $\mu = 80$ with $\sigma = 10$. To test the effectiveness of the training program, a random sample of 6-year-old children is selected. The data for the sample are as follows: 85, 69, 90, 77, 74, 76, 86, 93, 97, 88, 97, 80, 75, 98, 79, 75, 87, 94. Can the experimenter conclude that the program has an effect? Test with alpha set at .05.

a. Using symbols, state the hypotheses. Explain what the hypotheses predict in terms of the independent and dependent variables used in this experiment.

b. Sketch the distribution and locate the critical region.

c. Compute the test statistic.

d. What decision should be made regarding H_0? What conclusions can be drawn?

e. Would the same decision have been made if alpha had been set at .01?

*7. A researcher is trying to assess some of the physical changes that occur in addicts during drug withdrawal. For the population, suppose the average body temperature is $\mu = 98.6°F$ with $\sigma = 0.56$. The following data consist of the body temperatures of a sample of heroin addicts during drug withdrawal:

98.6, 99.0, 99.4, 100.1, 98.7, 99.3, 99.9, 101.0, 99.6, 99.5, 99.4, 100.3. Is there a significant change in body temperature during withdrawal? Test at the .01 level of significance.

a. Using symbols, state the hypotheses.

b. Locate the critical region.

c. Compute the test statistic.

d. Make a decision about the null hypothesis. Is there a significant change in temperature during withdrawal?

8. Suppose the U.S. Army tested thousands of recruits for their hearing thresholds of high-pitched (10,000-hertz) tones and determined that the average threshold is $\mu = 20$ decibels with $\sigma = 4.4$ and that this distribution is normal. Doctors are interested in the effects of the noise of rifle practice on high-pitched hearing. Following are the hearing thresholds (in decibels) for a 10,000-hertz tone for a sample of individuals that completed the rifle training: 26, 20, 32, 25, 24, 24, 23, 29, 20, 32, 27, 33, 22, 24, 28, 37, 26, 17, 25, 28, 26, 25, 19, 29. Do the trainees need protective ear covers? Test at the .05 level of significance.

a. Using symbols, state the hypotheses. What do these hypotheses predict in terms of the independent and dependent variables for this particular study?

b. Locate the critical region.

c. Compute the test statistic.

d. Make a decision about the null hypothesis. Is protective gear needed?

*9. A researcher would like to know if oxygen deprivation at the time of birth has a permanent effect on IQ. It is known that scores on a standard intelligence exam are normally distributed for the population with $\mu = 100$ and $\sigma = 15$. The researcher takes a random sample of individuals for whom complications at birth indicate moderate oxygen deprivation. The sample data are as follows: 92, 100, 106, 78, 96, 94, 98, 91, 83, 81, 86, 89, 87, 91, 89. Is there evidence for an effect? Test with alpha set at .05.

a. State the hypotheses in symbols and explain what they predict.

b. Locate the critical region.

c. Compute the test statistic.

d. What decision should be made about H_0? What conclusion should be drawn about the effect of the independent variable?

e. What would the decision be if the .01 level of significance is used instead of the .05 level?

10. For statistics sections during the past 12 years, an instructor has determined that the final exam scores average $\mu = 61.7$ with $\sigma = 14.6$. These scores are normally distributed. This semester the instructor has acquired two microcomputers and has set them up in a statistics laboratory so that the students in his current class can practice exercises and quiz themselves on the computer. Their final exam scores are as follows: 66, 92, 61, 70, 50, 81, 48, 53, 90, 72, 72, 32, 90, 39, 41, 60, 81, 83, 60, 67, 57, 84, 58, 72, 62, 86, 62, 62, 73, 77, 75. Does it appear that the computerized laboratory has had an effect on their understanding of the course material? Test at the .05 level of significance.

   a. State the hypotheses in symbols and explain what they predict for this study.

   b. Locate the critical region.

   c. Compute the test statistic.

   d. What decision and conclusion can be made?

   e. What are the independent and dependent variables for this study?

*11. A psychologist develops a new inventory to measure depression. Using a very large standardization group of "normal" individuals, the mean score on this test is $\mu = 55$ with $\sigma = 12$, and the scores are normally distributed. To determine if the test is sensitive in detecting those individuals that are severely depressed, a random sample of patients who are described as depressed by a therapist is selected and given the test. Presumably, the higher the score on the inventory, the more depressed the patient is. The data are as follows: 59, 60, 60, 67, 65, 90, 89, 73, 74, 81, 71, 71, 83, 83, 88, 83, 84, 86, 85, 78, 79. Do patients score significantly different on the test? Test with the .01 level of significance.

   a. State the hypotheses using symbols.

   b. Locate the critical region.

   c. Compute the test statistic.

   d. What is your conclusion?

12. On the General Aptitude Test Battery (GATB), scores of engineering graduates are normally distributed with $\mu = 134$ and $\sigma = 15$. The Dean of the School of Engineering at a large university is in the process of assessing the engineering program. For part of the assessment, a sample of the current graduates takes the GATB. The data are as follows: 136, 119, 143, 139, 150, 152, 144, 141, 121, 149, 139, 163, 147, 143, 148, 133, 140. Is there a significant difference between the performance of these graduates and those of the standardization group? Test with alpha set at .05.

*13. On a vocational/interest inventory that measures interest in several categories, a very large standardization group of adults has an average score on the "literary" scale of $\mu = 22$ with $\sigma = 4$. A researcher would like to determine if scientists differ from the general population in terms of writing interests. A random sample of scientists is selected from the directory of a national scientific society. The scientists are given the inventory, and their test scores on the literary scale are as follows: 21, 20, 23, 28, 30, 24, 23, 19. Do scientists differ from the general population in their writing interests? Test at the .05 level of significance.

14. Suppose that the average birth weight for the population is $\mu = 2.9$ kilograms with $\sigma = 0.65$. An investigator would like to see if the birth weights of infants are significantly different for mothers that smoked cigarettes throughout their pregnancy. A random sample of women who smoke is selected, and the birth weight of their infants is recorded. The data (in kilograms) are as follows: 2.3, 2.0, 2.2, 2.8, 3.2, 2.2, 2.5, 2.4, 2.4, 2.1, 2.3, 2.6, 2.0, 2.3. What should the scientist conclude? Use the .01 level of significance.

*15. Patients recovering from an appendix operation normally spend an average of $\mu = 6.3$ days in the hospital. The distribution of recovery times is normal with $\sigma = 1.2$ days. The hospital is trying a new recovery program that is designed to shorten the time patients spend in the hospital. The first 10 appendix patients in this new program were released from the hospital in an average of 5.5 days. On the basis of these data, can the hospital conclude that the new program has a significant effect on recovery time. Test at the .05 level of significance.

16. For the past 2 years the vending machine in the psychology department has charged 40 cents for a soft drink. During this time, company records indicate that an average of $\mu = 185$ cans of soft drinks were sold each week. The distribution of sales is approximately normal with $\sigma = 23$. Recently, the company increased the price to 50 cents a can. The weekly sales for the first 8 weeks after the price increase are as follows: 148, 135, 142, 181, 164, 159, 192, 173. Do these data indicate that there was a significant change in sales after the price increase? Test at the .05 level of significance.

*17. IQ scores for the general population form a normal distribution with $\mu = 100$ and $\sigma = 15$. However, there are data which indicate that children's intelligence can be affected if their mothers have German measles during pregnancy. Using hospital records, a researcher obtained a sample of $n = 20$ school children whose mothers all had German measles during their pregnancies. The average IQ for this sample was $\overline{X}$ = 97.3. Do these data indicate that German measles have a significant effect on IQ? Test with α = .05.

18. For the past 12 years, an instructor in the Psychology Department has taught a course called "Thinking and Problem Solving." During this time the average enrollment for the course was μ = 28.6 students with σ = 8.2. The distribution of enrollments is normal. For this semester, the instructor has changed the title of the course to "Higher Mental Processes" and has only 16 students enrolled. Can the instructor conclude that the change in the course title has caused a significant change in enrollment? Test with α = .05.

*19. In 1965 a nationwide survey revealed that American grade school children spent an average of μ = 8.4 hours per week doing homework. The distribution of homework times was normal with σ = 3.3. Last year a sample of n = 200 students was given the same survey. For this sample, the average number of homework hours was $\overline{X}$ = 7.1.

a. Do these data indicate a significant change in the amount of homework hours for American grade school children? Test at the .01 level of significance.

b. If there had been only n = 20 students in the sample, would the data still indicate a significant change? Use the same sample mean, $\overline{X}$ = 7.1, and use α = .01.

20. The following sample of n = 10 scores was obtained from a normal population with σ = 12:

    78, 90, 54, 77, 71, 99, 85, 74, 93, 84.

a. Use these data to test the hypothesis that the population mean is μ = 75. Use α = .05 for your test.

b. Use these data to test the hypothesis that the population mean is μ = 85. Use α = .05 for your test.

c. In parts a and b of this problem you should find that μ = 75 and μ = 85 are both acceptable hypotheses. Explain how two different values can both be acceptable.

CHAPTER 9

Estimation, Directional Tests, and Power

TOOLS
YOU WILL
NEED

The following items are considered essential background material for this chapter. If you doubt your knowledge of any of these items, you should review the appropriate chapter or section before proceeding.

1. Distribution of sample means (Chapter 7)
2. Hypothesis tests (Chapter 8)
   a. Type I error
   b. Type II error
   c. Critical region

It should be obvious that a lot of planning and preparation go into the design of an experiment. Researchers do not blindly collect data and perform hypothesis tests to see whether or not a treatment has any effect. Part of this planning and preparation can be aided by the statistical techniques that will be presented in this chapter.

For example, researchers have access to results of earlier experimental work related to the particular treatment being examined. Almost always there are published research reports that provide some background, and, occasionally, a researcher will conduct some miniexperiments (pilot studies) to gather information about the treatment's effect. This information allows the researcher to predict in advance the magnitude of the treatment effect and the direction (increase or decrease) of the effect. Thus, a researcher is able to plan an experiment with a very detailed and specific hypothesis in mind. For example, a researcher may expect that the treatment will cause scores to increase by an average of approximately 12 points.

With a detailed prediction in mind, it is then possible for a researcher to anticipate the chances of the experiment being successful. It is very discouraging to invest time and money in a major experiment only to find that the final statistical result says "Fail to reject the null hypothesis—there is no evidence for a treatment effect." It would be valuable for a researcher to know in advance that the experiment has a 75% chance of successfully rejecting the null hypothesis. Although there is still some risk, at least you know the odds.

In this chapter we will examine three statistical topics that are relevant to planning experiments and evaluating data. First is the technique of estimation, which allows a researcher to use sample data to estimate the magnitude of a treatment's effect. Second is the topic of directional tests, which allow a researcher to incorporate a directional prediction (increase or decrease) into the hypothesis testing procedure. Finally, we will examine the topic of power, which provides the researcher with an opportunity to compute the probability of success for an experiment.

9.1

Introduction

The goal of inferential statistics is to use sample data to answer questions about populations. Hypothesis testing is perhaps the most commonly used inferential procedure, but there are others. Also, the format for hypothesis testing that was introduced in Chapter 8 often is modified to produce a slightly different kind of test. In this chapter we will consider some of the alternatives to hypothesis testing and some modifications and expansions of the standard hypothesis testing procedure.

9.2
Estimation

The basic principle underlying all of inferential statistics is that samples are representative of the populations from which they come. The most direct application of this principle is the use of sample values as estimators of the corresponding population values; that is, using statistics to estimate parameters. This process is called estimation.

DEFINITION

The inferential process of using sample data to estimate population parameters is called *estimation*.

The use of samples to estimate populations is quite common. For example, you often hear news reports such as "Sixty percent of the general public approves of the president's new budget plan." Clearly, the percentage that is reported was obtained from a sample (they don't ask everyone's opinion), and this sample statistic is being used as an estimate of the population parameter.

We already have encountered estimation in earlier sections of this book. For example, the formula for sample standard deviation was developed so that the sample value would give an accurate and unbiased estimate of the population. Now we will examine the process of using the sample mean $\overline{X}$ as an estimator of the population mean μ.

Precision and Confidence in Estimation

Before we begin the actual process of estimation, there are a few general points that should be kept in mind. First, a sample will not give a perfect picture of the whole population. A sample is expected to be representative of the population, but there always will be some differences between the sample and the entire population. These differences are referred to as *sampling error*. Second, there are two distinct ways of making estimates. Suppose, for example, you are asked to estimate the weight of this book. You could pick a single value (say, 2 pounds), or you could choose a range of values (say, between 1.5 pounds and 2.5 pounds). The first estimate, using a single number, is called a point estimate. Point estimates have the advantage of being very precise; they specify a particular value. On the other hand, you generally do not have much confidence that a point estimate is correct. You would not bet on it, for example.

For a *point estimate*, you use a single number as your estimate of an unknown quantity. For example, you might estimate that this textbook weighs exactly 2 pounds.

The second type of estimate, using a range of values, is called an interval estimate. Interval estimates do not have the precision of point estimates, but they do give you more confidence. You would feel more comfortable, for example, saying that this book weighs "around 2 pounds." At the extreme, you would be very confident in estimating that this book weighs between 0.5 and 10 pounds. Notice that there is a trade-off between precision and confidence. As the interval gets wider and wider, your confidence grows. But, at the same time, the precision of the estimate gets worse. We will be using samples to make both point and interval estimates of a population mean. Because the interval estimates are associated with confidence, they usually are called confidence intervals.

For an *interval estimate*, you use a range of numbers as your estimate of an unknown quantity. For example, you might estimate that the weight of this textbook is between 1.5 and 2.5 pounds.

When an interval estimate is accompanied with a specific level of confidence (or probability), it is called a *confidence interval*.

Estimation is used in situations where you have a population with an unknown mean (μ = ?). Often this is a population that has received some treatment. Suppose you are examining the effect of a special summer reading program for grade school children. Using a standard reading achievement test, you know that the scores for second-graders in the city school district form a normal distribution with $\mu = 80$ and $\sigma = 10$. It is reasonable to assume that a special reading program would increase the students' scores. The question is, "How much?"

The example we are considering is shown graphically in Figure 9.1. Notice that we have assumed that the effect of the treatment (the special program) is to add a constant amount to each student's reading score. As a result, after the summer reading program the entire distribution would be shifted to a new location with a larger mean. This new mean is what we want to estimate.

Because it would not be reasonable to put all of the students in the special program, we cannot measure this mean directly. However, we

Figure 9.1

A population distribution before the treatment is administered and the same population after treatment. Note that the effect of the treatment is to add a constant amount to each score. The goal of estimation is to determine how large the treatment effect is; i.e., what is the new population mean $\mu = $?

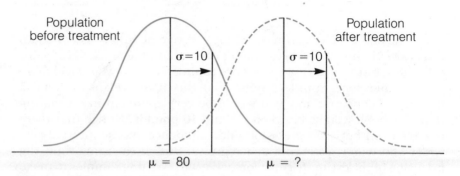

If the treatment simply adds a constant to each score, the standard deviation will not be changed. Although it is common practice to assume that a treatment will add a constant amount, you should realize that in most real-life situations there is a general tendency for variability to increase when the mean increases.

can get a sample and use the sample mean to estimate the population value. Suppose, for example, a random sample of $n = 25$ students is selected to participate in the summer program. At the end of the summer, each student takes the reading test and we compute a mean reading score of $\overline{X} = 88$. Note that this sample represents the population after the special program. The goal of estimation is to use this sample mean as the basis for estimating the unknown population mean.

Using a Sample Mean to Estimate the Population Mean

The procedure for estimating μ is based on the distribution of sample means (see Chapter 7). You should recall that this distribution is the set of all the possible $\overline{X}$ values for a specified sample size (n). The parameters of this distribution are the following:

1. The mean (called expected value) is equal to the population mean.
2. The standard deviation for this distribution (called standard error) is equal to $\sigma/\sqrt{n}$.
3. The distribution of sample means will be normal if either
   a. The population is normal, or
   b. The sample size is at least $n = 30$.

For the example we are considering, the distribution of sample means for $n = 25$ will be normal (because the population is normal), it will have a standard error of $\sigma/\sqrt{n} = 10/\sqrt{25} = \frac{10}{5} = 2$, and it will have a mean that is equal to the unknown population mean ($\mu = $?). This distribution is shown in Figure 9.2.

Our sample mean, $\overline{X} = 88$, is somewhere in this distribution; that

Figure 9.2

The distribution of sample means based on $n = 25$. Samples were selected from the unknown population (after treatment) shown in Figure 9.1.

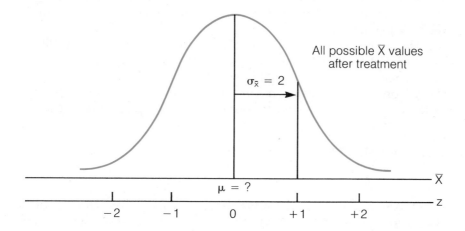

is, we have one value out of all the possible sample means. Unfortunately, we do not know where our sample mean is located in the distribution. Nonetheless, we can specify different locations by using z-scores. The z-score values and their locations have been identified in Figure 9.2.

Our sample mean, $\overline{X} = 88$, has a z-score given by the formula

$$z = \frac{\overline{X} - \mu}{\sigma_{\overline{x}}}$$

Because our goal is to find the population mean (μ), we will solve this z-score equation for μ. The result is

(9.1) $\mu = \overline{X} - z\sigma_{\overline{x}}$

We still do not know the value of μ, but now we have an equation to use. This is the basic equation for estimation. Note that it is simply the z-score formula with some rearrangement of terms.

To use this equation, we begin with the values we know: $\overline{X} = 88$ and $\sigma_{\overline{x}} = 2$. If we also knew the value of z (the location of $\overline{X}$ in the distribution), we would have all the necessary information to compute the value of μ. But we still do not know the z-score value. The solution to this problem is to estimate the z-score value for our sample mean. More precisely, we are estimating the location of our sample mean within the distribution of sample mean. The estimated position will determine a z-score value which can be used in the equation to compute μ. It is important to note that the z-score value we will be using is an *estimate* and that therefore the population mean that we compute will also be an estimate.

Point Estimates

For a point estimate, you must select a single value for the z-score. Remember, you are not simply picking a z-score; you are estimating the position of our sample mean ($\overline{X} = 88$) in the distribution of sample means. Looking at Figure 9.2., where would you estimate our sample mean is located?

It should be clear that your best bet is to select the exact middle of the distribution, that is, $z = 0$. It would be unwise to pick an extreme value such as $z = 2$ because there are relatively few samples that far away from the population mean. Most of the sample means pile up around $z = 0$, so this is your best choice. When this z-value is used in the equation, we get

$$\mu = \overline{X} - z\sigma_{\overline{x}}$$
$$\mu = 88 - 0(2)$$
$$= 88$$

This is our point estimate of the population mean. You should notice that this final result is exactly what would be predicted by common sense; we simply have used the sample mean $\overline{X}$ to estimate the population mean μ. Our conclusion is that the special summer program will increase reading scores from an average of $\mu = 80$ to an average of $\mu = 88$. We are estimating that the program will have an eight-point effect on reading scores.

Interval Estimates

To make an interval estimate, you select a range of z-score values rather than a single point. Looking again at the distribution of sample means in Figure 9.2, where would you estimate our sample mean is located? Remember, you now can pick a range of values. As before, your best bet is to predict that the sample mean is located somewhere in the center of the distribution. There is a good chance, for example, that our sample mean is located somewhere between $z = +1$ and $z = -1$. You would be almost certain that $\overline{X}$ is between $z = +3$ and $z = -3$. How do you know what range to use? Because several different ranges are possible and each range has its own degree of confidence, the first step is to determine the amount of confidence we want and then use this value to determine the range. Commonly used levels of confidence start at about 60% and go up. For this example, we will use 90%. This means that we want to be 90% confident that our interval estimate of μ is correct.

There are no strict rules for choosing a level of confidence. Researchers must decide how much precision and how much confidence are needed in each specific situation.

To be 90% confident, we simply estimate that our sample mean is somewhere in the middle 90% of the distribution of sample means. This section of the distribution is bounded by z-scores of $z = +1.65$ and $z = -1.65$ (check the table). We are 90% confident that our particular sample mean ($\overline{X} = 88$) is in this range because 90% of all the possible means are there.

The next step is to use this range of z-score values in the estimation equation. We use the two ends of the z-score range to compute the two ends of the interval estimate for μ.

At one extreme, $z = +1.65$, which gives

$$\mu = \overline{X} - z\sigma_{\overline{x}}$$
$$= 88 - 1.65(2)$$
$$= 88 - 3.30$$
$$= 84.70$$

At the other extreme, $z = -1.65$, which gives

$$\mu = \overline{X} - z\sigma_{\overline{x}}$$
$$= 88 - (-1.65)(2)$$
$$= 88 + 3.30$$
$$= 91.30$$

The result is an interval estimate for μ. We are estimating that the population mean after the special summer program is between 84.70 and 91.30. If the mean is as small as 84.70, then the effect of the special program would be to increase reading scores by an average of 4.70 points (from $\mu = 80$ to $\mu = 84.70$). If the mean is as large as 91.30, the program would have increased scores by an average of 11.30 points (from $\mu = 80$ to $\mu = 91.70$). Thus, we conclude that the special summer program will increase reading scores, and we estimate that the magnitude of the increase will be between 4.7 and 11.3 points. We are 90% confident that this estimate is correct because the only thing that was estimated was the z-score range, and we were 90% confident about that. Again, this interval estimate is called a confidence interval. In this case, it is the 90% confidence interval for μ.

Notice that the confidence interval sets up a range of values with the sample mean in the middle. As with point estimates, we are using the sample mean to estimate the population mean, but now we are saying that the value of μ should be *around* $\overline{X}$ rather than exactly equal to $\overline{X}$. Because the confidence interval is built around $\overline{X}$, adding in one direction and subtracting in the other, we will modify the estimation equation in order to simplify the arithmetic:

(9.2) $\quad \mu = \overline{X} \pm z\sigma_{\overline{x}}$

To build the confidence interval, start with the sample mean and add $z\sigma_{\overline{x}}$ to get the boundary in one direction; then subtract $z\sigma_{\overline{x}}$ to get the other boundary. Translated into words, the formula says that

population mean = sample mean $\pm$ some error

The sample mean is expected to be representative of the population mean with some margin of error. Although it may seem obvious that the sample mean is used as the basis for estimating the population mean, you should not overlook the reason for this result. Sample means, on the average, provide an accurate, unbiased representation of the population mean. You should recognize this fact as one of the characteristics of the distribution of sample means: The mean (expected value) of the distribution of sample means is μ.

Interpreting a Confidence Interval

In the preceding example we constructed a 90% confidence interval that extended from 84.70 to 91.30. The purpose of the interval is to provide an estimate of the unknown population mean. This estimate was obtained by building an interval around the sample mean:

$$\mu = \overline{X} \pm z\sigma_{\overline{x}}$$
$$= 88 \pm 1.65(2)$$
$$= 88 \pm 3.30$$

Notice that if we had obtained a different sample mean, for example, $\overline{X} = 90$, we would have obtained a different interval:

$$\mu = \overline{X} \pm z\sigma_{\overline{x}}$$
$$= 90 \pm 1.65(2)$$
$$= 90 \pm 3.30$$

Each individual sample mean will generate its own individual confidence interval. However, these confidence intervals will have some common characteristics. First, they all will have exactly the same width, extending from 3.30 points above $\overline{X}$ to 3.30 points below $\overline{X}$. This width is determined by the z-score ($z = 1.65$) and the standard error ($\sigma_{\overline{x}} = 2$). You also should note that this width corresponds to the middle 90% of the distribution of sample means. Figure 9.3 shows the distribution of sample means and the confidence intervals associated with several different samples. Notice that as long as the sample mean comes from the middle 90% of this distribution, the population mean ($\mu = ?$) will be included in the interval. Although we do

---

Figure 9.3

Confidence intervals for three separate samples selected from the distribution of sample means. Notice that although the three confidence intervals are different, each includes the value of the population mean. As long as the sample mean comes from the middle 90% of the distribution, its 90% confidence interval will include the population mean.

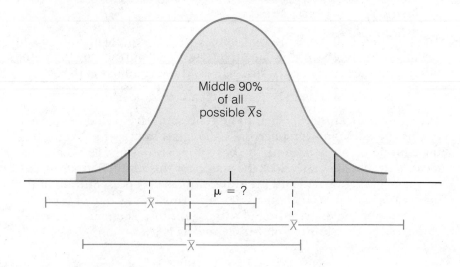

not know exactly where our sample is located in this distribution, we can be 90% confident that it is somewhere in the middle 90%. Thus, we can be 90% confident that the population mean is included in our confidence interval.

Factors Affecting the Width of a Confidence Interval

There are two characteristics of the confidence interval that should be noted. First, notice what happens to the width of the interval when you change the level of confidence (the percent confidence). To gain more confidence in your estimate, you must increase the width of the interval. Conversely, to have a smaller interval, you must give up confidence. This is the basic trade-off between precision and confidence that was discussed earlier. In the estimation formula, the percent confidence influences the width of the interval by way of the z-score value. For example, if you increase the level of confidence from 90% to 95%, the z-score value increases from 1.65 to 1.96. As confidence gets greater, the z-score gets bigger, and the interval gets wider.

Second, notice what would happen to the interval width if you had a different sample size. This time, the basic rule is as follows: The bigger the sample (n), the smaller the interval. This relation is straightforward if you consider the sample size as a measure of the amount of information. A bigger sample gives you more information about the population and allows you to make a more precise estimate (a narrower interval). The sample size controls the magnitude of the standard error in the estimation formula. As the sample size increases, the standard error decreases, and the interval gets smaller.

Comparison of Hypothesis Tests and Estimation

In many ways hypothesis testing and estimation are similar. They both make use of sample means and z-scores to find out about an unknown population. But these two inferential procedures are designed to answer different questions. The example we considered earlier, examining the effect of the special summer reading program, can be used to illustrate the similarities and differences between estimation and hypothesis testing.

For this example, we could have used a hypothesis test to evaluate the effect of the special program. The test would determine whether or not the program has any effect. Notice that this is a yes/no question. The test result would be either

> Yes, the treatment has an effect (reject H_0)

or

> No, the treatment does not appear to have an effect (fail to reject H_0)

The hypothesis test is done by using the basic z-score formula:

$$z = \frac{\overline{X} - \mu}{\sigma_{\overline{x}}}$$

To calculate the z-score, you use the known values of $\overline{X}$ and $\sigma_{\overline{x}}$ and the hypothesized value of μ (from H_0). The question is whether or not the hypothesized value of μ produces a reasonable z-score.

Estimation, on the other hand, determines *how much* effect the special training has. Our point estimate, for example, is that the population mean after the summer program is $\mu = 88$. This is eight points higher than the original population mean.

The estimation procedure uses the same z-score formula as the hypothesis test, but the terms in the formula are rearranged:

$$\mu = \overline{X} \pm z\sigma_{\overline{x}}$$

As before, you use the known values of $\overline{X}$ and $\sigma_{\overline{x}}$, but now you include the estimated z-score and calculate the value of μ. If you use a reasonable estimate of z, you expect to get a reasonable estimate for μ.

When to Use Estimation

There are three situations where estimation commonly is used.

1. Estimation is used after a hypothesis test where H_0 is rejected. Remember that when H_0 is rejected, the conclusion is that the treatment does have an effect. The next logical question would be, "How much effect?" This is exactly the question that estimation is designed to answer.

2. Estimation is used when you already know that there is an effect and simply want to find out how much. For example, the city school board probably knows that a special reading program will help students. However, they want to be sure that the effect is big enough to justify the cost. Estimation is used to determine the size of the treatment effect.

3. Estimation is used when you simply want some basic information about an unknown population. Suppose, for example, you want to know about the political attitudes of students at your college. You could use a sample of students as the basis for estimating the population mean.

LEARNING
CHECK

1. A cattle rancher is interested in using a newly developed hormone to increase the weight of his beef cattle. Before investing in this hormone, he would like to obtain some

estimate of its effect. He knows that his cattle weigh an average of $\mu = 1250$ pounds when they are sold at 8 months. The distribution of weights is approximately normal with $\sigma = 80$. A sample of 16 calves is selected to test the hormone. At age 8 months, the average weight for this sample is $\overline{X} = 1340$ pounds.

   a. Use these data to make a point estimate of the population mean weight if all the cattle were given the hormone.

   b. Make an interval estimate of the population mean so that you are 95% confident that the true mean is in your interval.

2. If the rancher in Problem 1 had used a sample of $n = 64$ calves and obtained a sample mean of $\overline{X} = 1340$ pounds, what range of values could be obtained for the 95% confidence interval?

ANSWERS

1. a. For a point estimate, use the sample mean: $\overline{X} = 1340$ pounds.

   b. For the 95% confidence interval, $z = +1.96$ and $\sigma_{\overline{x}} = 20$. The interval would be

$$\mu = 1340 \pm 39.20$$

The interval ranges from 1300.80 to 1379.20 pounds.

2. With $n = 64$ the standard error would be 10, so the interval is

$$\mu = 1340 \pm 19.60$$

This interval ranges from 1320.40 to 1359.60 pounds.

9.3
Directional (One-Tailed) Hypothesis Tests

The hypothesis testing procedure presented in Chapter 8 was the standard, or *two-tailed*, test format. The term *two-tailed* comes from the fact that the critical region is located in both tails of the distribution. This format is by far the most widely accepted procedure for hypothesis testing. Nonetheless, there is an alternative that will be discussed in this chapter.

Almost always a researcher begins an experiment with a specific prediction about the direction of the treatment effect. For example, a special training program is expected to *increase* student performance, or alcohol consumption is expected to *slow* reaction times. In these situations, it is possible to state the statistical hypotheses in a manner that incorporates the directional prediction into the statement of H_0 and H_1. The result is a directional test, or what commonly is called a one-tailed test.

In a *directional hypothesis test*, or a *one-tailed test*, the statistical hypotheses (H_0 and H_1) specify either an increase or a decrease in the population mean score.

Suppose, for example, a researcher is using a sample of $n = 16$ laboratory rats to examine the effect of a new diet drug. It is known that under regular circumstances these rats eat an average of 10 grams of food each day. The distribution of food consumption is normal with $\sigma = 4$. The expected effect of the drug is to reduce food consumption. The purpose of the experiment is to determine whether or not the drug really works. This experimental situation is shown graphically in Figure 9.4.

The Hypotheses for a Directional Test

Because there is a specific direction expected for the treatment effect, it is possible for the researcher to perform a directional test. The first step (and the most critical step) is to state the statistical hypotheses. Remember that the null hypothesis states that there is no treatment effect and that the alternative hypothesis says that there is an effect. For directional tests, it is easier to begin with the alternative hypothesis. In words, this hypothesis says that with the drug the mean food consumption is less than 10 grams per day; that is, the drug does reduce food consumption. In symbols, H_1 would say the following:

$$H_1: \quad \mu < 10 \quad \text{(mean food consumption is reduced)}$$

The null hypothesis is the opposite of the alternative. In words, the null hypothesis says that even with the diet drug the rats still will eat at least 10 grams per day. That is, the drug does not reduce food consumption. In symbols,

$$H_0: \quad \mu \geq 10 \quad \text{(the mean is at least 10 grams per day)}$$

Figure 9.4

Graphic representation of an experiment testing a new diet pill. Note that the pill is expected to reduce food consumption, i.e., to subtract a constant amount from each animal's score.

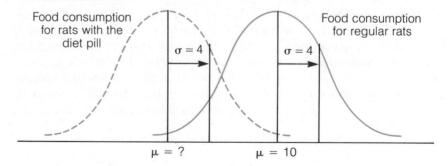

The Critical Region for Directional Tests

After stating the hypotheses, the next step is to locate the critical region. The critical region is defined as the most unlikely outcomes (probability less than alpha) if H_0 is true. To find the critical region, you begin by looking at all the possible results that could be obtained if H_0 were true. For our example this is the distribution of sample means for $n = 16$. This distribution is normal (because the population is normal), it has a standard error of $\sigma_{\bar{x}} = 4/\sqrt{16} = \frac{4}{4} = 1$, and it has a mean of $\mu = 10$ if H_0 is true. This distribution is pictured in Figure 9.5. If the null hypothesis is true and the drug does not reduce food consumption, you will expect the rats in the sample to average at least 10 grams of food per day. Therefore, a sample mean around 10 or higher would support H_0. The only value that would tend to refute H_0 would be a sample mean substantially less than 10. The result is that the entire critical region is located in one tail of the distribution (see Figure 9.5). This is why the directional test commonly is called *one-tailed*. A complete example of a one-tailed test is presented here.

EXAMPLE 9.1

A psychologist would like to examine the effect of background music on productivity at a local factory. Over the past 2 years it has been determined that the average daily output from this factory is $\mu = 210$ units. The daily output varies with $\sigma = 20$, and the distribution is approximately normal. The psychologist expects that the introduction of background music will improve the work environment and result in increased productivity. To test this hypothesis, a music system is installed, and productivity is measured for a sample period of $n = 25$ days. During this time the aver-

Figure 9.5

The distribution of sample means for $n = 16$ if H_0 is true. The null hypothesis states that the diet pill has no effect, so the population mean will still be $\mu = 10$ or larger.

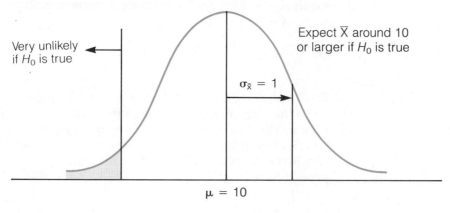

Very unlikely if H_0 is true

Expect $\bar{X}$ around 10 or larger if H_0 is true

$\sigma_{\bar{x}} = 1$

$\mu = 10$

age output is $\overline{X} = 217$ units per day. The psychologist wants to use these sample data to test the hypothesis about the music's effect.

Simply because you can do a directional test does not mean that you must use a directional test. A two-tailed test is always acceptable and generally preferred.

STEP 1.   *State the Hypotheses:* Because the psychologist is predicting an increase in productivity, it is possible to do a directional test. We begin with H_1, the alternative hypothesis, which states that there is a treatment effect. In symbols,

H_1: $\mu > 210$ (an increase in mean productivity)

The null hypothesis is the opposite of H_1 and states that

H_0: $\mu \leq 210$ (productivity is no greater with the music)

STEP 2.   *Locate the Critical Region:* To find the critical region, we look at all the possible results that could be obtained if H_0 were true and then locate the outcomes that would be extremely unlikely. The set of all possible outcomes is the distribution of sample means for $n = 25$. This distribution will be normal (because the population is normal), it will have a standard error of $\sigma_{\overline{x}} = 20/\sqrt{25} = \frac{20}{5} = 4$, and it will have a mean of $\mu = 210$ if H_0 is true. This distribution is shown in Figure 9.6.

If H_0 is true, we expect the sample to average around 210 units per day or less. It would be very unlikely to obtain a sample mean much greater than 210. Therefore, it is only large values that compose the critical region. With $\alpha = .05$, the most likely 95% of the distribution is separated from the most unlikely 5% by a z-score of $z = +1.65$ (see Figure 9.6.).

STEP 3.   *Obtain the Sample Data:* The obtained sample mean is $\overline{X} = 217$. This value corresponds to a z-score of

$$z = \frac{\overline{X} - \mu}{\sigma_{\overline{x}}} = \frac{217 - 210}{4} = \frac{7}{4} = 1.75$$

STEP 4.   *Statistical Decision:* A z-score of $z = +1.75$ indicates that our sample mean is in the critical region. This is a very unlikely outcome if H_0 is true, so the statistical decision is to reject H_0. The conclusion is that the music does increase productivity.

Figure 9.6
The distribution of sample means for $n = 25$ if H_0 is true. The null
hypothesis says that the music will not increase productivity, so
we still expect the mean to be around 210 or smaller.

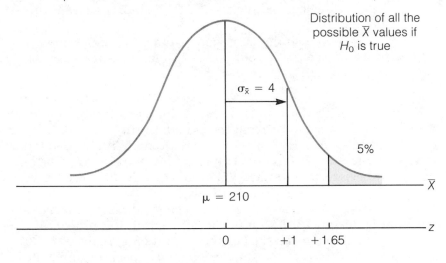

The Problem with One-Tailed Tests

You should understand the rationale and the procedure for conducting directional hypothesis tests, but you also should be aware that
these tests generally are considered to be improper. The reason that
most researchers frown on one-tailed tests is discussed in this section.

   The general goal of hypothesis testing is to determine whether or
not a particular treatment has any effect on a population. The test is
performed by selecting a sample, administering the treatment to the
sample, and then comparing the result with the original population.
If the treated sample is noticeably different from the original population, then we conclude that the treatment has an effect, and we
reject H_0. On the other hand, if the treated sample is still similar to
the original population, then we conclude that there is no evidence
for a treatment effect, and we fail to reject H_0. The critical factor in
this decision is the *size of the difference* between treated sample and
the original population. A large difference is evidence that the treatment worked; a small difference is not sufficient to say that the treatment has any effect.

   The problem with one-tailed tests is that they allow you to reject
H_0 even when the difference between the sample and the population
is relatively small. This point is illustrated in the following example.

> EXAMPLE 9.2
> Consider again the experiment examining background
> music and factory productivity (see Example 9.1). If we had
> used a standard, two-tailed test, then the hypotheses would
> have been

$$H_0: \quad \mu = 210 \quad \text{(no change in productivity)}$$
$$H_1: \quad \mu \neq 210 \quad \text{(there is a change)}$$

With $\alpha = .05$, the critical region would consist of any z-score value beyond the $z = \pm 1.96$ boundaries (see Figure 9.7).

If we obtained the same sample data, $\overline{X} = 217$, which corresponds to a z-score of $z = +1.75$, our statistical decision would be "fail to reject H_0."

Notice that with the standard test (Example 9.2), the difference between the data ($\overline{X} = 217$) and the hypothesis ($\mu = 210$) is not big enough to conclude that the hypothesis is wrong. With the one-tailed test (Example 9.1), these same data caused us to reject H_0. The one-tailed test permits you to reject H_0 even when the distance between the data and the hypothesis is relatively small.

If you consider only the distance between the data and the hypothesis (and ignore the direction of the difference), the probability of obtaining a sample mean farther than $z = 1.65$ is really $P = 10\%$. This means that 10% of the time you would expect a sample mean this far from the population mean just by chance. Although the stated α level for a one-tailed test may be only 5%, the effective α level is 10%. The result of using a one-tailed test is to double the α level and, therefore, double the risk of a type I error. For this reason, most researchers consider that one-tailed tests make it too easy to reject H_0 and make it too easy to make a type I error (reject a true H_0).

A less serious problem with one-tailed tests comes from the fact that they look for a treatment effect in one direction only. For the

Figure 9.7

The distribution of sample means for $n = 25$ if H_0 is true. The null hypothesis says that the music will not change productivity, so we expect the mean still to be around 210.

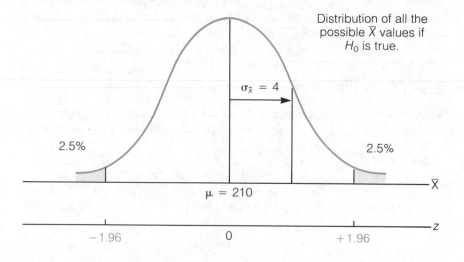

example we have been considering, suppose that the background music interfered with workers' concentration and caused productivity to fall. Because the one-tailed test has no critical region on the left-hand side of the mean, it would not detect a significant decrease in productivity; the test is looking only for an increase (see Figure 9.7). The two-tailed test, on the other hand, is sensitive to a change in either direction. For the reasons outlined, most researchers do not use one-tailed tests. Even though most experiments are designed with an expectation that the treament effect will be in a specific direction, this directional prediction is not included in the statement of the statistical hypotheses.

LEARNING CHECK

1. A psychologist is examining the effects of early sensory deprivation on the development of perceptual discrimination. A sample of $n = 9$ newborn kittens is obtained. These kittens are raised in a completely dark environment for 4 weeks, after which they receive normal visual stimulation. At age 6 months, the kittens are tested on a visual discrimination task. The average score for this sample is $\overline{X} = 32$. It is known that under normal circumstances cats score an average of $\mu = 40$ on this task. The distribution of scores is normal with $\sigma = 12$. The researcher is predicting that the early sensory deprivation will reduce the kittens' performance on the discrimination task. Use a one-tailed test with $\alpha = .01$ to test this hypothesis.

ANSWER

1. The hypotheses are $H_0: \mu \geqslant 40$ and $H_1: \mu < 40$. The critical region is determined by z-scores less than -2.33. The z-score for these sample data is $z = -2.00$. Fail to reject H_0.

9.4
Power for a Statistical Test

The purpose of a hypothesis test is to determine whether or not a particular treatment has an effect. The null hypothesis states that there is no effect, and the researcher is hoping that the data will provide evidence to reject this hypothesis. In Chapter 8 we saw that the hypothesis testing procedure is structured to minimize the risk of reaching a wrong conclusion. Specifically, the researcher selects an alpha level, generally 5% or 1%, that determines the maximum probability of committing a type I error (rejecting a true null hypothesis). You also should recall that every hypothesis test has the potential for resulting in a type II error, failing to reject a false null hypothesis. In everyday terms, a type II error means that the treatment really does have an effect but that the hypothesis test failed to discover it.

In this section we will reverse our perspective on hypothesis testing; rather than examining the potential for making an error, we will examine the probability of reaching the correct decision. Remember that the researcher's goal is to demonstrate that the experimental treatment actually does have an effect. This is the purpose of conducting the experiment in the first place. When a researcher is correct and the treatment does have an effect, what is the probability that the hypothesis test will correctly identify it? This is a question about the strength or power of the statistical test.

DEFINITION

The *power* of a statistical test is the probability that the test will correctly reject a false null hypothesis.

It should be clear that the concept of power and the concept of a type II error are closely related. When a treatment effect exists, the hypothesis test can have one of two conclusions:

1. It can fail to discover the treatment effect (a type II error), or
2. It can correctly identify the treatment effect (rejecting a false null hypothesis).

We already have defined the probability of a type II error as β (beta), so the probability of correctly rejecting a false null hypothesis must be $1 - \beta$. If, for example, a hypothesis test has a 20% chance of failing to identify a treatment effect, then it must have an 80% chance of correctly identifying it. Thus, the power of a statistical test is determined by

$$(9.3) \quad \text{power} = P(\text{reject a false } H_0) = 1 - \beta$$

Relation Between Power and the Treatment Effect

Although we now have a definition and an equation for power, we still do not have a value for this probability. The difficulty comes from the fact that power depends on the size of the treatment effect and therefore does not have a single value. When a treatment has a large effect, it is easy to see, and power will be high. On the other hand, when the treatment effect is very small, it can be difficult to discover, and power will be low. Rather than talking about power as a single value, we must examine the different values of power associated with different magnitudes of treatment effect. For example,

What is the power if the treatment produces a 5-point difference?

What is the power if the treatment produces a 10-point difference?

Because the hypothesis test is more likely to detect a 10-point treatment effect, the power will be greater than it would be for a 5-point treatment effect.

One more reminder is necessary before we actually begin the calculation of power. Remember, the null hypothesis is rejected whenever sample data are in the critical region. With this in mind, we can restate the definition of power as follows:

DEFINITION

Power is the probability of obtaining sample data in the critical region when the null hypothesis is false. (Because "data in the critical region" is equivalent to "rejecting the null hypothesis," this definition is equivalent to our original definition of power.)

The following example demonstrates the calculation of power for a statistical test.

EXAMPLE 9.3
A researcher is interested in whether cigarette smoke inhaled by pregnant females can affect their offspring. It is known that under normal circumstances newborn rats weigh an average of $\mu = 200$ milligrams with $\sigma = 40$. The distribution of birth weights is approximately normal. A random sample of $n = 25$ pregnant rats is obtained. These animals are placed in closed containers and exposed to cigarette smoke for 4 hours each day. When the pups are born, the researcher plans to randomly select one pup from each litter. The average weight $(\overline{X})$ for this sample of $n = 25$ rats will be used to test the researcher's hypothesis.

The researcher predicts that the cigarette smoke will cause a reduction in birth weight of approximately 20 milligrams. If this is correct, what is the probability that the statistical test will detect this treatment effect and correctly reject H_0? In other words, what is the power of the test if the treatment has a 20-point effect?

Because we want to know the probability of obtaining data in the critical region, the first step is to identify the critical region. This is done by following the usual hypothesis testing procedure.

STEP 1. *State the Hypotheses:*

H_0: $\mu = 200$ (no effect)

H_1: $\mu \neq 200$ (there is an effect)

We will use $\alpha = .05$.

STEP 2.   *Locate the Critical Region:* If the null hypothesis is true and the smoke has no effect, then we can determine the distribution of all possible sample means for $n = 25$. This distribution of sample means is shown in Figure 9.8. The distribution has an expected value of $\mu = 200$ (if H_0 is true), and it has a standard error of

$$\sigma_{\bar{x}} = \frac{\sigma}{\sqrt{n}} = \frac{40}{5} = 8$$

As usual, the critical region is determined by the most unlikely 5% of all the possible sample means. This region is bounded by z-scores of $+1.96$ and -1.96. To obtain a more general description of the critical region, we will find the $\overline{X}$ value that corresponds to each of these z-scores:

At the Lower Boundary	At the Upper Boundary
$z = \dfrac{\overline{X} - \mu}{\sigma_{\bar{x}}}$	$z = \dfrac{\overline{X} - \mu}{\sigma_{\bar{x}}}$
$-1.96 = \dfrac{\overline{X} - 200}{8}$	$+1.96 = \dfrac{\overline{X} - 200}{8}$
$-15.68 = \overline{X} - 200$	$+15.68 = \overline{X} - 200$
$184.32 = \overline{X}$	$215.68 = \overline{X}$

Thus, any sample mean less than 184.32 or greater than 215.68 will be in the critical region and will result in rejecting the null hypothesis.

Figure 9.8

The distribution of sample means assuming that the null hypothesis is true. The critical region (most extreme 5%) is determined by sample means less than 184.32 or greater than 215.68.

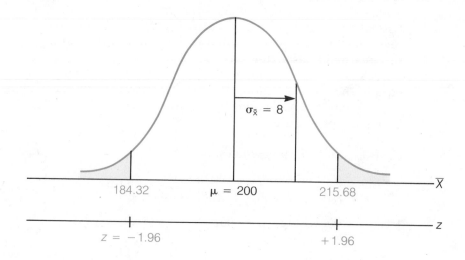

Now we are ready to begin the calculation of power. If the treatment has a 20-point effect, then the average birth weight of rats would be reduced from $\mu = 200$ to $\mu = 180$ milligrams. In this case the distribution of sample means should be centered at $\mu = 180$. Figure 9.9 shows this distribution along with the distribution predicted from the null hypothesis. The figure also shows the critical region that we determined earlier using the null hypothesis and $\alpha = .05$.

Remember, the distribution on the left in Figure 9.9 shows all the possible sample means if the treatment has a 20-point effect. Notice that most of this distribution is located in the critical region (shaded portion). Thus, if the treatment does have a 20-point effect, there is a high probability that our sample mean will be in the critical region (less than 184.32). This probability is the power of the statistical test. To find the exact probability, we convert the critical boundary (184.32) into a z-score and then find the probability in the unit normal table.

In this example, we are ignoring the critical region in the other tail of the distribution because the probability of obtaining a sample mean greater than 215.68 would be essentially zero.

If the treatment has reduced the population mean to $\mu = 180$, the z-score corresponding to $\overline{X} = 184.32$ is

$$z = \frac{\overline{X} - \mu}{\sigma_{\overline{x}}} = \frac{184.32 - 180}{8} = \frac{4.32}{8} = +0.54$$

From the unit normal table, the probability of obtaining a z-score smaller than this value is 0.7054. Thus, the power of the statistical test is 0.7074 (70.54%).

In summary,

Figure 9.9

The distribution of sample means that would be obtained if H_0 were true and the distribution of sample means that would be obtained if the treatment were to reduce the mean by 20 points. Notice that if the treatment does have a 20-point effect, most of the sample means will be in the critical region.

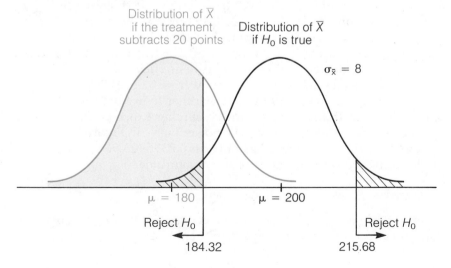

1. The hypothesis test established the critical region as sample means less than 184.32 or greater than 215.68.
2. If the treatment has a 20-point effect, then the distribution of sample means will be centered at $\mu = 180$ with a standard error of 8.
3. The proportion of this distribution that is located in the critical region is 0.7054.
4. Therefore, if the treatment has a 20-point effect, the probability of obtaining a sample mean in the critical region is 0.7054. The power of the test is 0.7054.

Power and Type II Errors

In Example 9.3, we found that the power of the hypothesis test was 0.7054. By assuming that the treatment has a 20-point effect, we calculated a 0.7054 probability of obtaining sample data in the critical region and correctly rejecting H_0. However, you should note that this means there is an 0.2944 probability that the sample data will not be in the critical region. In this event we would fail to reject the null hypothesis even though the treatment has a 20-point effect. This is a type II error, failing to reject a false null hypothesis. Just as power $(1 - \beta)$ measures the probability that the experiment will be successful, β measures the probability that the experiment will fail and result in a type II error. These two probabilities always will total 1.00 or 100%.

The Power Function

Note that the lowest level of the power function is α. If the treatment effect is zero, then the null hypothesis is true, and the probability of rejecting a true H_0 is α.

In Example 9.3 we computed power for a single, specific treatment value (a 20-point effect). To provide a complete description of power, you could compute the probability for every possible treatment effect and construct a graph showing the relation between power and the size of the treatment effect. The resulting graph is called a *power function*. An example of a power function graph is shown in Figure 9.10. This graph shows the power function for the cigarette smoke experiment described in Example 9.3. Notice that power increases as the size of the treatment effect increases. The hypothesis test is much more likely to detect a 20-point treatment effect (power = 0.7054) than it is to detect a 2-point effect (power = 0.0572). The value of a power function is that it allows a researcher to predict the success of an experiment. If, for example, the researcher expected the cigarette smoke to have a 10-point effect, the power curve in Figure 9.10 would specify that the experiment has only an 0.2396 (23.96%) probability of detecting a treatment effect of this magnitude.

Factors Affecting Power

There are three factors under the direct control of a researcher that have an effect on the power of a statistical test:

Figure 9.10

The power function for the hypothesis test described in Example 9.3. Notice that the power increases regularly as the magnitude of the treatment effect increases. The hypothesis test is more likely to detect a large effect than a small treatment effect.

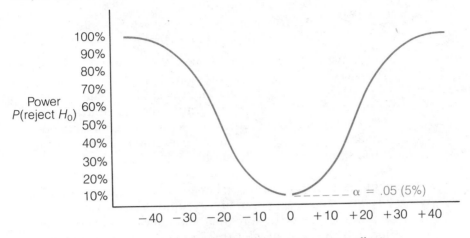

1. The alpha level
2. The choice of a one-tailed or a two-tailed test
3. The size of the sample

Each of these factors will be discussed briefly.

The Alpha Level   Reducing the alpha level reduces the risk of a type I error (reject a true H_0) by making it more difficult to reject H_0. Because a small alpha level generally reduces the probability of rejecting the null hypothesis, it also reduces the power of the test. This fact is demonstrated in the following example.

> EXAMPLE 9.4
> We will use the same experimental situation described in Example 9.3, but now the alpha level will be reduced from .05 to .01.
> As before, the researcher wants to determine the effect of cigarette smoke on birth weight. A sample of $n = 25$ rats will be used in the experiment. If the null hypothesis is true, the distribution of sample means will have an expected value of $\mu = 200$ (no effect) and a standard error of 8.
> With $\alpha = .01$, the critical region is determined by z-scores of $+2.58$ and -2.58. These z-scores correspond to sample means of

At the Lower Boundary	At the Upper Boundary

$$z = \frac{\overline{X} - \mu}{\sigma_{\overline{x}}} \qquad z = \frac{\overline{X} - \mu}{\sigma_{\overline{x}}}$$

$$-2.58 = \frac{\overline{X} - 200}{8} \qquad +2.58 = \frac{\overline{X} - 200}{8}$$

$$-20.64 = \overline{X} - 200 \qquad +20.64 = \overline{X} - 200$$

$$179.36 = \overline{X} \qquad 220.64 = \overline{X}$$

Thus, any sample mean less than 179.36 or greater than 220.64 will be in the critical region.

If the researcher is correct and the smoke reduces the mean birth weight by 20 milligrams, the distribution of sample means will be centered at $\mu = 180$. This distribution, along with the distribution from the null hypothesis, is shown in Figure 9.11. The problem is to find what proportion of the distribution is in the critical region if the treatment has a 20-point effect (shaded area in Figure 9.11).

To find this proportion, first compute the z-score corresponding to the critical region boundary of $\overline{X} = 179.36$ and then find the percentage value in the unit normal table. If the population mean has been reduced to $\mu = 180$, the z-score value is

Remember, power is the probability of rejecting a false H_0. H_0 is false if the treatment does have a real effect.

$$z = \frac{\overline{X} - \mu}{\sigma_{\overline{x}}} = \frac{179.36 - 180}{8} = \frac{-0.64}{8} = -0.08$$

Figure 9.11

The distribution of sample means that would be obtained if H_0 were true and the distribution of sample means that would be obtained if the treatment were to reduce the mean by 20 points. With $\alpha = .01$, if the treatment has a 20-point effect, only about half of the possible sample means will be in the critical region.

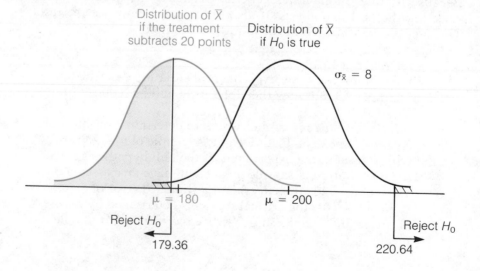

Distribution of $\overline{X}$ if the treatment subtracts 20 points

Distribution of $\overline{X}$ if H_0 is true

$\sigma_{\overline{x}} = 8$

$\mu = 180$ $\mu = 200$

Reject H_0 Reject H_0

179.36   220.64

The area to the left of this z-score is 0.4681 (46.81%) of the distribution. Thus, the probability of obtaining a sample mean in the critical region if the treatment has a 20-point effect is 0.4681. This is the power of the test.

Notice that the power of this test with $\alpha = .01$ is substantially less than the 0.7054 we obtained when alpha was .05.

One-Tailed Versus Two-Tailed Tests   You should recall that one-tailed tests make it easier to reject the null hypothesis. Because one-tailed tests increase the probability of rejecting H_0, they also increase the power of the test. This is demonstrated in the following example.

Using a one-tailed test will increase power only if the treatment effect is in the direction that is specified in the scientific hypothesis (H_1).

EXAMPLE 9.5
Once again, we will use the experimental situation from Example 9.3. If the researcher were using a one-tailed test, the hypotheses would be

$$H_0: \quad \mu \geqslant 200 \qquad \text{(the mean is at least 200)}$$
$$H_1: \quad \mu < 200 \qquad \text{(the smoke reduces birth weight)}$$

With a one-tailed test, the critical region will be located entirely in the lower tail of the distribution. With $\alpha = .05$, the z-score value defining the critical region will be $z = -1.64$. If the null hypothesis is true ($\mu = 200$), this z-score corresponds to a sample mean of

$$z = \frac{\overline{X} - \mu}{\sigma_{\overline{x}}}$$

$$-1.64 = \frac{\overline{X} - 200}{8}$$

$$13.12 = \overline{X} - 200$$

$$186.88 = \overline{X}$$

Thus, any sample mean less han 186.88 will be in the critical region.

If the smoke reduces average birth weight by 20 milligrams, the distribution of sample means will be centered at $\mu = 180$. This distribution, together with the distribution from H_0, is shown in Figure 9.12. As before, the problem is to find the proportion of this distribution that is located in the critical region (shaded area in Figure 9.12).

To find this proportion, we first convert the critical region boundary (186.88) into a z-score. If the population mean has been reduced to $\mu = 180$, the z-score will be

$$z = \frac{\overline{X} - \mu}{\sigma_{\overline{x}}} = \frac{186.88 - 180}{8} = \frac{6.88}{8} = +0.86$$

The proportion of the distribution to the left of this z-score is 0.8051 (80.51%). Thus, if the treatment has a 20-point

Figure 9.12

The distribution of sample means that would be obtained if H_0 were true and the distribution of sample means that would be obtained if the treatment were to reduce the mean by 20 points. With a one-tailed test, if the treatment does have a 20-point effect, the majority of the sample means will be in the critical region.

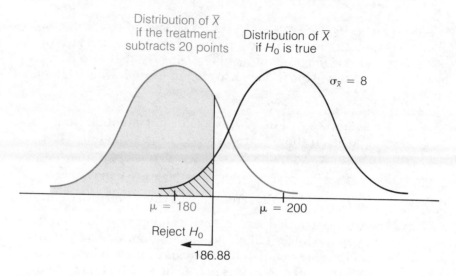

effect, the probability of obtaining a sample mean in the critical region is 0.8051. This is the power of the test.

Notice that the power for this one-tailed test is greater than the 0.7054 we obtained for the two-tailed test in Example 9.3.

Sample Size   In general, the larger the sample, the better the sample will represent the population. If there is a real treatment effect in the population, a large sample will be more likely to find it than a small sample. Thus, the power of a test can be increased by increasing the size of the sample. This fact is demonstrated in the following example.

EXAMPLE 9.6

We will use the cigarette smoke example one more time. In this case, however, we will increase the researcher's sample from $n = 25$ to $n = 64$. The larger sample should increase the power of the test.

If the null hypothesis is true, the distribution of sample means with $n = 64$ will have a mean of $\mu = 200$ and a standard error of

$$\sigma_{\bar{x}} = \frac{\sigma}{\sqrt{n}} = \frac{40}{\sqrt{64}} = \frac{40}{8} = 5$$

By using $\alpha = .05$, the z-score boundaries for the critical region are $+1.96$ and -1.96. These z-scores correspond to sample means of

At the Lower Boundary	At the Upper Boundary
$z = \dfrac{\overline{X} - \mu}{\sigma_{\overline{x}}}$	$z = \dfrac{\overline{X} - \mu}{\sigma_{\overline{x}}}$
$-1.96 = \dfrac{\overline{X} - 200}{5}$	$+1.96 = \dfrac{\overline{X} - 200}{5}$
$-9.80 = \overline{X} - 200$	$+9.80 = \overline{X} - 200$
$190.20 = \overline{X}$	$209.80 = \overline{X}$

Thus, any sample mean less than 190.20 or greater than 209.80 will be in the critical region.

If the researcher is correct and the smoke reduces the mean birth weight by 20 milligrams, the distribution of sample means will be centered at $\mu = 180$. This distribution is shown in Figure 9.13 along with the distribution predicted by the null hypothesis. As before, the problem is to find the proportion of the distribution that is located in the critical region (shaded portion in Figure 9.13).

If the treatment reduces the population mean to $\mu = 180$, the z-score corresponding to the critical region boundary (190.20) is

$$z = \frac{\overline{X} - \mu}{\sigma_{\overline{x}}} = \frac{190.20 - 180}{5} = \frac{10.20}{5} = +2.04$$

Figure 9.13

The distribution of sample means that would be obtained if H_0 were true and the distribution of sample means that would be obtained if the treatment were to reduce the mean by 20 points. With $n = 64$, a 20-point treatment effect will cause almost all of the possible sample means to be located in the critical region.

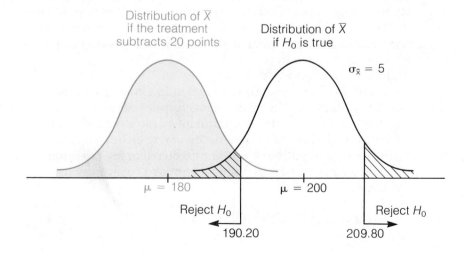

From the unit normal table, the area to the left of this boundary is 0.9793 (97.93%). Thus, we are almost guaranteed to get a sample mean in the critical region if the treatment has a 20-point effect. The power for this test is 0.9793.

Notice that the power with a sample size of 64 is much greater than the value of 0.7054 we obtained with $n = 25$.

Using Power to Determine Sample Size

Earlier in this chapter we noted that increasing the sample size will increase the power of a hypothesis test. The increased power results from the fact that a larger sample size has the effect of increasing the separation between the null distribution and the alternative distribution. If you compare Figure 9.9 and Figure 9.13 this effect should be clear. In both figures there is a 20-point difference between the two population means. However, in Figure 9.9 the standard error is 8 and the 20-point difference amounts to only two and one-half standard errors. In Figure 9.13 the standard error is 5 so the 20-point difference corresponds to four standard errors. In general, a larger sample will produce a smaller standard error which has the effect of increasing the separation between the two distributions, and thereby increases power.

This relation between sample size, standard error, and power can be used when planning experiments. Specifically, a researcher can decide how much power he/she would like for a hypothesis test and then compute the sample size needed to produce this level of power. In this way it is possible for a researcher to determine how large a sample is needed to ensure that an experiment has a reasonable chance for success. The process of using power to compute sample size is demonstrated in the following example.

EXAMPLE 9.7
A researcher is planning an experiment to demonstrate that increased salt intake will produce a corresponding increase in fluid consumption. It is known that under regular circumstances laboratory rats drink an average of $\mu = 80$ milliliters of water each day. The distribution of water consumption scores is normal with $\sigma = 10$. Based on previous data, the researcher predicts that increased salt will produce an 8 milliliter increase in fluid consumption. The researcher is planning to obtain a sample of rats, add extra salt to their food, and then measure water consumption. How large a sample is needed for this experiment to have an 80% chance of success? That is, what n is necessary to ensure that the hypothesis test will have power of 0.80 or larger? Assume that the researcher is planning a standard two-tailed test with $\alpha = .05$.

The first step is to sketch the two distributions and locate the critical region. If the null hypothesis is true, the distribution of sample means will be centered at $\mu = 80$. Within this distribution the critical region consists of z-score values greater than $+1.96$ or less than -1.96. On the other hand, if the treatment (more salt) increases the mean by 8 points, the distribution of sample means will be centered at $\mu = 88$. These two distributions are shown in Figure 9.14.

The second step is to specify the desired level of power. For this example, the researcher wants power equal to 80% or more. To achieve this level of power, at least 80% of the alternative distribution must be in the critical region (see the shaded portion in Figure 9.14). Therefore, in the alternative distribution the boundary for the critical region must have a z-score of $z = -0.84$ (check the unit normal table).

Looking at Figure 9.14 you will see that the distance between the two population means can be described in two different ways:

1. The distance is equal to 8 points ($\mu = 80$ versus $\mu = 88$).
2. The distance is equal to 2.80 standard errors. This description comes from the fact that the critical boundary is 1.96 standard errors above $\mu = 80$ (the z-score is $+1.96$) and this same boundary is 0.84 standard errors below $\mu = 88$ (z-score is -0.84). Thus, the total distance between the means is $1.96\sigma_{\bar{x}} + 0.84\sigma_{\bar{x}} = 2.80\sigma_{\bar{x}}$.

Figure 9.14

The distribution of sample means that would be obtained if H_0 were true (left) and the distribution that would be obtained if the treatment adds 8 points to each score (right). To have power = 0.80 it is necessary that 80% of the alternative distribution be located in the critical region.

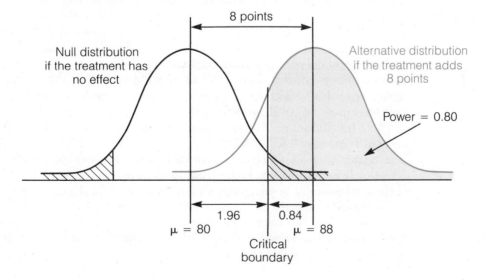

Because these two distances are identical, we can incorporate them into an equation.

$$2.80\sigma_{\bar{x}} = 8 \text{ points}$$

Solving this equation, we obtain $\sigma_{\bar{x}} = 2.86$. Finally, we use the formula for the standard error and solve for the value of n.

$$\sigma_{\bar{x}} = \frac{\sigma}{\sqrt{n}}$$

$$2.86 = \frac{10}{\sqrt{n}}$$

$$\sqrt{n} = \frac{10}{2.86}$$

$$n = 12.22$$

Thus, the researcher must use a sample of $n = 12.22$ or larger (actually $n = 13$ or larger) to ensure that the power of the hypothesis test is at least 0.80.

---

1. A researcher knows that a population of learning scores is approximately normal with $\mu = 50$ and $\sigma = 8$. This researcher plans to use a sample of $n = 16$ to evaluate a particular treatment that is expected to affect learning. Assuming the researcher uses a two-tailed test with $\alpha = .05$,
   a. What is the power of the statistical test if the treatment adds six points to each person's learning score?
   b. What is the power of the test if the treatment adds only two points to each person's score? (Be careful; both tails of the critical region will contribute to the power in this case.)

ANSWERS

1. a. With a standard error of 2, the critical region consists of sample means greater than 53.92 or less than 46.08. If the treatment adds six points, the distribution of sample means will have $\mu = 56$. In this distribution, the critical boundary of 53.92 has a z-score of $z = -1.04$. The power (area in the critical region) is 0.8508 (85.08%).
   b. The critical region consists of sample means greater than 53.92 or less than 46.08. If the treatment adds two points, the distribution of sample means will have $\mu = 52$. In this distribution, the critical boundary of 53.92 has a z-score of $z = +0.96$, and the boundary of 46.08 has a z-score of $z = -2.96$. The power (total area in the critical region) is 0.1700 (0.1685 + 0.0015).

Summary

1. Estimation is a procedure that uses sample data to obtain an estimate of a population mean. The estimate can be either a point estimate (single value) or an interval estimate (range of values). Point estimates have the advantage of precision, but they do not give much confidence. Interval estimates provide confidence, but you lose precision as the interval grows wider.

2. The formula for estimation is

$$\mu = \overline{X} \pm z\sigma_{\overline{x}}$$

This is the basic z-score formula with the terms rearranged. To use the formula, you first plug in the value of $\overline{X}$ from your sample and the value of $\sigma_{\overline{x}}$ (from the sample size n and the known value of σ). Next, you estimate the value of z. Note that you are using the z value to estimate the location of your particular sample mean within the distribution of sample means. For point estimates, use $z = 0$. For interval estimates, select a level of confidence (percent confidence); then use this percentage to determine the range of z-score values (for example, 80% confidence gives $+1.28$ to -1.28). Finally, plug in the estimate of z and calculate the estimate of μ.

3. The width of a confidence interval is an indication of its precision: A narrow interval is more precise than a wide interval. The interval width is influenced by sample size and the level of confidence.
   a. As sample size (n) gets larger, the interval width gets smaller (greater precision).
   b. As the percent confidence increases, the interval width gets greater (less precision).

4. Estimation and hypothesis testing are similar processes: Both use sample data to answer questions about populations. However, these two procedures are designed to answer different questions. Hypothesis testing will tell you whether or not a treatment effect exists (yes or no). Estimation will tell you how much treatment effect there is.

5. When a researcher predicts that a treatment effect will be in a particular direction (increase or decrease), it is possible to do a directional or one-tailed test. The first step in this procedure is to state the alternative hypothesis (H_1). This hypothesis states that the treatment works and, for directional tests, specifies the direction of the predicted treatment effect. The null hypothesis is the opposite of H_1. To locate the critical region, you must identify the kind of experimental outcome that refutes the null hypothesis and demonstrates that the treatment works. These outcomes will be located entirely in one tail of the distribution.

The entire critical region (5% or 1%, depending on α) will be in one tail.

6. Most researchers consider directional tests to be improper. These tests allow H_0 to be rejected when the data are relatively close to the null hypothesis and, thereby, increase the likelihood of a type I error.

7. The power of a statistical test is defined as the probability that the test will correctly reject the null hypothesis. Power is identified as

$$power = 1 - \beta$$

where β is the probability of a type II error.

8. To compute the power for a statistical test, you must first identify a specific alternative to the null hypothesis. That is, you must specify the magnitude of the treatment effect. Next, you locate the critical region as if you were doing a regular hypothesis test. Finally, you construct the distribution of all possible sample outcomes using the specified treatment effect. The power of the test is the portion of this distribution that is located in the critical region.

9. The power of a test is affected by several factors that can be controlled by the experimenter:
   a. Increasing the alpha level will increase power.
   b. A one-tailed test will have greater power than a two-tailed test.
   c. A large sample will result in more power than a small sample.

Key Terms

estimation	directional hypothesis test
point estimate	one-tailed test
interval estimate	two-tailed test
confidence interval	power

Problems for Chapter 9:
Estimation, Directional Tests, and Power

*1. An extensive survey in 1970 revealed that preschool children spend an average of $\mu = 6.3$ hours per day watching television. The distribution of TV times is normal with $\sigma = 2$. Last year a sample of $n = 100$ preschool children gave a mean of $\overline{X} = 5.8$ hours of television per day.

a. Use these sample data to make a point estimate of the population mean for last year.

b. Based on your point estimate, how much change has occurred in children's television habits since 1970?

c. Make an interval estimate of last year's population mean so that you are 80% confident that the true mean is in your interval.

2. Performance scores on a motor skills task form a normal distribution with $\mu = 20$ and $\sigma = 4$. A psychologist is using this task to determine the extent to which increased self-awareness affects performance. The prediction for this experiment is that increased self-awareness will reduce a subject's concentration and result in lower performance scores. A sample of $n = 16$ subjects is obtained, and each subject is tested on the motor skills task while seated in front of a large mirror. The purpose of the mirror is to make the subjects more self-aware. The average score for this sample is $\overline{X} = 15.5$. Use a one-tailed test with $\alpha = .05$ to test the psychologist's prediction.

*3. Use the data from Problem 2 to estimate how much performance is reduced by the presence of the mirror.

a. Make a point estimate of the population mean performance score with the mirror present.

b. Make an interval estimate of the population mean so that you are 95% confident that the true mean is in your interval.

4. Researchers have developed a filament that should add to the life expectancy of light bulbs. The standard 60-watt bulb burns for an average of $\mu = 750$ hours with $\sigma = 20$. A sample of $n = 100$ bulbs is prepared using the new filament. The average life for this sample is $\overline{X} = 820$ hours.

a. Use these sample data to make a point estimate of the mean life expectancy for the new filament.

b. Make an interval estimate so that you are 80% confident that the true mean is in your interval.

c. Make an interval estimate so that you are 99% confident that the true mean is in your interval.

*5. Scores on the Scholastic Aptitude Test (SAT) form a normal distribution with $\mu = 500$ and $\sigma = 100$. A school counselor has proposed a special training program for high school juniors that is intended to improve performance on the SAT. The counselor expects the program to improve scores by an average of 40 points. This year a sample of $n = 25$ students will participate in the program in order to evaluate its effectiveness.

a. If the counselor uses a one-tailed hypothesis test with $\alpha = .05$, what is the probability that the sample data will lead to rejecting H_0? Assume that the program does produce a 40-point increase in the mean score.

b. What would the power of the test be if the counselor used a standard two-tailed hypothesis test?

6. Suppose that the sample of $n = 25$ students described in Problem 5 achieved an average SAT score of $\overline{X} = 535$ after completing the training program.

a. Use a one-tailed test with $\alpha = .05$ to determine whether or not these data provide sufficient evidence to conclude that the program is successful.

b. What decision would be made if the counselor used a two-tailed test with these data?

*7. After years of working in the area of animal learning, a psychologist has observed that laboratory rats that have participated in several experiments tend to perform much better on a new task than rats with no previous experience. To determine the magnitude of this effect, the psychologist selects a random sample of $n = 9$ experienced rats and tests each rat on a standardized maze. On the maze, the error scores for naive rats form a normal distribution with $\mu = 55$ and $\sigma = 18$. Although none of the rats in the sample has seen this particular maze before, they solve the maze with an average of $\overline{X} = 46$ errors. Using a one-tailed test with $\alpha = .05$, can the psychologist conclude that previous experience results in a significant decrease in errors?

8. The psychologist in Problem 7 failed to demonstrate a significant effect. Nonetheless, he is convinced that experience does have an effect on performance. If the psychologist is right, the data from the first experiment can provide some useful information.

a. Based on the sample data from Problem 7, make a point estimate of the mean error rate for the population of experienced rats.

b. Based on this point estimate, the psychologist concludes that previous experience reduces errors on the maze by an average of 9 (from $\mu = 55$ for naive rats to $\mu = 46$ for experienced rats). If there really is a nine-point effect, then compute the power for a statistical test based on a sample of $n = 25$ rats. Assume a two-tailed test with $\alpha = .05$.

c. If the effect really is nine points, compute the power for the test in the psychologist's original experiment (Problem 7).

*9. The manufacturers of a gasoline additive would like to include some statistical data in their advertisements. Specifically, they would like to claim that their product significantly increases gas mileage, and they would like to make a statement concerning the magnitude of this increase. Based on published EPA figures, they know that the average mileage for a particular model car is $\mu = 24$ miles per gallon with $\sigma = 4$. They obtain a sample of $n = 16$ of these cars and measure the mileage obtained with their gasoline additive. The average for this sample is $\overline{X} = 26.5$ miles per gallon.

a. In using a one-tailed test with $\alpha = .05$, does the additive produce a significant increase in mileage?

b. Use these data to make a point estimate of the average mileage with the additive. Based on this estimate, how much effect does the additive have?

10. A psychological theory predicts that individuals who grow up as an only child will have above-average IQs. A sample of $n = 64$ people from single-child families is obtained. The average IQ for this sample is $\overline{X} = 104.9$. In the general population, IQs form a normal distribution with $\mu = 100$ and $\sigma = 15$.

a. Use a one-tailed test with $\alpha = .01$ to evaluate the theory.

b. Use these sample data to construct a 90% confidence interval for the mean IQ of the population of single children.

*11. A psychologist is interested in the long-term effects of a divorce on the children in a family. A sample is obtained of $n = 10$ children whose parents were divorced at least 5 years ago. Each child is given a personality questionnaire measuring depression. In the general population, the scores on this questionnaire form a normal distribution with $\mu = 80$ and $\sigma = 12$. The scores for this sample are as follows: 83, 81, 75, 92, 84, 107, 63, 112, 92, 88. The psychologist is predicting that children from divorced families will be more depressed than children in the general population. Use a one-tailed test with $\alpha = .05$ to test this hypothesis.

12. Use the data from Problem 11 to estimate the population mean depression score for children from divorced families.

a. Make a point estimate of the population mean.

b. Make an interval estimate so that you are 95% confident that the true mean is in your interval.

*13. A psychologist is examining the effect of chronic alcoholism on memory. In this experiment, a standardized memory test will be used. Scores on this test for the general population form a normal distribution with $\mu = 50$ and $\sigma = 5$. The psychologist expects alcoholics to average at least five points below the general population. The proposed experiment will use a sample of $n = 20$ alcoholics.

   a. Compute the power for a two-tailed hypothesis test with $\alpha = .05$. Assume that alcoholism does lower memory scores by an average of five points.

   b. Compute the power for a one-tailed hypothesis test with $\alpha = .05$. Again, assume alcoholism lowers memory scores by an average of five points.

   c. What is the probability that the two-tailed test will result in a type II error?

   d. What is the probability that the one-tailed test will result in a type II error?

14. A poultry farm supplies chickens to a fast-food restaurant chain. The chickens are sold by weight and average $\mu = 65$ ounces. The distribution of weights is normal with $\sigma = 4.9$ ounces. The farmer is interested in changing to a new brand of chicken food. However, the new food is more expensive and will not be economically feasible unless it results in an average weight increase of at least 3 ounces per chicken. A sample of $n = 30$ chicks is selected to be tested on the new food. At maturity, the weights for these chickens are as follows: 74, 72, 65, 79, 75, 73, 68, 75, 78, 69, 72, 75, 79, 81, 73, 63, 69, 73, 77, 73, 64, 73, 63, 78, 72, 71, 62, 72, 71, 74.

   a. Construct an 80% confidence interval for the population mean weight for chickens raised on the new feed.

   b. Based on your confidence interval, should the farmer switch to the new food? Explain your answer.

*15. A state inspector is checking the machinery at a canning factory. The canning machine is supposed to put an average of $\mu = 16$ ounces in each can. There is some variability, so the distribution of actual weights is normal with $\sigma = 0.15$ ounce. The inspector selects a random sample of 15 cans and carefully weighs the contents of each. The weights from this sample are as follows: 15.8, 16.1, 15.9, 15.8, 16.0, 15.9, 15.7, 16.2, 15.8, 15.7, 15.9, 16.1, 16.0, 15.9, 15.9. Use a one-tailed test with $\alpha = .05$ to determine whether the machine is averaging below 16 ounces per can.

16. Suppose that the canning machine described in Problem 15 is really averaging only 15.9 ounces per can. If the inspector uses a one-tailed test with a sample of 20 cans, what is the probability that this error will be detected? Assume that α is set at .05.

*17. A psychologist is investigating the degree to which personality disorders are familial. The psychologist selects a sample of 40 adolescents who have at least one parent with a history of personality disorder. Each individual in the sample is given a personality inventory questionnaire. For the general population, scores on this questionnaire are known to have a mean of $\mu = 100$ with $\sigma = 20$. The average score for the sample is $\overline{X} = 93.7$. Use a one-tailed statistical test with $\alpha = .05$ to determine whether a family history of personality disorder results in personality scores significantly lower than the general population.

18. In a nationwide survey, women were asked to use a 20-point scale to rate the personal importance of their jobs as well as other aspects of their lives (such as family, money, children, etc.). In this survey, the average rating for jobs was $\mu = 7.5$ with $\sigma = 2$. A psychologist suspects that women who were "tomboys" as children will have attitudes that are different from average. For a sample of $n = 28$ of these women, the average rating for job importance was $\overline{X} = 9.2$. Do these data indicate that former tomboys rate their jobs higher than the rating given by the national survey? Use a one-tailed test with $\alpha = .05$.

*19. Calculating the power of a statistical test can help a researcher plan the number of subjects needed for an experiment. For example, a researcher is testing a drug that is expected to lower blood pressure by five points. It is known that under regular conditions the distribution of blood pressure scores is normal with $\mu = 120$ and $\sigma = 10$. Assuming that the drug works as expected, how large a sample should the researcher use to obtain power of at least 75%. The researcher plans a standard two-tailed test with $\alpha = .05$. (*Hint:* See Example 9.7.)

20. In 1970 a nationwide survey measured the attitudes of college students concerning appropriate behavior for women. Each student was given a checklist of adjectives describing traditionally masculine behaviors (aggressive, assertive, competitive, etc.). The students had to rate on a scale from 1 to 100 how appropriate the behavior was for women. In 1970 the average rating was $\mu = 52$ with $\sigma = 13.5$. Last year the same survey was given to a sample of $n = 35$ students. The average rating for this sample was $\overline{X} = 59$.

a. On the basis of these data, has there been a significant increase in the appropriateness of these behaviors for women? Use a one-tailed test with $\alpha = .05$.

b. Use the sample data to estimate the magnitude of the change in attitude. Make a point estimate and a 90% confidence interval estimate.

CHAPTER 10

Introduction to the *t* Statistic

TOOLS
YOU WILL
NEED

The following items are considered essential background material for this chapter. If you doubt your knowledge of any of these items, you should review the appropriate chapter or section before proceeding.

1. Sample standard deviation (Chapter 4)
2. Degrees of freedom (Chapter 4)
3. Hypothesis testing (Chapter 8)
4. Estimation (Chapter 9)

Numerous accounts suggest that for many animals, including humans, a direct stare from another animal is aversive (e.g., Cook, 1977). Try it out for yourself. Make direct eye contact with a stranger in a cafeteria. Chances are the person will display avoidance by averting his or her gaze or turning away from you. Some insects, such as moths, have even developed eye-spot patterns on the wings or body to ward off predators (mostly birds) who may have a natural fear of eyes (Blest, 1957). Suppose a comparative psychologist is interested in determining whether or not the birds that feed on these insects show an avoidance of eye-spot patterns.

Using methods similar to those of Scaife (1976), the researcher performed the following experiment. A sample of n = 16 moth-eating birds is selected. The animals are tested in an apparatus that consists of a two-chambered box. The birds are free to roam from one side of the box to the other through a doorway in the partition that separates the two chambers. In one chamber, there are two eye-spot patterns painted on the wall. The other side of the box has plain walls. One at a time, the researcher tests each bird by placing it in the doorway between the chambers. Each subject is left in the apparatus for 60 minutes, and the amount of time spent in the plain chamber is recorded.

What kind of data should the experimenter expect if the null hypothesis is true? If the animals show no aversion to the eye spots, they should spend, on average, half of the time in the plain side. Therefore, the null hypothesis would predict that

$$H_0: \quad \mu_{\text{plain side}} = 30 \text{ minutes}$$

Suppose the researcher collected data for the sample and found that the average amount of time spent on the plain side was $\overline{X} = 35$ minutes. The researcher now has two of the needed pieces of information to compute a z-score test statistic—the sample data ($\overline{X}$) and the hypothesized mean (according to H_0). All that is needed is the population standard deviation, so that the standard error can be computed. Note that the investigator does not have this information about the population. All that is known is that the population of animals should, on average, spend half of the 60-minute period in the plain chamber if the eye spots have no effect on behavior. Without complete information about the population, how can the comparative psychologist test the hypothesis with a z-score? The answer is simple—z cannot be used for the test statistic because the standard error cannot be computed. However, it is possible to estimate the standard error using the sample data and to compute a test statistic that is similar in structure to the z-score. This new test statistic is called the t statistic.

10.1

Introduction

In the preceding two chapters we presented the statistical procedures that permit researchers to use a sample mean to draw inferences about a population. These statistical procedures were based on a few basic notions which we summarize as follows:

1. A sample mean $\overline{X}$ is expected to more or less approximate its population mean μ. This permits us to use the sample mean to test a hypothesis about the population mean or to estimate its value.

Remember, the expected value of the distribution of sample means is μ, the population mean.

2. The amount of variability among sample means can be described by the standard error $\sigma_{\overline{x}}$ of the distribution of sample means:

$$\sigma_{\overline{x}} = \frac{\sigma}{\sqrt{n}}$$

The standard error provides a measure of how well a sample mean approximates the population mean.

3. To quantify our inferences about the population, we convert each sample mean to a z-score using the formula

$$z = \frac{\overline{X} - \mu}{\sigma_{\overline{x}}}$$

When the z-scores form a normal distribution, we are able to use the unit normal table (Appendix B) to find the probabilities that are needed to relate the sample to the population, be it for the test of a hypothesis or for the estimation of μ.

The shortcoming of using the z-score as an inferential technique is that researchers usually have little or no knowledge about the population other than the information that is provided by the sample. That is, z-scores require that we know the value of the population standard deviation, which is needed to compute the standard error. Most often the standard deviation of the population is not known, and the standard error for sample means cannot be computed. Without the standard error, we have no way of quantifying the expected amount of distance (or error) between $\overline{X}$ and μ. We have no way of making precise, quantitative inferences about the population based on z-scores.

The *t* Statistic—a Substitute for *z*

Fortunately, there is a relatively simple solution to the problem of not knowing the population standard deviation. When the value of σ is not known, we use the sample standard deviation in its place. In Chapter 4 (p. 127), the sample standard deviation was developed specifically to be an unbiased estimate of the population standard deviation. The formula for the sample standard deviation is

$$s = \sqrt{\frac{SS}{n-1}}$$

Using this sample statistic, we can now estimate the standard error. The estimated standard error $s_{\bar{x}}$ is obtained by the formula

(10.1) $\quad s_{\bar{x}} = \dfrac{s}{\sqrt{n}}$

Notice that we have substituted the sample standard deviation (s) in place of the unknown population standard deviation (σ). Also notice that the symbol for the estimated standard error is $s_{\bar{x}}$ instead of $\sigma_{\bar{x}}$, indicating that the value is computed from sample data rather than from the population parameter.

The *estimated standard error* is used as an estimate of $\sigma_{\bar{x}}$ when the value of σ is unknown. It is computed from the sample standard deviation.

Now we can substitute the estimated standard error in the denominator of the z-score formula. This new test statistic is called a t statistic:

(10.2) $\quad t = \dfrac{\overline{X} - \mu}{s_{\bar{x}}}$

The only difference between the t formula and the z-score formula is that the z-score formula uses the actual population standard deviation (σ) and the t statistic uses the sample standard deviation as an estimate when σ is unknown:

$$z = \frac{\overline{X} - \mu}{\sigma_{\bar{x}}} = \frac{\overline{X} - \mu}{\dfrac{\sigma}{\sqrt{n}}}$$

$$t = \frac{\overline{X} - \mu}{s_{\bar{x}}} = \frac{\overline{X} - \mu}{\dfrac{s}{\sqrt{n}}}$$

Structurally, these two formulas have the same form:

$$z \text{ or } t = \frac{\text{sample mean} - \text{population mean}}{\text{(estimated) standard error}}$$

Both formulas are used for hypothesis testing and for estimation of μ. There is only one rule to remember:

When you know the value of σ, use a z-score. If σ is unknown, use the t statistic.

The *t statistic* is similar in structure to a *z*-score except that it uses the estimated standard error because the value for σ is not known.

Degrees of Freedom and the *t* Distribution

When using *z*-scores for making inferences about a population mean, we consulted the unit normal table to find the critical region or to determine a confidence interval. Our attention now turns to a *t* distribution to perform these tasks. However, we can no longer use the same table because a *t* distribution is not normal. Under certain conditions, it will approximate a normal distribution. How well a *t* distribution approximates a normal distribution of *z*-scores is determined by how well the sample standard deviation approximates the population standard deviation. Remember, to calculate a *t* statistic, *s* is substituted in place of σ. How well the sample standard deviation estimates the population standard deviation depends mainly on sample size, which is described in terms of degrees of freedom.

You will recall that the sample mean places a restriction on sample variability such that $n - 1$ scores in the sample are free to vary (Chapter 4, p. 130):

$$(10.3) \quad \text{degrees of freedom} = df = n - 1$$

The value $n - 1$ is called the *degrees of freedom* for the sample standard deviation. The more degrees of freedom a sample has (that is, the larger *n* is), the better *s* will estimate σ. This makes sense because a large sample will generally give us a "better picture" of the population than a small sample.

Degrees of freedom describe the number of scores in a sample that are free to vary. Because the sample mean places a restriction on the value of one score in the sample, there are $n - 1$ degrees of freedom for the sample (see Chapter 4).

Because the computation of the *t* statistic is ultimately based on the estimation of σ using the sample standard deviation, the greater the number of degrees of freedom (denoted *df*) for the sample data, the more closely the *t* distribution will approximate a normal *z*-score distribution (see Box 10.1 for examples). Let us examine the relationship between degrees of freedom and the shape of the *t* distribution in more detail.

The Shape of the *t* Distribution

The exact shape of a *t* distribution changes with degrees of freedom. In fact, statisticians speak of a "family" of *t* distributions. That is, there is a different sampling distribution of *t* (a distribution of all possible sample *t* values) for each possible number of degrees of freedom. As *df* gets very large, the *t* distribution gets closer in shape to a normal *z*-score distribution (see Box 10.1). A quick glance at Figure 10.1 reveals that distributions of *t* are bell-shaped and symmetrical and have a mean of zero. However, the *t* distribution has more variability than a normal *z* distribution, especially when *df* values are small (Figure 10.1). The *t* distribution tends to be flatter and more spread out, whereas the normal *z* distribution has more of a central peak.

Why is the *t* distribution flatter and more variable than a normal *z* distribution? For a particular population, the top of the *z*-score formula, $\overline{X} - \mu$, can take on different values because $\overline{X}$ will vary from one sample to another. However, the value of the bottom of the *z*-score formula, $\sigma_{\overline{x}}$, is constant. The standard error will not vary from sample to sample because it is derived from the population standard deviation. The implication is that samples which have the same value for $\overline{X}$ should also have the same *z*-score.

On the other hand, the standard error in the *t* formula is not a constant because it is estimated. That is, $s_{\overline{x}}$ is based on the sample standard deviation, which will vary in value from sample to sample.

Figure 10.1

Distributions of the *t* statistic for different values of degrees of freedom are compared to a normal *z*-score distribution. Like the normal distribution, *t* distributions are bell-shaped and symmetrical and have a mean of zero. However, *t* distributions have more variability, indicated by the flatter and more spread-out shape. The larger the value of *df*, the more closely the *t* distribution approximates a normal distribution.

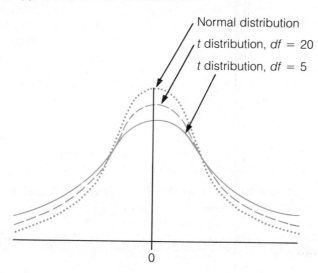

Normal distribution

t distribution, *df* = 20

t distribution, *df* = 5

0

The result is that samples can have the same value for $\overline{X}$ yet different values of t because the estimated standard error will vary from one sample to another. Therefore, a t distribution will have more variability than the normal z distribution. It will look flatter and more spread out. When the value of df increases, the variability in the t distribution decreases, and it more closely resembles the normal distribution, because with greater df, $s_{\overline{x}}$ will more closely estimate $\sigma_{\overline{x}}$, and when df is very large, they are nearly the same.

BOX 10.1 | **The Critical Values in a Normal z Distribution and a t Distribution: The Influence of Degrees of Freedom**

As previously noted, a t distribution approximates a normal z distribution. How well it approximates a normal distribution depends on the value of df. This can be seen by simply comparing critical values for z with critical values of t at various degrees of freedom. For example, if we test a hypothesis with a z-score using a two-tailed test and $\alpha = .05$, the critical z-scores will be $+1.96$ and -1.96. However, suppose the population standard deviation were not known and we conducted this hypothesis test with a t statistic. For a sample of $n = 4$, the t statistic would have $df = 3$. For three degrees of freedom, the critical values of t would be $+3.182$ and -3.182 (with alpha still set at .05). When df is small, the t distribution is flatter and more spread out. Consequently, the tails have a greater area for the t distribution compared to a normal distribution (see Figure 10.1). The extreme 5% of the distribution will be farther from the mean and have a larger critical value in the t distribution. If, however, we use a sample of $n = 31$, then $df = 30$, and the critical t values will be $+2.042$ and -2.042. These values are very close to the critical z-score values (± 1.96). If the sample is made even larger, say $n = 121$, the critical values get even closer to the z values. For 120 degrees of freedom, the critical values of t are $+1.980$ and -1.980 when $\alpha = .05$. Thus, the differences between a t distribution and a normal z distribution become negligible when a sample of more than 30 individuals is used.

10.2

Hypothesis Tests with the t Statistic

The t statistic formula is used in exactly the same way that the z-score formula is used to test a hypothesis about a population mean. Once again, the t formula and its structure are

$$t = \frac{\overline{X} - \mu}{s_{\overline{x}}} = \frac{\text{sample mean} - \text{population mean}}{\text{estimated standard error}}$$

In the hypothesis testing situation, we have a population with an unknown mean, often a population that has received some treatment (Figure 10.2). The goal is to use a sample from the treated population as the basis for determining whether or not the treatment has any effect. As always, the null hypothesis states that the treatment has no effect. Specifically, H_0 predicts that the population mean is unchanged. The hypothesized value for the population mean is put into the t formula along with the sample mean (from the obtained data) and the estimated standard error (also computed from the sample data). When the resulting t statistic is near zero, we can conclude that the sample mean is not significantly different from the hypothesized value and the decision is "fail to reject H_0." In other words, there is no support for a treatment effect. If there is a substantial difference between the sample mean and the hypothesized μ, we will obtain a large value for t (large positive or large negative value). In this case, we would conclude that the data are not consistent with the null hypothesis and our decision would be to "reject H_0." The evidence suggests the existence of a treatment effect. The basic steps of the hypothesis testing procedures will now be reviewed.

Figure 10.2
The basic experimental situation for using the t statistic or the z-score is presented. The parameter (μ) for the known population is taken from the previous example. The purpose of the experiment is to determine whether or not the treatment (exposure to eye-spot patterns) has an effect on time spent on the plain side of the test box. We ask, Is the population mean after treatment the same as or different from the mean before treatment? A sample is selected from the treated population to help answer this question.

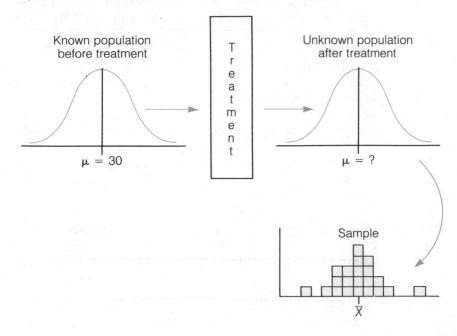

Steps and Procedures

For hypothesis tests with a t statistic, we use the same steps that were used with z-scores (Chapter 8). The major difference is that we are now required to estimate standard error because σ is unknown. Consequently, we compute a t statistic rather than a z-score and consult the t distribution table rather than the unit normal table to find the critical region.

STEP 1.   The hypotheses are stated, and the alpha level is set. The experimenter states the null hypothesis, that is, what should happen if no treatment effect exists. On the other hand, the alternative hypothesis predicts the outcome if an effect does occur. These hypotheses are always stated in terms of the population parameter μ. By testing hypotheses about the population, it is our goal to be able to make a general statement about how a treatment affects the population. Finally, a level of significance (α) is selected for the statistical test.

STEP 2.   The critical region is located. To find the critical region in a t distribution, it is necessary to determine the value for degrees of freedom. The exact shape of the distribution and therefore the critical t values vary with degrees of freedom. For the t test,

$$df = n - 1$$

After the value of df is determined, the critical region is located by consulting the t distribution table (Appendix B, p. A-30). Table 10.1 depicts a portion of the t distribution table. The two top rows of the table contain probabilities. These rows represent the proportions contained in either one or two tails, depending on which row is used. Therefore, these proportions may be conveniently used as alpha levels (levels of significance) for hypothesis tests. The first column of the table contains values of degrees of freedom for the sample. The numbers entered in the body of the table are the t values that mark off the critical region. Suppose a sample of $n = 6$ subjects is used to test a hypothesis, with the alpha level set at .05 for two tails. For this sample, degrees of freedom equal 5 ($df = n - 1 = 5$), and the critical region consists of t values greater than $+2.571$ or less than -2.571 (Figure 10.3).

Careful! The sample standard deviation uses n − 1 in the denominator to provide an unbiased estimate of σ (Chapter 4).

STEP 3.   The test statistic is computed. When σ is unknown, the test statistic is a t statistic. To calculate t, the sample standard deviation is used as an unbiased estimate of σ:

$$s = \sqrt{\frac{SS}{n - 1}}$$

From this value, the estimated standard error can be obtained:

$$s_{\bar{x}} = \frac{s}{\sqrt{n}}$$

Finally, the t statistic can be computed:

$$t = \frac{\overline{X} - \mu}{s_{\bar{x}}}$$

Table 10.1
A Portion of the t Distribution Table

	Proportion in One Tail					
	.25	.10	.05	.025	.01	.005
	Proportion in Two Tails					
df	.50	.20	.10	.05	.02	.01
1	1.000	3.078	6.314	12.706	31.821	63.657
2	0.816	1.886	2.920	4.303	6.965	9.925
3	0.765	1.638	2.353	3.182	4.541	5.841
4	0.741	1.533	2.132	2.776	3.747	4.604
5	0.727	1.476	2.015	2.571	3.365	4.032
6	0.718	1.440	1.943	2.447	3.143	3.707
7	0.711	1.415	1.895	2.365	2.998	3.499
8	0.706	1.397	1.860	2.306	2.896	3.355
9	0.703	1.383	1.833	2.262	2.821	3.250
10	0.700	1.372	1.812	2.228	2.764	3.169
11	0.697	1.363	1.796	2.201	2.718	3.106

The numbers in the table are the values of t that separate the tail from the main body of the distribution. Proportions for one or two tails are listed at the top of the table and df values for t are listed in the first column.

Figure 10.3
For $df = 5$ and $\alpha = .05$ with two tails, the critical values of t are $+2.571$ and -2.571. An obtained t that is more extreme than either critical t value warrants rejecting the null hypothesis.

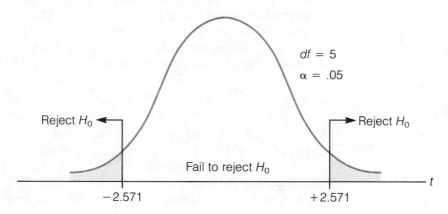

STEP 4. The null hypothesis is evaluated. If the t statistic we obtained in step 3 falls within the critical region (exceeds the value of a critical t), then H_0 is rejected. It can be concluded that a treatment effect exists. However, if the obtained t value does not lie in the critical region, then we fail to reject H_0, and we conclude that we failed to observe evidence for an effect in our study.

Hypothesis Testing Example

Let us return to the research problem posed in the beginning of the chapter to demonstrate the procedures of hypothesis testing. Recall that direct eye contact is avoided by many animals. Some animals, such as moths, have even developed large eye-spot patterns, presumably to ward off predators that avoid a direct gaze. The experiment will assess the effect of exposure to eye-spot patterns on the behavior of moth-eating birds.

EXAMPLE 10.1

To test the effectiveness of eye-spot patterns in deterring predation, a sample of $n = 16$ insectivorous birds is selected. The animals are tested in a box that has two separate chambers. The birds are free to roam from one chamber to another through a doorway in a partition. On the wall of one chamber, two large eye-spot patterns have been painted. The other chamber has plain walls. The birds are tested one at a time by placing them in the doorway in the center of the apparatus. Each animal is left in the box for 60 minutes, and the amount of time spent in the plain chamber is recorded. Suppose that the sample of $n = 16$ birds spent an average of $X = 35$ minutes in the plain side, with $SS = 1215$. Can we conclude that eye-spot patterns have an effect on behavior? Note that while it is possible to predict a value for μ, we have no information about the population standard deviation.

STEP 1. State the hypotheses and select an alpha level. If the null hypothesis were true, then the eye-spot patterns would have no effect on behavior. The animals should show no preference for either side of the box. That is, they should spend half of the 60-minute test period in the plain chamber. In symbols the null hypothesis would state that

$$H_0: \quad \mu_{\text{plain side}} = 30 \text{ minutes}$$

The alternative hypothesis would state that the eye patterns have an effect on behavior. There are two possibilities: (1) The animals may avoid staying in the chamber with the eye spots as we suspect, or (2) maybe for some reason the animals may show a preference for the patterns painted on the wall. A nondirectional hypothesis (for a two-tailed test) would be represented in symbols as follows:

$$H_1: \quad \mu_{\text{plain} \atop \text{side}} \neq 30 \text{ minutes}$$

We will set the level of significance at $\alpha = .05$ for two tails.

STEP 2. Locate the critical region. The test statistic is a t statistic because the population standard deviation is not known. The exact shape of the t distribution and therefore the proportions under the t distribution depend on the number of degrees of freedom associated with the sample. To find the critical region, df must be computed:

$$df = n - 1 = 16 - 1 = 15$$

For a two-tailed test at the .05 level of significance and with 15 degrees of freedom, the critical region consists of t values greater than $+2.131$ or less than -2.131. Figure 10.4 depicts the critical region in this t distribution.

STEP 3. Calculate the test statistic. To obtain the value for the t statistic, we first must compute s and then $s_{\bar{x}}$. The sample standard deviation is

$$s = \sqrt{\frac{SS}{n-1}}$$
$$= \sqrt{\frac{1215}{15}}$$
$$= \sqrt{81}$$
$$= 9$$

Figure 10.4
The critical region in the t distribution for $\alpha = .05$ and $df = 15$.

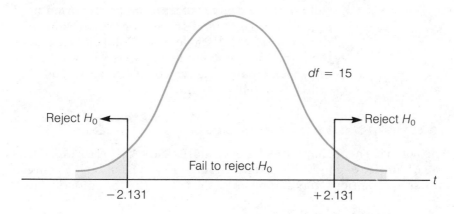

$df = 15$

Reject H_0 ←   → Reject H_0

Fail to reject H_0

-2.131 $+2.131$ t

The estimated standard error is

$$s_{\bar{x}} = \frac{s}{\sqrt{n}}$$

$$= \frac{9}{\sqrt{16}}$$

$$= 2.25$$

Finally, we can compute the t statistic for these sample data:

$$t = \frac{\bar{X} - \mu}{s_{\bar{x}}}$$

$$= \frac{35 - 30}{2.25}$$

$$= \frac{5}{2.25}$$

$$= 2.22$$

STEP 4. Make a decision regarding H_0. The obtained t statistic of 2.22 falls into the critical region on the right-hand side of the t distribution (Figure 10.4). Our statistical decision is to reject H_0 and conclude that the presence of eye-spot patterns does influence behavior. As can be seen from the sample mean, there is a tendency for animals to avoid the eyes and spend more time on the plain side of the box. For this example, alpha was set at .05. Therefore, the probability that a type I error has been committed is $p < .05$. It is common practice in scientific literature to report the results of the t test in the following manner:

The data suggest that the birds spent significantly more time in the chamber without eye-spot patterns; $t(15) = +2.22, p < .05$, two tailed.

Note that the degrees of freedom are reported in parentheses right after the symbol t. The value for the obtained t statistic follows (2.22) and next is the probability of committing a type I error (less than 5%). Finally, the type of test (one- versus two-tailed) is noted.

Assumptions of the t Test

As noted earlier (Chapter 8), for each statistical test it is assumed that a certain set of conditions exists. Severe violations of one or more of these assumptions may compromise the validity of the statistical test.

Of course, for a *t* test it is assumed that the sample has been randomly selected. This condition helps to ensure that the sample is representative of the population so that valid generalizations can be made from sample to population. Another important assumption for the *t* test is that the population distribution of scores is normal. If this condition is not met, the *t* distribution table cannot be used to locate the critical region. It is difficult to determine the exact *t* distribution which will be appropriate for the test when the population is not normally distributed.

Some statisticians have suggested that the *t* test is "robust." By robust, they mean the *t* test will still be a valid statistical test even when there are departures from the assumption of normality. However, the *t* statistic is more likely to be robust to violations of normality when large samples (for example, $n > 30$) are used. It should be noted that the assumption of normality is a condition that applies to all types of *t* tests that follow in later chapters.

The Versatility of the *t* Test

The obvious advantage of hypothesis testing with the *t* statistic (as compared to *z*-scores) is that you do not need to know the value of the population standard deviation. This means that we still can do a hypothesis test even though we have little or no information about the population. One result of this extra versatility is that it is possible to do *t* tests in circumstances where hypothesis tests with *z*-scores would not even allow for the statement of a null hypothesis.

Both the *t* statistic and *z*-score tests have been introduced as a means of determining whether or not a treatment has any effect on the dependent variable. Recall that the null hypothesis states that the treatment has no effect. That is, the population mean after treatment has the same value that it had before treatment. Notice that this experimental situation requires that we know the value of the population mean before the treatment. This requirement is often unrealistic and limits the usefulness of *z*-score tests. Although the *t* statistic often is used in this before-and-after type of experiment (Figure 10.2), the *t* test also permits hypothesis testing in situations where we do not have a "known" population to serve as a before-treatment standard. Specifically, the *t* test can be used in situations where the value for the null hypothesis can come from a theory, a prediction, or just wishful thinking. Some examples follow. Notice in each example that the hypothesis is not dependent on knowing the actual population mean before treatment and that the rest of the *t* statistic can be computed entirely from the obtained sample data.

1. A researcher would like to examine the accuracy of people's judgment of time when they are distracted. Individuals are placed in a waiting room where many distracting events occur for a period of 12 minutes. The researcher then asks each person to judge how much time has passed. The null hypothesis would state that

distraction has no effect and that time judgments are accurate. That is,

H_0: $\mu = 12$ minutes

2. A local fund-raising organization has set a goal of receiving $25 per contributor. After 1 week, a sample of contributions is selected to see if they deviate significantly from the goal. The null hypothesis would state that the contributions do not deviate from the goal of the organization. In symbols, it is

H_0: $\mu = \$25.00$

3. A psychology professor would like to see how familiar freshmen enrolled in psychology courses are with psychological theories and concepts. A sample of freshmen enrolled in Psychology 101 is given a multiple-choice examination containing 100 questions at the beginning of the semester. Each question has four choices. The null hypothesis would state that the freshmen, having never taken a psychology course before, are unfamiliar with the subject matter and guess on all of the questions on the test. Because there are 100 four-choice questions, the null hypothesis would predict that guessing results in an average of 25 correct responses. That is,

H_0: $\mu = 25$ correct items

---

1. A professor of philosophy hypothesizes that an introductory course in logic will help college students with their other studies. To test this hypothesis, a random sample of $n = 25$ freshmen is selected. These students are required to complete a logic course during their freshman year. At the time of graduation, the final grade point average is computed for each of these students. The mean GPA for this sample is $\overline{X} = 2.83$ with $SS = 6$. Can the professor conclude that the grades for the sample were significantly different from the rest of the graduating class, which had an average GPA of $\mu = 2.58$? Test with a two-tailed test at $\alpha = .05$.
   a. State the hypotheses.
   b. Determine the value for df and locate the critical region.
   c. Compute the test statistic.
   d. Make a decision regarding H_0.

ANSWERS

1. a.

H_0: $\mu_{\text{with logic course}} = 2.58$ (even with the logic course, the population mean GPA will still be 2.58)

H_1: $\mu_{\text{with logic course}} \neq 2.58$ (for the population, the logic course has an effect on GPA)

    b. $df = 24$; the critical region begins at t values of $+2.064$ and -2.064.

    c. $s = 0.5$; $s_{\bar{x}} = 0.1$; $t = +2.5$.

    d. Reject H_0.

10.3
Estimation of the Population Mean

The t statistic not only can be used for hypothesis testing but also for estimating the value of a population mean. Hypothesis testing addresses the question of whether or not a treatment effect exists. Estimation asks, "How much?" Therefore, estimation is not only useful to estimate the value of μ, but may also be used to determine the approximate size of a treatment effect (estimate the value of μ *after* treatment). Applications of the estimation procedure are discussed in Chapter 9.

The estimation procedure is used when we want to determine the average value for a population of scores (the average income for women lawyers, the average IQ scores for U.S. college students, etc.) but we do not have access to the entire population to find μ. Thus, a sample is selected from the population, and the goal is to use the sample mean as the basis for estimating the population mean. In Chapter 9, we used z-scores to assist in this estimation. That is, we selected z-score values to estimate the location of $\bar{X}$ in the distribution of sample means. The z-score formula was solved for μ, and the values of z, $\bar{X}$, and $\sigma_{\bar{x}}$ were used in the formula to obtain our estimate of μ.

In instances where σ is unknown, we cannot perform estimation with z-scores because $\sigma_{\bar{x}}$ cannot be computed. Just as we saw with hypothesis testing, when σ is unknown, we must use the t statistic. Because the purpose of estimation is to find the approximate value for the population mean μ, we begin by solving the t statistic equation for μ. The algebra in this process is as follows:

$$t = \frac{\bar{X} - \mu}{s_{\bar{x}}}$$

$$ts_{\bar{x}} = \frac{\bar{X} - \mu}{s_{\bar{x}}} \, s_{\bar{x}}$$

$$\mu = \bar{X} - ts_{\bar{x}}$$

Because t can have a positive or negative value in interval estimates, we can simplify the arithmetic of the formula:

(10.4) $\mu = \bar{X} \pm ts_{\bar{x}}$

This is the basic formula for estimation using the t statistic. You should notice that this formula is very similar to the z-score formula used for estimation in Chapter 9 (p. 265). Also note that either formula (using t or z) can be expressed conceptually in words as

population mean = sample mean ± some error

In the case of estimation when σ is unknown, we are using a t value to estimate the location of $\overline{X}$ in the distribution of sample means and the *estimated* standard error rather than $\sigma_{\overline{x}}$.

Procedures of Estimation Using a *t* Statistic

To obtain an estimate using Formula (10.4), we must select a level of confidence (for example, 95% or 99%) and find the value for the sample mean (from the data) and the estimated standard error (also computed from the sample data). Then we estimate the location of $\overline{X}$ in the distribution of sample means by selecting reasonable values (determined in part by the level of confidence) of t. Finally, these three values, namely $\overline{X}$, $s_{\overline{x}}$, and t, are substituted into the equation, and we compute the value for μ. Because we estimated the location of $\overline{X}$ (using t values), the result we obtain is an estimate for the value of μ. The process of estimation using both a point estimate and an interval estimate is nearly identical to previous accounts (Chapter 9) and is demonstrated in the following example.

EXAMPLE 10.2

A marketing researcher for a major U.S. jeans manufacturer would like to estimate the mean age for the population of people who buy its products. This information will be valuable in making decisions about how to spend advertising dollars. For example, should the company place more advertisements in *Seventeen* magazine or in *Cosmopolitan*? These represent publications that are directed at different age groups. It would be too costly and time consuming to record the age of every person in the population of their consumers, so a random sample is taken to estimate the value of μ. A sample of $n = 30$ people is drawn from the consumers who purchase the jeans from several major clothing outlets. The mean age of this sample is $\overline{X} = 30.5$ years, with $SS = 709$. The marketing researcher wishes to make a point estimate and to determine the 95% confidence interval for μ.

In this example we are simply trying to estimate the value of μ. Because no particular treatment is involved here, we are not trying to determine the size of a treatment effect.

Notice that nothing is known about the population parameters. Estimation of the value for μ will be based solely on the sample data. Because σ is unknown, a t statistic will be used for the estimation. The confidence level has been selected (95%), and the sample data have been collected. Now we can turn our attention to the computational steps of estimation.

Compute s and $s_{\overline{x}}$. The population standard deviation is not known; therefore, to estimate μ, it is necessary to use the estimated standard error. To obtain $s_{\overline{x}}$, we must first compute the sample standard deviation. Using the information provided, we obtain

$$s = \sqrt{\frac{SS}{n-1}}$$

$$= \sqrt{\frac{709}{29}}$$

$$= \sqrt{24.45}$$

$$= 4.94$$

For estimated standard error we obtain

$$s_{\bar{x}} = \frac{s}{\sqrt{n}}$$

$$= \frac{4.94}{\sqrt{30}}$$

$$= \frac{4.94}{5.48}$$

$$= 0.90$$

Compute the Point Estimate. The value for *t* that is used depends on the type of estimate being made. A single *t* value is used for a point estimate and an interval of values for the confidence interval. Just as we observed with the *z*-score distribution, *t* values are symmetrically distributed with a mean of zero. For a point estimate, the average *t* value is used to estimate the location of $\bar{X}$, namely, $t = 0$. In estimating the value of μ with $\bar{X}$, it would be unwise to use extreme *t* values such as $t = 3$ because relatively few samples are that far away from the population mean. Most of the sample means pile up around μ, so $t = 0$, the center of the distribution, is the best choice. By using the sample data, the estimation formula yields a point estimate of

$$\mu = \bar{X} \pm ts_{\bar{x}}$$

$$= 30.5 + 0(0.90)$$

$$= 30.5 + 0$$

$$= 30.5$$

As noted before (Chapter 9), the sample mean is the most appropriate point estimate of the population mean.

Construct an Interval Estimate. In constructing an estimate for μ, we estimate an interval around the sample mean in which the value for μ probably falls. We now use a range of *t* values to define this interval. For example, there is a good chance that the sample mean has a *t* value somewhere between $t = +2$ and $t = -2$ and even a much better chance it is between $t = +4$ and $t = -4$. The level of confidence (percent confidence) will determine the t values that mark off the boundaries of this interval. However, unlike the normal z distribution, there is a family of t distributions in which the exact shape of the distribution depends on the value of degrees of freedom. Therefore, the value of df that is associated with the sample is another determining factor of the t values to be used in the interval estimate. For this example,

$$df = n - 1 = 30 - 1 = 29$$

The marketing researcher selected the 95% confidence interval. Figure 10.5 depicts the t distribution for $df = 29$. To obtain the t values associated with the 95% confidence interval, we must consult the t distribution table. We look under the heading of proportions in *two tails*. If the middle 95% of the distribution is of interest to us, then both tails outside of the interval together will contain 5% of the t values. Therefore, to find the t values associated with the 95% confidence interval, we look for the entry under $p = .05$, two tails, for $df = 29$. The values of t used for the boundaries of this confidence interval are -2.045 and $+2.045$ (Figure 10.5). Using these values in the formula for μ, we obtain

$$\mu = \overline{X} - ts_{\overline{x}}$$
$$= 30.5 - 2.045(0.90)$$
$$= 30.5 - 1.84$$
$$= 28.66$$

for one end of the confidence interval and

$$\mu = \overline{X} + ts_{\overline{x}}$$
$$= 30.5 + 2.045(0.90)$$
$$= 30.5 + 1.84$$
$$= 32.34$$

for the other end of the interval. Therefore, the marketing researcher can be 95% confident that the population mean age for consumers of his product is between 28.66 and 32.34 years. The confidence level (%) determines the range of t values used in constructing the interval. That is, we used the middle 95% of the t distribution to estimate the location of $\overline{X}$. As long as the obtained sample mean really does have a t value that falls within the estimated range of t values, the population mean will be included in the confidence interval.

Figure 10.5
The 95% confidence interval for $df = 29$ will have boundaries that range from $t = -2.045$ to $+2.045$. Because the t distribution table presents proportions in both tails of the distribution, for the 95% confidence interval you find the t values under $p = 0.05$ (proportions of t-scores in two tails) for $df = 29$.

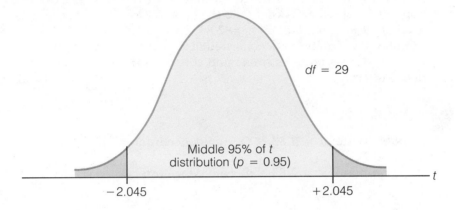

$df = 29$

Middle 95% of t distribution ($p = 0.95$)

-2.045 $+2.045$

Factors Affecting the Width of the Confidence Interval

As noted in Chapter 9, increasing the confidence level for an interval estimate will result in a larger interval width. In Example 10.2, suppose the marketing researcher had wanted to construct the 99% confidence interval instead of 95%. For the 99% confidence interval, 1% (or $p = .01$) of the distribution would fall in the two tails outside of the interval. For Example 10.2, $df = 29$, and therefore the t values for the 99% confidence interval are $+2.756$ and -2.756. Note that the t values are more extreme than those for the 95% confidence interval (± 2.045). These larger t values will result in a wider interval (try to compute the 99% confidence interval for Example 10.2). As the confidence level gets greater, the values of t that define the boundaries of the interval get bigger. As a result, the interval is wider.

When a larger sample (n) is used, the interval tends to be smaller. All other factors being held constant, increasing n will reduce the size of the estimated standard error used in the estimation formula. Less error will result in a narrower interval width. There is another aspect of sample size to consider. As the sample size gets larger, the value of degrees of freedom ($n - 1$) gets larger. Remember that the exact shape of the t distribution depends on degrees of freedom. As df gets larger, the t values associated with the boundaries of the interval get smaller. For a 95% confidence ($p = .05$ in two tails) interval with $df = 11$, the t values are $+2.201$ and -2.201. However, for $df = 20$ the t values for the interval are $+2.086$ and -2.086. As df increases, the range of t values decreases, and the width of the confidence interval gets smaller.

1. In the previous Learning Check (p. 310), the effect of a course in logic on grade point average was examined. The statistical decision was to reject H_0, indicating there was evidence for an effect. Using the sample data in that problem, estimate how much of an effect the professor can expect. Specifically, make a point estimate and an interval estimate for the mean GPA of the population of students that take the course. Use a confidence level of 99%. Sample data: $\overline{X} = 2.83$, $SS = 6$, and $n = 25$.

2. Suppose the sample data consisted of $\overline{X} = 2.83$, $SS = 6$, and $n = 16$. Make a point estimate and construct the 99% confidence interval.

ANSWERS

1. Point estimate: $\mu = 2.83$. 99% confidence interval: μ is between 3.11 and 2.55.

2. Point estimate: $\mu = 2.83$. 99% confidence interval: $s = 0.63$; $s_{\overline{x}} = 0.16$; μ is between 3.30 and 2.36.

Summary

1. When σ is unknown, the standard error cannot be computed, and a hypothesis test based on a z-score is impossible.

2. In order to test a hypothesis about μ when σ is unknown, σ must first be estimated using the sample standard deviation s:

$$s = \sqrt{\frac{SS}{n-1}}$$

Next, the standard error is estimated by substituting s for σ in the standard error formula. The estimated standard error ($s_{\overline{x}}$) is calculated in the following manner:

$$s_{\overline{x}} = \frac{s}{\sqrt{n}}$$

Finally, a t statistic is computed using the estimated standard error. The t statistic serves as a substitute for a z-score, which cannot be computed because σ is unknown.

$$t = \frac{\overline{X} - \mu}{s_{\overline{x}}}$$

3. The structure of the t formula is similar to that of the z-score in that

$$z \text{ or } t = \frac{\text{sample mean} - \text{population mean}}{\text{(estimated) standard error}}$$

4. The *t* distribution is an approximation of the normal *z* distribution. To evaluate a *t* statistic that is obtained for a sample mean, the critical region must be located in a *t* distribution. There is a family of *t* distributions, with the exact shape of a particular distribution of *t* values depending on degrees of freedom $(n - 1)$. Therefore, the critical *t* values will depend on the value for *df* associated with the *t* test. As *df* increases, the shape of the *t* distribution approaches a normal distribution.

5. Estimation of the value of the population mean can be performed when σ is unknown by solving the *t* formula for μ:

$$\mu = \overline{X} \pm ts_{\overline{x}}$$

6. For a point estimate, $t = 0$ is the best value to use in the estimation formula. The result is that the sample mean $\overline{X}$ is the best point estimate for μ.

7. For confidence intervals, a range of *t* values is used in the estimate. The *t* values that form the boundaries of the interval are determined by the selected level (percent) of confidence and the number of degrees of freedom associated with the sample.

8. Increasing the level of confidence results in an increase in the width of the confidence interval. Increasing sample size (n) or the *df* associated with the sample decreases the interval width.

Key Terms

t statistic
estimated standard error

degrees of freedom
t distribution

Problems for Chapter 10:
Introduction to the *t* Statistic

*1. For a standard set of discrimination problems that have been used for years in primate research, it is known that monkeys require an average of $\mu = 20$ trials before they can successfully reach the criterion (five consecutive correct solutions). A psychologist hypothesizes that the animals can learn the task vicariously—that is, simply by watching other animals perform the task. To test this hypothesis, the researcher selects a random sample of $n = 4$ monkeys. These animals are placed in neighboring enclosures from which they can watch another animal learn the task. After a week of viewing other animals, the four monkeys in the sample are tested on the problem. These animals require an average of $\overline{X} = 15$ trials to solve the problem, with $SS = 300$. On the basis of these data, can the psychologist conclude that there is evidence that the animals perform significantly better after viewing others. Test at the .05 level of significance.

a. State the hypotheses using symbols. Explain what they predict for this experiment.

b. Sketch the distribution and locate the critical region.

c. Calculate the test statistic.

d. Make a decision regarding H_0 and state your conclusion.

2. A group of students recently complained that all of the statistics classes are offered early in the morning. They claim that they "think better" later in the day and therefore would do better in the course had it been offered in the afternoon. To test this claim, the instructor scheduled the course this past semester for 3 p.m. The afternoon class was given the same final exam that has been used in previous semesters. The instructor knows that for previous students the scores are normally distributed with a mean of 70. The afternoon class with 16 students had an average score on the final of $\overline{X} = 76$ with $SS = 960$. Do the students perform significantly better in the afternoon section? Test with alpha set at .05 and with a one-tailed test.

a. State the hypotheses in symbols.

b. Locate the critical region.

c. Compute the test statistic.

d. What is your conclusion?

e. Identify the independent and dependent variables.

*3. A psychologist has developed a new personality questionnaire for measuring self-esteem and would like to estimate the population parameters for the test scores. The questionnaire is administered to a sample of $n = 25$ subjects. This sample has an average score of $\overline{X} = 43$ with $SS = 2400$.

a. Provide an unbiased estimate for the population standard deviation.

b. Make a point estimate for the population mean.

c. Make an interval estimate of μ so that you are 90% confident that the value for μ is in your interval.

4. A toy manufacturer asks a developmental psychologist to test children's responses to a new product. Specifically, the manufacturer wants to know how long, on average, the toy captures children's attention. The psychologist tests a sample of $n = 9$ children and measures how long they play with the toy before they get bored. This sample had a mean of $\overline{X} = 31$ minutes with $SS = 648$.

a. Make a point estimate for μ.

b. Make an interval estimate for μ using a confidence level of 95%.

*5. Why is a t distribution generally more variable than a normal distribution?

6. What is the relationship between the value for degrees of freedom and the shape of the t distribution? What happens to the critical value of t for a particular alpha level when df increases in value?

*7. What factors affect the width of the confidence interval? How is the width affected by each of these factors?

8. A recent national survey reports that the general population gives the president an average rating of $\mu = 62$ on a scale of 1 to 100. A researcher suspects that college students are likely to be more critical of the president than people in the general population. To test his suspicions, he selects a random sample of college students and has them rate the president. The data for this sample are as follows: 44, 52, 24, 45, 39, 57, 20, 38, 78, 74, 61, 56, 49, 66, 53, 49, 47, 88, 38, 51, 65, 47, 35, 59, 23, 41, 50, 19.

a. On the basis of this sample, can the researcher conclude that college students rate the president differently? Test at the .01 level of significance, two tails.

b. Use these data to estimate the average rating for the population of college students. In addition to a point estimate, determine the 95% confidence interval for μ.

*9. A fund raiser for a charitable organization has set a goal of averaging $20 per donation. To see if the goal is being met, a random sample of recent donations is selected. The data from this sample are as follows: 20, 5, 10, 15, 25, 5, 8, 10, 30, 10, 15, 24, 50, 10, 7, 15, 10, 5, 5, 15.

a. Do the contributions differ significantly from the goal of the fund raiser? Test at the .05 level of significance.

b. Would you reach the same conclusion had the .01 level of significance been used?

10. A random sample of $n = 11$ scores is selected from a population with unknown parameters. The scores in the sample are as follows: 12, 5, 9, 9, 10, 14, 7, 10, 14, 13, 8.

a. Provide an unbiased estimate of the population standard deviation.

b. Use the sample data to make a point estimate for μ and to construct the 95% confidence interval for μ.

*11. A researcher would like to examine the effect of labor unions on the average pay of workers. The investigator obtains information from the National Carpenters Union which states that the average pay for union carpenters is μ = $7.80 per hour. The researcher then obtains a random sample of eight carpenters who do not belong to a union and records the pay for each. The data from this sample are as follows: 6.25, 7.50, 6.75, 6.90, 7.10, 7.15, 8.00, 6.15.

a. Does the average pay of nonunion carpenters differ significantly from union members? Test at the .01 level of significance.

b. Make a point estimate and an interval estimate at the 95% confidence level for the population average pay of nonunion carpenters.

12. After many studies of memory, a psychologist has determined that when a standard list of 40 words is presented at a rate of 2 words per second college students can recall an average of μ = 17.5 words from the list. The psychologist would like to determine if the rate of presentation affects memory. He selects a random sample of n = 15 students, and each is given the standard list of words at a rate of only 1 word per second. At the end of the presentation of the list, each student is tested for recall. The number of words recalled is as follows: 14, 21, 23, 19, 17, 20, 24, 16, 27, 17, 20, 21, 18, 20, 19.

a. Is there evidence for an effect of presentation rate? Test at the .05 level of significance and with two tails.

b. Would you arrive at the same conclusion had the .01 level of significance been used?

c. Find the 99% confidence interval for μ with the 1-word-per-second presentation rate.

*13. A researcher knows that the average weight of American men between the ages of 30 and 50 is μ = 166 pounds. The researcher would like to determine if men who have heart attacks between those ages are heavier than the average male. For a random sample of heart patients, body weights are recorded. The data are as follows: 153, 176, 201, 188, 157, 182, 208, 186, 163, 187, 230, 196, 167, 193, 171, 198, 191, 193, 233, 197, 196.

a. Are these patients significantly heavier than expected? Use a two-tailed test at the .01 level of significance.

b. Make an interval estimate of the population mean weight for this class of patient using the 99% level of confidence.

14. A psychologist assesses the effect of distraction on time perception. Subjects are asked to judge the length of time between signals given by the experimenter. The actual inter-

val of time is 10 minutes. During this period, the subjects are distracted by noises, conversation between the experimenter and his assistant, and questions from the assistant. The experimenter expects that the subjects' judgments will average around 10 minutes if the distraction has no effect. The data are as follows:

11	9.5	14	8
8	14	15	15
12	7.5	15	18
15	12	11	10
20	10	9	14

Is there a significant effect? Test at the .05 level of significance. What conclusion can be made?

*15. A researcher would like to determine whether humidity can have an effect on eating behavior. It is known that under regular circumstances laboratory rats eat an average of $\mu = 10$ grams of food each day. The researcher selects a random sample of $n = 15$ rats and places them in a controlled atmosphere room where the relative humidity is maintained at 90%. The daily food consumption for each of these rats is as follows:

Food Consumption				
9.1	8.3	7.6	10.2	8.4
6.9	9.3	10.7	11.2	9.8
8.5	12.1	8.4	7.7	9.2

On the basis of these data, can the researcher conclude that humidity affects eating behavior? Test with $\alpha = .05$.

16. A manufacturer of office furniture is designing a new computer table. Although it is known that the standard height for typing tables is 26 inches, the manufacturer is concerned that the best height for a computer might be different. A sample of $n = 30$ computer operators is obtained, and each is asked to position the height of an adjustable table at its most comfortable level. The heights for this sample are as follows:

Heights (Inches)				
27.50	26.25	25.75	27.00	25.75
29.50	26.50	29.00	27.75	25.00
27.25	26.00	28.25	26.50	27.00
26.25	28.00	26.25	28.75	30.25
26.75	27.00	27.50	25.50	28.75
28.00	26.25	25.75	26.00	27.25

a. On the basis of this sample, should the company conclude that the best height for a computer table is different from 26 inches? Test with $\alpha = .05$.

b. Use these data to estimate the average "best height" for the general population. Make a point estimate and a 90% confidence interval estimate.

*17. Recently the college newspaper conducted a survey to assess student attitudes toward spending student government money to help support college athletic teams. Student responses were recorded on a scale from 0 (totally opposed) to 10 (completely in favor). A value of 5 on this scale represented a neutral point. The results from $n = 327$ students gave an average opinion score of $\overline{X} = 6.3$ with $SS = 1343$. Do these data indicate that the general student opinion is significantly different from neutral. Test with $\alpha = .01$.

18. A vocabulary skills test designed for 6-year-old children has been standardized to produce a mean score of $\mu = 50$. A researcher would like to use this test in an experiment with 5-year-old children. Before beginning the experiment, however, the researcher would like some indication of how well 5-year-olds can perform on this test. Therefore, a sample of $n = 30$ 5-year-old children is given the test. The data for this sample are as follows:

Vocabulary Test Scores

42	56	49	37	43	46	47	47	52	55
48	57	39	40	51	49	50	37	58	43
36	45	52	47	49	40	53	51	44	51

a. Use the data to make a point estimate of the population mean for 5-year-old children.

b. Make an interval estimate of the mean so that you are 95% confident that the true mean is in your interval.

c. On the basis of your confidence interval, can the researcher be 95% confident that the population mean for 5-year-olds is lower than the mean for 6-year-olds?

*19. For several years the members of the faculty in the Department of Psychology have been teaching small sections of the introductory statistics course because they believe that students learn better in small classes. For these small classes, the average score on the standardized final exam is $\mu = 73.5$. This year, for the first time, the department offered one large section. For the 81 students in this large class, the scores on the final exam averaged $\overline{X} = 71.2$ with $SS = 9647$. The psychologist would like to use these data to determine whether there is any difference between students' performance in large versus small classes. Perform the appropriate test with $\alpha = .05$.

20. A curious student would like to know the average number of books owned by college professors. A random sample of 12 professors is selected, and the student counts the number of

books owned by each professor. The data obtained by the student are as follows:

Professor	Number of Books
1	346
2	134
3	208
4	640
5	276
6	318
7	211
8	453
9	152
10	281
11	109
12	334

a. Use these sample data to make a point estimate of the population mean.

b. Use the data to make an interval estimate of the population mean so that you are 95% confident that the mean is in your interval.

c. Based on these data, the 80% confidence interval for the population mean extends from 229.87 to 347.13. Does this mean that 80% of all college professors own between 229.87 and 347.13 books? Explain your answer.

CHAPTER 11

Statistical Inference with Two Independent Samples

The following items are considered essential background material for this chapter. If you doubt your knowledge of any of these items, you should review the appropriate chapter or section before proceeding.

1. Sample variance (Chapter 4)
2. The *t* statistic (Chapter 10)
   a. Distribution of *t* values
   b. *df* for the *t* statistic
   c. Estimated standard error

In a classic study in the area of problem solving, Katona (1940) compared the effectiveness of two methods of instruction. One group of subjects was shown the exact, step-by-step procedure for solving a problem, and then these subjects were required to memorize the solution. This method was called *learning by memorization* (later called the *expository* method). Subjects in a second group were encouraged to study the problem and find the solution on their own. Although these subjects were given helpful hints and clues, the exact solution was never explained. This method was called *learning by understanding* (later called the *discovery* method).

Katona's experiment included the problem shown in Figure 11.1. This figure shows a pattern of five squares made of matchsticks. The problem is to change the pattern into exactly four squares by moving only three matches. (All matches must be used, none can be removed, and all the squares must be the same size.) Two groups of subjects learned the solution to this problem. One group learned by understanding, and the other group learned by memorization. After 3 weeks both groups returned to be tested again. The two groups did equally well on the matchstick problem they had learned earlier. But when they were given two new problems (similar to the matchstick

Figure 11.1

A pattern of five squares made of matchsticks. The problem is to change the pattern into exactly four squares by moving only three matchsticks.

Katona, G. (1940) *Organizing and Memorizing*. New York: Columbia University Press. Reprinted by permission.

problem), the *understanding* group performed much better than the *memorization* group.

The outcome of Katona's experiment probably is no surprise. However, you should realize that the experimental design is different from any we have considered before. This experiment involved *two separate samples*. Previously we have examined statistical techniques for evaluating the data from only one sample. In this chapter we will present the statistical procedures that allow a researcher to use two samples to evaluate the difference between two experimental treatment conditions.

Incidentally, if you still haven't discovered the solution to the matchstick problem, keep trying. According to Katona's results, it would be very poor teaching strategy for us to give you the answer.

11.1
Introduction

Until this point, all of the inferential statistics we have considered have involved using one sample as the basis for drawing conclusions about one population. Although these *single-sample* techniques are used occasionally in real research, most of the interesting experiments require two (or more) sets of data in order to compare two (or more) populations. For example, a social psychologist may want to compare attitudes toward abortion for men versus women, or an educational psychologist may want to compare two methods for teaching mathematics. In both of these examples, the basic question concerns a mean difference between two populations or between two treatments. Is the average attitude for men any different from the average attitude for women? Do children who are taught math by method A score higher than children who are taught by method B?

To answer these questions with the single-sample techniques, it is necessary that we know in advance the population parameters for one of the two distributions. For example, we might know that students taught by method A have math-achievement scores that form a normal distribution with $\mu = 60$ and $\sigma = 10$. When one of the two populations is known, the problem simplifies to a question about only one unknown population. To find out about one population, you need only one sample. (See Figure 11.2.)

In most situations, it is not reasonable to expect a researcher to have prior knowledge about either of the two populations being compared. In this case, the researcher has a question about two unknown populations. To find out about two separate populations, it will be necessary to take two separate samples. (See Figure 11.3.)

The remainder of this chapter will present the statistical techniques that permit a researcher to examine the data obtained from two separate samples. More specifically, our goal is to use the data from two samples as the basis for evaluating the mean difference between two populations.

Figure 11.2

Do the achievement scores for children taught by method A differ from the scores for children taught by method B? In statistical terms, is the mean for population A different from the mean for population B? If you already know that the mean for population A is $\mu = 60$, then the only question is whether or not the mean for population B also is equal to 60. This is a question about one population, so you would need only one sample.

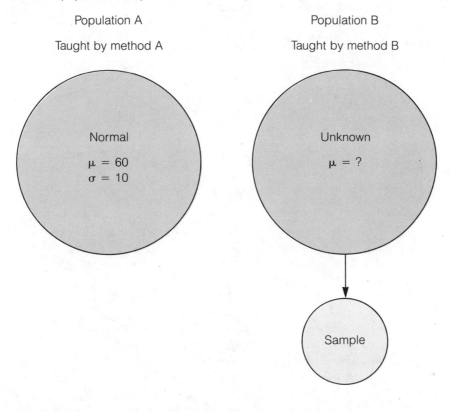

Population A

Taught by method A

Normal

$\mu = 60$
$\sigma = 10$

Population B

Taught by method B

Unknown

$\mu = ?$

Sample

DEFINITION

An experiment that uses a separate sample for each treatment condition (or each population) is called an *independent measures* experimental design.

The term *independent measures* comes from the fact that the experimental data consist of two *independent* sets of measurements, that is, two separate samples. On occasion, you will see an independent measures experiment referred to as a *between subjects* or a *between groups* design. This terminology reflects the fact that in an independent measures design differences between treatments are evaluated by looking at differences between the groups of subjects.

Figure 11.3

Do the achievement scores for children taught by method A differ from the scores for children taught by method B? In statistical terms, are the two population means the same or different? Because neither of the two population means is known, it will be necessary to take two samples, one from each population. The first sample will provide information about the mean for the first population, and the second sample will provide information about the second population mean.

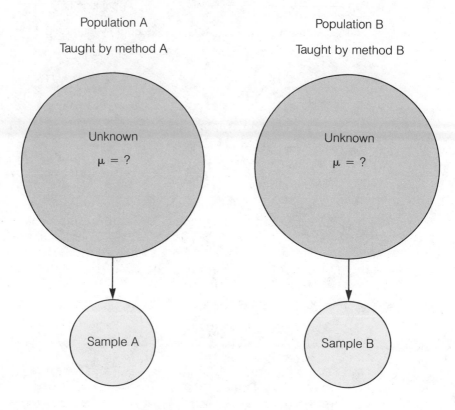

11.2
The *t* Statistic for an Independent Measures Experiment

Because an independent measures experiment involves two separate samples, we will need some special notation to help specify which data go with which sample. This notation involves the use of subscripts, which are small numbers written beside each sample statistic. For example, the number of scores in the first sample would be identified by n_1; for the second sample, the number of scores would be n_2. The sample means would be identified by $\overline{X}_1$ and $\overline{X}_2$. The sums of squares would be SS_1 and SS_2.

Recall that our goal is to evaluate the mean difference between two populations (or between two treatment conditions). In symbols, the mean difference between the two populations can be written as $\mu_1 - \mu_2$. For hypothesis tests we will hypothesize a value for this mean difference. Generally, the null hypothesis says there is no difference between the two population means: $\mu_1 - \mu_2 = 0$. For estimation, we will use the two samples to estimate the size of this mean difference.

The basis for either hypothesis tests or estimation will be a t statistic. The formula for this t statistic will have the same general structure as the single-sample t formula that was introduced in Chapter 10:

$$t = \frac{\overline{X} - \mu}{s_{\overline{x}}} = \frac{\text{sample data} - \text{population parameter}}{\text{estimated standard error}}$$

However, the details of the formula must be modified to accommodate the independent measures experimental design. Now the population parameter of interest is the difference between the two population means ($\mu_1 - \mu_2$). The corresponding sample data would be the difference between the two sample means ($\overline{X}_1 - \overline{X}_2$). The standard error in the denominator of the formula measures the standard distance between the sample data ($\overline{X}_1 - \overline{X}_2$) and the population parameter ($\mu_1 - \mu_2$). As always, standard error tells how well a sample value is expected to approximate the corresponding population value. In this case, the standard error tells how well the sample mean difference should approximate the population mean difference. The symbol for this standard error is $s_{\overline{x}_1 - \overline{x}_2}$. The s indicates an estimated standard distance and the lowercase $\overline{x}$s simply indicate that our sample value is the difference between two sample means. Substituting these values into the general t formula gives

$$t = \frac{(\overline{X}_1 - \overline{X}_2) - (\mu_1 - \mu_2)}{s_{\overline{x}_1 - \overline{x}_2}}$$

This is the t formula that will be used with data from an independent measures experiment. You should note that this is still a t statistic; it has the same basic structure as the original t formula that was introduced in Chapter 10. However, to distinguish between these two t formulas, we will occasionally refer to the original formula as the *single-sample t statistic* and this new formula as the *independent measures t statistic*. To complete the independent measures t formula, we must define more precisely the calculations needed for the standard error $s_{\overline{x}_1 - \overline{x}_2}$.

The Standard Error for a Sample Mean Difference

In general, the purpose of standard error is to provide a measure of how accurately a sample statistic approximates the population parameter. In the independent measures t formula, the sample statistic consists of two sample means, and the population parameter consists of two population means. We expect the sample data ($\overline{X}_1 -$

$\overline{X}_2$) to be close to the population parameter ($\mu_1 - \mu_2$), but there will be some error. Our goal is to determine how much error. To develop the formula for this standard error, we will consider two points:

1. First, we know that each of the two sample means provides an estimate of its own population mean:

    $\overline{X}_1$ approximates μ_1 with some error.
    $\overline{X}_2$ approximates μ_2 with some error.

    The amount of error from each sample is defined by the standard error of $\overline{X}$,

    See Equation (10.1).

    $$s_{\overline{x}} = \frac{s}{\sqrt{n}}$$

    which measures how accurately a sample mean approximates the population mean.

2. We want to know the total amount of error involved in using two sample means to approximate two population means. To do this, we will find the error from each sample separately and then add the two errors together.

As noted in point 1, the standard error between $\overline{X}$ and μ is specified by

$$s_{\overline{x}} = \frac{s}{\sqrt{n}}$$

Before we continue, we will change the appearance of this standard error formula. To accomplish this change, we first will square the standard error:

$$s_{\overline{x}}^2 = \frac{s^2}{n}$$

Then we take the square root of this squared value:

$$s_{\overline{x}} = \sqrt{\frac{s^2}{n}}$$

Note that by squaring and then taking the square root, we are right back where we started from. The value of the standard error is the same, but the appearance of the formula has changed. The reason for constructing this new appearance is that it helps to introduce the standard error for the independent measures t statistic. Because we now have two sample means approximating two population means, we now have two sources of error. The formula for this independent measures standard error is

$$s_{\overline{x}_1 - \overline{x}_2} = \sqrt{\frac{s^2}{n_1} + \frac{s^2}{n_2}}$$

Note that this standard error simply adds together the error from the first sample mean and the error from the second sample mean. (See Box 11.1.)

Before we continue, let's pause to compare the formula for the single-sample t statistic with the formula for the new independent measures t statistic. For the single-sample case,

$$t = \frac{\overline{X} - \mu}{s_{\overline{x}}} = \frac{\overline{X} - \mu}{s/\sqrt{n}} = \frac{\overline{X} - \mu}{\sqrt{s^2/n}}$$

For the independent measures case,

$$t = \frac{(\overline{X}_1 - \overline{X}_2) - (\mu_1 - \mu_2)}{\sqrt{\dfrac{s^2}{n_1} + \dfrac{s^2}{n_2}}}$$

The relationship between the two formulas should be obvious. The single-sample formula has one sample mean, one population mean, and one standard error. The independent measures formula simply doubles everything; there are two sample means, two population means, and two sources of error.

BOX 11.1 **The Variability of Difference Scores**

It may seem odd that the independent measures t statistic *adds* together the two sample errors when it *subtracts* to find the difference between the two sample means. The logic behind this apparently unusual procedure is demonstrated here.

We begin with two populations, I and II (see Figure 11.4). The scores in population I range from a high of 70 to a low of 50. The scores in population II range from 30 to 20. We will use the range as a measure of how spread out (variable) each population is:

> For population I, the scores cover a range of 20 points.

> For population II, the scores cover a range of 10 points.

continued

Figure 11.4

Two population distributions. The scores in population I vary from 50 to 70 (a 20-point spread), and the scores in population II range from 20 to 30 (a 10-point spread). If you select one score from each of these two populations, the closest two values would be $X_1 = 50$ and $X_2 = 30$. The two values that are farthest apart would be $X_1 = 70$ and $X_2 = 20$.

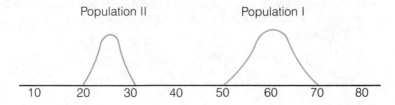

Population II   Population I

10   20   30   40   50   60   70   80

BOX 11.1 *continued*

If we randomly select a score from population I and a score from population II and compute the difference between these two scores $(X_1 - X_2)$, what range of values is possible for these differences? To answer this question, we need to find the biggest possible difference and the smallest possible difference. Look at Figure 11.4; the biggest difference occurs when $X_1 = 70$ and $X_2 = 20$. This is a difference of $X_1 - X_2 = 50$ points. The smallest difference occurs when $X_1 = 50$ and $X_2 = 30$. This is a difference of $X_1 - X_2 = 20$ points. Notice that the differences go from a high of 50 to a low of 20. This is a range of 30 points:

range for population I $(X_1$ scores) $= 20$ points

range for population II $(X_2$ scores) $= 10$ points

range for the differences $(X_1 - X_2) = 30$ points

The variability for the difference scores is found by *adding* together the variabilities for the two populations.

In the independent measures t statistic we are computing the variability (standard error) for a sample mean difference. To compute this value, we add together the variability for each of the two sample means.

Pooled Variance

One more detail must be addressed in order to complete the t formula. You should recall that the original t statistic was developed to be used in situations where the population variability is unknown. The general strategy of the t statistic is to use the sample data to compute an estimate of the variability in the population. With an independent measures experiment, we have two samples which are combined to obtain a single estimate of population variance. The result is called the *pooled variance* because it is obtained by averaging or "pooling" the two sample variances. To compute this pooled variance, we will find the average of the two sample variances, but we will allow the bigger sample to carry more weight in determining the average. This process is demonstrated in the following example.

EXAMPLE 11.1

Suppose we have two samples from the same population. The first sample has $n = 4$ scores and $SS = 36$. For the second sample, $n = 8$ and $SS = 56$. From these data, we can compute a variance for each sample.

For sample 1,

$$s^2 = \frac{SS}{n-1} = \frac{36}{3} = 12$$

For sample 2,

$$s^2 = \frac{SS}{n-1} = \frac{56}{7} = 8$$

Because these two samples are from the same population, each of the sample variances provides an estimate of the same population variance. Therefore, it is reasonable to somehow average these two estimates together in order to get a better estimate. Before we average the two variances, however, you should notice that one of the samples is much bigger than the other. Because bigger samples tend to give better estimates of the population, we would expect the sample variance based on $n = 8$ to be a better value than the variance based on $n = 4$. When we pool the two variances, we will let the "better" value carry more weight.

To compute the pooled variance, we will weight each of the sample variances by its degrees of freedom ($df = n - 1$). The degrees of freedom indicate how well the sample variance approximates the population variance (the bigger the sample, the bigger the df, and the better the estimate). To find the pooled variance, or the weighted mean for two sample variances, you follow two steps:

1. Multiply each s^2 by its df and then add the results together (this weights each variance).
2. Divide this total by the sum of the two df values.

The equation for this process is

$$\text{pooled variance} = s_p^2 = \frac{df_1 s_1^2 + df_2 s_2^2}{df_1 + df_2}$$

For this example, the calculation can be described in words as follows: You take 3 of the first variance ($df = 3$) and 7 of the second variance ($df = 7$). This gives you a total of 10 variances ($df_1 + df_2 = 10$). To find the average, you must divide by 10. For this example,

$$\text{pooled variance} = \frac{3(12) + 7(8)}{3 + 7} = \frac{36 + 56}{10} = 9.2$$

Notice that the value we obtained is not halfway between the two sample variances. Rather it is closer to $s^2 = 8$ (the big sample) than it is to $s^2 = 12$ (the small sample), because the larger sample carried more weight in computing the average.

You may have noticed that the calculation of the pooled variance in Example 11.1 can be simplified greatly. In the numerator of the formula, each sample variance is multiplied by its df. When you do this, you always obtain SS:

$$df(s^2) = df \frac{SS}{df} = SS$$

Therefore, we can use SS in place of $df(s^2)$ in the formula. The simplified result is

$$\text{pooled variance} = s_p^2 = \frac{SS_1 + SS_2}{df_1 + df_2}$$

The Final Formula and Degrees of Freedom

The complete equation for the independent measures t statistic is as follows:

(11.1)
$$t = \frac{(\overline{X}_1 - \overline{X}_2) - (\mu_1 - \mu_2)}{s_{\overline{x}_1 - \overline{x}_2}} = \frac{(\overline{X}_1 - \overline{X}_2) - (\mu_1 - \mu_2)}{\sqrt{\frac{s_p^2}{n_1} + \frac{s_p^2}{n_2}}}$$

with the pooled variance s_p^2 defined as

(11.2) $$s_p^2 = \frac{SS_1 + SS_2}{df_1 + df_2}$$

The degrees of freedom for this t statistic are determined by the df values for the two separate samples:

(11.3)
$$df = df \text{ for first sample} + df \text{ for second sample}$$
$$= df_1 + df_2$$

Remember, we pooled the two sample variances to compute the t *statistic. Now we combine the two* df *values to obtain the overall* df *for the* t *statistic.*

Occasionally, you will see degrees of freedom written in terms of the number of scores in each sample:

(11.4)
$$df = (n_1 - 1) + (n_2 - 1)$$
$$= n_1 + n_2 - 2$$

This t formula will be used for hypothesis testing and for estimation. In each case, we will use the sample data $(\overline{X}_1 - \overline{X}_2)$ as the basis for drawing inferences about the population parameter $(\mu_1 - \mu_2)$.

11.3
Hypothesis Tests with the Independent Measures t Statistic

The independent measures t statistic can be used to test a hypothesis about the mean difference between two populations (or between two treatments). As always, the null hypothesis states that there is no difference:

H_0: $\mu_1 - \mu_2 = 0$

The alternative hypothesis says that there is a mean difference:

H_1: $\mu_1 - \mu_2 \neq 0$

The hypothesis test procedure will determine whether or not the data provide evidence for a mean difference between the two populations. At the conclusion of the hypothesis test, we will decide either to

a. Reject H_0: We conclude that the data indicate a significant difference between the two populations, or to
b. Fail to reject H_0: The data do not provide sufficient evidence to conclude that a difference exists.

For hypothesis tests, we will use the t formula as follows:

$$t = \frac{\text{sample data} - \text{hypothesized population parameter}}{\text{estimated standard error}}$$

Notice that we simply take the value from the null hypothesis $(\mu_1 - \mu_2 = 0)$ and use it in the formula along with the data from the experiment. When the sample data are close to the hypothesis, we should get a t statistic near zero, and our decision will be to fail to reject H_0 (see Figure 11.5). On the other hand, when the data are very different from the hypothesis, we should obtain a large value for t (large positive or large negative), and we will reject H_0.

A complete example of a hypothesis test with two independent samples follows. Notice that the hypothesis testing procedure follows the same four steps that we have used before:

1. State the hypotheses H_0 and H_1 and select an alpha level. For the independent measures t test, the

---

Figure 11.5
The distribution of t values. For the independent measures t-score, when the sample data are close to the hypothesized value, you will get a t statistic near zero. In this case we conclude that the data "support" the H_0 and we fail to reject H_0. On the other hand, when there is a big difference between the data and the hypothesis, we will obtain a large value for t (either large positive or large negative). In this case, the data disagree with the hypothesis, and our decision is to reject H_0.

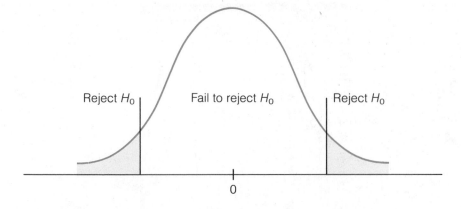

hypotheses concern the difference between two population means.

2. Locate the critical region. The critical region is defined as sample data that would be extremely unlikely ($p < \alpha$) if the null hypothesis were true. In this case, we will be locating extremely unlikely t values.

3. Get the data and compute the test statistic. Here we compute the t value for our data using the value from H_0 in the formula.

4. Make a decision. If the t statistic we compute is in the critical region, we reject H_0. Otherwise we conclude that the data do not provide sufficient evidence that the two populations are different.

EXAMPLE 11.2

In recent years psychologists have demonstrated repeatedly that using mental images can greatly improve memory. A hypothetical experiment, designed to examine this phenomenon, is presented here.

The psychologist first prepares a list of 40 pairs of nouns (for example, dog/bicycle, grass/door, lamp/piano, etc.). Next, two groups of subjects are obtained (two separate samples). Subjects in the first group are given the list for 5 minutes and instructed to memorize the 40 noun pairs. Subjects in the second group receive the same list of words, but in addition to the regular instructions these people are told to form a mental image for each pair of nouns (imagine a dog riding a bicycle, for example). Notice that the two samples are identical except that the second group is using mental images to help learn the list.

Later each group is given a memory test, and the psychologist records the number of words correctly recalled for each individual. The data from this experiment are as follows. On the basis of these data, can the psychologist conclude that mental images affected memory?

Data (Number of Words Recalled)

Group 1 (No Images)		Group 2 (Images)	
24	13	18	31
23	17	19	29
16	20	23	26
17	15	29	21
19	26	30	24
$n = 10$		$n = 10$	
$\overline{X} = 19$		$\overline{X} = 25$	
$SS = 160$		$SS = 200$	

STEP 1. State the hypothesis and select α.

H_0: $\mu_1 - \mu_2 = 0$ (no difference; imagery has no effect)

H_1: $\mu_1 - \mu_2 \neq 0$ (imagery produces a difference)

We will set α = .05.

STEP 2. This is an independent measures design. The t statistic for these data will have degrees of freedom determined by

$$df = df_1 + df_2$$
$$= (n_1 - 1) + (n_2 - 1)$$
$$= 9 + 9$$
$$= 18$$

Remember, an independent measures design means that there are separate samples for each treatment condition.

The distribution of all the possible t values with $df = 18$ is presented in Figure 11.6. The middle 95% of this distribution is separated from the extreme 5% by values of $t = +2.101$ and $t = -2.101$. These values determine the critical region. In simple terms, we are almost guaranteed to obtain a t statistic between these two extremes (95% of the time). On the other hand, it is almost impossible (only 5% likely) to obtain a t value beyond these extremes.

STEP 3. Obtain the data and compute the test statistic. The data are as given, so all that remains is to compute the t statistic. Because the independent measures t formula is relatively complex, the calculations can be simplified by dividing the process into three parts.

First, find the pooled variance for the two samples:

$$s_p^2 = \frac{SS_1 + SS_2}{df_1 + df_2}$$
$$= \frac{160 + 200}{9 + 9}$$
$$= \frac{360}{18}$$
$$= 20$$

Caution: The pooled variance combines the two samples to obtain a single estimate of variance. In the formula the two samples are combined in a single fraction.

Second, use the pooled variance to compute the standard error:

Caution: *The standard error adds the errors from two separate samples. In the formula these two errors are added as two separate fractions.*

$$s_{\bar{x}_1 - \bar{x}_2} = \sqrt{\frac{s_p^2}{n_1} + \frac{s_p^2}{n_2}}$$

$$= \sqrt{\frac{20}{10} + \frac{20}{10}}$$

$$= \sqrt{4}$$

$$= 2$$

Third, compute the t statistic:

$$t = \frac{(\overline{X}_1 - \overline{X}_2) - (\mu_1 - \mu_2)}{s_{\bar{x}_1 - \bar{x}_2}} = \frac{(19 - 25) - 0}{2}$$

$$= \frac{-6}{2}$$

$$= -3.00$$

STEP 4.   Make a decision. The obtained value ($t = -3.00$) is in the critical region. This result is very unlikely if H_0 is true. Therefore, we reject H_0 and conclude that using mental images produced a significant difference in memory performance. More specifically, the group using images recalled significantly more words than the group with no images.

In the scientific literature it is common to report the results of a hypothesis test in a concise, standardized format. For the test described in Example 11.2, the report would state the following: $t(18) = -3.00$; $p < .05$. This statement indicates that the t statistic has $df = 18$, the value obtained from these sample data is $t = -3.00$; and this value is in the critical region with $\alpha = .05$.

Figure 11.6

The distribution of t values with $df = 18$. Note that 95% of the values are between $+2.101$ and -2.101.

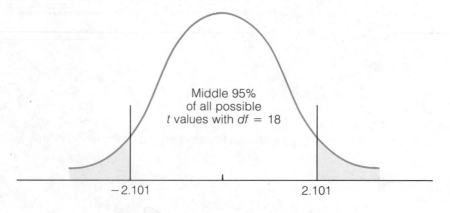

Middle 95%
of all possible
t values with $df = 18$

-2.101 2.101

The *t* Statistic as a Ratio

You should note that the magnitude of the *t* statistic is determined not only by the mean difference between the two samples but also by the sample variability. The bigger the difference between the sample means (the numerator of the *t* formula), the bigger the *t* value. This relation is reasonable because a big difference between the samples is a clear indication of a difference between the two populations. However, the sample variability (in the denominator of the *t* formula) is just as important. If the variability is large, *t* will tend to be small. The role of variability becomes clearer if you consider a simplified version of the *t* formula:

$$t = \frac{\text{sample mean difference}}{\text{variability}}$$

Notice that we have left out the population mean difference because the null hypothesis says that this is zero. Also, we have used the general term variability in place of standard error. In this simplified form, *t* becomes a ratio involving only the sample mean difference and the sample variability. It should be clear that large variability will make the *t* value smaller (or small variability will make *t* larger). The importance of sample variability is demonstrated in the following example.

EXAMPLE 11.3
The following two hypothetical experiments demonstrate the influence of variability in the computation and interpretation of an independent measures *t* statistic. Each of these experiments compares attitude scores for men versus women. Both experiments use a sample of $n = 7$ individuals from each of the populations, and both experiments obtain the same sample mean values ($\overline{X} = 8$ for the men and $\overline{X} = 12$ for the women). The only difference between the two experiments is in the amount of sample variability.

The data from experiment I are pictured in Figure 11.7. In this experiment the scores in each sample are clustered around the mean, so the sample variability is relatively small. The hypothesis test using these data gives a *t* statistic of $t = 9.16$. With $df = 12$, this value is in the critical region, so we would reject H_0 and conclude that the population mean for men is different from the population mean for women.

If you look at the data in Figure 11.7, the statistical decision should be easy to understand. The two samples look like they come from different populations. By visually examining a graph of the data, you often can predict the outcome of a statistical test.

Now consider the data from experiment II, which are shown in Figure 11.8. Do these two samples look like they came from two separate populations? It should be clear that

Figure 11.7

Data from experiment I comparing attitude scores for men versus women. The independent measures *t* test for these data gives a *t* statistic of *t* = 9.16. This value is in the critical region, so we reject H_0 and conclude that the two samples come from different populations.

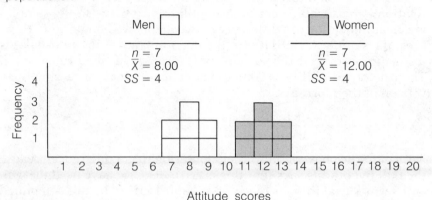

it is no longer easy to see a difference between the two samples. The scores completely overlap, and it appears likely that all 14 scores could have come from the same population.

The impression that the two samples do not look different is supported by the hypothesis test. The data from experiment II give a *t* statistic of *t* = 1.18. This value is not in the critical region so we fail to reject H_0. In this case, we conclude that there is not enough evidence to say that the samples come from two different populations.

There are two general points to be made from this example. First, variability plays an important role in the independent measures hypothesis test. In both experiments there was a four-point difference between the two sample means. In experiment I this difference was easy to see, and it was statistically significant. In experiment II this four-point difference gets lost in all the variability.

The second point is that the *t* statistic you obtain from a hypothesis test should be intuitively reasonable. In the first experiment, it looks like there are two separate populations, and the *t* statistic supports this appearance. In the second experiment, there does not appear to be any difference, and the *t* statistic says that there is no difference. The *t* value should not be a mysterious number; it simply is a precise, mathematical way of determining whether or not it "looks like" there is a difference between two samples.

Figure 11.8

Data from experiment II comparing attitude scores for men versus women. The independent measures t test for these data gives a t statistic of $t = 1.18$. This value is not in the critical region, so we fail to reject H_0 and conclude that there is not sufficient evidence to say that the two samples come from different populations.

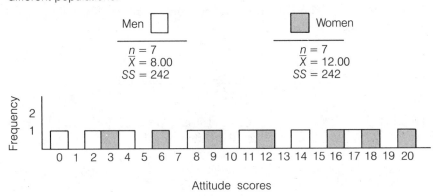

Men ☐

$n = 7$
$\overline{X} = 8.00$
$SS = 242$

Women ◼

$n = 7$
$\overline{X} = 12.00$
$SS = 242$

Attitude scores

1. A developmental psychologist would like to examine the difference in mathematical skills for 10-year-old boys versus 10-year-old girls. A sample of 10 boys and 10 girls is obtained, and each child is given a standardized mathematical abilities test. The data from this experiment are as follows:

Boys	Girls
$\overline{X} = 37$	$\overline{X} = 31$
$SS = 150$	$SS = 210$

Do these data indicate a significant difference in mathematical skills for boys versus girls? Test at the .05 level of significance.

2. A psychologist is interested in the effect of aging on memory. A sample of 10 college graduates is obtained. Five of these people are between 30 and 35 years old. The other 5 are between 60 and 65 years old. Each person is given a list of 40 words to memorize. A week later each person is asked to recall as many of the words as possible. The data from this experiment are as follows:

30-Year-Olds	60-Year-Olds
$\overline{X} = 21$	$\overline{X} = 16$
$SS = 130$	$SS = 190$

Do these data provide evidence for a significant decline in recall ability with age? Test at the .05 level of significance.

1. Pooled variance = 20; standard error = 2; t = 3.00. With df = 18, this value is in the critical region, so the decision is to reject H_0: There is a significant difference.
2. Pooled variance = 40; standard error = 4; t = 1.25. With df = 8, this value is not in the critical region, so the decision is to fail to reject H_0. These data do not provide evidence for a significant difference.

11.4

Estimation

The independent measures t statistic can be used for estimation as well as for hypothesis testing. In either case, the t statistic provides a means for using sample data to draw inferences about the difference between two population means. For the hypothesis test, the goal is to answer a yes/no question: Is there any mean difference between the two populations? For estimation, the goal is to determine *how much* difference.

Recall that the basic structure of the independent measures t formula is the same as we observed for the initial z-score or single-sample t:

$$t = \frac{\text{sample data} - \text{population parameter}}{\text{estimated standard error}}$$

Because we are interested in finding the population parameter, we will rewrite this equation as follows:

$$\text{population parameter} = \text{sample data} \pm t(\text{estimated standard error})$$

This is the basic formula for estimation. With an independent measures experimental design, the specific formula is

(11.5) $\mu_1 - \mu_2 = (\overline{X}_1 - \overline{X}_2) \pm ts_{\overline{x}_1 - \overline{x}_2}$

In words, we are using the sample mean difference, plus or minus some error, to estimate the population mean difference. To use this equation to estimate $\mu_1 - \mu_2$ requires two steps:

1. Use the sample data to compute the sample mean difference $(\overline{X}_1 - \overline{X}_2)$ and the standard error $(s_{\overline{x}_1 - \overline{x}_2})$.

2. The sample data could be used to calculate a t statistic using Formula (11.1). However, you do not know the value for the population mean difference $(\mu_1 - \mu_2)$, so the precise value of t cannot be determined. Nonetheless you can estimate where this t statistic would be located within the t distribution. You can either make a point estimate $(t = 0)$ or select a level of confidence and determine a range of values. With 90% confidence, for exam-

ple, you would estimate that the t statistic is located somewhere in the middle 90% of the t distribution.

At this point you have all of the values on the right-hand side of the equation [Formula (11.5)], and you can compute the value for $\mu_1 - \mu_2$. If you have used a single number to estimate the location of t, you will get a single, point estimate for $\mu_1 - \mu_2$. If you have used a range of values for t, you will compute a confidence interval for $\mu_1 - \mu_2$. A complete example of this estimation procedure follows.

EXAMPLE 11.4

Recent studies have allowed psychologists to establish definite links between specific foods and specific brain functions. For example, lecithin (found in soybeans, eggs, liver) has been shown to increase the concentration of certain brain chemicals that help regulate memory and motor coordination. This experiment is designed to demonstrate the importance of this particular food substance.

The experiment involves two separate samples of newborn rats (an independent measures experiment). The 10 rats in the first sample are given a normal diet containing standard amounts of lecithin. The 5 rats in the other sample are fed a special diet which contains almost no lecithin. After 6 months, each of the rats is tested on a specially designed learning problem that requires both memory and motor coordination. The purpose of the experiment is to demonstrate the deficit in performance that results from lecithin deprivation. The data from this experiment are as follows: The score for each animal is the number of errors before the learning problem was solved.

Regular Diet	No-Lecithin Diet
$n = 10$	$n = 5$
$\overline{X} = 25$	$\overline{X} = 33$
$SS = 250$	$SS = 140$

Because we fully expect that there will be a significant difference between these two treatments, we will not do the hypothesis test (although you should be able to do it). We want to use these data to obtain an estimate of the size of the difference between the two population means; that is, how much does lecithin affect learning performance? The basic equation for estimation with an independent measures experiment is

$$\mu_1 - \mu_2 = (\overline{X}_1 - \overline{X}_2) \pm ts_{\overline{x}_1 - \overline{x}_2}$$

The first step is to obtain the known values from the sample data. The sample mean difference is easy; one group averaged $\overline{X} = 25$, and the other averaged $\overline{X} = 33$, so there is an eight-point difference. Notice that it is not important whether you call this a $+8$ or a -8 difference. In either case the size of the difference is eight points, and the regular diet group scored lower. Because it is easier to do arithmetic with positive numbers, we will use

$$\overline{X}_1 - \overline{X}_2 = 8$$

To find the standard error, you first must pool the two variances:

$$s_p^2 = \frac{SS_1 + SS_2}{df_1 + df_2} = \frac{250 + 140}{9 + 4}$$

$$= \frac{390}{13}$$

$$= 30$$

Next, the pooled variance is used to compute the standard error:

$$s_{\overline{x}_1 - \overline{x}_2} = \sqrt{\frac{s_p^2}{n_1} + \frac{s_p^2}{n_2}} = \sqrt{\frac{30}{10} + \frac{30}{5}} = \sqrt{3 + 6} = \sqrt{9} = 3$$

You should recall that this standard error combines the error from the first sample and the error from the second sample. Because the first sample is much larger, $n = 10$, it should have less error. This difference shows up in the formula. The larger sample contributes an error of three points, and the smaller sample contributes six points, which combine for a total error of nine points under the square root.

Sample 1 has df = 9, and sample 2 has df = 4. The t statistic has df = 9 + 4 = 13.

The final value needed on the right-hand side of the equation is t. The data from this experiment would produce a t statistic with $df = 13$. With 13 degrees of freedom, we can sketch the distribution of all the possible t values. This distribution is shown in Figure 11.9. The t statistic for our data is somewhere in this distribution. The problem is to estimate where. For a point estimate, the best bet is to use $t = 0$. This is the most likely value, located exactly in the middle of the distribution. To gain more confidence in the estimate, you can select a range of t values. For 80% confidence, for example, you would estimate that the t statistic is somewhere in the middle 80% of the distribution. Checking the table, you find that the middle 80% is bounded by values of $t = +1.350$ and $t = -1.350$.

Using these t values and the sample values computed earlier, we now can estimate the magnitude of the performance deficit caused by lecithin deprivation.

For a point esimate, use the single-value (point) estimate of $t = 0$:

$$\mu_1 - \mu_2 = (\overline{X}_1 - \overline{X}_2) + ts_{\overline{x}_1 - \overline{x}_2}$$

$$= 8 + 0(3)$$

$$= 8$$

Notice that the result simply uses the sample mean difference to estimate the population mean difference. The conclusion is that lecithin deprivation produces an average of 8 more errors on the learning task. (Based on the fact that the normal animals averaged around 25 errors, an 8-point increase would mean a performance deficit of approximately 30%.)

For an interval estimate, or confidence interval, use the range of t values. With 80% confidence, at one extreme,

$$\mu_1 - \mu_2 = (\overline{X}_1 - \overline{X}_2) + ts_{\overline{x}_1 - \overline{x}_2}$$

$$= 8 + 1.350(3)$$

$$= 8 + 4.05$$

$$= 12.05$$

and at the other extreme,

$$\mu_1 - \mu_2 = (\overline{X}_1 - \overline{X}_2) - ts_{\overline{x}_1 - \overline{x}_2}$$

$$= 8 - 1.350(3)$$

$$= 8 - 4.05$$

$$= 3.95$$

Figure 11.9
The distribution of t values with $df = 13$. Note that t values pile up around zero and that 80% of the values are between $+1.350$ and -1.350.

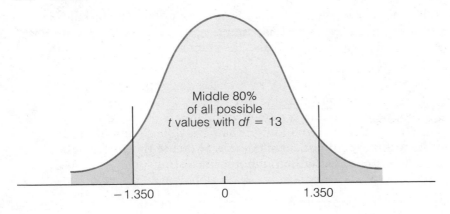

Middle 80%
of all possible
t values with $df = 13$

−1.350   0   1.350

This time we are concluding that the effect of lecithin deprivation is to increase errors with an average increase somewhere between 3.95 and 12.05 errors. We are 80% confident of this estimate because the only thing estimated was the location of the t statistic and we used the middle 80% of all the possible t values.

Note that the result of the point estimate is to say that lecithin deprivation will increase errors by exactly 8. To gain confidence, you must lose precision and say that errors will increase by around 8 (for 80% confidence, we say that the average increase will be 8 ± 4.05).

1. In families with several children, the first-born children tend to be more reserved and serious, while the last-born children tend to be more outgoing and happy-go-lucky. A psychologist is using a standardized personality inventory to measure the magnitude of this difference. A sample of eight first-born and eight last-born children is obtained. Each child is given the personality test. The results of this test are as follows:

First-Born	Last-Born
$\bar{X} = 11.4$	$\bar{X} = 13.9$
$SS = 26$	$SS = 30$

   a. Use these sample data to make a point estimate of the population mean difference in personality for first-born versus last-born children.
   b. Make an interval estimate of the population mean difference so that you are 80% confident that the true mean difference is in your interval.

ANSWERS

1. a. For a point estimate, use the sample mean difference: $\bar{X}_1 - \bar{X}_2 = 2.5$ points.
    b. With $df = 14$, the middle 80% of all possible t statistics is bounded by $t = +1.345$ and $t = -1.345$. For these data the pooled variance is 4, and the standard error is 1. The 80% confidence interval is 1.155 to 3.845.

11.5

Assumptions Underlying the t Formula

There are two assumptions that should be satisfied before you use the independent measures t formula for either hypothesis testing or estimation:

   1. The distribution of the sample mean differences should be normal.

2. The two populations from which the samples are selected must have the same variance.

The first assumption should be very familiar by now. In both the z-score formula and the single-sample t formula, it was necessary that the sample data come from a normal distribution. For an independent measures experiment, the sample data consist of a mean difference $(\overline{X}_1 - \overline{X}_2)$, and, once again, these data should form a normal distribution. To satisfy this assumption, it is necessary that the distribution of sample means for both samples ($\overline{X}_1$ and $\overline{X}_2$) be normal. You should recall from Chapter 7 that these sampling distributions do tend to be normal. Specifically, these distributions will be normal and the assumption will be satisfied if either

a. The two populations are normal or
b. Both samples are relatively large (n around 30 or more).

In general, this assumption is satisfied easily and is not a cause for concern in most research. When there is reason to suspect that the populations are far from normal in shape, you should compensate by ensuring that samples are relatively large.

The second assumption is referred to as *homogeneity of variance* and states that the two populations being compared must have the same variance. You may recall a similar assumption for both the z-score and the single-sample t. For those tests, we assumed that the effect of the treatment was to add (or subtract) a constant amount to each individual score. As a result, the population standard deviation after treatment was the same as it had been before treatment. We now are making essentially the same assumption but phrasing it in terms of variances.

Remember, adding (or subtracting) a constant to each score does not change the standard deviation.

You should recall that the pooled variance in the t statistic formula is obtained by averaging together the two sample variances. It makes sense to average these two values only if they both are estimating the same population variance, i.e., if the homogeneity of variance assumption is satisfied. If the two sample variances represent different population variances, then the average would be meaningless. (*Note:* There is no meaning to the value obtained by averaging two unrelated numbers. For example, what is the significance of the number obtained by averaging your shoe size and the last two digits of your social security number?)

The homogeneity of variance assumption is quite important because violating this assumption can negate any meaningful interpretation of the data from an independent measures experiment. Specifically, when you compute the t statistic in a hypothesis test, all of the numbers in the formula come from the data except for the population mean difference which you get from H_0. Thus, you are sure of all the numbers in the formula except for one. If you obtain an extreme result for the t statistic (a value in the critical region), you conclude that the hypothesized value was wrong. But consider what happens when you violate the homogeneity of variance assumption. In this case, you have two questionable values in the formula (the hypothesized population value and the meaningless average of the two variances). Now if you obtain an extreme t statistic, you do not know which of these two values is responsible. Specifically, you cannot reject the hypothesis because it may have been the pooled variance that produced the extreme t statistic. Without satisfying the homogeneity of variance requirement, you cannot accurately interpret a t statistic, and the hypothesis test becomes meaningless.

How do you know whether or not the homogeneity of variance requirement is satisfied? There are statistical tests that can be used to determine if the two population variances are the same or different (see Box 11.2), but there is a simple rule of thumb that works most of the time. If the two population variances are the same, then the two sample variances should be very similar. You can just look at the two sample variances to see whether or not they are close. If one of the sample variances is more than four times larger than the other, you probably have violated the homogeneity of variance requirement. Otherwise the two population variances are close enough to proceed with the hypothesis test.

BOX 11.2 | **Hartley's *F*-Max Test for Homogeneity of Variance**

Although there are many different statistical methods for determining whether or not the homogeneity of variance assumption has been satisfied, Hartley's *F*-max test is one of the simplest to compute and to understand. An additional advantage is that this test can be used to check homogeneity of variance with two or more independent samples. In later chapters we will examine statistical methods involving several samples, and Hartley's test will be useful again.

The *F*-max test is based on the principle that a sample variance provides an unbiased estimate of the population variance. Therefore, if the population variances are the same, the sample variances should be very similar. The procedure for using the *F*-max test is as follows:

1. Compute the sample variance, $s^2 = SS/df$, for each of the separate samples.

2. Select the largest and the smallest of these sample variances and compute

$$F\text{-max} = \frac{s^2 \, (\text{largest})}{s^2 \, (\text{smallest})}$$

A relatively large value for *F*-max indicates a large difference between the sample variances. In this case, the data suggest that the population variances are different and that the homogeneity assumption has been violated. On the other hand, a small value of *F*-max (near 1.00) indicates that the sample variances are

BOX 11.2 *continued*

similar and that the homogeneity assumption is reasonable.

3. The *F*-max value computed for the sample data is compared with the critical value found in Table B3 (Appendix B, page A-31). If the sample value is larger than the table value, then you conclude that the variances are different and that the homogeneity assumption is not valid.

To locate the critical value in the table, you need to know

a. k = number of separate samples. (For the independent measures *t* test, $k = 2$.)
b. $df = n - 1$ for each sample variance. The Hartley test assumes that all samples are the same size.
c. The α level. The table provides critical values for $\alpha = .05$ and $\alpha = .01$. Generally, a test for homogeneity would use the larger alpha level.

Example: Two independent samples each have $n = 10$. The sample variances are 12.34 and 9.15. For these data,

$$F\text{-max} = \frac{s^2 \,(\text{largest})}{s^2 \,(\text{smallest})} = \frac{12.34}{9.15} = 1.35$$

With $\alpha = .05$, $k = 2$, and $df = n - 1 = 9$, the critical value from the table is 4.03. Because the obtained *F*-max is smaller than this critical value, you conclude that the data do not provide evidence that the homogeneity of variance assumption has been violated.

Summary

1. The independent measures *t* statistic is used to draw inferences about the mean difference between two populations or between two treatment conditions. The term *independent* is used because this *t* statistic requires data from two separate (or independent) samples.

2. The formula for the independent measures *t* statistic has the same structure as the original *z*-score or the single-sample *t:*

$$t = \frac{\text{sample data} - \text{population parameter}}{\text{estimated standard error}}$$

For the independent measures statistic, the data consist of the difference between the two sample means ($\overline{X}_1 - \overline{X}_2$). The population parameter of interest is the difference between the two population means ($\mu_1 - \mu_2$). The standard error is computed by combining the errors for the two sample means.

The resulting formula is

$$t = \frac{(\overline{X}_1 - \overline{X}_2) - (\mu_1 - \mu_2)}{s_{\overline{x}_1 - \overline{x}_2}} = \frac{(\overline{X}_1 - \overline{X}_2) - (\mu_1 - \mu_2)}{\sqrt{\dfrac{s_p^2}{n_1} + \dfrac{s_p^2}{n_2}}}$$

The pooled variance in the formula, s_p^2, is the weighted mean of the two sample variances:

$$s_p^2 = \frac{SS_1 + SS_2}{df_1 + df_2}$$

This t statistic has degrees of freedom determined by the sum of the df values for the two samples:

$$df = df_1 + df_2$$
$$= (n_1 - 1) + (n_2 - 1)$$

3. For hypothesis testing, the formula has the following structure:

$$t = \frac{\text{sample data} - \text{hypothesized population parameter}}{\text{estimated standard error}}$$

The null hypothesis normally states that there is no difference between the two population means:

$$H_0: \quad \mu_1 = \mu_2 \quad \text{or} \quad \mu_1 - \mu_2 = 0$$

4. For estimation, the formula is solved for the value of $\mu_1 - \mu_2$:

$$\mu_1 - \mu_2 = (\overline{X}_1 - \overline{X}_2) \pm ts_{\overline{x}_1 - \overline{x}_2}$$

To use this formula, you first decide on a degree of precision and a level of confidence desired for the estimate. If your primary concern is precision, use $t = 0$ to make a point estimate of the mean difference. Otherwise you select a level of confidence (percent confidence) that determines a range of t values to be used in the formula.

5. Appropriate use and interpretation of the t statistic requires that the data satisfy the homogeneity of variance assumption. This assumption stipulates that the two populations have equal variances. An informal test of this assumption can be made by simply comparing the two sample variances: If the two sample variances are approximately equal, the t test is justified. Hartley's F-max test provides a statistical technique for determining whether or not the data satisfy the homogeneity assumption.

Key Terms

independent measures
  experimental design
between subjects experimental
  design

pooled variance
homogeneity of variance

Problems for Chapter 11:
Statistical Inference with Two Independent Samples

*1. A psychologist would like to compare the amount of information that people get from television versus newspapers. A random sample of 20 people is obtained. Ten of these people agree to get all of their news information from TV (no newspapers) for 4 weeks. The other 10 people agree to get all of their news information from newspapers. At the end of 4 weeks all 20 people are given a test on current events. The average score for the TV group was $\overline{X} = 41$ with $SS = 200$. The average for the newspaper group was $\overline{X} = 49$ with $SS = 160$. On the basis of these data, can the psychologist conclude that there is a significant difference between TV news and newspapers? Test at the .05 level of significance.

2. A local politician would like to compare the political attitudes for the older people and the younger people in his district. He develops a questionnaire which measures political attitude on a scale from 0 (very conservative) to 100 (very liberal) and administers this questionnaire to a sample of 10 young voters and a sample of 10 elderly voters. The data from these two samples are as follows:

Old	Young
$\overline{X} = 39$	$\overline{X} = 52$
$SS = 4200$	$SS = 4800$

On the basis of these data, should the politician conclude that there is a significant difference between political attitudes for younger voters and older voters? Test with $\alpha = .05$.

*3. A psychologist is studying the relation between weight and hormone levels. A random sample of rats is selected, and the sample is divided into two groups of five rats each. The rats in one group are given daily injections of a "growth" hormone, and the rats in the second group are injected with a harmless salt solution. During a 2-week test period, the psychologist records the amount of weight gained by each rat. The data are as follows:

Hormone	Control
$\overline{X} = 22$	$\overline{X} = 8$
$SS = 140$	$SS = 180$

a. Use these data to determine whether the hormone injections have any significant effect on weight gain. Test at the .05 level.

b. Use the data to estimate how much extra weight gain the hormone produces. Make a point estimate and an interval estimate so that you are 80% confident that the true mean difference is in your interval.

4. In an experiment designed to examine the effect that personality can have on practical decisions, a psychologist selects a random sample of $n = 5$ people who are classified as "impulsive" and a sample of $n = 10$ people who are classified as "reflective." Each person is given a brief description of a crime and then is asked for his/her judgment of a reasonable prison sentence for the criminal. The impulsive people gave an average sentence of 14 years with $SS = 130$, and the reflective people gave an average sentence of 12.5 years with $SS = 260$. On the basis of these samples, can the psychologist conclude that there is a significant difference in the harshness of judgment for impulsive versus reflective people? Test with $\alpha = .01$.

*5. A researcher has done a series of experiments to determine whether there is any significant difference between two treatments. The data from three of these experiments are as follows:

Experiment I		Experiment II		Experiment III	
A	B	A	B	A	B
$n = 5$	$n = 5$	$n = 5$	$n = 5$	$n = 5$	$n = 5$
$\overline{X} = 40$	$\overline{X} = 35$	$\overline{X} = 40$	$\overline{X} = 35$	$\overline{X} = 40$	$\overline{X} = 38$
$SS = 36$	$SS = 44$	$SS = 120$	$SS = 200$	$SS = 36$	$SS = 44$

a. Use the data from each experiment to determine whether there is any significant difference between treatment A and treatment B. Test at the .05 level of significance.

b. How do you explain the fact that the results of experiments I and II lead to different conclusions? Notice that the sample means are identical for these two experiments.

c. How do you explain that experiments I and III lead to different conclusions? Note that the sample SS values are identical for these two experiments.

6. A local hospital is planning a fund-raising campaign to raise money for the expansion of their pediatrics ward. Part of the campaign will involve visits to local industries to present their case to employees and to solicit contributions. One factory is selected as a test site to compare two different campaign strategies. Within this factory the employees are randomly divided into two groups. The individuals in one group are presented the "hard facts" (number of people served, costs, etc.) about the hospital. The individuals in the second group receive an "emotional appeal" that describes in detail the personal histories of two children recently treated at the hospital. The aver-

age contribution for the 20 employees in the hard facts group was $21.50 with $SS = 970$. The average for the 20 employees in the emotional group was $29.80 with $SS = 550$.

    a. On the basis of these sample data, should the hospital conclude that one strategy is significantly better than the other? Test at the .05 level of significance.

    b. Use Hartley's F-max test to determine whether these data satisfy the homogeneity of variance assumption.

*7. A psychologist would like to know how much difference there is between the problem-solving ability of 8-year-old children versus 10-year-old children. A random sample of 10 children is selected from each age group. The children are given a problem-solving test, and the results are summarized as follows:

8-Year-Olds	10-Year-Olds
$n = 10$	$n = 10$
$\bar{X} = 36$	$\bar{X} = 43$
$SS = 110$	$SS = 250$

    a. Use the sample data to make a point estimate of the mean difference between 8-year-olds' and 10-year-olds' problem-solving ability.

    b. Make an interval estimate of the mean difference so that you are 90% confident that the real difference is in your interval.

8. Do the data in Problem 7 satisfy the homogeneity of variance assumption? Use Hartley's F-max test with $\alpha = .05$.

*9. A psychologist would like to examine the effects of fatigue on mental alertness. An attention test is prepared which requires subjects to sit in front of a blank TV screen and press a response button each time a dot appears on the screen. A total of 110 dots are presented during a 90-minute period, and the psychologist records the number of errors for each subject. Two groups of subjects are selected. The first group ($n = 5$) is tested after they have been kept awake for 24 hours. The second group ($n = 10$) is tested in the morning after a full night's sleep. The data for these two samples are as follows:

Awake 24 Hours	Rested
$\bar{X} = 35$	$\bar{X} = 24$
$SS = 120$	$SS = 270$

On the basis of these data, can the psychologist conclude that fatigue has a significant effect on attention? Test at the .05 level of significance.

10. A school psychologist would like to examine cheating behavior for 10-year-old children. A standardized achievement test is used. One sample of $n = 8$ children is given the test under unsupervised conditions where cheating is possible. A second sample of 8 children receives the same test under very strict supervision. The test scores for these children are summarized as follows:

Unsupervised	Supervised
$\overline{X} = 78$	$\overline{X} = 65$
$SS = 3000$	$SS = 2600$

Can the psychologist conclude that the unsupervised (cheating?) group did significantly better than the strictly supervised group? Test at the .05 level of significance.

*11. A psychologist would like to measure the effects of air pollution on life expectancy. Two samples of newborn rats are selected. The first sample of 10 rats is housed in cages where the atmosphere is equivalent to the air in a severely polluted city. The second sample with $n = 20$ is placed in cages with clean air. The average life span for the first group is $\overline{X} = 478$ days with $SS = 5020$ and for the second group $\overline{X} = 511$ with $SS = 10,100$.

   a. Does pollution cause a difference in life expectancy? Test with $\alpha = .01$.

   b. Make a point estimate of the mean difference in life span for polluted versus clean air.

   c. Make an interval estimate of the mean difference so that you are 95% confident that the true difference is in your interval.

*12. A psychologist studying human memory would like to examine the process of forgetting. One group of subjects is required to memorize a list of words in the evening just before going to bed. Their recall is tested 10 hours later in the morning. Subjects in the second group memorize the same list of words in the morning, and then their memories are tested 10 hours later after being awake all day. The psychologist hypothesizes that there will be less forgetting during sleep than during a busy day. The recall scores for two samples of college students are as follows:

Asleep Scores				Awake Scores			
15	13	14	14	15	13	14	12
16	15	16	15	14	13	11	12
16	15	17	14	13	13	12	14

   a. Sketch a frequency distribution polygon for the "asleep" group. On the same graph (in a different color) sketch the distribution for the "awake" group. Just by looking at these two distributions, would you predict a significant difference between the two treatment conditions?

b. Use the independent measures t statistic to determine whether there is a significant difference between the treatments. Conduct the test with $\alpha = .05$.

13. The experiment described in Problem 12 was repeated using samples of 6-year-old children. The data for this experiment are as follows:

Asleep Scores				Awake Scores			
15	13	8	10	6	8	5	8
7	10	6	9	4	7	12	9
14	11	5	12	3	10	13	11

a. Again, sketch a frequency distribution polygon for each group on the same graph. Does there appear to be a significant difference between the two treatments?

b. Use the independent measures t statistic to test for significance with $\alpha = .05$.

c. Note that the data from Problem 12 and the data here show the same mean difference. Explain why the statistical analysis produces different conclusions for these two problems.

*14. An instructor would like to evaluate the effectiveness of a new programmed learning course in statistics. The class is randomly divided in half. One group gets the regular lecture series and textbook, while the other group takes the programmed course. At the end of the semester all students take the same final exam. The scores are as follows:

Regular Course Grades			Programmed Course Grades		
82	73	93	92	82	97
61	89	99	81	80	62
73	91	84	72	74	68
71	68	81	84	81	71
75	72	69	63	65	73

Use these data to determine whether there is any significant difference between the programmed course and the regular course. Test at the .05 level.

15. Although the instructor from Problem 14 found no significant difference in grades for the two different statistics courses, it is possible that the students preferred one teaching method over the other. At the end of the course, each student was given a course-evaluation questionnaire that included a question about how much he/she enjoyed the course. The responses range from 1 (not at all) to 5 (very much). The data for the two sections of students are as follows:

Regular Course				Programmed Course			
4	4	3	4	3	4	2	3
4	2	4	5	4	4	2	2
3	4	5	5	4	3	2	2
4	5	5		3	2	5	

Do these data indicate a significant preference between the two teaching methods? Test with $\alpha = .05$.

16. A researcher is interested in testing the opinions of college students concerning the value of their college education. She suspects that seniors will place more value on their education than will sophomores. A sample of 20 seniors and 20 sophomores is selected, and each subject is given an opinion questionnaire. The data for each sample are as follows:

Sophomores				Seniors			
18	21	24	21	25	19	23	22
20	19	23	26	23	21	21	18
19	24	19	28	27	18	28	21
22	17	27	18	26	25	22	16
25	22	14	17	21	29	18	20

With $\alpha = .05$, do these data indicate a significant difference in opinion between seniors and sophomores?

*17. A principal for a city high school would like to determine parents' attitudes toward a proposed sex education program. A sample of 15 families is selected, and each set of parents is requested to fill out an opinion questionnaire. Part of this questionnaire requires the parents' names and occupations. Looking over the data, the principal noticed that the opinions seemed to be a lot more favorable than had been expected. The principal suspected that the parents might have felt "forced" into stating a favorable opinion because they were required to identify themselves. They might have responded more honestly if the questionnaire had been anonymous. Therefore, a second sample of 15 families was selected, and they were requested to complete the same questionnaire without reporting their names or occupations. The data from both questionnaires are as follows:

First Questionnaire					Second Questionnaire				
60	56	54	58	63	51	50	53	48	42
61	52	49	57	58	52	57	47	49	50
65	59	42	51	67	51	43	48	53	41

Use these data to test the principal's hypothesis. Set $\alpha = .05$.

18. In a test of cognitive dissonance theory, Festinger and Carlsmith (1959) had college students participate in a really boring experiment. Later these students were asked to recruit

other subjects for the same experiment by pretending that it was an interesting experience. Some of these students were paid $20 to recruit others, and some were paid only $1. Afterward, each student was asked to report how he/she really felt about the experiment. Hypothetical data representing these reports are as follows:

Students Paid $1					Students Paid $20			
3	3	4	6		1	2	5	2
5	5	5	7		3	5	4	5
8	5	4	8		2	3	4	4
2	6	4	4		1	2	3	3
6	7	5	5		5	1	1	3

Cognitive dissonance theory predicts that those paid only $1 would come to believe that the experiment really was interesting. It must have been, or they wouldn't have worked so hard for only $1. The students paid $20 were working for money, not for the experiment, so they should have no reason to change their opinions. Do the preceding data support this prediction? Test for a significant difference between the two groups with $\alpha = .01$.

*19. a. Sketch a frequency distribution polygon showing the following samples. Use a different color for each set of scores.

Sample 1				Sample 2		
14	18	12		15	21	16
11	18	15		22	14	12
15	17	16		19	20	18
15	18	14		20	21	17
16	14	15		22	19	20
16	17	13		20	19	18

   b. By just looking at your polygon, does it appear that these two samples came from different populations, or from the same population?

   c. Calculate the independent measures t statistic for these data. Does the t statistic indicate that the samples came from different populations? Set $\alpha = .05$.

20. The following data came from an independent measures experiment comparing two different treatment conditions. The score for each subject is the amount of time (measured in minutes) required to complete a set of math problems.

Treatment 1 (Sample 1)		Treatment 2 (Sample 2)	
2.5	3.2	1.8	2.1
3.4	2.9	2.0	1.6
2.4	2.6	1.9	2.3
2.5	3.0	2.2	2.5
2.7	3.1	1.8	2.1

a. Use an independent measures t statistic to determine whether or not there is a significant difference between the two treatments. Use $\alpha = .05$.

b. The experimenter would like to convert each subject's score from minutes to seconds. To do this, each value must be multiplied by 60. After each value is multiplied, what will happen to the sample means? What will happen to the sample standard deviations? What do you expect will happen to the t statistic for these data?

c. Multiply each of the original scores by 60 (i.e., change them from minutes to seconds). Now compute the independent measures t statistic for the new scores? How does this t statistic compare with the t statistic for the original data?

CHAPTER 12

The Repeated Measures *t* Statistic

The following items are considered essential background material for this chapter. If you doubt your knowledge of any of these items, you should review the appropriate chapter or section before proceeding.

1. Introduction to the *t* statistic (Chapter 10)
   a. Estimated standard error
   b. Degrees of freedom
   c. *t* Distribution
   d. Hypothesis tests with the *t* statistic
   e. Estimation using the *t* statistic
2. Independent measures design (Chapter 11)

Sometimes a researcher is specifically interested in how a treatment changes behavior for the *same set* of subjects. For example, Davison (1968) studied the effects of a variety of treatments on anxiety and avoidance provoked by aversive stimuli. Among the many questions addressed, he tested the effectiveness of systematic desensitization on the avoidance of snakes. In one part of the study, Davison used a sample of subjects that was first tested for the amount of avoidance behavior displayed in the presence of a snake. These same individuals then received the desensitization treatment, which consisted of combining relaxation training with exposure to increasingly aversive snake-related stimuli. After the desensitization program, the subjects were tested once again for their avoidance of snakes.

When a single sample of individuals is tested more than once on a dependent variable, the experimenter is using a repeated measures design. Often in this design the sample provides control data in the form of a pretreatment test. These initial scores may serve as a baseline against which subsequent measurements can be compared. In this experiment, the sample of individuals was tested more than once, both before and after the treatment. The researcher looked for a mean difference (that is, a mean change) between the first and second measures. By comparing initial avoidance scores to those displayed after treatment, Davison (1968) found evidence that systematic desensitization reduced avoidance of snakes. In this chapter, we will develop and use the *t* statistic that is used for the repeated measures study.

12.1
Introduction to Repeated Measures

Previously we discussed inferential techniques using two separate samples to examine the mean difference between two populations. Usually, our goal was to evaluate the difference between two treatment conditions. For example, if a researcher would like to assess the effect of a new drug on depression, he/she might use two treatment conditions: a drug treatment and a no-drug treatment. With an independent measures design (Chapter 11), one sample of patients receives the drug, and the other sample receives an ineffective placebo. Depression can be measured by the subjects' scores on a depression inventory. Differences in the severity of depression between these two samples may then be used to test the effectiveness of the new drug. This independent measures design can be recognized by the assignment of separate, or "independent," samples of subjects for each treatment condition.

It should be obvious that there is a different experimental technique that could be used to evaluate the drug. Specifically, you could use a single sample of subjects and measure their depression scores before they receive the drug and then repeat the measurements after they have received the drug. This experimental design is called *repeated measures* because you are repeating measurements on a single sample of subjects.

DEFINITION

A *repeated measures* study is one in which a single sample of individuals is tested more than once on the dependent variable. The same subjects are used for every treatment condition.

Let us examine the statistical techniques that allow a researcher to use the sample data from a repeated measures experiment to draw inferences about the general population.

Difference Scores

Table 12.1 presents hypothetical data for a drug evaluation study. The first score for each person (X_1) is the score obtained on the depression inventory before the drug treatment. The second score (X_2) was obtained after the drug treatment. Because we are interested in how much change occurs as a result of the treatment, each person's scores are summarized as a single difference score. This is accomplished by subtracting the first score (before treatment) from the second score (after treatment) for each person:

(12.1) difference score = D-score = $X_2 - X_1$

The difference scores, or D-scores, are shown in the last column of the table. Note that the sign of the D-scores tells you the direction of change. For example, person A showed a decrease in depression, as indicated by the negative difference score.

The researcher's goal is to use this sample of difference scores to answer questions about the general population. Notice that the population we are interested in is a population of difference scores. This is the population that would be obtained if we measured every individual before and after receiving the drug and recorded the entire population of difference scores. Because populations usually are too large to test in an experiment, investigators must rely on the data from samples. Do these data indicate that the drug has a significant effect (more than chance)? How big is the effect? Our problem is to use the limited data from a sample to draw inferences about the population. This problem is diagrammed in Figure 12.1.

Table 12.1

Scores on a Depression Inventory Before and After Drug Treatment

Person	Before Treatment, X_1	After Treatment, X_2	D
A	72	64	−8
B	68	60	−8
C	60	50	−10
D	71	66	−5
E	55	56	+1

$$\Sigma D = -30$$

$$\overline{D} = \frac{\Sigma D}{n} = \frac{-30}{5} = -6$$

Figure 12.1

Because populations are usually too large to test in a study, the researcher selects a random sample from the population. The sample data are used to make inferences (hypothesis tests or estimation) about the population mean μ_D. The data of interest in the repeated measures study are difference scores (D-scores) for each subject.

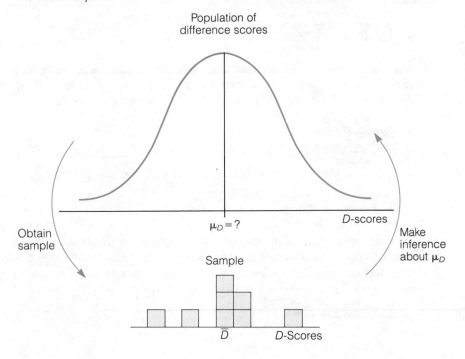

Notice that the problem we are facing here is essentially identical to the situation we encountered in Chapter 10. We have a single sample of scores that must be used to draw inferences about a single population. In Chapter 10 we introduced a t statistic that allowed us to use the sample mean as a basis for testing hypotheses about the population mean and for estimating the population mean. This t statistic formula will be used again here to develop the repeated measures t test.

The t Statistic for Repeated Measures

To refresh your memory, the single-sample t statistic (Chapter 10) is defined by the formula

$$t = \frac{\overline{X} - \mu}{s_{\overline{x}}}$$

The sample mean $\overline{X}$ comes from the data. The population mean μ is the unknown value for which we hypothesize a value. The standard error $s_{\overline{x}}$ (also computed from the sample data) gives a measure of the error between the sample mean and the expected population mean.

For the repeated measures experiment, the sample data are difference scores and are identified by the letter D rather than X. Therefore, we will substitute Ds in the formula in place of Xs to emphasize that we are dealing with D-scores instead of X values. Also, the population mean that is of interest to us is the population mean difference (the mean amount of change for the entire population), so we will identify this parameter with the symbol μ_D. With these simple changes, the t formula for the repeated measures design becomes

(12.2) $\quad t = \dfrac{\overline{D} - \mu_D}{s_{\overline{D}}}$

The standard error in this formula, $s_{\overline{D}}$, is computed exactly as it was in the original single-sample t statistic. First, we compute the standard deviation for the sample (this time a sample of D-scores):

$$s = \sqrt{\frac{SS}{n-1}}$$

Then we divide this value by the square root of the sample size:

(12.3) $\quad s_{\overline{D}} = \dfrac{s}{\sqrt{n}}$

Notice that the sample data we are using consist of the D-scores and that there is only one D-score for each subject. Because there are only n difference scores in the sample, our t statistic will have degrees of freedom equal to

(12.4) $\quad df = n - 1$

Note that this formula is identical to the *df* equation used for the single-sample *t* statistic (Chapter 10). However, *n* refers to the number of *D*-scores, not the number of *X* values.

12.2
Hypothesis Tests with the Repeated Measures *t* Test

The Hypotheses

In a repeated measures experiment we are interested in whether or not any change occurs between scores in the first treatment and scores in the second treatment. In statistical terms, we are interested in the population mean difference μ_D. Is the population mean difference equal to zero (no change), or has a change occurred? For hypothesis tests, we first must hypothesize how much mean change is expected for the population. Specifically, we must hypothesize a value for μ_D, the population mean of *D*-scores. As always, the null hypothesis states that there is no treatment effect. In symbols, this is

$$H_0: \quad \mu_D = 0$$

The alternative hypothesis states that there is a difference between the treatments. In symbols, this is

$$H_1: \quad \mu_D \neq 0$$

The two examples that follow will illustrate the repeated measures experiment in situations where (1) the null hypothesis is true and (2) the null hypothesis is false.

When H_0 Is True In the first example, a researcher is examining whether or not the IQ scores for ninth graders are affected by a course in speed reading. For the sake of argument, we will assume that the course actually has no effect on IQ; that is, the null hypothesis is true. This experiment would require measuring each individual's IQ before and after taking the speed-reading course. Even though the course has no effect, you generally will find some difference between the first score and the second score for individual subjects. For some cases there will be a slight increase in IQ; in others a decrease will occur. These differences are due to chance and represent the influence of uncontrolled variables. Some subjects, for example, might have a sleepless night between the first and second test and show a temporary decrease in IQ score caused by fatigue. Others may be more rested and more alert for the second test and, therefore, show an increase in IQ. Because these and similar changes are random and unsystematic, they will average zero for the entire population. (See Figure 12.2.) You also should note that even though the population mean difference is zero, the sample mean probably will not be exactly

Figure 12.2
For the population of difference scores, $\mu_D = 0$ when the null hypothesis is true (no treatment effect). Notice that the mean for the sample of D-scores is not exactly zero (the value of the population mean). However, the sample mean, $\overline{D} = +1.20$, is close to zero.

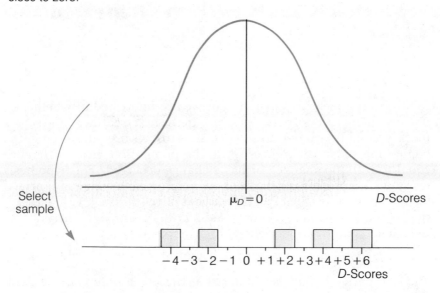

equal to zero. Remember, samples are not expected to be exactly the same as the populations they come from. The sample mean should be close to the population mean but probably will not be identical.

When H_0 Is False   For our second example, we will assume that H_0 actually is false and that the speed-reading course does work. Suppose it has the effect of adding 10 points to each individual's IQ score. Now we expect an average increase in IQ of approximately 10 points. Notice that the difference score for any particular subject probably will not be exactly equal to 10. In addition to the systematic change caused by the course, we still have the random changes caused by uncontrolled variables. For example, one subject who failed to have breakfast before the second IQ test might be fatigued and hungry and show an increase of only 8 points: a 10-point increase caused by the course and a 2-point decrease resulting from no breakfast. Again, this random variability should average to zero so that the mean change in IQ for the population will be 10 points. (See Figure 12.3.) As in the first example, you should realize that a sample selected from this population probably will not have a mean difference of exactly 10 points. However, the sample mean is expected to be close to the population mean.

As we saw in previous tests, the level of significance defines what values are sufficiently "far away" to reject H_0.

As a statistician, your job is to determine whether the sample data support or refute the null hypothesis. In simple terms, we must decide whether sample mean difference is close to zero (indicating no change) or far from zero (indicating there is a change). The t statistic helps us determine if the sample data are "close to" or "far from" zero.

Figure 12.3

For this example, the null hypothesis is false. The treatment effect for the population is reflected by its mean, $\mu_D = +10$. Notice that the mean for the sample of D-scores, $\overline{D} = 11.2$, is not identical to the mean of the population.

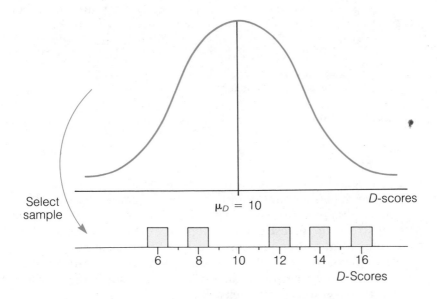

Procedures and Steps

The repeated measures t test procedure follows the same outline we have used in other situations. The basic steps for hypothesis testing are reviewed here.

STEP 1. The hypotheses are stated, and an alpha level is selected. For the repeated measures experiment, the null hypothesis is stated symbolically as

H_0: $\mu_D = 0$

The alternative hypothesis is

H_1: $\mu_D \neq 0$

Directional hypotheses can be used as well and would predict whether μ_D is greater or smaller than zero. A one-tailed test is used in those instances (Chapter 9).

STEP 2. The critical region is located. As before, the critical region is defined as values that would be very unlikely (probability less than alpha) if H_0 is true. Because the repeated measures test uses a t statistic with $df = n - 1$, we simply compute df and look up the critical values in the t distribution table.

STEP 3. Compute the test statistic, in this case the t statistic for repeated measures. We first must find the sample mean $\overline{D}$ and the SS for the set of D-scores. From the SS, we compute the sample standard deviation s and then the estimated standard error $s_{\overline{D}}$. These values are then plugged into the t formula.

STEP 4. If the obtained value falls in the critical region, we reject H_0 and conclude that there is a significant treatment effect. Remember, it is very unlikely for the t value to be in the critical region if H_0 is true. On the other hand, if the obtained t is not in the critical region, then we fail to reject H_0 and conclude that the sample data do not provide sufficient evidence for a treatment effect.

The complete hypothesis procedure is demonstrated in Example 12.1.

EXAMPLE 12.1

A researcher in behavioral medicine believes that stress often makes asthma symptoms worse for people who suffer from this respiratory disorder. Because of the suspected role of stress, the investigator decides to examine the effect of relaxation training on the severity of asthma symptoms. A sample of five patients is selected for the study. During the week before treatment, the investigator records the severity of their symptoms by measuring how many doses of medication are needed for asthma attacks. Then the patients receive relaxation training. For the week following training, the researcher once again records the number of doses required by each patient. Table 12.2 shows the data and summarizes the findings. Do these data indicate that relaxation training alters the severity of symptoms?

Table 12.2

The Number of Doses of Medication Needed for Asthma Attacks Before and After Relaxation Training

Patient	Week Before Training	Week After Training	D	D^2
A	9	4	−5	25
B	4	1	−3	9
C	5	5	0	0
D	4	0	−4	16
E	5	1	−4	16

$$\Sigma D = -16 \qquad \Sigma D^2 = 66$$

$$\overline{D} = \frac{\Sigma D}{n} = \frac{-16}{5} = -3.2$$

$$SS = \Sigma D^2 - \frac{(\Sigma D)^2}{n} = 66 - \frac{(-16)^2}{5}$$

$$= 66 - 51.2 = 14.8$$

STEP 1.   State hypotheses and select alpha:

H_0: $\mu_D = 0$ (no change in symptoms)
H_1: $\mu_D \neq 0$ (there is a change)

The level of significance is set at $\alpha = .05$ for a two-tailed test.

STEP 2.   Locate the critical region. For this example, $n = 5$, so the t statistic will have $df = n - 1 = 4$. From the t distribution table, you should find that the critical values are $+2.776$ and -2.776. These values are shown in Figure 12.4.

STEP 3.   Calculate the repeated measures t statistic. The mean for this sample is $\overline{D} = -3.2$. To compute the SS for the D-scores, we will use the computational formula:

$$SS = \Sigma X^2 - \frac{(\Sigma X)^2}{n}$$

Because we are using difference scores (D values) in place of X scores, this formula can be rewritten as

$$SS = \Sigma D^2 - \frac{(\Sigma D)^2}{n}$$

Remember, the computations for SS and s are based on the D-scores for the subjects in the sample.

For our data, the SS is

$$SS = 66 - \frac{(-16)^2}{5}$$
$$= 66 - 51.2$$
$$= 14.8$$

Next, use the SS value to compute the sample standard deviation:

$$s = \sqrt{\frac{SS}{n - 1}} = \sqrt{\frac{14.8}{4}} = \sqrt{3.7} = 1.92$$

Finally, the estimated standard error is computed:

$$s_{\overline{D}} = \frac{s}{\sqrt{n}} = \frac{1.92}{\sqrt{5}} = \frac{1.92}{2.24} = 0.86$$

Now these values are used to calculate the value of t:

$$t = \frac{\overline{D} - \mu_D}{s_{\overline{D}}} = \frac{-3.2 - 0}{0.86} = -3.72$$

STEP 4. The t value we obtained falls in the critical region (see Figure 12.4). The investigator rejects the null hypothesis and concludes that relaxation training does affect the amount of medication needed to control the asthma symptoms. For this example, a journal report might summarize the conclusion as follows:

> Relaxation training resulted in a significant reduction in the dose of medication needed to control asthma symptoms, $t(4) = -3.72$, $p < .05$, two tails.

As is customary, the number of degrees of freedom is contained in parentheses after the t, followed by the obtained value. The probability of a type I error (the alpha level) and the type of test (one or two tails) also are reported.

A researcher would like to examine the effect of hypnosis on cigarette smoking. A sample of smokers ($n = 8$) is selected for the study. The number of cigarettes smoked on the day prior to treatment is recorded. The subjects are then hypnotized and given the posthypnotic suggestion that each time they light a cigarette they will experience a horrible taste and feel nauseous. The data are as follows.

The Number of Cigarettes Smoked Before and After Hypnosis

Subject	Before Treatment	After Treatment
1	19	24
2	35	26
3	18	11
4	20	16
5	22	19
6	15	15
7	29	31
8	30	26

Do these data indicate that hypnosis has a significant effect on cigarette smoking? Test with $\alpha = .05$.

ANSWER

The hypotheses are, H_0: $\mu_D = 0$ and H_1: $\mu_D \neq 0$. With $df = 7$ the critical region consists of t values greater than $+2.365$ or less than -2.365. For these data $\overline{D} = -2.5$, $SS = 150$, $s = 4.63$, $s_{\overline{D}} = 1.64$, and $t = -1.52$. The null hypothesis cannot be rejected; there is no evidence for an effect of hypnosis in this experiment.

Figure 12.4

The critical regions with α = .05 and *df* = 4 begin at +2.776 and −2.776 in the *t* distribution. Obtained values of *t* that are more extreme than these values will lie in a critical region. In that case, the null hypothesis would be rejected.

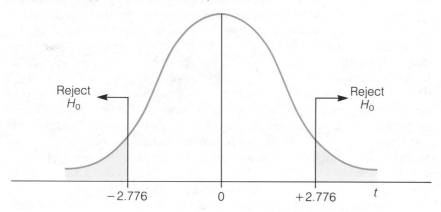

12.3
A Closer Look at the Repeated Measures *t* Test

Assumptions of the Repeated Measures *t* Test

As in the previous statistical tests, it is required that the sample of individuals is randomly selected from the population. This requirement helps ensure that the sample is representative of the population from which it was selected. There is also an assumption of normality for the repeated measures *t* test. Specifically, the population distribution of difference scores (*D*) should be normal. Ordinarily, researchers do not worry about this assumption unless there is ample reason to suspect a violation of this requirement of the test. In the case of severe departure from normality, the validity of the *t* test may be compromised. However, as noted before, the *t* statistic is robust to violations of normality when large samples (*n* > 30) are used.

Uses of Repeated Measures Studies

The repeated measures experiment differs from an independent measures study in a fundamental way. In the latter type of study, a separate sample is used for each treatment. In the repeated measures design, only one sample of subjects is used, and measurements are repeated for the same sample in each treatment (see Box 12.1). There are many situations where it is possible to examine the effect of a treatment by using either type of study. However, there are situations where one type of experimental design is more desirable or appropriate than the other. For example, if a researcher would like to study a particular type of subject (a rare species, people with an unusual illness, etc.) that is not commonly found, a repeated measures study will be more economical in the sense that fewer subjects are needed. Rather than selecting several samples for the study (one sample per treatment), a single sample can be used for the entire experiment.

Another factor in determining the type of experimental design is the specific question being asked by the experimenter. Some questions are better studied with a repeated measures design, especially those concerning changes in response across time. For example, a psychologist may wish to study the effect of practice on how well a person performs a task. To show that practice is improving a person's performance, the experimenter would typically measure the person's responses very early in the experiment (when there is little or no practice) and repeat the measurement later when the person has had a certain amount of practice. Most studies of skill acquisition examine practice effects by using a repeated measures design. Another situation where a repeated measures study is useful is in developmental psychology. By repeating observations of the same individuals at various points in time, an investigator can watch behavior unfold and obtain a better understanding of developmental processes. Developmental psychologists call this approach a longitudinal study. It involves assessing the same people at many different ages. The independent measures counterpart to this experiment is called a cross-sectional study. In this approach, several separate samples of children are studied, with each sample consisting of children of a particular age. For example, the psychologist might compare a sample of 4-year-olds to a sample of 10-year-olds in terms of their language skills. There are situations where a repeated measures design cannot or should not be used. Specifically, when you are comparing two different populations (men versus women, first-born versus last-born children, etc.), you must use an independent measure design with separate samples from each population.

Finally, it should be noted that there are certain statistical advantages to repeated measures designs, particularly when you are studying a population with large differences from one individual to the next. One of the sources of variability that contributes to the standard error is due to these individual differences—that is, subjects all respond differently because they enter the experiment with different abilities, experiences, and the like. Large amounts of individual differences would produce larger standard errors, which might mask a mean difference. A repeated measures design reduces the amount of this error variability in the analysis by using the same subjects for every treatment. The result is that the size of the standard error is reduced, and the t test will be more likely to detect the presence of a treatment effect. That is, the repeated measures t test is more powerful than an independent measures test when individual differences are large. The statistical advantage of a repeated measures design will be more evident in Chapter 14, when we examine the components of variability in an experiment.

BOX 12.1 **Matched Samples and the Repeated *t* Statistic**

We have described situations in which a researcher uses the repeated measures *t* test. All of these involved using just one sample and then testing the same individuals for every treatment. However, the repeated measures *t* test is also appropriate when two separate *but related* samples are used.

For example, suppose a researcher tests the effectiveness of a reading program on comprehension. One sample of fourth-graders take the reading course, and a second sample serves as the control group. The researcher will later compare the two groups in terms of reading comprehension. However, to reduce the possibility that differences in intelligence will confound the findings or mask an effect, the researcher first *matches* people in each sample for intelligence. That is, if a person assigned to the treatment group has an IQ of 120, the experimenter assigns another individual with the same IQ score to the control group (Table 12.3). This matching is done for all assignments of subjects to the groups. Thus, at the start of the experiment, the researcher has managed to reduce error variability due to individual differences by matching the samples in terms of IQ.

Table 12.3

Group Assignment of Subjects Matched for IQ

Control		Reading Program	
Subject	IQ	Subject	IQ
A	120	E	120
B	105	F	105
C	110	G	110
D	95	H	95

Statistically, the advantage of matched (also called related) samples is the same as that of the repeated measures design—the reduction of error variability due to individual differences. Note that even though there are two samples, the independent measures *t* test is *not* appropriate because these samples are not independent. The repeated *t* test should be used with a matched sample design.

Another type of related sample design consists of studies using identical twins. One twin can be assigned to one treatment group, while the other is assigned to the second condition. This assignment is done for all pairs of twins. The result is the ultimate in matched samples, because identical twins are exactly alike genetically and are typically raised in the same environment. Again, a repeated measures *t* test would be appropriate for examining the differences between the treatments because the two samples are *not* independent.

Some statisticians call the repeated t *test the related* t *test. This general term indicates that this* t *statistic is appropriate for both repeated measures and matched samples designs.*

Carry-over Effects in Repeated Measures Experiments

Sometimes the outcome of a repeated measures study is contaminated by the presence of a carry-over effect. This will occur when a subject's response in the second treatment is altered by lingering aftereffects of the first treatment. As a result, the outcome of the study may be uninterpretable. A common type of carry-over effect is fatigue. For example, suppose an experimenter studies the effects of distraction on task performance with a repeated measures design. Two treatment conditions are used: a no-distraction treatment and a distraction treatment. A sample of four subjects work on math problems requiring multiplication of large numbers. For the first 30 minutes, the subjects work on the problems in the no-distraction condition in a quiet room. Then the subjects are moved to the distraction condition. Now they must work on a similar set of math problems in the presence of loud background noise. The experimenter records the number of errors made by each subject. Table 12.4 summarizes the results.

Table 12.4

The Number of Errors Made Under Conditions of No Distraction and Distraction

Person	No Distraction	Distraction	D
A	6	15	+9
B	5	15	+10
C	11	17	+6
D	6	13	+7

$$\overline{D} = +8$$

Notice that the subjects in the experiment made an average of eight more errors in the distraction condition, $\overline{D} = +8$. A repeated measures t test would confirm that the mean difference between treatments is statistically significant, $t(3) = 8.79, p < .05$ for two tails. The experimenter might conclude that distraction has an effect on task performance. However, there may be another explanation of the effect. It is possible that the mean difference was observed because of a carry-over effect rather than a treatment effect. Perhaps the subjects became fatigued during the no-distraction condition. After all, they had to work on a boring, tedious task for 30 minutes. By the time the subjects are switched to the distraction condition, they might be bored, tired, and poorly motivated to do any more multiplication problems. Therefore, the increase in errors may have nothing to do with the introduction of distraction. It may have simply been due to the buildup of boredom and fatigue during the first condition. This buildup would in turn affect performance in (that is, "carry over" to) the second condition. If the significant mean difference were due solely to a carry-over effect of fatigue, then providing the subjects with a rest period between the two treatment conditions would lead to a different outcome. As shown in Table 12.5, the introduction of a rest period would eliminate the influence of fatigue on the second treatment. With the carry-over effect prevented, the data show no systematic effect, and the mean difference between treatments is negligible. On the other hand, if the effect were not due to fatigue, the significant mean difference would still be found when a rest period is introduced.

Table 12.5
The Number of Errors Made Under Conditions of No Distraction and Distraction with a Rest Period Between the Treatments

Person	No Distraction	Rest	Distraction	D
A	6	Rest	7	+1
B	5	Rest	4	−1
C	11	Rest	11	0
D	6	Rest	5	−1

$$\overline{D} = -0.25$$

Another way a researcher can reduce the contribution of a carry-over effect is to balance the order of presentation of treatments. That is, the treatments can be presented in one order for some subjects and in the reverse order for others. This procedure may eliminate a systematic contribution of a carry-over effect to any one treatment condition.

LEARNING
CHECK

1. What assumptions must be satisfied for the repeated measures t test to be valid?
2. Describe some situations for which a repeated measures design is well suited?
3. How is a matched sample design similar to a repeated measures design? How do they differ?
4. What is a carry-over effect?

ANSWERS

1. The sample must be randomly selected from the population. The population distribution of D-scores is assumed to be normal.
2. The repeated measures design is suited to situations where a particular type of subject is not readily available for study. This design is helpful because it uses fewer subjects (only one sample is needed). Certain questions are addressed more adequately by

a repeated measures design—for example, anytime one would like to study changes across time in the same individuals. Also, when individual differences are large, a repeated measures design is helpful because it reduces the amount of this type of error in the statistical analysis.

3. They are similar in that the role of individual differences in the experiment is reduced. They differ in that there are two samples in a matched sample design and only one in a repeated measures study.

4. A carry-over effect occurs in a repeated measures study when lingering aftereffects of the first treatment alter performance on the second—for example, fatigue.

12.4

Estimation with the Repeated Measures *t* Statistic

Introduction

The hypothesis testing procedure addresses the question of whether or not any mean difference exists. Occasionally, a researcher is interested in approximating *how much* difference can be expected for the population. This is a question for estimation. The repeated measures *t* statistic allows researchers to use sample data to estimate the value of μ_D, that is, to estimate the magnitude of the mean difference for the general population. Once again, the repeated measures *t* formula is

$$t = \frac{\overline{D} - \mu_D}{s_{\overline{D}}}$$

Because we want to estimate the value of the population mean difference, this formula is solved for μ_D:

(12.5) $\mu_D = \overline{D} \pm t s_{\overline{D}}$

In words, this formula may be stated as

> population mean difference = sample mean difference plus or minus *t*(estimated standard error)

That is, to estimate the mean difference for the population, we use the sample mean difference plus or minus some error.

Procedures for Estimation of μ_D

Remember, in estimation we use values of t and the estimated standard error to define an interval around the sample mean that probably contains μ.

In estimating μ_D, we first select a level of confidence (such as 95%) and determine the values for the sample mean of the *D*-scores ($\overline{D}$) and the estimated standard error of mean differences ($s_{\overline{D}}$). We then approximate the location of $\overline{D}$ in the distribution of sample means by choosing reasonable values for *t*. You will recall that these "reasonable" values are determined in part by the level of confidence selected for the interval estimate. The values for $\overline{D}$, $s_{\overline{D}}$, and t are used in the formula, and we compute the estimated value of μ_D. Our estimate of μ_D, therefore, is based on an estimation of the location of $\overline{D}$ plus or minus a margin of error. The estimation of μ_D involves essentially the same process that we used in Chapter 10, except the sample data in this case consist of difference scores.

EXAMPLE 12.2

A school psychologist has determined that a remedial reading course increases scores on a reading comprehension test. He now would like to estimate how much improvement might be expected for the whole population of students in his city. A random sample of $n = 16$ children is obtained. These children are first tested for level of reading comprehension and then enrolled in the course. At the completion of the remedial reading course, the students are tested again, and the difference between the second score and the first score is recorded for each child. For this sample, the average difference was $\overline{D} = +21$, and the SS for the D-scores was $SS = 1215$. The psychologist would like to use these data to make a point estimate and a 90% confidence interval estimate of μ_D.

STEP 1. The formula for estimation requires that we know the values of $\overline{D}$, $s_{\overline{D}}$, and t. We know that $\overline{D} = +21$ points for this sample, so all that remains is to compute $s_{\overline{D}}$ and look up the value of t in the t distribution table.

To find the standard error, we first must compute the sample standard deviation:

$$s = \sqrt{\frac{SS}{n-1}} = \sqrt{\frac{1215}{15}} = \sqrt{81} = 9$$

Now the estimated standard error is

$$s_{\overline{D}} = \frac{s}{\sqrt{n}} = \frac{9}{\sqrt{16}} = \frac{9}{4} = 2.25$$

To complete the estimate of μ_D, we must identify the value of t. We will consider the point estimate (step 2) and the interval estimate (step 3) separately.

STEP 2. *Point Estimation of* μ_D. To obtain a point estimate, a single value of t is selected to approximate the location of $\overline{D}$. Remember that the t distribution is symmetrical and bell-shaped with a mean of zero (see Figure 12.5). Because $t = 0$ is the most frequently occurring value in the distribution, this is the t value that is used for the point estimate.

Remember, we are not simply choosing a t value but are estimating the location of $\overline{D}$ with the distribution of sample means. Thus, for a point estimate, we should use a t value that is in the middle of the distribution. Using this value in the estimation formula gives

$$\mu_D = \overline{D} \pm ts_{\overline{D}}$$
$$= 21 \pm 0(2.25)$$
$$= 21$$

As noted several times before, the sample mean, $\overline{D} = 21$, provides the best point estimate of μ_D.

STEP 3.   *Interval Estimation of μ_D.* The psychologist also wanted to make an interval estimate so that he can be 90% confident that the interval contains the value of μ_D. To get the interval, it is necessary to determine what t values form the boundaries of the middle 90% of the t distribution. To use the t distribution table, we first must determine the proportion associated with the tails of this distribution. With 90% in the middle, the remaining area in both tails must be 10%, or $p = 0.10$. Also note that our sample has $n = 16$ scores, so the t statistic will have $df = n - 1 = 15$. Using $df = 15$ and $p = 0.10$ for two tails, you should find the values $+1.753$ and -1.753 in the t table. These values form the boundaries for the middle 90% of the t distribution. (See Figure 12.5.) We are confident that the t value for our sample mean $(\overline{D})$ is in this range because 90% of all the possible t values are there. Using these values in the estimation formula, we obtain the following: On one end of the interval,

$$\mu_D = \overline{D} - ts_{\overline{D}}$$
$$= 21 - 1.753(2.25)$$
$$= 21 - 3.94$$
$$= 17.06$$

and on the other end of the interval,

$$\mu_D = 21 + 1.753(2.25)$$
$$= 21 + 3.94$$
$$= 24.94$$

Therefore, the school psychologist can be 90% confident that the average amount of improvement in reading comprehension for the population (μ_D) will be somewhere between 17.04 and 24.94 points.

Figure 12.5
The t values for the 90% confidence interval are obtained by consulting the t table for $df = 15$, $p = 0.10$.

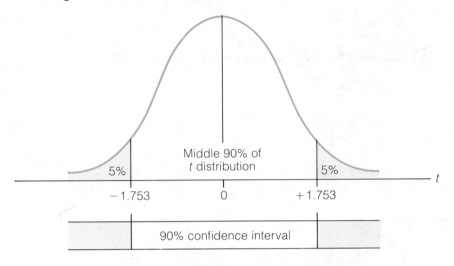

1. A government researcher believes that driving and automotive tips will result in energy-saving habits. A sample of nine subjects is given a brochure containing energy-saving tips and is asked to follow this advice. Before and after using the tips, the subjects maintain gasoline consumption records for their automobiles. The following data consist of the amount of improvement in gasoline mileage (in miles per gallon) for each subject: D-scores: 8, 10, 3, 11, 9, 12, 6, 9, 10. A repeated measures t test indicated that the mean change was statistically significant. However, before the government prints millions of copies of the brochure, the researcher is requested to estimate how much mean change can be expected for the population of drivers. The investigator decides to report the 95% confidence interval. What will this interval be?

ANSWER

1. $\overline{D} = +8.67$; $SS = 60$; $s = 2.74$; $s_{\overline{D}} = 0.91$; for the 95% confidence interval with $df = 8$, $t = \pm 2.306$; the 95% confidence interval for μ_D is from 6.57 to 10.77.

Summary

1. In a repeated measures experiment, a single sample of subjects is randomly selected, and measurements are repeated on this sample for each treatment condition. This type of experiment may take the form of a before-and-after study.

2. The data analysis for a repeated measures t test is done on the basis of the difference between the first and second measurement for each subject. These difference scores (D-scores) are obtained by

$$D = X_2 - X_1$$

3. The formula for the repeated measures t statistic is

$$t = \frac{\overline{D} - \mu_D}{s_{\overline{D}}}$$

where the sample mean is

$$\overline{D} = \frac{\Sigma D}{n}$$

the estimated standard error is

$$s_{\overline{D}} = \frac{s}{\sqrt{n}}$$

and the value of degrees of freedom is obtained by

$$df = n - 1$$

4. A repeated measures design may be more useful than an independent measures study when one wants to observe changes in behavior in the same subjects, as in learning or developmental studies. The repeated measures design has the advantage of reducing error variability due to individual differences. A potential problem with repeated measures studies is the presence of carry-over effects that can cloud the interpretation of the findings.

5. Estimation of the amount of mean change for the population is accomplished by solving the t statistic formula for μ_D:

$$\mu_D = \overline{D} \pm t s_{\overline{D}}$$

For a point estimate, a t value of zero is used. A range of t values is used to construct an interval around $\overline{D}$. As in previous estimation problems, the t values that mark the interval boundaries are determined by the confidence level that is selected and by degrees of freedom.

Key Terms

repeated measures design
repeated measures t statistic
difference scores
estimated standard error for $\overline{D}$

individual differences
matched sample design
carry-over effects

Problems for Chapter 12:
The Repeated Measures *t* Statistic

*1. A researcher arguing for stricter laws for drunk driving argues that even one can of beer can produce a significant effect on reaction time. In an attempt to prove his claim, he selects a random sample of $n = 4$ people and measures their baseline reaction times. This is accomplished by having the subjects view a stimulus display and press a button as fast as they can when a light flashes on. The subjects then consume a 12-ounce can of beer. After 30 minutes, they are tested again on the task. The researcher computed the difference scores and determined that for this sample $\overline{D} = 32$ milliseconds. That is, on average it took the group of subjects 32 milliseconds longer to respond. Also, the sample had $SS = 1200$. Do the data support the investigator's claim? Test at the .05 level of significance.

*2. For the data in Problem 1, estimate the amount of mean change in reaction time for the population as a result of drinking a single can of beer. Make an interval estimate at the 90% level of confidence.

3. What is a carry-over effect? Give an example of one.

4. A psychologist would like to know if there are any changes in personality during imprisonment. She selects a random sample of $n = 25$ people who have been sentenced to at least 5 years of prison. The psychologist interviews each of these people during their first week in prison and administers a personality test which measures introversion/extroversion on a scale from 0 to 50 (low scores indicate introversion). After 1 year, the investigator returns for a second interview with the prisoners and again administers the personality test. For each person, she calculates the difference between their initial score and the score after 1 year of confinement. The average for this sample of difference scores is $\overline{D} = -5$ with $SS = 2400$.

   a. Test the hypothesis that imprisonment changes personality variables. Set alpha at .05.

   b. Would the same decision be made had alpha been set at .01?

   c. Estimate how much change in personality is caused by 1 year of confinement for the population of prisoners. Make a point estimate and an interval esimate at the 80% level of confidence.

*5. A college professor performed a study to assess the effectiveness of computerized exercises in teaching mathematics. She decides to use a *matched sample design*. One group of subjects is assigned to the regular lecture section of introductory mathematics. A second group must attend a computer laboratory in addition to the lecture. These students work on computerized exercises for additional practice and instruction. Both samples are matched in terms of general mathematics ability, as measured by mathematical SAT scores. At the end of the semester, both groups are given the same final exam. For $n = 16$ matched pairs of subjects, the professor found a mean improvement of $\overline{D} = 9.3$ points for the computer group. The SS for the D-scores was 2160. Does the computerized instruction lead to a significant improvement? Test at the .01 level of significance.

*6. For the study in Problem 5, estimate the amount of mean change for the population (μ_D) using the 95% level of confidence.

7. What is the advantage of a matched sample design over an independent measures design?

*8. A psychologist for NASA examines the effect of cabin temperature on reaction time. A random sample of $n = 10$ astronauts and pilots is selected. Each person's reaction time is measured in a simulator where the cabin temperature is maintained at 70°F and again the next day at 95°F. The subjects are run through a launch simulation. Their reaction time (in milliseconds) is measured when an emergency indicator flashes and they must quickly press the appropriate switch. The data from this experiment are as follows:

Experiment 1

70°	95°	D
180	190	10
176	201	25
204	220	16
216	240	24
194	217	23
183	206	23
207	228	21
229	255	26
231	245	14
210	228	18

a. Using the results from this experiment, can the psychologist conclude that temperature has a significant effect on reaction time? Test at the .05 level of significance.

b. To verify the results of the first experiment, the psychologist repeats the experiment with another sample of $n = 10$. The data for the replication are as follows:

Experiment 2

70°	95°	D
178	252	74
194	244	50
217	200	−17
186	231	45
242	218	−24
212	214	2
221	201	−20
194	236	42
187	247	60
219	207	−12

Again, test for a significant difference at the .05 level of significance.

c. Both experiments showed reaction times that were on average 20 milliseconds longer with the hotter cabin temperature. Why are the results of one experiment significant and of the other not significant? [*Hint:* Compare the two experiments in terms of the consistency of the effect for all subjects. How does the consistency (or inconsistency) of the effect affect the analysis?]

9. A high school counselor has developed a course designed to help students with the mathematics portion of the SAT. A random sample of students is selected for the study. These students take the SAT at the end of their junior year. During the summer, they take the SAT review course. When they begin their senior year, they all take the SAT again. The data for the sample are as follows:

SAT Scores (Mathematics)

Before	After
402	468
486	590
543	625
516	553
475	454
403	447
522	543
480	416
619	652
493	495
485	496
551	585
573	610
437	491
472	544
409	492
444	521
502	485
419	466

SAT Scores (Mathematics)

Before	After
472	510
464	507
512	583
417	497
422	465
505	626

Did the students perform significantly better on the SAT after taking the special course? Set alpha at .05.

10. For the data in Problem 9, estimate how much improvement (μ_D) can be expected for the population. Use the 95% level of confidence for the interval estimate.

*11. A psychologist tests a new drug for its pain-killing effects. Pain threshold is measured for a sample of subjects by determining the intensity (in milliamperes) of electric shock that causes discomfort. After the initial baseline is established, subjects receive the drug, and their thresholds are once again measured. The data are as follows:

Pain Thresholds (Milliamperes)

Before	After
2.1	3.2
2.3	2.9
3.0	4.6
2.7	2.7
1.9	3.1
2.1	2.9
2.9	2.9
2.7	3.4
3.2	5.3
2.5	2.5
3.1	4.9
1.5	3.8
2.3	4.4
1.4	1.4

Is there an effect of the drug treatment? Test with an alpha of .01.

*12. Estimate the mean amount of change (μ_D) in threshold for the population for the study in Problem 11. Use a confidence level of 90% for the interval estimate.

13. A researcher examines the effects of sensitization on cigarette smoking in habitual smokers. A random sample of $n = 12$ smokers is selected. The number of cigarettes smoked per day is first determined for these people. The subjects are then sensitized to the effects of smoking by having them view a film

that graphically shows the harm caused by cigarette smoke. A week later, the subjects are asked to count the number of cigarettes they smoke that day. The data are as follows:

Number of Cigarettes Smoked

Before	One Week Later
19	15
22	7
32	31
17	10
37	28
20	12
23	23
24	17
28	19
21	24
15	11
18	16

Did sensitization cause a reduction in smoking? Use the .05 level of significance.

14. Estimate the average amount of reduction (μ_D) that sensitization will produce for the population using the data in Problem 13. Use a confidence level of 90% for the interval estimate.

*15. A researcher tests the effectiveness of a drug called Ritalin on hyperkinetic children. The researcher uses a sample of $n = 12$ hyperkinetic children ranging in age from 8 to 9 years of age. The children are told several brief stories. After each story, the experimenter asks the children questions about the story. The total number of questions answered correctly for all of the stories is recorded as the child's score. Because hyperkinetic children have attentional deficits, they should not perform well on this task when they are not treated. The researcher tests all of the children under two conditions: following administration of a sugar pill (placebo condition) and after receiving Ritalin. For the following data, determine if the drug treatment has an effect on performance. Use an alpha level of .01.

Subject	Placebo	Ritalin
A	10	15
B	8	15
C	11	13
D	6	17
E	7	8
F	9	17
G	6	18
H	8	3
I	5	14
J	10	20
K	7	18
L	2	19

*16. For the data in Problem 15, estimate the mean amount of change in performance (μ_D) for the population due to Ritalin treatment. Use the 95% level of confidence for the interval estimate.

17. A statistics instructor was unable to decide between two potential textbooks. To help with this decision, a random sample of 12 students was obtained, and each student was to rate both books using a scale from 1 (very bad) to 10 (excellent). The data from these 12 students are as follows:

Student	Book 1	Book 2
1	3	5
2	6	7
3	8	7
4	7	8
5	5	6
6	3	5
7	8	6
8	6	3
9	2	5
10	5	6
11	7	5
12	4	7

Do these data indicate that students perceive a significant difference between the books? Test at the .05 level of significance.

*18. Although psychologists do not completely understand the phenomenon of dreaming, it does appear that people need to dream. One experiment demonstrating this fact shows that people who are deprived of dreaming one night will tend to have extra dreams the following night, as if they were trying to make up for the lost dreams. In a typical version of this experiment, the psychologist first records the number of dreams [by monitoring rapid eye movements (REMs)] during a normal night's sleep. The next night, each subject is prevented from dreaming by being awakened as soon as he/she begins a dream. During the third night, the psychologist once again records the number of dreams. Hypothetical data from this experiment are as follows:

Subject	First Night	Night After Deprivation
1	4	7
2	5	5
3	4	8
4	6	7
5	4	10
6	5	7
7	4	7
8	4	6

Do these data indicate a significant increase in dreams after one night of dream deprivation? Test at the .05 level of significance.

19. A pharmaceutical company would like to test the effectiveness of a new antidepressant drug. A sample of 15 depressed patients is obtained, and each patient is given a mood inventory questionnaire before and after receiving the drug treatment. The data for this experiment are as follows:

Patient	Before	After
1	18	23
2	21	20
3	16	17
4	19	20
5	14	13
6	23	22
7	16	18
8	14	18
9	21	21
10	18	16
11	17	19
12	14	20
13	16	15
14	14	15
15	20	21

On the basis of these data, can the company conclude that the drug has a significant effect on mood? Test with $\alpha = .01$.

*20. A consumer protection agency is testing the effectiveness of a new gasoline additive that claims to improve gas mileage. A sample of 10 cars is obtained, and each car is driven over a standard 100-mile course with and without the additive. The researchers carefully record the miles per gallon for each test drive. The results of this test are as follows:

Car	With Additive	Without Additive
1	23.0	21.6
2	20.2	19.8
3	17.4	17.5
4	19.6	20.7
5	22.8	23.1
6	20.4	19.8
7	26.8	26.4
8	23.7	24.0
9	17.2	15.9
10	18.5	18.3

Does the new gasoline additive have a significant effect on gas mileage? Test at the .05 level of significance.

CHAPTER 13

Introduction to Analysis of Variance

TOOLS
YOU WILL
NEED

The following items are considered essential background material for this chapter. If you doubt your knowledge of any of these items, you should review the appropriate chapter or section before proceeding.

1. Variability (Chapter 4)
   a. Sum of squares
   b. Sample variance
   c. Degrees of freedom
2. Introduction to hypothesis testing (Chapter 8)
   a. The logic of hypothesis testing
3. Independent measures t statistic (Chapter 11)

"But I read the chapter four times! How could I possibly have failed the exam?"

Most of you probably have had the experience of reading a textbook and suddenly realizing that you have no idea of what was said on the past few pages. Although you have been reading the words, your mind has wandered off, and the meaning of the words never reaches memory. In an influential paper on human memory, Craik and Lockhart (1972) proposed a *levels of processing* theory of memory that can account for this phenomenon. In general terms, this theory says that all perceptual and mental processing leaves behind a memory trace. However, the quality of the memory trace depends on the level or the depth of the processing. If you superficially skim the words in a book, your memory also will be superficial. On the other hand, when you think about the meaning of the words and try to understand what you are reading, the result will be a good, substantial memory that should serve you well on exams. In general, deeper processing results in better memory.

Rogers, Kuiper, and Kirker (1977) conducted an experiment demonstrating the effect of levels of processing. Subjects in this experiment were shown lists of words and asked to answer questions about each word. The questions were designed to require different levels of processing, from superficial to deep. In one experimental condition, subjects were simply asked to judge the physical characteristics of each printed word ("Is it printed in capital letters or small letters?") A second condition asked about the sound of each word ("Does it rhyme with 'boat'?"). In a third condition, subjects were required to process the meaning of each word ("Does it have the same meaning as 'attractive'?"). The final condition required subjects to understand each word and relate its meaning to themselves ("Does this word describe you?"). After going through the complete list, all subjects were given a surprise memory test. As you can see in Figure 13.1, deeper processing resulted in better memory. Remember, none of these sub-

Figure 13.1
Mean recall as a function of the level of processing. Rogers, T. B., Kuiper, N. A., & Kirker, W. S. (1977). Self-reference and the encoding of personal information. *Journal of Personality and Social Psychology*, 35, 677-688. Copyright (1977) by the American Psychological Association. Adapted by permission of the author.

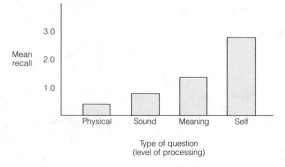

389

jects was trying to memorize the words; they were simply reading through the list answering questions. However, the more they processed and understood the words, the better they recalled the words on the test.

In terms of human memory the Rogers et al. experiment is notable because it demonstrates the importance of "self" in memory. You are most likely to remember material that is directly related to you. In terms of statistics, however, this study is notable because it compares four different treatment conditions in a single experiment. Although it may seem like a small step to go from two treatments (as in the *t* tests in Chapters 11 and 12) to four treatments, there is a tremendous gain in experimental sophistication. Suppose, for example, the Rogers et al. had decided to examine only two levels of processing: one based on physical characteristics and one based on sound. In

this simplified experiment, they would have made only *one* comparison: physical versus sound. In the real experiment, however, they used four conditions and were able to make *six* different comparisons:

> Physical versus sound
> Physical versus meaning
> Physical versus self
> Sound versus meaning
> Sound versus self
> Meaning versus self

To gain this experimental sophistication, there is some cost. Specifically, you no longer can use the familiar *t* tests we encountered in Chapters 11 and 12. Instead, you now must learn a new statistical technique which is designed for experiments consisting of two or more sets of data. This new, general-purpose procedure is called analysis of variance.

13.1
Introduction

Analysis of variance is a statistical technique that is used to compare two or more treatments (or two or more populations) to determine whether there are any mean differences among them. Like the *t* tests in Chapters 11 and 12, analysis of variance (ANOVA) will use a sample of scores from each of the treatments to test a hypothesis about the populations. Suppose, for example, you are given the following three separate samples:

Sample 1 (Treatment X)	Sample 2 (Treatment Y)	Sample 3 (Treatment Z)
0	1	4
2	4	6
4	7	8
$\bar{X} = 2$	$\bar{X} = 4$	$\bar{X} = 6$

Although you are told that these data come from three separate treatment conditions, your task (as a statistician) is to decide between the following two alternatives:

1. All three of the samples actually come from the same population; that is, the treatments are all the same.
2. The three samples come from different populations; that is, the treatments really do produce mean differences.

The purpose of analysis of variance is to help you decide between these two alternatives. In statistics terminology, analysis of variance tests a null hypothesis which states that there are no differences among the treatment means versus an alternative hypothesis that says the treatment means are different. These two alternatives are illustrated in Figure 13.2.

It may appear that analysis of variance and *t* tests are simply two different ways of doing exactly the same job: testing for a mean difference. In some respects this is true. Later in this chapter, we will show that there is a very close relationship between ANOVA and *t* tests. However, there are situations where analysis of variance has a tremendous advantage over *t* tests. Specifically, *t* tests have limited application because they are designed for situations where there are only two treatments to compare. This limitation severely restricts the kinds of experiments that can be done. For example, a psychologist

---

Figure 13.2

The two alternative conclusions for an analysis of variance.

Alternative 1: All three samples come from the same population
(H₀ is true; there is no treatment effect)

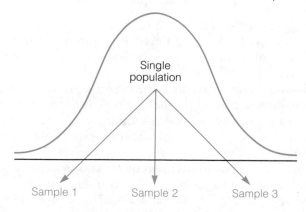

Alternative 2: The three samples come from three different populations
(H₀ is false; the treatments have different effects)

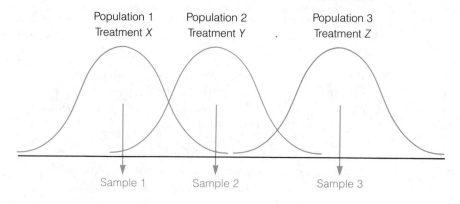

may want to examine learning performance under a series of temperature conditions: 50 degrees, 60 degrees, 70 degrees, and 80 degrees. Does the room temperature affect learning? In this experiment, the psychologist is comparing four different treatment conditions. You should notice that it is possible to examine the data from this experiment using t statistics. For example, you could use a t test to compare the 50-degree condition with the 60-degree condition, then use another t statistic to compare 50 versus 70, then another t to compare 50 versus 80, etc. Using t statistics, you need a total of six different hypothesis tests to make all of the possible comparisons. There are two problems with this procedure. First, it obviously is going to take a lot of work just to do the calculations. But there is a second problem that is much more serious. Remember, each time you do a hypothesis test, you risk a type I error. The more tests you do, the more risk there is. For this experiment, you would need six separate hypothesis tests, each with a risk of a type I error. By the time you finish, you would have a high probability of making an error. (See Box 13.1.)

BOX 13.1 **Experiment-Wise Alpha and Multiple t Tests**

Because complex experiments often require a number of statistical tests (each with a risk of a type I error), researchers differentiate between what is called the *test-wise* alpha level and the *experiment-wise* alpha level. The test-wise level is simply the α level you select for each individual hypothesis test. The experiment-wise alpha level is the total probability of a type I error that is accumulated from all of the separate tests in the experiment. It is the experiment-wise alpha level that is most important when an experiment is testing several different hypotheses. As you have seen in the preceding temperature experiment, it would require six different t tests to make all the comparisons among four treatment conditions. This would result in a relatively large experiment-wise alpha level. You can compute the experiment-wise alpha level by the formula

$$\text{overall } \alpha \text{ level} = 1 - (1 - \alpha)^N$$

where N is the number of separate tests in the experiment and each test has the same α level (α). The logic behind this formula is as follows:

The calculation of P(no error) is determined by the multiplication rule for probabilities (Chapter 6).

1. If $\alpha = P(\text{type I error})$, then $1 - \alpha = P(\text{no error})$.
2. The probability of no error on the first test *and then* no error on the second test would be $(1 - \alpha)(1 - \alpha)$. Continuing for all N tests would give

$$P(\text{no errors}) = (1 - \alpha)(1 - \alpha)(1 - \alpha) \cdots = (1 - \alpha)^N$$

3. If the experiment-wise probability of no error is $(1 - \alpha)^N$, then the probability of an error would be

BOX 13.1 *continued*

$$P(\text{at least one error}) = 1 - P(\text{no errors})$$
$$= 1 - (1 - \alpha)^N$$

For an experiment with six separate tests with $\alpha = .05$, the experiment-wise alpha level would be

$$1 - (.95)^6 = 1 - .735$$
$$= .265 \quad \text{or} \quad 26.5\%$$

The advantage of analysis of variance is that it allows you to keep the risk of a type I error small even when you are comparing several different treatments. In simple terms, the analysis of variance performs all of the treatment comparisons simultaneously in one single test. More importantly, it allows you to select one single alpha level that determines the total risk of a type I error for all of these simultaneous tests.

[handwritten margin note: advantages of ANOVA]

The Special Vocabulary of ANOVA

As noted earlier, analysis of variance is a general-purpose statistics procedure that can be used with two or more treatment conditions. Because the ANOVA procedure is so flexible, there is a special vocabulary that is used to specify the exact experimental situation where analysis of variance is being used.

The first term we will need from this vocabulary is the word *factor*.

DEFINITION

In analysis of variance, a *factor* is an independent variable.

[handwritten margin note: factor]

For example, suppose a researcher is examining learning performance under four different temperature conditions. The design of this experiment is shown graphically in Figure 13.3. For this experiment, the independent variable is temperature. (The dependent variable, the score for each individual, would be learning performance.) Because there is only one independent variable (temperature), this would be called a *single-factor experiment*.

It is possible to have more than one factor in an experiment. Suppose, for example, our researcher was interested in the effects of temperature on learning performance for males and females. Now the researcher is interested in comparing performance for males versus females as well as comparing the different temperature conditions.

Figure 13.3

The structure of a single-factor experiment. The factor (independent variable) is temperature.

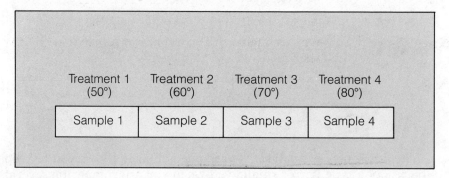

This experimental design is shown graphically in Figure 13.4. Notice that we now have two independent variables: sex and temperature. This would be called a *two-factor experiment*.

Each independent variable, or factor, in an experiment is made up of at least two different values or conditions. For example, the learning experiment we are considering uses four values of temperature. These different treatment values are called levels of the factor. In our example, the temperature factor has four levels, and the sex factor has two levels (see Figure 13.4).

DEFINITION

The individual treatment conditions that make up a factor are called *levels* of the factor.

Figure 13.4

The structure of a two-factor experiment. The factors (independent variables) are temperature and sex.

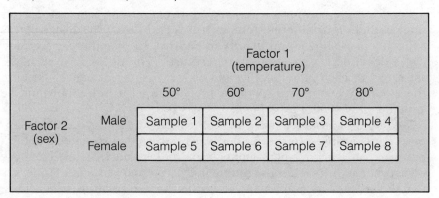

Finally, the analysis of variance procedure can be used with either an independent measures or a repeated measures experimental design. You should recall that an independent measures experiment uses a separate sample for each treatment condition. In a repeated measures experiment, the same sample is used in all of the treatment conditions.

With this special vocabulary in mind, the rest of this chapter will cover analysis of variance as it is applied to single-factor, independent measures experimental designs. Chapter 14 will look at single-factor, repeated measures designs, and Chapter 15 will introduce two-factor, independent measures experimental designs.

13.2

The Logic of Analysis of Variance

The formulas and calculations required in analysis of variance are somewhat complicated, but the logic that underlies the whole procedure is fairly straightforward. Therefore, this section will attempt to give a general picture of analysis of variance before we start looking at the details. We will introduce the logic of ANOVA with the help of the hypothetical data in Table 13.1. These data represent the results of an independent measures experiment comparing learning performance under four different temperature conditions.

Table 13.1

Hypothetical Data from an Experiment Examining Learning Performance Under Four Temperature Conditions[a]

Treatment 1, 50° (Sample 1)	Treatment 2, 60° (Sample 2)	Treatment 3, 70° (Sample 3)	Treatment 4, 80° (Sample 4)
0	1	4	1
1	3	3	2
3	2	6	2
1	2	3	0
0	2	4	0

[a]Note that there are four separate samples (four groups of subjects) with $n = 5$ in each sample. The dependent variable is the number of problems solved correctly.

Statistical Hypotheses for ANOVA

The purpose of this experiment is to determine whether temperature has any effect on learning performance. In statistical terms, we want to decide between two hypotheses: the null hypothesis (H_0) which says temperature has no effect and the alternative hypothesis which says temperature does affect learning. In symbols, these two hypotheses are

H_0: $\mu_1 = \mu_2 = \mu_3 = \mu_4$ (no differences)

H_1: at least one mean is different from the others

Notice that we have not given any specific alternative hypothesis. This is because there are many different alternatives possible, and it would be difficult and nonproductive to list them all. One alternative, for example, would be that the first three populations are identical but that the fourth is different. Another alternative states that the last three means are the same but that the first is different. Other alternatives would be

$$H_1: \quad \mu_1 = \mu_2 \neq \mu_3 = \mu_4$$
$$H_1: \quad \mu_1 = \mu_2 \text{ but } \mu_3 \text{ and } \mu_4 \text{ are different}$$

It should be pointed out that a researcher typically entertains only one (or at most a few) of these alternative hypotheses. Usually a theory or the outcomes of previous studies will dictate a more specific prediction concerning the treatment effect. For example, previous research has demonstrated that most tasks are performed best with a room temperature between 60 and 70 degrees. With this in mind, our researcher probably would predict that performance would be better in the two intermediate temperature treatments (60 and 70 degrees) and worse at the extreme temperatures (50 and 80 degrees). In symbols, this alternative would be

$$H_1: \quad \mu_1 < \mu_2 = \mu_3 > \mu_4$$

For the sake of simplicity, we will state a general alternative hypothesis rather than try to list all the possible specific alternatives.

The Process of Analyzing Variability

Although the purpose of ANOVA is to determine if there are any mean differences among the treatments, the calculations for ANOVA will be based on variances. The rationale for using variances will be presented now.

One obvious characteristic of the data in Table 13.1 is that the scores are not all the same. In everyday language, the scores are different; in statistical terms, the scores are variable. Our goal is to measure the amount of variability (the size of the differences) and to explain where it comes from.

The first step is to determine the total amount of variability for the entire set of data. Once we have measured this total amount, we can begin to break it apart into separate components. The word *analysis* means dividing into smaller parts. Because we are going to analyze the variability, the process is called *analysis of variance*.

After we have measured the total variability in the data, it can be divided into two basic components:

1. *Between Treatments Variability*. A lot of the variability in the scores is due to general differences between treatment conditions. For example, the scores in the 70-degree condition tend to be a lot higher than the scores in the 50-degree condition. This variability

between treatments is actually a measure of mean differences between treatments.

2. *Within Treatments Variability*. In addition to the general differences between the treatments, there is variability inside each of the groups. For example, the scores in the 70-degree condition are not all the same; they are variable.

within (handwritten)

Each of these variance components will now be examined.

Between Treatments Variability

If you select a score from treatment 1 and a score from treatment 2 (see Table 13.1), the two scores probably will be different. Why are they different? There are three possible answers to this question:

1. *Treatment Effect.* The score you picked from treatment 1 is a measure of learning performance with a room temperature of 50 degrees. The second score is a measure of performance when the temperature is 60 degrees. If temperature affects learning performance, then the difference between the two scores would be caused by the different temperatures. In more general terms, it is possible that the treatment effect has caused the two scores to be different.

 due to (handwritten)

2. *Individual Differences.* The subjects enter the experiment with different backgrounds, abilities, and attitudes; that is, they are unique individuals. Because this is an independent measures experiment, we have a separate sample (different individuals) for each of the treatment conditions. Therefore, the scores you selected from different treatments also represent two different individuals, and this fact could explain why the two scores are not the same.

3. *Experimental Error.* Whenever you make a measurement, there is a chance of error. The error could be caused by poor equipment, lack of attention, or unpredictable changes in the event you are measuring. Even though you are measuring the same individual under the same conditions, the scores can be different. This kind of unexplained and uncontrolled difference is called experimental error. (*Note:* Researchers try to keep experimental error as small as possible, but it cannot be eliminated entirely.)

Within Treatments Variability

Now we will examine the variability inside each of the treatment conditions. First, select one of the temperature conditions and then choose two scores from within that group. Again, the two scores you select probably will be different. Why are they different? This time there are only two possible answers to the question:

1. *Individual Differences.* The two scores come from two different individuals, and this could explain why they are not identical.
2. *Experimental Error.* There always is a chance that the difference is caused by experimental error. Even when you measure the same individual under the exact same conditions, you can get two different scores.

due to

Notice that we have not listed treatment effect as one of the possible explanations for differences (variability) inside a treatment condition. This is because all the individuals within the group receive exactly the same treatment. For example, all of the individuals in treatment 2 were tested in a 60-degree room. Because the temperature is the same for everyone, the differences between scores cannot be caused by differences in temperature. The analysis, or partitioning, of variability is diagrammed in Figure 13.5.

The Structure of the *F*-Ratio Statistic

Once we have analyzed the total variability into two basic components (between treatments and within treatments variability), we simply compare them. The comparison is made by computing a statistic called an *F*-ratio. For the independent measures, single-factor analysis of variance, the *F*-ratio is computed by dividing the between treatments variance by the within treatments variance:

$$F = \frac{\text{variance between treatments}}{\text{variance within treatments}} = \frac{MS\ between}{MS\ win}$$

Figure 13.5

The independent measures analysis of variance partitions, or analyzes, the total variability into two components: variability between treatments and variability within treatments.

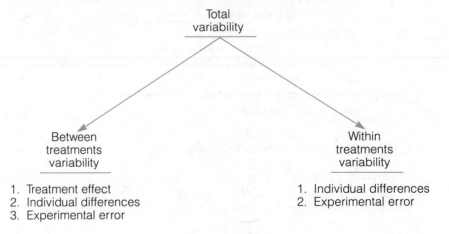

When we express each of these variances in terms of its sources (see Figure 13.5), the structure of the F-ratio is

(13.1) $$F = \frac{\text{treatment effect} + \text{individual diff's.} + \text{experimental error}}{\text{individual diff's.} + \text{experimental error}}$$

You should note that the between treatments variability and the within treatments variability differ in only one respect: the variability (mean differences) caused by the treatment effect. This single difference between the numerator and denominator of the F-ratio is crucial in determining if a treatment effect has occurred. Remember, the whole purpose for doing the experiment and the analysis is to find out whether or not the treatment has any effect. Let's consider the two possibilities:

(handwritten: under H_0 = true, F ratio = 1)

1. H_0 is true, and there is no treatment effect. In this case, the numerator and denominator of the F-ratio are measuring the same variance:

$$F = \frac{0 + \text{individual differences} + \text{experimental error}}{\text{individual differences} + \text{experimental error}}$$

   When H_0 is true and the treatment effect is zero (or negligible), the F-ratio is expected to be nearly equal to 1.

2. If H_0 is false, then a treatment effect does exist, and the F-ratio becomes

$$F = \frac{\text{treatment effect} + \text{individual diff's.} + \text{experimental error}}{\text{individual diff's.} + \text{experimental error}}$$

(handwritten: H_0 false, $F > 1$)

   Now the numerator of the ratio should be larger than the denominator, and the F-ratio is expected to be larger than 1.00. Ordinarily, the presence of a large treatment effect is reflected in a large value for the F-ratio.

In more general terms, the denominator of the F-ratio measures only uncontrolled and unexplained (often called *unsystematic*) variability. For this reason, the denominator of the F-ratio is called the *error term*. The numerator of the F-ratio always includes this same error variability, but it also includes any systematic differences caused by the treatment effect. The goal of analysis of variance is to find out whether or not a treatment effect exists.

(handwritten: unsystematic = denom.)

13.3
ANOVA Notation and Formulas

Because analysis of variance most often is used to examine data from several different treatment conditions and from several different samples, we will need a fairly sophisticated notation system to help keep track of all the individual scores and totals. To help introduce this notation system, we will use the hypothetical data from Table 13.1 once again. The basic data are reproduced in Table 13.2 along with some of the notation and statistics that will be described.

Table 13.2

Hypothetical Data from an Experiment Examining Learning Performance Under
Four Temperature Conditions[a]

	Temperature Conditions			
1 50°	2 60°	3 70°	4 80°	
0	1	4	1	$\Sigma X^2 = 128$
1	3	3	2	$G = 40$
3	2	6	2	$N = 20$
1	2	3	0	$k = 4$
0	2	4	0	
$T_1 = 5$	$T_2 = 10$	$T_3 = 20$	$T_4 = 5$	
$SS_1 = 6$	$SS_2 = 2$	$SS_3 = 6$	$SS_4 = 4$	
$n_1 = 5$	$n_2 = 5$	$n_3 = 5$	$n_4 = 5$	
$\overline{X}_1 = 1$	$\overline{X}_2 = 2$	$\overline{X}_3 = 4$	$\overline{X}_4 = 1$	

[a]Summary values and notation for an analysis of variance also are presented.

1. The letter k is used to identify the number of treatment
   conditions, that is, the number of levels of the factor.
   For an independent measures experiment, k also
   specifies the number of separate samples. For the data
   in Table 13.2, there are four treatments, so $k = 4$.

2. The number of scores in each treatment is identified by
   a lowercase letter n. For the example in Table 13.2,
   $n = 5$ for all the treatments. If the samples are of different sizes, you can identify a specific sample by using a
   subscript. For example, n_2 is the number of scores in
   treatment 2.

3. The total number of scores in the entire experiment is
   specified by a capital letter N. When all of the samples
   are the same size (n is constant), $N = kn$. For the data in
   Table 13.2, there are $n = 5$ scores in each of the $k = 4$
   treatments, so $N = 4(5) = 20$.

4. The total (ΣX) for each treatment condition is identified
   by the capital letter T. The total for a specific treatment
   can be identified by adding a numerical subscript to the
   T. For example, the total for the second treatment in
   Table 13.2 is $T_2 = 10$.

5. The sum of all the scores in the experiment (the grand
   total) is identified by G. You can compute G by adding
   up all N scores or by adding up the treatment totals:
   $G = \Sigma T$.

6. Although there is no new notation involved, we also
   have computed SS and $\overline{X}$ for each sample, and we have
   calculated ΣX^2 for the entire set of $N = 20$ scores in the

experiment. These values are given in Table 13.2 and will be important in the formulas and calculations for ANOVA.

ANOVA Formulas

The process of analyzing variability will proceed in two parts. First, we will analyze SS (the sum of squared deviations), and then we will analyze *df* (the degrees of freedom). You should recall that variance for a sample is defined as

$$\text{sample variance} = s^2 = \frac{SS}{n-1} = \frac{SS}{df}$$

In the final *F*-ratio, we will be comparing the variance between treatments with the variance within treatments. To compute these values, we will need an SS and a *df* for each of the two variances.

Analysis of Sum of Squares (SS)

The ANOVA requires that we first compute a total variability and then partition this value into two components: between treatments and within treatments. This analysis is outlined in Figure 13.5. We will examine each of the three components separately.

1. *Total Sum of Squares, SS_{total}.* As the name implies, SS_{total} is simply the sum of squares for the entire set of *N* scores. We calculate this value by using the computational formula for *SS:*

$$SS = \Sigma X^2 - \frac{(\Sigma X)^2}{N}$$

To make this formula consistent with the ANOVA notation, we substitute the letter *G* in place of ΣX and obtain

(13.2) $SS_{total} = \Sigma X^2 - \dfrac{G^2}{N}$

Applying this formula to the set of data in Table 13.2, we obtain

$$SS_{total} = 128 - \frac{40^2}{20}$$

$$= 128 - 80$$

$$= 48$$

2. *Within Treatments Sum of Squares, SS_{within}.* Now we are looking at the variability inside each of the treatment conditions. We already have computed the SS within each of the four treatment conditions: $SS_1 = 6$, $SS_2 = 2$,

$SS_3 = 6$, and $SS_4 = 4$. To find the overall within treatment sum of squares, we simply add these values together:

(13.3) $\quad SS_{within} = \Sigma SS_{inside\ each \atop treatment}$

For the data in Table 13.2, this formula gives

$$SS_{within} = 6 + 2 + 6 + 4$$

$$= 18$$

SS w/in [handwritten note]

3. *Between Treatments Sum of Squares, $SS_{between}$.* Before we introduce the equation for $SS_{between}$, consider what we have found so far. The total variability for the data in Table 13.2 is $SS_{total} = 48$. We intend to partition this total into two parts (see Figure 13.5). One part, SS_{within}, has been found to be equal to 18. This means that $SS_{between}$ must be equal to 30 in order for the two parts (18 and 30) to add up to the total (48). The equation for the between treatments sum of squares should produce a value of $SS_{between} = 30$. You should recall that the variability between treatments is measuring the differences between treatment means. Conceptually, the most direct way of measuring the amount of variability among the treatment means is simply to compute the sum of squares for the set of means. To do this, we begin with the calculational formula for *SS*:

SS between [handwritten note]

$$SS = \Sigma X^2 - \frac{(\Sigma X)^2}{N}$$

Then we substitute the sample means ($\overline{X}$ values) in place of scores (X values). The resulting formula is

Note that k *is the number of sample means.*

$$SS_{means} = \Sigma \overline{X}^2 - \frac{(\Sigma \overline{X})^2}{k}$$

Because each treatment mean is representing a sample of n scores, we multiply SS_{means} by n to obtain the between treatments sum of squares:

(13.4) $\quad SS_{between} = nSS_{means} = n\left[\Sigma \overline{X}^2 - \frac{(\Sigma \overline{X})^2}{k} \right]$

Applying this formula to the data in Table 13.2, we obtain

$$SS_{between} = 5\left(1^2 + 2^2 + 4^2 + 1^2 - \frac{8^2}{4} \right)$$

$$= 5(22 - 16)$$

$$= 5(6)$$

$$= 30$$

Notice that the result, $SS_{between} = 30$, is exactly what we predicted. The two parts from the analysis (between and within) add up to the total:

$$SS_{total} = SS_{within} + SS_{between}$$

$$48 = 18 + 30$$

Although Formula (13.4) is conceptually the most direct way of computing the amount of variability among the treatment means, this formula can be awkward to use, especially when the means are not whole numbers. For this reason, we generally will use an algebraically equivalent formula that uses the treatment totals (T values) instead of the means:

(13.5) $SS_{between} = \Sigma \dfrac{T^2}{n} - \dfrac{G^2}{N}$

For the derivation of this formula, see Box 13.2

Using this new formula with the data in Table 13.2, we obtain

$$SS_{between} = \frac{5^2}{5} + \frac{10^2}{5} + \frac{20^2}{5} + \frac{5^2}{5} - \frac{40^2}{20}$$
$$= 5 + 20 + 80 + 5 - 80$$
$$= 110 - 80$$
$$= 30$$

Notice that this result is identical to the value we obtained using Formula (13.4).

The formula for each SS and the relationships among these three values are shown in Figure 13.6.

Figure 13.6

Partitioning the sum of squares (SS) for the independent measures analysis of variance.

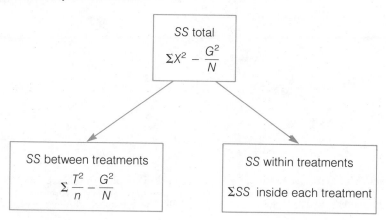

BOX 13.2 Alternative Formulas for ANOVA

Part I: Formulas for $SS_{between}$. We have presented two different formulas for $SS_{between}$. To show that these formulas are equivalent, we begin with Formula (13.4) and derive Formula (13.5):

$$SS_{between} = n\left[\Sigma\bar{X}^2 - \frac{(\Sigma\bar{X})^2}{k}\right]$$

$$= n\left[\Sigma\left(\frac{T}{n}\right)^2 - \frac{\left(\Sigma\frac{T}{n}\right)^2}{k}\right] \quad \left(\text{substituting}\frac{T}{n} = \bar{X}\right)$$

$$= n\left[\Sigma\frac{T^2}{n^2} - \frac{(\Sigma T)^2}{n^2 k}\right]$$

$$= n\left[\Sigma\frac{T^2}{n^2} - \frac{G^2}{n^2 k}\right] \quad (\text{substituting } G = \Sigma T)$$

$$= \Sigma\frac{T^2}{n} - \frac{G^2}{nk} \quad (\text{multiplying both terms by } n)$$

$$= \Sigma\frac{T^2}{n} - \frac{G^2}{N} \quad (\text{substituting } N = nk)$$

Part II: Formulas for SS_{within}. You also should know that there is an alternative formula for finding SS_{within}. This formula is developed briefly in the following three steps:

1. First, recall that the two components add up to the total:

$$SS_{within} + SS_{between} = SS_{total}$$

2. By simple algebra we obtain the relation

$$SS_{within} = SS_{total} - SS_{between}$$

3. Finally, substituting the equations for SS_{total} and $SS_{between}$, we obtain

$$SS_{within} = \Sigma X^2 - \frac{G^2}{N} - \left(\Sigma\frac{T^2}{n} - \frac{G^2}{N}\right)$$

$$= \Sigma X^2 - \frac{G^2}{N} - \Sigma\frac{T^2}{n} + \frac{G^2}{N}$$

$$= \Sigma X^2 - \Sigma\frac{T^2}{n}$$

Note: This alternative formula for SS_{within} can help simplify the calculations for ANOVA. To find all three SS values, you must compute only three numbers: ΣX^2, $\Sigma T^2/n$, and G^2/N. These three values are sufficient to satisfy the three SS formulas.

1. Calculate SS_{total}, $SS_{between}$, and SS_{within} for the following set of data:

Treatment 1	Treatment 2	Treatment 3	
$n = 10$	$n = 10$	$n = 10$	$N = 30$
$T = 10$	$T = 20$	$T = 30$	$G = 60$
$SS = 27$	$SS = 16$	$SS = 23$	$\Sigma X^2 = 206$

ANSWER

1. $SS_{total} = 86$; $SS_{between} = 20$; $SS_{within} = 66$.

The Analysis of Degrees of Freedom (*df*)

The analysis of degrees of freedom (*df*) follows the same pattern as the analysis of SS. First, we will find *df* for the total set of N scores, and then we will partition this into two components: degrees of freedom between treatments and degrees of freedom within treatments. In computing degrees of freedom, there are two important considerations to keep in mind:

1. Each *df* value is associated with a specific SS value.
2. Normally, the value of *df* is obtained by counting the number of items that were used to calculate SS and then subtracting 1. For example, if you compute SS for a set of *n* scores, then $df = n - 1$.

With this in mind, we will examine the degrees of freedom for each part of the analysis:

1. *Total Degrees of Freedom, df_{total}.* To find the *df* associated with SS_{total}, you must first recall that this SS value measures variability for the entire set of N scores. Therefore, the *df* value will be

    (13.6) $df_{total} = N - 1$

    For the data in Table 13.2, the total number of scores is $N = 20$, so the total degrees of freedom would be

    $df_{total} = 20 - 1$

    $= 19$

2. *Within Treatments Degrees of Freedom, df_{within}.* To find the *df* associated with SS_{within}, we must look at how this SS value is computed. Remember, we first find SS inside each of the treatments and then add these values together. Each of the treatment SS values measures variability for the *n* scores in the treatment, so each SS will have $df = n - 1$. When all these individual treatment values are added together, we obtain

    (13.7) $df_{within} = \Sigma(n - 1)$

For the experiment we have been considering, each treatment has $n = 5$ scores. This means there are $n - 1 = 4$ degrees of freedom inside each treatment. Because there are four different treatment conditions, this gives a total of 16 for the within treatment degrees of freedom. Notice that this formula for df simply adds up the number of scores in each treatment (the n values) and subtracts 1 for each treatment. If these two stages are done separately, you obtain

(13.8) $df_{within} = N - k$

(Adding up all the n values gives N. If you subtract 1 for each treatment, then altogether you have subtracted k because there are k treatments.) For the data in Table 13.2, $N = 20$ and $k = 4$, so

$$df_{within} = 20 - 4$$
$$= 16$$

3. *Between Treatments Degrees of Freedom, $df_{between}$.* The df associated with $SS_{between}$ can be found by considering the SS formula. This SS formula measures the variability among the treatment means or totals. To find $df_{between}$, simply count the number of T values (or means) and subtract 1. Because the number of treatments is specified by the letter k, the formula for df is

(13.9) $df_{between} = k - 1$

For the data in Table 13.2, there are four different treatment conditions (four T values), so the between treatments degrees of freedom are

$$df_{between} = 4 - 1$$
$$= 3$$

Notice that the two parts we obtained from this analysis of degrees of freedom add up to equal the total degrees of freedom:

$$df_{total} = df_{within} + df_{between}$$
$$19 = 16 + 3$$

The complete analysis of degrees of freedom is shown in Figure 13.7.

Calculation of Variances (*MS*) and the *F*-Ratio

The final step in the analysis of variance procedure is to compute the variance between treatments and the variance within treatments in order to calculate the *F*-ratio. You should recall (from Chapter 4) that variance is defined as the average squared deviation. For a sample, you compute this average by the following formula:

$$\text{variance} = \frac{SS}{n-1}$$

$$= \frac{SS}{df}$$

In ANOVA it is customary to use the term *mean square* or simply *MS* in place of the term *variance*. Note that variance is the *mean squared deviation*, so this terminology is quite sensible. For the final *F*-ratio you will need an *MS* between treatments and an *MS* within treatments. In each case,

(13.10) $MS = \dfrac{SS}{df}$

For the data we have been considering,

$$MS_{between} = \frac{SS_{between}}{df_{between}} = \frac{30}{3} = 10$$

and

$$MS_{within} = \frac{SS_{within}}{df_{within}} = \frac{18}{16} = 1.125$$

We now have a measure of the variance (or differences) between the treatments and a measure of the variance within the treatments. The *F*-ratio simply compares these two variances:

(13.11) $F = \dfrac{MS_{between}}{MS_{within}}$

Figure 13.7
Partitioning degrees of freedom (*df*) for the independent measures analysis of variance.

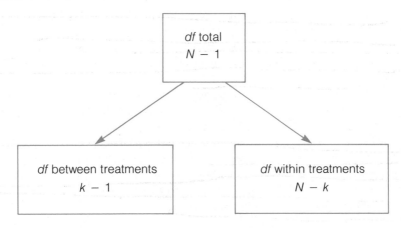

For the experiment we have been examining, the data give an F-ratio of

$$F = \frac{10}{1.125} = 8.89$$

The obtained value of $F = 8.89$ indicates that the numerator of the F-ratio is substantially bigger than the denominator. This is a clear indication that a treatment effect or mean difference really exists [see Formula (13.1)]. Stated in terms of the experimental variables, it appears that the temperature does have an effect on learning performance. However, to properly evaluate the F-ratio, we must examine the F distribution.

13.4
The Distribution of *F*-Ratios

In analysis of variance, the F-ratio is constructed so that the numerator and denominator of the ratio are measuring exactly the same variance when the null hypothesis is true [see Formula (13.1)]. In this situation we expect the value of F to be around 1.00. The problem now is to define precisely what we mean by "around 1.00." What values are considered to be close to 1.00, and what values are far away? To answer this question, we need to look at all the possible F values, that is, the distribution of F-ratios.

Before we examine this distribution in detail, you should note two obvious characteristics:

1. Because F-ratios are computed from two variances (the numerator and denominator of the ratio), F values always will be positive numbers. Remember, variance is always positive.
2. When H_0 is true, the numerator and denominator of the F-ratio are measuring the same variance. In this case, the two sample variances should be about the same size, so the ratio should be near 1. In other words, the distribution of F-ratios should pile up around 1.00.

With these two factors in mind we can sketch the distribution of F-ratios. The distribution is cut off at zero (all positive values), piles up around 1.00, and then tapers off to the right (see Figure 13.8). The exact shape of the F distribution depends on the degrees of freedom for the two variances in the F-ratio. You should recall that the precision of a sample variance depends on the number of scores or the degrees of freedom. In general, the variance for a large sample (large df) provides a more accurate estimate of the population variance. Because the precision of the MS values depends on df, the shape of the F distribution also will depend on the df values for the numerator and denominator of the F-ratio. With very large df values, nearly all the F-ratios will be clustered very near to 1.00. With smaller df values, the F distribution is more spread out.

Figure 13.8
A typical *F* distribution. *F*-ratios are always positive and form a
positively skewed distribution that peaks around a value of 1.00.

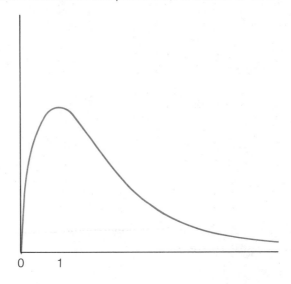

For analysis of variance we expect *F* near 1.00 if H_0 is true, and we
expect a large value for *F* if H_0 is not true. In the *F* distribution, we
need to separate those values that are reasonably near 1.00 from the
values that are significantly greater than 1.00. These critical values
are presented in an *F* distribution table in Appendix B, page A-32. To
use the table, you must know the *df* values for the *F*-ratio (numerator
and denominator), and you must know the alpha level for the hypothesis test. It is customary for an *F* table to have the *df* values for the
numerator of the *F*-ratio printed across the top of the table. The *df*
values for the denominator of *F* are printed in a column on the left-
hand side. A portion of the *F* distribution table is shown in Table 13.3.
For the temperature experiment we have been considering, the
numerator of the *F*-ratio (between treatments) has *df* = 3 and the
denominator of the *F*-ratio (within treatments) has *df* = 16. This *F*-
ratio is said to have "degrees of freedom equal to 3 and 16." The
degrees of freedom would be written as *df* = 3, 16. To use the table,
you would first find *df* = 3 across the top of the table and *df* = 16 in
the first column. When you line up these two values, they point to a
pair of numbers in the middle of the table. These numbers give the
critical cutoffs for α = .05 and α = .01. With *df* = 3, 16, for example,
the numbers in the table are 3.24 and 5.29. These values indicate that
the most unlikely 5% of the distribution (α = .05) begins at a value
of 3.24. The most extreme 1% of the distribution begins at a value of
5.29 (see Figure 13.9).

In the temperature experiment we obtained an *F*-ratio of 8.89.
According to the critical cutoffs in Figure 13.9, this value is extremely

Table 13.3

A Portion of the *F* Distribution Table. Entries in roman type are critical values for the .05 level of significance and bold type values are for the .01 level of significance.

	Degrees of Freedom: Numerator														
Degrees of Freedom Denominator	1	2	3	4	5	6	7	8	9	10	11	12	14	16	20
10	4.96 **10.04**	4.10 **7.56**	3.71 **6.55**	3.48 **5.99**	3.33 **5.64**	3.22 **5.39**	3.14 **5.21**	3.07 **5.06**	3.02 **4.95**	2.97 **4.85**	2.94 **4.78**	2.91 **4.71**	2.86 **4.60**	2.82 **4.52**	2.77 **4.41**
11	4.84 **9.65**	3.98 **7.20**	3.59 **6.22**	3.36 **5.67**	3.20 **5.32**	3.09 **5.07**	3.01 **4.88**	2.95 **4.74**	2.90 **4.63**	2.86 **4.54**	2.82 **4.46**	2.79 **4.40**	2.74 **4.29**	2.70 **4.21**	2.65 **4.10**
12	4.75 **9.33**	3.88 **6.93**	3.49 **5.95**	3.26 **5.41**	3.11 **5.06**	3.00 **4.82**	2.92 **4.65**	2.85 **4.50**	2.80 **4.39**	2.76 **4.30**	2.72 **4.22**	2.69 **4.16**	2.64 **4.05**	2.60 **3.98**	2.54 **3.86**
13	4.67 **9.07**	3.80 **6.70**	3.41 **5.74**	3.18 **5.20**	3.02 **4.86**	2.92 **4.62**	2.84 **4.44**	2.77 **4.30**	2.72 **4.19**	2.67 **4.10**	2.63 **4.02**	2.60 **3.96**	2.55 **3.85**	2.51 **3.78**	2.46 **3.67**
14	4.60 **8.86**	3.74 **6.51**	3.34 **5.56**	3.11 **5.03**	2.96 **4.69**	2.85 **4.46**	2.77 **4.28**	2.70 **4.14**	2.65 **4.03**	2.60 **3.94**	2.56 **3.86**	2.53 **3.80**	2.48 **3.70**	2.44 **3.62**	2.39 **3.51**
15	4.54 **8.68**	3.68 **6.36**	3.29 **5.42**	3.06 **4.89**	2.90 **4.56**	2.79 **4.32**	2.70 **4.14**	2.64 **4.00**	2.59 **3.89**	2.55 **3.80**	2.51 **3.73**	2.48 **3.67**	2.43 **3.56**	2.39 **3.48**	2.33 **3.36**
16	4.49 **8.53**	3.63 **6.23**	3.24 **5.29**	3.01 **4.77**	2.85 **4.44**	2.74 **4.20**	2.66 **4.03**	2.59 **3.89**	2.54 **3.78**	2.49 **3.69**	2.45 **3.61**	2.42 **3.55**	2.37 **3.45**	2.33 **3.37**	2.28 **3.25**
17	4.45 **8.40**	3.59 **6.11**	3.20 **5.18**	2.96 **4.67**	2.81 **4.34**	2.70 **4.10**	2.62 **3.93**	2.55 **3.79**	2.50 **3.68**	2.45 **3.59**	2.41 **3.52**	2.38 **3.45**	2.33 **3.35**	2.29 **3.27**	2.23 **3.16**
18	4.41 **8.28**	3.55 **6.01**	3.16 **5.09**	2.93 **4.58**	2.77 **4.25**	2.66 **4.01**	2.58 **3.85**	2.51 **3.71**	2.46 **3.60**	2.41 **3.51**	2.37 **3.44**	2.34 **3.37**	2.29 **3.27**	2.25 **3.19**	2.19 **3.07**

Figure 13.9

The distribution of F-ratios with $df = 3, 16$. Of all the values in the distribution, 95% are less than $F = 3.24$, and 99% are less than $F = 5.29$.

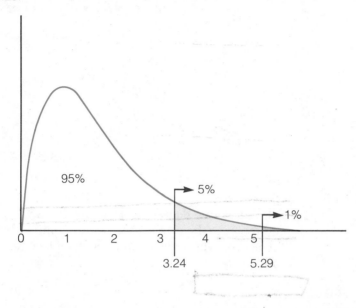

unlikely (it is in the most extreme 1%). Therefore, we would reject H_0 with $\alpha = .01$ and conclude that the temperature does have a significant effect on learning performance.

13.5
Examples of Hypothesis Testing with ANOVA

EXAMPLE 13.1

The data depicted in Table 13.4 were obtained from an independent measures experiment designed to measure the effectiveness of three pain relievers (A, B, and C). A fourth group that received a placebo (sugar pill) also was tested.

The purpose of the analysis is to determine whether these sample data provide evidence of any significant differences among the four drugs. The dependent variable is the amount of time (in seconds) that subjects can withstand a painfully hot stimulus.

STEP 1. The first step is to state the hypotheses and select an alpha level:

H_0: $\mu_1 = \mu_2 = \mu_3 = \mu_4$ (no treatment effect)

H_1: At least one of the treatment means is different

We will use $\alpha = .05$.

Table 13.4

The Effect of Drug Treatment on the Amount of Time (in Seconds) Stimulus Is Endured

Placebo	Drug A	Drug B	Drug C	
0	1	3	7	$N = 12$
0	2	4	4	$G = 36$
3	3	5	4	$\Sigma X^2 = 154$
$T = 3$	$T = 6$	$T = 12$	$T = 15$	
$SS = 6$	$SS = 2$	$SS = 2$	$SS = 6$	

STEP 2.   To locate the critical region for the F-ratio, we first must determine degrees of freedom for $MS_{between}$ and MS_{within} (the numerator and denominator of F). For these data, the total degrees of freedom would be

$$df_{total} = N - 1$$
$$= 12 - 1$$
$$= 11$$

Analyzing this total into two components, we obtain

Note that the two df components (between and within) add up to equal df_{total}.

$$df_{between} = k - 1$$
$$= 4 - 1$$
$$= 3$$
$$df_{within} = N - k$$
$$= 12 - 4$$
$$= 8$$

The F-ratio for these data will have $df = 3, 8$. The distribution of all the possible F-ratios with $df = 3, 8$ is presented in Figure 13.10. Almost always (95% of the time) we should obtain an F-ratio less than 4.07 if H_0 is true.

STEP 3.   We already have the data for this experiment, so it now is time for the calculations.

Analysis of SS: First we will compute the total SS and then the two components as indicated in Figure 13.6:

Figure 13.10

The distribution of F-ratios with $df = 3, 8$. The critical value for $\alpha = .05$ is $F = 4.07$.

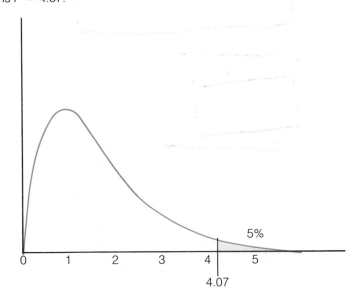

$$SS_{total} = \Sigma X^2 - \frac{G^2}{N}$$

$$= 154 - \frac{36^2}{12}$$

$$= 154 - 108$$

$$= 46$$

$$SS_{within} = \Sigma SS_{inside\ each\ treatment}$$

$$= 6 + 2 + 2 + 6$$

$$= 16$$

$$SS_{between} = \Sigma \frac{T^2}{n} - \frac{G^2}{N}$$

$$= \frac{3^2}{3} + \frac{6^2}{3} + \frac{12^2}{3} + \frac{15^2}{3} - \frac{36^2}{12}$$

$$= 3 + 12 + 48 + 75 - 108$$

$$= 30$$

Note that the two variability components (between and within) add up to equal SS_{total}.

Calculation of Mean Squares. Now we must compute the variance or MS for each of the two components:

$$MS_{between} = \frac{SS_{between}}{df_{between}} = \frac{30}{3} = 10$$

$$MS_{within} = \frac{SS_{within}}{df_{within}} = \frac{16}{8} = 2$$

Calculation of F. Finally, we compute the *F*-ratio:

$$F = \frac{MS_{between}}{MS_{within}} = \frac{10}{2} = 5.00$$

STEP 4. *Statistical Decision.* The *F* value we obtained, $F = 5.00$, is in the critical region (see Figure 13.10). It is very likely ($p < .05$) that we will obtain a value this large if H_0 is true. Therefore, we reject H_0 and conclude that there is a significant treatment effect.

Example 13.1 demonstrated the complete, step-by-step application of the ANOVA procedure. There are three additional points that can be made using this example.

First, you should look carefully at the statistical decision. We have rejected H_0 and concluded that not all the treatments are the same. But we have not determined which ones are different. Is drug A different from the placebo? Is drug A different from drug B? Unfortunately, these questions remain unanswered. We do know that at least one difference exists (we rejected H_0), but additional analysis is necessary to find out exactly where this difference is. This problem is addressed later in Section 13.6.

Second, it is common in experimental reports to present the obtained *F*-ratio, the degrees of freedom, and the alpha level in one concise phrase. For the data in Example 13.1, this phrase would be

$F(3, 8) = 5.00, p < .05$

This phrase indicates that our *F*-ratio has $df = 3, 8$, we obtained a value of $F = 5.00$ from the data, and the *F* value was in the critical region with alpha equal to .05.

Third, all of the parts of the analysis (the *SS, df, F,* etc.) can be presented together in one table called an analysis of variance summary table. Although these tables are no longer commonly used in published research reports, they do provide a concise means for presenting the results of an analysis. The summary table for the analysis in Example 13.1 is as follows:

Source	df	SS	MS	
Between treatments	3	30	10	F = 5.00
Within treatments	8	16	2	
Total	11	46		

EXAMPLE 13.2 A Computer Analysis

Because ANOVA requires extensive calculations, this hypothesis testing procedure is often conducted on a computer using one of several statistical *packages* that have been developed for data analysis (for example, BMDP, SPSS, SAS, OMNITAB). In addition to performing all of the basic calculations, most of these computer programs also will produce a detailed printout summarizing the ANOVA and providing general information about the data and the results. We have used one of these statistical packages, called MINITAB, to perform an ANOVA using the same data that were presented in Example 13.1. The printout from this program is shown in Table 13.5.

Most of the content of this printout is explained in the table, but one feature deserves special comment. The printout shows 95% confidence intervals for the population means of each of the four treatments. The sample mean, marked by *, is at the center of each interval, and the boundaries are marked by parentheses. For example, treatment 4 has a sample mean of 5.0, and the confidence interval extends from approximately 3.2 to 6.8. You can be 95% confident that the population mean is actually located somewhere within this interval.

You should notice that most of these confidence intervals overlap. For example, the range of values covered by the confidence interval for treatment 1 is almost the same as the range covered by the interval for treatment 2. This indicates that there is a good probability that these two population means are located in the same region. In statistical terms, these two population means are not significantly different. If you look closely at all four confidence intervals, you will notice that the only ones which do not overlap are the interval from treatment 1 and the interval from treatment 4. There is a high probability that these two population means are different. In fact, this is the mean difference, $\mu_1 \neq \mu_4$, that caused us to reject the null hypothesis in this ANOVA.

Examples with Zero Variance

The next two examples are intended to give you a better understanding of exactly what is measured by the between treatments and the within treatments variances. By creating extreme data sets, we will demonstrate how these two variance components are related to the actual scores from an experiment.

EXAMPLE 13.3

We will start with the same set of scores that was used in Example 13.1. However, we will adjust the scores so that each of the four treatment conditions has exactly the same

Table 13.5
MINITAB Analysis for Example 13.1[a]

```
MINITAB RELEASE 82.1 *** COPYRIGHT - PENN STATE UNIV. 1982
MAY 31, 1984 *** S.U.N.Y. BROCKPORT - ACADEMIC COMPUTING SERVICES
STORAGE AVAILABLE 1079344
There is HELP on new features of Rel. 82.1.  Type NEWS for details.
MTB > READ C1 C2 C3 C4
    3 ROWS READ
  ROW   C1   C2   C3   C4

    1    0    1    3    7
    2    0    2    4    4
    3    3    3    5    4


MTB > AOVONEWAY C1-C4

ANALYSIS OF VARIANCE
  SOURCE      DF       SS       MS        F
  FACTOR       3    30.00    10.00     5.00
  ERROR        8    16.00     2.00
  TOTAL       11    46.00

                          INDIVIDUAL 95 PCT CI'S FOR MEAN
                          BASED ON POOLED STDEV
  LEVEL      N     MEAN    STDEV   ----+---------+---------+---------+---
  C1         3    1.000    1.732   (-------*-------)
  C2         3    2.000    1.000      (-------*-------)
  C3         3    4.000    1.000              (-------*-------)
  C4         3    5.000    1.732                 (-------*-------)

POOLED STDEV = 1.414                ----+---------+---------+---------+---
MTB > END                           0.0      2.4      4.8      7.2
MTB > PRINT
MTB > STOP


*** MINITAB *** STATISTICS DEPT * PENN STATE UNIV. * RELEASE 82.1 *
STORAGE AVAILABLE 1079344
```

[a]Explanation of printout:
1. The Original Data. The four treatments from the experiment appear as four columns (C1, C2, C3, C4) of scores.
2. A Summary Table. The overall results of the ANOVA are presented in a summary table. Note that the between treatments source of variability is labeled "FACTOR." The within treatment variability is simply called "ERROR," indicating it is the error term of the F-ratio.
3. Sample Statistics. Summary statistics, including the number of scores (n), the mean, and the standard deviation, are provided for each of the four treatments (C1–C4). In addition, a 95% confidence interval is displayed for the population mean of each of the treatments (see the text for further explanation). The pooled standard deviation ("POOLED STDEV") is similar to the pooled variance we used in the independent t statistic. This measure is the square root of the error term, $MS_{within\ treatment}$.

total. In the placebo group, for example, we add two points to each score. For drug A, we add one point to each score. For drug B, we subtract one point, and for drug C, we subtract two points. The resulting data are as follows:

Placebo	Drug A	Drug B	Drug C	
2	2	2	5	$N = 12$
2	3	3	2	$G = 36$
5	4	4	2	$\Sigma X^2 = 124$
$T = 9$	$T = 9$	$T = 9$	$T = 9$	
$SS = 6$	$SS = 2$	$SS = 2$	$SS = 6$	

Before we start the calculation, you should notice that the treatment totals are no longer variable. Because there are no mean differences in these data, the between treatments variability should be zero.

Instead of working through the entire analysis of variance with these data, we simply will compute the total SS and then partition it into its two components:

$$SS_{total} = \Sigma X^2 - \frac{G^2}{N}$$

$$= 124 - \frac{36^2}{12}$$

$$= 124 - 108$$

$$= 16$$

$$SS_{within} = \Sigma SS_{inside}$$

$$= 6 + 2 + 2 + 6$$

$$= 16$$

$$SS_{between} = \Sigma \frac{T^2}{n} - \frac{G^2}{N}$$

$$= \frac{9^2}{3} + \frac{9^2}{3} + \frac{9^2}{3} + \frac{9^2}{3} - \frac{36^2}{12}$$

$$= 27 + 27 + 27 + 27 - 108$$

$$= 108 - 108$$

$$= 0$$

You should note that SS_{within} is the same now as it was for the original data in Example 13.1. The adjustment to the scores did not change any of the variability inside the treatment conditions. But now the variance inside the treatments accounts for all of the variability in the data. Because there are no differences between treatments, $SS_{between} = 0$.

EXAMPLE 13.4
Once again, we will start with the data that were used in Example 13.1, but this time we will adjust the scores to get rid of all variability inside the treatments. In the placebo group, for example, we will make all the scores $X = 1$. This group still totals $T = 3$, but now it has no variability. For drug A, we make all values $X = 2$. For drug B, all scores

become $X = 4$, and for drug C, all scores are now $X = 5$. The resulting data are as follows:

Placebo	Drug A	Drug B	Drug C	
1	2	4	5	$N = 12$
1	2	4	5	$G = 36$
1	2	4	5	$\Sigma X^2 = 138$
$T = 3$	$T = 6$	$T = 12$	$T = 15$	
$SS = 0$	$SS = 0$	$SS = 0$	$SS = 0$	

Comparing these data with the values in Example 13.1, you should notice that the adjustment has not changed any of the treatment totals; the differences between treatments are the same as they were before. However, we now have no variability inside the treatments.

Once again, we will analyze only the SS for these data:

$$SS_{total} = \Sigma X^2 - \frac{G^2}{N}$$

$$= 138 - \frac{36^2}{12}$$

$$= 138 - 108$$

$$= 30$$

$$SS_{within} = \Sigma SS_{inside\ each\ treatment}$$

$$= 0 + 0 + 0 + 0$$

$$= 0$$

$$SS_{between} = \Sigma \frac{T^2}{n} - \frac{G^2}{N}$$

$$= \frac{3^2}{3} + \frac{6^2}{3} + \frac{12^2}{3} + \frac{15^2}{3} - \frac{36^2}{12}$$

$$= 3 + 12 + 48 + 75 - 108$$

$$= 138 - 108$$

$$= 30$$

You should note that $SS_{between}$ is the same for these data as it was for the original set of scores in Example 13.1. But now the differences between the treatments account for all of the total variability.

There are several points to be drawn from the previous two examples. First, the variability within treatments and the variability between treatments are completely independent. This means that the value of one variance has no influence on the value of the other. In the preceding two examples, we were able to completely eliminate one of these variance components without having any effect on the other. The importance of this fact becomes clearer if you look once again at the F-ratio formula:

$$F = \frac{\text{variance between treatments}}{\text{variance within treatments}}$$

If we simplify matters by assuming that you always will get at least a medium amount of variance between and within treatments, then there are two ways that you can end up with a large F-ratio (i.e., a significant difference between treatments):

1. The F-ratio will be large if the numerator of the ratio ($MS_{between}$) is very large:

$$F = \frac{\text{large value}}{\text{medium value}} = \text{large value} \qquad \text{(greater than 1.00)}$$

2. The F-ratio will be large if the denominator of the ratio (MS_{within}) is very small:

$$F = \frac{\text{medium value}}{\text{small value}} = \text{large value} \qquad \text{(greater than 1.00)}$$

In designing an experiment, it is possible for a researcher to exert some control over these two variance components. Specifically, you can increase the chances that $MS_{between}$ will be large and that MS_{within} will be small. In this way the researcher can increase the chances of obtaining a large (significant) value for F. For example, a researcher investigating the effects of a drug may want to increase the dosage in order to maximize the chances of finding a large treatment effect, that is, increase $MS_{between}$. In addition, this researcher probably would test all the experimental subjects in a quiet laboratory setting in order to avoid external distractions. This should help to reduce the amount of variability within the treatment conditions. Once again, the important consideration is that the two variance components (the two parts of the F-ratio) are independent. An experimental manipulation that affects one will not necessarily affect the other.

The second point is that whenever you look at a set of data, you should be able to make a rough estimate of the amount of variability within and between treatments. To judge the amount of variability between treatments, you must examine the treatment totals (or means). Are the totals all around the same value (little variability), or are there big differences between the totals (large variability)? Remember, $SS_{between}$ essentially is measuring the mean differences from one treatment to the next. In Example 13.3, the treatment totals were all the same, there were no mean differences, and $SS_{between}$ was zero.

To judge the variability within treatments, you must look at the scores inside each treatment individually. If these scores are all clustered together, variability is low. If the scores are spread out, variability is large. In Example 13.4 the scores inside each treatment were identical, there was no variability, and SS_{within} was zero. Obviously you will not be able to judge these two variance components with great precision, but you should be able to make rough estimates (is the variance big or small?). Remember, if you can estimate the relative size of these two variance components, then you can estimate the size of the F-ratio.

An Example with Unequal Sample Sizes

In each example considered thus far all of the samples were exactly the same size (equal ns). However, the formulas for ANOVA can be used when the sample size varies within an experiment. With unequal sample sizes you must take care to be sure that each value of n is matched with the proper T value in the equations. You also should note that the general ANOVA procedure is most accurate when used to examine experimental data with equal sample sizes. Therefore, researchers generally try to plan experiments with equal ns. However, there are circumstances where it is impossible or impractical to have an equal number of subjects in every treatment condition. In these situations, ANOVA still provides a valid test, especially when the samples are relatively large and when the discrepancy between sample sizes is not extreme.

EXAMPLE 13.5
A psychologist conducts an experiment to compare learning performance for three species of monkeys. The animals are tested individually on a delayed-response task. A raisin is hidden in one of three containers while the animal is viewing from its cage window. A shade is then pulled over the window for 1 minute to block the view. After this delay period, the monkey is allowed to respond by tipping over one container. If its response is correct, the monkey is rewarded with the raisin. The number of trials it takes before the animal makes five consecutive correct responses is recorded. The experimenter used all of the available animals from each species, which resulted in unequal sample sizes (n). The data are summarized in Table 13.6.

Table 13.6
The Performance of Different Species of Monkeys on a Delayed-Response Task

Vervet	Rhesus	Baboon	
$n = 4$	$n = 10$	$n = 6$	$N = 20$
$\overline{X} = 9$	$\overline{X} = 14$	$\overline{X} = 4$	$G = 200$
$T = 36$	$T = 140$	$T = 24$	$\Sigma X^2 = 3400$
$SS = 200$	$SS = 500$	$SS = 320$	

STEP 1. *State Hypothesis and Select Alpha.*

H_0: $\mu_1 = \mu_2 = \mu_3$

H_1: At least one population is different from the others

$\alpha = .05$

STEP 2. *Locate the Critical Region.* To find the critical region, we first must determine the *df* values for the *F*-ratio:

$$df_{total} = N - 1 = 20 - 1 = 19$$
$$df_{between} = k - 1 = 3 - 1 = 2$$
$$df_{within} = N - k = 20 - 3 = 17$$

The *F*-ratio for these data will have $df = 2, 17$. With $\alpha = .05$, the critical value for the *F*-ratio is 3.59.

STEP 3. *Compute the F-ratio.* First compute *SS* for all three parts of the analysis:

$$\begin{aligned}
SS_{total} &= \Sigma X^2 - \frac{G^2}{N} \\
&= 3400 - \frac{200^2}{20} \\
&= 3400 - 2000 \\
&= 1400
\end{aligned}$$

$$\begin{aligned}
SS_{between} &= \Sigma \frac{T^2}{n} - \frac{G^2}{N} \\
&= \frac{36^2}{4} + \frac{140^2}{10} + \frac{24^2}{6} - \frac{200^2}{20} \\
&= 324 + 1960 + 96 - 2000 \\
&= 380
\end{aligned}$$

$$\begin{aligned}
SS_{within} &= \Sigma SS_{inside\ each\ treatment} \\
&= 200 + 500 + 320 \\
&= 1020
\end{aligned}$$

Finally, compute the *MS* values and the *F*-ratio:

$$\begin{aligned}
MS_{between} &= \frac{SS}{df} \\
&= \frac{380}{2} \\
&= 190
\end{aligned}$$

$$MS_{within} = \frac{SS}{df}$$

$$= \frac{1020}{17}$$

$$= 60$$

$$F = \frac{MS_{between}}{MS_{within}} = \frac{190}{60} = 3.17$$

STEP 4. *Make Decision.* Because the obtained F-ratio is not in the critical region, we fail to reject H_0 and conclude that these data do not provide evidence of significant differences among the three populations of monkeys in terms of average learning performance.

---

1. The following data summarize the results of an experiment using three separate samples to compare three treatment conditions:

Treatment 1	Treatment 2	Treatment 3	
$n = 5$	$n = 5$	$n = 5$	
$T = 5$	$T = 10$	$T = 30$	$\Sigma X^2 = 325$
$SS = 45$	$SS = 25$	$SS = 50$	

Do these data provide evidence of any significant mean differences among the treatments? Test with $\alpha = .05$.

ANSWER

1. The following summary table presents the results of the analysis:

Source	df	SS	MS	
Between	2	70	35	$F = 3.5$
Within	12	120	10	
Total	14	190		

13.6
Post Hoc Tests

In analysis of variance, the null hypothesis states that there is no treatment effect:

$$H_0: \quad \mu_1 = \mu_2 = \mu_3 \cdots$$

When you reject the null hypothesis, you conclude that the means are not all the same. Although this appears to be a simple conclusion, in most cases it actually creates more questions than it answers. For example, when there are only two treatments in an experiment, H_0 will state that $\mu_1 = \mu_2$. If you reject this hypothesis, the conclusion is quite straightforward; i.e., the two means are not equal ($\mu_1 \neq \mu_2$). However, when you have more than two treatments, the situation immediately becomes more complex. With $k = 3$, for example, rejecting H_0 indicates that not all the means are the same. Now you must decide which ones are different. Is μ_1 different from μ_2? Is μ_2 different from μ_3? Is μ_1 different from μ_3? Are all three different? The purpose of post hoc tests is to answer these questions.

As the name implies, post hoc tests are done after an analysis of variance. More specifically, these tests are done after ANOVA when

1. You reject H_0 and
2. There are three or more treatments ($k \geqslant 3$).

Rejecting H_0 indicates that at least one difference exists among the treatments. With $k = 3$ or more, the problem is to find where the differences are.

In general, a post hoc test enables you to go back through the data and compare the individual treatments two at a time. In statistical terms, this is called making *pairwise comparisons*. For example, with $k = 3$, we would compare μ_1 versus μ_2, then μ_2 versus μ_3, and then μ_1 versus μ_3. In each case, we are looking for a significant mean difference. You should notice that in order to test all of these pairwise comparisons, we will be doing several different hypothesis tests. As we discussed at the beginning of the chapter, this creates a problem. Specifically, the more tests you do, the more risk there is of a type I error. Even though the ANOVA has indicated that at least one significant difference exists, this does not mean that you can completely forget about alpha levels and go on a "fishing expedition" looking for treatment differences. When doing post hoc tests, you still must be concerned about type I errors.

Many different post hoc test procedures have been developed because there are many different ways of controlling the alpha level. However, these tests can be classified into two broad categories: *a priori* or planned comparisons and *a posteriori* or unplanned comparisons.

DEFINITION

A priori tests are intended to compare specific treatment conditions that are identified before the experiment begins. These tests generally make little attempt to control the alpha level. They should be used cautiously and only when you have a small number of preplanned comparisons. Planned comparisons can be made even when the overall F-ratio is not significant.

The rationale for these tests is that the researcher has a specific small experiment (comparing two treatments) contained within a larger experiment. Because the investigator has specific hypotheses for just this portion of the experiment, it is reasonable to test its results separately.

DEFINITION

A *posteriori tests* are used for treatment comparisons that were not necessarily planned at the beginning of the experiment. These tests attempt to control the overall alpha level by making adjustments for the number of different samples (potential comparisons) in the experiment. To justify a posteriori tests, the *F*-ratio from the overall ANOVA must be significant.

Tukey's Honestly Significant Difference (HSD) Test

We will examine only one of the many possible post hoc tests. We have selected Tukey's HSD test because it is a good representative of a posteriori tests, and it is a commonly used test in psychological research. Tukey's test allows you to compute a single value that determines the minimum difference between treatment means that is necessary for significance. This value, called the honestly significant difference, or HSD, is then used to compare any two treatment conditions. If the mean difference exceeds Tukey's HSD, you conclude that there is a significant difference between the treatments. Otherwise you cannot conclude that the treatments are significantly different. The formula for Tukey's HSD is

$$(13.12) \quad HSD = q\sqrt{\frac{MS_{within}}{n}}$$

The q value used in Tukey's HSD test is called a Studentized range statistic.

where the value of q is found in Table B5 (Appendix B, page A-35), MS_{within} is the within treatment variance from the ANOVA, and n is the number of scores in each treatment. To locate the appropriate value of q, you must know the number of treatments in the overall experiment (k) and the degrees of freedom for MS_{within} (the error term in the *F*-ratio) and select an alpha level (generally the same α used for the ANOVA).

EXAMPLE 13.6
To outline the procedure for conducting post hoc tests with Tukey's HSD, we will use the data from the pain-reliever study in Example 13.1. The data are reproduced here in summary form:

	1, Placebo	2, Drug A	3, Drug B	4, Drug C
	$n = 3$	$n = 3$	$n = 3$	$n = 3$
	$T = 3$	$T = 6$	$T = 12$	$T = 15$
	$\overline{X} = 1$	$\overline{X} = 2$	$\overline{X} = 4$	$\overline{X} = 5$

The within treatments variance for these data is $MS_{within} =$ 2.00 with $df = 8$.

With $\alpha = .05$ and $k = 4$, the value of q for these data is $q = 4.53$. Tukey's HSD is

$$HSD = q \sqrt{\frac{MS_{within}}{n}}$$

$$= 4.53 \sqrt{\frac{2.00}{3}}$$

$$= 3.70$$

Therefore, the mean difference between any two samples must be at least 3.70 to be significant. Using this value, we can make the following conclusions:

1. Drug A is not significantly different from the placebo ($\overline{X} = 2$ versus $\overline{X} = 1$).
2. Drug B is not significantly different from the placebo ($\overline{X} = 4$ versus $\overline{X} = 1$).
3. Drug C is significantly different from the placebo ($\overline{X} = 5$ versus $\overline{X} = 1$).

Thus, drug C is the only one that produced significantly more pain relief than the placebo.

You also may notice that Tukey's HSD test can lead to the conclusion that there are no significant differences among the drugs (check the mean differences). This may seem to contradict the finding that drug C is the only one different from the placebo. However, you should recall that saying "no significant difference" is not equivalent to saying "no difference." There may be differences among the three drugs; however, these differences are not large enough to satisfy the criterion of statistical significance. For these data, the only mean difference large enough to be statistically significant is between drug C ($\overline{X} = 5$) and the placebo ($\overline{X} = 1$).

LEARNING
CHECK

1. The following data summarize the results of an independent measures experiment comparing three treatments with samples of $n = 5$ in each treatment:

Treatment 1	Treatment 2	Treatment 3
$\overline{X} = 3.5$	$\overline{X} = 10.0$	$\overline{X} = 18.0$

The overall ANOVA produced a significant F-ratio with MS_{within} = 20. Use Tukey's HSD test to determine which treatment conditions are statistically different at the .05 level of significance.

ANSWER

1. With $\alpha = .05$, $k = 3$, and $df_{within} = 12$, the critical value of q is 3.77. This gives an HSD of 7.54. The comparisons between means are as follows:

> 1 versus 2 (6.5-point difference): not significant
>
> 2 versus 3 (8-point difference): significant
>
> 1 versus 3 (14.5-point difference): significant

13.7
The Relation Between ANOVA and t Tests

When you have data from an independent measures experiment with only two treatment conditions, you can use either a t test (Chapter 11) or independent measures ANOVA. In practical terms, it makes no difference which you choose. These two statistical techniques always will result in the same statistical decision. In fact, the two methods use many of the same calculations and are very closely related in several other respects. The basic relation between t statistics and F-ratios can be stated in an equation:

$$F = t^2$$

The details of this relationship are presented in Example 13.7, but we will discuss some of the more general aspects of the relation before looking at the example.

1. First, it should be obvious that you will be testing the same hypotheses whether you choose a t test or ANOVA. With only two treatments, the hypotheses for either test are

$$H_0: \quad \mu_1 = \mu_2$$
$$H_1: \quad \mu_1 \neq \mu_2$$

2. The degrees of freedom for the t statistic and the df for the denominator of the F-ratio (df_{within}) are identical. For example, if you have two samples, each with six scores, the independent measures t statistic will have $df = 10$, and the F-ratio will have $df = 1, 10$. In each case, you are adding the df from the first sample ($n - 1$) and the df from the second sample.

3. The distribution of t and the distribution of F-ratios match perfectly if you take into consideration the relation $F = t^2$. Consider the t distribution with $df = 10$ and the corresponding F distribution with $df = 1, 10$ that are presented in Figure 13.11. Notice the following relationships:

a. If each of the t values is squared, then all of the negative values will become positive. As a result, the whole left-hand side of the t distribution (below zero) will be

Figure 13.11

The distribution of t-scores with $df = 10$ and the corresponding F distribution with $df = 1, 10$. Notice that squaring the t values produces the F values. For $\alpha = .05$, the critical value for t is ±2.228, and the critical value for F is $2.228^2 = 4.96$. At $\alpha = .01$, the critical value for t is ±3.169, and the corresponding critical value for F is $3.169^2 = 10.04$.

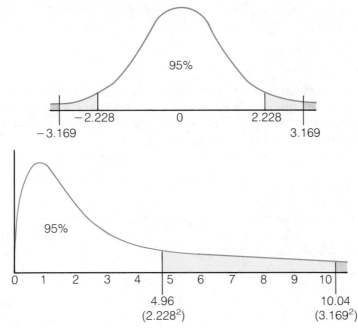

flipped over to the positive side. This creates a nonsymmetrical, positively skewed distribution, that is, the F distribution.

b. For $\alpha = .05$, the critical region for t is determined by values greater than $+2.228$ or less than -2.228. When these boundaries are squared, you get

$$\pm2.228^2 = 4.96$$

Notice that 4.96 is the critical value for $\alpha = .05$ in the F distribution. Any value that is in the critical region for t will end up in the critical region for F-ratios after it is squared.

c. For $\alpha = .01$, the critical cutoffs for t are ±3.169. Squaring this value gives 10.04, which is the $\alpha = .01$ cutoff for the F distribution.

4. Finally, the relation between F and t becomes clearer if you look at the structure of the two formulas. The independent measures t formula is

$$t = \frac{(\overline{X}_1 - \overline{X}_2) - (\mu_1 - \mu_2)}{s_{\overline{x}-\overline{x}}}$$

When the null hypothesis is true ($\mu_1 - \mu_2 = 0$), the formula becomes

$$t = \frac{\overline{X}_1 - \overline{X}_2}{s_{\overline{x} - \overline{x}}}$$

Note that the numerator and denominator of the t formula both are measuring distance. The distance between the two sample means is in the numerator. The standard error, or standard distance, is in the denominator. For the F-ratio the formula is

$$F = \frac{MS_{between}}{MS_{within}}$$

The numerator and denominator of this formula both measure variance, or mean squared deviation. Both parts of the F-ratio are measuring squared distance. With the t statistic based on distances and the F-ratio based on squared distances, we have the basic relation between F and t: $F = t^2$. This relation is presented in detail in Example 13.7.

EXAMPLE 13.7
We will use the following data to examine the relation between ANOVA and the t test when there are only two treatments being compared.

Hormone	Control
$n = 10$	$n = 10$
$SS = 40$	$SS = 50$
$\overline{X} = 3$	$\overline{X} = 7$

The data represent the results of an experiment designed to examine whether hormone levels in a pregnant rat can affect the intelligence of the offspring. A psychologist selects two groups of pregnant rats. The animals in one group receive regular injections of the hormone, and the rats in the second group serve as a control (no hormone injections). When the pups are 2 months old, one is randomly selected from each litter and tested on a problem-solving task. The dependent variable is the number errors.

STEP 1.   The hypotheses are the same for the t test and the analysis of variance:

H_0: $\mu_1 = \mu_2$ (no difference)
H_1: $\mu_1 \neq \mu_2$ (there is an effect)

We will use $\alpha = .05$.

STEP 2.   For these data, the t statistic will have $df = 18$, and the F-ratio will have $df = 1, 18$. With $\alpha = .05$, the critical values for t are ± 2.101. For the F-ratio, the critical value is 4.41. Notice that 4.41 = 2.101^2. The t statistic and the F-ratio distributions are shown in Figure 13.12.

STEP 3. To compute the t statistic for these data, we first need the pooled variance:

$$s_p^2 = \frac{SS_1 + SS_2}{df_1 + df_2} = \frac{40 + 50}{9 + 9} = \frac{90}{18} = 5$$

Then the standard error is computed:

$$s_{\bar{x}-\bar{x}} = \sqrt{\frac{s_p^2}{n_1} + \frac{s_p^2}{n_2}} = \sqrt{\frac{5}{10} + \frac{5}{10}} = \sqrt{1} = 1$$

Finally, t is

$$t = \frac{(\overline{X}_1 - \overline{X}_2) - (\mu_1 - \mu_2)}{s_{\bar{x}-\bar{x}}} = \frac{4 - 0}{1} = 4$$

To compute the F-ratio for these data, we will need $MS_{between}$ and MS_{within}. (Note that we do not have the individual scores, so we cannot compute

---

Figure 13.12

The distribution of t-scores with $df = 18$ and the corresponding distribution of F-ratios with $df = 1, 18$. Notice that the critical values for $\alpha = .05$ are $t = \pm 2.101$ and that $F = 2.101^2 = 4.41$.

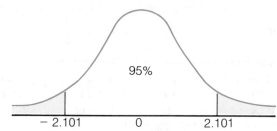

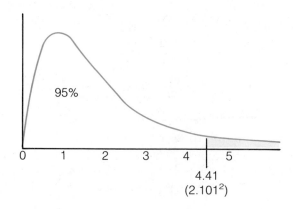

the total sum of squares directly. However, this value is not essential in order to find the F-ratio.)

For MS_{within} we need values for SS and df:

$$SS_{within} = \Sigma SS_{inside\ each\ treatment}$$
$$= 40 + 50$$
$$= 90$$
$$df_{within} = N - k$$
$$= 20 - 2 = 18$$

These two values give

$$MS_{within} = \frac{SS_{within}}{df_{within}}$$
$$= \frac{90}{18}$$
$$= 5$$

(Note that MS_{within} is the same value we computed earlier as the pooled variance for the t statistic.)

To compute $SS_{between}$ we need the treatment totals (Ts) and the grand total (G). Although these values are not given explicitly in the data, they are easy to find. In the hormone group, for example, we have $n = 10$ scores with an average of $\overline{X} = 3$. If the 10 scores average 3, the total must be $T = 10(3) = 30$. Similarly, the total for the control group would be $T = 70$. With these two values you can compute the grand total, $G = 30 + 70 = 100$.

$$SS_{between} = \Sigma \frac{T^2}{n} - \frac{G^2}{N} = \frac{30^2}{10} + \frac{70^2}{10} - \frac{100^2}{20}$$
$$= 90 + 490 - 500$$
$$= 80$$
$$df_{between} = k - 1$$
$$= 2 - 1 = 1$$

With the SS and the df values we can compute

$$MS_{between} = \frac{SS_{between}}{df_{between}}$$
$$= \frac{80}{1} = 80$$

Finally, the F-ratio for this analysis is

$$F = \frac{MS_{between}}{MS_{within}}$$

$$= \frac{80}{5}$$

$$= 16$$

(Notice that the value for F and the value for t are related by the formula $F = t^2$.)

STEP 4. The t test and the analysis of variance both reach the same decision. In each case, the data fall in the critical region, and we reject H_0. These data provide evidence that hormone levels in the mother affect the intelligence of the offspring.

13.8
Assumptions for Analysis of Variance

For analysis of variance, as well as other inferential techniques, there is the requirement that the samples be randomly selected from the population. There are two other basic assumptions that must be satisfied for the independent measures ANOVA to be valid. The first assumption is that the population distribution for each treatment condition is normal. For the other assumption to be met, the population variances for all treatments should be equal (homogeneity of variance). These conditions are the same as those required for the independent measures t test (Chapter 11).

Ordinarily, researchers are not overly concerned with the assumption of normality, especially when large samples are used, unless there are strong reasons to suspect the assumption has not been satisfied. The assumption of homogeneity of variance is an important one. If a researcher suspects it has been violated, it can be tested by Hartley's F-max test for homogeneity of variance (Chapter 11, page 348).

Summary

1. Analysis of variance is a statistical technique that is used to test for mean differences among two or more treatment conditions or among two or more populations. The null hypothesis for this test states that there are no differences among the population means. The alternative hypothesis states that at least one mean is different from the others. Although analysis of variance can be used with either an independent or a repeated measures experiment, this chapter examined only independent measures designs, that is, experiments with a separate sample for each treatment condition.

2. The test statistic for analysis of variance is a ratio of two variances called an F-ratio. The F-ratio is structured so that the numerator and denominator measure the same variance when

the null hypothesis is true. In this way, the existence of a significant treatment effect is apparent if the data produce an "unbalanced" F-ratio. The variances in the F-ratio are called mean squares or MS values. Each MS is computed by

$$MS = \frac{SS}{df}$$

3. For the independent measures analysis of variance the F-ratio is

$$F = \frac{MS_{between}}{MS_{within}}$$

The $MS_{between}$ measures differences among the treatments by computing the variability of the treatment means or totals. These differences are assumed to be produced by three factors:

a. Treatment effects (if they exist)
b. Individual differences
c. Experimental error

The MS_{within} measures variability inside each of the treatment conditions. This variability is assumed to be produced by two factors:

a. Individual differences
b. Experimental error

With these factors in mind, the F-ratio has the following structure

$$F = \frac{\text{treatment effect} + \text{individual diff's.} + \text{experimental error}}{\text{individual diff's.} + \text{experimental error}}$$

When there is no treatment effect (H_0 is true), the numerator and denominator of the F-ratio are measuring the same variance, and the obtained ratio should be near 1.00. If there is a significant treatment effect, the numerator of the ratio should be larger than the denominator, and the obtained F value should be much greater than 1.00.

4. The formulas for computing each SS, df, and MS value are presented in Figure 13.13, which also shows the general structure for the analysis of variance.

5. The F-ratio has two values for degrees of freedom, one associated with the MS in the numerator and one associated with the MS in the denominator. These df values are used to find the critical value for the F-ratio in the F distribution table.

6. When the decision from an analysis of variance is to reject the null hypothesis and when the experiment contained more than two treatment conditions, it is necessary to continue the analysis with post hoc tests such as Tukey's HSD test. The purpose of these tests is to determine exactly which treatments are significantly different and which are not.

Figure 13.13

The complete structure and formulas for the independent measures analysis of variance.

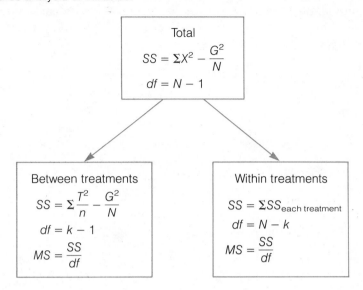

$$\text{Total}$$
$$SS = \Sigma X^2 - \frac{G^2}{N}$$
$$df = N - 1$$

$$\text{Between treatments}$$
$$SS = \Sigma \frac{T^2}{n} - \frac{G^2}{N}$$
$$df = k - 1$$
$$MS = \frac{SS}{df}$$

$$\text{Within treatments}$$
$$SS = \Sigma SS_{\text{each treatment}}$$
$$df = N - k$$
$$MS = \frac{SS}{df}$$

$$F\text{-ratio} = \frac{MS \text{ between treatments}}{MS \text{ within treatments}}$$

Key Terms

analysis of variance (ANOVA)
factor
levels
between treatments variability
within treatments variability
treatment effect
individual differences
experimental error
F-ratio

error term
mean squares
distribution of F-ratios
ANOVA summary table
post hoc tests
a priori tests
a posteriori tests
Tukey's HSD test

Problems for Chapter 13:
Introduction to Analysis of Variance

*1. A social psychologist would like to examine the relationship between personal appearance and authority. A special questionnaire is prepared which requires very careful attention to instructions in order to fill it in correctly. Three random samples of college students are obtained. For the first group the psychologist dresses very casually (blue jeans and T-shirt) when the questionnaire is administered. For the second sample, the psychologist wears a suit, and for the third sample the psychologist wears a very "scientific" laboratory coat. The psychologist records the number of errors made by each individual while completing the questionnaire. These data are as follows:

Blue Jeans	Suit	Lab Coat	
5	3	1	
2	3	0	$G = 30$
2	0	1	$\Sigma X^2 = 86$
4	2	2	
2	2	1	
$T = 15$	$T = 10$	$T = 5$	
$SS = 8$	$SS = 6$	$SS = 2$	

Should the psychologist conclude that appearance had an influence on the amount of attention people paid to the instructions? Test at the .05 level of significance.

2. A psychologist would like to examine how the rate of presentation affects people's ability to memorize a list of words. A list of 20 words is prepared. For one group of subjects the list is presented at the rate of one word every $\frac{1}{2}$ second. The next group gets one word every second. The third group has one word every 2 seconds, and the fourth group has one word every 3 seconds. After the list is presented, the psychologist asks each person to recall the entire list. The dependent variable is the number of errors in recall. The data from this experiment are as follows:

$\frac{1}{2}$ Second	1 Second	2 Seconds	3 Seconds	
4	0	3	0	$G = 32$
6	2	1	2	$\Sigma X^2 = 104$
2	2	2	1	
4	0	2	1	
$T = 16$	$T = 4$	$T = 8$	$T = 4$	
$SS = 8$	$SS = 4$	$SS = 2$	$SS = 2$	

a. Can the psychologist conclude that the rate of presentation has a significant effect on memory? Test at the .05 level.

b. Use Tukey's HSD test to determine which rates of presentation are statistically different and which are not.

*3. A psychologist would like to show that background noise can interfere with a student's concentration and therefore cause poorer performance on complex mental tasks. A sample of 12 students is obtained, and the psychologist randomly assigns these students to three separate groups. Each group is given a standard problem-solving task. One group works on this task under quiet conditions, one group works with soft background music, and the third group works with a loud radio tuned to a popular rock station. For each student the psychologist measures the number of errors on the task. The results from this experiment are summarized as follows:

Quiet	Soft Music	Loud Music	
$n = 4$	$n = 4$	$n = 4$	
$T = 4$	$T = 6$	$T = 14$	$\Sigma X^2 = 71$
$SS = 2$	$SS = 4$	$SS = 3$	

Can the psychologist conclude that the background noise had an effect on performance? Test at the .05 level of significance.

4. A psychologist using an independent measures experimental design to compare different teaching methods reports an F-ratio of $F = 3.87$ with $df = 3, 28$.

   a. How many teaching methods (treatments) were being compared?

   b. How many subjects participated in the total experiment?

   c. Were there significant differences among the teaching methods?

*5. Use an analysis of variance with $\alpha = .05$ to determine whether the following data provide evidence of any significant differences among the three treatments:

Treatment 1	Treatment 2	Treatment 3	
$n = 4$	$n = 5$	$n = 6$	$N = 15$
$T = 2$	$T = 10$	$T = 18$	$G = 30$
$SS = 13$	$SS = 21$	$SS = 26$	$\Sigma X^2 = 135$

6. A psychologist administers an art appreciation questionnaire to a group of five science students and a group of five English majors. The average score for the science students was $\overline{X} = 6$ with $SS = 200$, and the average score for the English majors was $\overline{X} = 8$ with $SS = 120$.

   a. Use an analysis of variance to determine whether or not these two populations differ significantly in art appreciation. Use $\alpha = .05$.

   b. Use a t test to compare the two groups. You should find that $F = t^2$.

*7. A pharmaceutical company has developed a drug which is expected to reduce hunger. To test the drug, three samples of rats are selected with $n = 10$ in each sample. The first sample receives the drug every day. The second sample is given the drug once a week, and the third sample receives no drug at all. The dependent variable is the amount of food eaten by each rat over a 1-month period. These data are analyzed by an analysis of variance, and the results are reported in the following summary table. Fill in all missing values in the table. (*Hint:* Start with the *df* column.)

Source	SS	df	MS	
Between treatments	24	——	——	$F =$ ——
Within treatments	——	——	2	
Total	——	——		

8. A developmental psychologist is examining problem-solving ability for grade school children. Random samples of 5-year-old, 6-year-old, and 7-year-old children are obtained with $n = 3$ in each sample. Each child is given a standardized problem-solving task, and the psychologist records the number of errors. These data are as follows:

5-Year-Olds	6-Year-Olds	7-Year-Olds	
5	6	0	$G = 30$
4	4	1	$\Sigma X^2 = 138$
6	2	2	
$T = 15$	$T = 12$	$T = 3$	
$SS = 2$	$SS = 8$	$SS = 2$	

a. Use these data to test whether there are any significant differences among the three age groups. Use $\alpha = .05$.

b. Use Tukey's HSD test to determine which groups are different.

9. A researcher would like to know whether infants can be affected by alcohol consumed by a mother during pregnancy. A sample of 24 pregnant rats is obtained. The researcher randomly divides these rats into four groups with $n = 6$ in each group. All groups receive the same diet of rat chow but during the last 2 weeks of pregnancy one group has $\frac{1}{4}$ ounce of vodka mixed with their food. The second group receives $\frac{1}{2}$ ounce, the third group receives 1 ounce, and the final group has no alcohol. One of the offspring of each rat is randomly selected to be weighed at birth. The data were examined using an ANOVA, and the results are summarized in the following table. Fill in all missing values.

Source	SS	df	MS	
Between treatments	——	——	10	$F =$ ——
Within treatments	40	——	——	
Total	——	——		

*10. A psychologist would like to demonstrate that the combination of two drugs can often produce much different effects than either of the drugs taken separately. Four random samples are selected with $n = 5$ in each sample. One group is given a sugar pill (no drug), one group is given drug A, another group is given drug B, and the final group is given drugs A and B together. Each person is then given a logic test measuring basic reasoning ability. The data are summarized as follows:

Sugar Pill	Drug A	Drug B	Drugs A and B	
$T = 0$	$T = 5$	$T = 5$	$T = 20$	$\Sigma X^2 = 122$
$SS = 7$	$SS = 8$	$SS = 7$	$SS = 10$	

   a. Can the psychologist conclude that there are any significant differences among the treatments? Test at the .05 level.

   b. Use Tukey's HSD test to determine which treatments are different.

11. In an avoidance-learning experiment, rats are required to move from one side of a cage to the other in order to escape an electric shock. A warning signal is presented a few seconds before the shock, so after a few trials the animals learn to move as soon as the warning occurs and thus escape before the shock starts. A psychologist is interested in how the strength of the shock affects the time it takes the animals to learn to respond to the warning. Three samples of rats are selected. The first group receives a mild shock, the second gets a medium shock, and the third group receives a strong shock. The dependent variable is the number of trials required before the animal learns to respond to the warning and avoid the shock. On the basis of the following data, can the psychologist conclude that the strength of the shock affects the speed of learning? Test at the .05 level of significance.

Mild	Medium	Strong	
$n = 10$	$n = 10$	$n = 10$	
$\overline{X} = 3$	$\overline{X} = 2$	$\overline{X} = 4$	$\Sigma X^2 = 560$
$SS = 90$	$SS = 85$	$SS = 95$	

*12. Several studies indicate that handedness (left-handed/right-handed) is related to differences in brain function. Because different parts of the brain are specialized for specific behaviors, this means that left- and right-handed people should show different skills or talents. To test this hypothesis, a psychologist tested pitch discrimination (a component of musical ability) for three groups of subjects: left-handed, right-handed, and ambidextrous. The data from this study are as follows:

Right-Handed	Left-Handed	Ambidextrous	
6	1	2	$G = 30$
4	0	0	$\Sigma X^2 = 102$
3	1	0	
4	1	2	
3	2	1	
$T = 20$	$T = 5$	$T = 5$	
$SS = 6$	$SS = 2$	$SS = 4$	

Each score represents the number of errors during a series of pitch discrimination trials.

a. Do these data indicate any differences among the three groups. Test with $\alpha = .05$.

b. Use the F-max test to determine whether these data satisfy the homogeneity of variance assumption.

13. In a paired-associate learning task, subjects are required to learn pairs of words. The first word in each pair is called the stimulus word, and the second is the response word. On each trial, the experimenter presents the stimulus word and asks the subject to recall the correct response. If the subject fails, the correct response word is given, and the experimenter continues through the list. The dependent variable is the number of times the experimenter must go through the entire list before the subject can recall all response words perfectly. This task often is used to demonstrate the effectiveness of mental imagery as an aid to memory. In a typical experiment, subjects in one group are instructed to form a mental image combining the two words in each pair. A second group is instructed to form a sentence that uses both of the words. A third group receives no special instructions. The data from this experiment are as follows:

use only the 1st 4 scores for each group

No Instructions	Images	Sentences
6	3	5
5	5	4
8	4	5
4	3	6

a. Compute the mean for each treatment. Draw a bar graph of these means. (See Chapter 2 for assistance.)

b. Do the data indicate significant differences among the instruction groups? Test with alpha set at .05.

c. Use Tukey's HSD test to determine which groups are different.

d. In a few sentences, explain what happened in this study.

*14. A researcher would like to systematically evaluate the effects of food deprivation on learning. Five groups of rats are selected with each group receiving a different level of deprivation before testing. The scores for these rats are as follows:

Hours of Deprivation

6	12	18	24	30
9	10	18	14	7
7	8	16	12	9
10	17	23	17	13
12	14	24	20	16
13	18	21	19	15

a. Can the researcher conclude that the level of deprivation has an effect on learning performance? Test at the .05 level of significance.

b. Sketch a graph showing the mean learning score for each treatment condition. Describe the relation between hours of deprivation and learning.

c. Use Tukey's HSD test to determine which treatment conditions are different.

*15. A school administrator would like to know whether students tend to select college majors that are consistent with their skills. A sample of $n = 12$ psychology majors and a sample of $n = 12$ English majors are selected. Each of these students completed a verbal abilities test when he/she first entered college. The scores for these two samples are as follows:

Psychology			English		
18	14	21	19	23	16
17	20	19	22	19	21
15	18	13	20	18	15
16	21	14	19	16	23

a. Use an analysis of variance to determine whether these data indicate any significant difference in verbal ability for English versus psychology majors. Test with $\alpha = .05$.

b. Use a t test to determine whether there is any mean difference between the two populations. Again, test at the .05 level of significance. (*Note:* You should find $F = t^2$.)

*16. Betz and Thomas (1979) have reported a distinct connection between personality and health. They identified three personality types who differ in their susceptibility to serious, stress-related illness (heart attack, high blood pressure, etc.). The three personality types are Alphas, who are cautious and steady; Betas, who are carefree and outgoing; and Gammas, who tend toward extremes of behavior such as being overly cautious or very careless. Sample data representing general health scores for each of these three groups are as follows. A low score indicates poor health.

Alphas		Betas		Gammas	
43	44	41	52	36	29
41	56	40	57	38	36
49	42	36	48	45	42
52	53	51	55	25	40
41	21	52	39	41	36
46	40	48	46	39	47
48	36	59	43	50	32

a. Compute the mean for each personality type. Do these data indicate a significant difference among the three types? Test with $\alpha = .05$.

b. Use Tukey's HSD test to determine which groups are different. Explain what happened in this study.

17. Do weather conditions affect people's moods? To examine this question, a researcher selected three samples of college students and administered a mood inventory questionnaire to each student. One group was tested on a dreary, overcast, and drizzly day. The second group was tested during a violent thunderstorm, and the third group was tested on a bright sunny day. The data are as follows:

Dreary		Stormy		Bright	
6	9	8	12	13	10
10	12	10	6	6	13
5	7	8	9	10	8
12	8	14	10	9	12
7	10	7	7	15	11
9	14	8	12	13	16
13	10	16	8	14	9
8	8	10	11	18	14

Do these data indicate that weather has an effect on mood? Test at the .05 level of significance.

*18. A psychologist is interested in the extent to which physical attractiveness can influence judgment of other personal characteristics such as intelligence or ability. The psychologist selected three groups of subjects who were to play the role of a company personnel manager. Each subject was given a stack of job applications which included a photograph of the applicant. One of these applications was previously selected as the test stimulus. For one group of subjects, this application contained a photograph of a very attractive woman. For the second group, the photograph was of an average-looking woman. For the third group, a photo of a very unattractive woman was attached to the application. The subjects were instructed to rate the quality of each job applicant (0 = "very poor" to 10 = "excellent"). The psychologist recorded the rating of the test stimulus for each subject. These data are as follows:

Attractive			Average			Unattractive		
5	4	4	6	5	3	4	3	1
3	5	6	6	6	7	3	1	2
4	3	8	5	4	6	2	4	3
3	5	4	8	7	8	2	1	2

a. Compute the means of the groups and draw a graph showing the results.

b. Use an ANOVA with $\alpha = .05$ to determine whether there are any significant differences among these three groups.

c. Use Tukey's HSD test to determine which groups are different.

d. Based on the results of the post hoc test, describe the relation between physical attractiveness and the job ratings.

19. Does coffee help people become sober more quickly after drinking too much? The ensuing data represent results from an experiment designed to answer this question. A sample of volunteers is randomly divided into four groups. One of these groups serves as a control and receives no alcohol. Subjects in each of the other three groups drink a fixed amount of alcohol in a 1-hour period. During the next $\frac{1}{2}$ hour, subjects in the second group drink two cups of decaffeinated coffee, subjects in another group drink two cups of regular coffee, and subjects in the final group drink two cups of water. Finally, all subjects are given a reaction-time test to determine mental alertness. The data from this experiment are as follows:

Control	Decaffeinated Coffee	Regular Coffee	Water
184	221	189	196
197	218	219	201
189	226	206	215
207	230	214	198
179	205	221	229
215	216	192	228
201	195	215	209
193	216	199	192
188	191	231	231
196	205	225	216

a. Compute the mean for each treatment group.

b. Are there any differences among these four groups? Use ANOVA with an alpha level of .01.

c. Use Tukey's HSD test to determine which groups are different.

d. Describe the findings of this experiment based on the analyses you have just completed.

*20. A researcher evaluating the effects of a drug designed an experiment using three different drug doses (small, medium, and large). A separate sample of subjects was tested for each drug dose, and the researcher obtained the following scores:

Small	Medium	Large
14	16	24
19	20	18
13	15	20
17	18	18
18	19	22
21	23	24

a. Use an analysis of variance to determine whether there are any significant differences among these three drug doses. Set $\alpha = .05$.

b. Suppose the researcher had collected data only for the small-dose and the large-dose conditions. If an analysis of variance is used only on the data from these two conditions, is there evidence for a significant difference between the two drug doses? Test with $\alpha = .05$.

c. You should find that there is a significant difference between the small dose and the large dose in part b but no significant difference in part a. How would you explain this apparent contradiction? (*Hint:* Analysis of variance evaluates mean differences. Compute all the mean differences among treatments when all three drug doses are included in the experiment. Now compute the mean difference between treatments when only two drug doses are used.)

CHAPTER 14

Repeated Measures Analysis of Variance (ANOVA)

TOOLS
YOU WILL
NEED

The following items are considered essential background material for this chapter. If you doubt your knowledge of any of these items, you should review the appropriate chapter or section before proceeding.

1. Introduction to analysis of variance (Chapter 13)
   a. The logic of analysis of variance
   b. ANOVA notation and formulas
   c. Distribution of F-ratios

In Chapter 13, we saw that partitioning total variability into separate components that reflect the treatment effect and sources of error provides the basis for determining whether or not any differences exist among the treatment groups. The same sort of analysis of variability components may be applied, with some modification, to a study that uses a repeated measures design. Recall that the repeated measures study differs from the independent measures design in that it uses only one sample of subjects. This single sample is tested repeatedly at each level of a treatment factor. A repeated measures design, therefore, is especially useful when a researcher wants to examine how behavior changes across time or treatments in the *same* individuals.

This approach was used in a study that examined changes in pain threshold during the course of pregnancy (Gintzler, 1980). In the early and mid-1970s, it was discovered that the brain manufactures and releases morphine-like substances called endorphins (see Snyder, 1977). Among many possible functions, these substances are thought to act as natural pain killers. For example, acupuncture may relieve pain because the acupuncture needles stimulate a release of endorphins in the brain. Gintzler (1980) studied changes in pain threshold during pregnancy and to what extent, if any, these changes were related to endorphin activity.

An experiment that uses repeated measures is well suited for this question in that changes in response are documented *within* the same individuals across a period of time (the duration of the pregnancy). Gintzler tested pregnant rats in several sessions that were spaced at regular intervals throughout their pregnancy (a rat's pregnancy lasts only 3 weeks). In a test session, a rat received a series of foot shocks that increased in intensity. The intensity of shock that elicited a jump response was recorded as the index of pain threshold. Note that each rat is observed *repeatedly*—each provides several threshold measures during the course of pregnancy. In general, the rats showed less sensitivity to shock (increased thresholds) as the pregnancy progressed. The change in threshold from one session to another was gradual, up until just a day or two before birth of the pups. At that point there was an abrupt increase in pain threshold. Gintzler also found evidence that the decrease in pain sensitivity was due to enhanced activity of endorphins. Perhaps a natural pain-killing mechanism prepares these animals for the stress of giving birth.

Analysis of variance can be used in situations when repeated measures are used to assess changes in response in the same sample of individuals. It examines these changes by partitioning variability into components that reflect systematic (*MS* between treatment) and unsystematic (the error term) sources of variability. As noted in Chapter 13, when the number of levels of a treatment (k) is greater than 2, ANOVA should be performed rather than

445

multiple t tests. The multiple t tests may result in an unacceptably large experiment-wise alpha level, making the probability of a type I error for the entire set of t tests undesirably high. The ANOVA, on the other hand, provides a single test statistic (the F-ratio) for the experiment.

In this chapter we will examine how the repeated measures design is analyzed with ANOVA. As we shall see, many of the notational symbols and computations are the same as those used for the independent measures ANOVA. However, there is a fundamental difference in the error term that is used for the F-ratio. We will examine this difference in detail.

14.1

The Logic of Repeated Measures ANOVA

Notation

We will first review the notation of ANOVA with an example. Then we will review and extend the logic of ANOVA as it applies to the repeated measures design.

EXAMPLE 14.1
An investigator would like to examine the effect of practice on the performance of people working on a spatial abilities task. The task involves the assembly of puzzles that form various visual patterns when completed. A sample of $n = 4$ subjects is tested in three practice sessions. For each session, the researcher measures the number of puzzles completed for each subject. Note that the treatment consists simply of test sessions and that the same sample of people is used throughout the experiment to determine if there is a practice effect. The data for this study are summarized in Table 14.1.

Table 14.1

The Number of Puzzles Completed as a Function of Amount of Practice (Test Session)

Person	Session 1	Session 2	Session 3	P
A	3	3	6	12
B	2	2	2	6
C	1	1	4	6
D	2	4	6	12
	$T_1 = 8$	$T_2 = 10$	$T_3 = 18$	
	$SS_1 = 2$	$SS_2 = 5$	$SS_3 = 11$	

$G = 36$ $\quad \Sigma X^2 = 140$ $\quad k = 3$ $\quad n = 4$ $\quad N = 12$

The notation for a repeated measures study is the same as was used for an independent measures design with the addition of one symbol. The data in Table 14.1 reveal that the total for each treatment is signified by the letter T and a subscript indicating the treatment. For example, the total of the scores in the first test session is $T_1 = 8$. As with the independent measures design, we can find the sum of squares for the set of scores in each treatment. In the present example, the sum of squares for the scores in the second test session is $SS_2 = 5$. The number of people in the sample is $n = 4$, and for the number of levels of the treatment, $k = 3$. The number of scores in the entire experiment, N, may be obtained by multiplying k by n, or

$$N = kn = 3(4) = 12$$

The sum of all N scores is signified by the letter G for grand total. This value may be determined by adding up all 12 scores in the experiment or by finding the sum of the three treatment totals:

$$G = \Sigma T = 8 + 10 + 18 = 36$$

For ΣX^2, all (N) scores in the experiment are first squared, and then the total of the squared values is obtained. For this example, $\Sigma X^2 = 140$. Up to this point, all of these terms are found exactly as we have done for the independent measures ANOVA.

As noted before, there is one departure in the notation for the repeated measures design; namely, we must find the total for each person's set of scores. This is signified by the letter P, for "person total." For each person, we obtain the P value by adding up that person's score for each test session. For example, person C has a P value of 6. Note that the sum of P values also equals the grand total G. This is because all of the P values and the grand total are based on the same 12 scores. Table 14.1 provides all of the necessary information to perform the calculations of the repeated measures ANOVA. To develop the logic of the analysis, attention will be turned to the components of variability used in the analysis.

The Initial Partitioning of Variability

Analysis of variance begins with the partitioning of the total variability in the experiment into two separate components, between treatments variability and within treatments variability. This procedure was also done with the independent measures ANOVA. While the procedure is the same, there is a fundamental difference in the analysis of a repeated measures study. This difference can best be seen in the sources of variability that contribute to between treatments variability.

What might cause a score in one treatment to be different from a score in another treatment? Why is there any variability between treatments? One possibility is that a treatment effect has occurred. In Example 14.1, the scores for one person may differ from one test session to the next as a result of practice in a previous session. Another possibility is that a person's scores will vary across treatments due to experimental error. Anytime a measurement is made of behavior,

error may be introduced. The error might be inherent in the accuracy of the tools used for measurement, or it might be introduced by the experimenter. Uncontrolled conditions in the laboratory, such as noises or changes in room temperature, may also cause experimental error. The main point is that experimental error is uncontrolled and unsystematic. Individual differences, however, do not play a role in between treatments variability. This fact contrasts with the independent measures ANOVA. For a repeated measures design, the *same sample* of persons is used for each level of the independent variable. If the same people serve in every treatment, then variability between the treatments cannot be due to individual differences. Therefore, there are two sources of variability that contribute to between treatments variability:

1. Treatment effect
2. Experimental error

Because the ANOVA initially partitions total variability into between treatments and within treatments variability, let us now look at the sources that contribute to within treatments variability.

Why might scores within any treatment vary? Examine the data in session 1 for Table 14.1. The scores do not have the same value. What accounts for this variability? First, the four scores within session 1 (or within any session) may vary because four different people are generating those scores. That is, the subjects may come into the experiment with different levels of spatial abilities or different experiences that will affect their performance on the puzzle task. These initial differences between the subjects (that is, individual differences) may account for the variability within treatments. Another factor that influences within treatments variability is experimental error. This is introduced anytime the experimenter makes a measurement of the dependent variable. Note that the treatment effect does not contribute to within treatments variability because the set of scores are within the same treatment group. For example, the set of four scores within session 3 vary from each other but not because of a treatment effect. They are within the same test session. The sums of squares for session 3, SS_3, reflects variability due to individual differences and experimental error within that particular session. The variability within treatments is therefore accounted for by

1. Individual differences
2. Experimental error

Figure 14.1 illustrates the partitioning of total variability into its separate components and the sources that account for the variability in each of these components.

The Structure of the *F*-Ratio

The purpose of the analysis of variance is to determine whether or not the data indicate the presence of a treatment effect. Although it may be tempting to simply look at the treatment means to see whether

Figure 14.1

The partitioning of total variability into separate components of variability, between treatments and within treatments variability.

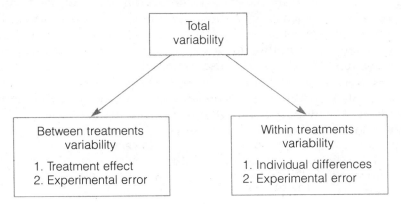

they are the same or different, this procedure is not acceptable. Remember, differences between treatments (measured by between treatments variability) may also be caused by experimental error. The problem is to find out how much of the between treatments variability is due to treatment effect and how much is due to error. The solution to this problem comes from the structure of the F-ratio.

The F-ratio is constructed so that the numerator and denominator of the ratio have identical sources of variability whenever the treatment effect is zero. In this way, the F-ratio is balanced when H_0 is true so that you should obtain an F value equal to or near 1.00 if the treatment has no effect. On the other hand, when a significant treatment effect does exist, the ratio becomes unbalanced and produces a value greater than 1.00. For a repeated measures experiment, the variability between treatments (the numerator of the ratio) contains two sources of variability:

1. Treatment effect
2. Experimental error

To balance the ratio, the denominator, or the *error term*, should have only experimental error. This would produce the following structure:

$$F = \frac{\text{treatment effect} + \text{experimental error}}{\text{experimental error}}$$

Notice that the value for this F-ratio is expected to be 1.00 if the treatment effect is zero (H_0 is true). If a significant treatment effect exists, this F-ratio should be large (as defined by the level of significance).

Unfortunately, the analysis shown in Figure 14.1 does not produce a measure of variability that is due solely to experimental error. To obtain this value for the denominator of the F-ratio, additional calculations are necessary. We begin these calculations with the within treatments variability.

Partitioning Within Treatments Variability

Fortunately, it is possible to statistically remove the influence of individual differences from the error term (denominator) of the F-ratio. This is accomplished by partitioning within treatments variability into two separate components: (1) variability due to individual differences and (2) variability due to experimental error. Variability due to individual differences may also be called between subjects variability. Because the same sample of subjects is used for every treatment in a repeated measures study, it is possible to measure individual differences by computing the amount of variability between subjects. If there are large amounts of individual differences in how subjects respond in the study, then between subjects variability will be quite large. When between subjects variability has been determined, it can be subtracted from within treatments variability. The remainder is error variability. It is used to compute the error term of the F-ratio for a repeated measures study. When a variance (MS) based on this residual is used, we obtain

$$F = \frac{MS_{between\ treatments}}{MS_{error}} = \frac{\text{treatment effect} + \text{experimental error}}{\text{experimental error}}$$

As noted before, if the null hypothesis is true and there is no treatment effect, then the F-ratio should equal 1.00.

Figure 14.2 summarizes the partitioning of variability for repeated measures design. Note that it consists of a two-stage process. In the first stage, total variability is partitioned into two components: (1) between treatments variability and (2) within treatments variability. Between treatments variability is the basis for the variance that is used in the numerator of the F-ratio, and it is influenced by the treatment effect and experimental error. Within treatments variability is influenced by both individual differences and experimental error and therefore is not suitable as an error term for the F-ratio. Remember, the expected F-ratio should equal 1.00 when H_0 is true. The second stage of the analysis is designed to eliminate the influence of individual differences. This is accomplished by determining the amount of between subjects variability and subtracting it from within treatments variability. The residual, error variability, reflects the amount of experimental error in the study and is suitable to use in the error term of the F-ratio.

LEARNING
CHECK

1. What sources contribute to between treatments variability for the repeated measures design?
2. What sources of variability contribute to within treatments variability?
3. (a) Describe the structure of the F-ratio for a repeated measures ANOVA. (b) Compare it to the F-ratio structure for the independent measures ANOVA (Chapter 13). How do they differ?

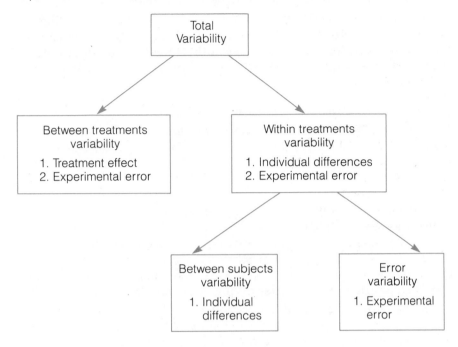

4. In the second stage of analysis, within treatments variability is partitioned into _____ variability and _____ variability.

ANSWERS

1. Treatment effect, experimental error.
2. Individual differences, experimental error.
3. a. $F = \dfrac{\text{treatment effect} + \text{experimental error}}{\text{experimental error}}$
   b. For the independent measures ANOVA, individual differences contribute variability to both between treatments variability and the error term of the F-ratio.
4. Between subjects variability, error variability.

14.2

The Computations for Repeated Measures ANOVA

Formulas for Sums of Squares

The ANOVA for a repeated measures study initially proceeds like the independent measures analysis. The sum of squares for total variability (SS_{total}) is first computed. This SS is then partitioned into

$SS_{between\ treatments}$ and $SS_{within\ treatments}$. Just as we noted in Chapter 13, SS_{total} equals the sum of these two components, or

$$SS_{total} = SS_{between\ treatments} + SS_{within\ treatments}$$

For the repeated measures ANOVA, a second stage of partitioning is performed. Between subjects variability ($SS_{between\ subjects}$) is calculated to measure the amount of variability due to individual differences. Because within treatments variability is composed of individual differences and experimental error, we may state that

$$SS_{within\ treatments} = SS_{between\ subjects} + SS_{error}$$

To obtain SS_{error}, which will be needed to find the error term of the F-ratio, $SS_{between\ subjects}$ is subtracted from $SS_{within\ treatments}$:

$$SS_{error} = SS_{within\ treatments} - SS_{between\ subjects}$$

Figure 14.3 depicts a chart of the partitioning of sum of squares for a repeated measures design. The chart is a useful guide to follow during the course of a repeated measures analysis.

The formulas for the first stage of the analysis, the partitioning of SS_{total} into $SS_{between\ treatments}$ and $SS_{within\ treatments}$, are identical to those of the independent measures ANOVA. Let us return to the example of the effect of practice on puzzle-solving performance. Recall that subjects were given three practice sessions (treatments) in which they

Figure 14.3
The partitioning of variability for a repeated measures design with the formula for each SS component.

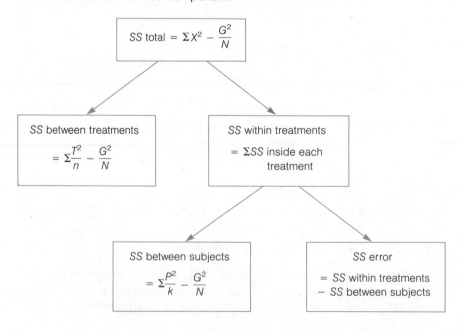

worked on a spatial abilities task consisting of assembling puzzles that form various visual patterns. The experimenter measured the number of puzzles completed by each person in each test session (Table 14.1).

We begin the analysis with SS_{total}, the measurement of total variability in the experiment. The total sum of squares is based on all (N) of the scores in the experiment, and its formula is

(14.1) $SS_{total} = \Sigma X^2 - \dfrac{G^2}{N}$

Using this formula for the data in Table 14.1, we obtain

$$SS_{total} = 140 - \frac{36^2}{12} = 140 - \frac{1296}{12}$$
$$= 140 - 108 = 32$$

Now we will look at $SS_{within\ treatments}$. This component consists of the amount of variability inside of each treatment condition. In Table 14.1 the variability inside of each treatment is provided by $SS_1 = 2$, $SS_2 = 5$, and $SS_3 = 11$. The $SS_{within\ treatments}$ for the experiment is determined by adding the variability that is present inside each treatment, or

(14.2) $SS_{within\ treatments} = \Sigma SS_{inside\ each\ treatment}$

Therefore, for the data in Table 14.1,

$$SS_{within\ treatments} = 2 + 5 + 11$$
$$= 18$$

In Chapter 13, we saw that the between treatments SS is based on the amount of variability among the treatment means but that it can be computed using the treatment totals (T). This formula for between treatments SS is

(14.3) $SS_{between\ treatments} = \Sigma \dfrac{T^2}{n} - \dfrac{G^2}{N}$

For the example, we obtain

$$SS_{between\ treatments} = \frac{8^2}{4} + \frac{10^2}{4} + \frac{18^2}{4} - \frac{36^2}{12}$$
$$= 16 + 25 + 81 - 108$$
$$= 122 - 108$$
$$= 14$$

The computations can be quickly checked by determining if the between treatments and within treatments components of variability equal total variability when added:

$$SS_{total} = SS_{between\ treatments} + SS_{within\ treatments}$$
$$32 = 14 + 18$$
$$32 = 32$$

Notice that the formulas and computations up to this point are identical to those of the independent measures ANOVA. The analysis will now depart from the procedures used for the independent measures design. The $SS_{within\ treatments}$ cannot be used to obtain the error term of the F-ratio because it is influenced by individual differences in addition to experimental error. The solution is to compute a sum of squares for individual differences and subtract it from $SS_{within\ treatments}$. The residual will be SS_{error}. Individual differences may be assessed in a repeated measures design because the same people are serving in every treatment condition. We accomplish this by finding out how much between subjects variability exists, or, specifically, how much variability exists among the person totals (P values). The formula for $SS_{between\ subjects}$ is

(14.4) $SS_{between\ subjects} = \Sigma \dfrac{P^2}{k} - \dfrac{G^2}{N}$

Notice that the formula for $SS_{between\ subjects}$ is similar in structure to the formula for $SS_{between\ treatments}$. The person totals (P values) are used instead of treatment totals (T values). Each P value is divided by the number of scores that were added together to obtain P, or by k. Remember, each person was measured repeatedly, once for each treatment. There are k treatment conditions, and thus k scores are used to get a person total. For the example, $SS_{between\ subjects}$ is

$$
\begin{aligned}
SS_{between\ subjects} &= \Sigma \frac{P^2}{k} - \frac{G^2}{N} \\[2mm]
&= \frac{12^2}{3} + \frac{6^2}{3} + \frac{6^2}{3} + \frac{12^2}{3} - \frac{36^2}{12} \\[2mm]
&= 48 + 12 + 12 + 48 - 108 \\[2mm]
&= 120 - 108 \\[2mm]
&= 12
\end{aligned}
$$

Now we can determine SS_{error}. From Figure 14.3 it is evident that

$$SS_{within\ treatments} = SS_{between\ subjects} + SS_{error}$$

Therefore,

(14.5) $SS_{error} = SS_{within\ treatments} - SS_{between\ subjects}$

The values for SS_{within} and $SS_{between\ subjects}$ have already been calculated. By substituting these values into the formula, we obtain

$$
\begin{aligned}
SS_{error} &= 18 - 12 \\
&= 6
\end{aligned}
$$

Subtracting the variability due to individual differences from $SS_{within\ treatments}$ is the easiest way to compute SS_{error}. There is, however, a more complicated formula that can be used to directly compute this value (see Box 14.1).

BOX 14.1 **Derivation of Formula for SS$_{error}$**

It is possible to derive a formula for SS_{error} based on the information and formulas that have been reviewed for the repeated measures ANOVA. First, we saw that (Figure 14.3)

$$SS_{total} = SS_{between\ treatments} + SS_{within\ treatments}$$

and that

$$SS_{within\ treatments} = SS_{between\ subjects} + SS_{error}$$

By substituting for $SS_{within\ treatments}$, the equation for SS_{total} becomes

$$SS_{total} = SS_{between\ treatments} + SS_{between\ subjects} + SS_{error}$$

If we now solve the equation for SS_{error}, we obtain

$$SS_{error} = SS_{total} - SS_{between\ treatments} - SS_{between\ subjects}$$

The actual computational formulas for SS_{total}, $SS_{between\ treatments}$, and $SS_{between\ subjects}$ may be placed in the equation for SS_{error}. These substitutions yield

$$SS_{error} = \left(\Sigma X^2 - \frac{G^2}{N}\right) - \left(\Sigma \frac{T^2}{n} - \frac{G^2}{N}\right) - \left(\Sigma \frac{P^2}{k} - \frac{G^2}{N}\right)$$

$$= \Sigma X^2 - \frac{G^2}{N} - \Sigma \frac{T^2}{n} + \frac{G^2}{N} - \Sigma \frac{P^2}{k} + \frac{G^2}{N}$$

$$= \Sigma X^2 - \Sigma \frac{T^2}{n} - \Sigma \frac{P^2}{k} + \frac{G^2}{N}$$

For the data in Table 14.1, this formula yields

$$SS_{error} = 140 - 122 - 120 + 108$$
$$= 248 - 242$$
$$= 6$$

This formula may seem more difficult to use than

$$SS_{error} = SS_{within\ treatments} - SS_{between\ subjects}$$

However, many researchers prefer to use it because it eliminates the need to compute SS_{within} and $SS_{between\ subjects}$.

Formulas for Degrees of Freedom

You should recall from Chapter 4 that variance for sample data is computed by

$$variance = \frac{SS}{df}$$

Because the F-ratio is calculated from variances, called mean squares or *MS* values, it is necessary to find the degrees of freedom associated with each of the *SS* values in the analysis.

Degrees of freedom may be partitioned into components that parallel the partitioning of variability. First we determine the total *df* for the experiment, and then we partition this value into two components: (1) the between treatments *df* and (2) the within treatments *df*. For the repeated measures ANOVA, there is a second stage to this analysis. The within treatments *df* is broken down into two components: (1) the between subjects *df* and (2) the error *df*. Note that there is a *df* value for every *SS* in the analysis (Figure 14.4). It was noted in Chapter 13 that the *df* value is usually obtained by counting the number of items that was used to determine the *SS* and then subtracting 1 from this number. The *df* formulas for the first part of the analysis are identical to those of the independent measures ANOVA.

Total *df* is computed by

(14.6) $df_{total} = N - 1$

Remember, the entire set of *N* scores was used to compute the total *SS*. For the data in Table 14.1,

$$df_{total} = N - 1$$
$$= 12 - 1$$
$$= 11$$

In Chapter 13, the formula for within treatments *df* was derived:

(14.7) $df_{within\ treatments} = N - k$

Figure 14.4

The partitioning of degrees of freedom for a repeated measures experiment.

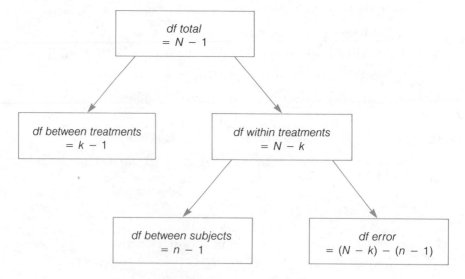

This formula was ultimately based on the sum of *df* within each treatment condition (Chapter 13). For the example,

$$df_{within\ treatments} = 12 - 3$$
$$= 9$$

As noted before, because between treatments *SS* is based on *k* treatment totals (*T*), $df_{between\ treatments}$ is obtained by subtracting 1 from the number of treatments:

(14.8) $df_{between\ treatments} = k - 1$

For the data in Table 14.1,

$$df_{between\ treatments} = 3 - 1$$
$$= 2$$

This completes the first stage of partitioning for the ANOVA. Much like we observed with sum of squares, total *df* should equal between treatments *df* and within treatments *df*. A quick computation confirms this statement:

$$df_{total} = df_{between\ treatments} + df_{within\ treatments}$$
$$11 = 2 + 9$$
$$11 = 11$$

In the second stage of the analysis, within treatments *df* is broken down into its components, namely, between subjects *df* and error *df*. The between subjects *SS* is determined using the person totals (*P* values). How many *P* values are used to compute this *SS*? This is determined by the size of the sample, or *n*. Therefore, if the number of *P* values used is *n*, then

(14.9) $df_{between\ subjects} = n - 1$

For the example, this value is

$$df_{between\ subjects} = 4 - 1$$
$$= 3$$

Finally, we must determine the value for error *df*. We have seen that

$$df_{within\ treatments} = df_{between\ subjects} + df_{error}$$

When this equation is solved for df_{error}, we obtain

$$df_{error} = df_{within\ treatments} - df_{between\ subjects}$$

For our example,

$$df_{error} = 9 - 3$$
$$= 6$$

A formula can be derived for the error *df* by substituting the formulas for within treatments *df* and between subjects *df* into the equation:

(14.10) $df_{error} = (N - k) - (n - 1)$

Calculation of the Variances (*MS*) and the *F*-ratio

The *F*-ratio is a ratio of two variances. These variances, also called mean squares (*MS*), are obtained by dividing a sum of squares by degrees of freedom. The *MS* in the numerator of the *F*-ratio, in part, is influenced by the amount of treatment effect that is present. This is the between treatments *MS*, and it is calculated by dividing the between treatments *SS* by between treatments *df:*

$$(14.11) \quad MS_{between\ treatments} = \frac{SS_{between\ treatments}}{df_{between\ treatments}}$$

The error term of the *F*-ratio consists of MS_{error} for a repeated measures ANOVA. This *MS* is computed by dividing the error *SS* by the error *df:*

$$(14.12) \quad MS_{error} = \frac{SS_{error}}{df_{error}}$$

The *F*-ratio therefore consists of

$$(14.13) \quad F = \frac{MS_{between\ treatments}}{MS_{error}}$$

Notice that the repeated measures *F*-ratio uses MS_{error} as an error term in place of MS_{within}. The new error term is used because it maintains the expected *F*-ratio of 1.00 if the null hypothesis is true. This is confirmed when the structure of the repeated measures *F*-ratio is examined:

$$F = \frac{treatment\ effect + error}{error}$$

When H_0 is true, the treatment effect will be zero, and the *F*-ratio should equal 1.00. Alternatively, when H_0 is false, the presence of a treatment effect in the numerator of the *F*-ratio should give us a large value that falls in the critical region.

For the data in Table 14.1, we obtain the following *MS* values:

$$MS_{between\ treatments} = \frac{SS_{between\ treatments}}{df_{between\ treatments}}$$
$$= \frac{14}{2}$$
$$= 7$$

$$MS_{error} = \frac{SS_{error}}{df_{error}}$$
$$= \frac{6}{6}$$
$$= 1$$

The F-ratio for the example is obtained by dividing the between treatments MS by the error MS:

$$F = \frac{MS_{between\ treatments}}{MS_{error}}$$

$$= \frac{7}{1}$$

$$= 7$$

The df values associated with the repeated measures F-ratio are the between treatments df and error df. These values are reported in the form of

$$df = \text{between treatments } df, \text{ error } df$$

Therefore, the df values associated with the repeated measures F-ratio in our example are

$$df = 2, 6$$

The obtained F-ratio is evaluated by the same general procedure used for the independent measures ANOVA. The experimenter must consult the F distribution table (page A-32) to find the critical value of F. The df values printed across the top of the table are values for the df associated with the numerator of the F-ratio (between treatments df). The column on the left-hand side of the table contains df values associated with the denominator of the F-ratio. For a repeated measures ANOVA, this value is the error df.

Caution! A very common mistake is to use the value of within treatments df *instead of error* df. *Remember, the error term for a repeated measures ANOVA is not the same as that of an independent measures ANOVA.*

LEARNING CHECK

1. $SS_{within\ treatments} - SS_{between\ subjects} = $ _____ .
2. What two df components are associated with the repeated measures F-ratio? How are they computed?
3. For the following set of data, compute all of the SS components for a repeated measures ANOVA:

	Treatment			
Subject	1	2	3	4
A	2	2	2	2
B	4	0	0	4
C	2	0	2	0
D	4	2	2	4

4. Which two MS components are used to form the F-ratio of the repeated measures ANOVA? How are they computed?

ANSWERS

1. SS_{error}
2. Between treatments df and error df; $df_{between\ treatments} = k - 1$; $df_{error} = (N - k) - (n - 1)$.

3. $SS_{total} = 32, SS_{between\ treatments} = 10, SS_{within\ treatments} = 22, SS_{between\ subjects} = 8, SS_{error} = 14.$

4. Between treatments MS and error MS;

$$MS_{between\ treatments} = \frac{SS_{between\ treatments}}{df_{between\ treatments}}$$

$$MS_{error} = \frac{SS_{error}}{df_{error}}$$

14.3
Testing Hypotheses with the Repeated Measures ANOVA

Let us consider a complete example of hypothesis testing with a repeated measures study. This task will be accomplished in the four steps that should be familiar by now: (1) State hypotheses and set the alpha level, (2) compute df and locate the critical region, (3) compute the test statistic, and (4) evaluate the hypotheses.

EXAMPLE 14.2
A school psychologist would like to test the effectiveness of a behavior modification technique in controlling classroom outbursts of unruly children. A teacher is instructed to use the response-cost technique. Every time a child disrupts the class, he/she is told that the behavior has cost him/her 10 minutes of free time. That is, the free time period is shortened for each unruly act. For a sample of $n = 4$ children, the number of outbursts is measured for a day before the treatment is initiated and again 1 week, 1 month, and 6 months after the response-cost technique began. Note that the measurements taken after the response-cost technique is administered serve as a long-term follow-up on the effectiveness of the treatment. This underscores the usefulness of the repeated measures design in evaluating the effectiveness of clinical treatments. The data are summarized in Table 14.2.

STEP 1. State the Hypotheses and Select an Alpha Level. According to the null hypothesis, the response-cost technique will be ineffective in producing a change in the number of classroom disruptions. In symbols the null hypothesis states that

H_0: $\mu_{before} = \mu_{1\ week} = \mu_{1\ month} = \mu_{6\ months}$

The alternative hypothesis may take on many forms. Somewhere among the four levels of the treatment there will be a difference. Because there are a number of possibilities, the alternative hypothesis states that

H_1: At least one mean is different from the others

Table 14.2

The Effect of Response-Cost Treatment on the Number of
Outbursts in Class After Different Periods of Time

Subject	Before Treatment	One Week After	One Month After	Six Months After	P
A	8	2	1	1	12
B	4	1	1	0	6
C	6	2	0	2	10
D	8	3	4	1	16
	$T_1 = 26$	$T_2 = 8$	$T_3 = 6$	$T_4 = 4$	
	$SS_1 = 11$	$SS_2 = 2$	$SS_3 = 9$	$SS_4 = 2$	
	$n = 4$ $k = 4$	$N = 16$	$G = 44$	$\Sigma X^2 = 222$	

For the level of significance, the experimenter selects $\alpha = .05$. In other words, the researcher is willing to take only a 5% chance of committing a type I error.

STEP 2. Find df and Locate the Critical Region. For a repeated measures study, the degrees of freedom associated with the F-ratio are between treatments df and error df. In this example between treatments df is

$$\text{between treatments } df = k - 1$$
$$= 4 - 1$$
$$= 3$$

For error df we obtain

$$\text{error } df = (N - k) - (n - 1)$$
$$= (16 - 4) - (4 - 1)$$
$$= 12 - 3$$
$$= 9$$

We have computed only those df *values that are needed to evaluate the F-ratio. However, it is useful to compute all* df *components of ANOVA in order to check the computations (see Figure 14.4).*

Therefore, for this F-ratio $df = 3, 9$. Consulting the F distribution table for $\alpha = .05$, we observe that the critical region begins with $F = 3.86$. Figure 14.5 illustrates the distribution. An obtained F-ratio that exceeds this critical value justifies rejecting H_0.

STEP 3. Compute the Test Statistic. To compute the F-ratio, we must first calculate the values for SS, df,

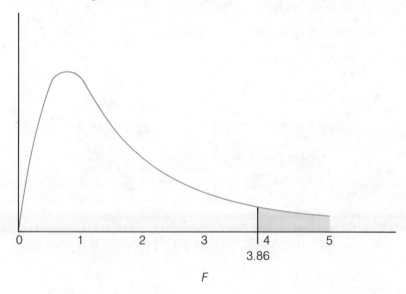

and *MS*. This analysis begins by finding the value for total *SS:*

$$\text{total } SS = \Sigma X^2 - \frac{G^2}{N}$$

$$= 222 - \frac{44^2}{16}$$

$$= 222 - 121$$

$$= 101$$

Total variability is partitioned into between treatments *SS* and within treatments *SS*. For between treatments variability, we get

$$\text{between treatments } SS = \Sigma \frac{T^2}{n} - \frac{G^2}{N}$$

$$= \frac{26^2}{4} + \frac{8^2}{4} + \frac{6^2}{4} + \frac{4^2}{4} - \frac{44^2}{16}$$

$$= 169 + 16 + 9 + 4 - 121$$

$$= 77$$

The first stage of the partitioning of variability is completed by computing within treatments *SS:*

$$\text{within treatments } SS = \Sigma SS_{inside\ each\ treatment}$$

$$= 11 + 2 + 9 + 2$$

$$= 24$$

At this point of the analysis, the work may be checked to see if total SS equals between treatments SS plus within treatments SS:

total SS = between treatments SS +
within treatments SS

$101 = 77 + 24$

$101 = 101$

In the second stage of the analysis, within treatments SS is partitioned into between subjects SS and error SS. This analysis is accomplished by first calculating between subjects SS and then subtracting it from within treatments SS. The residual will be error SS:

$$\text{between subjects } SS = \Sigma \frac{P^2}{k} - \frac{G^2}{N}$$

$$= \frac{12^2}{4} + \frac{6^2}{4} + \frac{10^2}{4} + \frac{16^2}{4} - \frac{44^2}{16}$$

$$= 36 + 9 + 25 + 64 - 121$$

$$= 13$$

error SS = within treatments SS −
between subjects SS

$$= 24 - 13$$

$$= 11$$

Finally, we can compute the MS values and then the F-ratio. The repeated measures F-ratio uses between treatments MS in the numerator and error MS in the denominator. These are readily obtained by dividing SS by the appropriate number of degrees of freedom:

$$\text{between treatments } MS = \frac{\text{between treatments } SS}{\text{between treatments } df}$$

$$= \frac{77}{3}$$

$$= 25.67$$

$$\text{error } MS = \frac{\text{error } SS}{\text{error } df}$$

$$= \frac{11}{9}$$

$$= 1.22$$

$$F = \frac{\text{between treatments } MS}{\text{error } MS}$$

$$= \frac{25.67}{1.22}$$

$$= 21.04$$

STEP 4. Evaluate the Hypotheses. The obtained F-ratio is 21.04. This value falls in the critical region that begins at 3.86. The statistical decision is to reject the null hypothesis. The school psychologist may conclude that the response-cost technique had an effect on the number of disruptions. A report might state:

There was a significant effect of response-cost training on the number of outbursts exhibited by the children, $F(3, 9) = 21.04, p < .05$.

The complete results of the analysis are summarized in Table 14.3.

Table 14.3

Analysis of Variance Summary

Source	SS	df	MS	F
Between treatments	77	3	25.67	21.04
Within treatments	24	12		
Between subjects	13	3		
Error	11	9	1.22	
Total	101	15		

Post Hoc Tests with Repeated Measures

Recall that ANOVA provides an overall test of significance for the treatment. When the null hypothesis is rejected, it only indicates that there is a difference between at least two of the treatment means. If $k = 2$, it is obvious where the difference lies in the experiment. However, when k is greater than 2, the situation becomes more complex. To determine exactly where significant differences exist, the researcher must follow the ANOVA with post hoc tests. In Chapter 13, we used Tukey's HSD test to make these multiple comparisons among treatment means. As an unplanned comparison, this test attempts to control the overall alpha level by making adjustments for the number of potential comparisons.

For a repeated measures ANOVA, Tukey's HSD and similar tests can be used in the exact same manner as was done for the independent measures ANOVA *provided* that you substitute MS_{error} in place of MS_{within} in the formula and use df_{error} in place of df_{within} when locating the critical value in a statistical table. For example, with a repeated measures design Tukey's HSD is computed by

$$\text{HSD} = q \sqrt{\frac{MS_{error}}{n}}$$

where q is the appropriate studentized range statistic found in Table B.5 on page A-35. When locating the q value in the table, remember to use df_{error}. Tukey's HSD determines the minimum difference between two treatment means that is necessary for significance.

It should be noted that statisticians are not in complete agreement about the appropriate error term in post hoc tests for repeated measures designs (for an excellent discussion, see Keppel, 1973).

14.4
Advantages of the Repeated Measures Design

When we first encountered the repeated measures design (Chapter 12), it was noted that this type of experiment has certain advantages and disadvantages. On the bright side, a repeated measures study may be desirable if the supply of subjects is limited. A repeated measures experiment is economical in that the experimenter can get by using fewer subjects. However, the disadvantages may be very great. These take the form of carry-over effects, such as fatigue, that can make the interpretation of the data very difficult.

Now that we have examined the repeated measures ANOVA, we can introduce another advantage, namely, the elimination of the role of variability due to individual differences. Consider the structure of the F-ratio for both the independent and repeated measures designs. For the independent measures design the F-ratio takes the following form:

$$F = \frac{\text{treatment effect} + \text{individual diff's.} + \text{experimental error}}{\text{individual diff's.} + \text{experimental error}}$$

The structure of the repeated measures F-ratio reveals that the influence of individual differences has been eliminated altogether:

$$F = \frac{\text{treatment effect} + \text{experimental error}}{\text{experimental error}}$$

The removal of individual differences from the analysis becomes an advantage in situations where very large individual differences exist among the subjects being studied. When individual differences are extraordinarily large, the presence of a treatment effect may be masked if an independent measures study is performed. In this case, a repeated measures design would be more sensitive in detecting a treatment effect, because individual differences do not influence the value of the F-ratio.

This point will become evident in the following example. Suppose an experiment is performed in two ways, with an independent measures design and a repeated measures experiment. Also, let's suppose that we know how much variability is accounted for by the different sources of variance. For example,

$$\text{treatment effect} = 10 \text{ units of variance}$$
$$\text{individual differences} = 1000 \text{ units of variance}$$
$$\text{experimental error} = 1 \text{ unit of variance}$$

Notice that a very large amount of the variability in the experiment is due to individual differences. By comparing the F-ratios of both types of experiments, we will be able to see a fundamental difference between the two types of experimental designs. For the independent measures experiment, we obtain

$$F = \frac{\text{treatment effect} + \text{individual diff's.} + \text{experimental error}}{\text{individual diff's.} + \text{experimental error}}$$

$$= \frac{10 + 1000 + 1}{1000 + 1}$$

$$= \frac{1011}{1001}$$

$$= 1.01$$

However, the repeated measures F-ratio provides a different outcome:

$$F = \frac{\text{treatment effect} + \text{experimental error}}{\text{experimental error}}$$

$$= \frac{10 + 1}{1}$$

$$= \frac{11}{1}$$

$$= 11$$

All things (sources of variability) being equal, the repeated measures F-ratio is larger. In this example, the F-ratio is much larger for the repeated measures study because the individual differences, which are extremely large, have been removed (see Box 14.2). In the independent ANOVA, the presence of a treatment effect is obscured by the influence of individual differences. This problem is remedied by the repeated measures design in which variability due to individual differences has been partitioned out of the analysis. When the amount of individual differences is great, a repeated measures experiment may provide a more sensitive test for a treatment effect.

14.5
Assumptions of the Repeated Measures ANOVA

In Chapter 11, we introduced the F-max test for the assumption of homogeneity of variance.

Of course, random sampling is a requirement for the repeated measures ANOVA. Also, it is assumed that the population distribution for each treatment is normal. As we noted in Chapter 13, homogeneity of variance is required for analysis of variance. That is, the variances of the population distributions for each treatment should be equivalent. These assumptions are essentially the same as those for the independent measures ANOVA.

For the repeated measures ANOVA, there is an additional assumption, called homogeneity of covariance. Basically, it refers to the requirement that the relative standing of each subject is maintained

BOX 14.2 | **Data that Produce a Large MS_{error}**

To get some idea of a situation that results in a large MS_{error}, it is useful to examine hypothetical data in the form of a graph. Suppose an experimenter examines the effect of amount of reward on maze performance in rats. A sample of $n = 4$ rats that have learned to solve a maze is subsequently tested in all four reward conditions: 1, 2, 4, and 8 grams of food reward. The experimenter measures the speed with which they solve the maze after experiencing the new amount of reward. Figure 14.6 shows a graph of the means of each treatment. The speed of maze running seems to increase with amount of reward.

Figure 14.6

The effect of amount of reward on running speed. Each point on the graph represents the mean speed at that level of the treatment.

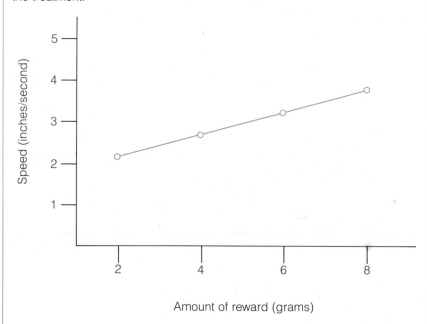

Figure 14.7 graphs a set of hypothetical data for each individual subject that would produce the data shown in Figure 14.6. Notice that there are individual differences in these data. The subject totals (*P* values) differ, indicating that some subjects generally run faster than others. Also note that the individual differences are consistent from one treatment to the next. For example, in all four treatment conditions subject 1 is fastest, and subject 2 is slowest. This means

continued

BOX 14.2 *continued*

that much of the variability within treatments is due to consistent, predictable individual differences. When the individual differences are subtracted out of the analysis, the result will be a very small value for MS_{error}. Remember that a small value for MS_{error} will tend to produce a large value for the F-ratio, indicating a significant difference between treatments. The consistency in these data can be described in another way that may help you to understand the F-ratio. For the data in Figure 14.7 the effect of the treatment is consistent for all subjects: Every rat shows an increase in speed when the amount of reward is increased. Because the treatment effect is very consistent, you should expect to find a significant difference between treatments.

Figure 14.7

The effect of amount of reward on running speed. Individual scores for each subject at each level of reward are shown by solid lines. The treatment means depicted by the broken line are the same as shown in Figure 14.6.

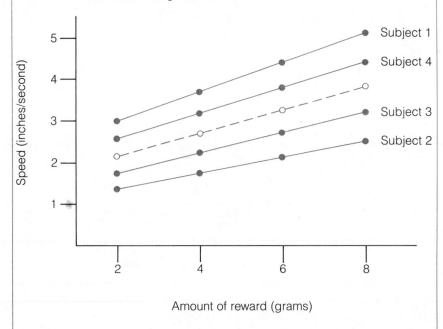

Figure 14.8 depicts another possibility for individual subjects. Although these data will produce the same treatment means as the previous example (Figure 14.6), the treatment effect is no longer consistent across subjects. Now when the amount of reward is increased, some subjects run faster, and some run slower. Because the treatment effect is not consistent, you should not expect to find significant differences between treatments. Also note that the data in Figure 14.8 do not show consistent individual differences from

BOX 14.2

one treatment to another. For example, subject 2 is the slowest rat in the first treatment but is the fastest in the second treatment. Because there are no consistent individual differences, most of the variability within treatments is due to experimental error. As a result, MS_{error} will be large and will tend to produce a relatively small F-ratio.

Figure 14.8

The effect of amount of reward on running speed. Individual scores for each subject at each level of reward are shown by solid lines. The treatment means depicted by the broken line are the same as shown in Figure 14.6.

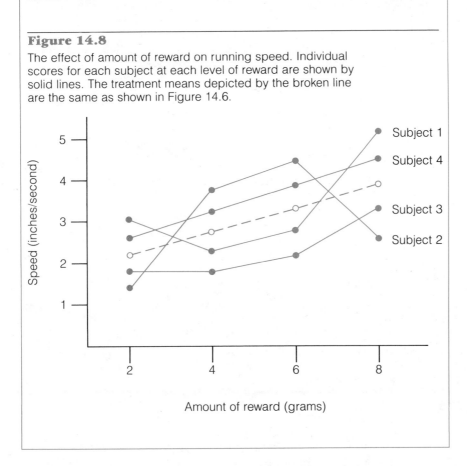

in each treatment condition. This assumption will be violated if the effect of the treatment is not consistent for all of the subjects or if carry-over effects exist for some but not other subjects. This issue is a very complex one and beyond the scope of this book. However, methods do exist for dealing with violations of this assumption (for a discussion, see Keppel, 1973).

LEARNING
CHECK

1. It has been suggested that pupil size increases during emotional arousal. A researcher, therefore, would like to see if the increase in pupil size is a function of the type of arousal (pleasant versus

aversive). A random sample of five subjects is selected for the study. Each subject views *all* three stimuli: neutral, pleasant, and aversive photographs. The neutral photograph portrays a plain brick building. The pleasant photograph consists of a young man and woman sharing a large ice cream cone. Finally, the aversive stimulus is a graphic photograph of an automobile accident. Upon viewing each stimulus, the pupil size is measured (in millimeters) with sophisticated equipment. The data are as follows. Perform an ANOVA and make a conclusion about the findings.

		Stimulus	
Subject	Neutral	Pleasant	Aversive
A	4	8	3
B	3	6	3
C	2	5	2
D	3	3	6
E	3	8	1

ANSWER

1.

Source	SS	df	MS	F
Between treatments	30	2	15	4.29
Within treatments	34	12		
Between subjects	6	4		
Error	28	8	3.5	
Total	64	14		

$F(2, 8) = 4.29$. For an alpha level of .05, the obtained F-ratio fails to reach statistical significance. The null hypothesis cannot be rejected. There is not sufficient evidence for an effect of stimulus type on pupil size.

Summary

1. Analysis of variance for a repeated measures design initially partitions total variability into between treatments SS and within treatments SS.

2. Between treatments SS is influenced by the treatment effect and experimental error. Individual differences do not play a role in this source of variability because the same sample of subjects serves in all treatments.

3. Within treatments SS is affected by individual differences and experimental error.

4. The structure of the repeated measures F is

$$F = \frac{\text{treatment effect} + \text{experimental error}}{\text{experimental error}}$$

5. To obtain the error term for the F-ratio, within treatments SS is partitioned into between subjects SS and error SS.

6. Degrees of freedom are partitioned in a similar fashion. That is, there is a df value for each SS value in the analysis.

7. The estimated variances, or MS values, are computed by dividing each SS used in the F-ratio by the appropriate df value. For the repeated measures ANOVA,

$$MS_{between\ treatments} = \frac{SS_{between\ treatments}}{df_{between\ treatments}}$$

$$MS_{error} = \frac{SS_{error}}{df_{error}}$$

8. The F-ratio for the repeated measures ANOVA is computed by

$$F = \frac{between\ treatments\ MS}{error\ MS}$$

9. When the obtained F-ratio is significant (that is, H_0 is rejected), it indicates that a significant difference lies between at least two of the treatment conditions. To determine exactly where the difference lies, unplanned, post hoc comparisons may be made. Unplanned tests, such as Tukey's HSD, use MS_{error} rather than $MS_{within\ treatments}$ and df_{error} instead of $df_{within\ treatments}$.

10. A repeated measures ANOVA eliminates the influence of individual differences from the analysis. If individual differences are extremely large, a treatment effect might be masked in an independent measures experiment. In this case, a repeated measures design might be a more sensitive test for a treatment effect.

Key Terms

between treatments variability
within treatments variability
between subjects variability
error variability
treatment effect

individual differences
experimental error
mean squares
F-ratio

Problems for Chapter 14:
Repeated Measures Analysis of Variance (ANOVA)

*1. It has been demonstrated that when subjects must memorize a list of words serially (in the order of presentation) words at the beginning and end of the list are remembered better than words in the middle. This observation has been called the *serial-position effect*. The following data represent the number of errors made in recall of the first eight, second eight, and last eight words in the list:

Person	Serial Position		
	First	Middle	Last
A	1	5	0
B	3	7	2
C	5	6	1
D	3	2	1

a. Compute the mean number of errors for each position and draw a graph of the data.

b. Is there evidence for a significant effect of serial position? Test at the .05 level of significance. Based on the ANOVA, explain the results of the study.

2. The following data were obtained to compare three experimental treatments:

Treatments		
1	2	3
2	4	6
5	5	5
1	2	3
0	1	2

a. If these data were obtained from an *independent measures design*, then could you conclude that there is a significant difference among the treatment conditions? Test with alpha set at .05.

b. If these data were obtained from a *repeated measures design*, so that each row of scores represents data from a single subject, then could you conclude that there is a significant difference among the treatments? Test at the .05 level of significance.

c. Explain the difference in the results of part a and part b.

*3. To determine the long-term effectiveness of relaxation training on anxiety, a researcher uses a repeated measures study. A random sample of $n = 10$ subjects is first tested for the severity of anxiety with a standardized test. In addition to this pretest, subjects are tested again 1 week, 1 month, 6 months, and 1 year after treatment. The investigator used ANOVA to evaluate these data, and portions of the results are presented in the following summary table. Fill in the missing values. (*Hint:* Start with the *df* values.)

Source	SS	df	MS	
Between treatments	_____	_____	_____	F = 5
Within treatments	500	_____		
Between subjects	_____	_____		
Error	_____	_____	10	
Total	_____	_____		

4. A company researcher examines the sales performance of $n = 5$ new employees at the real estate firm. To see if there is a significant trend toward improvement, the number of homes sold is recorded each month for the first 3 months of employment. The data are as follows:

Person	Month 1	Month 2	Month 3
A	1	3	4
B	4	6	8
C	3	3	5
D	2	4	7
E	0	4	6

a. Compute the mean number of sales that were made in each month.

b. Is there a significant change in sales performance with more experience? Test at the .05 level of significance.

The researcher examines the role of experience on sales performance at another branch office. Again, a sample of $n = 5$ new employees is studied, and the number of sales is noted for each of the first 3 months of employment:

Person	Month 1	Month 2	Month 3
A	4	0	10
B	0	10	0
C	0	6	4
D	6	0	14
E	0	4	2

c. Compute the mean number of sales that were made in each month. Compare these values to those obtained in part a.

d. Is there a significant change in sales across months? Set the alpha level of .05.

e. Compare the results of the ANOVA for the first branch office (part b) to those of the second branch (part d). Even though the means are the same at each branch (part a versus part c), why are the results of the ANOVA so different?

5. A teacher studies the effectiveness of a reading skills course on comprehension. A sample of $n = 20$ students is studied. The instructor assesses their comprehension with a standardized reading test. The test is administered at the beginning of the

course, at midterm, and at the end of the course. The instructor uses analysis of variance to determine whether or not a significant change has occurred in the students' reading performance. The following summary table presents a portion of the ANOVA results. Provide the missing values in the table. (Start with df values.)

Source	SS	df	MS	
Between treatments	_____	_____	18	$F = 9.0$
Within treatments	170	_____		
Between subjects	_____	_____		
Error	_____	_____	_____	
Total	_____	_____		

*6. A psychologist studies the effect of practice on maze learning in rats. Rats are tested in the maze in one daily session for 4 days. The psychologist records the number of errors made in the trials of each daily sesion. The data are as follows:

	Session			
Rat	1	2	3	4
1	3	1	0	0
2	3	2	2	1
3	6	3	1	2

Is there evidence for a practice effect? Use the .05 level of significance.

*7. A researcher studies the interference of old habits on new tasks in the following manner: He presents three types of stimuli, one at a time, on a slide projector. In the first type, the subject views the name of a color, such as "green," printed in the same color ink as the name. For the second type of stimulus the name of a color, such as "red," is printed in ink that is *different* in color from the name. The third type of stimulus is a random string of consonants printed in ink of one of several possible colors (such as blue ink). The task for the subject is to name the color of the ink as soon as possible. The reaction time (the latency of response to the stimulus presentation) is recorded for each type of stimulus. Because reading words is such a strong habit, subjects should have difficulty in quickly naming the color of ink for the second type of stimulus. This method of studying interference effects is known as a Stroop task. A random sample of $n = 8$ subjects is selected for this study. The data are as follows:

| Subject | Type of Stimulus | | |
	1 Same Color (msec)	2 Different Color (msec)	3 Consonants (msec)
1	180	220	190
2	198	233	201
3	174	218	187
4	185	221	193
5	207	240	209
6	191	215	189
7	198	235	193
8	173	210	177

a. Compute the means for each stimulus type.

b. Perform an ANOVA to determine if there is an effect of stimulus type on reaction time. Test at the .01 level of significance.

c. In a few sentences, interpret the findings in light of the ANOVA. What happened in the experiment?

8. When a stimulus is presented continuously and it does not vary in intensity, the individual will eventually perceive the stimulus as less intense or not perceive it at all. This phenomenon is known as sensory adaptation. Years ago Zigler (1932) studied adaptation for skin (cutaneous) sensation by placing a small weight on part of the body and measuring how much time lapsed until subjects reported they felt nothing at all. Zigler compared cutaneous adaptation on the back of the hand, forearm, forehead, and cheek. Suppose a researcher does a similar study, comparing adaptation on the back of the hand, the lower back, the middle of the palm, and the chin just below the lower lip. A 500-milligram weight is gently placed on the region, and the latency (in seconds) for a report that it is no longer felt is recorded for each subject. A sample of $n = 9$ subjects is used, and each subject is tested for adaptation in each of the four regions. The data are as follows:

| Subject | Area of Stimulation | | | |
	Back of Hand	Lower Back	Middle of Palm	Chin Below Lower Lip
1	6.5	4.6	10.2	12.1
2	5.8	3.5	9.7	11.8
3	6.0	4.2	9.9	11.5
4	6.7	4.7	8.1	10.7
5	5.2	3.6	7.9	9.9
6	4.3	3.5	9.0	11.3
7	7.4	4.8	10.8	12.6
8	5.4	3.1	9.3	11.0
9	6.6	4.0	11.7	13.9

Is there a significant effect of area of stimulation on the latency of adaptation? Set the alpha level to .01.

*9. A psychologist has $n = 7$ subjects fitted with glasses containing prisms that make everything look upside down. The psychologist has the subjects wear these glasses for 5 days to see if they eventually learn to compensate for the inversion of their visual field. On each of the 5 days, the subjects must assemble a wooden puzzle, and the experimenter measures the amount of time to completion (in seconds). The data are as follows:

| Subject | Day | | | | |
	1	2	3	4	5
1	112	107	83	87	69
2	135	130	110	74	46
3	89	33	27	36	29
4	37	60	62	32	19
5	73	66	54	43	37
6	56	58	51	59	60
7	95	89	125	70	31

Is there an effect of practice? Test at the .05 level of significance.

10. A psychologist is asked by a dog food manufacturer to determine if animals will show a preference among three new food mixes recently developed. The psychologist takes a sample of $n = 6$ dogs. They are deprived of food overnight and presented simultaneously with three bowls of the mixes on the next morning. After 10 minutes, the bowls are removed, and the amount of food (in ounces) consumed is determined for each type of mix. The data are as follows:

| Subject | Mix | | |
	1	2	3
1	3	2	1
2	0	5	1
3	2	7	3
4	1	6	5
5	1	2	3
6	3	0	3

Is there evidence for a significant preference? Test at the .05 level of significance.

*11. A psychologist performs an experiment to demonstrate a generalization gradient in instrumental conditioning. Pigeons are trained to peck a key for food reward whenever a 1000-hertz tone is presented. The animals are trained until they satisfactorily learn that the discriminative stimulus (the tone) signals the availability of reward and until their response rates are high and stable. The experimenter then tests the pigeons for stimulus generalization by presenting tones of 200, 600, 1000, 1400, and 1800 hertz to all of the animals. The number of responses are recorded in each of these generalization tests. In a generalization gradient, the more difference between the test stimulus and the original stimulus, the less the animal will respond. The data from the experiment are as follows:

Number of Responses in a Test Session

Pigeon	Test Tone (Hz)				
	200	600	1000	1400	1800
1	63	129	356	240	94
2	95	110	123	120	90
3	45	190	251	154	33
4	80	181	180	75	30
5	68	135	277	124	65
6	32	79	286	174	81

a. Compute the mean number of responses for each test tone. Draw a graph of these means.

b. Perform an ANOVA on the results. Is there an effect of the frequency (hertz) of the test tone? Set alpha at .01.

c. Based on the "picture" of the results in part a and the analysis in part b, explain what occurred in this experiment.

12. A scientist tests two drugs for their effects on insomnia. A sample of $n = 10$ insomniacs is pretested with a placebo before bedtime, and the latency to onset of sleep is measured to serve as a baseline. A week later, the subjects receive the first drug before bedtime, and the time that lapses between drug administration and sleep onset is measured again. Finally, a week later the second drug is tested in the same fashion. The latency to sleep onset (in minutes) is presented for each subject on every test. The data are as follows:

Subject	Pretest	Drug 1	Drug 2
E.B.	136	24	33
K.F.	92	107	21
T.Z.	117	98	111
J.R.	65	51	49
R.E.	129	29	37
A.G.	172	112	70
P.S.	89	122	145
D.W.	84	22	16
L.K.	140	95	27
C.Y.	73	67	77

Is there a significant effect on latency? Test at the .05 level of significance.

*13. A sample of 14-week-old infants is studied in a perception experiment. The infants are presented with three line drawings successively for 5 minutes each. The designs vary in their complexity. The researcher records how much time (in seconds) is spent viewing each of the stimuli. The data are as follows:

Infant	Low	Moderate	High
A	63	112	39
B	210	73	80
C	94	314	83
D	219	232	115
E	54	396	76
F	120	352	100
G	195	409	206

Amount of Complexity

Is there a significant preference among the three stimuli? Test at the .01 level of significance.

14. An industrial psychologist examines the effect of hourly wages and piecework pay on productivity. A random sample of $n = 12$ workers is studied. These workers are assembling small circuit boards for appliances and are getting paid at an hourly rate. The psychologist records the number of circuit boards assembled in 1 day for this pay schedule. The workers are later switched to a piecework rate in which they get paid according to the number of circuit boards assembled, not the number of hours worked. Again, the number of boards assembled is recorded for 1 day. The results are as follows:

Subject	Hourly Rate	Piecework
1	74	82
2	59	70
3	70	63
4	67	91
5	79	87
6	61	75
7	80	96
8	72	68
9	69	60
10	57	67
11	70	74
12	71	79

a. Perform an ANOVA to determine if a significant effect occurred. Use the .05 level of significance.

b. Use a repeated measures t test to analyze the data. Again, set alpha to .05. Compare the results of parts a and b. Remember, $F = t^2$ (Chapter 13).

*15. The following data are from an experiment comparing three different treatment conditions:

A	B	C
0	1	2
2	5	5
1	2	6
5	4	9
2	8	8

a. If the experiment uses an *independent measures design*, then can the researcher conclude that the treatments are significantly different? Test at the .05 level of significance.

b. If the experiment were done with a *repeated measures design*, should the researcher conclude that the treatments are significantly different? Set alpha at .05 again.

c. Explain why the results are different in the analyses of parts a and b.

16. A researcher is examining the effect of sleep deprivation on basic mental processes. A sample of eight subjects is obtained. These subjects agree to stay awake for a total of 48 hours. Every 12 hours the researcher gives each subject a series of arithmetic problems as a test of mental alertness. The number of problems worked correctly in 10 minutes is recorded for each subject. The data are as follows:

	Hours Awake			
Subject	12	24	36	48
1	8	7	8	6
2	10	12	9	11
3	9	9	8	10
4	7	8	6	6
5	12	10	10	8
6	10	9	12	8
7	7	7	6	8
8	9	10	11	11

On the basis of these data can the researcher conclude that sleep deprivation has a significant effect on basic mental processing? Test with $\alpha = .05$.

*17. The researcher in Problem 16 also wanted to examine the subjects' own perceptions of their mental functioning. Immediately before the subjects started each set of arithmetic problems, they were asked to rate their own abilities using a scale from 10 (normal) to 1 (severely impaired). The data from this part of the experiment are as follows:

Hours Awake

Subject	12	24	36	48
1	10	9	6	2
2	9	8	5	5
3	10	8	7	3
4	10	9	6	4
5	9	7	6	2
6	8	9	4	1
7	9	8	7	2
8	9	7	6	4

a. Do these data indicate that subjects perceive a change in performance as they become more tired? Test with $\alpha = .05$.

b. Write a brief description of the results of the entire experiment, combining the data from Problem 16 and Problem 17.

18. A researcher used an analysis of variance to evaluate the results from a single-factor repeated measures experiment. The reported F-ratio was $F(2, 28) = 6.35$.

a. How many different treatments were compared in this experiment?

b. How many subjects participated in the experiment?

*19. A manufacturer of business machines would like to compare the four most popular brands of electric typewriters. A sample of eight typists is selected, and each typist spends 15 minutes testing each of the four typewriters and then rates its performance. The manufacturer would like to know if there are any significant differences among the four brands. The data from this study were examined using an analysis of variance. The results are shown in the following summary table. Fill in all missing values.

Source	SS	df	MS	
Between treatments	270	____	____	$F = 9.00$
Within treatments	____	____		
Between subjects	____	____		
Error	____	____	____	
Total	680	____		

20. A psychology professor would like to determine whether or not the introductory course in psychology has any effect on students' opinions concerning the field of psychology. At the beginning of the semester a random sample of 16 students is selected, and each student is asked to rate psychology in terms

of how interesting and relevant it is. At the end of the semester these same 16 students are asked again for their opinions. The results are as follows:

Student	Beginning	End
1	13	14
2	16	16
3	10	13
4	17	16
5	15	18
6	19	18
7	12	15
8	17	16
9	10	18
10	8	12
11	11	12
12	9	13
13	12	10
14	13	15
15	17	17
16	7	12

a. Use an analysis of variance to determine whether the introductory course has any effect on students' opinions. Test at the .05 level of significance.

b. Use a t test to determine whether there is any change in opinion. Again, test at the .05 level of significance. *Note:* You should find that $F = t^2$.

CHAPTER 15

Two-Factor Analysis of Variance (Independent Measures)

TOOLS
YOU WILL
NEED

The following items are considered essential background material for this chapter. If you doubt your knowledge of any of these items, you should review the appropriate chapter or section before proceeding.

1. Introduction to analysis of variance (Chapter 13)
   a. The logic of analysis of variance
   b. ANOVA notation and formulas
   c. Distribution of F-ratios

Imagine that you seated at your desk, ready to take the final exam in statistics. Just before the exams are handed out, a television crew appears and sets up a camera and lights aimed directly at you. They explain that they are filming students during exams for a television special. You are told to ignore the camera and go ahead with your exam.

Would the presence of a TV camera affect your performance on an exam? For some of you, the answer to this question is "definitely yes" and for others, "probably not." In fact, both answers are right; whether or not the TV camera affects performance depends on your personality. Some of you would become terribly distressed and self-conscious, while others really could ignore the camera and go on as if everything were normal.

In an experiment that duplicates the situation we have described, Shrauger (1972) tested subjects on a concept formation task. Half the subjects worked alone (no audience), and half the subjects worked with an audience of people who claimed to be interested in observing the experiment. Shrauger also divided the subjects into two groups on the basis of personality: those high in self-esteem and those low in self-esteem. The dependent variable for this experiment was the number of errors on the concept forma-

tion task. Data similar to those obtained by Shrauger are shown in Figure 15.1. Notice that the audience had no effect on the high-self-esteem subjects. However, the low-self-esteem subjects made nearly twice as many errors with an audience as when working alone.

We have presented Shrauger's study as an introduction to experiments that have two independent variables. In this study, the independent variables are

1. Audience (present or absent)
2. Self-esteem (high or low)

The results of this study indicate that the effect of one variable (audience) depends on another variable (self-esteem).

You should realize that it is quite common to have experimental variables that interact in this way. For example, a particular drug may have a profound effect on some patients and have no effect whatsoever on others. Some children develop normally in a single-parent home, while others show serious difficulties. In general, the effects of a particular treatment often depend on other factors. To determine whether two variables are interdependent, it is necessary to examine both variables together in a single experiment. In this chapter we will introduce the experimental techniques that are used for experiments with two independent variables.

Figure 15.1

Results of an experiment examining the effect of an audience on the number of errors made in a concept formation task for subjects who are rated either high or low in self-esteem. Notice that the effect of the audience depends on the self-esteem of the subjects.

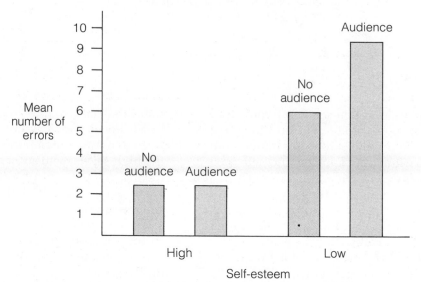

Shrauger, J. S. (1972). Self-esteem and reactions to being observed by others. *Journal of Personality and Social Psychology, 23*, 192–200. Copyright (1972) by the American Psychological Association. Adapted by permission of the author.

15.1

Introduction

Often a two-factor design is specified by the size of the matrix. For example, Table 15.1 depicts a 2 × 3 factorial design and Figure 15.2 a 2 × 2 factorial design. The numbers reflect the levels of each factor.

An example of an experiment that combines two independent variables is presented in Figure 15.2. The independent variables in this experiment are age (one group of animals is tested at 1 month and another group at 8 months) and drug (one group receives the drug before testing, and the other does not). The dependent variable is the learning score obtained for each animal. Notice that this experiment will allow the researcher to examine several different questions:

1. What is the effect of the drug on learning?
2. How does learning performance depend on age (1 month versus 8 months)?
3. Does the effect of the drug depend on the age of the animals?

An experiment of this type is called a *two-factor* experiment. Notice that the data for a two-factor experiment always can be presented in a matrix listing the values for one factor across the top and the other factor down the first column. Each box in the matrix corresponds to exactly one value for each factor. These boxes are called *cells*, and each cell identifies a specific treatment condition. For example, the lower left-hand cell in Figure 15.2 would contain scores for those animals who received no drug and were tested at age 1 month.

The different values for each factor are called the *levels* of the factor. For example, the age factor has two levels, 1 month and 8 months. The drug factor also has two levels, drug and no drug.

15.2
Advantages of a Two-Factor Experiment

You may have noticed that the experiment described in Figure 15.2 could have been done as two separate experiments (see Figure 15.3). One experiment could evaluate the drug effect, and the other experiment could examine the age difference. What is the advantage of combining these two different questions into a single experiment? In fact, there are several advantages:

1. <u>Fewer Subjects.</u> The two-factor experiment pictured in Figure 15.2 uses a total of 30 subjects in the drug condition and 30 subjects in the no-drug condition. The mean difference between these two groups of 30 will be used to evaluate the drug's effect. At the same time, the two-factor experiment tests a group of 30 subjects at age 1 month versus a second group of 30 subjects tested at age 8 months. Both of these tests are done with the same overall group of 60 subjects. If the two experiments were done separately (see Figure 15.3), it would require a total of 120 subjects (60 in each experiment).

Figure 15.2

Matrix showing the experimental treatment combinations for a two-factor experiment. The factors are age and drug. There are two levels for each factor, resulting in four different treatment combinations, or cells, in the matrix.

Factor 1 (age)

	1 month	8 months
Drug	Scores for $n = 15$ subjects given the drug and tested at age 1 month	Scores for $n = 15$ subjects given the drug and tested at age 8 months
No drug	Scores for $n = 15$ subjects given no drug and tested at age 1 month	Scores for $n = 15$ subjects given no drug and tested at age 8 months

Factor 2 (drug)

Figure 15.3

Two separate experiments that duplicate the two factors shown in Figure 15.2. Notice that it would take a total of $N = 120$ subjects to complete these two experiments, compared to a total of only $N = 60$ subjects for the two-factor experiment in Figure 15.2.

Experiment I: Evaluating the drug effect

Drug	Scores for all $n = 30$ subjects who are given the drug before testing
No drug	Scores for all $n = 30$ subjects who are given no drug before testing

Experiment II: Evaluating the effect of age

1 month	8 months
Scores for all $n = 30$ subjects who are tested at age 1 month	Scores for all $n = 30$ subjects who are tested at age 8 months

2. **Experimental Control.** Often it is possible for an experimental treatment to have a positive effect on one group of subjects and no effect (or a negative effect) on others. For example, the drug we are testing could improve learning performance for the young animals but have no effect on the older animals. If we tested only the young animals, we would observe a strong effect. But if we tested a mixed group of young and old together, we would observe a mixed and inconsistent drug effect. Whenever separate groups of individuals are combined into a single sample, there is a risk that the treatment will show mixed effects. This is often called *noise* in the data because it can mask the treatment effect. The two-factor experiment allows you to control some of this noise. In the example we are considering, the two distinct groups of animals (young and old) have been separated by using age as a factor. A more detailed example showing how a second factor can be used for experimental control is given in Example 15.2 at the end of this chapter.

3. **Interaction.** The greatest advantage of a two-factor experiment is the opportunity to examine the *interaction* between the two separate factors. As already noted, it is possible for a treatment to affect one group differently than it does another. Also, it is possible for the effect of a

By noise the experimenter is referring to variability that cannot be explained by the treatment effect.

treatment to depend on the specific circumstances under which it is administered. When the effects of one treatment depend on a second treatment, you have an interaction. The two-factor experiment allows you to look at this interaction as well as each of the two treatments separately.

Main Effects and Interactions

It is possible to look at the data from a two-factor experiment as if they represented two separate single-factor experiments. In Figure 15.2, for example, you could ignore the age groups and look at the data as if the experiment were only comparing the drug group versus the no-drug group (the 30 subjects in the first row versus the 30 subjects in the second row). A comparison of this type is called a main effect.

DEFINITION

The mean differences among the levels of one factor are referred to as the *main effect* of that factor. If the design of the experiment is represented as a matrix with one factor determining the rows and the second factor determining the columns, then the main effect for the first factor would evaluate the mean differences among the rows, and the main effect for the second factor would evaluate the mean differences among the columns.

For our example, we could evaluate the main effect for the drug (ignoring age), or we could evaluate the main effect for age (ignoring the drug). When discussing a general two-factor experiment, we will identify the factors as factor A and factor B. The main effect for factor A commonly is called the A-effect. Similarly, the main effect for factor B is called the B-effect. The evaluation of main effects will be one part of the two-factor data analysis procedure.

DEFINITION

There is an *interaction* between two factors if the effect of one factor depends on the levels of the second factor. When the two factors are identified as A and B, the interaction is identified as the $A \times B$ interaction.

The examples in Figure 15.4 should make this definition a bit more concrete. Figure 15.4(a) shows results with no interaction. If you look at the main effect for the drug in these data, you should see that the

Figure 15.4

(a) Data showing drug effect and no interaction. (b) Data showing drug effect and an interaction. (c) Data showing no drug effect but an interaction.

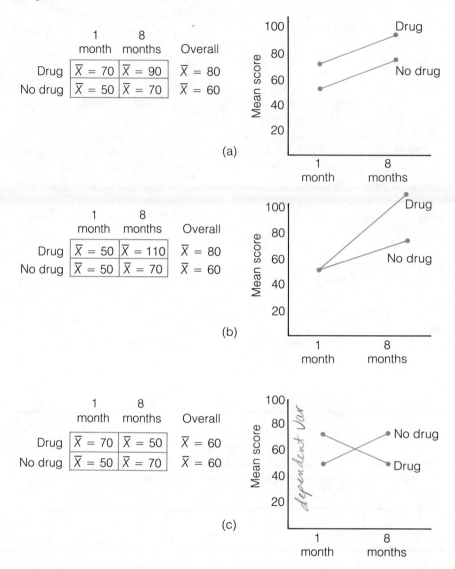

	1 month	8 months	Overall
Drug	$\overline{X} = 70$	$\overline{X} = 90$	$\overline{X} = 80$
No drug	$\overline{X} = 50$	$\overline{X} = 70$	$\overline{X} = 60$

(a)

	1 month	8 months	Overall
Drug	$\overline{X} = 50$	$\overline{X} = 110$	$\overline{X} = 80$
No drug	$\overline{X} = 50$	$\overline{X} = 70$	$\overline{X} = 60$

(b)

	1 month	8 months	Overall
Drug	$\overline{X} = 70$	$\overline{X} = 50$	$\overline{X} = 60$
No drug	$\overline{X} = 50$	$\overline{X} = 70$	$\overline{X} = 60$

(c)

overall average score for the drug group is $\overline{X} = 80$. The overall average score for the no-drug group is $\overline{X} = 60$. This means that the drug has a 20-point effect (from 60 to 80). Does this drug effect (one factor) depend on age (the levels of the second factor)? To answer, look at each age group separately. For the animals tested at 1 month, the drug effect is exactly 20 points (50 versus 70). For the animals tested at 8 months, the drug effect is still 20 points (70 versus 90). The drug effect does not depend on age. Therefore, there is no interaction. Notice that when the effect of one treatment is constant across all levels of the other factor (no interaction) there will be a constant distance between the two lines in the graph. Therefore, when there is no inter- action, a graph of the data will always have parallel lines (a constant distance apart). On the other hand, an easy way to spot an interaction is to look for lines that are not parallel; that is, look for lines that converge or cross.

Now look at Figure 15.4(b). Again, the overall drug effect is 20 points ($\overline{X} = 60$ for the no-drug group versus $\overline{X} = 80$ for the drug group). But when you look at each age group separately, you find a 40-point drug effect for the animals tested at 8 months and no drug effect for the animals tested at 1 month. In this case, the effect of the drug does depend on the age of the animals. Now there is an interaction.

One final example should help solidify the concept of an interaction. Look at the data in Figure 15.4(c). For these data, the overall drug effect is zero. The drug group and the no-drug group both show an overall mean of $\overline{X} = 60$. Does this mean that the drug has no effect? The answer is *no*: The drug produces a 20-point increase in scores for the young animals and a 20-point decrease for the old animals. In this case the effect of the drug depends on which age group you are exam- ining; that is, there is an interaction. Notice that when there is an interaction, the main effects may be misleading. In general, whenever an interaction exists, you must interpret the effects of each factor in terms of its interaction with the other factor. For this example, it would be wrong to conclude that the drug has no effect. Instead, you should interpret the drug effect for each age group separately.

15.3
Logic of the Analysis

The two-factor analysis of variance actually is composed of three dis- tinct hypothesis tests. The analysis will evaluate the following:

1. *The Main Effect of Factor* A. The null hypothesis for this test states that there are no population mean differences among the different levels of factor *A*. In symbols,

   H_0: $\mu_{A_1} = \mu_{A_2} = \mu_{A_3}$

2. *The Main Effect of Factor* B. The null hypothesis for this test states that there are no population mean differences among the levels of factor *B*. In symbols,

   H_0: $\mu_{B_1} = \mu_{B_2} = \mu_{B_3}$

3. *The* A $\times$ B *Interaction*. The null hypothesis for this test simply states that there is no interaction. That is, the effect of either factor is independent of the other factor.

In each case we are looking for treatment differences that are larger than would be expected by chance. For each of the three tests, the magnitude of the treatment effect will be evaluated by an *F*-ratio. Notice that there will be three *F*-ratios, one for each main effect and one for the interaction. Each of these *F*-ratios will have the same basic structure:

$$F = \frac{\text{variance between treatments}}{\text{variance within treatments}}$$

The between treatments variance is assumed to be caused by three things:

1. Treatment effect (either factor *A*, or factor *B*, or *A* × *B* interaction)
2. Individual differences (there are different subjects for each treatment condition)
3. Experimental error (there always is a margin of error in measurements)

The variability within treatments will provide a measure of the variability expected by chance. Differences within treatments are assumed to be caused by

1. Individual differences
2. Experimental error

With these components of variability in mind, the three *F*-ratios will all have the basic form:

The level of significance helps us decide if the value for the F-ratio is sufficiently larger than 1.00.

$$F = \frac{\text{treatment effect} + \text{individual diffs.} + \text{experimental error}}{\text{individual diffs.} + \text{experimental error}}$$

As always, a value of *F* near 1.00 indicates that there is no treatment effect (the numerator and denominator of *F* are nearly the same). A value of *F* much greater than 1.00 indicates that the treatment effect is real.

15.4
Notation and Formulas

The general format for any two-factor experiment is shown in Figure 15.5. Notice that we have identified the factors by using the letters *A* and *B*. By convention, the number of levels of factor *A* is specified by the symbol *p* and the number of levels of factor *B* is specified by *q*. The *A* × *B* matrix gives a picture of the total experiment, with each cell corresponding to a specific treatment condition. In the example shown in Figure 15.5, *p* = 2 and *q* = 3, so we have a total of *pq* = 2 × 3 = 6 different treatment conditions.

It is possible to use either an independent or a repeated measures experimental design with a two-factor experiment. In this chapter, we will only look at independent measures designs. By definition, independent measures means that there is a separate group of subjects for each treatment condition, i.e., a separate sample for each cell in the experimental design. For the experiment shown in Figure 15.5, there are six treatment conditions, so we would need six different groups of subjects.

Figure 15.5

Matrix showing the general design of a two-factor experiment. The factors are identified by the letters A and B. The levels of each factor are identified by adding numerals to the factor letters; for example, the third level of factor B is identified by B_3.

Factor B

	Level B_1	Level B_2	Level B_3
Level A_1	Treatment (cell) A_1B_1	Treatment (cell) A_1B_2	Treatment (cell) A_1B_3
Level A_2	Treatment (cell) A_2B_1	Treatment (cell) A_2B_2	Treatment (cell) A_2B_3

Factor A (labels the rows Level A_1 and Level A_2)

To develop the formulas for the two-factor analysis of variance, we must be able to specify all the totals, numbers, and SS values in the data. The notation system for the two-factor design is as follows:

1. G = the grand total of all the scores in the experiment.
2. N = the total number of scores in the entire experiment.
3. p = the number of levels of factor A.
4. q = the number of levels of factor B.
5. n = the number of scores in each treatment condition (in each cell of the $A \times B$ matrix).
6. The totals for each treatment condition will be specified by using the capital letters (A and B) that represent that condition. For example, A_1B_2 would represent the total of the scores in the cell where the level of A is 1 and the level of B is 2. When we want to talk in general about the cell totals, we will refer to the AB totals (without specifying a particular cell). Notice that there are n scores in each AB total.

In addition, A_1 will refer to the total of all the scores for subjects in the first level of factor A (all the scores in the first row of the $A \times B$ matrix). A_2 refers to the total for the second row, etc. When speaking in general about the row totals, we will refer to the A totals. Notice that there are qn scores in each A total. In a similar way, B_1 will refer to the total of all the scores in the first column. In general, the column totals will be called B totals. Note that you add pn scores to obtain each B total.

Formulas

The general structure for the analysis of a two-factor experiment is shown in Figure 15.6. At the first level of the analysis, the total variability is separated into two components: between treatments variability and within treatments variability. You should notice that this

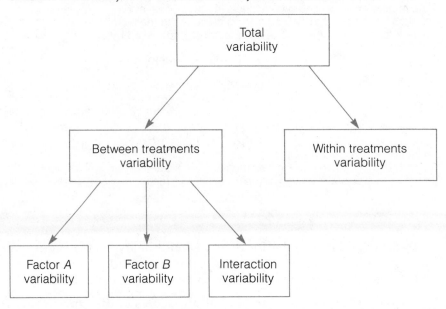

first stage is identical to the structure used for the single-factor analysis of variance in Chapters 13 and 14 (see Figures 13.5 and 14.1). The second level of the analysis partitions the between treatments variability into separate components. With a two-factor experiment, the differences between treatment conditions (cells) could be caused by either of the two factors (A or B) or by the interaction. These three components are examined individually in the second stage of the analysis.

The goal of this analysis is to compute the variance values needed for the three F-ratios. We will need three between treatments variances (one for factor A, one for factor B, and one for the interaction), and we will need a within treatments variance. Each of these variances (or mean squares) will be determined by a sum of squares value (SS) and a degrees of freedom value (df):

$$\text{mean square} = MS = \frac{SS}{df}$$

The actual formulas for the two-factor analysis of variance are almost identical to the formulas for the single-factor analysis (Chapters 13 and 14). You may find it useful to refer to these chapters for a more detailed explanation of the formulas. To help demonstrate the use of the formulas, we will use the data in Table 15.1. You should notice that the analysis consists of two parts; we must analyze the SS values as well as the df values. We will begin with the analysis of the sum of squares (SS).

Table 15.1

Hypothetical Data for a Two-Factor Experiment with Two Levels of Factor A and Three Levels of Factor B.[a]

		Factor B			
		B_1	B_2	B_3	
		1	7	3	
		6	7	1	
		1	11	1	
A_1		1	4	6	$A_1 = 60$
		1	6	4	
		$AB = 10$	$AB = 35$	$AB = 15$	
		$SS = 20$	$SS = 26$	$SS = 18$	
		0	0	0	
		3	0	2	
		7	0	0	
A_2		5	5	0	$A_2 = 30$
		5	0	3	
		$AB = 20$	$AB = 5$	$AB = 5$	
		$SS = 28$	$SS = 20$	$SS = 8$	
		$B_1 = 30$	$B_2 = 40$	$B_3 = 20$	

Factor A (row label, left)

$G = 90$
$\Sigma X^2 = 520$

[a]The individual scores are given for each treatment cell ($n = 5$), along with the cell totals (AB values) and the SS for each cell.

Analysis of Sum of Squares

Total Sum of Squares, SS_{total} SS_{total} computes the sum of squares for the total set of N scores:

$$(15.1) \quad SS_{total} = \Sigma X^2 - \frac{G^2}{N}$$

You should notice that this formula is identical to the SS formula that was used for single-factor ANOVA in Chapters 13 and 14 [see Formulas (13.2) and (14.1)].

For the data in Table 15.1, this total sum of squares would be

$$SS_{total} = 520 - \frac{90^2}{30}$$
$$= 520 - 270$$
$$= 250$$

Within Treatments Sum of Squares, SS_{within} The variability within, or "inside," the treatments is found by simply calculating SS for each individual cell and then adding up these SS values. The formula is

$$(15.2) \quad SS_{within} = \Sigma SS_{inside\ each\ treatment\ cell}$$

For the data in Table 15.1, SS_{within} is

$$SS_{within} = 20 + 26 + 18 + 28 + 20 + 8$$
$$= 120$$

Between Treatments Sum of Squares, $SS_{between}$ In the single-factor analysis of variance the formula for computing sum of squares between treatments focused on the treatment totals (T values) and computed SS for these totals:

$$SS_{between} = \Sigma \frac{T^2}{n} - \frac{G^2}{N}$$

In the two-factor design, each treatment corresponds to a particular cell, and the cell totals are identified by AB rather than T, so the between treatments formula becomes

This SS is also called $SS_{between\ cells}$. It measures between cell variability.

(15.3) $SS_{between} = \Sigma \dfrac{AB^2}{n} - \dfrac{G^2}{N}$

Applying this formula to the data in Table 15.1 gives

$$SS_{between} = \frac{10^2}{5} + \frac{35^2}{5} + \frac{15^2}{5} + \frac{20^2}{5} + \frac{5^2}{5} + \frac{5^2}{5} - \frac{90^2}{30}$$

$$= 20 + 245 + 45 + 80 + 5 + 5 - 270$$

$$= 400 - 270$$

$$= 130$$

This completes the first level of the analysis. When you are performing the calculations for a two-factor analysis of variance, you should stop at this stage and be sure that the two components add up to the total:

$$SS_{total} = SS_{between} + SS_{within}$$

$$250 = 120 + 130$$

We now move to the second level of the analysis. Remember, we are still measuring treatment effects or differences between treatments. But now we want to determine how much of the overall treatment effect can be attributed to factor A, how much is due to factor B, and how much is due to the interaction between these two factors. To compute the SS for each of the two separate factors, we will continue to use the same basic formula for sum of squares between treatments. The first part of this formula uses the total for each treatment condition and the number of scores in each condition [see Formula (15.3)]. For factor A, the totals are identified by As, and the number of scores in each level of A is given by qn. Thus, the formula for SS between the levels of factor A would be

To get an A total, we must sum scores across the levels of factor B. Therefore, qn (or 15) scores are added to obtain an A total.

(15.4) $SS_A = \Sigma \dfrac{A^2}{qn} - \dfrac{G^2}{N}$

The A totals for the data in Table 15.1 are $A_1 = 60$ and $A_2 = 30$. Each of these totals is obtained by adding up a set of $3(5) = 15$ scores. Therefore, the sum of squares for factor A would be

$$SS_A = \frac{60^2}{15} + \frac{30^2}{15} - \frac{90^2}{30}$$

$$= 240 + 60 - 270$$

$$= 30$$

For factor B, the totals are identified by Bs, and the number of scores in each B total is determined by pn. The formula for sum of squares for factor B is

$$(15.5) \quad SS_B = \Sigma \frac{B^2}{pn} - \frac{G^2}{N}$$

To get a B total, we must sum across levels of factor A. Therefore, pn (or 10) scores are added to find the B total.

For the data in Table 15.1, this SS would be

$$SS_B = \frac{30^2}{10} + \frac{40^2}{10} + \frac{20^2}{10} - \frac{90^2}{30}$$

$$= 90 + 160 + 40 - 270$$

$$= 20$$

Finally, the SS for the interaction is found by subtraction. According to Figure 15.6, the between treatments variability is partitioned into three parts: factor A, factor B, and the interaction. Therefore, if you start with $SS_{between}$ and subtract out SS_A and SS_B, the amount that is left will be the SS for the interaction. Thus, the "formula" for the interaction is

$$(15.6) \quad SS_{A \times B} = SS_{between} - SS_A - SS_B$$

Using this formula on the data from Table 15.1 gives

$$SS_{A \times B} = 130 - 30 - 20$$

$$= 80$$

The complete analysis of SS for the data in Table 15.1 is presented in Figure 15.7. Notice that the separate parts at each level of the analysis add up to the total amount of variability at the level above. For example, the SS for factor A, factor B, and the $A \times B$ interaction add up to the $SS_{between}$.

Analysis of Degrees of Freedom

Each SS value in the analysis of variance has a corresponding degrees of freedom. Normally, SS measures the amount of variability (or differences) among a number of things. The corresponding df value is found by counting the number of things and subtracting 1. For a set of n scores, for example, $df = n - 1$. Using this general principle, we will define the df value associated with each of the SSs in the analysis.

Total Degrees of Freedom, df_{total}　The df_{total} is simply the degrees of freedom associated with the SS_{total}. When we computed this SS, we used all N scores. Therefore,

$$(15.7) \quad df_{total} = N - 1$$

For the data in Table 15.1, there are a total of $N = 30$ scores, so $df_{total} = 29$.

Figure 15.7

Analysis of the sum of squares (SS) for a two-factor experiment.
The values are those obtained from the data in Table 15.1.

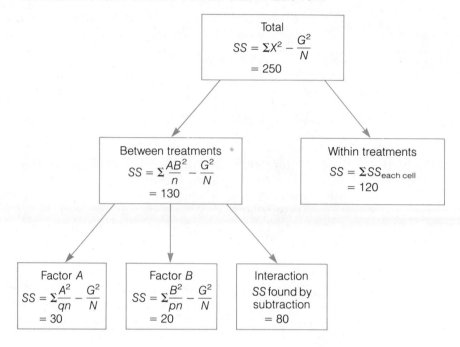

Degrees of Freedom Within Treatments, df_{within} To compute SS_{within}, we added up the SS values inside each of the treatment conditions. Because there are n scores inside each treatment, each SS value has $df = n - 1$. When these are added up, you get

(15.8) $df_{within} = \Sigma(n - 1)$

$= N - pq$

For the data in Table 15.1, there are $n = 5$ scores in each treatment condition. Therefore, $df = 4$ inside each treatment. Summing over the six treatments gives an overall within treatments df of 24. This same value is obtained if we start with $N = 30$ scores and subtract $pq = 6$ treatments.

Degrees of Freedom Between Treatments, $df_{between}$ $SS_{between}$ was computed using the AB totals from each of the treatment cells. Because there are pq separate cells,

(15.9) $df_{between} = pq - 1$

The example we are considering has a total of six treatment conditions (two levels of factor A and three levels of factor B). Therefore, the between treatment $df = 3 \times 2 - 1 = 6 - 1 = 5$.

Notice that the analysis of the df values follows the same pattern shown in Figure 15.6. Specifically, the $df_{between}$ and the df_{within} will combine to equal the df_{total}:

$$df_{total} = df_{between} + df_{within}$$
$$29 = 5 + 24$$

Degrees of Freedom for Factor A, df_A The SS for factor A measures the variability among the A totals. Because the number of levels of factor A is identified by p,

(15.10) $df_A = p - 1$

Because there are two levels of factor A ($p = 2$) in Table 15.1, this factor would have $df = 1$.

Degrees of Freedom for Factor B, df_B There are q different levels for factor B, and the SS for factor B is computed by using these totals. Therefore,

(15.11) $df_B = q - 1$

For the data we are considering, factor B has three levels ($q = 3$), so factor B would have $df = 2$.

Degrees of Freedom for the Interaction, $df_{A \times B}$ The df for the $A \times B$ interaction can be computed two different ways. First, you can use the structure of the analysis shown in Figure 15.6 to find $df_{A \times B}$ by subtraction. If you start with $df_{between}$ and subtract out the df values for factors A and B, the value that is left will be df for the interaction:

(15.12) $df_{A \times B} = df_{between} - df_A - df_B$

The data in Table 15.1 have $df_{between}$ equal to 5, df_A equal to 1, and df_B equal to 2. Therefore, the df for the interaction would be

$$df_{A \times B} = 5 - 1 - 2$$
$$= 2$$

An easy shortcut for finding df for the interaction is to notice that

(15.13) $df_{A \times B} = df_A df_B$

Using this shortcut formula for the data in Table 15.1, the $A \times B$ interaction would have $df = 1 \times 2 = 2$. An intuitive explanation of this formula for df is presented in Box 15.1.

The complete analysis of df values is shown in Figure 15.8. Again, notice that the separate components always add up to the total. For example, the $df_{between}$ (5) and the df_{within} (24) add up to the df_{total} (29).

Mean Squares (*MSs*) and *F*-Ratios

The final step in the analysis is to compute the mean square values and the *F*-ratios. Recall that each mean square (*MS*) is actually a sample variance and is computed from the SS and df values:

$$MS = \frac{SS}{df}$$

Figure 15.8

Analysis of the degrees of freedom for a two-factor analysis of variance. The values are those obtained from the data in Table 15.1.

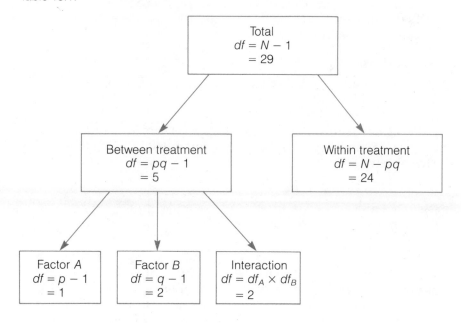

For the example we are considering,

$$MS \text{ for } A \quad = MS_A = \frac{SS_A}{df_A} = \frac{30}{1} = 30$$

$$MS \text{ for } B \quad = MS_B = \frac{SS_B}{df_B} = \frac{20}{2} = 10$$

$$MS \text{ for } A \times B = MS_{A \times B} = \frac{SS_{A \times B}}{df_{A \times B}} = \frac{80}{2} = 40$$

The denominator of each F-ratio will have MS_{within}:

$$MS_{within} = \frac{SS_{within}}{df_{within}} = \frac{120}{24} = 5$$

For factor A, the F-ratio is

$$F = \frac{MS_A}{MS_{within}} = \frac{30}{5} = 6.00$$

This F-ratio has $df = 1, 24$ ($df = 1$ for the numerator of the ratio and $df = 24$ for the denominator). Commonly, this would be written as

$$F(1, 24) = 6.00$$

For factor B,

$$F(2, 24) = \frac{MS_B}{MS_{within}}$$

$$= \frac{10}{5}$$

$$= 2.00$$

And for the $A \times B$ interaction,

$$F(2, 24) = \frac{MS_{A \times B}}{MS_{within}}$$

$$= \frac{40}{5}$$

$$= 8.00$$

To determine whether or not these values fall in the critical region and thereby indicate a significant treatment effect, it is necessary to look at the distribution of F-ratios. The F distributions for $df = 1, 24$ and for $df = 2, 24$ are shown in Figure 15.9. The critical values are shown for the .05 level of significance (check the table on page A-32).

Figure 15.9

Distribution of F for $df = 1, 24$ for evaluating the F-ratio for factor A and the distribution with $df = 2, 24$ for evaluating factor B and the $A \times B$ interaction. In each case, the critical value for $\alpha = .05$ is shown.

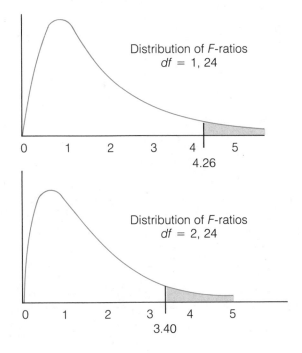

Caution: *Be sure to check the appropriate critical region. Factors A and B have different critical values because these factors have different values for degrees of freedom in this example.*

Note that for factor A our obtained F-ratio of $F(1, 24) = 6.00$ is in the critical region. This indicates that the obtained difference between treatments (the numerator of the ratio) is significantly greater than what would be expected by chance (the denominator of the ratio). We conclude that factor A does have a significant effect.

On the other hand, the obtained F-ratio for factor B, $F(2, 24) = 2.00$, is not in the critical region. According to these data, factor B does not have a significant effect; that is, the difference we obtained is not larger than would be expected by chance.

Finally, the F-ratio for the $A \times B$ interaction, $F(2, 24) = 8.00$, is in the critical region. This indicates that there is a significant interaction. There are several equivalent ways of expressing this result. You could say that the specific combinations of factors A and B produce significant differences. Or you could say that the effect of factor A depends on the different levels of factor B. Or you could say that the effect of factor B depends on the different levels of factor A.

To make these conclusions more concrete, the data from the experiment are graphed in Figure 15.10. The significant main effect for factor A is seen in the fact that the line for A_1 is generally higher than the line for A_2. The average difference between these lines is the A-effect.

To visualize the B-effect, imagine a point midway between the two dots above B_1 on the graph. Do the same thing for the two dots above B_2 and for the dots above B_3. Now draw a line connecting these three

Figure 15.10

Graph of the data from Table 15.1, showing the means for each of the six different treatment combinations (cells) in the experiment.

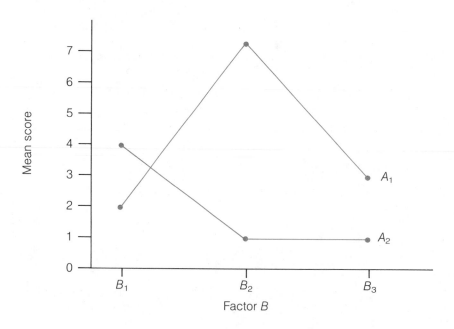

imaginary points. You should find that this line is nearly horizontal; as you move across the line from B_1 to B_2 to B_3, there is not much change in the mean score. This indicates that factor B does not have much effect and supports our conclusion that the main effect for B is not significant.

The interaction is easy to see because the two lines in the graph are not parallel. You can describe this interaction by focusing on the distance between the lines at each level of factor B. At B_1, for example, the A_1 line is lower. But at B_2, the A_1 line goes considerably higher than A_2, etc. This description is equivalent to saying that the A-effect (the distance between the lines) depends on the levels of B.

A concise summary of the formulas and structure for the two-factor analysis of variance is presented in Figure 15.11. This figure contains nearly all of the information you need to conduct the analysis and should help you to understand the relationships among all the parts.

Figure 15.11

The complete analysis of variance for an independent measures two-factor design.

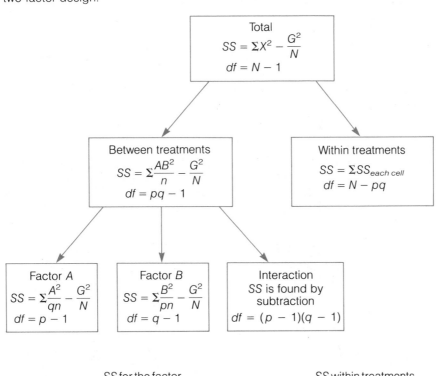

$$MS_{factor} = \frac{SS \text{ for the factor}}{df \text{ for the factor}} \qquad MS_{error\ term} = \frac{SS \text{ within treatments}}{df \text{ within treatments}}$$

This MS is computed for A, B, and the interaction.

The same MS is used as the error term for all three F-ratios.

BOX 15.1 | **Additive and Multiplicative Relations Between Factors**

One way to think about interactions is to consider the difference between factors that multiply together and factors that add together.

When there is no interaction, the effect of one factor simply adds to the effect of the other factor. This situation is shown in Figure 15.12. Notice that the effect of factor A is to add three points to each mean (the means in A_2 are each three points greater than the corresponding means in A_1). When these means are placed in a graph, the lines for A_1 and A_2 are parallel. There is no interaction. When an additive relation exists between the two factors, there is no interaction.

Figure 15.12

Treatment means for a two-factor experiment showing an additive relation between the two factors. Notice that there is no $A \times B$ interaction.

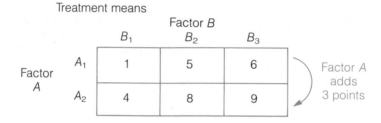

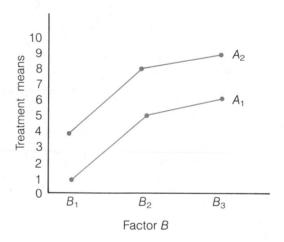

Alternatively, when the relation between the two factors is multiplicative, an interaction will be present. Consider the data shown in Figure 15.13. In this case, the effect of factor A is to multiply

BOX 15.1 *continued*

Figure 15.13

Treatment means for a two-factor experiment showing a multiplicative relation between the two factors. Notice that there is a large $A \times B$ interaction.

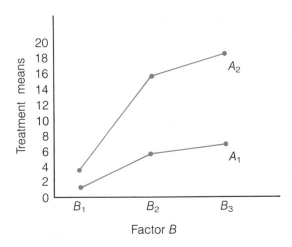

each mean by three points (each mean in A_2 is three times greater than the corresponding mean in A_1). When these means are placed in a graph, the lines for A_1 and A_2 are not parallel. This time there is an interaction.

The notation used to represent an interaction is consistent with this idea of a multiplicative relation between two factors. For example, an interaction is identified as $A \times B$. Also, you can find the degrees of freedom for an interaction by multiplication:

$$df \text{ for } A \times B = df \text{ for } A \times df \text{ for } B$$

The notion that an interaction can be described as a multiplicative relation is common in areas other than statistics. For example, pharmacists often speak of "drug interactions." This term is

(continued)

BOX 15.1

continued

used when the effects of one drug multiply the effects of another. You should note that in some cases the multiplication produces a much greater effect than would be expected by simply "adding" the two drugs together. In other cases, two drugs can cancel each other so that the combination is less effective than would be expected by simple addition.

LEARNING
CHECK

1. The following data summarize the results from a two-factor, independent measures experiment.

| | | Factor B | | |
		B_1	B_2	B_3
Factor A	A_1	$n = 10$ $AB = 0$ $\overline{X} = 0$ $SS = 30$	$n = 10$ $AB = 10$ $\overline{X} = 1$ $SS = 40$	$n = 10$ $AB = 20$ $\overline{X} = 2$ $SS = 50$
	A_2	$n = 10$ $AB = 40$ $\overline{X} = 4$ $SS = 60$	$n = 10$ $AB = 30$ $\overline{X} = 3$ $SS = 50$	$n = 10$ $AB = 20$ $\overline{X} = 2$ $SS = 40$

$\Sigma X^2 = 610$

a. Sketch a graph similar to those in Figure 15.4 to show the results of this experiment.

b. Looking at your graph, does there appear to be a main effect for factor A? Does factor B have an effect? Is there an interaction?

c. Use an analysis of variance with $\alpha = .05$ to evaluate the effects of factor A, factor B, and the $A \times B$ interaction for these data.

ANSWERS

1. a. Your graph should show two converging lines similar to Figure 15.4(b).

b. The points for level 1 of factor A are much lower than the means for level 2. This mean difference indicates a main effect for factor A. There is no main effect for factor B. The fact that the lines are not parallel indicates an interaction.

c. The results of the ANOVA are summarized in the following table:

Source	SS	df	MS	
Between treatments	100	5		
Factor A	60	1	60	$F = 12.00$
Factor B	0	2	0	$F = 0$
$A \times B$ interaction	40	2	20	$F = 4.00$
Within treatments	270	54	5	
Total	370	59		

(*Note:* The fact that $SS_B = 0$ should be clear from looking at the data. The B totals are all the same; they are not variable.)

15.5
Examples of the Two-Factor ANOVA

Example 15.1 presents the complete hypothesis testing procedure for a two-factor independent measures experiment.

EXAMPLE 15.1

In 1968 Stanley Schachter published an article in *Science* reporting a series of experiments on obesity and eating behavior. One of these studies examined the hypothesis that obese individuals do not respond to internal, biological signals of hunger. In simple terms, this hypothesis says that obese individuals tend to eat whether or not their bodies are actually hungry.

In Schachter's experiment subjects were led to believe that they were taking part in a "taste test." All subjects were told to come to the experiment without eating for several hours beforehand. The experiment used two independent variables or factors:

1. Weight (obese versus normal subjects)
2. Full stomach versus empty stomach (half the subjects were given a full meal, as much as they wanted, after arriving at the experiment, and half were left hungry)

All subjects were then invited to taste and rate five different types of crackers. The dependent variable was the number of crackers eaten by each subject.

The prediction for this study was that the obese subjects would eat the same amount of crackers whether or not they were full. The normal subjects were expected to eat more with empty stomachs and less with full stomachs. Notice that the primary prediction of this study is that there will be an interaction between weight and fullness.

Hypothetical data similar to those obtained by Schachter are presented in Table 15.2.

Table 15.2

Results from an Experiment Examining the Eating Behavior of Normal and Obese Individuals Who Have Either a Full or an Empty Stomach.[a]

		Factor B (Fullness)		
		Empty Stomach	Full Stomach	
Factor A (Weight)	Normal	$n = 20$ $\overline{X} = 22$ $AB = 440$ $SS = 1540$	$n = 20$ $\overline{X} = 15$ $AB = 300$ $SS = 1270$	$A_1 = 740$
	Obese	$n = 20$ $\overline{X} = 17$ $AB = 340$ $SS = 1320$	$n = 20$ $\overline{X} = 18$ $AB = 360$ $SS = 1266$	$A_2 = 700$
		$B_1 = 780$	$B_2 = 660$	$G = 1440$ $\Sigma X^2 = 31{,}836$ $N = 80$

[a] The dependent variable is the number of crackers eaten in a taste test (hypothetical data).

For this analysis, we will identify weight as factor A and fullness as factor B.

STEP 1. State Hypotheses and Select α. For factor A the null hypothesis states that there is no difference in the amount eaten for normal versus obese subjects. In symbols,

H_0: $\mu_{A_1} = \mu_{A_2}$

H_1: $\mu_{A_1} \neq \mu_{A_2}$

For factor B the null hypothesis states that the amount eaten will be the same for full-stomach subjects as for empty-stomach subjects. In symbols,

H_0: $\mu_{B_1} = \mu_{B_2}$

H_1: $\mu_{B_1} \neq \mu_{B_2}$

For the $A \times B$ interaction the null hypothesis can be stated two different ways. First, if there is a difference in eating between the full-stomach and empty-stomach conditions, it will be the same for normal and obese subjects. Second, if there is a difference in eating between the normal and obese subjects, it will be the same for the full-stomach and empty-stomach conditions. In more general terms,

H_0: The effect of factor A does not depend on factor B (and B does not depend on A)

H_1: The effect of one factor does depend on the other factor

We will use $\alpha = .05$ for all tests.

STEP 2. Locate the Critical Region. To locate the critical values for each of the three F-ratios, we first must determine the df values. For these data (Table 15.2),

$$df_{total} = N - 1 = 79$$
$$df_{between} = pq - 1 = 3$$
$$df_{within} = N - pq = 76$$
$$df_A = p - 1 = 1$$
$$df_B = q - 1 = 1$$
$$df_{A \times B} = df_A df_B = 1$$

Thus, all three F-ratios will have $df = 1, 76$. With $\alpha = .05$, the critical F value is 3.98 for all three tests.

Notice that the F distribution table has no entry for df = 1, 76. A close and conservative estimate of this critical value may be obtained by using df = 1, 70 (critical F = 3.98). Whenever there is no entry for the df value of the error term, use the nearest smaller value in the table.

STEP 3. Use the Data to Compute the F-Ratios. First, we will analyze the SS values:

$$SS_{total} = \Sigma X^2 - \frac{G^2}{N} = 31{,}836 - \frac{1440^2}{80}$$
$$= 31{,}836 - 25{,}920$$
$$= 5916$$

$$SS_{between} = \Sigma \frac{AB^2}{n} - \frac{G^2}{N}$$
$$= \frac{440^2}{20} + \frac{300^2}{20} + \frac{340^2}{20} + \frac{360^2}{20} - \frac{1440^2}{80}$$
$$= 26{,}440 - 25{,}920$$
$$= 520$$

$$SS_{within} = \Sigma SS_{inside\ each\ cell}$$
$$= 1540 + 1270 + 1320 + 1266$$
$$= 5396$$

$$SS_A = \Sigma \frac{A^2}{qn} - \frac{G^2}{N}$$
$$= \frac{740^2}{40} + \frac{700^2}{40} - \frac{1440^2}{80}$$

$$= 25{,}940 - 25{,}920$$
$$= 20$$
$$SS_B = \Sigma \frac{B^2}{pn} - \frac{G^2}{N}$$
$$= \frac{780^2}{40} + \frac{660^2}{40} - \frac{1440^2}{80}$$
$$= 26{,}100 - 25{,}920$$
$$= 180$$
$$SS_{A \times B} = SS_{between} - SS_A - SS_B$$
$$= 520 - 20 - 180$$
$$= 320$$

The MS values needed for the F-ratios are

$$MS_A = \frac{SS_A}{df_A} = \frac{20}{1} = 20$$

$$MS_B = \frac{SS_B}{df_B} = \frac{180}{1} = 180$$

$$MS_{A \times B} = \frac{SS_{A \times B}}{df_{A \times B}} = \frac{320}{1} = 320$$

$$MS_{within} = \frac{SS_{within}}{df_{within}} = \frac{5396}{76} = 71$$

Finally, the F-ratios are

$$F_A = \frac{MS_A}{MS_{within}} = \frac{20}{71} = 0.28$$

$$F_B = \frac{MS_B}{MS_{within}} = \frac{180}{71} = 2.54$$

$$F_{A \times B} = \frac{MS_{A \times B}}{MS_{within}} = \frac{320}{71} = 4.51$$

STEP 4. Make Decisions. For these data, factor A (weight) has no significant effect; $F(1, 76) = 0.28$. Statistically, there is no difference in the number of crackers eaten by normal versus obese subjects.

Similarly, factor B (fullness) has no significant effect; $F(1, 76) = 2.54$. Statistically, the number of crackers eaten by full subjects is no different from the number eaten by hungry subjects. (*Note:* This conclusion concerns the combined group of normal and obese subjects. The interaction concerns these two groups separately.)

These data produce a significant interaction; $F(1, 76) = 4.51, p < .05$. This means that the effect of fullness does depend on weight. Specifically, the degree of fullness did affect the normal subjects, but it had no effect on the obese subjects.

Reduction of Uncontrolled Variance by a Two-Factor Design

We mentioned at the beginning of this chapter that one advantage of a two-factor experiment is that it allows you to "control" some of the variability within an experiment. The following example demonstrates how you can "add" a second factor to a single-factor experiment in order to reduce the error variability and thereby increase the chances of obtaining a significant treatment effect. The rationale for this technique comes from the fact that the independent measures analysis of variance uses the variability within treatments (MS_{within}) as the denominator of the F-ratio. This variance inside the treatments provides a measure of how much variability is expected just by chance, that is, how much variability is due to individual differences and experimental error.

Often the variability within treatments is not all unexplained and uncontrolled variance. For example, a researcher may notice that a particular treatment seems to have a large effect on the young animals in his sample but not much effect on the older animals. In this case, much of the variability within the treatment condition is caused by the age of the animals. Whenever variability can be explained or predicted in this way, it is possible to measure it and remove it from the F-ratio. The following example demonstrates this process.

EXAMPLE 15.2
The data in Table 15.3 represent the outcome of a single-factor experiment comparing two treatment conditions. Each

---

Table 15.3

Hypothetical Data from a Single-Factor Experiment Comparing Two Treatment Conditions.[a]

Treatment 1		Treatment 2
3		5
3		4
1		3
2		5
1	Males	3
7	̄ ̄ ̄Females̄ ̄ ̄	7
7		7
5		8
6		9
5		9
$T_1 = 40$		$T_2 = 60$
$SS_1 = 48$		$SS_2 = 48$

[a]Each treatment contains a sample of $n = 10$ subjects, 5 males and 5 females.

treatment condition contains $n = 10$ subjects, 5 males and 5 females.

Using a single factor analysis of variance on these data, the researcher obtains

$$SS_{between} = \Sigma \frac{T^2}{n} - \frac{G^2}{N}$$

$$= \frac{40^2}{10} + \frac{60^2}{10} - \frac{100^2}{20}$$

$$= 520 - 500$$

$$= 20$$

The within treatments SS for these data is

$$SS_{within} = \Sigma SS_{inside\ each\ treatment}$$

$$= 48 + 48$$

$$= 96$$

The MS values are

$$MS_{between} = \frac{SS}{df} = \frac{20}{1}$$

$$= 20$$

$$MS_{within} = \frac{SS}{df} = \frac{96}{18}$$

$$= 5.33$$

The resulting F-ratio is $F(1, 18) = 3.75$, which is not in the critical region. Therefore, the researcher must conclude that these data do not demonstrate a significant treatment effect.

The researcher noticed, however, that much of the variability inside the treatments appears to come from the fact that the females tend to have higher scores than the males. If this is true, then much of the within treatments variability (the denominator of the F-ratio) can be explained. Table 15.4 reproduces the data, but this time the scores for males and females are separated by using sex as a second factor. If we call the original treatments factor A and use sex as factor B, the two-factor analysis of variance gives the following results:

$$SS_A = \Sigma \frac{A^2}{qn} - \frac{G^2}{N}$$

$$= \frac{40^2}{10} + \frac{60^2}{10} - \frac{100^2}{20}$$

$$= 20$$

(Notice that the treatment effect is the same whether you use a one- or a two-factor analysis.)

$$SS_B = \Sigma \frac{B^2}{pn} - \frac{G^2}{N}$$

$$= \frac{30^2}{10} + \frac{70^2}{10} - \frac{100^2}{20}$$

$$= 80$$

(This is the variability due to sex differences.) The SS for the $A \times B$ interaction is zero for these data. (Check it for yourself.)

With the data arranged in a two-factor design, SS_{within} is

$$SS_{within} = SS_{inside\ each\ cell}$$

$$= 4 + 4 + 4 + 4$$

$$= 16$$

Finally, the mean square values are

$$MS_A = \frac{SS_A}{df_A} = \frac{20}{1}$$

$$= 20$$

$$MS_B = \frac{SS_B}{df_B} = \frac{80}{1}$$

$$= 80$$

$$MS_{within} = \frac{SS_{within}}{df_{within}} = \frac{16}{16}$$

$$= 1$$

The F-ratios are as follows:

$$\text{For factor } A: \quad F(1, 16) = \frac{20}{1} = 20$$

$$\text{For factor } B: \quad F(1, 16) = \frac{80}{1} = 80$$

Now the treatment effect (factor A) gives an F-ratio of 20, which is in the critical region. The researcher can conclude that there is a significant treatment effect.

The difference between the two analyses is entirely in the denominator of the F-ratios. In the two-factor analysis, much of the "error" variability is accounted for and removed from the denominator of the F-ratio. This makes it much more likely to obtain a significant result. You also should notice that the two-factor analysis provides additional information about the second factor and the interaction between the two factors.

Table 15.4

The Same Hypothetical Data Shown in Table 15.3 with a Second
Factor (Sex) Added to Create a Two-Factor Experiment

| | Factor A (Treatment) | |
	Treatment 1	Treatment 2

Factor B
(Sex)

	Treatment 1	Treatment 2	
Males	3 3 1 2 1 $AB = 10$ $SS = 4$	5 4 3 5 3 $AB = 20$ $SS = 4$	$B_1 = 30$
Females	7 7 5 6 5 $AB = 30$ $SS = 4$	7 7 8 9 9 $AB = 40$ $SS = 4$	$B_2 = 70$
	$A_1 = 40$	$A_2 = 60$	

15.6
Assumptions for the Two-Factor ANOVA

The validity of the analysis of variance presented in this chapter depends on the same two assumptions we have encountered with other hypothesis tests for independent measures experiments (the t test in Chapter 11 and the single-factor ANOVA in Chapter 13):

1. The population distribution should be normal.
2. The population variances should be equal (homogeneity of variance).

As before, the assumption of normality generally is not a cause for concern, especially when the sample size is relatively large. The homogeneity of variance assumption is more important, and if it appears that your data fail to satisfy this requirement, you should conduct a test for homogeneity before you attempt the ANOVA. Hartley's F-max test (see page 348) allows you to use the sample variances from your data to determine whether there is evidence for any differences among the population variances.

Summary

1. An experiment with two independent variables is called a two-factor experiment. Such an experiment can be diagrammed as a matrix by listing the levels of one factor across the top and the

levels of the other factor down the side. Each *cell* in the matrix corresponds to a specific combination of the two factors.

2. Traditionally, the two factors are identified as factor A and factor B. The purpose of the analysis of variance is to determine whether there are any significant mean differences among the treatment conditions or cells in the experimental matrix. These treatment effects are classified as follows:
    a. The A-effect: Differential effects produced by the different levels of factor A.
    b. The B-effect: Differential effects produced by the different levels of factor B.
    c. The $A \times B$ interaction: Differences that are produced by unique combinations of A and B. An interaction exists when the effect of one factor depends on the levels of the other factor.

3. The two-factor analysis of variance produces three F-ratios: one for factor A, one for factor B, and one for the $A \times B$ interaction. Each F-ratio has the same basic structure:

$$F = \frac{MS_{treatment\ effect}\ (\text{either factor } A \text{ or } B \text{ or the } A \times B \text{ interaction})}{MS_{within}}$$

The formulas for SS, df, and MS values for the two-factor analysis of variance are presented in Figure 15.11.

Key Terms

two-factor experiment	main effect
matrix	interaction
cells	

Problems for Chapter 15:
Two-Factor Analysis of Variance (Independent Measures)

*1. The following data are from a two-factor experiment with $n = 10$ subjects in each treatment condition (each cell):

Factor B

		B_1	B_2	
	A_1	$AB = 40$ $SS = 70$	$AB = 10$ $SS = 80$	
Factor A				$\Sigma X^2 = 588$
	A_2	$AB = 30$ $SS = 73$	$AB = 20$ $SS = 65$	

Test for a significant A-effect, B-effect, and $A \times B$ interaction using $\alpha = .05$ for all tests.

2. The following data are from an experiment examining the extent to which different personality types are affected by distraction. Individuals were selected to represent two different personality types: introverts and extroverts. Half the individuals in each group were tested on a monotonous task in a relatively quiet, calm room. The individuals in the other half of each group were tested in a noisy room filled with distractions. The dependent variable was the number of errors committed by each individual. The results of this experiment are as follows:

Factor B
(Personality)

		Introvert	Extrovert	
	Quiet	$n = 5$ $AB = 10$ $SS = 15$	$n = 5$ $AB = 10$ $SS = 25$	
Factor A (Distraction)				$\Sigma X^2 = 520$
	Noisy	$n = 5$ $AB = 20$ $SS = 10$	$n = 5$ $AB = 40$ $SS = 30$	

Use an ANOVA with $\alpha = .05$ to evaluate these results. Describe how distraction and personality affect performance.

*3. The following data were obtained from an independent measures experiment using $n = 5$ subjects in each treatment condition:

Factor B

		B_1	B_2	
	A_1	$AB = 15$ $SS = 80$	$AB = 25$ $SS = 90$	
Factor A				$\Sigma X^2 = 1100$
	A_2	$AB = 5$ $SS = 70$	$AB = 55$ $SS = 80$	

a. Compute the means for each cell and draw a graph showing the results of this experiment. Your graph should be similar to those shown in Figure 15.4.

b. Just from looking at your graph, does there appear to be a main effect for factor A? What about factor B? Does there appear to be an interaction?

c. Use an analysis of variance with $\alpha = .05$ to evaluate these data.

4. Many species of animals communicate using odors. A researcher suspects that specific chemicals contained in the urine of male rats can influence the behavior of other males in the colony. The researcher predicts that male rats will become anxious and more active if they think they are in territory that has been marked by another male. Also, it is predicted that these chemicals will have no effect on female rats. To test this theory, the researcher obtains samples of 15 male and 15 female rats. One-third of each group is tested in a sterile cage. Another one-third of each group is tested in a cage that has been painted with a small amount of the chemicals. The rest of the rats are tested in a cage that has been painted with a large amount of the chemicals. The dependent variable is the activity level of each rat. The data from this experiment are as follows:

		Factor B (Amount of Chemical)		
		None	Small	Large
Factor A (Sex)	Male	$n = 5$ $AB = 10$ $SS = 15$	$n = 5$ $AB = 20$ $SS = 19$	$n = 5$ $AB = 30$ $SS = 31$
	Female	$n = 5$ $AB = 10$ $SS = 19$	$n = 5$ $AB = 10$ $SS = 21$	$n = 5$ $AB = 10$ $SS = 15$

$\Sigma X^2 = 460$

Use an ANOVA with $\alpha = .05$ to test the researcher's predictions. Explain the results.

*5 It has been demonstrated in a variety of experiments that memory is best when the conditions at the time of testing are identical to the conditions at the time of learning. This phenomenon is called *encoding specificity* because the specific cues that you use to learn (or encode) new information are the best possible cues to help you recall the information at a later time. In an experimental demonstration of encoding specificity, Tulving and Osler (1968) prepared a list of words to be memorized. For each word on the list, they selected an associated word to serve as a cue. For example, if the word "queen" were on the list, the word "lady" would be a cue. Four groups of subjects participated in the experiment. One group was given the cues during learning and during the recall test. Another group received the cues only during recall. A third group received the cues only during learning, and the final group was not given any cues at all. The dependent variable was the number of words correctly recalled. Data similar to Tulving and Osler's results are as follows:

Cues at Learning

	Yes	No
Yes	$n = 10$ $\overline{X} = 3$ $SS = 22$	$n = 10$ $\overline{X} = 1$ $SS = 15$
No	$n = 10$ $\overline{X} = 1$ $SS = 16$	$n = 10$ $\overline{X} = 1$ $SS = 19$

Cues at Recall

$\Sigma X^2 = 192$

Use an ANOVA with $\alpha = .05$ to evaluate these data. Describe the results.

6. The following data summarize the results of a two-factor experiment with $n = 5$ in each treatment condition (each cell):

Factor B

	B_1	B_2	B_3	B_4
A_1	$AB = 5$ $SS = 40$	$AB = 5$ $SS = 50$	$AB = 5$ $SS = 30$	$AB = 5$ $SS = 40$
A_2	$AB = 5$ $SS = 30$	$AB = 15$ $SS = 30$	$AB = 15$ $SS = 50$	$AB = 25$ $SS = 50$

Factor A

$\Sigma X^2 = 560$

Use an ANOVA with $\alpha = .05$ to evaluate the results of this experiment.

*7. The following data show the results of a two-factor experiment with $n = 10$ in each treatment condition (cell):

Factor B

	B_1	B_2
A_1	$\overline{X} = 4$ $SS = 40$	$\overline{X} = 2$ $SS = 50$
A_2	$\overline{X} = 3$ $SS = 50$	$\overline{X} = 1$ $SS = 40$

Factor A

$\Sigma X^2 = 480$

a. Sketch a graph showing the results of this experiment. (See Figure 15.4 for examples.)

b. Looking at your graph, does there appear to be an $A \times B$ interaction? Does factor A appear to have any effect? Does factor B appear to have any effect?

c. Evaluate these data using an ANOVA with $\alpha = .05$.

8. Sketch a graph showing the results of a 2 × 2 factorial experiment for each of the following descriptions:

   a. There is an A-effect but no B-effect and no interaction.
   b. There is an A-effect and a B-effect but no interaction.
   c. There is an interaction but no A-effect and no B-effect.

*9. Individuals who are identified as having an antisocial personality disorder also tend to have reduced physiological responses to painful or anxiety-producing stimuli. In everyday terms, these individuals show a limited physical response to fear, guilt, or anxiety. One way of measuring this response is with the galvanic skin response (GSR). Normally, when a person is aroused, there is an increase in perspiration which causes a measurable reduction in the electrical resistance on the skin. The following data represent the results of an experiment measuring GSR for normal and antisocial individuals in regular and stress-provoking situations:

	Arousal Level	
	Baseline	Stress
Normal	22 18 27 25 26 23 19 24 27 26 21 19	18 19 15 21 20 18 14 21 19 24 13 17
Antisocial	24 26 28 29 23 27 25 22 21 25 23 26	29 22 27 25 22 20 20 29 28 21 23 24

Personality

   a. Compute the cell means and sketch a graph of the results.
   b. Use an ANOVA with $\alpha = .05$ to evaluate these data.
   c. Explain the findings of this study.

10. The following data are from an experiment examining the influence of a specific hormone on eating behavior. Three different drug doses were used, including a control condition (no drug), and the experiment measured eating behavior for males and females. The dependent variable was the amount of food consumed over a 48-hour period.

	No Drug	Small Dose	Large Dose
Males	1 6 1 1 1	7 7 11 4 6	3 1 1 6 4
Females	0 3 7 5 5	0 0 0 5 0	0 2 0 0 3

Use an ANOVA with $\alpha = .05$ to evaluate these data and describe the results (i.e., the drug effect, the sex difference, and the interaction).

*11. A psychologist would like to evaluate the effectiveness of a special counseling program for students with math anxiety. Students from a freshman math class are assessed as being either high or low in math anxiety. Half of each group participates in the counseling program, while the other students continue without any special counseling. Each student's performance in the course is measured by the grade on the final exam. These data are as follows:

Math Anxiety		Counseling		No Counseling	
	High	72 61 61 63 85 82 52 68 75 72		75 64 72 87 85 76 78 79 71 83	
	Low	64 87 89 94 92 75 61 73 85 82		75 93 78 71 90 84 84 86 81 75	

a. Use an analysis of variance to evaluate these data. Use the .05 level of significance for all tests.

b. Based on the results of your analysis, can the psychologist conclude that the counseling program has any effect? Is the effectiveness of the program different for students high in math anxiety versus students low in math anxiety?

12. Hyperactivity in children usually is treated by counseling, or by drugs, or by both. The following data are from an experiment designed to evaluate the effectiveness of these different treatments. The dependent variable is a measure of attention

span (how long each child was able to concentrate on a specific task).

	Drug		No Drug	
Counseling	14	10	8	6
	13	15	7	4
	15	12	5	10
	10	8	9	11
No Counseling	11	13	10	13
	12	10	9	6
	14	8	12	9
	15	9	7	13

a. Use an ANOVA with $\alpha = .05$ to evaluate these data.

b. Do the data indicate that the drug has a significant effect? Does the counseling have an effect? Describe these results in terms of the effectiveness of the drug and counseling and their interaction.

*13. A school psychologist is examining students' responses to a trial program in self-paced instruction. In this program, students are left on their own to determine how quickly (or slowly) they work through a set of required material. The psychologist suspects that self-motivated students will do well in this program but that other students may find it difficult. The psychologist identifies samples of students with "internal" personality types (self-motivated) and "external" personality types. Half of each group is placed in the self-paced program, and half remains in a normal, well-structured classroom. The final grades for these students are as follows:

	Internal		External	
Self-paced	84	64	71	86
	83	85	68	64
	91	93	75	72
	75	90	73	65
	72	81	81	73
Structured Class	86	85	76	90
	83	91	81	85
	92	76	78	83
	72	84	71	72
	81	78	64	85

a. Use an analysis of variance to evaluate these data. Make all tests at the .05 level of significance.

b. Describe the results of the ANOVA in terms of the two independent variables.

14. In addition to measuring classroom performance, the psychologist in Problem 13 also measured each student's attitude

toward his/her course. Attitudes were measured on a 10-point scale with 10 being best ("I completely enjoyed the course"). These attitude scores are as follows:

	Internal		External	
Self-paced	8	8	3	4
	10	10	5	3
	10	7	3	5
	9	8	7	6
	7	9	5	5
Structured Class	8	7	8	8
	6	6	9	7
	5	7	10	6
	10	5	7	9
	7	8	9	8

a. Use an ANOVA with $\alpha = .05$ to evaluate these data.

b. Describe the results. (Is one type of instruction preferred over the other? Is one personality type generally more positive or negative than the other? Does preference for the type of instruction depend on personality?

*15. In the preview section of this chapter we presented an experiment that examined the effect of an audience on the performance of two different personality types. Data from this experiment are as follows. The dependent variable is the number of errors made by each subject.

		Alone			Audience		
Self-esteem	High	2	5	5	3	5	1
		3	0	4	2	4	2
		0	3	2	4	0	0
		4	1	5	1	3	3
		2	0	1	5	1	2
	Low	6	8	2	11	13	9
		7	9	5	8	10	7
		3	4	3	7	8	11
		6	7	4	14	10	7
		5	9	6	7	12	10

Use an ANOVA with $\alpha = .05$ to evaluate these data. Describe the effect of the audience and the effect of personality on performance.

16. The general relation between performance and arousal level is described by the Yerkes-Dodson law. This law states that performance is best at a moderate level of arousal. When arousal is too low, people don't care about what they are doing, and performance is poor. At the other extreme, when arousal is too high, people become overly anxious, and performance suffers. In addition, the exact form of the relation between arousal and

performance depends on the difficulty of the task. The following data demonstrate the Yerkes-Dodson law. The dependent variable is a measure of performance.

		Arousal Level							
		Very Low		Low		Medium		High	
Task Difficulty	Easy	10	11	16	14	20	18	15	12
		12	10	16	15	19	21	14	13
		8	12	13	12	19	16	13	14
		9	10	15	14	21	20	16	14
	Hard	5	8	12	11	9	9	5	4
		6	4	13	14	8	7	4	3
		4	6	10	13	10	11	3	4
		5	5	12	11	9	8	6	5

a. Sketch a graph showing the mean level of performance for each treatment condition.

b. Use a two-factor ANOVA to evaluate these data.

c. Describe and explain the main effect for task difficulty.

d. Describe and explain the interaction between difficulty and arousal.

*17. The process of interference is assumed to be responsible for much of forgetting in human memory. New information going into memory interferes with the information that already is there. One demonstration of interference examines the process of forgetting while people are asleep versus while they are awake. Because there should be less interference during sleep, there also should be less forgetting. The following data are the results from an experiment examining four groups of subjects. All subjects were given a list of words to remember. Then half of the subjects went to sleep, and the others stayed awake. Within both the asleep and the awake groups, half of the subjects were tested after 2 hours, and the rest were tested after 8 hours. The dependent variable is the number of words correctly recalled.

	Delay of Memory Test			
	2 Hours		8 Hours	
Asleep	5	7	6	4
	6	10	8	4
	4	5	5	7
	3	8	10	8
	6	5	7	6
Awake	3	2	1	2
	4	3	0	1
	5	4	0	2
	3	2	1	0
	2	4	1	1

a. Use a two-factor ANOVA to examine these data.

b. Describe and explain the interaction.

18. Most adolescents experience a growth spurt when they are between 12 and 15 years old. This period of dramatic growth generally occurs earlier for girls than for boys. A psychologist studying the physical development of adolescents recorded the gain in height (in centimeters) over a 1-year period for boys and girls ranging in age from 11 to 15. Separate samples were used for each age group. The data are as follows:

	11 Years	12 Years	Age 13 Years	14 Years	15 Years
Males	4 5 6 5 4 5	4 5 4 6 4 6	6 7 5 4 7 6	8 7 10 9 10 7	9 8 6 7 6 7
Females	5 7 6 5 6 6	8 7 9 10 9 8	7 6 6 7 5 6	4 3 3 5 3 4	1 2 2 1 1 2

a. Compute the mean gain in height for each of these 10 groups and draw a graph showing the results of this study.

b. By just looking at your graph, how would you describe the difference between the growth spurt for boys and the growth spurt for girls?

c. Use an analysis of variance to evaluate these data. Perform all tests with $\alpha = .05$.

d. Do the results of the ANOVA support your description of these data?

*19. It has been demonstrated that children who watch violent television shows tend to be more aggressive than children who are not exposed to television violence. However, there is some question as to whether this effect exists only for shows with human characters or whether it also occurs for violent cartoons. A hypothetical experiment to address this question is presented here. A large sample of preschool children is obtained. One group from this sample watches a violent TV show with human characters for half an hour. A second group watches violent cartoons. Two other groups serve as control groups: One watches nonviolent human shows, and the other watches nonviolent cartoons. After watching these television shows, all four groups are placed together in a large playroom, and a psychologist records the number of aggressive actions for each child.

a. Identify the two independent variables (factors) and the dependent variable for this experiment.

b. Suppose that the psychologist is predicting that exposure to human violence will affect behavior but that cartoon violence will not. If the psychologist is correct, what outcomes are expected for the ANOVA? Predict both main effects and the interaction. (*Note:* It may help to sketch a graph of the predicted results.)

c. Suppose that the psychologist predicts that cartoon violence and human violence will affect behavior equally. In this case, what outcomes are expected for the ANOVA? Predict both main effects and the interaction.

20. The following hypothetical data represent one possible outcome of the experiment described in Problem 19:

	Violent		Nonviolent	
Human Characters	6	2	3	5
	3	4	2	3
	2	5	1	2
	5	4	4	4
	3	6	2	3
Cartoon Characters	5	2	1	3
	4	5	3	2
	3	3	2	2
	4	3	3	3
	3	4	4	4

a. Use an ANOVA to evaluate these data. Set $\alpha = .05$ for all tests.

b. Describe the results of this experiment.

CHAPTER 16

Correlation

TOOLS
YOU WILL
NEED

The following items are considered essential background material for this chapter. If you doubt your knowledge of any of these items, you should review the appropriate chapter or section before proceeding.

1. Sum of squares (SS) (Chapter 4)
   a. Computational formula
   b. Definitional formula
2. z-Scores (Chapter 5)

Having been a student and taken exams for much of your life, you probably have noticed a curious phenomenon. In every class there are some students who zip through exams and turn in their papers while everyone else is still on page 1. Other students cling to their exams and are still working frantically when the instructor announces that time is up and demands that all papers be turned in. Have you wondered what grades these students receive? Are the students who finish first the best in the class, or are they completely ignorant and simply accepting their failure? Are the A students the last to finish because they are compulsively checking and rechecking their answers? To help answer these questions, we carefully observed a recent exam and recorded the amount of time each student spent and the grade each student received. These data are shown in Figure 16.1. Note that we have listed time along the X-axis and grade on the Y-axis. Each students is identified by a point in the graph with the point located directly above the student's time and directly across from the student's grade.

The graph in Figure 16.1 shows that there is a relationship between time and grade. The best grades tend to go to the students who finished their exams early. Students who held their papers to the bitter end tended to have low grades.

In statistical terms, these data show a correlation between time and grade. In this chapter we will see how correlations are used to measure and describe relations. Just as a sample mean provides a concise description of an entire sample, a correlation will provide a description of a relationship. We also will look at how correlations are used and interpreted. For example, now that you have seen the relation between time and grades, don't you think it might be a good idea to start turning in your exam papers a little sooner? Wait and see.

Figure 16.1
The relationship between exam grade and time needed to complete the exam. Notice the general trend in these data: Students who finish the exam early tend to have better grades.

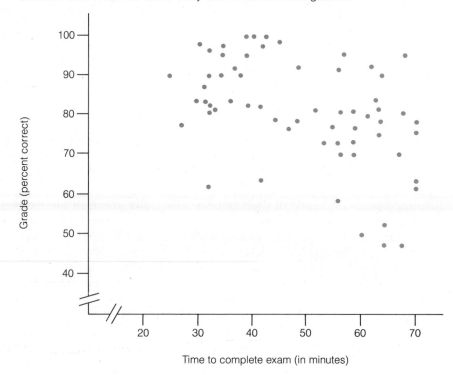

16.1
Introduction

Correlation is a statistical technique that is used to measure the relationship between two variables. Although correlation has a number of different applications, a few specific examples are presented below to give an indication of the value of this measure.

1. *Prediction.* If two variables are known to be related in some systematic way, it is possible to use one of the variables to make accurate predictions about the other. For example, when you applied for admission to college, you were required to submit a great deal of personal information, including your scores on the Scholastic Aptitude Test (SAT). College officials want this information so they can predict your chances of success in college. It has been demonstrated over several years that SAT scores and college grade point averages are

correlated. Students who do well on the SAT tend to do well in college; students who have difficulty with the SAT tend to have difficulty in college. Based on this relationship, the college admissions office can make a prediction about the potential success of each applicant. You should note that this prediction is not perfectly accurate. Not everyone who does poorly on the SAT will have trouble in college. That is why you also submit letters of recommendation, high school grades, and other information with your application.

2. *Validity.* Suppose a psychologist develops a new test for measuring intelligence. How could you show that this test truly is measuring what it claims; that is, how could you demonstrate the validity of the test? One common technique for demonstrating validity is to use a correlation. If the test actually is measuring intelligence, then the scores on the test should be related to other measures of intelligence, for example, standardized IQ tests, performance on learning tasks, problem-solving ability, etc. The psychologist could measure the correlation between the new test and each of these other measures of intelligence in order to demonstrate that the new test is valid.

3. *Theory Verification.* Many psychological theories make specific predictions about the relationship between two variables. For example, a theory may predict a relation between brain size and learning ability; a developmental theory may predict a relationship between the parents' IQs and the child's IQ; a social psychologist may have a theory predicting a relation between personality type and behavior in a social situation. In each case, the prediction of the theory could be tested by determining the correlation between the two variables.

The Data for a Correlation

To compute a correlation, it is necessary to have two scores for each individual (one score from each of the two variables involved). These scores normally are identified as X and Y. The pairs of scores can be listed in a table, or they can be presented graphically in a scatterplot (see Figure 16.2). In the scatterplot, the X values are placed on the horizontal axis of a graph, and the Y values are placed on the vertical axis. Each individual is then identified by a single point on the graph so that the coordinates of the point (the X and Y values) match the individual's X-score and Y-score. The value of the scatterplot is that it allows you to see the nature of the relationship (see Figure 16.2).

Figure 16.2

The same set of $n = 6$ pairs of scores (X and Y values) are shown in a table and in a scatterplot. Notice that the scatterplot allows you to see the relationship between X and Y.

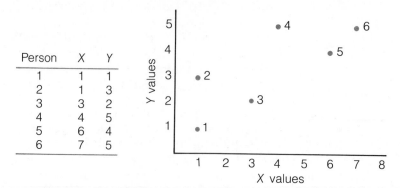

Person	X	Y
1	1	1
2	1	3
3	3	2
4	4	5
5	6	4
6	7	5

16.2
The Characteristics of a Relationship

The numerical value that is computed for a correlation measures three characteristics of the relation between X and Y. These three characteristics are as follows:

1. *The Direction of the Relationship.* Correlations can be classified into two basic categories: positive and negative. The following example provides a description of each. Suppose you run the drink concession at the football stadium. After several seasons you begin to notice a relationship between the temperature at game time and the beverages you sell. Specifically, you have noted that when the temperature is high, you tend to sell a lot of beer. When the temperature is low, you sell relatively little beer (see Figure 16.3). This is an example of a positive correlation.

DEFINITION

In a *positive correlation*, the two variables tend to move in the same direction: When the X variable increases, the Y variable also increases; if the X variable decreases, the Y variable also decreases.

At the same time, you have noted a relation between temperature and coffee sales: On cold days you sell much more coffee than on hot days (see Figure 16.4). This is an example of a negative relation.

Figure 16.3

An example of a positive relationship. Notice that temperature and beer tend to change in the same direction. As the temperature goes up, the amount of beer sold also goes up.

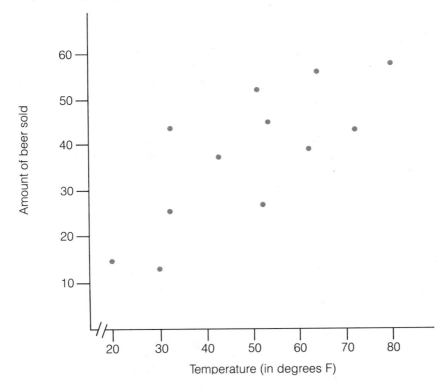

DEFINITION

In a *negative correlation*, the two variables tend to go in opposite directions. As the X variable increases, the Y variable decreases.

The direction of a relationship is identified by the sign of the correlation. A positive value ($+$) indicates a positive relationship; a negative value ($-$) indicates a negative relation.

2. *The Form of the Relation.* In the preceding coffee and-beer examples, the relationships are linear; that is, the points in the scatterplot tend to form a straight line. The most common use of correlation is to measure straight-line relations. However, you should note that other forms of relationship do exist and that there are special correlations used to measure them. For example, Figure

Figure 16.4

An example of a negative relationship. Notice that temperature and coffee tend to change in opposite directions. As the temperature goes up, the amount of coffee sold goes down.

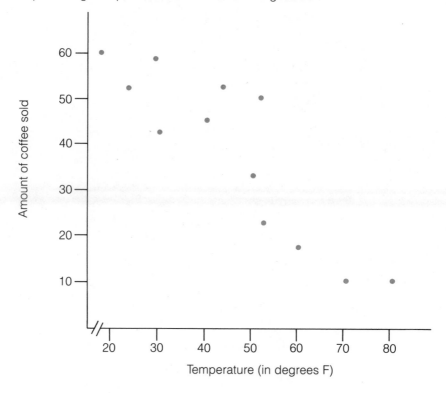

16.5(a) shows the relationship between reaction time and age. In this scatterplot there is a curved relation. Reaction time improves with age until the late teens when it reaches a peak; after that, reaction time starts to get worse. Figure 16.5(b) shows the typical relation between practice and performance. Again, this is not a straight-line relationship. In the early stages of practice, performance increases rapidly. But with a great deal of practice, the improvement in performance becomes less noticeable. (Ask anyone who has taken piano lessons for 10 years.) Many different types of correlations exist. In general, each type is designed to evaluate a specific form of relationship. In this text we will concentrate on the correlation that measures linear relations.

A correlation of −1.00 also indicates a perfect fit. The direction of the relation (positive or negative) should be considered separately from the degree of the relationship.

3. *The Degree of the Relationship.* Finally, a correlation measures how well the data fit the specific form being considered. For example, a linear correlation measures how well the data points fit on a straight line. A perfect fit always is identified by a correlation of 1.00, while a

Figure 16.5

Examples of relationships that are not linear. (a) Relationship between reaction time and age. (b) Relationship between performance and amount of practice.

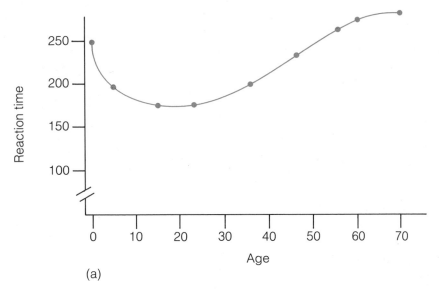

(a)

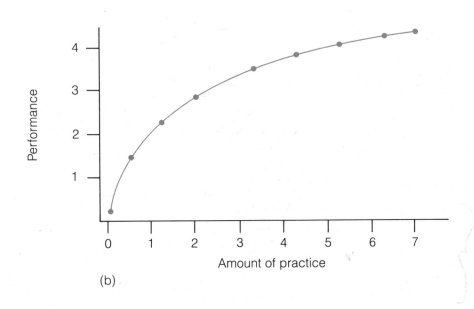

(b)

correlation of 0 indicates no fit at all. Intermediate values represent the degree to which the data points approximate the perfect form. Examples of different values for linear correlations are shown in Figure 16.6. Notice that in each example we have sketched a line around the data points. This line, called an *envelope* because it encloses the data, often helps you to see the overall trend in the data.

Figure 16.6

Examples of different values for linear correlations. Figure (a) shows a good, positive relation, approximately +0.90; figure (b) shows a relatively poor, negative correlation, approximately −0.40; figure (c) shows a perfect, negative correlation, −1.00; figure (d) shows no linear trend, 0.00.

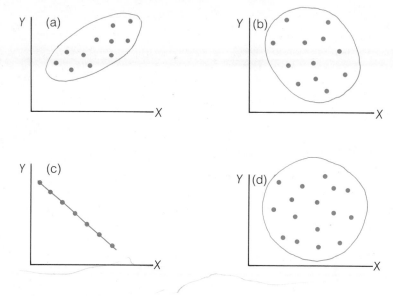

16.3
The Pearson Correlation

By far the most common correlation is the Pearson correlation (or the Pearson product-moment correlation).

DEFINITION

The *Pearson correlation* measures the degree and direction of linear relation between two variables.

The Pearson correlation is identified by the letter r and is computed by

$$r = \frac{\text{degree to which } X \& Y \text{ vary together}}{\text{degree to which } X \& Y \text{ vary separately}}$$

$$= \frac{\text{covariability of } X \& Y}{\text{variability of } X \& Y \text{ separately}}$$

When there is a perfect linear relation, every change in the X variable is accompanied by a corresponding change in the Y variable. In this case, the covariability perfectly reflects the total variability of X and Y separately. The result is a correlation of 1.00. At the other extreme, when there is no linear relation, a change in the X variable does not produce any predictable change in Y. In this case there is no covariability, and the resulting correlation is zero.

The Sum of Products of Deviations

To calculate the Pearson correlation, it is necessary to introduce one new concept: the sum of products of deviations. In the past we have used a similar concept, SS (the sum of squared deviations), to measure the amount of variability for a single variable. The sum of products, or SP, provides a parallel procedure for measuring the amount of covariability between two variables. The value for SP can be calculated with either a definitional formula or a computational formula.

The *definitional formula* for the sum of products is

$$\textbf{(16.1)} \quad SP = \Sigma(X - \overline{X})(Y - \overline{Y})$$

This formula instructs you to first find the product of each X deviation and Y deviation and then add up these products. Notice that the terms in the formula define the value being calculated: the sum of the products of the deviations.

The *computational formula* for the sum of products is

$$\textbf{(16.2)} \quad SP = \Sigma XY - \frac{\Sigma X \Sigma Y}{n}$$

Caution: *The* n *in this formula refers to the* number of pairs *of scores.*

Because this formula uses the original scores (X and Y values), it usually results in easier calculations than those required with the definitional formula. Before we demonstrate the use of these two formulas, you should note the similarity between the SP formulas and the corresponding formulas for SS that were presented in Chapter 4. The definitional formula for SS is

$$SS = \Sigma(X - \overline{X})^2$$

In this formula, you must square each deviation, which is equivalent to multiplying it by itself. With this in mind, the formula can be rewritten as

$$SS = \Sigma(X - \overline{X})(X - \overline{X})$$

The similarity between the SS formula and the SP formula should be

Similarity between SS & SP

obvious—the SS formula uses squares and the SP formula uses products. This same relationship exists for the computational formulas. For SS, the computational formula is

$$SS = \Sigma X^2 - \frac{(\Sigma X)^2}{n}$$

As before, each squared value can be rewritten so that the formula becomes

$$SS = \Sigma XX - \frac{\Sigma X \Sigma X}{n}$$

Again, you should note the similarity in structure between the SS formula and the SP formula. If you remember that SS uses squares and SP uses products, the two new formulas for the sum of products should be easy to learn. The following example demonstrates the calculation of SP with both of the formulas.

EXAMPLE 16.1

The same set of $n = 4$ pairs of scores will be used to calculate SP first using the definitional formula and then the computational formula.

For the definitional formula, you need deviation scores for each of the X values and each of the Y values. Note that the mean for the Xs is $\overline{X} = 3$ and that the mean for the Ys is $\overline{Y} = 5$. The deviations and the products of deviations are shown in the following table:

Scores		Deviations		Products
X	Y	$X - \overline{X}$	$Y - \overline{Y}$	$(X - \overline{X})(Y - \overline{Y})$
1	3	−2	−2	+4
2	6	−1	+1	−1
4	4	+1	−1	−1
5	7	+2	+2	+4
				+6 = SP

For these scores, the sum of the products of the deviations is $SP = +6$.

For the computational formula, you need the sum of the X values, the sum of the Y values, and the XY product for each pair. These values are as follows:

X	Y	XY	
1	3	3	
2	6	12	
4	4	16	
5	7	35	
12	20	66	Totals

Substituting the sums in the formula gives

$$SP = \Sigma XY - \frac{\Sigma X \Sigma Y}{n}$$

$$= 66 - \frac{12(20)}{4}$$

$$= 66 - 60$$

$$= 6$$

Note that both formulas produce the same result, $SP = 6$.

Calculation of the Pearson Correlation

By using the sum of products to measure the covariability between X and Y (see Box 16.1), the formula for the Pearson correlation becomes

$$(16.3) \quad r = \frac{SP}{\sqrt{SS_x SS_y}}$$

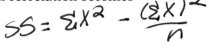
$$SS = \Sigma X^2 - \frac{(\Sigma X)^2}{n}$$

Notice that the variability for X is measured by the SS for the X-scores and the variability for Y is measured by SS for the Y-scores. The following example demonstrates the use of this formula with a simple set of scores.

EXAMPLE 16.2
The Pearson correlation is computed for the following set of $n = 5$ pairs of scores:

X	Y
0	1
10	3
4	1
8	2
8	3

Before starting any calculations, it is useful to put the data in a scatterplot and make a preliminary estimate of the correlation. These data have been graphed in Figure 16.7. Looking at the scatterplot, it appears that there is a very good (but not perfect) positive correlation. You should expect an approximate value of $r = +0.8$ or $+0.9$. To find the Pearson correlation, we will need SP, SS for X, and SS for Y. Each of these values is calculated using the definitional formula.

For the sum of products,

Scores		Deviations		Products
X	Y	$X - \bar{X}$	$Y - \bar{Y}$	$(X - \bar{X})(Y - \bar{Y})$
0	1	−6	−1	+6
10	3	+4	+1	+4
4	1	−2	−1	+2
8	2	+2	0	0
8	3	+2	+1	+2
				$+14 = SP$

Figure 16.7

Scatterplot of the data from Example 16.2.

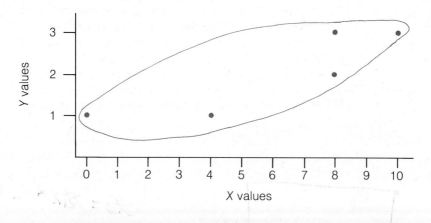

For the X values,

X	$X - \overline{X}$	$(X - \overline{X})^2$
0	−6	36
10	+4	16
4	−2	4
8	+2	4
8	+2	4
		64 = SS for X

For the Y values,

Y	$Y - \overline{Y}$	$(Y - \overline{Y})^2$
1	−1	1
3	+1	1
1	−1	1
2	0	0
3	+1	1
		4 = SS for Y

By using these values, the Pearson correlation is

$$r = \frac{SP}{\sqrt{SS_x SS_y}}$$

$$= \frac{14}{\sqrt{64(4)}}$$

$$= \frac{14}{16} = +0.875$$

Note that the value we obtained is in agreement with the prediction based on the scatterplot.

BOX 16.1 | The Role of *SP* in the Pearson Correlation

It should be obvious that the value of *SP* plays an important role in determining the sign (+ or −) and the magnitude of the Pearson correlation. The relation between *SP* and the actual *X*- and *Y*-scores is presented in Figure 16.8. In this figure we have drawn a vertical line at the mean of the *X* values. Scores to the right of this line have positive deviations (above the mean), and scores to the left have negative deviations. Similarly, the horizontal line separates the *Y* values into scores with a positive deviation (above the mean and above the line) and scores with a negative deviation (below the line). These two lines partition the scatterplot into four sections or quadrants. We will consider each quadrant separately, working clockwise through the four quadrants.

In the first quadrant (upper right), the *X* deviations and the *Y* deviations are both positive. Therefore, the products of deviations will be positive for individuals located in this quadrant.

Figure 16.8

The distribution of *X* and *Y* deviations and the products of deviations for each portion of the scatterplot.

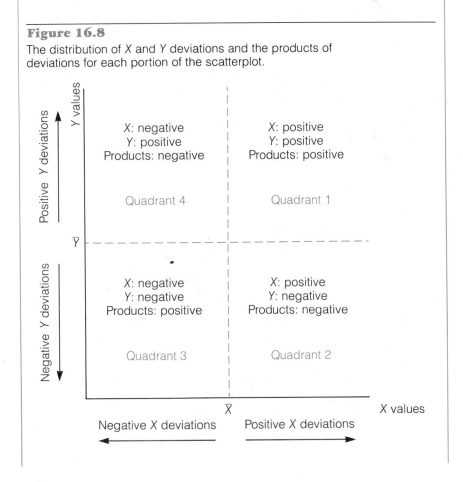

BOX 16.1 *continued*

In quadrant 2, the X deviations are positive, but the Y deviations are negative. Here the products of deviations will be negative.

In quadrant 3, X deviations are negative, and Y deviations are negative. Because both have the same sign, the products will be positive.

In quadrant 4, X deviations are negative, and Y deviations are positive. The products will be negative.

Now we will consider the location of the scores for three specific situations:

1. *A Strong Positive Correlation.* In this case, most of the scores will be located in the first and third quadrants (see Figure 16.8). The products of deviations are positive in both quadrants, so the sum of the products (SP) should be large and positive. This will produce a large, positive value for the correlation.

2. *A Strong Negative Correlation.* For a correlation near -1.00, the points tend to cluster around a line that slopes from the upper left down to the lower right. In this case, most of the scores will be located in the fourth and second quadrants (see Figure 16.8). In both of these quadrants the products of deviations are negative. When they are added, the sum should be a large, negative value for SP. This will produce a large, negative value for the correlation.

3. *A Correlation Near Zero.* With a correlation near zero, there is no linear trend, and the scores will be scattered through all four quadrants. This means that some of the products of deviations will be positive and some will be negative. When these products are summed (SP), the result will be a value near zero. When SP is near zero, the correlation will be near zero.

The Pearson Correlation and z-Scores

You should recall from Chapter 5 that the primary purpose of a z-score is to identify the exact location of an individual score within a distribution. You also should realize that the Pearson correlation measures the relationship between an individual's location in the X distribution and his/her location in the Y distribution. For example, a positive correlation means that individuals who score high on X also will tend to score high on Y. Similarly, a negative correlation indicates that individuals with high X-scores will tend to have low Y-

scores. Thus, correlations and z-scores are both concerned with locations within a distribution.

In the formula for the Pearson correlation, each individual's location in the X distribution and in the Y distribution is designated by his/her deviation scores, $X - \overline{X}$ and $Y - \overline{Y}$. The product of these two deviation scores depends on the relation between the two locations (see Box 16.1). If the X- and Y-scores in the data are transformed into z-scores, the Pearson correlation can be calculated by the following formula:

$$(16.4) \quad r = \frac{\Sigma z_x z_y}{n}$$

In this formula, z_x identifies each individual's position within the X distribution, and z_y identifies the position within the Y distribution. The product of the z-scores (like the product of the deviation scores) depends on the relationship between X and Y. For example, with a positive relation between X and Y, individuals will tend to have the same relative position in both the X and the Y distributions. In this case, the two z-scores for the individual will be similar (both positive or both negative), so the product of the z-scores will be positive, and the Pearson correlation will be positive. On the other hand, a negative relation means that an individual with a relatively high X-score (positive z_x) will tend to have a low Y-score (negative z_y). In this case, the z-score product will be negative, and the resulting correlation will be negative. Thus, whenever there is a consistent, predictable relation between the X positions and the Y positions, there will be a correlation between X and Y.

Because z-scores are considered to be the best way to describe a location within a distribution, Formula (16.4) often is considered to be the best way to define the Pearson correlation. However, you should realize that this formula requires a lot of tedious calculations (changing each score to a z-score), so it rarely is used to calculate a correlation.

LEARNING
CHECK

1. Calculate the sum of products of deviations (SP) for the following set of scores. Use the definitional formula and then the computational formula. Verify that you get the same answer with both formulas.

X	Y
1	0
3	1
7	6
5	2
4	1

2. Compute the Pearson correlation for the following data:

X	10
2	9
1	10
3	6
0	8
4	2

3. A recent study reports that the correlation between grade point average and the number of hours spent studying is $r = -0.58$. According to this study, who gets the best grades, students who study more or students who study less?

ANSWERS

1. $SP = 19$.
2. $r = -\frac{16}{20} = -0.80$
3. The negative correlation indicates that higher grades go with less studying.

16.4
Understanding and Interpreting Correlations

Whenever you encounter correlations, there are three additional considerations that you should bear in mind:

1. Correlation simply describes a relationship between two variables. It does not explain why the two variables are related. Specifically, a correlation should not and cannot be interpreted as proof of a cause/effect relation between the two variables.

2. The value of a correlation can be affected greatly by the range of scores represented in the data.

3. When judging "how good" a relationship is, it is tempting to focus on the numerical value of the correlation. For example, a correlation of $+0.5$ is halfway between 0 and 1.00 and therefore appears to represent a moderate degree of relation. However, a correlation should not be interpreted as a proportion. Although a correlation of 1.00 does mean that there is a 100% perfectly predictable relation between X and Y, a correlation of 0.5 does not mean that you can make predictions with 50% accuracy. To describe how accurately one variable predicts the other, you must square the correlation. Thus, a correlation of $r = 0.5$ provides only $r^2 = 0.5^2 = 0.25$ or 25% accuracy.

Each of these three points will now be discussed in detail.

Correlation and Causation

One of the most common errors in interpreting correlations is to assume that a correlation necessarily implies a cause-and-effect relation between the two variables. We constantly are bombarded with reports of relationships: Cigarette smoking is related to heart disease; alcohol consumption is related to birth defects; carrot consumption is related to good eyesight. Do these relationships mean that cigarettes cause heart disease or carrots cause good eyesight? The answer is *no*. Although there may be a causal relation, the simple existence of a correlation does not prove it. This point should become clear in the following hypothetical example.

EXAMPLE 16.3

Suppose we select a variety of different cities and towns throughout the United States and measure the number of serious crimes (X variable) and the number of churches (Y variable) for each. A scatterplot showing hypothetical data for this study is presented in Figure 16.9. Notice that this scatterplot shows a strong, positive correlation between churches and crime. You also should note that these are realistic data. It is reasonable that the smaller towns would have less crime and fewer churches and that the large cities would have large values for both variables. Does this relation mean that churches cause crime? Does it mean that crime causes churches? It should be clear that the answer is no. Although a good correlation exists between churches and crime, the real cause of the relationship is the size of the population.

Correlation and Restricted Range

Whenever a correlation is computed from scores that do not represent the full range of possible values, you should be cautious in interpreting the correlation. Suppose, for example, you are interested in the relationship between IQ and creativity. If you select a sample of your fellow college students, your data probably would represent only a limited range of IQ scores (most likely from 110 to 130). The correlation within this restricted range could be completely different from the correlation that would be obtained from a full range of IQ scores. Two extreme examples are shown in Figure 16.10.

Figure 16.10(a) shows an example where there is a strong positive relation between X and Y when the entire range of scores is considered. However, this relation is obscured when the data are limited to a restricted range. In Figure 16.10(b) there is no consistent relation between X and Y for the full range of scores. However, when the range of X values is restricted, the data show a strong positive relation.

Figure 16.9

Hypothetical data showing the logical relation between the number of churches and the number of serious crimes for a sample of U.S. cities.

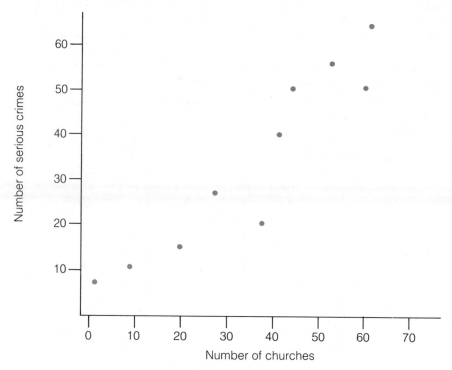

To be safe, you should not generalize any correlation beyond the range of data represented in the sample. For a correlation to provide an accurate description for the general population, there should be a wide range of X and Y values in the data.

Correlation and the Strength of the Relation

A correlation measures the degree of relation between two variables on a scale from 0 to 1.00. Although this number provides a measure of the degree of relationship, many researchers prefer to square the correlation and use the resulting value to measure the strength of the relationship. The reasons for squaring the correlation are discussed in Chapter 17, but a brief explanation is presented here.

One of the common uses of correlation is for prediction. If two variables are correlated, you can use the value of one variable to predict the other. For example, college admissions officers do not just guess which applicants are likely to do well; they use other variables (SAT scores, high school grades, etc.) to predict which students are most likely to be successful. These predictions are based on correlations. By using correlations, the admissions officers expect to make more accurate predictions than would be obtained by just guessing. In general, the squared correlation (r^2) measures the gain in accuracy that is obtained from using the correlation for prediction instead of just guessing.

Figure 16.10

(a) An example where the full range of X and Y values show a strong, positive correlation but the restricted range of scores produces a correlation near zero. (b) An example where the full range of X and Y values show a correlation near zero but the scores in the restricted range produce a strong, positive correlation.

(a)

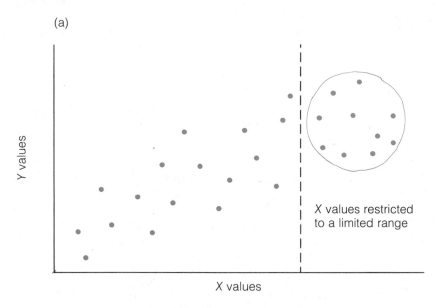

X values restricted to a limited range

X values

(b)

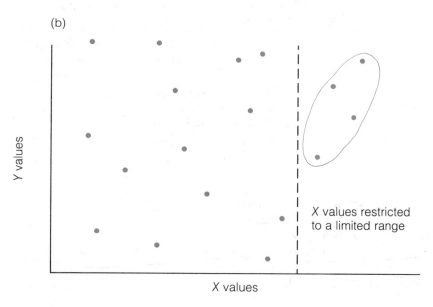

X values restricted to a limited range

X values

The value r^2 is called the _coefficient of determination_ because it measures the proportion of variability in one variable that is determined by the relationship with the other variable. A correlation of r = 0.80 (or −0.80), for example, means that r^2 = 0.64 (or 64%) of the variability in X is determined by Y.

Although the coefficient of determination will be defined and described in more detail in Chapter 17, a simple example should help make this concept more concrete. Suppose, for example, you are given the task of predicting the annual income for Mr. X. To help you with your task, we will provide three bits of information:

1. Mr. X wears a size 9 shoe.
2. Mr. X has been working in his profession for 2 months.
3. Mr. X has a monthly income of $1000.

It should be clear that the first bit of information (shoe size) is no help whatsoever. Because there is no correlation between shoe size and annual income, knowing shoe size will not improve your estimate of income. In this case, annual income is _not determined_ by shoe size, so the coefficient of determination is zero. However, the second bit of information (length of employment) does provide some useful information. You should recognize that annual income is _partially determined_ by seniority. Because Mr. X has been employed only 2 months, he probably is in an entry-level job and earning a relatively low salary. This information should improve the accuracy of your prediction. The amount of accuracy you gain depends on the strength of the correlation between salary and seniority. A correlation of 0.40, for example, would mean that r^2 = 0.16 or 16% of the variability in salary is determined by seniority. Finally, the third bit of information (monthly income) is extremely useful. Because there is a perfect correlation (r = +1.00) between monthly income and annual income, you now are able to predict annual income with perfect accuracy. In this case, annual income is _completely determined_ by monthly income, so the coefficient of determination is 1.00 (100%).

16.5
The Spearman Correlation

Often the relationship between two variables will show a good, consistent trend but not a linear trend. One example is the relation between amount of practice and level of performance (see Figure 16.11). In this example, there is a good positive relation between the two variables; more practice leads to better performance. Sometimes, however, performance reaches a plateau and does not change much with additional practice. At other times, a small amount of practice seems to result in a dramatic increase in performance. Although the relation shows consistency of direction, it is not a linear relation. Calculation of the Pearson correlation for such data would show only a moderate relationship (r about $+0.5$) when in fact there is a nearly perfect positive trend. The Spearman rank-order correlation is designed to measure the consistency of direction of a relation, independent of its specific form.

DEFINITION

The *Spearman correlation* measures the degree to which the relationship between two variables is generally one-directional or monotonic. The possible values for this measure of correlation range from 0 (no consistent direction) to 1.00 (a perfectly monotonic relation). In addition, Spearman measures the direction of trend as either positive or negative.

The term mono-tonic describes a sequence that is consistently increasing or decreasing. Like the word monot-onous, it means constant and unchanging.

Figure 16.11

Hypothetical data showing the relationship between practice and performance. Although this relation is not linear, there is a consistent positive relationship: An increase in performance tends to accompany an increase in practice.

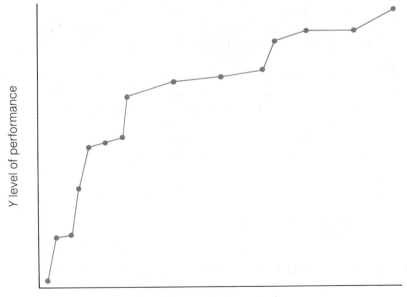

Calculation of the Spearman Correlation

The calculation of the Spearman correlation is based on a simple observation: If two variables are monotonically related, their ranks will be linearly related. For example, a perfect positive monotonic relationship means that every time X increases, Y also increases. This means that the smallest value of X is paired with the smallest value of Y, that the second smallest value of X is paired with the second smallest value of Y, and that this pairing continues for the third values, fourth values, fifth values, etc. Drawing a scatterplot of these ranks would produce a perfect straight line. This phenomenon is demonstrated in Figure 16.12.

The observation that a monotonic relation for scores produces a linear relation for ranks is valuable because we already know how to measure the linear relationship between two variables: The Pearson correlation measures the degree of linear relation. To measure the monotonic relation for a set of scores, we first will rank the scores and then measure the linear relation for the set of ranks. This results in a two-step procedure for calculating the Spearman correlation:

1. First, convert the X- and Y-scores into ranks. The smallest score is called 1, the next smallest is 2, etc. Note that the X- and Y-scores are ranked separately.
2. Compute the Pearson correlation using the ranks.

The resulting value is the Spearman rank-order correlation. By measuring the degree of linear relation for the ranks, we also have measured the degree of monotonic relation for the scores. The Spearman correlation is identified by the symbol r_s to differentiate it from the Pearson correlation. The complete process for computing the Spearman correlation is demonstrated in Example 16.4.

EXAMPLE 16.4

The following data show the results of an experiment examining human memory. Each of the $n = 8$ subjects memorized a grocery list of 40 items. The X value in the original data is the amount of time (in hours) between learning the list and the memory test. The Y value is the number of items correctly recalled. The researcher wants to use these data to demonstrate a general decline in memory as a function of time.

| Original Data | | Ranks | | |
X (Time)	Y (Memory)	X	Y	XY
1	39	1	8	8
6	25	2	6	12
12	26	3	7	21
18	20	4	3	12
24	23	5	5	25
30	21	6	4	24
36	18	7	1	7
42	19	8	2	16
				$125 = \Sigma XY$

Figure 16.12

A set of $n = 4$ scores (X and Y values) and the scatterplot for the scores are shown in the top half of this figure. Notice that there is a consistent positive relation between X and Y although this is not a linear relation. In the bottom half of the figure the scores have been ranked. Notice that the scatterplot of the ranks shows a perfect, linear relationship.

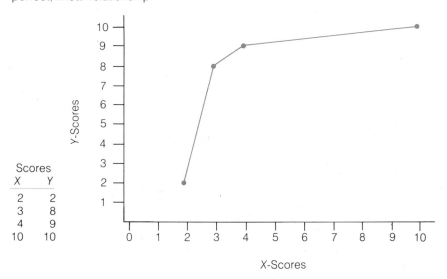

Scores	
X	Y
2	2
3	8
4	9
10	10

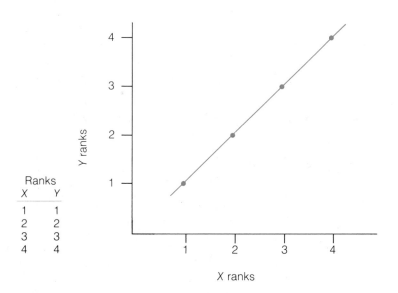

Ranks	
X	Y
1	1
2	2
3	3
4	4

Because the researcher is interested only in the directional trend in the data, we will use a Spearman correlation.

The scatterplots for the original data and the ranks are shown in Figure 16.13. To calculate the Spearman correla-

Figure 16.13

(a) Scatterplot of the original data from a memory experiment.
(b) Scatterplot of the memory experiment data after the original
scores have been converted to ranks.

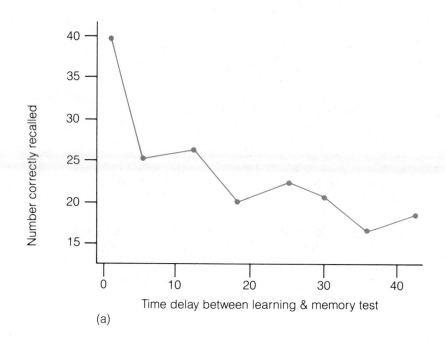

(a)

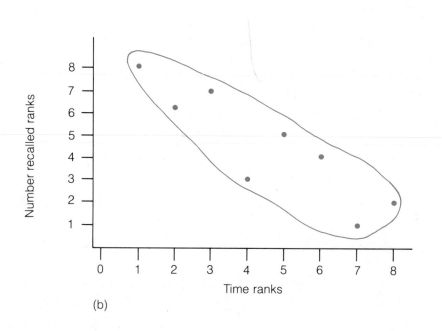

(b)

tion for these data, we simply calculate the Pearson correlation *using the ranks*. This computation will require SS for X, SS for Y, and SP.

The X ranks are simply the integers $1, 2, 3, \ldots, 8$. These values have $\Sigma X = 36$ and $\Sigma X^2 = 204$. The SS for the X ranks is

$$SS_x = X^2 - \frac{(\Sigma X)^2}{n}$$

$$= 204 - \frac{36^2}{8}$$

$$= 204 - 162$$

$$= 42$$

You should note that the ranks for Y are identical to the ranks for X; that is, they are the integers $1, 2, 3, \ldots, 8$. Therefore, SS for Y will be identical to SS for X:

$$SS_y = 42$$

To compute the SP value, we need the ΣX, ΣY, and ΣXY values for the ranks. The XY values are listed in the preceding table, and we already have found that both the Xs and the Ys have a sum of 36. Using these values, we obtain

$$SP = \Sigma XY - \frac{\Sigma X \Sigma Y}{n} = 125 - \frac{36(36)}{8}$$

$$= 125 - 162$$

$$= -37$$

The final Spearman correlation is

$$r_s = \frac{SP}{\sqrt{SS_x SS_y}}$$

$$= \frac{-37}{\sqrt{42(42)}}$$

$$= \frac{-37}{42} = -0.88$$

Remember, for a Spearman correlation SP, SS_x, and SS_y all are computed with the ranks, not the original scores.

These data show a strong, negative trend: As more time passes, memory grows worse.

When the Spearman Correlation Is Used

By far the most commonly used measure of relationship is the Pearson correlation. However, there are two situations where the Spearman is preferred:

1. Spearman is used when the researcher's primary interest is in the consistency of direction for a relation.

Specifically, when a researcher is not concerned with whether or not a relation is linear, the Spearman correlation is a better measure.

2. Because the Spearman correlation measures relationship between ranks, it is used whenever the original data are measured on an ordinal scale, that is, when the original data are ranks. You should recall that rank-order data are fairly common because they are often easier to obtain than interval or ratio data. For example, a teacher may feel confident about rank-ordering students' leadership abilities but would find it difficult to measure leadership on some other scale.

data measured ordinally

Ranking Tied Scores

When two (or more) scores have exactly the same value, their ranks should also be the same. This is accomplished by the following procedure:

1. List the scores in order from smallest to largest. Include tied values in this list.
2. Assign a rank (first, second, etc.) to each position in the ordered list.
3. When two (or more) scores are tied, compute the average of their ranked positions and assign this average value as the final rank for each score.

EXAMPLE 16.5
The process of finding ranks for tied scores is demonstrated here. Note that these scores have been listed in order from smallest to largest.

Scores	Rank Position	Final Rank	
3	1	1.5	} average of 1 and 2
3	2	1.5	
5	3	3	
6	4	5	
6	5	5	} average of 4, 5, and 6
6	6	5	
12	7	7	

Special Formula for the Spearman Correlation

After the original X values and Y values have been ranked, the calculations necessary for SS and SP can be greatly simplified. First, you should note that the X ranks and the Y ranks are really just a set of integers $1, 2, 3, 4, \ldots, n$. To compute the mean for these integers, you can locate the midpoint of the series by $\overline{X} = (n + 1)/2$. Similarly, the SS for this series of integers can be computed by

$$SS = \frac{n(n^2 - 1)}{12} \quad \text{(try it out)}$$

Also, because the X ranks and the Y ranks are the same values, SS for X will be identical to SS for Y.

Because calculations with ranks can be simplified and because the Spearman correlation uses ranked data, these simplifications can be incorporated into the final calculations for the Spearman correlation. Instead of using the Pearson formula after ranking the data, you can put the ranks directly into a simplified formula:

$$\textbf{(16.5)} \quad r_s = 1 - \frac{6\,\Sigma D^2}{n(n^2 - 1)}$$

where D is the difference between the X rank and the Y rank for each individual. This special formula will produce the same result that would be obtained from the Pearson formula. However, you should note that this special formula can be used only after the scores have been converted to ranks and only when there are no ties among the ranks. If there are relatively few tied ranks, the formula still may be used, but it loses accuracy as the number of ties increases. The application of this formula is demonstrated in Example 16.6.

Caution: *In this formula, you compute the value of the fraction and then subtract from 1. The "1" is not part of the fraction.*

EXAMPLE 16.6

To demonstrate the special formula for the Spearman correlation, we will use the same data that were presented in Example 16.4. The ranks for these data are shown again here:

Ranks		Difference	
X	Y	D	D^2
1	8	7	49
2	6	4	16
3	7	4	16
4	3	1	1
5	5	0	0
6	4	2	4
7	1	6	36
8	2	6	36
			158 $= \Sigma D^2$

Using the special formula for the Spearman correlation, we obtain

$$r_s = 1 - \frac{6\,\Sigma D^2}{n(n^2 - 1)}$$

$$= 1 - \frac{6(158)}{8(63)}$$

$$= 1 - 1.88$$

$$= -0.88$$

Relation Between the Spearman and Pearson Correlations

If you compute the Pearson correlation and the Spearman correlation for the same set of data, how will the two correlations be related? First, you should note that these two correlations are measuring different things and generally will produce different values. Pearson is measuring linear relationship, and Spearman is measuring monotonic relationship. In most cases, the value you obtain for Spearman will be larger (closer to 1.00 or −1.00) than the value you obtain for Pearson. This occurs because the Spearman correlation is less demanding than the Pearson correlation. In simple terms, it is easier to be perfect by Spearman's criteria than by Pearson's criteria. Spearman only measures monotonic relation, while Pearson measures linear relation (which includes monotonic as a prerequisite).

However, there is one situation where the Pearson correlation will produce a larger value than Spearman. When there is an extreme point in the data, this single point can have a large influence on the value of the Pearson correlation. The single extreme data point tends to exaggerate the magnitude of the correlation, bringing it much closer to 1.00 (or −1.00) than would be expected from the other data points. The exaggerated influence of an extreme point is eliminated with the Spearman correlation because the ranking process reduces the distance between adjacent scores to exactly one (first to second, second to third, etc.). Because these distances are all equal, it is impossible for one point to be extremely different from the rest. This phenomenon is demonstrated in the following example.

EXAMPLE 16.7
Figure 16.14 shows the scatterplot for a set of $n = 5$ data points. Notice that the single extreme point produces what appears to be a good, positive linear relation.

The Pearson correlation for these data is computed as follows:

Scores		Deviations		Squared Deviations		Products of Deviations
X	Y	$X - \bar{X}$	$Y - \bar{Y}$	$(X - \bar{X})^2$	$(Y - \bar{Y})^2$	$(X - \bar{X})(Y - \bar{Y})$
0	2	−4	−2	16	4	+8
1	0	−3	−4	9	16	+12
2	3	−2	−1	4	1	+2
3	1	−1	−3	1	9	+3
14	14	+10	+10	100	100	+100
				$SS_x = 130$	$SS_y = 130$	$SP = 125$

Figure 16.14

Scatterplot of the data from Example 16.7. Notice that the single extreme data point produces a strong, positive correlation. Without this extreme point, the correlation between X and Y would be zero.

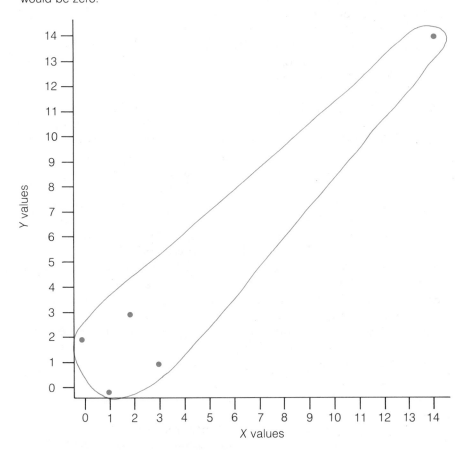

For these data, the Pearson correlation is

$$r = \frac{SP}{\sqrt{SS_x SS_y}} = \frac{125}{\sqrt{130(130)}}$$

$$= \frac{125}{130}$$

$$= +0.96$$

However, if the one extreme point is removed, the Pearson correlation becomes zero. You should check this fact for yourself. Notice that the single extreme data point transforms a zero correlation into a nearly perfect linear relation.

Now we will compute the Spearman correlation for the original set of $n = 5$ pairs of scores. You should notice that the influence of the extreme point is greatly reduced when the Spearman correlation is computed for these same data.

Scores		Ranks			
X	Y	X	Y	D	D^2
0	2	1	3	2	4
1	0	2	1	1	1
2	3	3	4	1	1
3	1	4	2	2	4
14	14	5	5	0	0
					10 $= \Sigma D^2$

Using the special Spearman formula, we obtain

$$r_s = 1 - \frac{6\,\Sigma D^2}{n(n^2 - 1)}$$

$$= 1 - \frac{6(10)}{5(24)}$$

$$= \tfrac{1}{2} = 0.50$$

For this set of data, the Pearson correlation is $r = +0.96$, and the Spearman correlation is only $r_s = 0.50$. The single extreme data point has inflated the value of the Pearson correlation.

LEARNING
CHECK

1. Rank the following scores, using tied ranks where necessary: 14, 3, 4, 0, 3, 5, 14, 3.
2. Calculate the Pearson correlation and the Spearman correlation for the following set of scores. Explain the difference between the two values you obtain.

X	Y
1	1
2	8
9	9

ANSWERS

1. Scores: 0 3 3 3 4 5 14 14
   Ranks: 1 3 3 3 5 6 7.5 7.5
2. $SS_x = 38$, $SS_y = 38$, $SP = 26$, Pearson $r = \frac{26}{38} = 0.68$, Spearman $r_s = 1.00$.

Summary

1. A correlation measures the relationship between two variables X and Y. The relationship is described by three characteristics:
    a. *Direction.* A relation can be either positive or negative. A positive relation means that X and Y vary in the same direction. A negative relation means that X and Y vary in opposite directions. The sign of the correlation ($+$ or $-$) specifies the direction.
    b. *Form.* The most common form for a relation is a straight line. However, special correlations exist for measuring other forms. The form is specified by the type of correlation used. For example, the Pearson correlation measures linear form.
    c. *Degree.* The magnitude of the correlation measures the degree to which the data points fit the specified form. A correlation of 1.00 indicates a perfect fit, and a correlation of 0 indicates no degree of fit.

2. The most commonly used correlation is the Pearson correlation, which measures the degree of linear relationship. The Pearson correlation is identified by the letter r and is computed by

    $$r = \frac{SP}{\sqrt{SS_x SS_y}}$$

    In this formula, SP is the sum of products of deviations and can be calculated either with a definitional formula or a computational formula:

    $$\text{Definitional formula:} \quad SP = \Sigma(X - \bar{X})(Y - \bar{Y})$$

    $$\text{Computational formula:} \quad SP = \Sigma XY - \frac{\Sigma X \Sigma Y}{n}$$

3. The Pearson correlation and z-scores are closely related because both are concerned with the location of individuals within a distribution. When X- and Y-scores are transformed into z-scores, the Pearson correlation can be computed by

    $$r = \frac{\Sigma z_x z_y}{n}$$

4. A correlation between two variables should not be interpreted as implying a causal relation. Simply because X and Y are related does not mean that X causes Y or that Y causes X.

5. When the X or Y values used to compute a correlation are limited to a relatively small portion of the potential range, you should exercise caution in generalizing the value of the correlation. Specifically, a limited range of values can either obscure a strong relation or exaggerate a poor relation.

6. To evaluate the strength of a relation, you should square the value of the correlation. The resulting value, r^2, is called the

coefficient of determination because it measures the portion of the variability in one variable that can be predicted using the relationship with the second variable.

7. The Spearman correlation (r_s) measures the consistency of direction in the relation between X and Y, that is, the degree to which the relation is one-directional or monotonic. The Spearman correlation is computed by a two-stage process:
   a. Rank the X-scores and the Y-scores.
   b. Compute the Pearson correlation using the ranks.

   Note: After the X and Y values are ranked, you may use a special formula to determine the Spearman correlation:

   $$r_s = 1 - \frac{6\Sigma D^2}{n(n^2 - 1)}$$

   where D is the difference between the X rank and the Y rank for each individual. This formula is accurate only when there are no tied scores in the data.

Key Terms

correlation   sum of products (SP)
positive correlation   restricted range
negative correlation   coefficient of determination
perfect correlation   Spearman correlation
Pearson correlation   monotonic relationship
linear relationship

Problems for Chapter 16:
Correlation

*1. For each of the following sets of scores, calculate SP using the definitional formula and then using the computational formula:

Set 1		Set 2		Set 3	
X	Y	X	Y	X	Y
1	3	0	7	1	5
2	6	4	3	2	0
4	4	0	5	3	1
5	7	4	1	2	6

*2. For the following set of data,

Data

X	Y
8	2
9	2
2	4
1	5
5	2

a. Sketch a graph showing the location of the five (X, Y) points.

b. Just looking at your graph, estimate the value of the Pearson correlation.

c. Compute the Pearson correlation for this data set.

3. For this problem we have used the same X and Y values that appeared in Problem 2, but we have changed the X, Y pairings:

Data

X	Y
8	4
9	5
2	2
1	2
5	2

a. Sketch a graph showing these reorganized data.

b. Estimate the Pearson correlation by just looking at your graph.

c. Compute the Pearson correlation. (*Note:* Much of the calculation for this problem was done already in Problem 2.)

If you compare the results of Problem 2 and Problem 3, you will see that the correlation measures the relation between X and Y. These two problems use the same X and Y values, but they differ in the way X and Y are related.

4. A psychology instructor asked each student to report the number of hours he/she had spent preparing for the final exam. In addition, the instructor recorded the number of incorrect answers on each student's exam. These data are as follows:

Hours	Number Wrong
4	8
0	6
1	3
2	2
4	5

What is the relation between study hours and number wrong?

*5. With a very small sample, a single point can have a large influence on the magnitude of a correlation. For the following data set,

X	Y
0	1
10	3
4	1
8	2
8	3

a. Sketch a graph showing the X, Y points.

b. Estimate the value of the Pearson correlation.

c. Compute the Pearson correlation.

d. Now we will change the value of one of the points. For the first individual in the sample ($X = 0$ and $Y = 1$), change the Y value to $Y = 6$. What happens to the graph of the X, Y points? What happens to the Pearson correlation? Compute the new correlation.

6. In the following data there are three scores (X, Y, and Z) for each of the $n = 5$ individuals:

X	Y	Z
3	5	5
4	3	2
2	4	6
1	1	3
0	2	4

a. Sketch a graph showing the relation between X and Y. Compute the Pearson correlation between X and Y.

b. Sketch a graph showing the relation between Y and Z. Compute the Pearson correlation between Y and Z.

c. Given the results of parts a and b, what would you predict for the correlation between X and Z?

d. Sketch a graph showing the relation between X and Z. Compute the Pearson correlation for these data.

e. What general conclusion can you make concerning relations among correlations? If X is related to Y and Y is related to Z, does this necessarily mean that X is related to Z?

*7. A professor in the Art Department would like to demonstrate that art classes make a real contribution to artistic ability. A random sample of $n = 6$ seniors is selected from a drawing class. The professor obtains a sample drawing from each student and the drawings are ranked (best to worst). In addition, the professor records the number of art courses that each student has completed. These data are as follows:

Rank of Student's Drawing	Number of Art Courses
3	2
4	1
6	0
1	7
5	1
2	4

Compute the correlation between drawing ability and education. (*Note:* First you must determine which correlation to use for these data.)

8. Rank the following scores and compute the Spearman correlation between X and Y:

X	Y
7	19
2	4
11	34
15	28
32	104

*9. If you obtain a random sample of $n = 2$ people and measure each person's annual salary and shoe size, what would you expect to obtain for the Pearson correlation? (Be careful. Try making up some data points to see what happens.) How would you interpret a correlation of $r = +1.00$ obtained for a sample of $n = 2$? Should you generalize this sample correlation and conclude that a strong relationship between X and Y exists in the population?

10. For the following set of data,

X	Y
1	2
2	4
3	1
4	3
5	3
6	9
7	10
8	7
9	8
10	9

a. Sketch a graph showing the X, Y points.

b. Compute the Pearson correlation for the full set of data.

c. Compute the Pearson correlation using only the first five individuals in the sample (the five smallest X values).

d. Compute the Pearson correlation for the final five individuals in the sample (the five largest X values).

e. Explain why the results from parts c and d are so different from the overall correlation obtained in part b.

*11. a. Compute the Pearson correlation for the following set of data:

X	Y
2	8
3	10
3	7
5	6
6	7
8	4
9	2
10	3

b. Add five points to each X value and compute the Pearson correlation again.

c. When you add a constant to each score, what happens to SS for X and Y? What happen to SP? What happens to the correlation between X and Y?

d. Now multiply each X in the original data by 3 and calculate the Pearson correlation once again.

e. When you multiply by a constant, what happens to SS for X and Y? What happens to SP? What happens to the correlation between X and Y?

12. There are several tied scores in the following data:

X	Y
9	6
9	14
12	14
12	14
26	14
26	18

a. Compute the Spearman correlation by first ranking and then using the Pearson formula.

b. Compute the Spearman correlation using the special Spearman formula on the ranks.

c. Compare the results from the two different formulas. In general, how do tied scores affect the results with the special formula?

*13. A researcher has developed a simple test that is intended to measure general intelligence. To evaluate the validity of this test, the researcher administers it to a class of 24 seventh grade students. In addition, the teacher for this class is asked to rank-order the students in terms of intelligence with 1 being

the smartest child in the class. The teacher's ranking and the test score for each child are as follows:

Teacher's Ranking	Test Score	Teacher's Ranking	Test Score
1	41	13	37
2	47	14	40
3	36	15	31
4	42	16	30
5	41	17	36
6	39	18	32
7	40	19	34
8	36	20	30
9	32	21	28
10	39	22	31
11	35	23	34
12	33	24	29

a. Compute the Spearman correlation for these data. (*Note:* You must change the test scores to ranks before you begin.)

b. On the basis of this correlation, does it appear that the researcher's test is a good measure of intelligence?

14. The local electric corporation has kept records of the demand for electric power and the daily high temperature during the summer months. These data are as follows:

High Temperature	Power Consumption
87	845
92	1030
79	820
84	915
98	1135
89	1005
81	870
75	810
83	905
86	960
93	1010
97	1085

a. Calculate the Pearson correlation for these data.

b. The electric corporation plans to use this correlation as the basis for predicting power consumption. They hope to use each day's weather forecast to predict the amount of power that will be needed. Use these data to compute the coefficient of determination. Remember, this coefficient provides an indication of the level of accuracy for predictions based on a correlation.

*15. An educational psychologist wanted to demonstrate that scores on the Scholastic Aptitude Test (SAT) provide a reasonably accurate indication of how a student will perform in college. A random sample of $n = 20$ students was selected. Each student's SAT score and his/her grade point average after four semesters are as follows:

Student	SAT	GPA	Student	SAT	GPA
1	650	3.12	11	745	3.84
2	680	3.06	12	590	2.18
3	710	3.55	13	605	2.43
4	440	1.98	14	520	2.10
5	660	3.25	15	635	2.72
6	485	2.23	16	750	3.88
7	590	2.76	17	490	2.31
8	780	4.00	18	700	3.49
9	620	3.52	19	460	2.45
10	480	3.01	20	670	3.20

a. Calculate the Pearson correlation for these data.

b. Does it appear that there is a reasonable relation between the SAT and grade point average?

16. A common concern for students (and teachers) is the assignment of grades for essays or term papers. Because there are no absolute right or wrong answers, these grades must be based on a judgment of quality. To demonstrate that these judgments actually are reliable, an English instructor asked a colleague to rank-order a set of term papers. The ranks and the instructor's grades for these papers are as follows:

Rank	Grade
1	A
2	B
3	A
4	B
5	B
6	C
7	D
8	C
9	C
10	D
11	E

a. Calculate the Spearman correlation for these data. (*Note:* You must convert the letter grades to ranks (A = 1, B = 2, etc.).

b. Based on this correlation, does it appear that there is reasonable agreement between these two instructors in their judgment of the papers?

*17. a. Calculate the Pearson correlation for the following set of data:

X	Y
7	18
12	11
1	20
18	10
3	15
9	16

b. Find the mean and standard deviation for the X-scores and transform each score into a z-score. Transform each of the Ys into a z-score. Now use Formula (16.4) to compute the Pearson correlation.

*18. A curious statistician would like to know whether there is any relation between IQ and salary for government employees. The personnel files are obtained for a random sample of $n = 16$ people and the statistician records the IQ and salary for each person. Calculate the Pearson correlation for the following data:

Employee	IQ	Salary (in $1000)	Employee	IQ	Salary (in $1000)
1	104	22.5	9	96	13.7
2	126	31.3	10	108	20.1
3	148	45.6	11	112	25.5
4	105	14.8	12	89	19.5
5	122	27.5	13	136	30.0
6	97	32.1	14	110	22.1
7	135	35.5	15	123	26.9
8	128	43.3	16	101	18.7

19. In the following data, X and Y are related by the equation $Y = X^2$:

X	Y
0	0
1	1
2	4
3	9
4	16
5	25

a. Sketch a graph showing the relation between X and Y. Describe the relationship shown in your graph.

b. Compute the Pearson correlation for these data.

c. Compute the Spearman correlation for these data.

*20. In the preview section of this chapter we presented a graph showing that students who turn in exams early tend to get better grades (see Figure 16.1). The data for this figure are as follows:

Student	Time (in Minutes)	Grade	Student	Time (in Minutes)	Grade
1	25	90	32	51	82
2	28	76	33	54	96
3	30	98	34	54	92
4	30	84	35	54	74
5	31	88	36	55	78
6	31	84	37	55	58
7	32	96	38	56	74
8	32	82	39	57	70
9	32	64	40	58	82
10	33	90	41	59	78
11	33	82	42	59	74
12	34	98	43	59	70
13	34	96	44	59	82
14	35	90	45	60	50
15	36	84	46	61	88
16	37	92	47	62	92
17	38	90	48	62	84
18	38	96	49	62	82
19	39	100	50	64	78
20	39	82	51	64	76
21	39	100	52	64	52
22	41	82	53	64	48
23	42	100	54	65	90
24	42	64	55	67	48
25	42	96	56	68	70
26	44	98	57	68	96
27	45	78	58	69	82
28	47	76	59	70	62
29	48	78	60	70	78
30	49	92	61	70	64
31	50	78	62	70	76

Calculate the Pearson correlation for these data.

21. A physiological psychologist is interested in the relationship between brain weight and learning ability. It is expected that there should be a consistent relationship, but the psychologist has no prediction concerning the form (linear or nonlinear) of the relation. The data for a sample of $n = 10$ animals are as follows:

Brain Weight	Learning Score
1.04	1.5
2.75	1.8
4.14	1.9
7.81	1.6
8.11	2.1
8.35	4.5
8.50	4.2
8.73	6.2
8.81	10.3
8.97	14.7

a. Calculate the Pearson correlation for these data.
b. Calculate the Spearman correlation for these data.

CHAPTER 17

Regression

The following items are considered essential background material for this chapter. If you doubt your knowledge of any of these items, you should review the appropriate chapter or section before proceeding.

1. Pearson correlation (Chapter 16)
   a. Sum of products, *SP*
2. Measures of variability (Chapter 4)
   a. Sample variance
   b. Sample standard deviation
3. Analysis of variance (Chapter 13)
   a. *F* Ratios
   b. The *F* distribution

"As the twig is bent, so grows the tree." Most psychologists agree that early childhood experiences do have an impact on later development. However, this does not necessarily mean that the skills, habits, and personality that exist in a 2-year-old child will still be there when the child becomes an adult. What is the relationship between childhood characteristics and adult characteristics? Can you use observations of a child to predict his/her adult potential? One area that has received extensive attention is the development of intelligence.

It is fairly common for parents to have their child's IQ tested at an early age. Do these early measures of IQ have any relation to the child's future intelligence? Can you use an IQ score for a 4-year-old child to predict his/her IQ at age 18? One of the original studies addressing these questions was reported by Honzik et al. (1948). By regularly measuring IQ for a group of individuals over a 16-year period, they found a correlation of only 0.31 between IQ measured at age 2 and IQ measured at age 18. You should recognize that a correlation of 0.31 is far from perfect. It indicates some relationship, but is this relation strong enough to permit reliable prediction? If you know the IQ score for a 2-year-old child, how accurately can you predict his/her IQ at age 18?

In this chapter we will examine the statistical methods that use correlations to help make predictions. The general procedure is called regression, and it will specify exactly when and how predictions can be made as well as providing a measure of how accurate the predictions are.

17.1

Introduction

In Chapter 16 we noted that one of the primary uses of correlation is for prediction. Whenever two variables are consistently related, it is possible to use a known value on one variable to predict the corresponding value on the other. Regression is the technical procedure by which these predictions are made. Before we introduce the detailed mathematics of regression, we will present a general example of how this procedure works and introduce the basic concepts of regression.

Figure 17.1 presents hypothetical data showing the relationship between SAT scores and college grade point average (GPA). Note that there is a good (but not perfect) positive correlation between these two variables. These data would be collected from a large group of college students. The SAT score is recorded for each individual when he/she enters college, and the GPA is recorded after 2 full years of college coursework. These data, collected from past students, will serve to define the relationship and will form the basis of prediction for new students.

Now suppose a high school senior with an SAT score of 620 applies to the college. The admissions officer first locates a score of 620 on the X-axis in the figure. The data points directly above this value correspond to the GPAs of previous students who entered the college with the same SAT score. These data points provide a description of

Figure 17.1

Scatterplot showing the relation between college grade point average and SAT scores for a set of hypothetical data. In this sample, three students had a SAT score of $X = 620$. Notice that these three students have relatively high grade point averages.

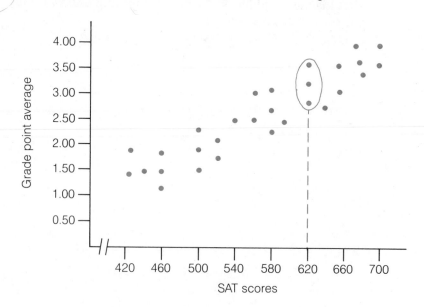

how well students with an SAT of 620 have done in the past, and they can be used to predict how well the new applicant will perform.

You should note that the prediction is not perfect. The data show that three students who entered with SAT scores of 620 earned GPAs of 3.62, 2.95, and 3.20. Although there is no single GPA that describes all of these students, it should be clear that they generally have performed above the collegewide average. The admissions officer could reasonably expect the new applicant to be similar to the previous students and therefore could predict that the applicant will be an above-average student with a relatively high GPA.

You also should note that the precision of the prediction depends on the value of the correlation. Figure 17.2 shows another set of data where the correlation between SAT and GPA is relatively poor. When an SAT score of 620 is located on this graph, the range of corresponding GPAs goes from 0.5 to 4.0. These data will not be a great help to the admissions officer in predicting performance for the new applicant.

Finally, you should note that the predictions we are making could be reversed; that is, we could use a student's GPA to predict his/her SAT score. Figure 17.1, for example, shows that students with a GPA of 2.00 entered college with relatively low SAT scores. The importance of this point is that prediction need not refer to future performance. Prediction is useful whenever it is difficult to obtain a direct measurement of performance. It does not matter whether you are pre-

Figure 17.2
Scatterplot showing the relation between college grade point average and SAT scores for a set of hypothetical data. For these data, there is a poor (near zero) relation between these two variables. Notice that three students in this sample had a SAT score of $X = 620$.

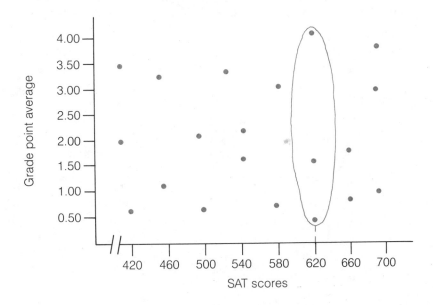

dicting future performance or past performance or simply predicting current performance on some variable for which you currently do not have a direct measurement.

17.2
Linear Relationships

The process of regression is based on the fact that the Pearson correlation measures the degree of linear relation between two variables. When two variables are linearly related, it is possible to describe the relation by a simple equation. For example, a local tennis club charges a fee of $5 per hour plus an annual membership fee of $25. Based on this information, you can compute the cost of playing tennis by using the following linear equation:

$$\text{total cost} = \$5 \times (\text{number of hours}) + \$25$$

This equation describes the relation between total cost and number of hours. In general, a linear relation between two variables X and Y can be expressed by the equation

$$(17.1) \quad Y = bX + a$$

where a and b are fixed constants. In this general equation, the value of b is called the *slope* of the line, and the value of a is called the *Y*-intercept. The value of b determines the slope or tilt of the line because it controls how much change there will be in Y whenever X changes by one point. For the tennis club example, $b = \$5$; your total cost goes up by $5 for each hour you play. The value of a is called the *Y-intercept* because it determines the *Y*-score when $X = 0$. (On a graph, the a value is where the line intercepts the *Y*-axis.) For the tennis club example, $a = \$25$; there is a $25 charge even if you never play tennis.

For any value of X, you can use this equation to compute the corresponding value of Y. If you planned on playing 20 hours of tennis, for example, your total cost would be

$$Y = bX + a$$
$$= \$5(20) + \$25$$
$$= \$100 + \$25$$
$$= \$125$$

Figure 17.3 shows the general relation between cost and number of hours. Notice that the relation results in a straight line. To obtain this graph, we picked any two values of X and then used the equation to compute the corresponding values for Y. For example, when $X = 10$,

$$Y = bX + a$$
$$= \$5(10) + \$25$$
$$= \$50 + \$25$$
$$= \$75$$

Figure 17.3

Relationship between total cost and number of hours playing tennis. The tennis club charges a $25 membership fee plus $5 per hour. The relation is described by a linear equation:

$$\text{total cost} = \$5(\text{number of hours}) + \$25$$
$$Y = bX + a$$

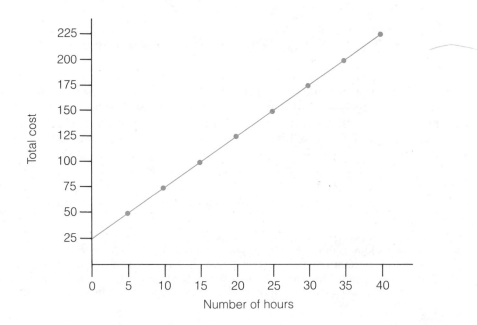

and when $X = 30$,

$$Y = bX + a$$
$$= \$5(30) + \$25$$
$$= \$150 + \$25$$
$$= \$175$$

When drawing a graph of a linear equation, it is wise to compute and plot at least three points to be certain you have not made a mistake.

Next, these two points are plotted on the graph: one point at $X = 10$ and $Y = 75$ and the other point at $X = 30$ and $Y = 175$. Because two points completely determine a straight line, we simply drew the line so that it passed through these two points.

Because there is a linear relation between cost and number of hours, the Pearson correlation between these two variables is $r = +1.00$.

With a perfect linear relation, you can make perfect predictions. For this example, the linear equation makes it possible for you to predict one variable (total cost) for any specific value of the other variable (number of hours).

In most real-life cases, the relation between two variables will not be perfectly linear. Nonetheless, it is possible to find the equation for the best fitting straight line and then use this equation to make predictions. Figure 17.4 shows another scatterplot of SAT scores and GPAs and includes a straight line drawn through the data points. If the equation for this line is known, it can be used to compute a predicted GPA (*Y* value) for any known SAT score (*X* value). The goal of regression is to find the equation for this best fitting line.

17.3
The Regression Equation: The Least-Squares Solution

The first problem in determining the "best fitting" linear equation is to define precisely what is meant by best fit. There are lots of possible straight lines that could be drawn through a set of data (see Figure 17.4). Each of the possible lines can be defined by the general linear equation

$$Y = bX + a$$

Figure 17.4
Scatterplot showing the relation between college grade point average and SAT scores for a set of hypothetical data. Notice that there is a linear relation between these two variables and that the data points fit reasonably well on a straight line. The equation for this line can be used to calculate a predicted grade point average (*Y* value) for any SAT score (*X* value).

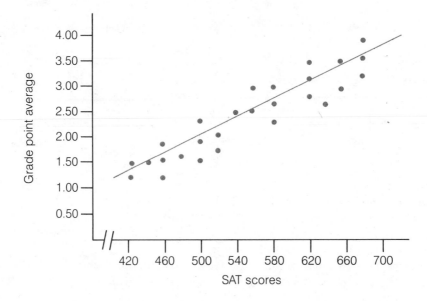

The specific values of *b* and *a* will be different for each of the different lines. The goal is to determine which line is closest to the actual data points.

To determine how well a line fits the data points, the first step is to mathematically define the distance between the line and each data point. For every *X* value in the data, the linear equation will determine a *Y* value on the line. This value is the predicted *Y* and is called $\hat{Y}$ ("*Y* hat"). The distance between this predicted value and the actual *Y* value in the data is determined by

$$\text{distance} = Y - \hat{Y}$$

Notice that we simply are measuring the vertical distance between the actual data point (*Y*) and the predicted point on the line. This distance measures the error between the line and the actual data (see Figure 17.5).

Because some of these distances will be positive and some will be negative, the next step is to square each distance in order to obtain a uniformly positive measure of error. Finally, to determine the total error between the line and the data, we sum the squared errors for all of the data points. The result is a measure of overall squared error between the line and the data:

$$\text{total squared error} = \Sigma(Y - \hat{Y})^2$$

Figure 17.5
The distance between the actual data point (*Y*) and the predicted point on the line($\hat{Y}$) is defined as $Y - \hat{Y}$. The goal of regression is to find the equation for the line that minimizes these distances.

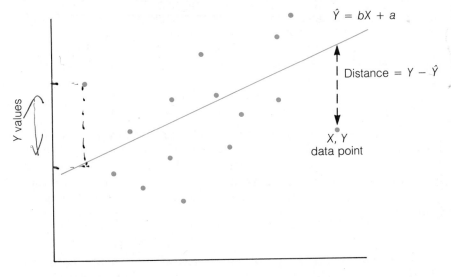

$\hat{Y} = bX + a$

Distance = $Y - \hat{Y}$

X, Y
data point

Y values

X values

Now we can define the *best fitting* line as the one that has the smallest total squared error. For obvious reasons, the resulting line is commonly called the *least squared error* solution.

In symbols, we are looking for a linear equation of the form

$$\text{predicted } Y = \hat{Y} = bX + a$$

For each value of X in the data, this equation will determine the point on the line ($\hat{Y}$) that gives the best prediction of Y. The problem is to find the specific values for a and b that will make this the best fitting line.

The calculations that are needed to find this equation require calculus and some sophisticated algebra, so we will not present the details of the solution. The results, however, are relatively straightforward, and the solutions for b and a are as follows:

A commonly used alternative formula for the slope is

$$b = r \frac{s_y}{s_x}$$

where s_x and s_y are the standard deviations for X and Y, respectively.

$$\textbf{(17.2)} \quad b = \frac{SP}{SS_x}$$

Where SP is the sum of products (see Chapter 16, p. 533) and SS_x is the sum of squares for the X-scores.

$$\textbf{(17.3)} \quad a = \overline{Y} - b\overline{X}$$

Note that these two formulas determine the linear equation that provides the best prediction of Y values. This equation is called the regression equation for Y.

DEFINITION

The *regression equation for Y* is the linear equation

$$\hat{Y} = bX + a$$

where the constants b and a are determined by Formulas (17.2) and (17.3), respectively. This equation results in the least squared error between the data points and the line.

You should notice that the values of SS and SP are needed in the formulas for b and a just as they are needed to compute the Pearson correlation. Relations between the correlation and the regression equation will appear repeatedly throughout this chapter. An example demonstrating the calculation and use of this best fitting line is presented now.

EXAMPLE 17.1
The following table presents X- and Y-scores for a sample of $n = 5$ individuals. These data will be used to demonstrate the procedure for determining the linear regression equation for predicting Y values.

Scores		Deviations		Products	SS
X	Y	$X - \bar{X}$	$Y - \bar{Y}$	$(X - \bar{X})(Y - \bar{Y})$	$(X - \bar{X})^2$
7	11	2	5	10	4
4	3	−1	−3	3	1
6	5	1	−1	−1	1
3	4	−2	−2	4	4
5	7	0	1	0	0
				16 = SP	10 = SS_x

For these data $\Sigma X = 25$, so $\bar{X} = 5$. Also, $\Sigma Y = 30$, so $\bar{Y} = 6$. These means have been used to compute the deviation scores for each X and Y value. The final two columns show the products of the deviation scores and the squared deviations for X. Based on these values,

$$SP = \Sigma(X - \bar{X})(Y - \bar{Y}) = 16$$
$$SS_x = \Sigma(X - \bar{X})^2 = 10$$

Our goal is to find the values for b and a in the linear equation so that we obtain the best fitting straight line for these data.

By using Formulas (17.2) and (17.3), the solutions for b and a are

$$b = \frac{SP}{SS_x} = \frac{16}{10} = 1.6$$
$$a = \bar{Y} - b\bar{X}$$
$$= 6 - 1.6(5)$$
$$= 6 - 8$$
$$= -2$$

The resulting regression equation is

$$\hat{Y} = 1.6X - 2$$

This regression equation can be used to determine a predicted Y value for any given value of X. (To predict X from Y see Box 17.1.) For example, an individual with an X-score of $X = 5$ would be predicted to have a Y-score of

$$\hat{Y} = 1.6X - 2$$
$$= 1.6(5) - 2$$
$$= 8 - 2$$
$$= 6$$

The Regression Equation with z-Scores

We noted in Chapter 16 that there is a close relation between the Pearson correlation and z-scores because both are concerned with the location of individuals within a distribution. In a similar way, there

BOX 17.1 Using Regression to Predict X

In this chapter we have presented formulas defining the regression equation that permit you to use X-scores to predict Y-scores. These formulas were developed by requiring that the best fitting line must minimize the error between the predicted Y values on the line and the actual Y values in the data. When the data points are shown on a graph, the regression equation minimizes the *vertical distance* between the line and the data points. If your goal is to predict X values, then you want to minimize the error between the predicted X and the actual X values. In this case, you must find the linear equation that minimizes *horizontal distance* between the line and the data points. Almost always, the regression equation for predicting X will be different from the equation for predicting Y.

Rather than develop a new set of formulas defining the regression equation for X, we will offer a very simple alternative: If you want to predict X values, just reverse the labels on your data so that the X-scores are renamed Y. Then use the formulas that determine the regression equation for Y.

To demonstrate this process we will use the same data that appeared in Example 17.1. Now, however, we will reverse the X and Y labels in order to compute the equation for predicting X. With X and Y reversed, the data are as follows:

X	Y	$X - \bar{X}$	$Y - \bar{Y}$	$(X - \bar{X})(Y - \bar{Y})$	$(X - \bar{X})^2$
11	7	5	2	10	25
3	4	−3	−1	3	9
5	6	−1	1	−1	1
4	3	−2	−2	4	4
7	5	1	0	0	1
				$16 = SP$	$40 = SS_x$

Using the standard formulas for the regression equation, we obtain

$$b = \frac{SP}{SS_x} = \frac{16}{40} = 0.4$$

$$a = \bar{Y} - b\bar{X}$$
$$= 5 - 0.4(6)$$
$$= 5 - 2.4$$
$$= 2.6$$

The resulting regression equation is

$$\hat{Y} = 0.4X + 2.6$$

Now you can replace the original labels for X and Y, so the final regression equation for predicting X is

$$\hat{X} = 0.4Y + 2.6$$

is a close relation between z-scores and the regression equation. Specifically, when the original X and Y values in the data are transformed into z-scores, the regression equation becomes

$$(17.4) \quad \hat{z}_y = rz_x$$

where $\hat{z}_y$ is the predicted z-score for Y, z_x is the z-score for X, and r is the Pearson correlation. This simplified equation is very easy to derive if you remember that z-scores always have a mean of 0 and a standard deviation of 1. The fact that all z-scores have the same standard deviation means that the z-scores for X and the z-scores for Y will have equal variances. For these two sets of scores to have the same variance, they also must have the same SS. Therefore, when the X- and Y-scores are both changed to z-scores,

$$SS_x = SS_y$$

The general regression equation takes the form

$$\hat{Y} = bX + a$$

where

$$b = \frac{SP}{SS_x}$$

and

$$a = \bar{Y} - b\bar{X}$$

When X and Y are both z-scores,

$$b = \frac{SP}{SS_x} = \frac{SP}{\sqrt{SS_x SS_x}}$$

$$= \frac{SP}{\sqrt{SS_x SS_y}} \quad (\text{because } SS_x = SS_y)$$

$$= r$$

Similarly,

$$a = \bar{Y} - b\bar{X}$$
$$= 0 - 0 \quad (\text{the mean for } z\text{-scores is } 0)$$
$$= 0$$

Substituting these solutions in the general equation, we obtain

$$\hat{z}_y = b z_x + a$$

$$= r z_x + 0$$

This is the regression equation defining the best fitting line when both the X values and the Y values have been transformed into z-scores.

LEARNING
CHECK

1. Sketch a scatterplot for the following data, that is, a graph showing the X, Y data points:

X	Y
1	4
3	9
5	8

Find the regression equation for predicting Y from X. Draw this line on your graph. Does it look like the best fitting line?

ANSWER

1. $SS_x = 8$, $SP = 8$, $\hat{Y} = X + 4$.

17.4

The Standard Error of Estimate

It is possible to determine a best fitting regression equation for any set of data by simply using the formulas already presented. The linear equation you obtain is then used to generate predicted Y values for any known value of X. However, it should be clear that the accuracy of this prediction depends on how well the points on the line correspond to the actual data points, that is, the amount of error between the predicted values $\hat{Y}$ and the actual scores, Y values. Figure 17.6 shows two different sets of data that have exactly the same regression equation. In one case there is a perfect correlation ($r = +1$) between X and Y, so the linear equation fits the data perfectly. For the second set of data, the predicted Y values on the line only approximate the real data points.

A regression equation, by itself, allows you to make predictions, but it does not provide any information about the accuracy of the predictions. To measure the precision of the regression, it is customary to compute a standard error of estimate.

DEFINITION

The *standard error of estimate* gives a measure of the standard distance between a regression line and the actual data points.

Figure 17.6

(a) Scatterplot showing data set 1 from Example 17.2. Notice that the data points fit perfectly on the regression equation, $\hat{Y} = 2X + 3$. (b) Scatterplot showing data set 2 from Example 17.2. In this case there is some error between the data points and the regression line.

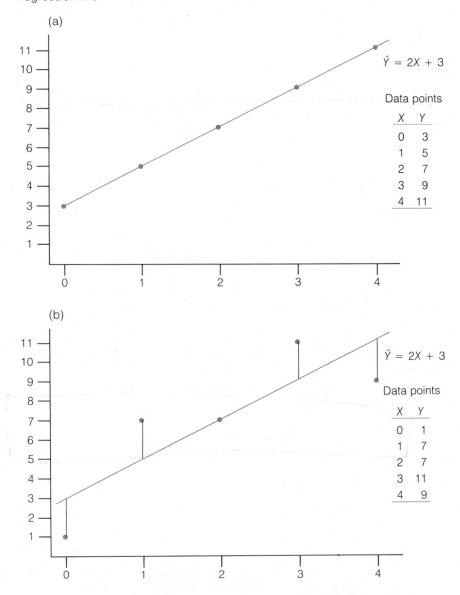

Conceptually, the standard error of estimate is very much like a standard deviation: Both provide a measure of standard distance. You also should note that the calculation of the standard error of estimate is very similar to the calculation of standard deviation.

To calculate the standard error of estimate, we first will find a sum of squared deviations (SS). Each deviation will measure the distance between the actual Y value (from the data) and the predicted Y value (from the regression line). This sum of squares is commonly called SS_{error} because it measures the sum of squared distances, or errors, between the actual data and the predicted values:

$$(17.5) \quad SS_{error} = \Sigma(Y - \hat{Y})^2$$

The obtained SS value is then divided by its degrees of freedom to obtain a measure of variance. This procedure should be very familiar:

$$\text{variance} = \frac{SS}{df}$$

The degrees of freedom for the standard error of estimate are $df = n - 2$. The reason for having $n - 2$ degrees of freedom, rather than the customary $n - 1$, is that we now are measuring deviations from a line rather than deviations from a mean. You should recall that it is necessary to know SP to find the slope of the regression line (the value of b in the equation). To calculate SP, you must know the means for both the X- and the Y-scores. Specifying these two means places two restrictions on the variability of the data with the result that the scores have only $n - 2$ degrees of freedom. (A more intuitive explanation for the fact that the SS_{error} has $df = n - 2$ comes from the simple observation that it takes exactly two points to determine a straight line. If there are only two data points, they must fit perfectly on a straight line so there will be no error. It is only when you have more than two points that there is some freedom in determining the best fitting line.)

The final step in the calculation of the standard error of estimate is to take the square root of the variance in order to obtain a measure of standard distance. The final equation is

$$(17.6) \quad \text{standard error of estimate} = \sqrt{\frac{SS_{error}}{df}} = \sqrt{\frac{\Sigma(Y - \hat{Y})^2}{n - 2}}$$

The following example demonstrates the calculation of this standard error.

EXAMPLE 17.2
The two sets of data in Figure 17.6 will be used to demonstrate the calculation of the standard error of estimate. Both of these data sets have the same regression equation:

$$\hat{Y} = 2X + 3$$

However, for the first set of scores there is a perfect correlation ($r = +1$) between X and Y; that is, the points fit perfectly on a straight line. For the second data set the correlation is $r = +0.845$, so there is some error between the predicted values on the line and the actual Y values.

For the first set of data, $SS_x = 10$, $SS_y = 40$, and $SP = 20$. The mean for X is $\overline{X} = 2$, and the mean for Y is $\overline{Y} = 7$. By using these values, the constants in the regression equation are

$$b = \frac{SP}{SS_x} = \frac{20}{10} = 2 \qquad \hat{Y} = bX + a$$

$$a = \overline{Y} - b\overline{X} \qquad \hat{Y} = 2X + 3$$
$$= 7 - 2(2)$$
$$= 7 - 4$$
$$= 3$$

Using this regression equation, we have computed the predicted Y value, the error, and the squared error for each individual in the data. Notice that in every case the predicted Y value is identical to the actual Y-score. All of the errors are equal to zero, so the SS for these errors also is zero:

Data		Predicted Y Value	Error	Squared Error
X	Y	$\hat{Y} = 2X + 3$	$Y - \hat{Y}$	$(Y - \hat{Y})^2$
0	3	3	0	0
1	5	5	0	0
2	7	7	0	0
3	9	9	0	0
4	11	11	0	0
				$0 = SS_{error}$

Because there is no error between the predicted values and the actual Y values, the standard error of estimate is zero: The regression line provides a perfect prediction:

$$\text{standard error of estimate} = \sqrt{\frac{SS_{error}}{df}} = \sqrt{\frac{0}{3}} = 0$$

For the second data set, $SS_x = 10$, $SS_y = 56$, and $SP = 20$. The mean for the X values is $\overline{X} = 2$, and the mean for the Y values is $\overline{Y} = 7$. By using these values, the constants in the regression equation are

$$b = \frac{SP}{SS_x} = \frac{20}{10} = 2 \qquad \hat{Y} = bX + a$$

$$a = \overline{Y} - b\overline{X} \qquad \hat{Y} = 2X + 3$$
$$= 7 - 2(2)$$
$$= 3$$

Again, we have used the regression equation to compute the predicted Y, the error, and the squared error for each individual:

Data		Predicted Y Value $\hat{Y} = 2X + 3$	Error $Y - \hat{Y}$	Squared Error $(Y - \hat{Y})^2$
X	Y			
0	1	3	−2	4
1	7	5	+2	4
2	7	7	0	0
3	11	9	+2	4
4	9	11	−2	4
				16 $= SS_{error}$

This time the data points do not fit exactly on the line. The sum of squared errors for these data is $SS_{error} = 16$. With $n = 5$, these data have $df = n - 2 = 3$, so the standard error of estimate is

$$\text{standard error of estimate} = \sqrt{\frac{SS_{error}}{df}} = \sqrt{\frac{16}{3}} = 2.31$$

Remember, the standard error of estimate provides a measure of how accurately the regression equation predicts the Y values. In this case, the standard distance between the actual data points and the regression line is measured by standard error of estimate = 2.31.

Relation Between Standard Error and the Correlation

It should be clear from Example 17.2 that the standard error of estimate is directly related to the magnitude of the correlation between X and Y. If the correlation is near 1.00 (or −1.00), the data points will be clustered close to the line, and the standard error of estimate will be small. As the correlation gets nearer to zero, the line will provide less accurate predictions, and the standard error of estimate will grow larger. In Chapter 16 (page 544) we observed that squaring the correlation provides a measure of the accuracy of prediction: r^2 is called the coefficient of determination because it determines what proportion of the variability in Y is predicted by the relationship with X. Because r^2 measures the predicted portion of the variability, we can use $1 - r^2$ to measure the unpredicted, or error, portion of the variability. The total variability in Y is measured by SS_y, so the error portion would be

(17.7) $\quad SS_{error} = (1 - r^2)SS_y$

Notice that when $r = 1.00$ there is no error (perfect prediction) and that as the correlation approaches zero the error will grow larger. By using this formula for SS_{error}, the standard error of estimate can be computed as

$$\text{standard error of estimate} = \sqrt{\frac{SS_{error}}{df}} = \sqrt{\frac{(1-r^2)SS_y}{n-2}}$$

The two data sets in Example 17.2 will be used to demonstrate this new formula. For the first data set there was a perfect correlation between X and Y, $r = +1.00$.

By using this value, the SS for the errors would be

$$SS_{error} = (1 - r^2)SS_y$$
$$= (1 - 1^2)(40)$$
$$= 0(40)$$
$$= 0$$

For the second set of data, $SS_y = 56$, and the correlation between X and Y is $r = 0.845$. By using the new formula, SS for the errors would be

$$SS_{error} = (1 - r^2)SS_y$$
$$= (1 - 0.845^2)(56)$$
$$= (1 - 0.714)(56)$$
$$= 0.286(56)$$
$$= 16.01$$

Notice that in each case the new formula for the SS produces the same value that was obtained in Example 17.2. Also note that this new formula is much easier to use because it requires only the correlation value (r) and the SS for Y.

LEARNING
CHECK

1. In the previous learning check, you found the regression equation for the following data:

X	Y
1	4
3	9
5	8

The equation is

$$\hat{Y} = X + 4$$

a. Use the regression equation to find the predicted Y value corresponding to each X in the data.
b. Find the error $(Y - \hat{Y})$ for each data point and compute SS_{error} and the standard error of estimate.
c. Compute the Pearson correlation for these data.
d. Use the Pearson correlation and SS_y to find the SS_{error} and the standard error of estimate.

ANSWERS

a. The predicted Y values are 5, 7, and 9.
b. The errors are -1, 2, and -1. $SS_{error} = 6$. The standard error of estimate is $\sqrt{\frac{6}{1}} = 2.45$.
c. $SS_x = 8$; $SS_y = 14$; $SP = 8$; $r = 0.756$.
d. $1 - r^2 = 0.428$; $SS_{error} = 0.428(14) = 5.99$; standard error of estimate $= 2.45$.

17.5
Analysis of Regression

Correlations and regression equations generally are computed for sample data. Quite often these sample values are used to provide information about populations. For example, a psychologist would like to know whether there is a relation between IQ and creativity. This is a general question concerning a population. To answer the question, a sample would be selected, and the sample data would be used to compute the correlation value. You should recognize this process as another example of inferential statistics: using samples to draw inferences about populations. In the past, we have been concerned primarily with using sample means as the basis for answering questions about population means. In this section we will examine the procedures for using sample correlations and regression equations as a means of obtaining information about the corresponding population values. The general process is called analysis of regression, and it is another example of hypothesis testing.

Hypotheses for the Analysis of Regression

The hypotheses for analysis of regression can be phrased in two different ways depending on whether your primary interest is in the population correlation or in the population regression equation. In terms of correlations, the basic question is whether or not a correlation exists in the population. The null hypothesis would say "No, the population correlation is zero." The alternative hypothesis is "Yes, there is a real, nonzero, correlation in the population." Because the population correlation is traditionally represented by the Greek letter rho, ρ, these hypotheses would be stated in symbols as

H_0: $\rho = 0$ (no population correlation)
H_1: $\rho \neq 0$ (there is a correlation)

The correlation from the sample data (r) will be used to evaluate these hypotheses. As always, samples are not expected to be identical to the populations from which they come. Specifically, you should note that it is possible to obtain a nonzero sample correlation even when the population value is zero. This is particularly true when you have a small sample (see Figure 17.7). The question for this hypothesis test is whether the obtained sample correlation provides sufficient evi-

Figure 17.7

Scatterplot of a population of X and Y values with a near zero correlation. However, a small sample of $n = 3$ data points from this population shows a relatively strong, positive correlation. Data points in the sample are circled.

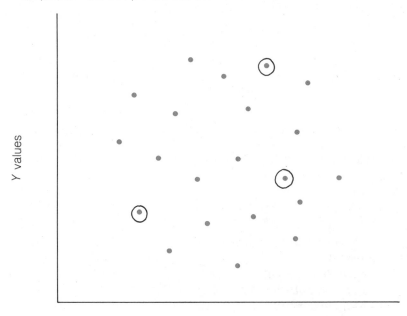

dence to conclude that a real, nonzero correlation exists in the population.

If your major interest is in the regression equation, the hypotheses for analysis of regression concern whether or not there is any linear trend in the population. Notice that this is the same as asking whether or not there is any correlation because the Pearson correlation measures the degree of linear relation. The null hypothesis says that no linear trend exists; the alternative hypothesis says that there is a real linear trend. For the population regression equation, the slope constant is identified by the Greek letter beta, β. The null hypothesis states that there is no trend, which can be stated in symbols as

$$H_0: \quad \beta = 0 \quad \text{(no positive trend and no negative trend)}$$

The alternative hypothesis is

$$H_1: \quad \beta \neq 0 \quad \text{(there is a real positive or negative trend)}$$

As before, sample data almost always will produce some nonzero value for the slope constant b in the regression equation. The question is whether this sample value provides sufficient evidence to conclude that a real, nonzero trend exists in the population.

The Structure of the Analysis of Regression

The hypothesis test for analysis of regression will use an F-ratio. You should recall from the chapters on analysis of variance that an F-ratio is comprised of two sample variances,

$$F = \frac{s^2}{s^2}$$

where each sample variance is computed by the basic formula

$$s^2 = \frac{SS}{df}$$

To obtain these two sample variances for the analysis, we will use the linear relationship between X and Y to analyze or partition the sample data. The general structure for this analysis is shown graphically in Figure 17.8. Notice that the total variability of the Y-scores is to be partitioned into two components:

A conceptual interpretation of this analysis is presented in Box 17.2.

1. The variability that is predicted from the linear relation. This component provides a measure of how well the correlation (or the regression equation) establishes a relation between X and Y.
2. The variability that is not predicted from the linear relation. This component provides a measure of unpredicted, or error, variability.

Figure 17.8

The general structure of the analysis of regression. The total variability in the Y-scores is partitioned into two components: the part that is predicted by the relation between X and Y and the part that cannot be predicted.

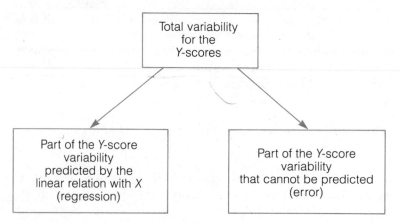

BOX 17.2 **Variability and Uncertainty**

The purpose of regression is to help make more accurate predictions. By using information about one variable X, it is possible to gain some knowledge about another variable Y. In this way, the college admissions officer uses a student's SAT score to predict future grade point average; a businessman uses current economic factors to predict sales for the company. In general, regression is used when there is uncertainty about the value of some variable. In statistical terms, the value being predicted is called Y, and the uncertainty comes from the fact that the Y-scores are variable (not all the same). Notice that the statistical concept of variability and the everyday concept of uncertainty are identical. The following two sets of scores should help demonstrate this equivalence:

Data Set 1		Data Set 2	
X	Y	X	Y
1	7	1	5
3	12	3	5
5	14	5	5
7	20	7	5
10	26	10	5
13	31	13	5
15	39	15	5

For each data set, I will randomly select one individual, and your job is to predict the Y-score for that person. It should be obvious that you would have more uncertainty with data set 1 than with data set 2. In data set 1 the Y-scores are variable. This variability means that you are uncertain about your prediction. However, the Y values have no variability in data set 2. Here there is no uncertainty about your prediction.

You also should notice that there is a good positive relationship between X and Y in data set 1. You could use this relationship to predict Y-scores for individuals who are not in the sample. For example, if an individual has a small value for X, you can be reasonably confident that he/she also will have a small value for Y. This is regression: using one variable (X) to help predict another (Y). With regression you can make a more accurate prediction; that is, you can reduce your uncertainty about Y. On the other hand, you should remember that regression usually does not produce perfect predictions; that is, you still have some uncertainty. In everyday terms, one part of your initial uncertainty is removed by regression, but another part remains. In statistical terms, regression predicts part of the variability in the Y-scores, but part of the variability remains. The analysis of regression shows how uncertainty is reduced by showing how the variability is partitioned.

These two components will be the two variances in the final F-ratio:

$$F = \frac{\text{variance predicted by regression}}{\text{error variance}}$$

Formulas for the Analysis of Regression

The analysis of regression is based on the fact that each Y value in the data can be partitioned into two parts:

$$Y = \text{predicted value} + \text{error}$$
$$= \hat{Y} + (Y - \hat{Y})$$

Note that the predicted value ($\hat{Y}$) is simply a point on the regression line. The error is the distance between the predicted value and the actual Y-score. This is the same measure of error that was used to find the standard error of estimate.

By computing the sum of squares (SS) for each of these components, it is possible to partition the SS for the Y-scores into two components: the portion predicted from the regression line and the portion from the error scores:

$$SS_y = SS_{regression} + SS_{error}$$

This analysis is demonstrated in the following example.

In analysis of regression the error component often is called residual *because it measures how much variability remains after you use the regression equation to predict the* Y *values.*

EXAMPLE 17.3
The following data consist of a set of $n = 5$ pairs of scores (X and Y values). For these data, the SS for X is 10, the SS for Y is 70, and the sum of products (SP) is -20. From these values we can compute the correlation between X and Y as

$$r = \frac{SP}{\sqrt{SS_x SS_y}} = \frac{-20}{\sqrt{10(70)}} = -0.756$$

The constants in the regression equation are

$$b = \frac{SP}{SS_x} = \frac{-20}{10} = -2$$
$$a = \overline{Y} - b\overline{X} = 8 - (-2)(3) = 14$$

The complete regression equation is

$$\hat{Y} = bX + a$$
$$= -2X + 14$$

Using this equation, we have computed the predicted value for each Y and the error ($Y - \hat{Y}$):

Data Points		Predicted Y	Error
X	Y	$\hat{Y}$	$Y - \hat{Y}$
1	10	12	-2
2	13	10	$+3$
3	6	8	-2
4	9	6	$+3$
5	2	4	-2

Notice that each Y in the data now has been partitioned into two parts:

$$Y = \text{predicted value} + \text{error value}$$

These two parts are the basic components of the analysis of regression. We now will compute SS for each component. For the predicted Y values, SS is computed using the computational formula as follows:

$\hat{Y}$	$\hat{Y}^2$
12	144
10	100
8	64
6	36
4	16

$$\Sigma\hat{Y} = 40$$

$$\Sigma\hat{Y}^2 = 360$$

$$SS = \Sigma\hat{Y}^2 - \frac{(\Sigma\hat{Y})^2}{n}$$

$$= 360 - \frac{40^2}{5}$$

$$= 360 - 320$$

$$= 40$$

Thus, $SS_{regression} = 40$ for this set of data.

Because the error scores sum to zero, the mean also is zero. Therefore, each error score is its own deviation score. To find the sum of the squared deviation scores (SS), all that is necessary is to find the sum of the squared error scores:

Error	Squared Error
-2	4
$+3$	9
-2	4
$+3$	9
-2	4
	$\overline{30}$ $= SS_{error}$

Notice that the two components combine to equal the total SS for the original Y-scores:

$$SS_y = SS_{regression} + SS_{error}$$
$$= 40 + 30$$
$$= 70$$

Using the Correlation in the Analysis of Regression

In Example 17.3, the SS values were computed directly from the predicted Y-scores and the error scores. In most cases, this direct method is a very inefficient way to compute these values. You should recall that the sample correlation (r) provides a simple means of partitioning the total variability into a predicted component and an error component. The predicted portion of the variability is measured by r^2, and the unpredicted, or error, portion is measured by $1 - r^2$. Using these two proportions, we can divide the total SS_y as follows:

$$SS_{error} = (1 - r^2)SS_y$$
$$SS_{regression} = r^2 SS_y$$

The value of these simpler equations can be demonstrated using the data from Example 17.3. For these data, SS for Y was 70, and the correlation between X and Y was $r = -0.756$. By using these numbers, the predicted portion of the SS_y is

$$SS_{regression} = r^2 SS_y$$
$$= (-0.756^2)70$$
$$= (0.5715)70$$
$$= 40.00$$

The error portion of the SS_y is

$$SS_{error} = (1 - r^2)SS_y$$
$$= (1 - 0.5715)70$$
$$= (0.4285)70$$
$$= 30.00$$

These are the same values that we obtained in Example 17.3, but it should be obvious that the calculations were much easier this time.

Notice that the value of the correlation, or more precisely the value of r^2, determines how the SS for Y is partitioned. When the correlation is large, most of the variability in the Y-scores is predicted by the regression equation. This is reasonable because a large correlation means that the data points are clustered very near to the regression line. Alternately, a small correlation (near zero) means that there is not a strong linear trend, so the regression line is not an accurate predictor of data points. You may recall from Chapter 16 that the value of r^2 was defined as the coefficient of determination and was used to evaluate the strength of a correlation. Now we can repeat this definition using terminology from the analysis of regression.

The value r^2 is called the *coefficient of determination* because it determines how the variability of the Y-scores is partitioned. Specifically, r^2 is the proportion of the Y variability that is determined or predicted by the regression equation. The remaining portion of the Y variability $(1 - r^2)$ is unpredicted or error variability.

Degrees of Freedom in Analysis of Regression

To complete the analysis of regression, we must determine the degrees of freedom for each of the SS components. As before, we will obtain the df value by partitioning the original Y-scores into two components (see Figure 17.8):

$$df_y = df_{regression} + df_{error}$$

We observed earlier that the error scores have $df = n - 2$. Because the original Y-scores have $df = n - 1$, it can be shown by simple algebra that the predicted Y values from the regression equation must have $df = 1$:

$$df_y = df_{regression} + df_{error}$$
$$n - 1 = df_{regression} + (n - 2)$$
$$(n - 1) - (n - 2) = df_{regression}$$
$$1 = df_{regression}$$

With the SS and df values it is possible to compute a variance for each component of the regression analysis. As in analysis of variance, these sample variances are called mean squares or MS values:

$$MS = \frac{SS}{df} = \text{variance}$$

For the predicted portion of the variability,

$$(17.8) \quad MS_{regression} = \frac{SS_{regression}}{df_{regression}} = \frac{r^2 SS_y}{1} = r^2 SS_y$$

For the error portion,

$$(17.9) \quad MS_{error} = \frac{SS_{error}}{df_{error}} = \frac{(1 - r^2)SS_y}{n - 2}$$

The final step in the analysis of regression is the calculation of the F-ratio:

$$(17.10) \quad F = \frac{MS_{regression}}{MS_{error}} = \frac{r^2 SS_y}{\dfrac{(1 - r^2)SS_y}{(n - 2)}}$$

Because SS_y appears in the numerator and in the denominator of this ratio, the two values cancel, and we are left with the following formula for F:

$$F = \frac{r^2}{\dfrac{(1 - r^2)}{(n - 2)}}$$

A large F-ratio indicates that a significant portion of the total variability is predicted by the regression equation; that is, the data provide evidence for a significant linear relation between X and Y. A small F-ratio, near 1.00, indicates that there is not sufficient evidence to conclude that a real relation exists; that is, the correlation obtained in the data could be due to chance. The complete set of formulas for the analysis of regression is shown in Figure 17.9.

A complete example of analysis of regression follows.

EXAMPLE 17.4

For this example we will use the same data that were used in Example 17.3. Now we are trying to determine whether or not these sample data provide sufficient evidence to conclude that a linear relation between X and Y exists in the population. The original data and some summary statistics are as follows:

X	Y	
1	10	
2	13	$SS_x = 10$
3	6	$SS_y = 70$
4	9	$SP = -20$
5	2	

For this sample the Pearson correlation is $r = -0.756$, and the regression equation is

$$\hat{Y} = -2X + 14$$

STEP 1. The null hypothesis states that there is no linear relationship:

$$H_0: \quad \rho = 0$$

The alternative is that a real relationship does exist:

$$H_1: \quad \rho \neq 0$$

We will use $\alpha = .05$.

Figure 17.9

The complete set of formulas for the analysis of regression. The final F-ratio is used to test whether or not the data provide sufficient evidence to conclude that there is a significant linear relation between X and Y.

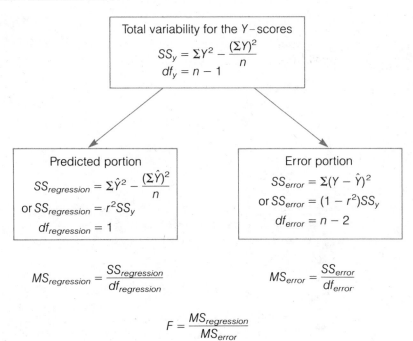

STEP 2. This is an analysis of regression. The total variability will be partitioned into two components, the predicted portion and the error portion. With a total of $n = 5$ pairs of scores, these two components will have

$$df_{regression} = 1$$
$$df_{error} = n - 2 = 3$$

Thus, the final F-ratio will have $df = 1, 3$. With $\alpha = .05$, the critical value is 10.13 (see Figure 17.10).

Use the F distribution table in Appendix B (page A-32) to look up the critical value.

STEP 3. The predicted portion of the variability is r^2. This portion has $df = 1$, so

$$MS_{regression} = \frac{r^2 SS_y}{1} = r^2 SS_y$$

The error portion is $1 - r^2$. This portion has $df = n - 2$, so

$$MS_{error} = \frac{(1 - r^2)SS_y}{n - 2}$$

Figure 17.10

The distribution of F-ratios with df = 1, 3. The critical region for α = .05 begins at an F value of 10.13.

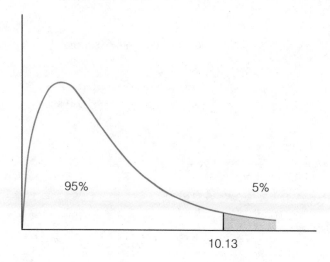

95% 5%

10.13

The final F-ratio is

$$F = \frac{MS_{regression}}{MS_{error}} = \frac{r^2 SS_y}{\dfrac{(1 - r^2)SS_y}{(n - 2)}} = \frac{r^2}{\dfrac{(1 - r^2)}{(n - 2)}}$$

With $r = -0.756$,

$$F = \frac{-0.756^2}{\dfrac{1 - (-0.756^2)}{3}}$$

$$= \frac{0.5715}{0.1428}$$

$$= 4.00$$

STEP 4. The F-ratio is not in the critical region. Therefore, we fail to reject the null hypothesis and conclude that these data do not provide sufficient evidence to establish a real linear relation between X and Y in the population.

Example 17.4 Continued—a Computer Analysis

As noted before, statistics that require extensive calculations often are done on a computer using one of the statistical packages such as BMDP, SPSS, or MINITAB. We have used the MINITAB program to perform the analysis of regression with the same data that were used in Example 17.4 and in Example 17.3. The printout from this program is shown in Figure 17.11. Because you are likely to encounter similar

Figure 17.11

A copy of the printout from the MINITAB analysis of regression program. The data used in this analysis are the same data that appeared in Examples 17.3 and 17.4.[a]

```
MINITAB RELEASE 82.1 *** COPYRIGHT - PENN STATE UNIV. 1982
MAY 31, 1984 *** S.U.N.Y. BROCKPORT - ACADEMIC COMPUTING SERVICES
STORAGE AVAILABLE 1079344
There is HELP on new features of Rel. 82.1.  Type NEWS for details.
MTB > READ C1 C2
     5 ROWS READ
  ROW   C1    C2

   1     1    10
   2     2    13          ────────────────────────────────────────►  1
   3     3     6
   4     4     9
   5     5     2

MTB > REGR C2 1 C1

THE REGRESSION EQUATION IS
C2 = 14.0 - 2.00 C1          ────────────────────────────────────►  2

                        ST. DEV.      T-RATIO =
COLUMN      COEFFICIENT  OF COEF.     COEF/S.D.
              14.000      3.317        4.22
C1            -2.000      1.000       -2.00

S = 3.162   ─────────────────────────────────────────────────────►  3

R-SQUARED = 57.1 PERCENT
R-SQUARED = 42.9 PERCENT, ADJUSTED FOR D.F.

ANALYSIS OF VARIANCE

  DUE TO      DF         SS      MS=SS/DF
REGRESSION    1        40.00      40.00
RESIDUAL      3        30.00      10.00    ──────────────────────►  4
TOTAL         4        70.00

                      Y    PRED. Y   ST.DEV.
ROW     C1     C2    VALUE  PRED. Y  RESIDUAL   ST.RES.
 1     1.00   10.00  12.00   2.45     -2.00     -1.00
 2     2.00   13.00  10.00   1.73      3.00      1.13   ──────────►  5
 3     3.00    6.00   8.00   1.41     -2.00     -0.71
 4     4.00    9.00   6.00   1.73      3.00      1.13
 5     5.00    2.00   4.00   2.45     -2.00     -1.00


DURBIN-WATSON STATISTIC = 3.33

MTB > END
MTB > STOP

*** MINITAB *** STATISTICS DEPT * PENN STATE UNIV. * RELEASE 82.1 *
STORAGE AVAILABLE 1079344
```

[a]Explanation of printout:
1. The original data with the X-scores in column 1 (C1) and the Y-scores in column 2.
2. The regression equation: Remember, C2 is Y and C1 is X.
3. S is the standard error of estimate.
4. A summary table for the analysis of regression. Note that the term *residual* is used to identify what we have called *error*.
5. A table showing the original data (X = C1 and Y = C2), the predicted Y values from the regression equation, and the residual or error for each value. Note that these are the same values we obtained in Example 17.3. The other two columns in this table show components of regression that are beyond the scope of this text.

computer output in the future, you should take a few minutes to look over this printout and compare the computer version of the analysis with the results we obtained in Examples 17.3 and 17.4.

LEARNING
CHECK

1. A researcher obtains a Pearson correlation of $r = +0.60$ for a sample of $n = 6$ pairs of X and Y values. Does this sample provide evidence for a significant correlation in the population? Test at the .05 level of significance.
2. A researcher obtains a Pearson correlation of $r = +0.10$ for a sample of $n = 902$ pairs of X and Y values. Does this sample provide evidence for a significant correlation in the population? Test at the .05 level of significance.
3. How do you explain the fact that the relatively large correlation in Problem 1 is not significant, while the relatively small correlation in Problem 2 is significant?

ANSWERS

1. For $r = 0.60$ and $n = 6$, the F-ratio is $F = 0.36/0.16 = 2.25$. This is not significant.
2. For $r = 0.10$ and $n = 902$, the F-ratio is $F = 0.01/0.0011 = 9.09$. This is significant at the .05 level.
3. A very large sample should provide a very accurate picture of the population. Therefore, even though the sample correlation is small in Problem 2, it is sufficient to indicate a correlation in the population. On the other hand, there is a large amount of error associated with a very small sample. Therefore, the correlation in Problem 1 is not sufficient to provide convincing evidence of a correlation in the population.

Summary

1. When there is a general linear relation between two variables X and Y, it is possible to construct a linear equation that allows you to predict the Y value corresponding to any known value of X:

    $$\text{predicted } Y \text{ value} = \hat{Y} = bX + a$$

    The technique for determining this equation is called regression. By using a *least-squares* method to minimize the error between the predicted Y values and the actual Y values, the best fitting line is achieved when the linear equation has

    $$b = \frac{SP}{SS_x} \quad \text{and} \quad a = \overline{Y} - b\overline{X}$$

2. The linear equation generated by regression (called the *regression equation*) can be used to compute a predicted Y value for

any value of X. The accuracy of the prediction is measured by the standard error of estimate, which provides a measure of the average distance (or error) between the predicted Y value on the line and the actual data point. The standard error of estimate is computed by

$$\text{standard error of estimate} = \sqrt{\frac{SS_{error}}{n-2}}$$

where SS_{error} may be computed directly from the error scores,

$$SS_{error} = \Sigma(Y - \hat{Y})^2$$

or as a proportion of the original Y variability,

$$SS_{error} = (1 - r^2)SS_y$$

3. Analysis of regression is a statistical technique that evaluates sample data to determine whether or not there is sufficient evidence to conclude that a linear relation exists in the population. Analysis of regression is based on the observation that each Y-score in the data can be partitioned into two components:

a. A predicted value ($\hat{Y}$) from the regression
b. An error component ($Y - \hat{Y}$)

By computing a variance (or MS) for each of these components, it is possible to construct an F-ratio that determines whether or not the predicted portion is significant:

$$F = \frac{\text{variance predicted by regression}}{\text{error variance}} = \frac{MS_{regression}}{MS_{error}}$$

The complete formulas for analysis of regression are shown in Figure 17.9.

Key Terms

linear equation	standard error of estimate
slope	analysis of regression
Y-intercept	coefficient of determination
regression equation for Y	

Problems for Chapter 17:
Regression

1. Sketch a graph showing the linear equation $Y = 3X - 2$.

*2. Two major companies supply laboratory animals for psychologists. Company A sells laboratory rats for $6 each and charges a $10 fee for delivery. Company B sells rats for only $5 each but has a $20 delivery charge. In each case the delivery fee is a one-time charge and does not depend on the number of rats in the order.

  a. For each company, what is the linear equation that defines the total cost (Y) as a function of the number of rats (X)? Each equation should be of the form

$$Y = bX + a$$

  b. What would the total cost be for an order of 10 rats from company A? From company B?

  c. If you were buying 20 rats, which company gives you the better deal?

3. For the following set of data, find the linear regression equation for predicting Y from X:

X	Y
0	9
2	9
4	7
6	3

*4. a. Find the regression equation for the following data:

X	Y
1	2
4	7
3	5
2	1
5	14
3	7

  b. Compute the predicted Y value for each X in the data.

  c. Compute the error $(Y - \hat{Y})$ for each individual and find SS_{error} for these data.

5. A set of $n = 6$ pairs of X and Y values has a Pearson correlation of $r = +0.60$ and $SS_y = 100$. If you are using these data as the basis for a regression equation,

  a. On the average, how much error would you expect if the regression equation were used to predict the Y-score for a specific individual? That is, find the standard error of ~~regression.~~ estimate.

  b. How much error would you expect if the sample size were $n = 102$ instead of $n = 6$?

  c. How much error would you expect if the sample correlation were $r = +0.80$ instead of 0.60?

*6. A high school counselor would like to know if there is a relation between mathematical skill and verbal skill. A sample of $n = 25$ students is selected, and the counselor records achievement test scores in mathematics and English for each student. The Pearson correlation for this sample is $r = +0.50$. Do these data provide sufficient evidence for a real relationship in the population? Test at the .05 level.

7. Find the regression equation and compute the standard error of estimate for the following data:

X	Y
3	12
0	8
4	18
2	12
1	8

*8. A photographer has noticed that a freshly mixed batch of chemicals will develop photographs faster than an old batch of chemicals. The photographer keeps records of the time needed to develop a print and the age of the chemicals:

Age of Chemicals (Days)	Time to Develop (Seconds)
1	35
4	38
6	40
9	44
12	49
14	52

a. Use these data to find the regression equation for predicting time as a function of age of the chemicals.

b. Using your regression equation, predict how long it should take to develop a print if the chemicals are 10 days old.

c. Calculate the standard error of estimate to determine a degree of accuracy for your prediction in part b.

*9. A psychologist would like to determine whether there is any consistent relationship between intelligence and creativity. A random sample of $n = 18$ people is obtained, and the psychologist administers a standardized IQ test and a creativity test to each individual. Using these data, the psychologist obtained a Pearson correlation of $r = +0.20$ between IQ and creativity. Do these sample data provide sufficient evidence to conclude that a correlation exists in the population? Test at the .05 level of significance.

10. The marketing division of a major breakfast cereal manufacturer prepared the following table showing the monthly advertising expenditure and sales figures for the company:

Advertising Expenditure (in Thousands)	Sales Figures (in Thousands)
14	218
23	237
27	241
17	214
29	243
15	218
19	232
25	230

Also plot scattergram + draw regression line.

a. Compute the Pearson correlation for these two variables.

b. Do these data indicate that there is a significant relation between the amount spent on advertising and the amount of sales? Test at the .05 level of significance.

c. Next month, the company plans to spend $20,000 on advertising. Find the regression equation and then use it to predict next month's sales.

*11. The man who runs the concession at the football stadium has noticed that he sells more coffee on cold days than on warm days. For several games he has kept records of the temperature and coffee sales. These data are as follows:

Temperature	Coffee Sales
52	147
73	43
40	253
61	120
28	359
38	261
25	341

a. Find the regression equation for predicting coffee sales based on temperature.

b. The weather center expects the temperature to be 34 degrees at game time tomorrow. Use the regression equation to predict how much coffee will be sold.

c. Compute the standard error of estimate to determine a level of accuracy for your prediction from part b.

12. A major appliance dealer has kept records of the monthly unemployment rate in his state and the number of color televisions he sells each month. These data are as follows. He would like to use the data to help predict each month's sales.

Unemployment Rate	Number of Televisions
10.3%	24
8.7%	31
8.1%	39
7.6%	47
8.3%	45
7.2%	56
6.5%	51
6.2%	58
7.3%	49
7.9%	40

a. Find the regression equation for predicting sales from the unemployment rate.

b. If the unemployment rate is announced as 7.5% for this month, predict the number of televisions that will be sold.

c. How accurate is your prediction in part b? That is, on the average, how much error do you expect when using the regression equation for prediction?

*13. At the beginning of this chapter we noted that the correlation between IQ measured at age 2 and IQ at age 18 was only $r = 0.31$. Assume that this correlation is based on a sample of 22 people.

a. Do these data provide evidence for a significant relation between IQ at age 2 and IQ at 18? Test at the .05 level of significance.

b. If the IQ scores for the 18-year-olds had $SS = 5220$, how accurately can you predict adult IQ based on the 2-year-old's score? (Find the standard error of estimate.)

14. A college professor claims that the scores on the first exam provide an excellent indication of how students will perform throughout the term. To test this claim, first-exam scores and final scores were recorded for a sample of $n = 12$ students in an introductory psychology class. The data are as follows:

First Exam	Final Grade
62	74
73	93
88	68
82	79
85	91
77	72
94	96
65	61
91	92
74	82
85	93
98	95

a. Is the professor right? Is there a significant relation between scores on the first exam and final grades? Test with $\alpha = .01$.

b. How accurately do the exam scores predict final grades? Compute the standard error of estimate.

*15. Sternberg (1966) reported results of a human memory experiment using regression. Sternberg presented subjects with a short list of digits to hold in memory. Then he flashed a single digit, and the subjects had to decide as quickly as possible whether or not this single digit was contained in the memory list. The results showed a linear relation between the number of items in memory and the reaction time; the more items in memory, the more time needed to respond. Data similar to those obtained by Sternberg are as follows:

Number of Items in Memory	Reaction Time (in Milliseconds)
1	430
2	471
3	505
4	543
5	578

Calculate the regression equation for predicting reaction time as a function of the number of items in memory. (Note that the slope of the regression equation corresponds to the amount of extra time needed for each additional item in memory. The Y-intercept is a measure of basic reaction time with zero items in memory.)

16. Data indicate that infants with low birth weight tend to lag behind in general development. The following data are infant birth weights and scholastic achievement scores at age 10 years for a sample of $n = 12$ children:

Birth Weight	Scholastic Achievement	Birth Weight	Scholastic Achievement
81 oz	58	127 oz	81
96 oz	65	108 oz	85
132 oz	78	76 oz	55
104 oz	76	86 oz	68
122 oz	81	113 oz	79
88 oz	62	110 oz	72

a. Calculate the Pearson correlation for these data.

b. Find the regression equation for predicting scholastic achievement from birth weight.

c. Find the regression equation for predicting birth weight on the basis of scholastic achievement scores.

*17. A researcher would like to determine whether or not there is a relation between aggressive behavior and television. A sample of $n = 14$ children, aged 3 to 5 years, is obtained. These children are observed in a day-care center to obtain a measure of aggression for each child. In addition, the parents of each child are asked to complete a questionnaire which includes a report of the number of hours the child spends watching TV each day. The data are as follows:

TV Time	Aggression	TV Time	Aggression
1.5	21	3.0	30
1.5	15	0	23
3.5	36	2.0	26
1.5	27	2.5	33
0.5	19	2.0	20
0	25	3.5	29
1.5	22	2.0	24

Do these data indicate a significant relationship between TV and aggression? Test with $\alpha = .05$.

18. You probably have read for years about the relation between years of education and salary potential. The following hypothetical data represent a sample of $n = 10$ men who have been employed for 5 years. For each person, we report the total number of years of higher education (high school plus college) and current annual salary.

Salary (in $1000)	Years of Higher Education
21.4	4
18.7	4
17.5	2
32.0	8
12.6	0
25.3	5
35.5	10
17.3	4
33.8	12
14.0	0

a. Find the regression equation for predicting salary from education.

b. How would you interpret the slope constant (b) in the regression equation?

c. How would you interpret the Y-intercept (a) in the equation?

*19. A social psychologist identified 10 national issues that currently are in the news. The psychologist recorded the amount of time that a TV network news program devoted to each issue. At the same time, a questionnaire was used to determine the perceived importance of each issue by the general public. These data are as follows:

Issue	Number of Seconds on TV News	Public Opinion Rating
1	23	35
2	65	92
3	32	50
4	56	70
5	45	75
6	15	25
7	90	96
8	20	38
9	82	65
10	25	41

a. Do these data indicate a significant relationship between news coverage and public opinion? Test with $\alpha = .05$.

b. Find the regression equation for using TV news time to predict the public's impression of importance.

c. A defensive politician might claim that these data show that the media are controlling public opinion. How would you answer this claim?

20. Pilots for public airlines face mandatory retirement at age 60. The airlines claim that this forced retirement is intended to ensure safety. To determine whether or not there is any relation between age and skill, a researcher collected data from a sample of $n = 11$ pilots. For each pilot, the researcher measured age and the pilot's score on a flight simulator test. The data are as follows:

Age	Skill
37	81
44	85
32	88
54	73
48	72
36	94
42	90
33	70
55	84
47	75
35	81

Do these data indicate a significant relation between age and flying skill? Test with $\alpha = .05$.

CHAPTER 18

The Binomial Distribution

TOOLS
YOU WILL
NEED

The following items are considered essential background material for this chapter. If you doubt your knowledge of any of these items, you should review the appropriate chapter or section before proceeding.

1. z-Scores (Chapter 5)
2. Probability (Chapter 6)
   a. Multiplication rule
   b. Addition rule
   c. The unit normal table
3. Hypothesis Tests (Chapter 8)

In 1960 Eleanor Gibson and Richard Walk designed a classic piece of apparatus to test depth perception (Gibson and Walk, 1960). Their device, called a *visual cliff*, consisted of a wide board with a deep drop (the cliff) to one side and a shallow drop on the other side. An infant was placed on the board and then observed to see whether he/she crawled off the shallow side or crawled off the cliff. (*Note*: Infants who moved to the deep side actually crawled onto a sheet of heavy glass which prevented them from falling. Thus, the deep side only appeared to be a cliff—hence the name *visual cliff*.)

Gibson and Walk reasoned that if infants are born with the ability to perceive depth, they would recognize the deep side and not crawl off the cliff. On the other hand, if depth perception is a skill that develops over time through learning and experience, then infants should not be able to perceive any difference between the shallow and the deep sides.

Out of 27 infants who moved off the board, only 3 ventured onto the deep side at any time during the experiment. Gibson and Walk interpreted these data as convincing evidence that depth perception is innate. The infants showed a systematic preference for the shallow side.

You should notice immediately that the data from this experiment are different from any we have encountered before. There aren't any scores. Gibson and Walk simply counted the number of infants who went off the deep end and the number who went to the shallow side. Still, we would like to use these data to make statistical decisions. Do these sample data provide sufficient evidence to make a confident conclusion about depth perception in the population? Suppose 8 of the 27 infants had crawled to the deep side. Would you still be convinced that there is a significant preference for the shallow side? What about 12 out of 27?

Notice that we are asking questions about probability and statistical significance. In this chapter we will examine the statistical techniques designed for use with data similar to those obtained in the visual cliff experiments. Each individual in the sample is classified into one of two possible categories (for example, deep or shallow), and we simply count the number in each category. These frequency data are then used to answer probability questions and to draw inferences about the general population.

18.1

Parametric and Nonparametric Statistical Tests

All of the statistical tests we have examined thus far are designed to test hypotheses about specific population parameters. For example, we used t tests to assess hypotheses about μ and later about $\mu_1 - \mu_2$. In addition, these tests typically make assumptions about the shape of the population distribution and about other population parameters. Recall that for analysis of variance the population distributions are assumed to be normal and homogeneity of variance is required. Because these tests all concern parameters and require assumptions about parameters, they are called *parametric tests*.

Another general characteristic of parametric tests is that they require a numerical score for each individual in the sample. The scores then are added, squared, averaged, and otherwise manipulated using basic arithmetic. In terms of measurement scales, parametric tests require data from an interval or a ratio scale (see Chapter 1).

Often, researchers are confronted with experimental situations that do not conform to the requirements of parametric tests. In these situations you should not attempt a parametric test. Remember, when the assumptions of a test are violated, the test may lead to an erroneous interpretation of the data. Fortunately, there are several hypothesis testing techniques that provide alternatives to parametric tests. These alternatives are called *nonparametric tests*.

In this chapter, and in the next two chapters, we will introduce some of the more commonly used nonparametric tests. You should notice that these nonparametric tests usually do not state hypotheses in terms of a specific parameter, and they make few (if any) assumptions about the population distribution. For the latter reason, nonparametric tests sometimes are called *distribution-free tests*. Another distinction is that nonparametric tests are well suited for data that are measured on nominal or ordinal scales. Finally, you should be warned that nonparametric tests generally do not have as much statistical power as parametric tests; nonparametric tests are more likely to fail in detecting a real difference between two treatments. Therefore, whenever the experimental data give you a choice between a parametric and a nonparametric test, you always should choose the parametric alternative.

Remember, statistical power is the probability that a test will reject a false null hypothesis.

18.2

Introduction to Binomial Tests

As mentioned earlier, parametric tests generally require data from an interval or a ratio scale. Occasionally, a researcher will find it inconvenient or impossible to obtain precise, numerical scores. Sometimes the best that can be done is to classify individuals into categories. This is measurement on a nominal scale.

In this chapter we will examine statistical procedures for use with nominal scales. The data will be the frequencies or number of individuals who end up in each category. To simplify things even further, we will look only at situations where there are exactly two categories. To summarize,

1. We have a nominal scale consisting of two separate categories.
2. Each individual in the sample is classified in one of the categories.
3. The sample data consist of the frequency or number of individuals in each category.

The statistical techniques we will be using are called *binomial tests*. The term *binomial* can be loosely translated as meaning "two names," referring to the two categories on the nominal scale. It may seem odd to have a special test developed for situations where the data consist of only two classifications, but quite often a researcher encounters an interesting situation where the data fit the binomial requirements exactly. Consider the following examples:

1. A school nurse has encountered 34 color-blind students in the past 5 years. Of these 34 students, 30 were males and only 4 were females. Is color blindness really more common for males than for females?
2. A college advisor has noticed that there are 6 psychology majors among the 10 student government officers. Is this an unusually large proportion?
3. A recent TV news program reported that 43% of Americans approve of the way the president is handling the economy. This report was based on a survey administered to a sample of 1000 people. Is this sample representative of the population?

Notice in each example that there are exactly two categories. The data reported are simply the frequencies corresponding to each category. Binomial data can occur when a variable naturally exists with only two categories. For example, people can be classified as male or female, and a coin toss results in either heads or tails. It also is common for a researcher to simplify data by collapsing them into two categories. For example, a company executive may classify employees by separating those who earn salaries above the state median income and those who earn below the median. In either case the resulting data are said to be *dichotomous*, consisting of exactly two categories. You also should notice that although the data are relatively simple, we are still asking the same statistical questions about probabilities and significance.

18.3
The Binomial Distribution

To answer probability questions or to perform hypothesis tests, we must know about the distribution of all possible outcomes. For the binomial tests, this means we must know about the binomial distribution. To define and describe this distribution, we first will introduce some notation:

1. The two categories are identified as A and B.
2. The probabilities (or proportions) associated with each category are identified as

$$p = P(A) = \text{the probability of } A$$
$$q = P(B) = \text{the probability of } B$$

Notice that $p + q = 1.00$ because A and B are the only two possible outcomes.
3. The number of individuals or observations in the sample is identified by n.
4. The variable X refers to the number of times category A occurs in the sample. Notice that X can have any value from 0 (none of the sample is in category A) to n (all of the sample is in category A).

DEFINITION

Using the notation presented, the *binomial distribution* shows the probability associated with each value of X from $X = 0$ to $X = n$.

A simple example of a binomial distribution is presented here.

EXAMPLE 18.1
Figure 18.1 shows the binomial distribution for the number of heads in four tosses of a balanced coin. This distribution

Figure 18.1
The binomial distribution showing the probability for the number of heads obtained in four tosses of a balanced coin.

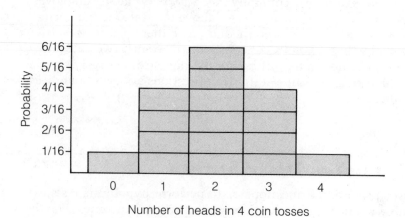

shows that it is possible to obtain as many as four heads or as few as zero heads in four tosses. The most likely outcome (highest probability) is to obtain exactly two heads in four tosses. The construction of this binomial distribution will now be discussed in detail.

Notice that the binomial distribution tends to form a normal shape.

For this example, the event we are considering is a coin toss. There are two possible outcomes, heads and tails. We assume the coin is balanced, so

$$p = P(\text{heads}) = \tfrac{1}{2}$$
$$q = P(\text{tails}) = \tfrac{1}{2}$$

We are looking at a sample of $n = 4$ tosses, and the variable of interest is

$$X = \text{number of heads}$$

To construct the binomial distribution, we will look at all the possible outcomes from tossing a coin four times. The complete set of 16 outcomes is as follows:

First Toss	Second Toss	Third Toss	Fourth Toss	
Heads	Heads	Heads	Heads	(all 4 heads)
Heads	Heads	Heads	Tails	(each sequence has exactly 3 heads)
Heads	Heads	Tails	Heads	
Heads	Tails	Heads	Heads	
Tails	Heads	Heads	Heads	
Heads	Heads	Tails	Tails	(each sequence has exactly 2 heads)
Heads	Tails	Heads	Tails	
Heads	Tails	Tails	Heads	
Tails	Heads	Heads	Tails	
Tails	Heads	Tails	Heads	
Tails	Tails	Heads	Heads	
Heads	Tails	Tails	Tails	(each sequence has exactly 1 head)
Tails	Heads	Tails	Tails	
Tails	Tails	Heads	Tails	
Tails	Tails	Tails	Heads	
Tails	Tails	Tails	Tails	(0 heads)

Notice that there are 16 possible outcomes (they have been organized systematically to ensure that all are listed). Only 1 of the 16 outcomes has all four heads, so the probability of obtaining four heads is $P = \tfrac{1}{16}$. Similarly, 4 of the 16 outcomes have exactly one head, so the probability of one head is $P = \tfrac{4}{16}$. The probability of two heads is $P = \tfrac{6}{16}$, the probability of three heads is $P = \tfrac{4}{16}$, and the probability of zero heads is $P = \tfrac{1}{16}$. These are the probabilities shown in Figure 18.1.

You should notice that this binomial distribution can be used to answer probability questions. For example, what is

Remember, probability corresponds to the area of the distribution.

the probability of obtaining more than two heads in four tosses? According to the distribution shown in Figure 18.1, the answer would be $P = \frac{5}{16}$.

18.4
Computing Probabilities in the Binomial Distribution

In most situations it would be extremely difficult to construct an entire binomial distribution like the one in Example 18.1. In addition, you rarely need the entire distribution in order to answer binomial questions. Most questions concern probabilities associated with individual values of X or with a specific range of X values. For example, you may want to know the probability of obtaining exactly seven heads in 10 tosses of a coin. Individual probabilities from a binomial distribution can be calculated using the binomial formula. Before we introduce this formula, we will briefly review some of the logic behind it.

In Example 18.1 we constructed a binomial distribution by looking at four tosses of a balanced coin and finding the probability associated with exactly zero heads, or one head, or two heads, etc. This example will serve as a model for the general process of computing probabilities with the binomial probability formula. Remember, in a binomial situation there are two possible outcomes A and B with probabilities

$$P(A) = p \qquad P(B) = q \qquad p + q = 1.00$$

Our goal is to find the probability that outcome A will occur exactly X times in a series of n events. To simplify the development of this probability formula, we first observe that each probability is obtained by a two-stage process.

Step 1. The first step is to identify all of the possible outcomes that result in exactly X occurrences of A in a sequence of n events. For example, there were four sequences that contain exactly one head ($X = 1$) in the series of $n = 4$ tosses:

H $\cdots$ T $\cdots$ T $\cdots$ T	(Note that the one head can occur either
T $\cdots$ H $\cdots$ T $\cdots$ T	first, second, third, or fourth in the set of
T $\cdots$ T $\cdots$ H $\cdots$ T	four tosses.)
T $\cdots$ T $\cdots$ T $\cdots$ H	

In general, the number of different sequences can be calculated by finding the number of *combinations* of X in n. This value is given by the formula

(18.1) number of combinations of X in n: $\quad C(X \text{ in } n) = \dfrac{n!}{(n-X)!\,X!}$

(*Note:* The "!" in the formula is called a factorial sign. This sign instructs you to compute a series of multiplications as in the following examples:

"six factorial" $= 6! = 6 \times 5 \times 4 \times 3 \times 2 \times 1 = 720$

"four factorial" $= 4! = 4 \times 3 \times 2 \times 1 = 24$

You also should know that by definition $0! = 1$.)

To demonstrate this formula, we will compute the number of different sequences that have $X = 1$ in $n = 4$:

$$C(1 \text{ in } 4) = \frac{4!}{(4-1)! \, 1!} = \frac{4 \times 3 \times 2 \times 1}{(3 \times 2 \times 1)(1)} = 4$$

(Note that this agrees with the fact that we found exactly four sequences that contained $X = 1$ head in $n = 4$ tosses.)

To compute the number of different sequences with $X = 2$ in $n = 4$,

$$C(2 \text{ in } 4) = \frac{4!}{(4-2)! \, 2!} = \frac{4 \times 3 \times 2 \times 1}{(2 \times 1)(2 \times 1)} = 6$$

(Note that this agrees with the fact that we found six sequences with $X = 2$ heads in $n = 4$ tosses in Example 18.1.)

Step 2. Next you must find the exact probability associated with each sequence of events. For the coin-toss example we are considering, the probability of heads is $p = \frac{1}{2}$, and the probability of tails is $q = \frac{1}{2}$. The probability of a sequence containing exactly one head and three tails would be

$$
\begin{aligned}
P(\text{H} \cdots \text{T} \cdots \text{T} \cdots \text{T}) &= P(\text{H}) \times P(\text{T}) \times P(\text{T}) \times P(\text{T}) \\
&= pqqq \\
&= \tfrac{1}{2}\left(\tfrac{1}{2}\right)\left(\tfrac{1}{2}\right)\left(\tfrac{1}{2}\right) \\
&= \tfrac{1}{16}
\end{aligned}
$$

The multiplication rule for probabilities (Chapter 6) states that the probability for a sequence of events is found by multiplying the probabilities for the individual events.

Notice that any sequence with one head and three tails will have this same probability.

In general, the probability for a specific sequence with X occurrences of A in a total of n events would be

$$P = pp \cdots pqq \cdots q$$

where p occurs X times (once for each A in the sequence) and q occurs $n - X$ times (once for each B in the sequence).

By using exponents to express the number of times p and q appear, this formula can be simplified to

$$P = p^X q^{n-X}$$

Remember, this is the probability of a specific sequence of n events that contains exactly X occurrences of A and exactly $n - X$ occurrences of B. For example, the sequence tails-heads-tails-tails contains one head and three tails. This sequence has a probability of

$$P = p^1 q^3 = \left(\tfrac{1}{2}\right)^1 \left(\tfrac{1}{2}\right)^3 = \tfrac{1}{2}\left(\tfrac{1}{8}\right) = \tfrac{1}{16}$$

The complete formula for the probability of X occurrences of A in a series of n events is obtained by combining the results of step 1 and step 2. For example, to obtain the exact probability of obtaining $X = 1$ head in $n = 4$ tosses, we simply combine the following facts:

1. There are exactly four sequences which contain one head and three tails.
2. Each of these sequences has a probability of $P = \frac{1}{16}$. Therefore,

$$P(X = 1) = (4\text{ sequences}) \times (P = \tfrac{1}{16}\text{ for each sequence})$$

$$= 4\left(\tfrac{1}{16}\right)$$

$$= \tfrac{4}{16}$$

DEFINITION

In general, the probability of obtaining X occurrences of event A in a series of n events is computed by the *binomial probability formula*:

(18.2) $\quad$ probability $= \dfrac{n!}{(n - X)!\,X!}\, p^X q^{n-X}$

Note that the first part of Formula (18.2) determines the number of different sequences of n events that contain exactly X occurrences of A. The second part of the formula determines the probability of each individual sequence. To construct the complete binomial distribution, you must compute the probability associated with every possible value of X.

18.5
Uses of the Binomial Distribution

The binomial distribution is used to answer two different types of statistical questions. First, this distribution can be used to determine the probability for a specific event if the values of p and q are known for a population. For example, a factory produces machine parts with a defective rate of $p = 0.003$ (three per thousand). What is the probability that a shipment of $n = 100$ parts will have no defective pieces? In this case, we are using known population values (p and q) to predict a sample. The second use of the binomial distribution is for inferential statistics, that is, using sample data to answer questions about unknown populations. The most commonly used inferential procedure is hypothesis testing, where a researcher uses sample data to evaluate a hypothesis about the values of p and q for a population.

Finding Probabilities

The use of the binomial distribution to find exact probability values is demonstrated in Example 18.2.

EXAMPLE 18.2

As noted earlier, it generally is not necessary to construct the entire binomial distribution to answer probability questions about specific events. In most cases, the probabilities can be obtained more efficiently by using the binomial probability formula.

Suppose, for example, you are taking a multiple-choice quiz. There are five questions, and each question has four choices for the answer. If you simply guessed at the answers, what is the probability that you would get exactly four questions right? For this example, the two possible outcomes are A = right and B = wrong. Because you are simply guessing among the four alternatives, the probabilities would be

$$P(\text{right}) = p = \tfrac{1}{4} \qquad P(\text{wrong}) = q = \tfrac{3}{4}$$

The quiz has a total of $n = 5$ questions, and we want the probability of getting exactly $X = 4$ correct. Using the binomial formula, we obtain

$$P(4 \text{ right out of } 5) = \frac{n!}{(n - X)!\,X!} p^X q^{n - X}$$

$$= \frac{5!}{1!\,4!} \left(\tfrac{1}{4}\right)^4 \left(\tfrac{3}{4}\right)^1$$

$$= 5(0.0039)(0.75)$$

$$= 0.1465$$

The probability of getting all five questions wrong would be

$$P(0 \text{ right out of } 5) = \frac{n!}{(n - X)!\,X!} p^X q^{n - X}$$

$$= \frac{5!}{5!\,0!} \left(\tfrac{1}{4}\right)^0 \left(\tfrac{3}{4}\right)^5$$

$$= 1(1)(0.2373)$$

$$= 0.2373$$

Note that $p^0 = 1$. Any value raised to the zero power is equal to 1.

Hypothesis Tests with the Binomial Distribution

Hypothesis tests using the binomial distribution follow the same structure as other hypothesis tests we have considered. As always, the procedure consists of four steps.

STEP 1.   *State the Hypotheses.* In the binomial test the null hypothesis will specify the population values for p and q. For example, a null hypothesis might state that a particular coin has $P(\text{heads}) = \tfrac{1}{2}$ and $P(\text{tails}) = \tfrac{1}{2}$. Note that the null hypothesis often states that there is "nothing wrong or unusual" about the probabilities. For example, our hypothesis states that the coin is balanced. Also note that the hypothesis refers to the population (for example, the set of all possible coin tosses). The data will consist of a small sample from this general population.

STEP 2. *Locate the Critical Region.* You should recall that the critical region is defined as those outcomes that are extremely unlikely if the null hypothesis is true. To locate the critical region, we construct the binomial distribution using the values of p and q from the null hypothesis. Then the critical region is identified as that portion of the distribution that has a probability value less than the alpha level.

STEP 3. *Obtain the Data.* At this stage you obtain a sample of n individuals (or events) and count how many times category A occurs in this set. The number of occurrences of A is the X value.

STEP 4. *Make Decision.* If the X value from the data is in the critical region, you should reject H_0. If the X value from the data is not in the critical region, you should fail to reject H_0.

A complete example of a hypothesis test with the binomial distribution follows.

EXAMPLE 18.3
In an experiment testing for extrasensory perception (ESP) a subject is required to predict the suit of a card that is randomly selected from a complete deck. In this experiment the subject is correct on five out of eight trials. Is this performance significantly better than would be expected by chance?

This is a binomial situation. On each trial there are two possible outcomes:

A = correct identification of the suit

B = incorrect identification

The actual values of $p = P(A)$ and $q = P(B)$ are unknown for this subject. However, if we hypothesize that there is no ESP and the subject is just guessing, then the probability of guessing correctly would be $p = \frac{1}{4}$, and the probability of guessing incorrectly would be $q = \frac{3}{4}$ (note that there are four suits in a deck of cards).

STEP 1. *State the Hypotheses*

H_0: $p = P(\text{correct}) = \frac{1}{4}$ (the subject has no ESP)

$q = P(\text{incorrect}) = \frac{3}{4}$

H_1: $p \neq \frac{1}{4}$ and $q \neq \frac{3}{4}$ (the subject is not performing at chance)

For this test we will use $\alpha = .05$.

STEP 2   and STEP 3. *Locate the Critical Region and Get the Data.* Because it is difficult and time-consuming to construct the entire binomial distribution, we will focus on the limited portion that is needed to make a statistical decision. Specifically, all we need to determine is whether or not the sample data (in this case, $X = 5$) are located in the critical region.

First make a rough sketch of the distribution. With $n = 8$ trials, you know that the possible X values range from $X = 0$ correct to $X = 8$ correct. Each of these X values has some probability value (as yet undetermined). Even though you do not know the exact probability associated with each X, you can draw a bar above each value, remembering that probabilities tend to be highest near the middle of the distribution. The result is a sketch of a distribution similar to the one in Figure 18.2.

With $\alpha = .05$, the critical region corresponds to the extreme 5% of this distribution. For a standard, nondirectional (two-tailed) test, this 5% would be divided equally between the two tails of the distribution with 2.5% ($P = 0.025$) in each tail. The problem is to determine the boundaries that sepa-

---

Figure 18.2

Rough sketch of the binomial distribution showing the number of cards guessed correctly in eight trials. Notice that the probability values are arbitrary—not precisely calculated. This is simply a sketch that can be used to help locate the critical region.

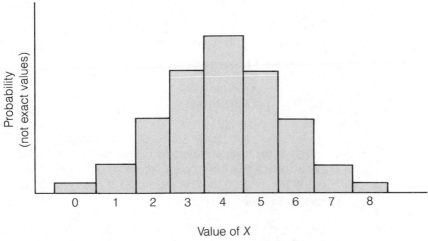

Value of X
(Number correctly identified in eight attempts)

rate the critical region from the rest of the distribution. To find these boundaries, we only need to compute probabilities for the extreme tails of the distribution. This should be much easier than computing all of the probability values.

Because the data, $X = 5$, are located toward the right-hand side of the distribution, we can simplify the calculations further by computing the critical region only for the right-hand tail of the distribution. We start with the most extreme score in the tail ($X = 8$) and calculate its probability. If this probability value is smaller than 0.025, we move to $X = 7$ and then $X = 6$ until we find the score that separates the extreme 2.5% from the rest of the distribution. This process will now be demonstrated.

$$P(X = 8) = \frac{8!}{0!\,8!}\, p^8 q^0$$
$$= 1\left(\tfrac{1}{4}\right)^8\left(\tfrac{3}{4}\right)^0$$
$$= 0.000015$$

Because this probability is substantially less than 0.025, the critical boundary must be located farther to the left. Therefore, we continue with $X = 7$:

$$P(X = 7) = \frac{8!}{1!\,7!}\, p^7 q^1$$
$$= 8\left(\tfrac{1}{4}\right)^7\left(\tfrac{3}{4}\right)^1$$
$$= 0.000366$$

Remember, the critical region consists of the total area in the tail of the distribution. Therefore, we will combine the probabilities for $X = 7$ and $X = 8$. Thus, the probability of obtaining a score at or beyond $X = 7$ is $0.000015 + 0.000366 = 0.000381$. This is less than 0.025, so we continue to move the boundary farther to the left:

$$P(X = 6) = \frac{8!}{2!\,6!}\, p^6 q^2$$
$$= 28\left(\tfrac{1}{4}\right)^6\left(\tfrac{3}{4}\right)^2$$
$$= 0.003842$$

The total area so far is found by combining the probability of 6 or 7 or 8 correct: $0.000015 + 0.000366 + 0.003842 = 0.004223$. This area is still less than 0.025, so continue:

$$P(X = 5) = \frac{8!}{3!\,5!}\, p^5 q^3$$

$$= 56\left(\tfrac{1}{4}\right)^5\left(\tfrac{3}{4}\right)^3$$
$$= 0.023066$$

Combining all of the values thus far gives a total probability of obtaining a score of 5 or more equal to $0.000015 + 0.000366 + 0.003842 + 0.023066 = 0.027289$.

Now we have moved the boundary too far; the total area in the tail exceeds the 0.025 (2.5%) that defines this critical region. Therefore, $X = 5$ cannot be included in the critical region. In this tail of the distribution, the critical region consists of scores $X = 6$ or greater.

STEP 4. *Make Decision*. Because the sample value, $X = 5$ correct out of 8, is not in the critical region, the decision is to fail to reject H_0.

In terms of the experimental variables, we conclude that the subject's performance in the experiment is not significantly different from what would be expected by chance.

LEARNING CHECK

1. What is the value of 5!?
2. If you are simply guessing on a multiple-choice test with four choices for each question, what is the probability that you would get exactly one out of three questions correct? (*Note*: If you are guessing, then the probability of guessing correctly is $P = \tfrac{1}{4}$ for each question.)
3. If you are simply guessing on a multiple-choice test with four choices for each question, what is the probability that you would get exactly two out of three questions wrong? (*Note*: If you are guessing, then the probability of guessing wrong is $P = \tfrac{3}{4}$ for each question.)
4. You should realize that Problems 2 and 3 are asking the same question. Did you get the same answer?
5. Under normal conditions there are equal numbers of males and females among newborn laboratory mice. A researcher is testing a new drug which claims to increase the chances of male offspring. The drug is given to a small sample of mice who then produce four newborn males and only one female. Are these data sufficient to conclude that the drug is effective. Test at the .05 level.

ANSWERS

1. 120.
2. $P = \tfrac{27}{64}$.
3. $P = \tfrac{27}{64}$.

4. One out of three right is the same as two out of three wrong.
5. If $p = q = \frac{1}{2}$, the probability of zero females in five births is $P = \frac{1}{32}$ and the probability of exactly one female out of five is $P = \frac{5}{32}$. Therefore, the probability of zero or one female is $\frac{6}{32} = 0.1875$, which is greater than the $0.025 = \alpha/2$ located in this tail of the distribution. Fail to reject H_0.

18.6
Normal Approximation of the Binomial Distribution

Although it is possible to compute the exact probabilities for a binomial distribution, it should be clear that these computations can be tedious and difficult. Fortunately, there is a very simple way to obtain precise estimates of the probability values for many binomial distributions. This simple procedure is based on the fact that the binomial distribution tends to approximate a normal distribution, particularly when the sample is relatively large and when both p and q are near $\frac{1}{2}$. Under these circumstances, the normal distribution can be used as an extremely accurate substitute for the binomial. The fact that the binomial distribution tends to have a normal shape can be seen in Figure 18.1.

It should not be surprising that the binomial distribution tends to be normal. Consider, for example, the distribution for the number of heads obtained in 100 tosses of a coin. Assuming the coin is fair so that $P(\text{heads}) = \frac{1}{2} = P(\text{tails})$, what would you expect to obtain in 100 tosses? Clearly, the most likely outcome would be around $X = 50$ heads. On the other hand, values far from 50 would be very unlikely. For example, you would not expect to get heads more than 80 times in 100 tosses. Notice that we have described a normal shaped distribution: The probabilities are highest in the middle (around $X = 50$), and they taper off as you move toward either extreme.

We have stated that the binomial distribution tends to approximate a normal distribution, particularly when n is large and when p and q are near $\frac{1}{2}$. To be more specific, the binomial distribution will be a nearly perfect normal distribution when pn and qn are both equal to or greater than 10. Under these circumstances, the binomial distribution will approximate a normal distribution with the following parameters:

Note: The value of 10 for pn *or* qn *is a general guide, not an absolute cutoff. Values slightly less than 10 still provide a good approximation. However, with smaller values the normal approximation becomes less accurate as a substitute for the binomial distribution.*

a. Mean: $\mu = pn$
b. Standard deviation: $\sigma = \sqrt{npq}$

Within this normal distribution, each value of X has a corresponding z-score:

$$(18.3) \quad z = \frac{X - \mu}{\sigma} = \frac{X - pn}{\sqrt{npq}}$$

The use of the normal distribution in place of the binomial distribution will greatly simplify the calculation of probabilities and hypothesis testing. With a normal distribution, probability values and alpha levels can be obtained directly from z-scores and the unit normal table without detailed calculation.

Finding Probabilities

Examples 18.4 and 18.5 demonstrate how the normal approximation to the binomial distribution can be used to compute probability values.

EXAMPLE 18.4

Suppose you are tossing a balanced coin 100 times. How many heads would you expect to obtain?

This is a question about a binomial distribution. We have two outcomes, heads and tails, with probabilities

$$p = P(\text{heads}) = \tfrac{1}{2}$$
$$q = P(\text{tails}) = \tfrac{1}{2}$$

With the sample of $n = 100$ it is unreasonable to compute probabilities for obtaining exactly one head, two heads, three heads, etc. Fortunately, this example meets the criteria for using the normal approximation to the binomial distribution.

With $n = 100$ tosses,

$$pn = \tfrac{1}{2}(100) = 50$$

and

$$qn = \tfrac{1}{2}(100) = 50 \quad \text{(both greater than 10)}$$

Therefore, the distribution for the number of heads out of 100 tosses will be normal with

$$\mu = pn = \tfrac{1}{2}(100) = 50$$

$$\sigma = \sqrt{npq} = \sqrt{100(\tfrac{1}{2})(\tfrac{1}{2})} = \sqrt{25} = 5$$

This distribution is shown in Figure 18.3.

The advantage of this normal distribution is that it is now possible to compute probabilities quickly and easily for any value of X. For example, what is the probability of obtaining more than 60 heads in a series of 100 tosses?

To answer the question, first locate the score $X = 60$ in the distribution. We want the probability, or proportion greater than this value (this portion has been shaded in Figure 18.3). The next step is to find the z-score corresponding to $X = 60$:

$$z = \frac{X - \mu}{\sigma} = \frac{60 - 50}{5} = \frac{10}{5} = +2.00$$

Figure 18.3

The binomial distribution (normal approximation) showing the number of heads obtained in 100 tosses of a balanced coin. The portion of the distribution corresponding to more than 60 heads has been shaded.

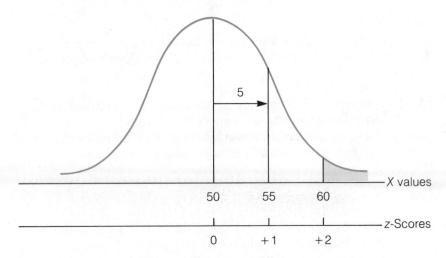

Now we look up the probability in the unit normal table. In this case, we want the proportion of the normal distribution that falls beyond a z-score of $+2.00$.

The value from the unit normal table is 0.0228. This is the answer we wanted; the probability of obtaining more than 60 heads in 100 tosses of a balanced coin is $P = 0.0228$ or 2.28%.

EXAMPLE 18.5

The normal approximation to the binomial distribution can be used to find the probability for any specific X value. However, you must remember that each X value actually corresponds to an interval in the normal distribution. For example, $X = 10$ actually is an interval from 9.5 to 10.5. The details of this process will now be demonstrated.

If you toss a balanced coin 16 times, what is the probability of obtaining exactly 10 heads?

For this example, the two outcomes are heads and tails and the two probabilities are

$$p = P(\text{heads}) = \tfrac{1}{2} = P(\text{tails}) = q$$

With $n = 16$, both pn and qn equal 8. Although the normal approximation will not be perfect, it should be reasonable. The normal distribution of the number of heads in 16 tosses is shown in Figure 18.4. Note that

$$\mu = pn = \tfrac{1}{2}(16) = 8$$

Figure 18.4

The binomial distribution (normal approximation) for the number of heads obtained in 16 tosses of a balanced coin. The shaded portion of the distribution corresponds to the probability of obtaining exactly $X = 10$ heads. Notice that the score $X = 10$ corresponds to an interval bounded by $X = 9.5$ and $X = 10.5$.

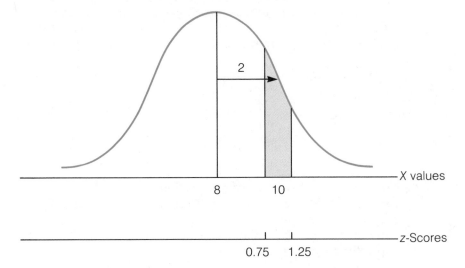

and

$$\sigma = \sqrt{npq} = \sqrt{16(\tfrac{1}{2})(\tfrac{1}{2})} = \sqrt{4} = 2$$

We want the proportion of this distribution that corresponds to $X = 10$, that is, the portion between $X = 9.5$ and $X = 10.5$. This portion is shaded in Figure 18.4.

To find the shaded portion, we first convert each X value into a z-score. For $X = 10.5$,

$$z = \frac{X - \mu}{\sigma} = \frac{10.5 - 8}{2} = \frac{2.5}{2} = 1.25$$

For $X = 9.5$,

$$z = \frac{X - \mu}{\sigma} = \frac{9.5 - 8}{2} = \frac{1.5}{2} = 0.75$$

Looking up these values in the unit normal table, we find that

    a. The area beyond $z = 1.25$ is 0.1056.
    b. The area beyond $z = 0.75$ is 0.2266.

Therefore, the area between these two values would be

    $0.2266 - 0.1056 = 0.1210$

Using the normal approximation to the binomial, we have found that

$$P(X = 10) = 0.1210$$

You should remember that this value is an approximation to the exact probability value. However, it is a reasonably accurate approximation. To demonstrate the accuracy of the normal approximation, we will use the binomial probability formula to find the precise value for this probability:

$$P(X = 10) = \frac{n!}{(n - X)!\,X!}\,p^X q^{n-X}$$

$$= \frac{16!}{6!\,10!}\left(\tfrac{1}{2}\right)^{10}\left(\tfrac{1}{2}\right)^6$$

$$= 8008(0.00097)(0.0156)$$

$$= 0.1222$$

Notice that the normal approximation value of 0.1210 is very close to the exact value of 0.1222. This is especially impressive because we were using a relatively small sample and did not strictly satisfy the criteria for using the normal approximation to the binomial.

Hypothesis Tests with the Normal Approximation

Example 18.6 demonstrates how the normal approximation can be used to test hypotheses about probability values p and q in a population.

EXAMPLE 18.6
In subliminal advertising, commercial messages are presented for extremely short periods of time so that subjects are unaware of having seen them. These messages often are flashed in the middle of TV shows or movies. Although people are not aware of seeing the messages, some researchers claim that the messages do affect behavior. To test this claim, the message "eat popcorn" is flashed subliminally during a movie. That evening, the theater owner counted 27 people who bought popcorn out of the total crowd of 100 people. Normally, only one-fifth of the theatergoers buy popcorn. Do these data indicate that the advertising worked? That is, are the sample data significantly different from what would be expected by chance?

This is a binomial hypothesis testing problem. The two categories are

A = buy popcorn
B = not buy

STEP 1. The null hypothesis would state that the advertising has no effect; the probability of any individual buying popcorn is still $\frac{1}{5}$. In symbols the hypotheses would be

H_0: $p = P(\text{buy popcorn}) = \frac{1}{5}$
    $q = P(\text{not buy}) = \frac{4}{5}$
H_1: $p \neq \frac{1}{5}$ and $q \neq \frac{4}{5}$ (the probabilities have changed)

We will use $\alpha = .05$.

STEP 2. To locate the critical region, we will need the binomial distribution. Because both pn and qn are greater than 10, we can use the normal approximation. This normal distribution is shown in Figure 18.5. Notice that

$$\mu = pn = \tfrac{1}{5}(100) = 20$$

and

$$\sigma = \sqrt{npq} = \sqrt{100(\tfrac{1}{5})(\tfrac{4}{5})} = \sqrt{16} = 4$$

The critical region consists of the most extreme 5% of this distribution. This portion is bounded by z-scores of $z = +1.96$ at one extreme and $z = -1.96$ at the other.

Figure 18.5
The binomial distribution (normal approximation) for the number of people buying popcorn ($p = 0.20$) out of a sample of $n = 100$. The most unlikely 5% of this distribution, the critical region, has been shaded.

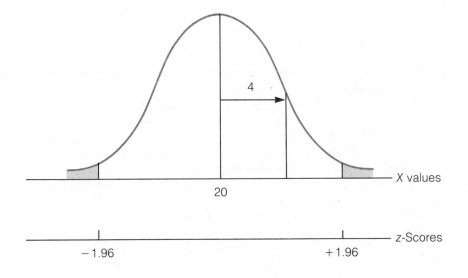

STEP 3. For this experiment, the data were $X = 27$ out of 100 people. These data correspond to a z-score of

$$z = \frac{X - \mu}{\sigma} = \frac{27 - 20}{4} = \frac{7}{4} = +1.75$$

STEP 4. Because the data are not in the critical region, our decision is to fail to reject H_0. These data do not provide sufficient evidence (with $\alpha = .05$) to conclude that the advertising produced any change in the proportion of people buying popcorn.

LEARNING CHECK

1. A multiple-choice test consists of 48 questions with four possible answers for each question. What is the probability that you would get more than half of the questions correct just by guessing?

2. If you toss a balanced coin 36 times, you would expect, on the average, to get 18 heads and 18 tails. What is the probability of obtaining exactly 18 heads in 36 tosses?

3. The makers of Brand X beer claim that people like their beer just as much as the leading brand. The basis for this claim is an experiment where 64 beer drinkers compared the two brands side by side. In this sample, 26 preferred Brand X and 38 preferred the leading brand. Do these data support the claim that there is no significant preference? Test at the .05 level.

ANSWERS

1. $p = \frac{1}{4}, q = \frac{3}{4}, z = 4, P = 0.00003$.
2. $z = \pm 0.17, P = 0.1350$.
3. $H_0: p = \frac{1}{2} = q, X = 26, z = -1.50$, fail to reject H_0. Conclude that there is no evidence for a significant preference.

18.7
The Sign Test

Although hypothesis tests with the binomial distribution are used in many situations, there is one specific case that merits special attention. Throughout this book we have observed that one of the basic experimental designs is repeated measures. You should recall that in a repeated measures experiment each subject is measured in several different experimental conditions; that is, you "repeat measurements" on the same subjects. The binomial distribution can use the data from a repeated measures experiment to test hypotheses about the difference between two treatment conditions. In this situation, the binomial test commonly is called a *sign test*.

The data for the sign test require that each individual be measured in two experimental conditions. The researcher then records the direction of the difference between the treatments. An example is as follows:

Subject	Treatment 1	Treatment 2	Difference
1	18	14	− (decrease)
2	23	10	− (decrease)
3	17	12	− (decrease)
4	31	33	+ (increase)
5	27	24	− (decrease)

Notice that the magnitude of the treatment effect is not important; the researcher records only the direction of the effect. Traditionally, increases and decreases in scores are noted by plus and minus signs in the data and hence the name sign test.

The null hypothesis for the sign test states that there is no difference between the two treatments. Therefore, any change in a subject's score is due to chance. In terms of probabilities, this means that increases and decreases are equally likely, so

$$p = P(\text{increase}) = \tfrac{1}{2}$$
$$q = P(\text{decrease}) = \tfrac{1}{2}$$

Because the data from the repeated measures experiment have been transformed into two categories (increases and decreases), we now have dichotomous data appropriate for a binomial test. The null hypothesis specifies probabilities for these two categories ($p = \tfrac{1}{2} = q$). A complete example of a sign test follows.

EXAMPLE 18.7

A researcher would like to test the effectiveness of a new antidepressant drug. A sample of 36 severely depressed patients is selected. These patients are clinically evaluated by a committee of psychiatrists before and after receiving the drug. In the judgment of the psychiatrists, 23 patients improved after being given the drug, and the remaining 13 patients worsened.

STEP 1. *State the Hypotheses*. The null hypothesis states that the drug has no effect. Any change in the patients is due to chance, so increases and decreases are equally likely. Expressed as probabilities, the hypotheses are

H_0: $p = P(\text{improve}) = \tfrac{1}{2}$
 $q = P(\text{worsen}) = \tfrac{1}{2}$

H_1: $p \neq q$ (changes are consistently in one direction or the other)

Set $\alpha = .05$.

STEP 2.   *Locate the Critical Region.* With $p = q = \frac{1}{2}$ and $n = 36$, the normal approximation to the binomial distribution is appropriate. This distribution is shown in Figure 18.6. Note that

$$\mu = pn = \tfrac{1}{2}(36) = 18$$

$$\sigma = \sqrt{npq} = \sqrt{36(\tfrac{1}{2})(\tfrac{1}{2})} = \sqrt{9} = 3$$

With $\alpha = .05$, the critical region is defined as the most extreme 5% of the distribution. This portion is bounded by z-scores of $z = +1.96$ at one extreme and $z = -1.96$ at the other.

STEP 3.   *Get the Data.* For this sample we have $X = 23$ patients who improved. This score corresponds to a z-score of

$$z = \frac{X - \mu}{\sigma} = \frac{23 - 18}{3} = \frac{5}{3} = 1.67$$

STEP 4.   *Make Decision.* Because the data are not in the critical region, we fail to reject H_0. These data do not provide sufficient evidence (with $\alpha = .05$) to conclude that the drug has any consistent effect on the patients.

Figure 18.6
The binomial distribution (normal approximation) for the sign test in Example 18.7.

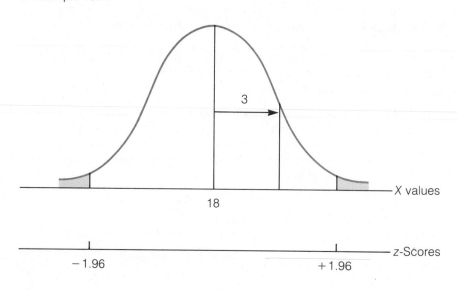

Zero Differences in the Sign Test

You should notice that the null hypothesis in the sign test refers only to those individuals who show some difference between treatment 1 versus treatment 2. The null hypothesis states that if there is any change in an individual's score then the probability of an increase is equal to the probability of a decrease. Stated in this form, the null hypothesis does not consider individuals who show zero difference between the two treatments. As a result, the usual recommendation is that these individuals be discarded from the data and the value of n be reduced accordingly. However, if the null hypothesis is interpreted more generally, it states that there is no difference between the two treatments. Phrased this way, it should be clear that individuals who show no difference actually are supporting the null hypothesis and should not be discarded. Therefore, an alternative approach to the sign test is to divide individuals who show zero differences equally between the positive and negative categories. (With an odd number of zero differences, discard one and divide the rest evenly.) This alternative results in a more conservative test; that is, the test is more likely to fail to reject the null hypothesis.

EXAMPLE 18.8
It has been demonstrated that stress or exercise causes an increase in the concentration of certain chemicals called endorphins in the brain. Endorphins are similar to morphine and produce a generally relaxed feeling and a sense of well-being. The endorphins may explain the "high" experienced by long-distance runners. To demonstrate this phenomenon, a researcher tested pain tolerance for 40 athletes before and after they completed a mile run. Immediately after running, the ability to tolerate pain increased for 21 of the athletes, decreased for 12, and showed no change for the remaining 7.

Following the standard recommendation for handling zero differences, you would use $n = 33$ for the sign test because only 33 subjects showed any difference between the two treatments. The other 7 athletes are eliminated from the sample. With the more conservative approach, only 1 of the 7 athletes who showed no difference would be discarded, and the other 6 would be divided equally between the two categories. This would result in a total of $n = 39$ in the sample data with 24 (21 + 3) in one category and 15 (12 + 3) in the other.

When to Use the Sign Test

In many cases, data from a repeated measures experiment can be evaluated using either a sign test or a repeated measures t test. In general, you should use the t test whenever possible. Because the t test uses the actual difference scores (not just the signs), it makes maximum use of the available information and results in a more powerful test. However, there are some cases where a *t* test cannot or should not be used, and in these situations the sign test can be valuable. Three specific cases where a *t* test is inappropriate or inconvient will now be described.

1. When you have infinite or undetermined scores, a *t* test is impossible, and the sign test is appropriate. Suppose, for example, you are evaluating the effects of a sedative drug on problem-solving ability. A sample of rats is obtained, and each animal's performance is measured before and after receiving the drug. Hypothetical data are as follows:

Before	After	Difference
20	23	+3
14	39	+25
27	Failed	+??
⋮	⋮	⋮

Note that the third rat in this sample failed to solve the problem after receiving the drug. Because there is no score for this animal, it is impossible to compute a sample mean, an *SS*, or a *t* statistic. But you could do a sign test because you know that the animal made more errors (an increase) after receiving the drug.

2. Often it is possible to describe the difference between two treatment conditions without precisely measuring a score in either condition. In a clinical setting, for example, a doctor can say whether a patient is improving, growing worse, or showing no change even though the patient's condition is not precisely measured by a score. In this situation, the data are sufficient for a sign test, but you could not compute a *t* statistic without individual scores.

3. Often a sign test is done as a preliminary check on an experiment before serious statistical analysis begins. For example, a researcher may predict that scores in treatment 2 should be consistently greater than scores in treatment 1. However, examination of the data after 1 week indicates that only 8 of 15 subjects showed the predicted increase. On the basis of these preliminary results, the researcher may choose to reevaluate the experiment before investing additional time.

1. A developmental psychologist is using a behavior modification program to help control the disruptive behavior of 40 children in a local school. After 1 month, 26 of these children have

improved, 10 are worse, and 4 show no change in behavior. On the basis of these data, can the psychologist conclude that the program is working? Test at the .05 level.

ANSWER

1. Discarding the 4 subjects who showed zero difference, $X = 26$ increases out of $n = 36$; $z = 2.67$; reject H_0; the program is working.

Summary

1. The binomial distribution is used with dichotomous data, that is, when each individual in the sample is classified in one of two categories. The two categories are identified as A and B, with probabilities of

   $$P(A) = p \quad \text{and} \quad P(B) = q$$

2. The binomial distribution gives the probability for each value of X, where X equals the number of occurrences of category A in a sequence of n events. For example, X equals the number of heads in $n = 10$ tosses of a coin.

3. The probability of obtaining exactly X occurrences of A in n events can be computed by the formula

   $$P(X) = \frac{n!}{(n - X)!\, X!}\, p^X q^{n - X}$$

4. When pn and qn are both at least 10, the binomial distribution is closely approximated by a normal distribution with

   $$\mu = pn$$
   $$\sigma = \sqrt{npq}$$

   By using this normal approximation, each value of X has a corresponding z-score:

   $$z = \frac{X - \mu}{\sigma} = \frac{X - pn}{\sqrt{npq}}$$

   With the z-score and the unit normal table, you can find probability values associated with any value of X.

5. When the population values for p and q are known, the binomial distribution (or the normal approximation) can be used to find the probability of obtaining any specific sample.

6. If p and q are unknown for a population, a sample can be used to test hypotheses about these probability values. The null hypothesis specifies p and q, and the binomial distribution (or the normal approximation) is used to determine the critical region.

7. One common use of the binomial distribution is for the sign test. This test evaluates the difference between two treatments using the data from a repeated measures design. The difference scores are coded as being either increases (+) or decreases (−). Without a consistent treatment effect, the increases and decreases should be mixed randomly so the null hypothesis states that

$$P(\text{increase}) = \tfrac{1}{2} = P(\text{decrease})$$

With dichotomous data and hypothesized values for p and q, this is a binomial test.

Key Terms

parametric statistical test
nonparametric statistical test
dichotomous data

binomial distribution
combinations of X in n
sign test

Problems for Chapter 18:
The Binomial Distribution

*1. Suppose you are tossing a balanced coin. If it comes up heads four times in a row, what is the probability that it will be heads on the fifth toss?

2. If you are tossing a balanced coin five times,
   a. How many different ways are there to obtain exactly one heads and four tails?
   b. How many different ways are there to obtain exactly two heads and three tails?
   c. Every possible sequence of heads and tails has exactly the same probability. What is this probability?

*3. An extensive survey 2 years ago indicated that 80% of the population of New York State favored income tax over sales tax as a means of increasing state revenue. In a recent sample of 100 people, 72 preferred income tax, and 28 preferred sales tax. Do these data indicate a significant change in opinion? Test at the .05 level of significance.

4. The National Weather Service reports that for the first 70 days of this year 42 days have had temperatures lower than last year, 22 days had higher temperatures, and 6 days show no difference. Do these data indicate that this year's temperatures are significantly different from last year's? Test at the .05 level.

*5. In a recent study examining color preference in infants, six babies were offered a choice between a red rattle and a green rattle. Five of the six selected the red rattle. Do these data provide evidence for a significant color preference? Test at the .05 level of significance.

6. A multiple-choice exam has 48 questions, each with four possible answers.

   a. Using the normal approximation to the binomial distribution, what is the probability that someone will get exactly 12 questions correct by just guessing? (Note that you must use the real limits for $X = 12$.)

   b. If a passing grade on this test is $X = 27$, what is the probability of obtaining a passing grade by just guessing?

*7. A sample of 40 children is selected for an experiment to evaluate the effect of teacher's sex on classroom performance. Each child is given a task while being observed by a male teacher and then a similar task while being observed by a female teacher. Of these 40 children, 20 were judged to work better for the female teacher, 8 worked better for the male teacher, and 12 worked equally well in the two situations. Do these results indicate that the teacher's sex has a significant influence on performance? Test with $\alpha = .05$.

8. An English professor conducts a special 1-week course in writing skills for freshmen who are poorly prepared for college-level writing. To test the effectiveness of this course, each student in a recent class of $n = 36$ was required to write a short paragraph describing a painting before the course started. At the end of the course, the students were once again required to write a paragraph describing the same painting. The students' paragraphs were then given to another instructor to be evaluated. For 25 students the writing was judged to be better after the course. For the rest of the class, the first paragraph was judged to be better. Do these results indicate a significant change in performance? Test at the .05 level.

*9. A college dormitory recently sponsored a taste comparison between two major soft drinks. Of the 64 students who participated, 39 selected Brand A, and only 25 selected Brand B. Do these data indicate a significant preference? Test at the .05 level of significance.

10. An automobile manufacturer is developing a computer for its cars. Among other things, the computer will "talk to" the driver to warn of open doors, unfastened seat belts, low fuel levels, etc. The company would like to know whether the computer should have a masculine or a feminine voice. When two

voices were tested with a sample of 36 people, 30 preferred the masculine voice, and only 6 preferred the feminine voice. Do these data represent a significant preference? Test at the .05 level of significance.

*11. A student recently got 24 out of 36 questions correct on a true/false quiz. Although the student got 67% correct, she was given a grade of E.

    a. On average, how many questions would a student get correct if he/she were simply guessing?

    b. What is the probability of getting 24 or more questions correct just by guessing?

    c. Is it reasonable for the instructor to conclude that a score of $X = 24$ does not provide convincing evidence of any knowledge? Explain your answer.

12. A trick coin has been weighted so that the probability of heads is 0.9 and the probability of tails is 0.1.

    a. If you toss this coin four times, what is the probability of obtaining all four heads?

    b. What is the probability of obtaining exactly three heads in four tosses?

    c. What is the probability of obtaining at least three heads in four tosses? (*Note*: "At least three" means either three or four.)

*13. Nationwide, only 4% of the population develops ulcers each year. In a sample of 200 executive vice presidents, 40 had developed ulcers during the previous 12 months. Do these data indicate that vice presidents have a higher incidence of ulcers than the general population? Test at the .05 level of significance.

14. A large manufacturing company produces automobile spark plugs with a defective rate of $P = 0.06$.

    a. If you buy a set of four plugs for your car, what is the probability that you will get no defective plugs?

    b. If you buy four plugs, what is the probability that you will get exactly one defective plug?

    c. If you buy eight plugs, what is the probability that none will be defective?

    d. If you buy eight plugs, what is the probability of getting exactly one defective plug?

*15. Use $\alpha = .05$ to answer each of the following questions. Use the normal approximation to the binomial distribution.

a. For a true/false test with 20 questions, how many would you have to get right to do significantly better than chance?

b. How many would you need to get right on a 40-question test?

c. How many would you need to get right on a 100-question test?

16. A television commercial claims that four out of five people prefer Brand X potato chips over Brand Y.

a. If this claim is based on a sample of $n = 5$, is the result sufficient to claim a significant preference at the .05 level of significance? Use the binomial probability formula.

b. If this claim is based on a sample of $n = 50$ (40 out of 50 preferred Brand X), is there evidence for a significant preference? Use the normal approximation to the binomial distribution and test with $\alpha = .05$.

*17. Biofeedback training often is used to help people who suffer migraine headaches. A recent study found that 29 out of 50 subjects reported a decrease in the frequency and severity of their headaches after receiving biofeedback training. Of the remaining subjects in this study, 10 reported that their headaches were worse, and 11 reported no change.

a. Discard the zero difference subjects and use a sign test with $\alpha = .05$ to determine whether or not the biofeedback produced a significant difference.

b. Divide the zero difference subjects between the two groups and use a sign test to evaluate the effect of biofeedback training.

18. In the general population, 8 out of 10 people can be hypnotized. A researcher suspects that the ability to be hypnotized is partially determined by an individual's personality. A sample of $n = 80$ subjects is obtained. All of these subjects are known to be *field independent*, which means that they tend to rely on internal cues rather than external cues for making judgments. The researcher finds that 51 of these 80 subjects can be hypnotized. Do these data indicate that field-independent people are different from the general population in terms of their ability to be hypnotized? Test at the .05 level of significance.

*19. The sense of smell plays an important role in the "taste" of food. A favorite demonstration of this fact involves having people hold their noses while tasting slices of apple and onion. Without smell, these two taste much the same. In a sample of 25 people who tried this demonstration, only 15 were able to correctly identify the onion. Is this significantly better than chance? Test at the .05 level of significance.

20. In a study of human memory, Sachs (1967) demonstrated that people recall the meaning of verbal material but tend to forget the exact word-for-word details. In this study, people read a passage of text. Then the people were shown a test sentence and asked whether or not the identical sentence had appeared in the text. In one condition the test sentence was phrased differently but had the same meaning as a sentence which was in the text. For example, the sentence in the text might be "The boy hit the ball," and the test sentence might be "The ball was hit by the boy." If only 27 out of 45 people correctly notice the change in the sentence, can you conclude that their performance is significantly better than chance? Test at the .05 level of significance.

*21. A psychologist examining the psychology of art appreciation selected an abstract painting that had no obvious top or bottom. Hangers were placed on the painting so that it could be hung with any one of the four sides at the top. This painting was shown to a sample of $n = 50$ undergraduates, and each was asked to hang the painting in whatever orientation "looked best." Twenty-three of the subjects in this sample placed the painting so that the correct side was up. Is this significantly better than would be expected by chance? Test with $\alpha = .05$.

22. In the preview section of this chapter, we noted that Gibson and Walk (1960) reported that only 3 of 27 infants crawled off the deep side of the visual cliff.
    a. With $\alpha = .01$, do these data indicate a significant preference for the shallow side?
    b. If 10 out of 27 had crawled to the deep side, would the data still indicate a significant preference? Use $\alpha = .01$.

CHAPTER 19

The Chi Square Statistic: Tests for Goodness of Fit and Independence

TOOLS
YOU WILL
NEED

The following items are considered essential background material for this chapter. If you doubt your knowledge of any of these items, you should review the appropriate chapter or section before proceeding.

1. Proportions (math review, Appendix A)
2. Parametric versus nonparametric tests (Chapter 18)

Once in a while we hear a horrifying report in which passersby observe a person in trouble and yet do not go to the victim's aid. While some people have attributed bystander apathy to the alienating and dehumanizing aspect of modern life, Darley and Latané (1968) suggested that the number of witnesses is the key variable in determining if aid will be given. Specifically, if *one* person observes someone in trouble, the observer tends to feel personally responsible for that individual and therefore is likely to assist. However, if there is a *group* of observers, the responsibility for the victim gets "spread thin" among the witnesses. That is, no one feels personally responsible for the victim, and the chances that someone will help is much smaller. This interpretation has been called *diffusion of responsibility*. Darley and Latané (1968) tested the effect of group size on bystander apathy to see if their interpretation was correct.

Subjects were asked to participate in group discussions concerning problems adjusting to college life. To ensure anonymity, each participant sat in a separate room, and the discussion was held over an intercom. In each discussion group, all but one of the subjects were actually "confederates," or research assistants posing as subjects. At one point during the experiment, the subject was led to believe that one of the participants was having an epileptic seizure by a recording that was played over the intercom. For the dependent variable, Darley and Latané noted how many people tried to help the victim and how many did not respond. The independent variable was the perceived size of the group of observers. The smallest group consisted of the subject and the "victim." In the other treatment conditions, the real subjects thought there were three or as many as six participants in the discussion. The findings are summarized in Table 19.1. Notice that the data consist of frequencies. Every subject is categorized according to group assignment and the type of response made. There is a frequency distribution for each treatment consisting of the number of people who did and did not help. For example, in group sizes of two (subject and victim), the distribution consists of 11 subjects helping and 2 not helping the victim. On the other hand, for groups of six, 4 subjects assisted and 9 did not. It appears as though group size has an effect on the likelihood that a person will aid the victim. To confirm this hypothesis, a statistical test is needed that is capable of testing hypotheses about entire frequency distributions. In this chapter, we will examine a statistical test called *chi square*, which can test hypotheses about the form and shape of frequency distributions. We will return to the bystander apathy study later in the chapter to determine if there is a relationship between the number of observers and aid-giving behavior.

Table 19.1
The Relationship Between the Size of Group and the Type of Response to the Victim

	Group Size		
	2	3	6
Assistance	11	16	4
No Assistance	2	10	9

J. M. Darley and B. Latané (1968). Bystander intervention in emergencies: Diffusion of responsibility. *Journal of Personality and Social Psychology, 8,* 377–383. Copyright (1968) by the American Psychological Association. Adapted with permission of the publisher and author.

19.1

Chi Square Test for Goodness of Fit

Rationale of the Test

In this chi square test, the researcher is testing a hypothesis about the shape of the population frequency distribution. The null hypothesis predicts a specific type of distribution for the population. Sample data are then collected to test the hypothesis. The chi square statistic then compares the frequency distribution obtained for the sample to the frequency distribution that is specified by the null hypothesis. The chi square test determines how well the sample data fit the hypothesis—hence the name of the test, *goodness of fit.* A large discrepancy (a poor fit) between the sample data and the hypothesized data would result in a decision to reject the null hypothesis. To explain the various components and mechanics of the goodness-of-fit test, let us begin with an example.

DEFINITION

The *goodness-of-fit test* determines how well a frequency distribution for a sample fits a distribution predicted by the null hypothesis.

EXAMPLE 19.1
A marketing researcher would like to determine if shoppers have a preference for one of three major department stores in a large suburban mall. Sixty shoppers are stopped at the mall and asked to select the store that they would like to

shop at the most if they were allowed to shop at only one. That is, the shoppers are placed in a *forced-choice* situation. They must respond by selecting one store. Their responses can then be classified into one of three categories: store A, store B, or store C.

The Null Hypotheses and Expected Frequencies

For the study described in Example 19.1, the null hypothesis might state that there is no preference among the three stores in the population of shoppers. For the chi square test for goodness of fit, the null hypothesis always specifies the proportion (or percentage) of the population that should be found in each category. In this example, we would expect that exactly one-third of the population will select store A, one-third will select store B, and one-third will select store C if no preference exists in the population. Notice that the null hypothesis predicts the shape of the frequency distribution for the population.

Once the null hypothesis has been stated, it can be used to predict a sample distribution for any size sample. For the example, the null hypothesis would predict that one-third of the sample should select store A, one-third should select store B, and one-third should select store C. Thus, for a sample of $n = 60$ people, we would expect 20 people (one-third of 60) to choose each of the three stores. The frequency values predicted from the null hypothesis are called *expected frequencies*. For each category on the scale of measurement, the expected frequency is computed by

(19.1) expected frequency $= f_e = pn$

where p is the hypothesized proportion or percentage for that category and n is the sample size. Note that the symbol for expected frequency is f_e. The expected frequencies for the study in Example 19.1 are shown in Table 19.2.

Table 19.2

Part A: Expected Frequencies (f_e) for Shoppers' Preference

	Store A	Store B	Store C	
f_e	20	20	20	$n = 60$

Part B: The Number (f_o) of Shoppers Selecting Each Store

	Store A	Store B	Store C	
f_o	24	22	14	$n = 60$

The *expected frequency* for each category is the frequency value specified by the null hypothesis.

Observed Frequencies

The actual frequencies that are obtained from the subjects' responses are called the *observed frequencies*. Table 19.2 summarizes the sample data for Example 19.1. Each cell contains the frequency of people who selected that store as the most preferred place to shop. Note that each person's response falls into one of three categories. Therefore, we are dealing with a nominal scale of measurement. It is important to also note that the frequencies in one category are independent of frequencies in the other categories. That is, individuals had to choose just *one store* as their preference. Therefore, the frequencies in one cell are made up of responses by people different from those in the other cells. The sum of the observed frequencies should always equal the sum of the expected frequencies. This rule provides a good way to check the accuracy of the expected frequencies that have been computed from the null hypothesis.

Note: $\Sigma f_e = \Sigma f_o$ $= n$.

The *observed frequency* is the actual frequency of responses obtained for a particular category.

The Chi Square Statistic

As stated earlier, the chi square test for goodness of fit determines how well the data (observed frequencies) fit the null hypothesis (expected frequencies). If there is a large discrepancy between f_o and f_e, we will conclude that the data do not fit the hypothesis, and H_0 will be rejected. On the other hand, when there is a reasonable fit between the data and the null hypothesis, we cannot reject H_0. The chi square statistic provides a method of measuring how good (or poor) the fit is.

The value of chi square is computed by following these steps:

1. First find the difference between the observed and expected frequency for each category, or

    $$f_o - f_e$$

    This difference measures how well the data (f_o) fit the hypothesis (f_e).

2. Because some of the differences will be positive and some will be negative, each is squared to eliminate negative signs, or

$$(f_o - f_e)^2$$

3. Next the value for each category is divided by its expected frequency. A justification for this step is given in Box 19.1. At this stage, we have a value computed for each category consisting of

$$\frac{(f_o - f_e)^2}{f_e}$$

This value provides a measure of how well the sample data (f_o) fit the hypothesized data (f_e) for a particular category.

4. The final step is to sum these values (from step 3) from all of the categories. This sum provides a measure of the total amount of discrepancy between the expected and observed frequencies. The complete formula for the four steps is

$$\textbf{(19.2)} \quad \text{chi square} = \chi^2 = \Sigma \frac{(f_o - f_e)^2}{f_e}$$

The symbol χ^2 is the Greek letter chi, and it is squared to reflect that the statistic is based on squared differences for each category.

For the data in Example 19.1 (Table 19.2) we obtain a chi square value of

$$\chi^2 = \Sigma \frac{(f_o - f_e)^2}{f_e}$$

$$= \frac{16}{20} + \frac{4}{20} + \frac{36}{20}$$

$$= 0.8 + 0.2 + 1.8 = 2.8$$

Distribution of Chi Square

It should be clear from the chi square equation that chi square will equal zero if the match between the sample data and hypothesized data is perfect. Of course, there is typically a small amount of discrepancy between f_o and f_e even when H_0 is true, resulting in a small nonzero value for chi square. When chi square values are small, we fail to reject H_0. On the other hand, a large chi square value indicates a real mismatch between the observed and expected frequencies. This outcome would cause us to reject H_0. To decide whether a particular chi square value is "large" or "small," we must refer to the chi square distribution. The chi square distribution consists of the chi square values for all possible random samples when H_0 is true. Much like

BOX 19.1 **The Chi Square Formula**

We have seen that the chi square formula compares observed frequencies to expected frequencies in order to assess how well the sample data match the hypothesized data. This function of the chi square statistic is easy to spot in the numerator of the equation, $(f_o - f_e)^2$. The difference between the observed and expected frequencies is found first. The greater this difference, the more discrepancy there is between what is observed and what is expected. The difference is then squared to remove the negative signs (large discrepancies may have negative signs as well as positive signs). The summation sign in front of the equation indicates that we must examine the amount of discrepancy for every category. Why, then, must we divide the squared differences by f_e for each category before we sum the category values? Basically, we would view the $f_o - f_e$ discrepancies in a different light if f_e were very small or very large.

Suppose you were going to throw a party and you *expected* 1000 people to show up. However, at the party you counted the number guests and *observed* that 1040 actually showed up. Forty more guests than expected are no major problem when all along you were planning for 1000. There will still probably be enough beer and potato chips for everyone. On the other hand, suppose you had a party and you expected 10 people to attend but instead 50 actually showed up. Forty more guests in this case spell big trouble. How "significant" the discrepancy is depends in part on what you were originally expecting. With very large expected frequencies, allowances are made for more error between f_o and f_e. This is accomplished in the chi square formula by dividing the squared discrepancy for each category, $(f_o - f_e)^2$, by its expected frequency.

other distributions we have examined (distribution of sample means, t distribution, F distribution), the chi square distribution is a theoretical distribution whose characteristics are well known. Some of these characteristics are easy to infer from the chi square formula.

First, it should be obvious that a chi square value can never be less than zero. It would be impossible to obtain a negative value for chi square because the $f_o - f_e$ differences are squared. Second, as noted earlier, when H_0 is true, we expect the chi square value to be relatively small. That is, the obtained data (f_o) should be relatively close to, if not the same as, the hypothesized data (f_e). These two characteristics suggest that when H_0 is true the chi square values will form a positively skewed distribution. It should begin at zero, show a peak for χ^2 values at or near zero, and then taper off so that large extreme values will be unlikely. An example of a chi square distribution is shown in Figure 19.1.

In locating the critical region for a chi square test, we will separate the main body of the distribution from the extreme values in the tail

Figure 19.1
Chi square distributions are positively skewed. The critical region is placed in the extreme tail, which reflects large chi square values.

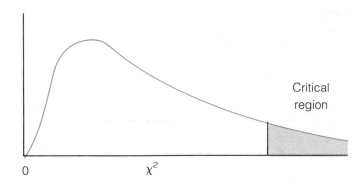

(Figure 19.1). With $\alpha = .05$, for example, we designate the most extreme 5% of the distribution as the critical region. Notice that if H_0 were true, it would be very unlikely to obtain sample data that will yield a chi square value which falls in this critical region. In fact, a value in this region indicates that the sample data do not fit the frequencies predicted by the null hypothesis. Therefore, a chi square value that falls in the extreme tail of the distribution will lead us to reject the null hypothesis.

Recall that we have always defined "unlikely" by the level of significance selected for the hypothesis test.

Degrees of Freedom

There is another factor that plays a role in the exact shape of the chi square distribution—the number of categories. You should recall that the chi square statistic sums values from every category. Therefore, even if H_0 were true, the more categories used, the larger the sum would be. That is, even when H_0 is true, there can be a small amount of error between f_o and f_e in each category. As we increase the number of categories used in the study, we will also increase the number of discrepancies that are added together to compute chi square. Therefore, the shape of the chi square distribution will change as the number of categories changes. This change can be seen at the peak of the distribution, the most likely (modal) chi square value when H_0 is true (it can also be seen at the tails; see Box 19.2). With only a few categories, the chi square value is expected to be very small (few discrepancies are being added together), and the distribution will peak at zero or slightly above zero. With 9 or 10 categories, the expected chi will be larger, because more category discrepancies are summed. The distribution will have a mode at a larger χ^2 value. Thus there is a family of chi square distributions, with the exact shape of each distribution depending on the number of categories used in the study.

The Number of Categories and the Size of the Critical Chi Square Value

It was noted that there is a family of chi square distributions and that the precise shape of each distribution depends on the number of degrees of freedom. It is useful to compare these distributions in order to get a better understanding of the chi square test. Specifically, what happens to the critical region of chi square distributions when the value for df is changed? In previous situations where a family of distributions exists, increasing the df value results in smaller critical values (t distributions, for example, in Chapter 10). In the chi square family, increases in the value of df are accompanied by *increases* in the critical value for χ^2. Note that for $df = 1$ and when alpha is .05, the critical chi square is 3.84. For $df = 9$ at the same level of significance, the critical value is much more extreme, namely $\chi^2 = 16.92$. The critical value increases because larger values of chi square are easier to obtain with larger df, even if H_0 is true. This point should become more obvious when you consider how χ^2 is computed.

Remember, the chi square is based on the $f_o - f_e$ difference for each category. The summation sign in the chi square formula indicates that every category contributes its $f_o - f_e$ discrepancy to the obtained chi square value. Even if H_0 is true, small discrepancies can exist between f_o and f_e for each category. When the chi square statistic is computed, a small nonzero value will be obtained. If $df = 1$, then these discrepancies ordinarily do not result in a large chi square value because there are only two categories contributing to the chi square value. However, when $df = 9$, a small amount of error between f_o and f_e in each of the 10 categories will yield a larger chi square value—even if H_0 is true. Therefore, the table of critical chi square values reflects the fact that it is easier to get larger values of chi square by chance (when H_0 is true) for studies in which df is large. The table provides larger critical values with increasing values of degrees of freedom.

Technically, degrees of freedom are used, instead of number of categories, to identify a specific chi square distribution. There is a df value associated with every chi square test. For the chi square statistic used in the goodness-of-fit test, the degrees of freedom are determined by

(19.3) degrees of freedom $= df = C - 1$

where C is the number of categories. Figure 19.2 depicts the shape of several chi square distributions for different df values.

The df value indicates how many categories are free to vary when determining the values for their expected frequencies. As the formula indicates, all but one category are free to vary. Consider the expected

Figure 19.2

The shape of the chi square distribution for different values of *df*. As the number of categories increase, the peak (mode) of the distribution has a larger chi square value.

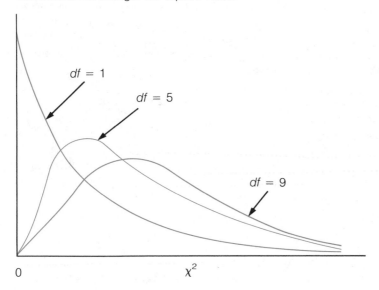

frequencies for Example 19.1 (Table 19.2). Out of $n = 60$ people who are asked to choose their favorite store, we expected one-third ($f_e = 20$) to choose store A and one-third (again, $f_e = 20$) to choose store B. Now that the f_e values for the first two categories are determined, the expected frequency for store C must be the remaining one-third of the distribution—also $f_e = 20$. In this example, there are two categories that are free to vary; therefore, $df = 2$. By using Formula (19.3), this value is confirmed:

$$df = C - 1$$
$$= 3 - 1$$
$$= 2$$

In general, the expected frequencies for all categories are free to vary *except for the last one to be determined*. This point can be demonstrated by considering how f_e values are computed. As noted previously, the null hypothesis provides proportions for determining the expected frequencies for each category. These proportions or percentages are applied to the sample size to compute f_e:

$$f_e = pn$$

Naturally, the sum of the percentages for the categories should always equal 100%. As we use up portions of this 100% in determining the expected frequencies, we finally get to the point where we must find f_e for the last category. Its f_e value is not free to vary and must be based on the remaining portion of 100%.

Caution! Unlike many of the statistical tests we have studied, the value of df for a chi square goodness-of-fit test is not based on the sample size n. Remember, it is based on the number of categories, C.

Locating the Critical Region

To evaluate the results of a chi square test, we must first locate the critical region and specifically the critical chi square value associated with that region. This task is accomplished by first selecting a level of significance, typically $\alpha = .05$ or $.01$. It is also necessary to compute the value of degrees of freedom, because the exact shape of the chi square distribution depends on this value. The critical χ^2 value is obtained from the table entitled The Chi Square Distribution (Appendix B) using the df value and the level of significance. Table 19.3 depicts a portion of these critical values. The left-hand margin lists df values, and the top column indicates the proportion of area in the critical region. For Example 19.1, there are two degrees of freedom. If the researcher uses $\alpha = .01$, then the critical region begins with the chi square value of 9.21. That is, to reject H_0, the obtained chi square must be greater than 9.21. Note that for Example 19.1 the obtained chi square is 2.8. Because this value does not fall in the critical region, we fail to reject H_0. For Example 19.1, there is no evidence for a store preference among the shoppers.

Steps for the Chi Square Test for Goodness of Fit

The steps for testing hypotheses with chi square are basically the same as those of other hypothesis tests. Generally speaking, the steps consist of stating the hypotheses, locating a critical region, computing the test statistic, and making a decision about H_0. These steps are summarized as follows.

Table 19.3

A Portion of the Table of Critical Values for the Chi Square Distribution

df	Proportion in Critical Region				
	0.10	0.05	0.025	0.01	0.005
1	2.71	3.84	5.02	6.63	7.88
2	4.61	5.99	7.38	9.21	10.60
3	6.25	7.81	9.35	11.34	12.84
4	7.78	9.49	11.14	13.28	14.86
5	9.24	11.07	12.83	15.09	16.75
6	10.64	12.59	14.45	16.81	18.55
7	12.02	14.07	16.01	18.48	20.28
8	13.36	15.51	17.53	20.09	21.96
9	14.68	16.92	19.02	21.67	23.59

STEP 1. *State Hypotheses and Select an Alpha Level*. For the chi square test for goodness of fit, the hypotheses concern the form of the frequency distribution rather than the value of a specific parameter. Therefore, we typically do not state the hypotheses in terms of symbols. Instead, we use a description of the type of distribution we expect. For Example 19.1, the hypotheses could have been stated as follows:

H_0: In the population, there is no preference among shoppers for store A, B, or C.

H_1: In the population, people display a preference in shopping patterns.

As always, hypotheses are stated in terms of the population. A traditional alpha level (.05, .01) is selected.

STEP 2. *Determine df and Locate the Critical Region*. For the goodness-of-fit test, degrees of freedom are obtained by subtracting 1 from the number of categories, C:

$$df = C - 1$$

The values for df and the alpha level are used to find the critical region by consulting the table for critical values for chi square.

STEP 3. *Compute the Expected Frequencies and Chi Square*. The expected frequencies are computed for all categories, and then the chi square statistic is computed using the formula

$$\chi^2 = \Sigma \frac{(f_o - f_e)^2}{f_e}$$

STEP 4. *Make a Decision About the Null Hypothesis*. If the obtained χ^2 value falls in the critical region, then H_0 is rejected. The experimenter may conclude that the observed frequency distribution differs significantly from the distribution predicted by H_0. On the other hand, if the obtained value does not exceed the critical value, then H_0 cannot be rejected.

EXAMPLE 19.2

A researcher is interested in the factors that are involved in course selection. A sample of 50 students is asked, "Which of the following factors is most important to you when selecting a course?" Students must choose one and only one of the following alternatives:

1. Interest in course topic
2. Ease of passing the course
3. Instructor for the course
4. Time of day course is offered

The frequency distribution of responses for this sample is summarized in Table 19.4. Do any of these factors play a greater role than others for course selection?

STEP 1. We must state the hypotheses and select a level of significance. The hypotheses may be stated as follows:

H_0: For the population of students, there is no difference in the importance of these four factors in determining which courses are selected.

H_1: In the population of students, one or more of these factors plays a greater role in course selection (the factor is named more frequently by students).

The level of significance is set at a standard value, $\alpha = .05$.

STEP 2. The value for degrees of freedom is determined, and then the critical region is located. For this example, the value for degrees of freedom is

$$df = C - 1 = 4 - 1 = 3$$

For $df = 3$ and $\alpha = .05$, the table for critical values of chi square indicates that the critical χ^2 has a value of 7.81. The critical region is sketched in Figure 19.3.

STEP 3. The expected frequencies for all categories must be determined, and then the chi square statistic can be calculated. If H_0 were true and the students display no response preference for the four alternatives, then the proportion of the population

---

Table 19.4

Part A: The Most Important Factor in Course Selection (Observed Frequencies)

	Interest in Topic	Ease of Passing	Course Instructor	Time of Day
f_o	18	17	7	8

Part B: The Expected Frequencies for Example 19.2

	Interest in Topic	Ease of Passing	Course Instructor	Time of Day
f_e	12.5	12.5	12.5	12.5

responding to each category would be $\frac{1}{4}$. Because the sample size (n) is 50, the null hypothesis predicts expected frequencies of 12.5 for all categories (Table 19.4):

$$f_e = pn = \tfrac{1}{4}(50) = 12.5$$

Using the observed and the expected frequencies from Table 19.4, the chi square statistic may now be calculated:

$$\chi^2 = \Sigma \frac{(f_o - f_e)^2}{f_e}$$
$$= \frac{(18 - 12.5)^2}{12.5} + \frac{(17 - 12.5)^2}{12.5}$$
$$+ \frac{(7 - 12.5)^2}{12.5} + \frac{(8 - 12.5)^2}{12.5}$$
$$= \frac{30.25}{12.5} + \frac{20.25}{12.5} + \frac{30.25}{12.5} + \frac{20.25}{12.5}$$
$$= 2.42 + 1.62 + 2.42 + 1.62$$
$$= 8.08$$

STEP 4.   The obtained chi square value lies in the critical region. Therefore, H_0 is rejected, and the researcher may conclude that the subjects mentioned some of the factors more than others in response to the question about course selection. In a research report, the investigator might state:

Figure 19.3
For Example 19.2, the critical region begins at a chi square value of 7.81.

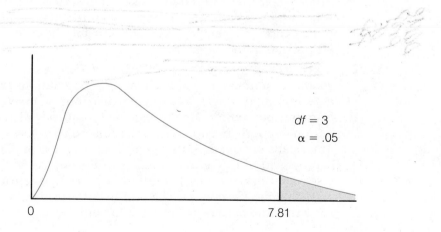

$df = 3$
$\alpha = .05$

0   7.81

"The students showed a significant response preference to the question concerning factors involved in course selection, $\chi^2(3, n = 50) = 8.08, p < .05$."

Note that the form of reporting the chi square value is similar to that of other statistical tests we have encountered. Degrees of freedom and the sample size are indicated in the parentheses after the χ^2 symbol. This information is followed by the obtained chi square value and then by the probability that a type I error has been committed.

More About the Null Hypothesis

Although the expected frequencies were equally distributed among categories in the previous two examples (Examples 19.1 and 19.2), the null hypothesis for a chi square goodness-of-fit test can specify any shape for the population distribution. Let us reconsider Example 19.1 for a moment. Suppose the president of a store (store C) made the advertising claim that twice as many shoppers prefer to shop there, compared to the two other major stores. The claim is that the frequency distribution for shoppers' preference looks like the following distribution:

Store A	Store B	Store C
25%	25%	50%

If you work for store A, you may wish to prove that the claim made by store C is wrong. Therefore, you could state their claim as your null hypothesis. You would then collect sample data and determine if they are sufficiently inconsistent with the hypothesis by a test for goodness of fit. If the discrepancy between the sample data and hypothesized data is large enough, you may reject H_0 and conclude that their claim is incorrect. Generally, the null hypothesis for a chi square test for goodness of fit will fall into one of the following categories.

1. *No Preference*. The null hypothesis often states that there is no response preference among the different categories. In this case, H_0 specifies that each category has the same proportion of the population.

2. *No Difference from a Comparison Population*. A test for goodness of fit can be used to compare populations by determining how well a frequency distribution taken from one population fits the expected frequency distribution of another. Suppose it is estimated that 40% of Americans are opposed to and 60% are in favor of the deployment of U.S. cruise missiles in Europe. A researcher may wonder if a different pattern of attitudes exists among Europeans. The null hypothesis would state that the pattern is the same for Europeans,

namely, 40% opposed to and 60% in favor of deployment. These percentages would be used to determine the f_e values. Sample data would then be collected to assess the attitudes of the European citizens. If the populations are different, there will be a large discrepancy between the sample and hypothesized data.

3. *No Change from a Past Distribution*. The test for goodness of fit can be used to determine if the form of a population distribution has changed over time. For example, a researcher may know that in 1970 the distribution for type of occupations consisted of 45% white-collar and 55% blue-collar workers. Considering the development of the "high-tech" industries and new service occupations, the researcher wonders if this pattern has changed. The 1970 proportions are used in the null hypothesis to determine the expected frequencies. The observed frequencies for a sample of present-day workers are used to see if the current distribution matches the 1970 distribution.

4. *No Difference from a Theoretical Population*. A theory may predict a particular distribution for a population. For example, a genetic theory may predict that crossbreeding two strains of mice will result in a distribution of offspring consisting of 25% that are prone to seizures and 75% that are normal. Of course, it is impossible to prove a hypothesis about the population (see Chapter 8, Box 8.1), but it is possible to disprove a hypothesis. Therefore, a researcher may try to determine if the theory is incorrect. The proportions predicted by the theory would be used for the null hypothesis. If there is a large discrepancy between the observed frequencies of offspring and the expected frequencies, then one might conclude that the theory is incorrect.

LEARNING CHECK

1. A researcher for an insurance company would like to know if high-performance, overpowered automobiles are more likely to be involved in accidents than other types of cars. For a sample of 50 insurance claims, the investigator classifies the automobiles as high-performance, subcompact, midsize, or full-size. The observed frequencies are as follows:

Observed Frequencies of Insurance Claims

High-Performance	Subcompact	Midsize	Full-Size	Total
20	14	7	9	50

In determining the f_e values, assume that only 10% of the cars in the population are the high-performance variety. However, subcompacts, midsize cars, and full-size cars make up 40%, 30%, and 20%, respectively. Can the researcher conclude that the observed pattern of accidents does not fit the predicted (f_e) values? Test with $\alpha = .05$.

a. In a few sentences, state the hypotheses.
b. Determine the value for df and locate the critical region.
c. Determine f_e values and compute chi square.
d. Make a decision regarding H_0.

ANSWERS

1. a. H_0: In the population, no particular type of car shows a disproportionate number of accidents. H_1: In the population, a disproportionate number of the accidents occur with certain types of cars.
   b. $df = 3$; the critical χ^2 value is 7.81.
   c. The f_e values for high-performance, subcompact, midsize, and full-size cars are 5, 20, 15, and 10, respectively. The obtained chi square is 51.17.
   d. Reject H_0.

19.2
Chi Square Test of Independence

The Concept of Independence

The chi square statistic may also be used to examine the extent to which two variables are related. In this situation, there are two sets of categories. Each observation must be classified in only one category for the first variable and in one category for the second variable. The null hypothesis states that the two variables are not related (are independent of each other) and makes predictions for the expected frequencies for all categories. If the two variables are independent, then the frequency distribution for one variable should not depend on nor be related to the categories of the second variable. When a relationship does exist, the frequency distribution for one variable will depend on the categories of the other variable. These points can be made clearer by looking at some hypothetical data.

DEFINITION

Two variables are *independent* when the distribution for one of the variables is not related to nor dependent on the categories of the second variable.

EXAMPLE 19.3

Suppose a researcher wants to see if there is a relationship between gender and attitudes about the Equal Rights Amendment (ERA). Two hundred people are asked if they are in favor of, against, or undecided about the ERA. The investigator classifies each response from this sample in terms of two variables: gender (male or female respondent) and attitude (for, against, or undecided). Two sets of hypothetical data are presented in Table 19.5.

First, you should notice that the data are organized in rows and columns (Table 19.5). Each column represents a different category for the attitude variable, and the rows depict the categories for the gender variable. Each "box," or cell, contains the observed frequencies for responses that fall into one category from each of the variables. For example, in Table 19.5, Part A, we can see that 40 of the 80 males in the sample were in favor of the ERA. The observed frequencies in each cell consist of responses from different people. A single individual cannot provide a frequency count for more than one cell.

It is common practice to show the column and row frequency totals in the margins of the table. These marginal frequencies are useful in forming first impressions of the data and are later necessary in determining the expected frequencies for each cell. The sum of the row totals equals the sum of the column totals, which in turn equals the sample size (n). Table 19.5, Part A, depicts data that suggest there is no relationship between gender and attitude. Notice that the form of the frequency distribution for males is the same as that for females.

Table 19.5

Attitudes About the Equal Rights Amendment (ERA) According to Gender (Observed Frequencies)

Part A: No Relationship Between Gender and Attitude

	In Favor of ERA	Against ERA	Undecided	Totals
Male	40	20	20	80
Female	60	30	30	120
Totals	100	50	50	

Part B: Relationship Between Gender and Attitude

	In Favor of ERA	Against ERA	Undecided	Totals
Male	20	40	20	80
Female	90	10	20	120
Totals	110	50	40	

That is, of 80 male respondents, 50% are in favor of the ERA, 25% are opposed to it, and 25% are undecided. Female respondents show the same pattern. The frequency distribution for attitude has the same form for both males and females. Therefore, gender and attitude are independent for these data. The frequency distribution of one variable does not depend on the categories of the other variable.

Table 19.5, Part B, shows an example of data in which there is a relationship between the two variables. Notice how the frequency distribution of attitudes differs markedly across the gender variable. The vast majority of female respondents are in favor of the ERA, while most male respondents are against it. The shape of the frequency distribution for attitude depends on which category of gender we consider.

The Null Hypothesis and Expected Frequencies

The expected frequencies are dictated by the null hypothesis. That is, we ask, What frequencies will be expected if the null hypothesis is true (if the variables are independent of each other)? To answer this question, we must first closely examine H_0. For Example 19.3 the null hypothesis states that

H_0: For the population, attitude toward the ERA and gender are independent.

What does this hypothesis imply for the data? It predicts that the distribution of attitudes *does not* depend on the gender of the respondents. In other words, the frequency distribution of attitudes should have the *same shape* for females and males if H_0 is true. In finding the f_e values for H_0, we must direct our attention to the marginal frequency totals for the columns and rows.

Let us assume that the investigator in Example 19.3 obtained the sample data shown in Table 19.6, Part A. What frequencies should be expected according to H_0? The column frequency totals at the bottom of Table 19.6, Part A, give us a clue. These totals reflect the overall frequency distribution for all subjects. Regardless of the respondent's sex, 110 people are in favor of, 50 are against, and 40 are undecided about the ERA. Because the sample consists of 200 people, the overall distribution consists of the following proportions:

In favor of the ERA: $p = \dfrac{110}{200} = 0.55$ or 55%

Against the ERA: $p = \dfrac{50}{200} = 0.25$ or 25%

Undecided: $p = \dfrac{40}{200} = 0.20$ or 20%

If H_0 were true and attitude were independent of gender, then these overall proportions should describe the frequency distributions for *both* females and males. In other words, 55% of the males should be

Table 19.6

Attitudes About the Equal Rights Amendment (ERA) According to Gender

Part A: Observed Frequencies

	In Favor of ERA	Against ERA	Undecided	Totals
Male	20	40	20	80
Female	90	10	20	120
Totals	110	50	40	

Part B: Expected Frequencies

	In Favor of ERA	Against ERA	Undecided	Totals
Male	44	20	16	80
Female	66	30	24	120
Totals	110	50	40	

in favor of, 25% against, and 20% undecided about the ERA. The same percentages would apply for the distribution of female respondents if the null hypothesis were true.

The row frequency totals (right-hand margin, Table 19.6, Part A) reveal that the sample of 200 people consists of 80 male and 120 female respondents. Therefore, the f_e values for each can be readily determined by applying the percentages from the overall frequency distribution to the number of female and male respondents. The expected frequencies for the data in Table 19.6 are computed as follows:

1. Males—in favor of the ERA:

   55% of 80   or $0.55 \times 80 = 44$

2. Males—against the ERA:

   25% of 80   or $0.25 \times 80 = 20$

3. Males–undecided:

   20% of 80   or $0.20 \times 80 = 16$

4. Females—in favor of the ERA:

   55% of 120   or $0.55 \times 120 = 66$

5. Females—against the ERA:

   25% of 120   or $0.25 \times 120 = 30$

6. Females—undecided:

   20% of 120   or $0.20 \times 120 = 24$

The marginal totals for the expected frequencies are the same as those for observed frequencies (Table 19.6). Comparing the marginal totals for f_e and f_o is a good way to be sure you have not made a mistake in computing f_e values.

These expected frequencies are shown in Table 19.6, Part B. Note that the form of the *expected* frequency distribution is the same for males and females. Recall that the null hypothesis states that attitude and gender are independent. Large discrepancies between f_o and f_e would result in a large chi square value. This outcome would suggest that H_0 is false and that a relationship exists between the two variables.

A Computational Formula for Expected Frequencies

It is not necessary to compute percentages in order to determine the value of expected frequencies. In fact, it is much quicker to compute f_e directly from a formula. So that you better understand the formula, let us first review the mechanics of computing f_e. Consider, for example, the males that are in favor of the ERA (Table 19.6, Part B). The f_e for this cell was obtained by taking 55% of 80. Where did we get the 55%? The marginal total for all people in favor of the ERA is 110 (Table 19.6, Part A), and this amount is 55% of the total number of observations ($n = 200$):

$$\text{proportion} = p = \frac{110}{200} = 0.55$$

Next we computed 55% of the 80 males, or

$$f_e = \frac{110}{200} \times 80$$
$$= 0.55 \times 80 = 44$$

This calculation may also be expressed in the following way:

$$f_e = \frac{110(80)}{200} = 44$$

That is, for the particular cell in question, we can determine f_e by multiplying the column frequency total by the row frequency total and then dividing by the sample size (n), or

(19.4) $\quad f_e = \dfrac{f_c f_r}{n}$

where f_c is the frequency total of the column and f_r is the frequency total of the row for a particular cell. For female respondents in favor of the ERA, the column frequency total is 110, and the row frequency total is 120 (Table 19.6, Part A). Using the formula to find f_e for this cell, we obtain

$$f_e = \frac{f_c f_r}{n} = \frac{110(120)}{200} = 66$$

This value is identical to the f_e we obtained by using the percentage method. Try the formula to check the remaining expected frequencies in Table 19.6.

Degrees of Freedom

For the chi square test of independence, the value for degrees of freedom is based on the number of cells for which you can freely choose the expected frequencies. Given the marginal frequency totals in Table 19.6, the f_e values for only two cells are free to vary. This point is illustrated in Table 19.7. Once the f_e values for any two cells are selected, the remaining f_e values are not free to vary because they are restricted by the marginal frequency totals. In general, the final value in each row and the final value in each column are determined by the previous f_e values. This means that we may freely choose only $(R - 1)(C - 1)$ values, where R is the number of rows and C is the number of columns:

$$(19.5) \quad df = (R - 1)(C - 1)$$

For the ERA example, degrees of freedom equal

$$df = (R - 1)(C - 1) = (2 - 1)(3 - 1) = 1(2)$$
$$= 2$$

As noted before, the degrees of freedom value is needed to locate the critical region in the chi square distribution. With $df = 2$ and alpha set at .05, the critical χ^2 value for the ERA example (Table 19.6) is 5.99.

Computing the Chi Square Value for the Test of Independence

The chi square formula for the test of independence is identical to the one used for the goodness-of-fit test. For each cell, the difference between the observed and expected frequencies is computed first. This difference is squared and then divided by the expected frequency for that cell. Finally, we sum this value for all of the cells. This sum provides a measure of the total amount of discrepancy between the sample data and hypothesized data:

$$\chi^2 = \Sigma \frac{(f_o - f_e)^2}{f_e}$$

Table 19.7[a]

	In Favor of ERA	Against ERA	Undecided	Totals
Male	44	20	?	80
Female	?	?	?	120
Totals	110	50	40	

[a]For the ERA study (Table 19.6), the expected frequencies for any two cells can be freely selected.

For the ERA example, we obtain the following chi square value from the frequencies in Table 19.6:

$$\chi^2 = \Sigma \frac{(f_o - f_e)^2}{f_e}$$

$$= \frac{(20 - 44)^2}{44} + \frac{(40 - 20)^2}{20} + \frac{(20 - 16)^2}{16} + \frac{(90 - 66)^2}{66}$$

$$+ \frac{(10 - 30)^2}{30} + \frac{(20 - 24)^2}{24}$$

$$= \frac{-24^2}{44} + \frac{20^2}{20} + \frac{4^2}{16} + \frac{24^2}{66} + \frac{-20^2}{30} + \frac{-4^2}{24}$$

$$= \frac{576}{44} + \frac{400}{20} + \frac{16}{16} + \frac{576}{66} + \frac{400}{30} + \frac{16}{24}$$

$$= 13.09 + 20 + 1 + 8.73 + 13.33 + 0.67$$

$$= 56.82$$

Notice that the obtained χ^2 value exceeds the critical value (5.99). Therefore, the experimenter should reject the null hypothesis. It can be concluded that there is a significant relationship between gender and attitude toward the ERA. As the data in Table 19.6 indicate, women were more likely to be in favor of and men against the ERA amendment.

Steps in Testing Hypotheses of Independence

The steps for the chi square test of independence should be familiar by now. First, the hypotheses must be stated and an alpha level selected. Second, the value for degrees of freedom is computed, and the critical region is located in the chi square distribution. Next the expected frequencies are determined, and the chi square statistic is computed. Finally, a decision is made regarding the null hypothesis.

EXAMPLE 19.4
Darley and Latané (1968) did a study which examined the relationship between the number of observers and aid-giving behaviors (see the preview for details). The group sizes consisted of two people (subject and victim), three people, or six people. The investigators categorized the response of a subject in terms of whether or not the observer exhibited any helping behaviors when the victim (actually another laboratory worker) staged an epileptic seizure. The data are presented again in Table 19.8. Do aid-giving behaviors depend on group size?

STEP 1. State the hypotheses and select a level of significance. According to the null hypothesis, group size and helping behavior are independent of each other in the population. That is, the absence or presence of aid-giving behavior should not be

Table 19.8

The Relationship Between the Size of Group and the Type of Response to the Victim

Part A: Observed Frequencies

Group Size

	2	3	6	Totals
Assistance	11	16	4	31
No Assistance	2	10	9	21
Totals	13	26	13	

Part B: Expected Frequencies

Group Size

	2	3	6	Totals
Assistance	7.75	15.5	7.75	31
No Assistance	5.25	10.5	5.25	21
Totals	13	26	13	

J. M. Darley and B. Latané (1968). Bystander intervention in emergencies: Diffusion of responsibility. *Journal of Personality and Social Psychology, 8,* 377–383. Copyright (1968) by the American Psychological Association. Adapted with permission of the publisher and author.

related to the number of observers. The alternate hypothesis would state that the absence or presence of helping behavior is dependent on group size for the population. The level of significance is set at $\alpha = .05$.

STEP 2. Calculate the degrees of freedom and locate the critical region. For the chi square test of independence,

$$df = (R - 1)(C - 1)$$

Therefore, for this study,

$$df = (2 - 1)(3 - 1) = 1(2) = 2$$

With two degrees of freedom and a level of significance of .05, the critical value for χ^2 is 5.99 (see table for critical values of chi square).

STEP 3. Determine the expected frequencies and calculate the chi square statistic. As noted before, it is quicker to use the computational formula to determine the f_e values, rather than the percentage method. The expected frequency for each cell is as follows:

1. Group size 2—showed aid-giving behavior:

$$f_e = \frac{f_c f_r}{n} = \frac{13(31)}{52} = 7.75$$

2. Group size 3—showed aid-giving behavior:

$$f_e = \frac{26(31)}{52} = 15.5$$

3. Group size 6—showed aid-giving behavior:

$$f_e = \frac{13(31)}{52} = 7.75$$

4. Group size 2—no aid-giving behavior:

$$f_e = \frac{13(21)}{52} = 5.25$$

5. Group size 3—no aid-giving behavior:

$$f_e = \frac{26(21)}{52} = 10.5$$

6. Group size 6—no aid-giving behavior:

$$f_e = \frac{13(21)}{52} = 5.25$$

The expected frequencies are summarized in Table 19.8, Part B. Using these expected frequencies along with the observed frequencies (Table 19.8, Part A), we can now calculate the value for the chi square statistic:

$$\chi^2 = \Sigma \frac{(f_o - f_e)^2}{f_e}$$

$$= \frac{(11 - 7.75)^2}{7.75} + \frac{(16 - 15.5)^2}{15.5} + \frac{(4 - 7.75)^2}{7.75}$$

$$+ \frac{(2 - 5.25)^2}{5.25} + \frac{(10 - 10.5)^2}{10.5} + \frac{(9 - 5.25)^2}{5.25}$$

$$= 1.363 + 0.016 + 1.815 + 2.012 + 0.024 + 2.679$$

$$= 7.91$$

STEP 4. Make a decision regarding the null hypothesis. The obtained chi square value exceeds the critical value (5.99). Therefore, the decision is to reject H_0 and conclude that there is a relationship between group size and the likelihood that someone will aid another person in trouble. For purposes of reporting the data, the researchers could state that there is a significant relationship between size of group and helping behavior, $\chi^2(2, n = 52) = 7.91$,

$p < .05$. By examining the observed frequencies in Table 19.8, Part A, we see that the likelihood of aid-giving behavior decreases as group size increases.

Example 19.4 Continued—a Computer Analysis

When cell frequencies are large, the computations of f_e values and the chi square statistic can be quite tedious. For this reason, it has become very common for researchers to use one of several computer software packages that are available for statistical analyses. Table 19.9 depicts the printout of an analysis for the data of Example 19.4. The MINITAB package was used, which like many of the statistical packages can be readily learned with little previous computer experience. Note that the printout displays the matrix of cells for observed and expected frequencies as well as the computations for chi square and degrees of freedom. Explanatory notes are provided in the table.

Table 19.9
MINITAB Analysis for Example 19.4[a]

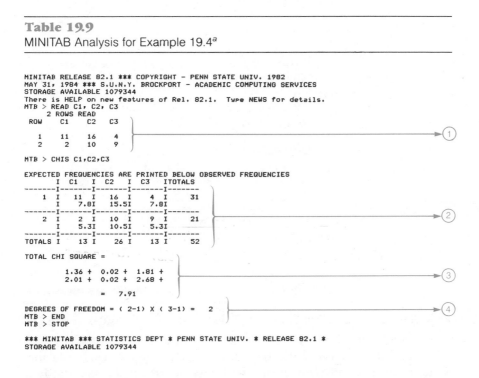

```
MINITAB RELEASE 82.1 *** COPYRIGHT - PENN STATE UNIV. 1982
MAY 31, 1984 *** S.U.N.Y. BROCKPORT - ACADEMIC COMPUTING SERVICES
STORAGE AVAILABLE 1079344
There is HELP on new features of Rel. 82.1.  Type NEWS for details.
MTB > READ C1, C2, C3
      2 ROWS READ
  ROW    C1    C2    C3
    1    11    16     4
    2     2    10     9

MTB > CHIS C1,C2,C3

EXPECTED FREQUENCIES ARE PRINTED BELOW OBSERVED FREQUENCIES
         I  C1    I  C2    I  C3    ITOTALS
-------I-------I-------I-------I-------
   1  I    11 I    16 I     4 I      31
      I   7.8I   15.5I   7.8I
-------I-------I-------I-------I-------
   2  I     2 I    10 I     9 I      21
      I   5.3I   10.5I   5.3I
-------I-------I-------I-------I-------
TOTALS I    13 I    26 I    13 I      52

TOTAL CHI SQUARE =

       1.36 +   0.02 +  1.81 +
       2.01 +   0.02 +  2.68 +

            =    7.91

DEGREES OF FREEDOM = ( 2-1) X ( 3-1) =   2
MTB > END
MTB > STOP

*** MINITAB *** STATISTICS DEPT * PENN STATE UNIV. * RELEASE 82.1 *
STORAGE AVAILABLE 1079344
```

[a]Explanation of printout:
1. The Original Data. The three group sizes used in the experiment (see Table 19.8) appear as three columns (C1, C2, C3) of frequencies. The type of response is coded into two rows.
2. The Cell Frequencies. The expected frequencies are printed below the observed frequencies for all of the cells. The marginal totals are provided for the rows and columns as well.
3. Computation of Chi Square. The chi square statistic is computed, showing the values obtained for each cell.
4. Degrees of Freedom. Finally, the df value for the test of independence is displayed.

1. A researcher suspects that color blindness is inherited by a sex-linked gene. This possibility is examined by looking for a relationship between gender and color vision. A sample of 1000 people is tested for color blindness, and then they are classified according to their sex and color vision status (normal, red-green blind, other color blindness). Is color blindness related to gender? The data are as follows:

Observed Frequencies of Color Vision Status According to Sex

	Normal Color Vision	Red-Green Color Blindness	Other Color Blindness	Totals
Male	320	70	10	400
Female	580	10	10	600
Totals	900	80	20	

a. State the hypotheses.
b. Determine the value for df and locate the critical region.
c. Compute the f_e values and then chi square.
d. Make a decision regarding H_0.

ANSWERS

1. a. H_0: In the population, there is no relationship between gender and color vision. H_1: In the population, gender and color vision are related.
   b. $df = 2$; critical $\chi^2 = 5.99$ for $\alpha = .05$.
   c. f_e values are as follows:

Expected Frequencies

	Normal	Red-Green	Other
Male	360	32	8
Female	540	48	12

Obtained $\chi^2 = 83.44$.
   d. Reject H_0.

19.3

Assumptions and Restrictions for Chi Square Tests

To use a chi square test for goodness of fit or a test of independence, several conditions must be satisfied. For any statistical test, violation of assumptions and restrictions will cast doubt on the results. For example, the probability of committing a type I error may be distorted when assumptions of statistical tests are not satisfied. Some important assumptions and restrictions for using chi square tests are the following:

1. *Random Sampling*. As we have seen with other inferential techniques, it is assumed that the sample

under study is selected randomly from the population of interest.

2. *Independence of Observations.* This is *not* to be confused with the concept of independence between *variables* as seen in the test of independence (Section 19.2). By independence of observations, it is assumed that each observed frequency is generated by a different subject. A chi square test would be inappropriate if a person could produce responses that can be classified in more than one category or contribute more than one frequency count to a single category.

3. *Size of Expected Frequencies.* The chi square statistic can be distorted when f_e is very small. Consider the chi square computations for a single cell. Suppose the cell has values of $f_e = 1$ and $f_o = 5$. The contribution of this cell to the total chi square value is

$$\text{cell} = \frac{(f_o - f_e)^2}{f_e} = \frac{(5 - 1)^2}{1} = \frac{4^2}{1} = 16$$

Now consider another instance, where $f_e = 10$ and $f_o = 14$. The difference between the observed and expected frequency is still 4, but the contribution of this cell of the total chi square value differs from that of the first case:

$$\text{cell} = \frac{(f_o - f_e)^2}{f_e} = \frac{(14 - 10)^2}{10} = \frac{4^2}{10} = 1.6$$

It should be clear that a small f_e value can have a great influence on the chi square value. This problem becomes serious when f_e values are less than 5. When f_e is very small, what would otherwise be a minor discrepancy between f_o and f_e will now result in large chi square values. The test is too sensitive when f_e values are extremely small. A chi square test should not be performed when the expected frequency of any cell is less than 5. One way to avoid small expected frequencies is to use large samples.

4. *Assumption of Continuity.* The illustrations of chi square distributions (Figure 19.2, for example) depict the graph as a smooth, continuous line. For the theoretical distribution, chi square values are assumed to be a continuous variable. This assumption is violated when there is only *one* degree of freedom. Specifically, when a chi square is computed for all possible samples of a given size, the resulting distribution of sample χ^2 values is not continuous. In the past, statisticians have suggested a correction for the chi square formula to be used only when there is one degree of freedom. *Yates' correction for*

continuity consists of subtracting 0.5 from the absolute value of the difference between f_o and f_e. The "absolute value" operation removes negative signs and is symbolized by two vertical lines surrounding the value to be changed. After this correction has been done for each cell, the remaining steps of the chi square computation are performed as usual:

$$(19.6) \quad \chi^2 = \Sigma \frac{(|f_o - f_e| - 0.5)^2}{f_e}$$

It should be noted that recent work (Camilli and Hopkins, 1978) has strongly argued that the Yates correction is not necessary. However, we suggest it be used (when $df = 1$) until these arguments gain wider acceptance.

Summary

1. Chi square tests are a type of nonparametric technique that test hypotheses about the form of the entire frequency distribution. Two types of chi square tests are the test for goodness of fit and the test for independence. The data for these tests consist of the frequency of observations that fall into various categories of a variable.

2. The test for goodness of fit compares the frequency distribution for a sample to the frequency distribution that is predicted by H_0. The test determines how well the observed frequencies (sample data) fit the expected frequencies (data predicted by H_0).

3. The expected frequencies for the goodness-of-fit test are determined by

   expected frequency $= f_e = pn$

   where p is the hypothesized proportion (according to H_0) of observations falling into a category and n is the size of the sample.

4. The chi square statistic is computed by

   chi square $= \chi^2 = \Sigma \dfrac{(f_o - f_e)^2}{f_e}$

   where f_o is the observed frequency for a particular category and f_e is the expected frequency for that category. Large values for χ^2 indicate that there is a large discrepancy between the observed (f_o) and expected (f_e) frequencies and may warrant rejection of the null hypothesis.

5. Degrees of freedom for the test for goodness of fit are

   $df = C - 1$

where C is the number of categories in the variable. Degrees of freedom measure the number of categories for which f_e values can be freely chosen. As can be seen from the formula, all but the last f_e value to be determined are free to vary.

6. The chi square distribution is positively skewed and begins at the value of zero. Its exact shape is determined by degrees of freedom.

7. The test for independence is used to assess the relationship between two variables. The null hypothesis states that the two variables in question are independent of each other. That is, the frequency distribution for one variable does not depend on the categories of the second variable. On the other hand, if a relationship does exist, then the form of the distribution for one variable will depend on the categories of the other variable.

8. The expected frequencies for H_0 can be directly calculated from the marginal frequency totals,

$$f_e = \frac{f_c f_r}{n}$$

where f_c is the total column frequency and f_r is the total row frequency for the cell in question.

9. Degrees of freedom for the test for independence are computed by

$$df = (R - 1)(C - 1)$$

where R is the number of row categories and C is the number of column categories.

10. For the test of independence, a large chi square value means there is a large discrepancy between the f_o and f_e values. Rejecting H_0 in this test provides support for a relationship between the two variables.

11. Both chi square tests (for goodness of fit and independence) are based on the assumption that the sample is randomly selected from the population. It is also assumed that each observation is independent of the others. That is, each observed frequency reflects a different individual, and no individual can produce a response that would be classified in more than one category or more than one frequency in a single category.

12. The chi square statistic is distorted when f_e values are small. Chi square tests, therefore, are restricted to situations where f_e values are 5 or greater. The test should not be performed when the expected frequency of any cell is less than 5.

13. It is assumed that the chi square distribution is continuous. However, this assumption is not satisfied in instances where

there is only one degree of freedom. Yates' correction for continuity is used when $df = 1$:

$$\chi^2 = \Sigma \frac{(|f_o - f_e| - 0.5)^2}{f_e}$$

For each cell the absolute value of the $f_o - f_e$ difference is taken, and 0.5 is subtracted from this value. The remaining steps of the computation are the same as for the regular chi square formula.

Key Terms

goodness-of-fit test

expected frequencies

observed frequencies

chi square statistic

distribution of chi square

test of independence

assumption of continuity

Yates correction for continuity

Problems for Chapter 19:
The Chi Square Statistic: Tests for Goodness of Fit and Independence

*1. An advertising researcher is trying to determine the criteria that people use when choosing a new car. The researcher selects a sample of $n = 100$ people and asks each person to select what they consider to be the "most important factor in selecting a new car" from a list of alternatives. The data are as follows:

Cost	Styling	Performance	Reliability
30	10	20	40

On the basis of these observed frequencies, can the researcher conclude that there is any specific factor (or factors) which is most often cited as being important? Test at the .05 level of significance.

2. A researcher would like to determine if any particular age group has a greater risk of influenza-related death. A sample of 50 such cases is categorized according to the victim's age. The observed frequencies are as follows:

Number of Flu-Related Deaths

Under 30	30 to 60	Over 60
5	5	40

It should be noted that in the city from which the sample was selected, 30% of the population is in the "under 30" bracket, 40% in "30 to 60," and 30% in "over 60." (This information should help in determining f_e values.) Can the investigator conclude the risk differs with age? Test with the .05 level of significance.

*3. A questionnaire given to last year's freshman class indicated that 30% intended to be science majors, 50% intended to major in social science or humanities, and 20% were interested in professional programs. A random sample of 100 students from the current freshman class yielded the following frequency distribution:

Intended Major

Sciences	Social Science or Humanities	Professional
35	40	25

a. On the basis of these data, should the university officials conclude that there has been a significant change in student interests? Test at the .05 level of significance.

b. If twice as many students had been sampled with the result that the observed frequencies were doubled in each of the three categories, would there be evidence for a significant change? Again, test with $\alpha = .05$.

c. How do you explain the different conclusions for parts a and b?

4. A researcher would like to determine whether there is any relationship between a person's age and his/her attitude toward a new law that would raise the drinking age to 21 years. He selects a random sample of 100 people and records each person's age and attitude toward the law. The observed frequencies are as follows:

	For the Law	Against the Law
Over 21	73	7
Under 21	2	18

Do the data indicate that these two variables are related? Use an alpha level of .05. (Note that $df = 1$ for this example. Be sure to use Yates' correction.)

*5. The U.S. Senate recently considered a controversial amendment for school prayer. The amendment did not get the required two-thirds majority, but the results of the vote are interesting when viewed in terms of the party affiliation of the senators. The data are as follows:

| | Prayer Amendment Vote (March 1984) | |
	Yes	No
Party Democrat	19	26
Republican	37	18

Is there a relationship between political party affiliation and prayer amendment vote? Test with $\alpha = .05$.

6. A random sample of 200 people is selected to determine if there is any relationship between an individual's educational background and his/her opinion concerning additional funding for higher education. Each person is classified according to the highest degree obtained and requested to give an opinion. Use the following data to determine if there is a relationship between the 2 variables. Set alpha to .05.

| | Attitude | | |
	For Funding	Against Funding	Undecided
No Degree	16	26	58
High School	4	2	34
College	30	2	28

*7. A psychologist would like to determine if there is a relationship between extroversion and cigarette smoking. A random sample of 150 people is selected. Each person is given a standard personality inventory to classify him/her as an introvert or extrovert. Each must also provide information about how much he/she smokes (never, less than a pack per day, more than a pack per day). The observed frequencies are as follows:

| | Number of Cigarettes Per Day | | |
	None	Less Than a Pack	More Than a Pack
Extrovert	50	12	28
Introvert	50	8	2

Can the psychologist conclude there is a relationship between these personality types and smoking behavior? Set alpha to .05.

8. A researcher would like to know if there is a relationship between a student's gender and choice of college major. To test this hypothesis, a sample of $N = 500$ students is selected and each person's sex and college major are recorded. The resulting data are as follows:

	Science	Humanities	Arts	Professional
Male	30	10	15	45
Female	80	120	45	155

Major

Is there a relationship between the two variables? Test at the .01 level of significance.

*9. A school board would like to study a proposal to eliminate the cost-of-living raises for next year and replace them with merit raises (raises based on evaluation of performance). The board decides to assess the attitudes toward the proposal among those individuals who are working in the school system. Specifically, the school board would like to know if attitude is related to the type of position the person holds. The observed frequencies are as follows:

Type of Position

	Teachers	Administration	Counselors
Approve of Merit Raises	265	14	33
Against Merit Raises	124	37	21

Is there a relationship between the two variables? Test at the .01 level of significance.

10. Friedman and Rosenman (1974) have suggested that personality type is related to heart disease. Specifically, Type A people who are competitive, driven, pressured, and impatient, are more prone to heart disease. On the other hand, Type B individuals, who are less competitive and more relaxed, are less likely to have heart disease. Suppose an investigator would like to examine the relationship between personality type and disease. For a random sample of individuals, personality type is assessed with a standardized test. These individuals are then examined and categorized according to the type of disorder they have. The observed frequencies are as follows:

Type of Disorder

	Heart	Vascular	Hypertension	None
Type A Personality	38	29	43	60
Type B Personality	18	22	14	126

Is there a relationship between personality and disorder? Test at the .05 level of significance.

*11. A researcher would like to determine if attitudes about career differ as a function of year in college. A random sample of college students is selected. The students fill out a questionnaire, specifying year in school and what they intend to do when they complete college. Their responses are classified and recorded in the following table:

Plans After College

Year	Work	Graduate School	Undecided
Freshman	22	20	48
Sophomore	37	26	29
Junior	58	31	15
Senior	56	35	9

Is there a relationship between year in college and attitude about career? Test with alpha set at .01.

12. McClelland (1961) suggested that the strength of a person's need for achievement can predict behavior in a number of situations, including risk-taking situations. This experiment is patterned after his work. A random sample of college students is given a standardized test that measures the need for achievement. On the basis of their test scores, they are classified into high achievers and low achievers. They are then confronted with a task for which they can select the level of difficulty. Their selections are classified as "cautious" (low risk of failure), "moderate" risk, or "high" risk of failure. The observed frequencies for this study are as follows:

Risk Taken by Subject

	Cautious	Moderate	High
High Achiever	8	24	6
Low Achiever	17	7	16

Can you conclude there is a relationship between the need for achievement and risk-taking behavior? Set alpha to .05. Describe the outcome of the study.

*13. A marketing researcher would like to determine if a preference exists among adult readers for one of the three leading weekly news magazines. In a telephone survey, a sample of $n = 1000$ people are asked to select the magazine they like the most: *Newsweek, Time,* or *U.S. News and World Report.* The observed frequencies are as follows:

Selection

	Newsweek	Time	U.S. News
f_o	342	355	303

Is there a significant preference? Test at the .05 level of significance.

14. It is known that blood type varies among different populations of people. In the United States, for example, types O, A, B, and AB blood make up 45%, 41%, 10%, and 4% of the population, respectively. Suppose blood type is determined for a sample of $n = 136$ individuals from a foreign country. The resulting frequency distribution is as follows:

Blood Type

	O	A	B	AB
f_o	43	38	41	14

Is there a significant difference between this distribution and what we would expect for the United States? Set alpha at .05.

*15. A scientist would like to see if there is a relationship between handedness and eye preference. A random sample of $n = 238$ subjects is selected. For each subject the researcher determines two things: (1) whether the person is left-handed or right-handed and (2) which eye the person prefers to use when looking through a camera viewfinder. The observed frequencies are as follows:

		Hand Preference	
		Left	Right
Eye Preference	Left	17	35
	Right	15	171

Is there a relationship between the two variables? Test at the .01 level of significance.

16. A researcher believes that people with low self-esteem will avoid situations that will focus attention on themselves. A random sample of $n = 72$ people is selected. Each person is given a standardized test that measures self-esteem and is classified as high, medium, or low in self-esteem. The subjects are then placed in a situation in which they must choose between performing a task in front of other people or by themselves. The researcher notes which task is chosen. The observed frequencies are as follows:

	Task Chosen	
	Audience	No Audience
Low Self-esteem	4	16
Medium Self-esteem	14	14
High Self-esteem	4	16

Is there a relationship between self-esteem and the task chosen? Use $\alpha = .05$.

*17. Suppose an opinion poll taken in 1970 revealed the following data regarding the legalization of marijuana: 15% in favor of, 79% against, and 6% no opinion regarding legalization. Suppose you took a random sample of $n = 220$ people today and obtained the following data:

Attitude Toward Legalization of Marijuana

	For	Against	No Opinion
f_o	38	165	17

Is there a significant difference between the current data and what were obtained in 1970? Use the .05 level of significance.

18. In a recent presidential election, voters were surveyed to determine preferences between the two major party candidates. A sample of 100 people was obtained from each geographical region of the country. The distribution of preferences is reported in the following table:

		North	South	East	West
Candidate Preferred	A	54	61	52	59
	B	46	39	48	41

Do these data indicate a significant relation between voter preferences and geographical region? Test with $\alpha = .05$.

*19. In a normal distribution, 6.68% of the scores have z-score values less than -1.50, 24.17% have z-scores between -1.50 and -0.50, 38.30% have z-scores between -0.50 and $+0.50$, 24.17% have z-scores between $+0.50$ and $+1.50$, and 6.68% have z-scores greater than $+1.50$. These percentages come from the unit normal table. A researcher obtained the following distribution of scores in an experiment with $n = 150$ subjects:

z Less than -1.50	z Between -1.50 and -0.50	z Between -0.50 and $+0.50$	z Between $+0.50$ and $+1.50$	z Greater than $+1.50$
15	42	58	28	7

Is the distribution for these data significantly different from normal? Test with $\alpha = .05$.

20. A social psychology experiment examined the effect of success or failure on people's willingness to help others. In this experiment, individual subjects were given a task that was either very easy or impossible to perform. Thus, some subjects were guaranteed to succeed, and some were doomed to fail. As subjects left the testing room, they encountered a student who was trying to reach a telephone from a wheel chair. The psy-

chologist recorded how many subjects stopped to help. The data from this experiment are presented in the following table:

	Success	Failure
Help	16	11
No Help	9	14

On the basis of these data, can the psychologist conclude that there is a significant relation between people's willingness to help and their personal experience of success or failure. Test at the .05 level of significance.

CHAPTER 20

Nonparametric Tests for Ordinal Data

Mann-Whitney and Wilcoxon Tests

TOOLS
YOU WILL
NEED

The following items are considered essential background material for this chapter. If you doubt your knowledge of any of these items, you should review the appropriate chapter or section before proceeding.

1. Nonparametric statistical tests (Chapter 18)
2. Probability (Chapter 6)
   a. The unit normal table
3. Introduction to hypothesis testing (Chapter 8)

Have you ever heard of the NFL? Even if you are not a sports fan, you probably are familiar with the National Football League, and you know that the teams in this league are divided into two conferences: the American Football Conference (AFC) and the National Football Conference (NFC). A source of constant debate among true football fanatics is the relative strength of these two conferences. Is one group of teams really better than the other? One way of addressing this question is to examine the end-of-season rankings for the entire set of 28 teams (see Table 20.1).

According to these data, the AFC teams finished the season with ranks of 2, 3, 8, 10, 12, 13, 14, 17, 18, 21, 22, 23, 24, and 28. The average rank for these teams is 15.36. Similarly, the NFC teams finished with an average rank of 13.64.

Time out! Wait just a minute!

The numbers we are working with are ranks, not regular scores. Is it legitimate to compute an average for ranks? Most statisticians would contend that you cannot treat ranks as if they were scores. The basis of this claim becomes more clear if you focus on a smaller set of data. Suppose we look at two teams from each conference: Washington and Green Bay from the NFC and New England and Cleveland from the AFC. For the sake of argument, let's assume most experts agree that Washington is vastly superior to all of the other three teams. Washington is ranked 1. On the other hand, Green Bay, New England, and Cleveland are

very similar teams. All three of these teams are considered "average," and the differences among them are very small.

Table 20.1
Ranking of the 28 teams in the National Football League at the end of the 1983 regular season

Rank	Team	Conference
1	Washington	NFC
2	Miami	AFC
3	L.A. Raiders	AFC
4	San Francisco	NFC
5	Dallas	NFC
6	Detroit	NFC
7	St. Louis	NFC
8	Seattle	AFC
9	L.A. Rams	NFC
10	Cincinnati	AFC
11	Chicago	NFC
12	New England	AFC
13	Pittsburgh	AFC
14	Cleveland	AFC
15	Atlanta	NFC
16	Green Bay	NFC
17	Denver	AFC
18	Kansas City	AFC
19	New Orleans	NFC
20	Minnesota	NFC
21	N.Y. Jets	AFC
22	San Diego	AFC
23	Buffalo	AFC
24	Baltimore	AFC
25	Philadelphia	NFC
26	N.Y. Giants	NFC
27	Tampa Bay	NFC
28	Houston	AFC

From the *New York Times*, December 23, 1983, page 18a. Copyright © 1983 by the New York Times Company. Reprinted by permission.

Within this group of four teams they are ranked as follows:

2. New England
3. Cleveland
4. Green Bay

In this simplified comparison, the two AFC teams are both average. The NFC pair, however, consists of one average team and one super team. Clearly the NFC pair is superior.

AFC
New England (average)
Cleveland (average)

NFC
Washington (super)
Green Bay (average)

Now look at the ranks for these four teams. The NFC teams have ranks of 1 and 4 for an average rank of 2.5. The AFC teams have ranks of 2 and 3 for an average of 2.5. The average rank does not detect any difference.

The problem with ranks is that they do not give any information about the magnitude of the difference between two individuals. Ranks tell which team is better, but they do not tell you how much better. You should recall that ranks are measurements on an ordinal scale (see Chapter 1). Because ordinal measurements provide only limited information, they must be used and interpreted carefully. Attempts to average ranks, for example, can produce misleading results.

The result of all this discussion is that you generally should not compute means with ranked data. Therefore, you cannot use the standard t tests or analysis of variance to compare treatments when data are measured on an ordinal scale. However, it still is possible to use ordinal data to answer statistical questions. Special procedures and techniques have been developed for use with ranked data. It is possible, for example, to use the football rankings in Table 20.1 to test whether or not there is a significant difference between the two conferences. In this chapter, we will examine two statistical tests that are designed specifically for use with ordinal data.

20.1
Introduction

When a researcher wishes to determine whether or not there is a difference between two treatment conditions, there are two basic experimental designs that can be used: independent measures and repeated measures. You should recall that in an independent measures experiment, a separate sample is obtained for each treatment condition. For a repeated measures experiment, the same sample is used in all treatment conditions. Under most circumstances, the data from these experiments would be evaluated by using the appropriate t test or analysis of variance. However, there are situations where these traditional, parametric tests are not appropriate. It is in these situations that the Mann-Whitney test and the Wilcoxon test are used. Both of these are nonparametric tests because they require no assumptions about the shape of the population distribution. The Mann-Whitney test is used to compare two treatment conditions with data from an independent measures design. The Wilcoxon test is used to compare two treatment conditions with data from a repeated measures design.

Before discussing these two tests in detail, we will look more closely at three situations where they might be used.

1. There are several statistical assumptions that underlie the *t* tests and analysis of variance. For example, all of these tests assume that the data come from populations with normal distributions. In addition, the independent measures tests assume that the different populations all have the same variance (the homogeneity of variance assumption). Occasionally a researcher knows that data do not satisfy these assumptions. More often, the researcher may suspect that the data do not meet the assumptions. In either case, the researcher may decide that the traditional, parametric test is not justified and may produce a misleading result. In this case, one of the nonparametric tests should be used.

2. The *t* tests and analysis of variance all require that the sample data undergo substantial manipulation with basic arithmetic. The scores are added, squared, averaged, etc. For these manipulations to produce meaningful results, you must begin with numerical data measured on an interval or a ratio scale (see Chapter 1). Occasionally, it is impossible or impractical to obtain measurements with this degree of sophistication. For example, a researcher may be able to rank-order subjects with respect to athletic ability, or leadership, or artistic talent even though there are no precise scores for these variables. When the sample data consist of ranks (an ordinal scale), the traditional parametric tests should not be used. In this situation, either the Mann-Whitney or the Wilcoxon test would be appropriate.

3. Occasionally sample data will include an infinite or an undetermined score. For example, a rat being tested on a problem-solving task continues to make errors and shows no sign of learning after days of testing. This animal has an infinite or undetermined score. It is impossible to compute a sample mean, or *SS*, or a *t* statistic with these data. However, the Wilcoxon or the Mann-Whitney test would be appropriate.

20.2
The Mann-Whitney *U*-Test

The Mann-Whitney test is designed to evaluate the difference between two treatments (or two populations) using data from an independent measures experiment. The calculations for this test require that the individual scores in the two samples be rank-ordered. The mathematics of the Mann-Whitney test is based on the following simple observation:

A real difference between the two treatments should cause the scores in one sample to be generally larger than the scores in the other sample. If the two samples are combined and all the scores placed in rank order on a line, then the scores from one sample should be concentrated at one end of the line, and the scores from the other sample should concentrate at the other end.

On the other hand, if there is no treatment difference, then large and small scores will be mixed evenly in the two samples because there is no reason for one set of scores to be systematically larger or smaller than the other.

This observation is demonstrated in Figure 20.1.

Calculation of the Mann-Whitney U

The first steps in the calculations for the Mann-Whitney test have already been discussed. To summarize,

1. A separate sample is obtained from each of the two treatments. We will use n_A to refer to the number of subjects in sample A and n_B to refer to the number in sample B.
2. These two samples are combined, and the total group of $n_A + n_B$ subjects is rank-ordered.

The remaining problem is to decide whether the scores from the two samples are mixed randomly in the rank ordering or whether they are systematically clustered at opposite ends of the scale. This is the familiar question of statistical significance: Are the data simply the result of chance, or has some treatment effect produced these results? We will answer this question exactly as we always have answered it. First, look at all the possible results that could have been obtained. Next, separate these outcomes into two groups:

1. Those results that are reasonably likely to occur by chance
2. Those results that are very unlikely to occur by chance (this is the critical region)

For the Mann-Whitney test, the first step is to identify each of the possible outcomes. This is done by assigning a numerical value to every possible set of sample data. This number is called the Mann-Whitney U. The value of U is computed as if the two samples were two teams of athletes competing in a sports event. Each individual in sample A (the A-team) gets one point whenever he is ranked ahead of an individual from sample B. The total number of points accumulated for sample A is called U_A. In the same way, a U value, or team total, is computed for sample B. The final Mann-Whitney U is the smaller of these two values. This process is demonstrated in the following example.

EXAMPLE 20.1
The following data are used to demonstrate the calculation of the Mann-Whitney U. The original data consist of two

samples with $n = 6$ in each. These two samples are combined, and all 12 scores are placed in rank order. Each individual in sample A is assigned one point for every score in sample B that is ranked beneath him. Finally, the points

---

Figure 20.1

In the top half of the figure there is a real difference between the two treatments. In this case, the scores from the two samples are clustered at opposite ends of the scale. The bottom half of the figure shows no difference between the two treatments. In this case, the two samples are intermixed evenly along the scale.

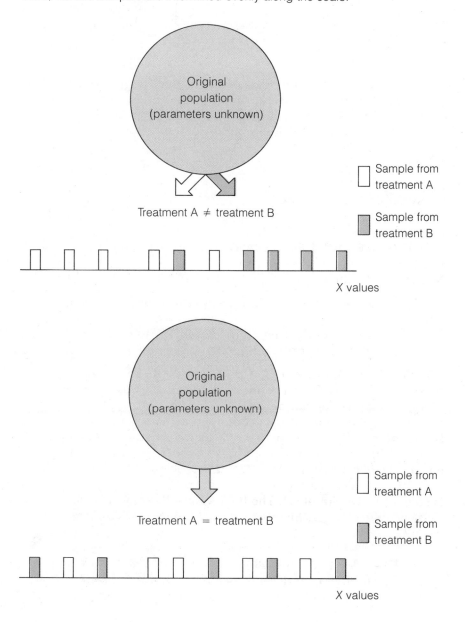

from all the individuals in sample *A* are combined, and the total number of points is computed for this sample.

Original Scores, Treatments (Samples)		Ordered Scores		Points for Sample A
1(*A*)	2(*B*)	Score	Sample	
27	71	2	(*A*)	6 points
2	63	6	(*A*)	6 points
9	18	8	(*B*)	
48	68	9	(*A*)	5 points
6	94	15	(*A*)	5 points
15	8	18	(*B*)	
		27	(*A*)	4 points
		48	(*A*)	4 points
		63	(*B*)	
		68	(*B*)	
		71	(*B*)	
		94	(*B*)	

In this example the total points or the U value for sample A is $U_A = 30$. In the same way you can compute the U value for sample B. You should obtain $U_B = 6$. As a simple check on your arithmetic, note that

To avoid errors, it is wise to compute both U *values and verify that the sum is equal to* $n_A n_B$.

$$(20.1) \quad U_A + U_B = n_A n_B$$

For these data,

$$30 + 6 = 6(6)$$

Formulas for the Mann-Whitney *U*

Because the process of counting points to determine the Mann-Whitney U can be tedious, especially with large samples, there is a formula that will generate the U value for each sample. To use this formula, you combine the samples and rank-order all the scores as before. Then you must find ΣR_A, which is the sum of the ranks for individuals in sample A and the corresponding ΣR_B for sample B. The U value for each sample is then computed as follows: For sample A,

$$(20.2) \quad U_A = n_A n_B + \frac{n_A(n_A + 1)}{2} - \Sigma R_A$$

and for sample B,

$$(20.3) \quad U_B = n_A n_B + \frac{n_B(n_B + 1)}{2} - \Sigma R_B$$

As noted before, the Mann-Whitney U is the smaller of these two values. These formulas are demonstrated in the following example.

EXAMPLE 20.2
The same scores that appeared in Example 20.1 are repeated here. This time we have included the rank of each individual.

Rank	Score	Sample	
1	2	A	
2	6	A	
3	8	B	For sample A,
4	9	A	$\Sigma R_A = 1 + 2 + 4 + 5 + 7 + 8$
5	15	A	$= 27$
6	18	B	
7	27	A	
8	48	A	
9	63	B	For sample B,
10	68	B	$\Sigma R_B = 3 + 6 + 9 + 10 + 11 + 12$
11	71	B	$= 51$
12	94	B	

By using the special formula, for sample A,

$$U_A = n_A n_B + \frac{n_A(n_A + 1)}{2} - \Sigma R_A$$

$$= 6(6) + \frac{6(7)}{2} - 27$$

$$= 36 + 21 - 27$$

$$= 30$$

For sample B,

$$U_B = n_A n_B + \frac{n_B(n_B + 1)}{2} - \Sigma R_B$$

$$= 6(6) + \frac{6(7)}{2} - 51$$

$$= 36 + 21 - 51$$

$$= 6$$

Notice that these are the same U values we obtained in Example 20.1 using the counting method. The Mann-Whitney U value is the smaller of these two,

$$U = 6$$

Hypothesis Tests with the Mann-Whitney U

Now that we have developed a method for identifying each rank order with a numerical value, the remaining problem is to decide whether the U value provides evidence for a real difference between the two treatment conditions. We will look at each possibility separately.

A large difference between the two treatments will cause all the ranks from sample A to cluster at one end of the scale and all the ranks from sample B to cluster at the other (see Figure 20.1). At the extreme, there will be no overlap between the two samples. In this case, the Mann-Whitney U will be zero because one of the samples will get no points at all. In general, a Mann-Whitney U of zero indicates the greatest possible difference between the two samples. As the two samples become more alike, their ranks begin to intermix, and the U becomes larger. If there is no consistent tendency for one treatment to produce larger scores than the other, then the ranks from the two samples should be intermixed evenly. In terms of a competition between the two samples (the A-team versus the B-team), a final score of 49 to 51 indicates that the two teams were nearly equal; a final score of 100 to 0 indicates a real difference between the two teams.

The null hypothesis for the Mann-Whitney test states that there is no difference between the two treatment conditions being compared; that is, the two samples are selected from identical populations. In this case, the most likely outcome is that the two samples would be similar and that the U value would be relatively large. On the other hand, a very small value of U, near zero, is evidence that the two samples are very different. Therefore, a U value near zero would tend to refute the null hypothesis. The distribution of all the possible U values has been constructed, and the critical values for $\alpha = .05$ and $\alpha = .01$ are presented in Table B.7 of Appendix B. When sample data produce a U that is *less than or equal to* the table value, we reject H_0.

A complete example of a hypothesis test using the Mann-Whitney U follows.

EXAMPLE 20.3

A local police expert claims to be able to judge an individual's personality on the basis of his/her handwriting. To test this claim, 10 samples of handwriting are obtained: 5 come from prisoners convicted of violent crimes, and 5 come from psychology majors at the college. The expert ranks the handwriting samples from first to tenth, with 1 representing the most antisocial personality. The rankings are as follows:

Ranking	Source
1	Prisoner
2	Prisoner
3	Student . . . 3 points
4	Prisoner
5	Prisoner
6	Student . . . 1 point
7	Prisoner
8	Student . . . 0 points
9	Student . . . 0 points
10	Student . . . 0 points

STEP 1. The null hypothesis states that there is no difference between the two populations. For this example, H_0 states that the police expert cannot differentiate the handwriting for prisoners from the handwriting for students.

The alternative hypothesis says there is a discernible difference.

STEP 2. For $\alpha = .05$ and with $n_A = n_B = 5$, the Mann-Whitney table gives a critical value of $U = 2$. If our data produce a U less than or equal to 2, we will reject the null hypothesis.

STEP 3. We will designate the students as sample A and the prisoners as sample B. Because the students tended to cluster at the bottom of the rankings, they should have the smaller U. Therefore, we have identified the points for this sample. The students' point total is $U_A = 4$.

Because we have found the smaller of the two U values, it is not necessary to compute U for the sample of prisoners. However, we will continue with this calculation to demonstrate the formula for U. The sample of prisoners has ranks 1, 2, 4, 5, and 7. The sum is $\Sigma R_B = 19$, so the U_B value is

$$U_B = n_A n_B + \frac{n_B(n_B + 1)}{2} - \Sigma R_B$$

$$= 5(5) + \frac{5(6)}{2} - 19$$

$$= 25 + 15 - 19$$

$$= 21$$

To check our calculations,

$$U_A + U_B = n_A n_B$$

$$4 + 21 = 5(5)$$

$$25 = 25$$

The final U is the smaller of the two values, so the Mann-Whitney U statistic is $U = 4$.

STEP 4. Because $U = 4$ is not in the critical region, we fail to reject the null hypothesis. With $\alpha = .05$, these data do not provide sufficient evidence to conclude that there is a discernible difference in handwriting between the two populations.

Assumptions and Cautions for the Mann-Whitney U

The Mann-Whitney U test is a very useful alternative to the independent measures t test. Because the Mann-Whitney test does not require homogeneity of variance or normal distributions, it can be used in situations where the t test would be inappropriate. However, the U test does assume that the dependent variable is continuous. You should recall from Chapter 1 that a continuous scale has an infinite number of distinct points. One consequence of this fact is that it is very unlikely for two individuals to have exactly the same score. This means that there should be few, if any, tied scores in the data. When sample data do have several tied scores, you should suspect that a basic assumption underlying the Mann-Whitney U test has been violated. In this situation, you should be cautious about using the Mann-Whitney U.

When there are relatively few tied scores in the data the Mann-Whitney test may be used, but you must follow the standard procedure for ranking tied scores. This procedure, which was presented in Chapter 16, page 550, is demonstrated in the following example.

EXAMPLE 20.4
The following eight scores have been placed in order from smallest to largest. Ranks from 1 to 8 have been assigned to the scores. When scores are tied, each individual is assigned the average of the tied ranks.

Scores:	7	12	12	24	35	35	35	55
Rank Position:	1	2	3	4	5	6	7	8
Final Ranks:	1	2.5	2.5	4	6	6	6	8

LEARNING CHECK

1. Do the football rankings in Table 20.1 indicate a significant difference between the AFC and the NFC? Test at the .05 level of significance. *Note:* The sum of the ranks for the AFC is 215, and the sum for the NFC is 191.

2. A developmental psychologist is examining social assertiveness for preschool children. Three- and four-year-old children are observed for 10 hours in a day-care center. The psychologist records the number of times each child initiates a social interaction with another child. The scores for the sample of four boys and nine girls are as follows:

   Boys' scores: 8, 17, 14, 21

   Girls' scores: 18, 25, 23, 21, 34, 28, 32, 30, 13

   Use a Mann-Whitney test to determine whether these data provide evidence for a significant difference in social assertiveness between preschool boys and girls. Test at the .05 level.

ANSWERS

1. For the AFC, $U = 86$. For the NFC, $U = 110$. The critical value in the table is 55, so fail to reject H_0.
2. For the boys, $U = 31.5$. For the girls, $U = 4.5$. The critical value in the table is 4, so fail to reject H_0.

Normal Approximation for the Mann-Whitney U

When samples are large (about $n = 20$), the distribution of the Mann-Whitney U statistic tends to approximate a normal shape. In this case the Mann-Whitney hypotheses can be evaluated using a z-score statistic and the unit normal distribution. You may have noticed that the table of critical values for the Mann-Whitney test does not list values for samples larger than $n = 20$. This is because the normal approximation typically is used with larger samples. The procedure for this normal approximation is as follows:

1. Find the U values for sample A and sample B as before. The Mann-Whitney U is the smaller of these two values.
2. When both samples are relatively large (around $n = 20$ or more), the distribution of the Mann-Whitney U statistic tends to form a normal distribution with

$$\mu = \frac{n_A n_B}{2}$$

and

$$\sigma = \sqrt{\frac{n_A n_B (n_A + n_B + 1)}{12}}$$

The Mann-Whitney U obtained from the sample data can be located in this distribution using a z-score:

$$(20.4) \quad z = \frac{X - \mu}{\sigma} = \frac{U - \dfrac{n_A n_B}{2}}{\sqrt{\dfrac{n_A n_B (n_A + n_B + 1)}{12}}}$$

This approximation is intended for data without tied scores or with very few ties. A special formula has been developed for data with many ties and can be found in most advanced statistics texts such as Hays (1981).

3. Use the unit normal table to establish the critical region for this z-score. For example, with $\alpha = .05$ the critical values would be ± 1.96.

An example of this normal approximation to the Mann-Whitney U follows.

EXAMPLE 20.5
To demonstrate the normal approximation, we will use the same data that were used in Example 20.1. This experiment tested the accuracy of handwriting evaluation using a sample of $n = 5$ prisoners and a sample of $n = 5$ college students. The data produced a final value of $U = 4$. (You should notice that these samples are too small to require using the normal approximation. With these data, you should use the Mann-Whitney table to decide whether or not H_0 is rejected. However, we will use these data as a demonstration in order to compare the outcome of the normal approximation test with the regular Mann-Whitney test.)

STEP 1.　The normal approximation does not affect the statement of hypotheses:

H_0:　There is no difference between the populations.

H_1:　There is a difference.

$\alpha = .05$.

STEP 2.　The critical region for this test is defined in terms of the normal distribution. The unit normal table states that the extreme 5% of this distribution is located beyond z-scores of ± 1.96 (see Figure 20.2).

STEP 3.　The sample value of $U = 4$ corresponds to a z-score of

$$z = \frac{U - \dfrac{n_A n_B}{2}}{\sqrt{\dfrac{n_A n_B (n_A + n_B + 1)}{12}}}$$

$$= \frac{4 - \dfrac{5 \times 5}{2}}{\sqrt{\dfrac{5 \times 5(11)}{12}}}$$

$$= \frac{4 - 12.5}{\sqrt{\dfrac{275}{12}}}$$

$$= -1.78$$

Figure 20.2

The normal distribution of z-scores used with the normal approximation to the Mann-Whitney U test. The critical region for $\alpha = .05$ has been shaded.

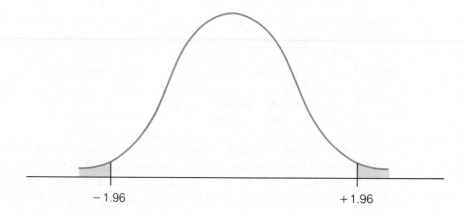

-1.96　　　　　　　$+1.96$

STEP 4. Because this z-score is not in the critical region, our decision is to fail to reject the null hypothesis.

Notice that we reach exactly the same decision whether we use the normal approximation or the original Mann-Whitney test. You also should notice that in both cases the data are close to the critical region but not quite sufficient to reject H_0. (The sample $U = 4$ is close to the critical value of 2, and the sample $z = -1.78$ is close to the critical value of -1.96.)

There is one final point that should be made comparing the normal approximation with the regular Mann-Whitney test. The table of significant values for the Mann-Whitney test customarily is constructed to identify critical values in terms of the smaller of the two sample Us. However, with the normal approximation, you may use either of the two sample U values. For example, the two samples in Example 20.1 produced U values of $U_A = 4$ and $U_B = 21$. In the preceding calculations, we found that $U_A = 4$ corresponds to $z = -1.78$. If we had used $U_B = 21$, we would have obtained

$$z = \frac{U - \dfrac{n_A n_B}{2}}{\sqrt{\dfrac{n_A n_B (n_A + n_B + 1)}{12}}}$$

$$= \frac{21 - \dfrac{5 \times 5}{2}}{\sqrt{\dfrac{5 \times 5(11)}{12}}}$$

$$= \frac{21 - 12.5}{\sqrt{\dfrac{275}{12}}}$$

$$= +1.78$$

The two samples always will produce z-scores that are identical except for the sign. If one sample value is significantly small (in the critical region), then the other sample will be significantly large. If the smaller U is not significant, then the larger U also will not be significant.

LEARNING CHECK

1. An experiment using $n = 25$ in one sample and $n = 10$ in the other produced a Mann-Whitney U of $U = 50$. Assuming that this is the smaller of the two U values, what was the value of U for the other sample?

Remember, the
normal approxi-
mation is not
intended for sam-
ples this small.

2. According to the Mann-Whitney table, a value of $U = 30$ is significant (in the critical region) with $\alpha = .05$ when both samples
have $n = 11$. If this value is used in the normal approximation,
does it produce a z-score in the critical region? The table also
indicates that a value larger than $U = 30$ is not significant. Use
the normal approximation to find the z-score for $U = 31$. Is this
value in the critical region?

ANSWERS

1. With $n_A = 25$ and $n_B = 10$, the two U values must total $n_A n_B = 25(10) = 250$. If the smaller value is 50, then the larger value
must be 200.

2. $U = 30$ produces a z-score of $z = -2.00$. This is in the critical
region. $U = 31$ produces a z-score of $z = -1.94$. This is not in
the critical region.

20.3
The Wilcoxon Signed-Ranks Test

The Wilcoxon test is designed to evaluate the difference between two
treatments using the data from a repeated measures experiment. The
data for the Wilcoxon test consist of the difference scores from the
repeated measures design. The test requires that these differences be
ranked from smallest to largest in terms of their *absolute values* (without regard to the sign). This process is demonstrated in the following
example.

EXAMPLE 20.6
The following data are from a repeated measures experiment using a sample of $n = 6$ subjects to compare two
treatment conditions:

Subject	Treatments 1	2	Difference	Rank	
1	18	43	+25	6	(largest)
2	9	14	+5	2	
3	21	20	−1	1	(smallest)
4	30	48	+18	5	
5	14	21	+7	3	
6	12	4	−8	4	

The null hypothesis for this test states that there is no difference
between the two treatments. If this hypothesis is true, any differences
that exist in the sample data must be due to chance. Therefore, we
would expect positive and negative differences to be intermixed evenly.
On the other hand, a consistent difference between the two treatments
should cause the scores in one treatment to be consistently larger than
scores in the other. This should produce difference scores that tend

to be consistently positive or consistently negative. The Wilcoxon test uses the signs and the ranks of the difference scores to decide whether or not there is a significant difference between the two treatments.

Calculation of the Wilcoxon T

As with most nonparametric tests, the calculations for the Wilcoxon are quite simple. After ranking the absolute values of the difference scores as in Example 20.6, you separate the ranks into two groups: those associated with positive differences and those associated with negative differences. Next, find the sum of the ranks for each group. The smaller of these two sums is the test statistic for the Wilcoxon test and is identified by the letter T. For the data in Example 20.6, the ranks for positive differences are 6, 2, 3, and 5. These ranks sum to $\Sigma R = 16$. The ranks for negative differences are 1 and 4, which sum to $\Sigma R = 5$. The smaller of these two sums is 5, so the Wilcoxon T for these data is $T = 5$.

Hypothesis Tests with the Wilcoxon T

We noted earlier that a strong treatment effect should cause the difference scores to be consistently positive or consistently negative. In the extreme case, all of the differences will be in the same direction. This will produce a Wilcoxon T of zero. For example, when all of the differences are positive, the sum of the negative ranks will be zero. On the other hand, when there is no treatment effect, the signs of the difference scores should be intermixed evenly. In this case, the Wilcoxon T will be relatively large. In general, a small value T (near zero) provides evidence for a real difference between the two treatment conditions. The distribution of all the possible T values has been constructed, and the critical values for $\alpha = .05$ and $\alpha = .01$ are given in Table B.8 of Appendix B. Whenever sample data produce a T that is *less than or equal to* this critical value, we will reject H_0.

See Box 20.1 for information concerning how the distribution of Wilcoxon T values is constructed.

Tied Scores and Zero Scores

Although the Wilcoxon test does not require normal distributions, it does assume that the dependent variable is continuous. As noted with the Mann-Whitney test, this assumption implies that tied scores should be very unlikely. When ties do appear in sample data, you should be concerned that the basic assumption of continuity has been violated, and the Wilcoxon test may not be appropriate. If there are relatively few ties in the data, most researchers assume that the data actually are continuous but have been crudely measured. In this case, the Wilcoxon test may be used, but the tied values must receive special attention in the calculations.

With the Wilcoxon test, there are two different types of tied scores:

1. When a subject has the same score in treatment 1 and treatment 2, resulting in a zero difference
2. When two or more subjects have identical difference scores

BOX 20.1 Critical Values for the Wilcoxon *T*

You may have wondered how statisticians develop all of the tables you find in the back of statistics books. The Wilcoxon test provides a good opportunity to demonstrate how one of these tables is constructed.

To determine the critical values for a statistical test, you first must look at the distribution of all the possible results that could be obtained. Next you determine the probability values for each portion of this distribution. In this way you can identify the results that are very unlikely; that is, results with probability less than .01 or less than .05 (for α = .01 or .05, respectively).

For the Wilcoxon test the number of possible results is limited, so it is relatively simple to construct the entire distribution. For example, suppose you are using a sample of $n = 7$ in a repeated measures experiment comparing two treatments. The results from this experiment would consist of a set of $n = 7$ difference scores. These differences are then classified as either positive or negative and rank-ordered from smallest to largest. For each position in the rank order there are only two alternatives (positive and negative). With two possibilities for the first position, two for the second, two for the third, etc., there is a total of

$$2 \times 2 \times 2 \times 2 \times 2 \times 2 \times 2 = 2^7 = 128$$

different outcomes. When the null hypothesis is true and there is no treatment effect, all of these 128 possibilities are equally likely. This set of 128 possibilities is the distribution of all possible results. The next step is to determine probabilities for each outcome.

Some of the 128 possible outcomes are listed in Table 20.2. Notice that we have concentrated on outcomes that produce small values for the Wilcoxon T. For example, there are only 2 outcomes that result in $T = 0$. Either the positive ranks sum to zero, or the negative ranks sum to zero. Thus, only 2 out of 128 possible results will give $T = 0$. In terms of probabilities,

$$P(T = 0) = \tfrac{2}{128} = 0.0156$$

Similarly, there are only two outcomes that produce $T = 1$. Either there is one positive difference with a rank of 1, or there is exactly one negative difference and it has a rank of 1. Again, there are 2 out of 128 possible results that produce $T = 1$:

$$P(T = 1) = \tfrac{2}{128} = 0.0156$$

Table 20.2 shows that there are only two possible outcomes that result in $T = 2$. Therefore,

$$P(T = 2) = \tfrac{2}{128} = 0.0156$$

For $T = 3$ the possibilities become a bit more interesting. To obtain $T = 3$, either the positive or the negative ranks must sum to 3. To obtain a sum of 3, you either can have one individual ranked

BOX 20.1 *continued*

Table 20.2

Partial listing of the 128 possible outcomes from a repeated measures experiment with $n = 7$ subjects[a]

			Rank				
1	2	3	4	5	6	7	
Pos.	Pos.	Pos.	Pos.	Pos.	Pos.	Pos.	$T = 0$
Neg.	Neg.	Neg.	Neg.	Neg.	Neg.	Neg.	$T = 0$
Pos.	Neg.	Neg.	Neg.	Neg.	Neg.	Neg.	$T = 1$
Neg.	Pos.	Pos.	Pos.	Pos.	Pos.	Pos.	$T = 1$
Pos.	Neg.	Pos.	Pos.	Pos.	Pos.	Pos.	$T = 2$
Neg.	Pos.	Neg.	Neg.	Neg.	Neg.	Neg.	$T = 2$
Pos.	Pos.	Neg.	Neg.	Neg.	Neg.	Neg.	$T = 3$
Neg.	Neg.	Pos.	Pos.	Pos.	Pos.	Pos.	$T = 3$
Neg.	Neg.	Pos.	Neg.	Neg.	Neg.	Neg.	$T = 3$
Pos.	Pos.	Neg.	Pos.	Pos.	Pos.	Pos.	$T = 3$

[a]The table assumes that the seven difference scores have been rank-ordered from smallest to largest and have been classified as either a positive difference (pos.) or a negative difference (neg.)

third or you can have two individuals who are ranked first and second. Thus, there are two outcomes that make the positive ranks sum to 3 and two outcomes that make the negative outcomes sum to 3 (see Table 20.2). In the 128 total possible outcomes, there are 4 that produce a T value of 3. Thus,

$$P(T = 3) = \tfrac{4}{128} = 0.0312$$

The table and the probability values could be continued in this manner until all the possible T values were examined. However, we already have the values needed to determine the critical region for this test. For example, there is no outcome that has probability less than 0.01. Even $T = 0$ has a probability of 0.0156. Thus, you could not use $\alpha = .01$ with the Wilcoxon test with a sample of $n = 7$. On the other hand, there are several outcomes that have probability less than 0.05. To find the exact critical cutoff for $\alpha = .05$, we start at the extreme end of the distribution ($T = 0$) and then accumulate larger values of T until we reach a probability value that goes over 0.05:

$$P(T = 0) = \tfrac{2}{128} = 0.0156 \quad (P < 0.05)$$

$$P(T = 0\,\text{or}\,1) = \tfrac{4}{128} = 0.0312 \quad (P < 0.05)$$

$$P(T = 0\,\text{or}\,1\,\text{or}\,2) = \tfrac{6}{128} = 0.0468 \quad (P < 0.05)$$

$$P(T = 0\,\text{or}\,1\,\text{or}\,2\,\text{or}\,3) = \tfrac{10}{128} = 0.0781 \quad (P > 0.05)$$

continued

BOX 20.1 _continued_

Notice that a T value of 2 or less has a probability smaller than 0.05. Therefore, $T \leq 2$ would be considered a very unlikely outcome and would result in rejecting H_0 at the .05 level of significance. If you check the Wilcoxon table (page A-42), you will find that $T = 2$ is given as the critical value for $\alpha = .05$ when $n = 7$.

Remember, the null hypothesis says there is no difference between the two treatments. Subjects with zero difference scores tend to support this hypothesis.

When the data include individuals with zero difference scores, some texts recommend that these subjects should be discarded from the analysis and the sample size (n) reduced. However, this procedure ignores the fact that a zero difference is evidence for retaining the null hypothesis. A better procedure is to divide the zero differences evenly between the positives and negatives. (If you have an odd number of zero differences, one should be discarded, and the rest divided evenly.) This second procedure will tend to increase ΣR for both the positive and the negative ranks, which increases the final value of T and makes it more likely that H_0 will be retained.

When you have ties among the difference scores, each of the tied scores should be assigned the average of the tied ranks. This procedure was presented in detail in an earlier section of this chapter (see page 686).

A complete example of the Wilcoxon test showing some tied scores will now be presented.

EXAMPLE 20.7

The local Red Cross has conducted an intensive campaign to increase blood donations. This campaign has been concentrated in 10 local businesses. In each company, the goal was to increase the percentage of employees who participate in the blood donation program. Figures showing the percent participation from last year (before the campaign) and from this year are as follows. We will use the Wilcoxon test to decide whether these data provide evidence that the campaign had a significant impact on blood donations. Note that the 10 companies are listed in rank order according to the absolute value of the difference scores.

Company	Percent Participation			Rank Discarding Zeros	Rank Including Zeros
	Before	After	Difference		
A	18	18	0	—	1.5
B	24	24	0	—	1.5
C	31	30	−1	1	3
D	28	24	−4	2	4
E	17	24	+7	3	5
F	16	24	+8	4	6
G	15	26	+11	5.5	7.5
H	18	29	+11	5.5	7.5
I	20	36	+16	7	9
J	9	28	+19	8	10

Note: We will conduct the Wilcoxon test using the recommendation that zero differences be discarded. Following this test, we will examine what would happen if the zero differences were included.

STEP 1. The null hypothesis states that the campaign had no effect. Therefore, any differences are due to chance, and there should be no consistent pattern.

STEP 2. The two companies with zero difference are discarded, and n is reduced to 8. With $n = 8$ and $\alpha = .05$, the critical value for the Wilcoxon test is $T = 3$. A sample value that is less than or equal to 3 will lead us to reject H_0.

STEP 3. For these data, the positive differences have ranks of 3, 4, 5.5, 5.5, 7, and 8:

$$\Sigma R_+ = 33$$

The negative differences have ranks of 1 and 2:

$$\Sigma R_- = 3$$

The Wilcoxon T is the smaller of these sums, so $T = 3$.

STEP 4. The T value from the data is in the critical region. This value is very unlikely to occur by chance ($p < .05$); therefore, we reject H_0 and conclude that there is a significant change in participation after the Red Cross campaign.

Note: If we include the zero differences in this test, then $n = 10$, and with $\alpha = .05$ the critical value for the Wilcoxon T is 8. Because the zero differences are tied for first and second in the ordering, each is given a rank of 1.5. One of these ranks is assigned to the positive group and one to the negative group. As a result, the sums are

$$\Sigma R_+ = 1.5 + 5 + 6 + 7.5 + 7.5 + 9 + 10$$
$$= 46.5$$

and

$$\Sigma R_- = 1.5 + 3 + 4$$
$$= 8.5$$

The Wilcoxon T is the smaller of these two sums, $T = 8.5$. Because this T value is larger than the critical value, we fail to reject H_0 and conclude that these data do not provide sufficient change in blood donor participation.

By including the zero differences in the test, we have changed the statistical conclusion. Remember, the zero differences are an indication that the null hypothesis is correct. When zero differences are considered, the test is more likely to retain H_0.

LEARNING CHECK

1. A physician is testing the effectiveness of a new arthritis drug by measuring patients' grip strength before and after they receive the drug. The difference scores for 10 patients are as follows: $+3$, $+46$, $+16$, -2, $+38$, $+14$, 0 (no change), -8, $+25$, and $+41$. Each score is the difference in strength, with a positive value indicating a stronger grip after receiving the drug. Use a Wilcoxon test to determine whether these data provide sufficient evidence to conclude that the drug has a significant effect. Test at the .05 level.

ANSWER

1. The Wilcoxon $T = 4$. Because one patient showed no change, n is reduced to 9, and the critical value is $T = 6$. Therefore, we reject H_0 and conclude that there is a significant effect.

Summary

1. The Mann-Whitney and Wilcoxon tests are nonparametric alternatives to the independent measures t and repeated measures t tests, respectively. These tests do not require normal distributions or homogeneity of variance. Both tests require that the data be rank-ordered, and they assume that the dependent variable is continuously distributed. For both tests, the null hypothesis states that there is no difference between the two treatments being compared.

2. The Mann-Whitney U can be computed either by a counting process or by a formula. A small value of U (near zero) is evidence of a difference between the two treatments. With the counting procedure, U is determined by the following:
   a. The scores from the two samples are combined and ranked from smallest to largest.
   b. Each individual in sample A is awarded one point for every member of sample B with a larger rank.
   c. U_A equals the total points for sample A. U_B is the total for sample B. The Mann-Whitney U is the smaller of these two values.
   In formula form,

   $$U_A = n_A n_B + \frac{n_A(n_A + 1)}{2} - \Sigma R_A$$

   $$U_B = n_A n_B + \frac{n_B(n_B + 1)}{2} - \Sigma R_B$$

3. For large samples, larger than those normally presented in the Mann-Whitney table, the normal distribution can be used to evaluate the difference between the two treatments. This normal approximation to the Mann-Whitney is used as follows:
   a. Find the value of U as before.
   b. The Mann-Whitney U is converted to a z-score by the formula

   $$z = \frac{U - \frac{n_A n_B}{2}}{\sqrt{\frac{n_A n_B (n_A + n_B + 1)}{12}}}$$

   c. If this z-score is in the critical region of the unit normal distribution, the null hypothesis is rejected.

4. The test statistic for the Wilcoxon test is called a T score. A small value of T (near zero) provides evidence of a difference between the two treatments. T is computed as follows:
   a. Compute a difference score (treatment 1 versus treatment 2) for each individual in the sample.
   b. Rank these difference scores from smallest to largest without regard to the signs.
   c. Sum the ranks for the positive differences, and sum the ranks for the negative differences. T is the smaller of these two sums.

Key Terms

Mann-Whitney U

Wilcoxon T

normal approximation to the Mann-Whitney U

Problems for Chapter 20:
Nonparametric Tests for Ordinal Data: Mann-Whitney and Wilcoxon Tests

*1. The following data are scores from two separate samples, each representing a different treatment condition:

Sample 1, Treatment 1	Sample 2, Treatment 2
8	22
10	16
15	20
12	24
17	14
9	23
13	19

a. Sketch a frequency distribution histogram for these data. Put both samples in the same histogram (use different colors or shading to differentiate the two treatments).

b. Just by looking at your frequency distribution sketch, does it appear that the two samples came from the same population or from two different populations?

c. Compute the Mann-Whitney U for these data. By using the .05 level of significance, do these data provide evidence of a significant difference between the two treatments?

2. An instructor teaches two sections of the same statistics course. All students take a common final exam, and the instructor receives a printout of the grades in rank order (lowest to highest). For the morning section with $n = 14$ students, the sum of the ranks is $\Sigma R = 192$. The afternoon section with $n = 10$ students has $\Sigma R = 108$. Do these data indicate a significant difference between the two sections? Test at the .05 level.

*3. A researcher is trying to determine which of two species of laboratory rats should be housed in the psychology department. A sample of $n = 10$ rats is obtained for each species, and the researcher records the amount of food each rat consumes during a 1-week period. The data are as follows:

Species A: 7, 9, 14, 20, 16, 18, 10, 22, 25, 13

Species B: 24, 19, 21, 26, 21, 29, 13, 28, 32, 17

Do these data indicate that one species eats significantly more than the other? Use a Mann-Whitney test with $\alpha = .05$.

4. A doctor has been collecting data on the birth weight of newborn children for smoking and nonsmoking mothers:

Smoking mothers: 92 oz, 111 oz, 108 oz, 120 oz, 101 oz

Nonsmoking mothers: 127 oz, 118 oz, 134 oz, 136 oz, 109 oz, 122 oz, 115 oz, 129 oz, 113 oz

Do these data indicate a significant difference in birth weight between these two groups? Use a Mann-Whitney U Test at the .05 level of significance.

*5. A psychologist studying problem-solving ability presents subjects with a set of five anagrams to unscramble. (An anagram is a word with the letters rearranged into a random order.) In one condition, the anagrams are all pronounceable sequences (e.g., CAWTH), and in a second condition the anagrams are unpronounceable (e.g., HTWCA). In each condition, the psychologist records the amount of time needed to solve all five anagrams:

Subject	Pronounceable	Unpronounceable
1	189	130
2	167	94
3	208	185
4	143	82
5	156	148
6	119	124
7	129	91
8	175	107

Do these data indicate a significant difference between the two conditions? Use a Wilcoxon test with $\alpha = .05$.

6. Monkeys raised in isolation tend to have difficulty adjusting to a social situation as adults. In an experimental demonstration of this phenomenon, a sample of 16 newborn monkeys was obtained. Eight of these monkeys were raised in isolation, and the other 8 were left to be reared in the colony. After 10 months, the 8 isolated monkeys were returned to the colony. Two months later, all 16 monkeys were ranked in terms of their position in the colony dominance hierarchy (number 1 being most dominant). These rankings are as follows:

Isolated Monkeys		Not Isolated	
Subject	Ranking	Subject	Ranking
1	13	9	3
2	7	10	12
3	10	11	5
4	16	12	1
5	6	13	4
6	14	14	2
7	11	15	8
8	15	16	9

Do these data provide evidence that isolation affects social dominance? Test at the .05 level of significance.

*7. As part of a product testing program, a paint manufacturer painted 12 houses in a suburban community. Six of the houses were painted with the company's own product, and the other 6 were painted with a competitor's paint. After 5 years a panel of home owners inspected the 12 houses and ranked them according to how well the paint was holding up. The rankings are as follows:

Ranks for company's paint: 1, 3, 4, 5, 7, 8

Ranks for competitor's paint: 2, 6, 9, 10, 11, 12

Do these data indicate a significant difference between the two brands of paint? Test with $\alpha = .05$.

8. In a hidden-figures task, subjects are required to find a specific shape that is contained within a more complex drawing. In an

experiment using this task, the same figure was presented twice to each subject. On one presentation the figure was oriented so that all the lines were vertical and horizontal. On the other presentation, the figure was rotated so that all the lines were oblique. The dependent variable was the amount of time needed to locate and identify the hidden figure. Use a Wilcoxon test to determine whether the following data indicate a significant difference between the two orientations:

Subject	Horizontal-Vertical	Oblique
1	8 seconds	13 seconds
2	10 seconds	35 seconds
3	7 seconds	12 seconds
4	3 seconds	11 seconds
5	12 seconds	10 seconds
6	17 seconds	29 seconds
7	8 seconds	9 seconds
8	14 seconds	38 seconds
9	5 seconds	21 seconds
10	13 seconds	9 seconds

*9. Hyperactive children often are treated with a stimulant such as Ritalin to improve their attention span. In one test of this drug treatment, hyperactive children were given a boring task to work on. A psychologist recorded the amount of time (in seconds) each child spent on the task before becoming distracted. Each child's performance was measured before he/she received the drug and again after the drug was administered. Because the scores on this task are extremely variable, the psychologist decided to convert the data to ranks. Use a Wilcoxon test with $\alpha = .05$ to determine whether the following data provide evidence that the drug has a significant effect:

Child	Treatment 1 (Without the Drug)	Treatment 2 (With the Drug)
1	28	135
2	15	309
3	183	150
4	48	224
5	30	25
6	233	345
7	21	43
8	110	188
9	12	15

10. Quite often you have a choice between a parametric and a nonparametric statistical test; for example, you could use either a *t* test or a Wilcoxon test for the same set of data. In general, the parametric test is the better choice because it uses more of the information available in the data and is more likely to produce a correct interpretation of the experimental outcome. The following data are difference scores from a repeated measures design: 11, 3, −1, 10, 17, 15, −6, −4, 5, 13. Using $\alpha = .05$, test

for a significant difference using both a *t* test and the Wilcoxon test. Explain why the two tests lead to different conclusions.

*11. One assumption for parametric tests with independent measures data is that the different treatment conditions have the same variance (homogeneity of variance assumption). However, a treatment effect that increases the mean often will also increase the variability. In this situation, the parametric *t* test or ANOVA is not justified and a Mann-Whitney test should be used. The following data represent an example of this situation:

Treatment 1 (Sample A)	Treatment 2 (Sample B)
1	8
5	20
0	14
2	27
4	6
2	10
3	19

a. Compute the mean and variance for each sample. Note the difference between the two sample variances.

b. Use a Mann-Whitney test, with $\alpha = .05$, to test for a significant difference between the two treatments.

12. A recent wine-tasting compared French and California wines. The 12 wines were ranked from best to worst with the French wines receiving ranks of 1, 2, 4, 10, 11, and 12. The California wines were ranked 3, 5, 6, 7, 8, and 9.

a. Use a Mann-Whitney U test with $\alpha = .05$ to determine whether these data indicate any significant difference between French and California wines.

b. By just looking at the rankings, how would you describe the French wines in terms of consistency of quality? How would you describe the California wines in terms of consistent quality.

c. You should find that the Mann-Whitney test in part a indicates no difference. How do you reconcile this fact with the obvious difference between the two samples that you described in part b?

*13. A new cold remedy contains a chemical that causes drowsiness and disorientation. Part of the testing for this drug involved measuring maze-learning performance for rats. Individual rats were tested with and without the drug. The dependent variable is the number of errors before the rat solves the maze. In the drug condition, two rats failed to solve the maze after 200 errors and were simply marked as "failed."

Subject	No Drug	Drug
1	28	125
2	43	90
3	37	(Failed)
4	16	108
5	47	40
6	51	75
7	23	91
8	31	23
9	26	115
10	53	55
11	26	(Failed)
12	32	87

Do these data indicate that the drug has a significant effect on maze-learning performance? Test at the .05 level of significance.

14. The American Automobile Club has classified states according to how strictly they enforce drinking-while-intoxicated (DWI) laws. The 20 states representing the 10 most strict and 10 most lax enforcers have been ranked by per capita traffic fatalities (1 = lowest). These data are as follows:

State	Traffic Fatalities Rank Position	DWI Enforcement
A	1	Strict
B	2	Strict
C	3	Strict
D	4	Lax
E	5	Strict
F	6	Strict
G	7	Lax
H	8	Strict
I	9	Lax
J	10	Lax
K	11	Strict
L	12	Strict
M	13	Lax
N	14	Strict
O	15	Lax
P	16	Strict
Q	17	Lax
R	18	Lax
S	19	Lax
T	20	Lax

Do these data indicate that DWI enforcement has a significant effect on traffic fatalities? Test at the .05 level of significance.

*15. A computer manufacturer is comparing two systems for word processing. A group of 60 subjects is obtained, all of whom have no experience with any word processor. Half of the subjects are assigned to system A and the other half to system B. The dependent variable is the amount of time each subject needs to learn the word-processing system (to type, store, and print out a letter). If subjects failed to complete the task within 4 hours, they were stopped and were given a score of "failed." The data from this study are as follows: Of the 30 subjects on system A, 3 failed to complete the task. The times (in minutes) for the other 27 subjects were as follows:

121	193	175	204
94	115	186	210
160	73	220	149
68	102	91	155
125	79	120	187
215	205	163	99
143	180	207	

Caution: Do not forget to rank the subjects who failed.

Of the 30 subjects on system B, 7 failed to complete the task. The times (in minutes) for the other 23 subjects were as follows:

183	215	225	168
193	86	130	179
212	195	229	208
153	182	95	107
218	230	165	81
194	151	219	

Do these data indicate a significant difference between the two systems? Test at the .05 level of significance.

16. A psychologist interested in the development of manual dexterity prepared a block manipulation task for 3-year-old children. A sample of 18 children was obtained, 10 boys and 8 girls. The psychologist recorded the amount of time required by each child to arrange the blocks in a specified pattern. These data are as follows:

Boys	Girls
23	37
18	21
39	104
26	48
29	25
42	85
56	123
34	62
20	
37	

Do these data indicate a significant difference in the development of manual dexterity for males versus females? Use a Mann-Whitney test with $\alpha = .01$.

*17. For the vast majority of right-handed people, language is controlled in the left hemisphere of the brain. The left hemisphere also manages motor control for the right side of the body.

Because language and fine motor control with the right hand are dependent on the same general area of the brain, these two activities can interfere with each other if an individual tries both at the same time. To demonstrate this fact, a psychologist asked subjects to balance a ruler on the index finger of their right hand. The psychologist recorded the amount of time the ruler was balanced under two conditions. In one condition the subject was allowed to concentrate on balancing the ruler. In the second condition, the subject was required to recite a nursery rhyme while balancing the ruler. The data for this experiment are as follows:

Subject	Just Balancing	Balancing and Reciting
1	43 seconds	15 seconds
2	127 seconds	21 seconds
3	18 seconds	25 seconds
4	28 seconds	6 seconds
5	21 seconds	10 seconds
6	47 seconds	9 seconds
7	12 seconds	14 seconds
8	25 seconds	6 seconds
9	53 seconds	24 seconds
10	17 seconds	11 seconds

On the basis of these data, can the psychologist conclude that the language task (nursery rhyme) significantly interferes with right-hand motor skill? Use a Wilcoxon test with $\alpha = .05$.

18. Psychosis such as schizophrenia often is expressed in the artistic work produced by patients. To test the reliability of this phenomenon, a psychologist collected 10 paintings done by schizophrenic patients and another 10 paintings done by normal college students. A professor in the art department was asked to rank-order all 20 paintings in terms of bizarreness. These ranks are as follows:

Ranks for schizophrenics: 1, 3, 4, 5, 6, 8, 9, 11, 12, 14

Ranks for students: 2, 7, 10, 13, 15, 16, 17, 18, 19, 20

On the basis of these data, can the psychologist conclude that there is a significant difference between the paintings for these two populations? Test at the .05 level of significance.

*19. Individuals who are rated high in need for achievement (nAch) tend to work harder and longer than individuals rated low in nAch. In a laboratory test, 12 individuals rated high in nAch and 8 individuals rated low in nAch were given a mechanical puzzle to solve. Unknown to the subjects, there was no solution to the puzzle. The psychologist observing these subjects recorded the amount of time each person persisted on the task before giving up. There was a 20-minute time limit for each subject. The scores (in minutes) for the 8 subjects rated low in nAch were 6, 3, 7, 3, 2, 10, 12, 8. Of the 12 subjects rated high in nAch, 3 worked for the full 20 minutes and had to be stopped by the psychologist. The scores for the other 9 subjects were 9, 17, 13, 8, 5, 15, 16, 18, 11. Do these data indicate a significant difference between two personality types in terms of their persistence? Test at the .05 level of significance.

20. Several studies suggest that prejudice between groups can be reduced if people are given an opportunity for interaction on an equal status basis. One of these studies involved a specially structured summer camp for children. In this camp, all of the administrative and counseling positions were divided equally between blacks and whites. Thus, the campers experienced a situation where blacks and whites were equal in number and in status. Each child's attitude toward opposite-race children was tested before and after the camp. These data are as follows:

Child	Before	After
1	6	13
2	10	10
3	8	9
4	11	10
5	7	15
6	12	15
7	4	6
8	10	17
9	12	10
10	9	12
11	14	18
12	7	12

Because the attitude scale used in this study was an ordinal scale, use a Wilcoxon test to determine whether or not these data indicate a significant change in attitude. Test at the .05 level.

Basic Mathematics Review

This appendix reviews some of the basic math skills that are necessary for the statistical calculations presented in this book. Many students already will know some or all of this material. Others will need to do extensive work and review. To help you assess your own skills, we are including a skills assessment exam here. You should allow approximately 30 minutes to complete the test. When you finish, grade your test using the answer key on page A-20.

Notice that the test is divided into four sections. If you miss more than three questions in any section of the test, you probably need help in that area. Turn to the section of this appendix that corresponds to your problem area. In each section, you will find a general review, some examples, and some additional practice problems. After reviewing the appropriate section and doing the practice problems, turn to the end of the appendix. You will find another version of the skills assessment exam. If you still miss more than three questions in any section of the exam, continue studying. Get assistance from an instructor or tutor if necessary. At the end of this appendix is a list of recommended books for individuals who need a more extensive review than can be provided here. We must stress that mastering this material now will make the rest of the course much easier.

Skills Assessment Exam

SECTION 1 (corresponding to Sections A.1 and A.2 of this appendix)

1. The fraction $\frac{3}{4}$ corresponds to a percentage of _____.
2. Express 30% as a fraction.
3. Convert $\frac{12}{40}$ to a decimal.
4. $\frac{2}{13} + \frac{8}{13} = ?$
5. $1.375 + 0.25 = ?$
6. $\frac{2}{5} \times \frac{1}{4} = ?$
7. $\frac{1}{8} + \frac{2}{3} = ?$
8. $3.5 \times 0.4 = ?$
9. $\frac{1}{5} \div \frac{3}{4} = ?$
10. $3.75/0.5 = ?$
11. In a group of 80 students, 20% are psychology majors. How many psychology majors are in this group?
12. A company reports that two-fifths of its employees are women. If there are 90 employees, how many are women?

SECTION 2 (corresponding to Section A.3 of this appendix)

1. $3 + (-2) + (-1) + 4 = ?$
2. $6 - (-2) = ?$
3. $-2 - (-4) = ?$
4. $6 + (-1) - 3 - (-2) - (-5) = ?$
5. $4 \times (-3) = ?$
6. $-2 \times (-6) = ?$

A-1

7. $-3 \times 5 = ?$
8. $-2 \times (-4) \times (-3) = ?$
9. $12 \div (-3) = ?$
10. $-18 \div (-6) = ?$
11. $-16 \div 8 = ?$
12. $-100 \div (-4) = ?$

SECTION 3 (corresponding to Section A.4 of this appendix)

For each equation, find the value of X.

1. $X + 6 = 13$
2. $X - 14 = 15$
3. $5 = X - 4$
4. $3X = 12$
5. $72 = 3X$
6. $X/5 = 3$
7. $10 = X/8$
8. $3X + 5 = -4$
9. $24 = 2X + 2$
10. $(X + 3)/2 = 14$
11. $(X - 5)/3 = 2$
12. $17 = 4X - 11$

SECTION 4 (corresponding to Section A.5 of this appendix)

1. $4^3 = ?$
2. $\sqrt{25 - 9} = ?$
3. If $X = 2$ and $Y = 3$, then $XY^3 = ?$
4. If $X = 2$ and $Y = 3$, then $(X + Y)^2 = ?$
5. If $a = 3$ and $b = 2$, then $a^2 + b^2 = ?$
6. $-3^3 = ?$
7. $-4^4 = ?$
8. $\sqrt{4} \times 4 = ?$
9. $36/\sqrt{9} = ?$
10. $(9 + 2)^2 = ?$
11. $5^2 + 2^3 = ?$
12. If $a = 3$ and $b = -1$, then $a^2 b^3 = ?$

The answers to the skills assessment exam are at the end of the appendix (page A-20).

A.1

Symbols and Notation

Table A.1 presents the basic mathematical symbols that you should know, and it provides examples of their use. Statistical symbols and notation will be introduced and explained throughout this book as they are needed. Notation for exponents and square roots is covered separately at the end of this appendix.

Table A.1

Symbol	Meaning	Example
$+$	Addition	$5 + 7 = 12$
$-$	Subtraction	$8 - 3 = 5$
$\times, (\ )$	Multiplication	$3 \times 9 = 27$, $3(9) = 27$
$\div, /$	Division	$15 \div 3 = 5$, $15/3 = 5$, $\frac{15}{3} = 5$
$>$	Greater than	$20 > 10$
$<$	Less than	$7 < 11$
$\neq$	Not equal to	$5 \neq 6$

Parentheses are a useful notation because they specify and control the order of computations. Everything inside the parentheses is calculated first. For example,

$$(5 + 3) \times 2 = 8 \times 2 = 16$$

Changing the placement of the parentheses also changes the order of calculations. For example,

$$5 + (3 \times 2) = 5 + 6 = 11$$

A.2
Proportions: Fractions, Decimals, and Percentages

A proportion is a part of a whole and can be expressed as a fraction, or a decimal, or a percentage. For example, in a class of 40 students, only 3 failed the final exam. The proportion of the class that failed can be expressed as a fraction,

$$\text{fraction} \quad = \frac{3}{40}$$

or as a decimal value,

$$\text{decimal} \quad = \quad 0.075$$

or a percentage,

$$\text{percentage} = \quad 7.5\%$$

In a fraction, the bottom value (the denominator) indicates the number of equal pieces the whole is split up into. Here the "pie" is split up into four equal pieces:

If the denominator has a larger value, say 8, then each piece of the whole pie is smaller:

A larger denominator indicates a smaller fraction of the whole.

The value on top of the fraction (the numerator) indicates how many pieces of the whole are being considered. Thus, the fraction $\frac{3}{4}$ indicates that the whole is split evenly into four pieces and that three of them are being used:

A fraction is simply a concise way of stating a proportion: "Three out of four" is equivalent to $\frac{3}{4}$. To convert the fraction to a decimal, you divide the numerator by the denominator:

$$\frac{3}{4} = 3 \div 4 = 0.75$$

To convert the decimal to a percentage, simply multiply by 100 and place a percent sign (%) after the answer:

$$0.75 \times 100 = 75\%$$

The U.S. money system is a convenient way of illustrating the relationship between fractions and decimals. "One quarter," for example, is one-fourth ($\frac{1}{4}$) of a dollar, and its decimal equivalent is 0.25. Other familiar equivalencies are as follows:

	Dime	Quarter	50-Cent Piece	75 Cents
Fraction	$\frac{1}{10}$	$\frac{1}{4}$	$\frac{1}{2}$	$\frac{3}{4}$
Decimal	0.10	0.25	0.50	0.75
Percentage	10%	25%	50%	75%

Fractions

1. Finding Equivalent Fractions. The same proportional value can be expressed by many equivalent fractions. For example,

$$\frac{1}{2} = \frac{2}{4} = \frac{10}{20} = \frac{50}{100}$$

To create equivalent fractions, you can multiply the numerator and denominator by the same value. As long as both the numerator and denominator of the fraction are multiplied by the same value, the new fraction will be equivalent to the original. For example,

$$\frac{3}{10} = \frac{9}{30}$$

because both the numerator and denominator of the original fraction have been multiplied by 3. Dividing the numerator and denominator of a fraction by the same value will also result in an equivalent fraction. By using division, you can reduce a fraction to a simpler form. For example,

$$\frac{40}{100} = \frac{2}{5}$$

because both the numerator and denominator of the original fraction have been divided by 20.

You can use these rules to find specific equivalent fractions. For example, find the fraction that has a denominator of 100 and is equivalent to $\frac{3}{4}$. That is,

$$\frac{3}{4} = \frac{?}{100}$$

Notice that the denominator of the original fraction must be multiplied by 25 to produce the denominator of the desired fraction. For the two fractions to be equal, both the numerator and the denominator must be multiplied by the same number. Therefore, we also multiply the top of the original fraction by 25 and obtain

$$\frac{3 \times 25}{4 \times 25} = \frac{75}{100}$$

2. Multiplying Fractions. To multiply two fractions, you first multiply the numerators and then multiply the denominators. For example,

$$\frac{3}{4} \times \frac{5}{7} = \frac{3 \times 5}{4 \times 7} = \frac{15}{28}$$

3. Dividing Fractions. To divide one fraction by another, you invert the second fraction and then multiply. For example,

$$\frac{1}{2} \div \frac{1}{4} = \frac{1}{2} \times \frac{4}{1} = \frac{1 \times 4}{2 \times 1} = \frac{4}{2}$$

4. Adding and Subtracting Fractions. Fractions must have the same denominator before you can add or subtract them. If the two fractions already have a common denominator, you simply add (or subtract as the case may be) *only* the values in the numerators. For example,

$$\frac{2}{5} + \frac{1}{5} = \frac{3}{5}$$

Suppose you divided a pie into five equal pieces (fifths). If you first ate two-fifths of the pie and then another one-fifth, the total amount eaten would be three-fifths of the pie:

If the two fractions do not have the same denominator, you must first find equivalent fractions with a common denominator before you can add or subtract. The product of the two denominators will always work as a common denominator for equivalent fractions (although it may not be the lowest common denominator). For example,

$$\frac{2}{3} + \frac{1}{10} = ?$$

Because these two fractions have different denominators, it is necessary to convert each into an equivalent fraction and find a common denominator. We will use $3 \times 10 = 30$ as the common denominator. Thus the equivalent fraction of each is

$$\frac{2}{3} = \frac{20}{30} \qquad \text{and} \qquad \frac{1}{10} = \frac{3}{30}$$

Now the two fractions can be added:

$$\frac{20}{30} + \frac{3}{30} = \frac{23}{30}$$

5. Comparing the Size of Fractions. When comparing the size of two fractions with the *same* denominator, the larger fraction will have the larger numerator. For example,

$$\frac{5}{8} > \frac{3}{8}$$

The denominators are the same, so the whole is partitioned into pieces of the same size. Five of these pieces is more than three of them:

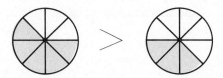

When two fractions have different denominators, you must first convert them to fractions with a common denominator to determine which is larger. Consider the following fractions:

$$\frac{3}{8} \quad \text{and} \quad \frac{7}{16}$$

If the numerator and denominator of $\frac{3}{8}$ are multiplied by 2, the resulting equivalent fraction will have a denominator of 16:

$$\frac{3}{8} = \frac{3 \times 2}{8 \times 2} = \frac{6}{16}$$

Now a comparison can be made between the two fractions:

$$\frac{6}{16} < \frac{7}{16}$$

Therefore,

$$\frac{3}{8} < \frac{7}{16}$$

Decimals

1. Converting Decimals to Fractions. Like a fraction, a decimal represents part of the whole. The first decimal place to the right of the decimal point indicates how many tenths are used. For example,

$$0.1 = \frac{1}{10} \qquad 0.7 = \frac{7}{10}$$

The next decimal place represents $\frac{1}{100}$, the next $\frac{1}{1000}$, the next $\frac{1}{10,000}$, and so on. To change a decimal to a fraction, just use the number without the decimal point for the numerator. Use the denominator that the last (on the right) decimal place represents. For example,

$$
\begin{aligned}
0.32 \quad &= \quad \frac{32}{100} \\
0.5333 \quad &= \quad \frac{5333}{10,000} \\
0.05 \quad &= \quad \frac{5}{100} \\
0.001 \quad &= \quad \frac{1}{1000}
\end{aligned}
$$

2. Addition and Subtraction. To add and subtract decimals, the only rule is that you must keep the decimal points in a straight vertical line. For example,

$$\begin{array}{r} .27 \\ +\ 1.326 \\ \hline 1.596 \end{array} \qquad \begin{array}{r} 3.595 \\ -\ .67 \\ \hline 2.925 \end{array}$$

3. Multiplying Decimals. To multiply two decimal values, you first multiply the two numbers ignoring the decimal points. Then you position the decimal point in the answer so that the number of digits to the right of the decimal point are equal to the total number of decimal places in the two numbers being multiplied. For example,

$$\begin{array}{r} 1.73 \\ \times\quad 0.251 \\ \hline 173 \\ 865 \\ 346 \\ \hline 0.43423 \end{array} \quad \begin{array}{l} \text{(two decimal places)} \\ \text{(three decimal places)} \\ \\ \\ \\ \text{(five decimal places)} \end{array}$$

$$\begin{array}{r} 0.25 \\ \times\quad 0.005 \\ \hline 125 \\ 00 \\ 00 \\ \hline 0.00125 \end{array} \quad \begin{array}{l} \text{(two decimal places)} \\ \text{(three decimal places)} \\ \\ \\ \\ \text{(five decimal places)} \end{array}$$

4. Dividing Decimals. The simplest procedure for dividing decimals is based on the fact that dividing two numbers is identical to expressing them as a fraction:

$$0.25 \div 1.6 \text{ is identical to } \frac{0.25}{1.6}$$

You now can multiply both the numerator and denominator of the fraction by 10, 100, 1000, or whatever number is necessary to remove the decimal places. Remember, multiplying both the numerator and denominator of a fraction by the *same* value will create an equivalent fraction. Therefore,

$$\frac{0.25}{1.6} = \frac{0.25 \times 100}{1.6 \times 100} = \frac{25}{160}$$

The result is a division problem without any decimal places in the two numbers.

Percentages

1. Converting a Percentage to a Fraction or Decimal. To convert a percentage to a fraction, remove the percent sign, place the number in the numerator, and use 100 for the denominator. For example,

$$52\% = \frac{52}{100} \qquad 5\% = \frac{5}{100}$$

To convert a percentage to a decimal, remove the percent sign and divide by 100, or simply move the decimal point two places to the left. For example,

$$83\% = 83. = 0.83$$

$$14.5\% = 14.5 = 0.145$$

$$5\% = 5. = 0.05$$

2. Arithmetic Operations with Percentages. There are situations when it is best to change percent values into decimals in order to perform certain arithmetic operations. For example, what is 45% of 60? This question may be stated as

$$45\% \times 60 = ?$$

The 45% should be converted to decimal form to find the solution to this question. Therefore,

$$0.45 \times 60 = 27$$

LEARNING CHECK

1. Convert $\frac{3}{25}$ to a decimal.
2. Convert $\frac{3}{8}$ to a percentage.
3. Next to each set of fractions, write "true" if they are equivalent and "false" if they are not:
    a. $\frac{3}{8} = \frac{9}{24}$ _____
    b. $\frac{7}{9} = \frac{17}{19}$ _____
    c. $\frac{2}{7} = \frac{4}{14}$ _____
4. Compute the following:
    a. $\frac{1}{6} \times \frac{7}{10}$ c. $\frac{9}{10} \div \frac{2}{3}$
    b. $\frac{7}{8} - \frac{1}{2}$ d. $\frac{7}{22} + \frac{2}{3}$
5. Identify the larger fraction of each pair:
    a. $\frac{7}{10}, \frac{21}{100}$
    b. $\frac{3}{4}, \frac{7}{12}$
    c. $\frac{22}{3}, \frac{19}{3}$
6. Convert the following decimals into fractions:
    a. 0.012   b. 0.77   c. 0.005
7. $2.59 \times 0.015 = ?$
8. $1.8 \div 0.02 = ?$
9. What is 28% of 45?

1. 0.12. 2. 37.5%. 3. a. True. b. False. c. True.
4. a. $\frac{7}{60}$. b. $\frac{3}{8}$. c. $\frac{27}{20}$. d. $\frac{65}{66}$. 5. a. $\frac{7}{10}$. b. $\frac{3}{4}$. c. $\frac{22}{3}$.
6. a. $\frac{12}{1000}$. b. $\frac{77}{100}$. c. $\frac{5}{1000}$. 7. 0.03885. 8. 90.
9. 12.6.

A.3
Negative Numbers

Negative numbers are used to represent values less than zero. Negative numbers may occur when you are measuring the difference between two scores. For example, a researcher may want to evaluate the effectiveness of a propaganda film by measuring people's attitude with a test both before and after viewing the film:

	Before	After	Amount of Change
Person A	23	27	+4
Person B	18	15	−3
Person C	21	16	−5

Notice that the negative sign provides information about the direction of the difference: a plus sign indicates an increase in value, and a minus sign indicates a decrease.

Because negative numbers are frequently encountered, you should be comfortable working with these values. This section reviews basic arithmetic operations using negative numbers. You should also note that any number without a sign (+ or −) is assumed to be positive.

1. Addition with Negative Numbers. When adding numbers that include negative values, simply interpret the negative sign as subtraction. For example,

$$3 + (-2) + 5 = 3 - 2 + 5 = 6$$

When adding a long string of numbers, it often is easier to add all the positive values to obtain the positive sum and then add all of the negative values to obtain the negative sum. Finally, you subtract the negative sum from the positive sum. For example,

$$-1 + 3 + (-4) + 3 + (-6) + (-2)$$
positive sum = 6   negative sum = 13
Answer: $6 - 13 = -7$

2. Subtraction with Negative Numbers. To subtract a negative number, change it to positive and add. For example,

$$4 - (-3) = 4 + 3 = 7$$

This rule is easier to understand if you think of subtraction as "taking away." In the preceding example, if you substitute $7 - 3$ in place of the original 4 (note that $7 - 3 = 4$), you obtain

$$4 - (-3)$$
$$7 - 3 - (-3) \quad \text{(substitution of } 7 - 3 \text{ for 4)}$$
$$7 - 3 \text{ "take away" } -3 \quad (-3 \text{ "take away" } -3 \text{ is zero)}$$
$$7 \quad \text{(7 is the remainder)}$$

3. Multiplying and Dividing Negative Numbers. When the two numbers being multiplied (or divided) have the same sign, the result is a positive number. When the two numbers have different signs, the result is negative. For example,

$$3 \times (-2) = -6$$
$$-4 \times (-2) = +8$$

The first example is easy to explain by thinking of multiplication as repeated addition. In this case,

$$3 \times (-2) = (-2) + (-2) + (-2) = -6$$

You take three negative 2s, which result in a total of negative 6. In the second example, we are multiplying by a negative number. This amounts to repeated subtraction. That is,

$$-4 \times (-2) = -(-2) - (-2) - (-2) - (-2)$$
$$= 2 + 2 + 2 + 2 = 8$$

By using the same rule for both multiplication and division, we ensure that these two operations are compatible. For example,

$$-6 \div 3 = -2$$

which is compatible with

$$3 \times (-2) = -6$$

Also,

$$8 \div (-4) = -2$$

which is compatible with

$$-4 \times (-2) = +8$$

LEARNING
CHECK

1. Complete the following calculations:
   a. $3 + (-8) + 5 + 7 + (-1) + (-3)$
   b. $5 - (-9) + 2 - (-3) - (-1)$
   c. $3 - 7 - (-21) + (-5) - (-9)$
   d. $4 - (-6) - 3 + 11 - 14$
   e. $9 + 8 - 2 - 1 - (-6)$
   f. $9 \times (-3)$
   g. $-7 \times (-4)$
   h. $-6 \times (-2) \times (-3)$
   i. $-12 \div (-3)$
   j. $18 \div (-6)$

A-10 Appendix A

A.4

Basic Algebra: Solving Equations

An equation is a mathematical statement which indicates that two quantities are identical. For example,

$$12 = 8 + 4$$

Often an equation will contain an unknown (or variable) quantity that is identified with a letter or symbol rather than a number. For example,

$$12 = 8 + X$$

In this event, your task is to find the value of X which makes the equation "true" or balanced. For this example, an X value of 4 will make a true equation. Finding the value of X is usually called *solving the equation*.

To solve an equation, there are two points to be kept in mind:

1. Your goal is to have the unknown value (X) isolated on one side of the equation. This means that you need to remove all of the other numbers and symbols that appear on the same side of the equation as the X.
2. The equation will remain balanced provided you treat both sides exactly the same. For example, you could add 10 points to *both* sides, and the solution (the X value) for the equation would be unchanged.

Finding the Solution for an Equation

We will consider four basic types of equations and the operations needed to solve them.

1. When X has a Value Added to It. An example of this type of equation is

$$X + 3 = 7$$

Your goal is to isolate X on one side of the equation. Thus, you must remove the $+3$ on the left-hand side. The solution is obtained by subtracting 3 from *both* sides of the equation:

$$X + 3 - 3 = 7 - 3$$
$$X = 4$$

The solution is $X = 4$. You should always check your solution by returning to the original equation and replacing X with the value you obtained for the solution. For this example,

$$X + 3 = 7$$
$$4 + 3 = 7$$
$$7 = 7$$

2. When *X* Has a Value Subtracted from It. An example of this type of equation is

$$X - 8 = 12$$

In this example, you must remove the -8 from the left-hand side. Thus, the solution is obtained by adding 8 to *both* sides of the equation:

$$X - 8 + 8 = 12 + 8$$
$$X = 20$$

Check the solution:

$$X - 8 = 12$$
$$20 - 8 = 12$$
$$12 = 12$$

3. When *X* Is Multiplied by a Value. An example of this type of equation is

$$4X = 24$$

In this instance, it is necessary to remove the 4 which is multiplied by *X*. This may be accomplished by dividing both sides of the equation by 4:

$$\frac{4X}{4} = \frac{24}{4}$$
$$X = 6$$

Check the solution:

$$4X = 24$$
$$4(6) = 24$$
$$24 = 24$$

4. When *X* Is Divided by a Value. An example of this type of equation is

$$\frac{X}{3} = 9$$

Now the *X* is divided by 3, so the solution is obtained by multiplying by 3. Multiplying both sides yields

$$3\left(\frac{X}{3}\right) = 9(3)$$
$$X = 27$$

For the check,

$$\frac{X}{3} = 9$$

$$\frac{27}{3} = 9$$

$$9 = 9$$

Solutions for More Complex Equations

More complex equations can be solved by using a combination of the preceding simple operations. Remember, at each stage you are trying to isolate X on one side of the equation. For example,

$$3X + 7 = 22$$

$3X + 7 - 7 = 22 - 7$ (remove $+7$ by subtracting 7 from both sides)

$$3X = 15$$

$\dfrac{3X}{3} = \dfrac{15}{3}$ (remove 3 by dividing both sides by 3)

$$X = 5$$

To check this solution, return to the original equation and substitute 5 in place of X:

$$3X + 7 = 22$$
$$3(5) + 7 = 22$$
$$15 + 7 = 22$$
$$22 = 22$$

Following is another type of complex equation that is frequently encountered in statistics:

$$\frac{X + 3}{4} = 2$$

First, remove the 4 by multiplying both sides by 4:

$$4\left(\frac{X + 3}{4}\right) = 2(4)$$
$$X + 3 = 8$$

Now remove the $+3$ by subtracting 3 from both sides:

$$X + 3 - 3 = 8 - 3$$
$$X = 5$$

To check this solution, return to the original equation and substitute 5 in place of X:

$$\frac{X + 3}{4} = 2$$

$$\frac{5 + 3}{4} = 2$$

$$\frac{8}{4} = 2$$

$$2 = 2$$

LEARNING CHECK

1. Solve for X and check the solutions:

   a. $3X = 18$

   b. $X + 7 = 9$

   c. $X - 4 = 18$

   d. $5X - 8 = 12$

   e. $\dfrac{X}{9} = 5$

   f. $\dfrac{X + 1}{6} = 4$

   g. $X + 2 = -5$

   h. $\dfrac{X}{5} = -5$

   i. $\dfrac{2X}{3} = 12$

   j. $\dfrac{X}{3} + 1 = 3$

ANSWERS

a. $X = 6$ b. $X = 2$ c. $X = 22$ d. $X = 4$ e. $X = 45$
f. $X = 23$ g. $X = -7$ h. $X = -25$ i. $X = 18$ j. $X = 6$

A.5
Exponents and Square Roots

Exponential Notation

A simplified notation is used whenever a number is being multiplied by itself. The notation consists of placing a value, called an exponent, on the right-hand side of and raised above another number called a base. For example,

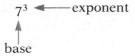

The exponent indicates how many times the base is multiplied by itself. Some examples are the following:

$7^3 = 7(7)(7)$ (read "7 cubed" or "7 raised to the third power")

$5^2 = 5(5)$ (read "5 squared")

$2^5 = 2(2)(2)(2)(2)$ (read "2 raised to the fifth power")

There are a few basic rules about exponents that you will need to know for this course. They are outlined here.

1. Numbers Raised to One or Zero. Any number raised to the first power equals itself. For example,

$$6^1 = 6$$

Any number (except zero) raised to the zero power equals 1. For example,

$$9^0 = 1$$

2. Exponents for Multiple Terms. The exponent applies only to the base that is just in front of it. For example,

$$XY^2 = XYY$$
$$a^2b^3 = aabbb$$

3. Negative Bases Raised to an Exponent. If a negative number is raised to a power, then the result will be positive for exponents that are even and negative for exponents that are odd. For example,

$$\begin{aligned} -4^3 &= -4(-4)(-4) \\ &= 16(-4) \\ &= -64 \end{aligned}$$

and

$$\begin{aligned} -3^4 &= -3(-3)(-3)(-3) \\ &= 9(-3)(-3) \\ &= 9(9) \\ &= 81 \end{aligned}$$

4. Exponents and Parentheses. If an exponent is present outside of parentheses, then the computations within the parentheses are done first, and the exponential computation is done last:

$$(3 + 5)^2 = 8^2 = 64$$

Notice that the meaning of the expression is changed when each term in the parentheses is raised to the exponent individually:

$$3^2 + 5^2 = 9 + 25 = 34$$

Therefore,

$$X^2 + Y^2 \neq (X + Y)^2$$

5. Fractions Raised to a Power. If the numerator and denominator of a fraction are each raised to the same exponent, then the entire fraction can be raised to that exponent. That is,

$$\frac{a^2}{b^2} = \left(\frac{a}{b}\right)^2$$

For example,

$$\frac{3^2}{4^2} = \left(\frac{3}{4}\right)^2$$

$$\frac{9}{16} = \frac{3}{4}\left(\frac{3}{4}\right)$$

$$\frac{9}{16} = \frac{9}{16}$$

Square Roots

The square root of a value equals a number which when multiplied by itself yields the original value. For example, the square root of 16 equals 4, because 4 times 4 equals 16. The symbol for the square root is called a radical, $\sqrt{\ }$. The square root is taken for a number under the radical. For example,

$$\sqrt{16} = 4$$

The square root is the inverse of raising a number to the second power (squaring). Thus,

$$\sqrt{a^2} = a$$

For example,

$$\sqrt{3^2} = \sqrt{9} = 3$$

Also,

$$(\sqrt{b})^2 = b$$

For example,

$$(\sqrt{64})^2 = 8^2 = 64$$

Computations under the same radical are performed *before* the square root is taken. For example,

$$\sqrt{9 + 16} = \sqrt{25} = 5$$

Note that with addition (or subtraction) separate radicals yield a different result:

$$\sqrt{9} + \sqrt{16} = 3 + 4 = 7$$

Therefore,

$$\sqrt{X} + \sqrt{Y} \neq \sqrt{X + Y}$$
$$\sqrt{X} - \sqrt{Y} \neq \sqrt{X - Y}$$

If the numerator and denominator of a fraction each have a radical, then the entire fraction can be placed under a single radical:

$$\frac{\sqrt{16}}{\sqrt{4}} = \sqrt{\frac{16}{4}}$$

$$\frac{4}{2} = \sqrt{4}$$

$$2 = 2$$

Therefore,

$$\frac{\sqrt{X}}{\sqrt{Y}} = \sqrt{\frac{X}{Y}}$$

Also, if the square root of one number is multiplied by the square root of another number, then the same result would be obtained by taking the square root of the product of both numbers. For example,

$$\sqrt{9} \times \sqrt{16} = \sqrt{9 \times 16}$$
$$3 \times 4 = \sqrt{144}$$
$$12 = 12$$

Therefore,

$$\sqrt{a} \times \sqrt{b} = \sqrt{ab}$$

---

1. Perform the following computations:

   a. -6^3

   b. $(3 + 7)^2$

   c. $a^3 b^2$ when $a = 2$ and $b = -5$

   d. $a^4 b^3$ when $a = 2$ and $b = 3$

   e. $(XY)^2$ when $X = 3$ and $Y = 5$

   f. $X^2 + Y^2$ when $X = 3$ and $Y = 5$

   g. $(X + Y)^2$ when $X = 3$ and $Y = 5$

   h. $\sqrt{5 + 4}$

   i. $(\sqrt{9})^2$

   j. $\dfrac{\sqrt{16}}{\sqrt{4}}$

Problems for Appendix A:
Basic Mathematics Review

1. Convert $\frac{7}{20}$ to a decimal.

2. Express $\frac{9}{25}$ as a percentage.

3. Convert 0.91 to a fraction.

4. Express 0.0031 as a fraction.

5. Next to each set of fractions, write "true" if they are equivalent and "false" if they are not:

   a. $\dfrac{4}{1000} = \dfrac{2}{100}$ _____

   b. $\dfrac{5}{6} = \dfrac{52}{62}$ _____

   c. $\dfrac{1}{8} = \dfrac{7}{56}$ _____

6. Perform the following calculations:

   a. $\dfrac{4}{5} \times \dfrac{2}{3} = ?$

   b. $\dfrac{7}{9} \div \dfrac{2}{3} = ?$

   c. $\dfrac{3}{8} + \dfrac{1}{5} = ?$

   d. $\dfrac{5}{18} - \dfrac{1}{6} = ?$

7. $2.51 \times 0.017 = ?$

8. $3.88 \times 0.0002 = ?$

9. $3.17 + 17.0132 = ?$

10. $5.55 + 10.7 + 0.711 + 3.33 + 0.031 = ?$

11. $2.04 \div 0.2 = ?$

12. $0.36 \div 0.4 = ?$

13. $5 + 3 - 6 - 4 + 3 = ?$

14. $9 - (-1) - 17 + 3 - (-4) + 5 = ?$

15. $5 + 3 - (-8) - (-1) + (-3) - 4 + 10 = ?$

16. $8 \times (-3) = ?$

17. $-22 \div (-2) = ?$

18. $-2 \times (-4) \times (-3) = ?$

19. $84 \div (-4) = ?$

Solve the equations in Problems 20–27 for X.

20. $X - 7 = -2$

21. $9 = X + 3$

22. $\frac{X}{4} = 11$

23. $-3 = \frac{X}{3}$

24. $\frac{X+3}{5} = 2$

25. $\frac{X+1}{3} = -8$

26. $6X - 1 = 11$

27. $2X + 3 = -11$

28. $-5^2 = ?$

29. $-5^3 = ?$

30. If $a = 4$ and $b = 3$, then $a^2 + b^4 = ?$

31. If $a = -1$ and $b = 4$, then $(a + b)^2 = ?$

32. If $a = -1$ and $b = 5$, then $ab^2 = ?$

33. $\frac{18}{\sqrt{4}} = ?$

34. $\sqrt{\frac{20}{5}} = ?$

Skills Assessment Exam: A Follow-up Test

SECTION 1

1. Express $\frac{14}{80}$ as a decimal.

2. Convert $\frac{6}{25}$ to a percentage.

3. Convert 18% to a fraction.

4. $\frac{3}{5} \times \frac{2}{3} = ?$

5. $\frac{5}{24} + \frac{5}{6} = ?$

6. $\frac{7}{12} \div \frac{5}{6} = ?$

7. $\frac{5}{9} - \frac{1}{3} = ?$

8. $6.11 \times 0.22 = ?$

9. $0.18 \div 0.9 = ?$

10. $8.742 + 0.76 = ?$

11. In a statistics class of 72 students, three-eights of the students received a B on the first test. How many Bs were earned?

12. What is 15% of 64?

SECTION 2

1. $3 - 1 - 3 + 5 - 2 + 6 = ?$

2. $-8 - (-6) = ?$

3. $2 - (-7) - 3 + (-11) - 20 = ?$

4. $-8 - 3 - (-1) - 2 - 1 = ?$

5. $8(-2) = ?$

6. $-7(-7) = ?$

7. $-3(-2)(-5) = ?$

8. $-3(5)(-3) = ?$

9. $-24 \div (-4) = ?$

10. $36 \div (-6) = ?$

11. $-56/7 = ?$

12. $-7/(-1) = ?$

SECTION 3 Solve for X.

1. $X + 5 = 12$

2. $X - 11 = 3$

3. $10 = X + 4$

4. $4X = 20$

5. $\dfrac{X}{2} = 15$

6. $18 = 9X$

7. $\dfrac{X}{5} = 35$

8. $2X + 8 = 4$

9. $\dfrac{X + 1}{3} = 6$

10. $4X + 3 = -13$

11. $\dfrac{X + 3}{3} = -7$

12. $23 = 2X - 5$

SECTION 4

1. $5^3 = ?$

2. $-4^3 = ?$

3. $-2^5 = ?$

4. $-2^6 = ?$

5. If $a = 4$ and $b = 2$, then $ab^2 = ?$

6. If $a = 4$ and $b = 2$, then $(a + b)^3 = ?$

7. If $a = 4$ and $b = 2$, then $a^2 + b^2 = ?$

8. $(11 + 4)^2 = ?$

9. $\sqrt{7^2} = ?$

10. If $a = 36$ and $b = 64$, then $\sqrt{a + b} = ?$

11. $\dfrac{25}{\sqrt{25}} = ?$

12. If $a = -1$ and $b = 2$, then $a^3 b^4 = ?$

Answer Key for Skills Assessment Exams
Preview Exam (p. A-1)

SECTION 1

1. 75%   **2.** $\dfrac{30}{100}$ or $\dfrac{3}{10}$ **3.** 0.3   **7.** $\dfrac{19}{24}$ **8.** 1.4   **9.** $\dfrac{4}{15}$

4. $\dfrac{10}{13}$ **5.** 1.625   **6.** $\dfrac{2}{20}$ **10.** 7.5   **11.** 16   **12.** 36

SECTION 2
1. 4　**2.** 8　**3.** 2　**4.** 9　**5.** -12
6. 12　**7.** -15　**8.** -24　**9.** -4
10. 3　**11.** -2　**12.** 25
SECTION 3
1. $X = 7$　**2.** $X = 29$　**3.** $X = 9$
4. $X = 4$　**5.** $X = 24$　**6.** $X = 15$

7. $X = 80$　**8.** $X = -3$　**9.** $X = 11$
10. $X = 25$　**11.** $X = 11$　**12.** $X = 7$
SECTION 4
1. 64　**2.** 4　**3.** 54　**4.** 25　**5.** 13
6. -27　**7.** 256　**8.** 8　**9.** 12
10. 121　**11.** 33　**12.** -9

Follow-up Exam

SECTION 1

1. 0.175　**2.** 24%　**3.** $\dfrac{18}{100}$ or $\dfrac{9}{50}$　**4.** $\dfrac{6}{15}$

5. $\dfrac{25}{24}$　**6.** $\dfrac{42}{60}$ or $\dfrac{7}{10}$　**7.** $\dfrac{2}{9}$　**8.** 1.3442

9. 0.2　**10.** 9.502　**11.** 27　**12.** 9.6
SECTION 2
1. 8　**2.** -2　**3.** -25　**4.** -13
5. -16　**6.** 49　**7.** -30　**8.** 45　**9.** 6
10. -6　**11.** -8　**12.** 7

SECTION 3
1. $X = 7$　**2.** $X = 14$　**3.** $X = 6$
4. $X = 5$　**5.** $X = 30$　**6.** $X = 2$
7. $X = 175$　**8.** $X = -2$　**9.** $X = 17$
10. $X = -4$　**11.** $X = -24$　**12.** $X = 14$
SECTION 4
1. 125　**2.** -64　**3.** -32　**4.** 64
5. 16　**6.** 216　**7.** 20　**8.** 225　**9.** 7
10. 10　**11.** 5　**12.** -16

Solutions to Selected Problems:
Appendix A: Basic Mathematics Review

1.　0.35

2.　36%

4.　$\dfrac{31}{10,000}$

5.　b.　False

6.　a.　$\dfrac{8}{15}$　b.　$\dfrac{21}{18}$　c.　$\dfrac{23}{40}$

7.　0.04267

9.　20.1832

12.　0.9

14.　5

16.　-24

17.　11

20.　$X = 5$

23.　$X = -9$

25.　$X = -25$

26.　$X = 2$

29.　-125

31.　9

32.　-25

34.　2

Suggested Review Books

There are many basic mathematics review books available if you need a more extensive review than this appendix can provide. The following books are but a few of the many that you may find helpful:

Barker, V. C., and Aufmann, R. N. (1982). *Essential Mathematics.* Boston: Houghton Mifflin.

Falstein, L. D. (1982). *Basic Mathematics for College Students.* Reading, Mass.: Addison-Wesley.

Washington, A. J. (1984). *Arithmetic and Beginning Algebra.* Menlo Park, Calif.: Benjamin/Cummings.

Statistical Tables

Table B.1
The Unit Normal Table*

*Column A lists the z-score values. Column B provides the proportion of area between the mean and the z-score value:

Column C provides the proportion of area beyond the z-score:

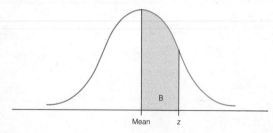

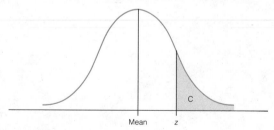

Note: Because the normal distribution is symmetrical, areas for negative z-scores are the same as those for positive z-scores.

Table B.1 *continued*

(A) z	(B) Area Between Mean and z	(C) Area Beyond z	(A) z	(B) Area Between Mean and z	(C) Area Beyond z
0.00	.0000	.5000	0.35	.1368	.3632
0.01	.0040	.4960	0.36	.1406	.3594
0.02	.0080	.4920	0.37	.1443	.3557
0.03	.0120	.4880	0.38	.1480	.3520
0.04	.0160	.4840	0.39	.1517	.3483
0.05	.0199	.4801	0.40	.1554	.3446
0.06	.0239	.4761	0.41	.1591	.3409
0.07	.0279	.4721	0.42	.1628	.3372
0.08	.0319	.4681	0.43	.1664	.3336
0.09	.0359	.4641	0.44	.1700	.3300
0.10	.0398	.4602	0.45	.1736	.3264
0.11	.0438	.4562	0.46	.1772	.3228
0.12	.0478	.4522	0.47	.1808	.3192
0.13	.0517	.4483	0.48	.1844	.3156
0.14	.0557	.4443	0.49	.1879	.3121
0.15	.0596	.4404	0.50	.1915	.3085
0.16	.0636	.4364	0.51	.1950	.3050
0.17	.0675	.4325	0.52	.1985	.3015
0.18	.0714	.4286	0.53	.2019	.2981
0.19	.0753	.4247	0.54	.2054	.2946
0.20	.0793	.4207	0.55	.2088	.2912
0.21	.0832	.4168	0.56	.2123	.2877
0.22	.0871	.4129	0.57	.2157	.2843
0.23	.0910	.4090	0.58	.2190	.2810
0.24	.0948	.4052	0.59	.2224	.2776
0.25	.0987	.4013	0.60	.2257	.2743
0.26	.1026	.3974	0.61	.2291	.2709
0.27	.1064	.3936	0.62	.2324	.2676
0.28	.1103	.3897	0.63	.2357	.2643
0.29	.1141	.3859	0.64	.2389	.2611
0.30	.1179	.3821	0.65	.2422	.2578
0.31	.1217	.3783	0.66	.2454	.2546
0.32	.1255	.3745	0.67	.2486	.2514
0.33	.1293	.3707	0.68	.2517	.2483
0.34	.1331	.3669	0.69	.2549	.2451

continued

(A) z	(B) Area Between Mean and z	(C) Area Beyond z		(A) z	(B) Area Between Mean and z	(C) Area Beyond z
0.70	.2580	.2420		1.05	.3531	.1469
0.71	.2611	.2389		1.06	.3554	.1446
0.72	.2642	.2358		1.07	.3577	.1423
0.73	.2673	.2327		1.08	.3599	.1401
0.74	.2704	.2296		1.09	.3621	.1379
0.75	.2734	.2266		1.10	.3643	.1357
0.76	.2764	.2236		1.11	.3665	.1335
0.77	.2794	.2206		1.12	.3686	.1314
0.78	.2823	.2177		1.13	.3708	.1292
0.79	.2852	.2148		1.14	.3729	.1271
0.80	.2881	.2119		1.15	.3749	.1251
0.81	.2910	.2090		1.16	.3770	.1230
0.82	.2939	.2061		1.17	.3790	.1210
0.83	.2967	.2033		1.18	.3810	.1190
0.84	.2995	.2005		1.19	.3830	.1170
0.85	.3023	.1977		1.20	.3849	.1151
0.86	.3051	.1949		1.21	.3869	.1131
0.87	.3078	.1922		1.22	.3888	.1112
0.88	.3106	.1894		1.23	.3907	.1093
0.89	.3133	.1867		1.24	.3925	.1075
0.90	.3159	.1841		1.25	.3944	.1056
0.91	.3186	.1814		1.26	.3962	.1038
0.92	.3212	.1788		1.27	.3980	.1020
0.93	.3238	.1762		1.28	.3997	.1003
0.94	.3264	.1736		1.29	.4015	.0985
0.95	.3289	.1711		1.30	.4032	.0968
0.96	.3315	.1685		1.31	.4049	.0951
0.97	.3340	.1660		1.32	.4066	.0934
0.98	.3365	.1635		1.33	.4082	.0918
0.99	.3389	.1611		1.34	.4099	.0901
1.00	.3413	.1587		1.35	.4115	.0885
1.01	.3438	.1562		1.36	.4131	.0869
1.02	.3461	.1539		1.37	.4147	.0853
1.03	.3485	.1515		1.38	.4162	.0838
1.04	.3508	.1492		1.39	.4177	.0823

STATISTICAL TABLES

(A) z	(B) Area Between Mean and z	(C) Area Beyond z	(A) z	(B) Area Between Mean and z	(C) Area Beyond z
1.40	.4192	.0808	1.75	.4599	.0401
1.41	.4207	.0793	1.76	.4608	.0392
1.42	.4222	.0778	1.77	.4616	.0384
1.43	.4236	.0764	1.78	.4625	.0375
1.44	.4251	.0749	1.79	.4633	.0367
1.45	.4265	.0735	1.80	.4641	.0359
1.46	.4279	.0721	1.81	.4649	.0351
1.47	.4292	.0708	1.82	.4656	.0344
1.48	.4306	.0694	1.83	.4664	.0336
1.49	.4319	.0681	1.84	.4671	.0329
1.50	.4332	.0668	1.85	.4678	.0322
1.51	.4345	.0655	1.86	.4686	.0314
1.52	.4357	.0643	1.87	.4693	.0307
1.53	.4370	.0630	1.88	.4699	.0301
1.54	.4382	.0618	1.89	.4706	.0294
1.55	.4394	.0606	1.90	.4713	.0287
1.56	.4406	.0594	1.91	.4719	.0281
1.57	.4418	.0582	1.92	.4726	.0274
1.58	.4429	.0571	1.93	.4732	.0268
1.59	.4441	.0559	1.94	.4738	.0262
1.60	.4452	.0548	1.95	.4744	.0256
1.61	.4463	.0537	1.96	.4750	.0250
1.62	.4474	.0526	1.97	.4756	.0244
1.63	.4484	.0516	1.98	.4761	.0239
1.64	.4495	.0505	1.99	.4767	.0233
1.65	.4505	.0495	2.00	.4772	.0228
1.66	.4515	.0485	2.01	.4778	.0222
1.67	.4525	.0475	2.02	.4783	.0217
1.68	.4535	.0465	2.03	.4788	.0212
1.69	.4545	.0455	2.04	.4793	.0207
1.70	.4554	.0446	2.05	.4798	.0202
1.71	.4564	.0436	2.06	.4803	.0197
1.72	.4573	.0427	2.07	.4808	.0192
1.73	.4582	.0418	2.08	.4812	.0188
1.74	.4591	.0409	2.09	.4817	.0183

STATISTICAL TABLES

(A) z	(B) Area Between Mean and z	(C) Area Beyond z	(A) z	(B) Area Between Mean and z	(C) Area Beyond z
2.10	.4821	.0179	2.45	.4929	.0071
2.11	.4826	.0174	2.46	.4931	.0069
2.12	.4830	.0170	2.47	.4932	.0068
2.13	.4834	.0166	2.48	.4934	.0066
2.14	.4838	.0162	2.49	.4936	.0064
2.15	.4842	.0158	2.50	.4938	.0062
2.16	.4846	.0154	2.51	.4940	.0060
2.17	.4850	.0150	2.52	.4941	.0059
2.18	.4854	.0146	2.53	.4943	.0057
2.19	.4857	.0143	2.54	.4945	.0055
2.20	.4861	.0139	2.55	.4946	.0054
2.21	.4864	.0136	2.56	.4948	.0052
2.22	.4868	.0132	2.57	.4949	.0051
2.23	.4871	.0129	2.58	.4951	.0049
2.24	.4875	.0125	2.59	.4952	.0048
2.25	.4878	.0122	2.60	.4953	.0047
2.26	.4881	.0119	2.61	.4955	.0045
2.27	.4884	.0116	2.62	.4956	.0044
2.28	.4887	.0113	2.63	.4957	.0043
2.29	.4890	.0110	2.64	.4959	.0041
2.30	.4893	.0107	2.65	.4960	.0040
2.31	.4896	.0104	2.66	.4961	.0039
2.32	.4898	.0102	2.67	.4962	.0038
2.33	.4901	.0099	2.68	.4963	.0037
2.34	.4904	.0096	2.69	.4964	.0036
2.35	.4906	.0094	2.70	.4965	.0035
2.36	.4909	.0091	2.71	.4966	.0034
2.37	.4911	.0089	2.72	.4967	.0033
2.38	.4913	.0087	2.73	.4968	.0032
2.39	.4916	.0084	2.74	.4969	.0031
2.40	.4918	.0082	2.75	.4970	.0030
2.41	.4920	.0080	2.76	.4971	.0029
2.42	.4922	.0078	2.77	.4972	.0028
2.43	.4925	.0075	2.78	.4973	.0027
2.44	.4927	.0073	2.79	.4974	.0026

Table B.1 *continued*

(A) z	(B) Area Between Mean and z	(C) Area Beyond z		(A) z	(B) Area Between Mean and z	(C) Area Beyond z
2.80	.4974	.0026		3.15	.4992	.0008
2.81	.4975	.0025		3.16	.4992	.0008
2.82	.4976	.0024		3.17	.4992	.0008
2.83	.4977	.0023		3.18	.4993	.0007
2.84	.4977	.0023		3.19	.4993	.0007
2.85	.4978	.0022		3.20	.4993	.0007
2.86	.4979	.0021		3.21	.4993	.0007
2.87	.4979	.0021		3.22	.4994	.0006
2.88	.4980	.0020		3.23	.4994	.0006
2.89	.4981	.0019		3.24	.4994	.0006
2.90	.4981	.0019		3.30	.4995	.0005
2.91	.4982	.0018		3.40	.4997	.0003
2.92	.4982	.0018		3.50	.4998	.0002
2.93	.4983	.0017		3.60	.4998	.0002
2.94	.4984	.0016		3.70	.4999	.0001
2.95	.4984	.0016		3.80	.49993	.00007
2.96	.4985	.0015		3.90	.49995	.00005
2.97	.4985	.0015		4.00	.49997	.00003
2.98	.4986	.0014				
2.99	.4986	.0014				
3.00	.4987	.0013				
3.01	.4987	.0013				
3.02	.4987	.0013				
3.03	.4988	.0012				
3.04	.4988	.0012				
3.05	.4989	.0011				
3.06	.4989	.0011				
3.07	.4989	.0011				
3.08	.4990	.0010				
3.09	.4990	.0010				
3.10	.4990	.0010				
3.11	.4991	.0009				
3.12	.4991	.0009				
3.13	.4991	.0009				
3.14	.4992	.0008				

Table B.2

The *t* Distribution

	Proportion in One Tail					
	0.25	0.10	0.05	0.025	0.01	0.005
	Proportion in Two Tails					
df	0.50	0.20	0.10	0.05	0.02	0.01
1	1.000	3.078	6.314	12.706	31.821	63.657
2	0.816	1.886	2.920	4.303	6.965	9.925
3	0.765	1.638	2.353	3.182	4.541	5.841
4	0.741	1.533	2.132	2.776	3.747	4.604
5	0.727	1.476	2.015	2.571	3.365	4.032
6	0.718	1.440	1.943	2.447	3.143	3.707
7	0.711	1.415	1.895	2.365	2.998	3.499
8	0.706	1.397	1.860	2.306	2.896	3.355
9	0.703	1.383	1.833	2.262	2.821	3.250
10	0.700	1.372	1.812	2.228	2.764	3.169
11	0.697	1.363	1.796	2.201	2.718	3.106
12	0.695	1.356	1.782	2.179	2.681	3.055
13	0.694	1.350	1.771	2.160	2.650	3.012
14	0.692	1.345	1.761	2.145	2.624	2.977
15	0.691	1.341	1.753	2.131	2.602	2.947
16	0.690	1.337	1.746	2.120	2.583	2.921
17	0.689	1.333	1.740	2.110	2.567	2.898
18	0.688	1.330	1.734	2.101	2.552	2.878
19	0.688	1.328	1.729	2.093	2.539	2.861
20	0.687	1.325	1.725	2.086	2.528	2.845
21	0.686	1.323	1.721	2.080	2.518	2.831
22	0.686	1.321	1.717	2.074	2.508	2.819
23	0.685	1.319	1.714	2.069	2.500	2.807
24	0.685	1.318	1.711	2.064	2.492	2.797
25	0.684	1.316	1.708	2.060	2.485	2.787
26	0.684	1.315	1.706	2.056	2.479	2.779
27	0.684	1.314	1.703	2.052	2.473	2.771
28	0.683	1.313	1.701	2.048	2.467	2.763
29	0.683	1.311	1.699	2.045	2.462	2.756
30	0.683	1.310	1.697	2.042	2.457	2.750
40	0.681	1.303	1.684	2.021	2.423	2.704
60	0.679	1.296	1.671	2.000	2.390	2.660
120	0.677	1.289	1.658	1.980	2.358	2.617
∞	0.674	1.282	1.645	1.960	2.326	2.576

Table B.3

Critical Values for the *F*-max Statistic*

*The critical values for $\alpha = .05$ are in lightface type, and for $\alpha = .01$ they are in boldface type.

n − 1	*k* = Number of Samples										
	2	3	4	5	6	7	8	9	10	11	12
4	9.60	15.5	20.6	25.2	29.5	33.6	37.5	41.4	44.6	48.0	51.4
	23.2	**37.**	**49.**	**59.**	**69.**	**79.**	**89.**	**97.**	**106.**	**113.**	**120.**
5	7.15	10.8	13.7	16.3	18.7	20.8	22.9	24.7	26.5	28.2	29.9
	14.9	**22.**	**28.**	**33.**	**38.**	**42.**	**46.**	**50.**	**54.**	**57.**	**60.**
6	5.82	8.38	10.4	12.1	13.7	15.0	16.3	17.5	18.6	19.7	20.7
	11.1	**15.5**	**19.1**	**22.**	**25.**	**27.**	**30.**	**32.**	**34.**	**36.**	**37.**
7	4.99	6.94	8.44	9.70	10.8	11.8	12.7	13.5	14.3	15.1	15.8
	8.89	**12.1**	**14.5**	**16.5**	**18.4**	**20.**	**22.**	**23.**	**24.**	**26.**	**27.**
8	4.43	6.00	7.18	8.12	9.03	9.78	10.5	11.1	11.7	12.2	12.7
	7.50	**9.9**	**11.7**	**13.2**	**14.5**	**15.8**	**16.9**	**17.9**	**18.9**	**19.8**	**21.**
9	4.03	5.34	6.31	7.11	7.80	8.41	8.95	9.45	9.91	10.3	10.7
	6.54	**8.5**	**9.9**	**11.1**	**12.1**	**13.1**	**13.9**	**14.7**	**15.3**	**16.0**	**16.6**
10	3.72	4.85	5.67	6.34	6.92	7.42	7.87	8.28	8.66	9.01	9.34
	5.85	**7.4**	**8.6**	**9.6**	**10.4**	**11.1**	**11.8**	**12.4**	**12.9**	**13.4**	**13.9**
12	3.28	4.16	4.79	5.30	5.72	6.09	6.42	6.72	7.00	7.25	7.48
	4.91	**6.1**	**6.9**	**7.6**	**8.2**	**8.7**	**9.1**	**9.5**	**9.9**	**10.2**	**10.6**
15	2.86	3.54	4.01	4.37	4.68	4.95	5.19	5.40	5.59	5.77	5.93
	4.07	**4.9**	**5.5**	**6.0**	**6.4**	**6.7**	**7.1**	**7.3**	**7.5**	**7.8**	**8.0**
20	2.46	2.95	3.29	3.54	3.76	3.94	4.10	4.24	4.37	4.49	4.59
	3.32	**3.8**	**4.3**	**4.6**	**4.9**	**5.1**	**5.3**	**5.5**	**5.6**	**5.8**	**5.9**
30	2.07	2.40	2.61	2.78	2.91	3.02	3.12	3.21	3.29	3.36	3.39
	2.63	**3.0**	**3.3**	**3.4**	**3.6**	**3.7**	**3.8**	**3.9**	**4.0**	**4.1**	**4.2**
60	1.67	1.85	1.96	2.04	2.11	2.17	2.22	2.26	2.30	2.33	2.36
	1.96	**2.2**	**2.3**	**2.4**	**2.4**	**2.5**	**2.5**	**2.6**	**2.6**	**2.7**	**2.7**

Table B.4

The *F* Distribution*

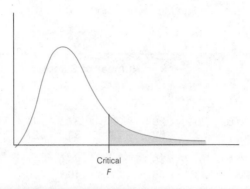

Critical
F

*Table entries in lightface type are critical values for the .05 level of significance.
Boldface type values are for the .01 level of significance.

Degrees of Freedom: Denominator	Degrees of Freedom: Numerator														
	1	2	3	4	5	6	7	8	9	10	11	12	14	16	20
1	161	200	216	225	230	234	237	239	241	242	243	244	245	246	248
	4052	**4999**	**5403**	**5625**	**5764**	**5859**	**5928**	**5981**	**6022**	**6056**	**6082**	**6106**	**6142**	**6169**	**6208**
2	18.51	19.00	19.16	19.25	19.30	19.33	19.36	19.37	19.38	19.39	19.40	19.41	19.42	19.43	19.44
	98.49	**99.00**	**99.17**	**99.25**	**99.30**	**99.33**	**99.34**	**99.36**	**99.38**	**99.40**	**99.41**	**99.42**	**99.43**	**99.44**	**99.45**
3	10.13	9.55	9.28	9.12	9.01	8.94	8.88	8.84	8.81	8.78	8.76	8.74	8.71	8.69	8.66
	34.12	**30.82**	**29.46**	**28.71**	**28.24**	**27.91**	**27.67**	**27.49**	**27.34**	**27.23**	**27.13**	**27.05**	**26.92**	**26.83**	**26.69**
4	7.71	6.94	6.59	6.39	6.26	6.16	6.09	6.04	6.00	5.96	5.93	5.91	5.87	5.84	5.80
	21.20	**18.00**	**16.69**	**15.98**	**15.52**	**15.21**	**14.98**	**14.80**	**14.66**	**14.54**	**14.45**	**14.37**	**14.24**	**14.15**	**14.02**
5	6.61	5.79	5.41	5.19	5.05	4.95	4.88	4.82	4.78	4.74	4.70	4.68	4.64	4.60	4.56
	16.26	**13.27**	**12.06**	**11.39**	**10.97**	**10.67**	**10.45**	**10.27**	**10.15**	**10.05**	**9.96**	**9.89**	**9.77**	**9.68**	**9.55**
6	5.99	5.14	4.76	4.53	4.39	4.28	4.21	4.15	4.10	4.06	4.03	4.00	3.96	3.92	3.87
	13.74	**10.92**	**9.78**	**9.15**	**8.75**	**8.47**	**8.26**	**8.10**	**7.98**	**7.87**	**7.79**	**7.72**	**7.60**	**7.52**	**7.39**
7	5.59	4.47	4.35	4.12	3.97	3.87	3.79	3.73	3.68	3.63	3.60	3.57	3.52	3.49	3.44
	12.25	**9.55**	**8.45**	**7.85**	**7.46**	**7.19**	**7.00**	**6.84**	**6.71**	**6.62**	**6.54**	**6.47**	**6.35**	**6.27**	**6.15**
8	5.32	4.46	4.07	3.84	3.69	3.58	3.50	3.44	3.39	3.34	3.31	3.28	3.23	3.20	3.15
	11.26	**8.65**	**7.59**	**7.01**	**6.63**	**6.37**	**6.19**	**6.03**	**5.91**	**5.82**	**5.74**	**5.67**	**5.56**	**5.48**	**5.36**
9	5.12	4.26	3.86	3.63	3.48	3.37	3.29	3.23	3.18	3.13	3.10	3.07	3.02	2.98	2.93
	10.56	**8.02**	**6.99**	**6.42**	**6.06**	**5.80**	**5.62**	**5.47**	**5.35**	**5.26**	**5.18**	**5.11**	**5.00**	**4.92**	**4.80**
10	4.96	4.10	3.71	3.48	3.33	3.22	3.14	3.07	3.02	2.97	2.94	2.91	2.86	2.82	2.77
	10.04	**7.56**	**6.55**	**5.99**	**5.64**	**5.39**	**5.21**	**5.06**	**4.95**	**4.85**	**4.78**	**4.71**	**4.60**	**4.52**	**4.41**
11	4.84	3.98	3.59	3.36	3.20	3.09	3.01	2.95	2.90	2.86	2.82	2.79	2.74	2.70	2.65
	9.65	**7.20**	**6.22**	**5.67**	**5.32**	**5.07**	**4.88**	**4.74**	**4.63**	**4.54**	**4.46**	**4.40**	**4.29**	**4.21**	**4.10**
12	4.75	3.88	3.49	3.26	3.11	3.00	2.92	2.85	2.80	2.76	2.72	2.69	2.64	2.60	2.54
	9.33	**6.93**	**5.95**	**5.41**	**5.06**	**4.82**	**4.65**	**4.50**	**4.39**	**4.30**	**4.22**	**4.16**	**4.05**	**3.98**	**3.86**
13	4.67	3.80	3.41	3.18	3.02	2.92	2.84	2.77	2.72	2.67	2.63	2.60	2.55	2.51	2.46
	9.07	**6.70**	**5.74**	**5.20**	**4.86**	**4.62**	**4.44**	**4.30**	**4.19**	**4.10**	**4.02**	**3.96**	**3.85**	**3.78**	**3.67**
14	4.60	3.74	3.34	3.11	2.96	2.85	2.77	2.70	2.65	2.60	2.56	2.53	2.48	2.44	2.39
	8.86	**6.51**	**5.56**	**5.03**	**4.69**	**4.46**	**4.28**	**4.14**	**4.03**	**3.94**	**3.86**	**3.80**	**3.70**	**3.62**	**3.51**

Table B.4 *continued*

Degrees of Freedom: Denominator	1	2	3	4	5	6	7	8	9	10	11	12	14	16	20
					Degrees of Freedom: Numerator										
15	4.54	3.68	3.29	3.06	2.90	2.79	2.70	2.64	2.59	2.55	2.51	2.48	2.43	2.39	2.33
	8.68	**6.36**	**5.42**	**4.89**	**4.56**	**4.32**	**4.14**	**4.00**	**3.89**	**3.80**	**3.73**	**3.67**	**3.56**	**3.48**	**3.36**
16	4.49	3.63	3.24	3.01	2.85	2.74	2.66	2.59	2.54	2.49	2.45	2.42	2.37	2.33	2.28
	8.53	**6.23**	**5.29**	**4.77**	**4.44**	**4.20**	**4.03**	**3.89**	**3.78**	**3.69**	**3.61**	**3.55**	**3.45**	**3.37**	**3.25**
17	4.45	3.59	3.20	2.96	2.81	2.70	2.62	2.55	2.50	2.45	2.41	2.38	2.33	2.29	2.23
	8.40	**6.11**	**5.18**	**4.67**	**4.34**	**4.10**	**3.93**	**3.79**	**3.68**	**3.59**	**3.52**	**3.45**	**3.35**	**3.27**	**3.16**
18	4.41	3.55	3.16	2.93	2.77	2.66	2.58	2.51	2.46	2.41	2.37	2.34	2.29	2.25	2.19
	8.28	**6.01**	**5.09**	**4.58**	**4.25**	**4.01**	**3.85**	**3.71**	**3.60**	**3.51**	**3.44**	**3.37**	**3.27**	**3.19**	**3.07**
19	4.38	3.52	3.13	2.90	2.74	2.63	2.55	2.48	2.43	2.38	2.34	2.31	2.26	2.21	2.15
	8.18	**5.93**	**5.01**	**4.50**	**4.17**	**3.94**	**3.77**	**3.63**	**3.52**	**3.43**	**3.36**	**3.30**	**3.19**	**3.12**	**3.00**
20	4.35	3.49	3.10	2.87	2.71	2.60	2.52	2.45	2.40	2.35	2.31	2.28	2.23	2.18	2.12
	8.10	**5.85**	**4.94**	**4.43**	**4.10**	**3.87**	**3.71**	**3.56**	**3.45**	**3.37**	**3.30**	**3.23**	**3.13**	**3.05**	**2.94**
21	4.32	3.47	3.07	2.84	2.68	2.57	2.49	2.42	2.37	2.32	2.28	2.25	2.20	2.15	2.09
	8.02	**5.78**	**4.87**	**4.37**	**4.04**	**3.81**	**3.65**	**3.51**	**3.40**	**3.31**	**3.24**	**3.17**	**3.07**	**2.99**	**2.88**
22	4.30	3.44	3.05	2.82	2.66	2.55	2.47	2.40	2.35	2.30	2.26	2.23	2.18	2.13	2.07
	7.94	**5.72**	**4.82**	**4.31**	**3.99**	**3.76**	**3.59**	**3.45**	**3.35**	**3.26**	**3.18**	**3.12**	**3.02**	**2.94**	**2.83**
23	4.28	3.42	3.03	2.80	2.64	2.53	2.45	2.38	2.32	2.28	2.24	2.20	2.14	2.10	2.04
	7.88	**5.66**	**4.76**	**4.26**	**3.94**	**3.71**	**3.54**	**3.41**	**3.30**	**3.21**	**3.14**	**3.07**	**2.97**	**2.89**	**2.78**
24	4.26	3.40	3.01	2.78	2.62	2.51	2.43	2.36	2.30	2.26	2.22	2.18	2.13	2.09	2.02
	7.82	**5.61**	**4.72**	**4.22**	**3.90**	**3.67**	**3.50**	**3.36**	**3.25**	**3.17**	**3.09**	**3.03**	**2.93**	**2.85**	**2.74**
25	4.24	3.38	2.99	2.76	2.60	2.49	2.41	2.34	2.28	2.24	2.20	2.16	2.11	2.06	2.00
	7.77	**5.57**	**4.68**	**4.18**	**3.86**	**3.63**	**3.46**	**3.32**	**3.21**	**3.13**	**3.05**	**2.99**	**2.89**	**2.81**	**2.70**
26	4.22	3.37	2.98	2.74	2.59	2.47	2.39	2.32	2.27	2.22	2.18	2.15	2.10	2.05	1.99
	7.72	**5.53**	**4.64**	**4.14**	**3.82**	**3.59**	**3.42**	**3.29**	**3.17**	**3.09**	**3.02**	**2.96**	**2.86**	**2.77**	**2.66**
27	4.21	3.35	2.96	2.73	2.57	2.46	2.37	2.30	2.25	2.20	2.16	2.13	2.08	2.03	1.97
	7.68	**5.49**	**4.60**	**4.11**	**3.79**	**3.56**	**3.39**	**3.26**	**3.14**	**3.06**	**2.98**	**2.93**	**2.83**	**2.74**	**2.63**
28	4.20	3.34	2.95	2.71	2.56	2.44	2.36	2.29	2.24	2.19	2.15	2.12	2.06	2.02	1.96
	7.64	**5.45**	**4.57**	**4.07**	**3.76**	**3.53**	**3.36**	**3.23**	**3.11**	**3.03**	**2.95**	**2.90**	**2.80**	**2.71**	**2.60**
29	4.18	3.33	2.93	2.70	2.54	2.43	2.35	2.28	2.22	2.18	2.14	2.10	2.05	2.00	1.94
	7.60	**5.42**	**4.54**	**4.04**	**3.73**	**3.50**	**3.33**	**3.20**	**3.08**	**3.00**	**2.92**	**2.87**	**2.77**	**2.68**	**2.57**
30	4.17	3.32	2.92	2.69	2.53	2.42	2.34	2.27	2.21	2.16	2.12	2.09	2.04	1.99	1.93
	7.56	**5.39**	**4.51**	**4.02**	**3.70**	**3.47**	**3.30**	**3.17**	**3.06**	**2.98**	**2.90**	**2.84**	**2.74**	**2.66**	**2.55**
32	4.15	3.30	2.90	2.67	2.51	2.40	2.32	2.25	2.19	2.14	2.10	2.07	2.02	1.97	1.91
	7.50	**5.34**	**4.46**	**3.97**	**3.66**	**3.42**	**3.25**	**3.12**	**3.01**	**2.94**	**2.86**	**2.80**	**2.70**	**2.62**	**2.51**
34	4.13	3.28	2.88	2.65	2.49	2.38	2.30	2.23	2.17	2.12	2.08	2.05	2.00	1.95	1.89
	7.44	**5.29**	**4.42**	**3.93**	**3.61**	**3.38**	**3.21**	**3.08**	**2.97**	**2.89**	**2.82**	**2.76**	**2.66**	**2.58**	**2.47**
36	4.11	3.26	2.86	2.63	2.48	2.36	2.28	2.21	2.15	2.10	2.06	2.03	1.98	1.93	1.87
	7.39	**5.25**	**4.38**	**3.89**	**3.58**	**3.35**	**3.18**	**3.04**	**2.94**	**2.86**	**2.78**	**2.72**	**2.62**	**2.54**	**2.43**
38	4.10	3.25	2.85	2.62	2.46	2.35	2.26	2.19	2.14	2.09	2.05	2.02	1.96	1.92	1.85
	7.35	**5.21**	**4.34**	**3.86**	**3.54**	**3.32**	**3.15**	**3.02**	**2.91**	**2.82**	**2.75**	**2.69**	**2.59**	**2.51**	**2.40**
40	4.08	3.23	2.84	2.61	2.45	2.34	2.25	2.18	2.12	2.07	2.04	2.00	1.95	1.90	1.84
	7.31	**5.18**	**4.31**	**3.83**	**3.51**	**3.29**	**3.12**	**2.99**	**2.88**	**2.80**	**2.73**	**2.66**	**2.56**	**2.49**	**2.37**
42	4.07	3.22	2.83	2.59	2.44	2.32	2.24	2.17	2.11	2.06	2.02	1.99	1.94	1.89	1.82
	7.27	**5.15**	**4.29**	**3.80**	**3.49**	**3.26**	**3.10**	**2.96**	**2.86**	**2.77**	**2.70**	**2.64**	**2.54**	**2.46**	**2.35**

continued

Degrees of Freedom: Denominator	Degrees of Freedom: Numerator														
	1	2	3	4	5	6	7	8	9	10	11	12	14	16	20
44	4.06	3.21	2.82	2.58	2.43	2.31	2.23	2.16	2.10	2.05	2.01	1.98	1.92	1.88	1.81
	7.24	**5.12**	**4.26**	**3.78**	**3.46**	**3.24**	**3.07**	**2.94**	**2.84**	**2.75**	**2.68**	**2.62**	**2.52**	**2.44**	**2.32**
46	4.05	3.20	2.81	2.57	2.42	2.30	2.22	2.14	2.09	2.04	2.00	1.97	1.91	1.87	1.80
	7.21	**5.10**	**4.24**	**3.76**	**3.44**	**3.22**	**3.05**	**2.92**	**2.82**	**2.73**	**2.66**	**2.60**	**2.50**	**2.42**	**2.30**
48	4.04	3.19	2.80	2.56	2.41	2.30	2.21	2.14	2.08	2.03	1.99	1.96	1.90	1.86	1.79
	7.19	**5.08**	**4.22**	**3.74**	**3.42**	**3.20**	**3.04**	**2.90**	**2.80**	**2.71**	**2.64**	**2.58**	**2.48**	**2.40**	**2.28**
50	4.03	3.18	2.79	2.56	2.40	2.29	2.20	2.13	2.07	2.02	1.98	1.95	1.90	1.85	1.78
	7.17	**5.06**	**4.20**	**3.72**	**3.41**	**3.18**	**3.02**	**2.88**	**2.78**	**2.70**	**2.62**	**2.56**	**2.46**	**2.39**	**2.26**
55	4.02	3.17	2.78	2.54	2.38	2.27	2.18	2.11	2.05	2.00	1.97	1.93	1.88	1.83	1.76
	7.12	**5.01**	**4.16**	**3.68**	**3.37**	**3.15**	**2.98**	**2.85**	**2.75**	**2.66**	**2.59**	**2.53**	**2.43**	**2.35**	**2.23**
60	4.00	3.15	2.76	2.52	2.37	2.25	2.17	2.10	2.04	1.99	1.95	1.92	1.86	1.81	1.75
	7.08	**4.98**	**4.13**	**3.65**	**3.34**	**3.12**	**2.95**	**2.82**	**2.72**	**2.63**	**2.56**	**2.50**	**2.40**	**2.32**	**2.20**
65	3.99	3.14	2.75	2.51	2.36	2.24	2.15	2.08	2.02	1.98	1.94	1.90	1.85	1.80	1.73
	7.04	**4.95**	**4.10**	**3.62**	**3.31**	**3.09**	**2.93**	**2.79**	**2.70**	**2.61**	**2.54**	**2.47**	**2.37**	**2.30**	**2.18**
70	3.98	3.13	2.74	2.50	2.35	2.23	2.14	2.07	2.01	1.97	1.93	1.89	1.84	1.79	1.72
	7.01	**4.92**	**4.08**	**3.60**	**3.29**	**3.07**	**2.91**	**2.77**	**2.67**	**2.59**	**2.51**	**2.45**	**2.35**	**2.28**	**2.15**
80	3.96	3.11	2.72	2.48	2.33	2.21	2.12	2.05	1.99	1.95	1.91	1.88	1.82	1.77	1.70
	6.96	**4.88**	**4.04**	**3.56**	**3.25**	**3.04**	**2.87**	**2.74**	**2.64**	**2.55**	**2.48**	**2.41**	**2.32**	**2.24**	**2.11**
100	3.94	3.09	2.70	2.46	2.30	2.19	2.10	2.03	1.97	1.92	1.88	1.85	1.79	1.75	1.68
	6.90	**4.82**	**3.98**	**3.51**	**3.20**	**2.99**	**2.82**	**2.69**	**2.59**	**2.51**	**2.43**	**2.36**	**2.26**	**2.19**	**2.06**
125	3.92	3.07	2.68	2.44	2.29	2.17	2.08	2.01	1.95	1.90	1.86	1.83	1.77	1.72	1.65
	6.84	**4.78**	**3.94**	**3.47**	**3.17**	**2.95**	**2.79**	**2.65**	**2.56**	**2.47**	**2.40**	**2.33**	**2.23**	**2.15**	**2.03**
150	3.91	3.06	2.67	2.43	2.27	2.16	2.07	2.00	1.94	1.89	1.85	1.82	1.76	1.71	1.64
	6.81	**4.75**	**3.91**	**3.44**	**3.14**	**2.92**	**2.76**	**2.62**	**2.53**	**2.44**	**2.37**	**2.30**	**2.20**	**2.12**	**2.00**
200	3.89	3.04	2.65	2.41	2.26	2.14	2.05	1.98	1.92	1.87	1.83	1.80	1.74	1.69	1.62
	6.76	**4.71**	**3.88**	**3.41**	**3.11**	**2.90**	**2.73**	**2.60**	**2.50**	**2.41**	**2.34**	**2.28**	**2.17**	**2.09**	**1.97**
400	3.86	3.02	2.62	2.39	2.23	2.12	2.03	1.96	1.90	1.85	1.81	1.78	1.72	1.67	1.60
	6.70	**4.66**	**3.83**	**3.36**	**3.06**	**2.85**	**2.69**	**2.55**	**2.46**	**2.37**	**2.29**	**2.23**	**2.12**	**2.04**	**1.92**
1000	3.85	3.00	2.61	2.38	2.22	2.10	2.02	1.95	1.89	1.84	1.80	1.76	1.70	1.65	1.58
	6.66	**4.62**	**3.80**	**3.34**	**3.04**	**2.82**	**2.66**	**2.53**	**2.43**	**2.34**	**2.26**	**2.20**	**2.09**	**2.01**	**1.89**
∞	3.84	2.99	2.60	2.37	2.21	2.09	2.01	1.94	1.88	1.83	1.79	1.75	1.69	1.64	1.57
	6.64	**4.60**	**3.78**	**3.32**	**3.02**	**2.80**	**2.64**	**2.51**	**2.41**	**2.32**	**2.24**	**2.18**	**2.07**	**1.99**	**1.87**

Table B.5

The Studentized Range Statistic (q)*

*The critical values for q corresponding to α = .05 (lightface type) and α = .01 (boldface type).

df for Error Term	k = Number of Treatments											
	2	3	4	5	6	7	8	9	10	11	12
5	3.64	4.60	5.22	5.67	6.03	6.33	6.58	6.80	6.99	7.17	7.32
	5.70	**6.98**	**7.80**	**8.42**	**8.91**	**9.32**	**9.67**	**9.97**	**10.24**	**10.48**	**10.70**
6	3.46	4.34	4.90	5.30	5.63	5.90	6.12	6.32	6.49	6.65	6.79
	5.24	**6.33**	**7.03**	**7.56**	**7.97**	**8.32**	**8.61**	**8.87**	**9.10**	**9.30**	**9.48**
7	3.34	4.16	4.68	5.06	5.36	5.61	5.82	6.00	6.16	6.30	6.43
	4.95	**5.92**	**6.54**	**7.01**	**7.37**	**7.68**	**7.94**	**8.17**	**8.37**	**8.55**	**8.71**
8	3.26	4.04	4.53	4.89	5.17	5.40	5.60	5.77	5.92	6.05	6.18
	4.75	**5.64**	**6.20**	**6.62**	**6.96**	**7.24**	**7.47**	**7.68**	**7.86**	**8.03**	**8.18**
9	3.20	3.95	4.41	4.76	5.02	5.24	5.43	5.59	5.74	5.87	5.98
	4.60	**5.43**	**5.96**	**6.35**	**6.66**	**6.91**	**7.13**	**7.33**	**7.49**	**7.65**	**7.78**
10	3.15	3.88	4.33	4.65	4.91	5.12	5.30	5.46	5.60	5.72	5.83
	4.48	**5.27**	**5.77**	**6.14**	**6.43**	**6.67**	**6.87**	**7.05**	**7.21**	**7.36**	**7.49**
11	3.11	3.82	4.26	4.57	4.82	5.03	5.20	5.35	5.49	5.61	5.71
	4.39	**5.15**	**5.62**	**5.97**	**6.25**	**6.48**	**6.67**	**6.84**	**6.99**	**7.13**	**7.25**
12	3.08	3.77	4.20	4.51	4.75	4.95	5.12	5.27	5.39	5.51	5.61
	4.32	**5.05**	**5.50**	**5.84**	**6.10**	**6.32**	**6.51**	**6.67**	**6.81**	**6.94**	**7.06**
13	3.06	3.73	4.15	4.45	4.69	4.88	5.05	5.19	5.32	5.43	5.53
	4.26	**4.96**	**5.40**	**5.73**	**5.98**	**6.19**	**6.37**	**6.53**	**6.67**	**6.79**	**6.90**
14	3.03	3.70	4.11	4.41	4.64	4.83	4.99	5.13	5.25	5.36	5.46
	4.21	**4.89**	**5.32**	**5.63**	**5.88**	**6.08**	**6.26**	**6.41**	**6.54**	**6.66**	**6.77**
15	3.01	3.67	4.08	4.37	4.59	4.78	4.94	5.08	5.20	5.31	5.40
	4.17	**4.84**	**5.25**	**5.56**	**5.80**	**5.99**	**6.16**	**6.31**	**6.44**	**6.55**	**6.66**
16	3.00	3.65	4.05	4.33	4.56	4.74	4.90	5.03	5.15	5.26	5.35
	4.13	**4.79**	**5.19**	**5.49**	**5.72**	**5.92**	**6.08**	**6.22**	**6.35**	**6.46**	**6.56**
17	2.98	3.63	4.02	4.30	4.52	4.70	4.86	4.99	5.11	5.21	5.31
	4.10	**4.74**	**5.14**	**5.43**	**5.66**	**5.85**	**6.01**	**6.15**	**6.27**	**6.38**	**6.48**
18	2.97	3.61	4.00	4.28	4.49	4.67	4.82	4.96	5.07	5.17	5.27
	4.07	**4.70**	**5.09**	**5.38**	**5.60**	**5.79**	**5.94**	**6.08**	**6.20**	**6.31**	**6.41**
19	2.96	3.59	3.98	4.25	4.47	4.65	4.79	4.92	5.04	5.14	5.23
	4.05	**4.67**	**5.05**	**5.33**	**5.55**	**5.73**	**5.89**	**6.02**	**6.14**	**6.25**	**6.34**

continued

STATISTICAL TABLES

df for Error Term	k = Number of Treatments										
	2	3	4	5	6	7	8	9	10	11	12
20	2.95	3.58	3.96	4.23	4.45	4.62	4.77	4.90	5.01	5.11	5.20
	4.02	**4.64**	**5.02**	**5.29**	**5.51**	**5.69**	**5.84**	**5.97**	**6.09**	**6.19**	**6.28**
24	2.92	3.53	3.90	4.17	4.37	4.54	4.68	4.81	4.92	5.01	5.10
	3.96	**4.55**	**4.91**	**5.17**	**5.37**	**5.54**	**5.69**	**5.81**	**5.92**	**6.02**	**6.11**
30	2.89	3.49	3.85	4.10	4.30	4.46	4.60	4.72	4.82	4.92	5.00
	3.89	**4.45**	**4.80**	**5.05**	**5.24**	**5.40**	**5.54**	**5.65**	**5.76**	**5.85**	**5.93**
40	2.86	3.44	3.79	4.04	4.23	4.39	4.52	4.63	4.73	4.82	4.90
	3.82	**4.37**	**4.70**	**4.93**	**5.11**	**5.26**	**5.39**	**5.50**	**5.60**	**5.69**	**5.76**
60	2.83	3.40	3.74	3.98	4.16	4.31	4.44	4.55	4.65	4.73	4.81
	3.76	**4.28**	**4.59**	**4.82**	**4.99**	**5.13**	**5.25**	**5.36**	**5.45**	**5.53**	**5.60**
120	2.80	3.36	3.68	3.92	4.10	4.24	4.36	4.47	4.56	4.64	4.71
	3.70	**4.20**	**4.50**	**4.71**	**4.87**	**5.01**	**5.12**	**5.21**	**5.30**	**5.37**	**5.44**
∞	2.77	3.31	3.63	3.86	4.03	4.17	4.29	4.39	4.47	4.55	4.62
	3.64	**4.12**	**4.40**	**4.60**	**4.76**	**4.88**	**4.99**	**5.08**	**5.16**	**5.23**	**5.29**

Table B.6
The Chi Square Distribution*

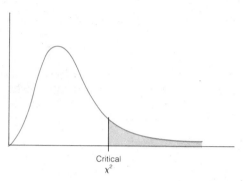

Critical
χ^2

*The table entries are critical values of χ^2.

df	Proportion in Critical Region				
	0.10	0.05	0.025	0.01	0.005
1	2.71	3.84	5.02	6.63	7.88
2	4.61	5.99	7.38	9.21	10.60
3	6.25	7.81	9.35	11.34	12.84
4	7.78	9.49	11.14	13.28	14.86
5	9.24	11.07	12.83	15.09	16.75
6	10.64	12.59	14.45	16.81	18.55
7	12.02	14.07	16.01	18.48	20.28
8	13.36	15.51	17.53	20.09	21.96
9	14.68	16.92	19.02	21.67	23.59
10	15.99	18.31	20.48	23.21	25.19
11	17.28	19.68	21.92	24.72	26.76
12	18.55	21.03	23.34	26.22	28.30
13	19.81	22.36	24.74	27.69	29.82
14	21.06	23.68	26.12	29.14	31.32
15	22.31	25.00	27.49	30.58	32.80
16	23.54	26.30	28.85	32.00	34.27
17	24.77	27.59	30.19	33.41	35.72
18	25.99	28.87	31.53	34.81	37.16
19	27.20	30.14	32.85	36.19	38.58
20	28.41	31.41	34.17	37.57	40.00
21	29.62	32.67	35.48	38.93	41.40
22	30.81	33.92	36.78	40.29	42.80
23	32.01	35.17	38.08	41.64	44.18
24	33.20	36.42	39.36	42.98	45.56
25	34.38	37.65	40.65	44.31	46.93
26	35.56	38.89	41.92	45.64	48.29
27	36.74	40.11	43.19	46.96	49.64
28	37.92	41.34	44.46	48.28	50.99
29	39.09	42.56	45.72	49.59	52.34
30	40.26	43.77	46.98	50.89	53.67
40	51.81	55.76	59.34	63.69	66.77
50	63.17	67.50	71.42	76.15	79.49
60	74.40	79.08	83.30	88.38	91.95
70	85.53	90.53	95.02	100.42	104.22
80	96.58	101.88	106.63	112.33	116.32
90	107.56	113.14	118.14	124.12	128.30
100	118.50	124.34	129.56	135.81	140.17

Table B.7A

Critical Values of the Mann-Whitney U^*

*Critical values are provided for a *one-tailed* test at $\alpha = .05$ (lightface type) and for a *two-tailed* test at $\alpha = .05$ (boldface type). To be significant for any given n_A and n_B, the obtained U must be *equal to* or *less than* the critical value in the table. Dashes (—) in the body of the table indicate that no decision is possible at the stated level of significance and values of n_A and n_B.

n_B \ n_A	1	2	3	4	5	6	7	8	9	10	11	12	13	14	15	16	17	18	19	20
1	—	—	—	—	—	—	—	—	—	—	—	—	—	—	—	—	—	—	0	0
	—	—	—	—	—	—	—	—	—	—	—	—	—	—	—	—	—	—	**—**	**—**
2	—	—	—	—	0	0	0	1	1	1	1	2	2	2	3	3	3	4	4	4
	—	—	—	—	—	—	—	**0**	**0**	**0**	**0**	**1**	**1**	**1**	**1**	**1**	**2**	**2**	**2**	**2**
3	—	—	0	0	1	2	2	3	3	4	5	5	6	7	7	8	9	9	10	11
	—	—	—	—	**0**	**1**	**1**	**2**	**2**	**3**	**3**	**4**	**4**	**5**	**5**	**6**	**6**	**7**	**7**	**8**
4	—	—	0	1	2	3	4	5	6	7	8	9	10	11	12	14	15	16	17	18
	—	—	—	**0**	**1**	**2**	**3**	**4**	**4**	**5**	**6**	**7**	**8**	**9**	**10**	**11**	**11**	**12**	**13**	**13**
5	—	0	1	2	4	5	6	8	9	11	12	13	15	16	18	19	20	22	23	25
	—	—	**0**	**1**	**2**	**3**	**5**	**6**	**7**	**8**	**9**	**11**	**12**	**13**	**14**	**15**	**17**	**18**	**19**	**20**
6	—	0	2	3	5	7	8	10	12	14	16	17	19	21	23	25	26	28	30	32
	—	—	**1**	**2**	**3**	**5**	**6**	**8**	**10**	**11**	**13**	**14**	**16**	**17**	**19**	**21**	**22**	**24**	**25**	**27**
7	—	0	2	4	6	8	11	13	15	17	19	21	24	26	28	30	33	35	37	39
	—	—	**1**	**3**	**5**	**6**	**8**	**10**	**12**	**14**	**16**	**18**	**20**	**22**	**24**	**26**	**28**	**30**	**32**	**34**
8	—	1	3	5	8	10	13	15	18	20	23	26	28	31	33	36	39	41	44	47
	—	**0**	**2**	**4**	**6**	**8**	**10**	**13**	**15**	**17**	**19**	**22**	**24**	**26**	**29**	**31**	**34**	**36**	**38**	**41**
9	—	1	3	6	9	12	15	18	21	24	27	30	33	36	39	42	45	48	51	54
	—	**0**	**2**	**4**	**7**	**10**	**12**	**15**	**17**	**20**	**23**	**26**	**28**	**31**	**34**	**37**	**39**	**42**	**45**	**48**
10	—	1	4	7	11	14	17	20	24	27	31	34	37	41	44	48	51	55	58	62
	—	**0**	**3**	**5**	**8**	**11**	**14**	**17**	**20**	**23**	**26**	**29**	**33**	**36**	**39**	**42**	**45**	**48**	**52**	**55**
11	—	1	5	8	12	16	19	23	27	31	34	38	42	46	50	54	57	61	65	69
	—	**0**	**3**	**6**	**9**	**13**	**16**	**19**	**23**	**26**	**30**	**33**	**37**	**40**	**44**	**47**	**51**	**55**	**58**	**62**
12	—	2	5	9	13	17	21	26	30	34	38	42	47	51	55	60	64	68	72	77
	—	**1**	**4**	**7**	**11**	**14**	**18**	**22**	**26**	**29**	**33**	**37**	**41**	**45**	**49**	**53**	**57**	**61**	**65**	**69**
13	—	2	6	10	15	19	24	28	33	37	42	47	51	56	61	65	70	75	80	84
	—	**1**	**4**	**8**	**12**	**16**	**20**	**24**	**28**	**33**	**37**	**41**	**45**	**50**	**54**	**59**	**63**	**67**	**72**	**76**
14	—	2	7	11	16	21	26	31	36	41	46	51	56	61	66	71	77	82	87	92
	—	**1**	**5**	**9**	**13**	**17**	**22**	**26**	**31**	**36**	**40**	**45**	**50**	**55**	**59**	**64**	**67**	**74**	**78**	**83**
15	—	3	7	12	18	23	28	33	39	44	50	55	61	66	72	77	83	88	94	100
	—	**1**	**5**	**10**	**14**	**19**	**24**	**29**	**34**	**39**	**44**	**49**	**54**	**59**	**64**	**70**	**75**	**80**	**85**	**90**

Table B.7A *continued*

n_B \ n_A	1	2	3	4	5	6	7	8	9	10	11	12	13	14	15	16	17	18	19	20
16	—	3	8	14	19	25	30	36	42	48	54	60	65	71	77	83	89	95	101	107
	—	**1**	**6**	**11**	**15**	**21**	**26**	**31**	**37**	**42**	**47**	**53**	**59**	**64**	**70**	**75**	**81**	**86**	**92**	**98**
17	—	3	9	15	20	26	33	39	45	51	57	64	70	77	83	89	96	102	109	115
	—	**2**	**6**	**11**	**17**	**22**	**28**	**34**	**39**	**45**	**51**	**57**	**63**	**67**	**75**	**81**	**87**	**93**	**99**	**105**
18	—	4	9	16	22	28	35	41	48	55	61	68	75	82	88	95	102	109	116	123
	—	**2**	**7**	**12**	**18**	**24**	**30**	**36**	**42**	**48**	**55**	**61**	**67**	**74**	**80**	**86**	**93**	**99**	**106**	**112**
19	0	4	10	17	23	30	37	44	51	58	65	72	80	87	94	101	109	116	123	130
	—	**2**	**7**	**13**	**19**	**25**	**32**	**38**	**45**	**52**	**58**	**65**	**72**	**78**	**85**	**92**	**99**	**106**	**113**	**119**
20	0	4	11	18	25	32	39	47	54	62	69	77	84	92	100	107	115	123	130	138
	—	**2**	**8**	**13**	**20**	**27**	**34**	**41**	**48**	**55**	**62**	**69**	**76**	**83**	**90**	**98**	**105**	**112**	**119**	**127**

Table B.7B

Critical Values of the Mann-Whitney U*

*Critical values are provided for a *one-tailed* test at $\alpha = .01$ (lightface type) and for a *two-tailed* test at $\alpha = .01$ (boldface type). To be significant for any given n_A and n_B, the obtained U must be *equal to* or *less than* the critical value in the table. Dashes (—) in the body of the table indicate that no decision is possible at the stated level of significance and values of n_A and n_B.

n_B \ n_A	1	2	3	4	5	6	7	8	9	10	11	12	13	14	15	16	17	18	19	20
1	—	—	—	—	—	—	—	—	—	—	—	—	—	—	—	—	—	—	—	—
2	—	—	—	—	—	—	—	—	—	—	—	—	0	0	0	0	0	0	1	1
													—	—	—	—	—	—	**0**	**0**
3	—	—	—	—	—	—	0	0	1	1	1	2	2	2	3	3	4	4	4	5
							—	—	**0**	**0**	**0**	**1**	**1**	**1**	**2**	**2**	**2**	**2**	**3**	**3**
4	—	—	—	—	0	1	1	2	3	3	4	5	5	6	7	7	8	9	9	10
					—	**0**	**0**	**1**	**1**	**2**	**2**	**3**	**3**	**4**	**5**	**5**	**6**	**6**	**7**	**8**
5	—	—	—	0	1	2	3	4	5	6	7	8	9	10	11	12	13	14	15	16
				—	**0**	**1**	**1**	**2**	**3**	**4**	**5**	**6**	**7**	**7**	**8**	**9**	**10**	**11**	**12**	**13**
6	—	—	—	1	2	3	4	6	7	8	9	11	12	13	15	16	18	19	20	22
				0	**1**	**2**	**3**	**4**	**5**	**6**	**7**	**9**	**10**	**11**	**12**	**13**	**15**	**16**	**17**	**18**
7	—	—	0	1	3	4	6	7	9	11	12	14	16	17	19	21	23	24	26	28
			—	**0**	**1**	**3**	**4**	**6**	**7**	**9**	**10**	**12**	**13**	**15**	**16**	**18**	**19**	**21**	**22**	**24**
8	—	—	0	2	4	6	7	9	11	13	15	17	20	22	24	26	28	30	32	34
			—	**1**	**2**	**4**	**6**	**7**	**9**	**11**	**13**	**15**	**17**	**18**	**20**	**22**	**24**	**26**	**28**	**30**
9	—	—	1	3	5	7	9	11	14	16	18	21	23	26	28	31	33	36	38	40
			0	**1**	**3**	**5**	**7**	**9**	**11**	**13**	**16**	**18**	**20**	**22**	**24**	**27**	**29**	**31**	**33**	**36**
10	—	—	1	3	6	8	11	13	16	19	22	24	27	30	33	36	38	41	44	47
			0	**2**	**4**	**6**	**9**	**11**	**13**	**16**	**18**	**21**	**24**	**26**	**29**	**31**	**34**	**37**	**39**	**42**
11	—	—	1	4	7	9	12	15	18	22	25	28	31	34	37	41	44	47	50	53
			0	**2**	**5**	**7**	**10**	**13**	**16**	**18**	**21**	**24**	**27**	**30**	**33**	**36**	**39**	**42**	**45**	**48**
12	—	—	2	5	8	11	14	17	21	24	28	31	35	38	42	46	49	53	56	60
			1	**3**	**6**	**9**	**12**	**15**	**18**	**21**	**24**	**27**	**31**	**34**	**37**	**41**	**44**	**47**	**51**	**54**
13	—	0	2	5	9	12	16	20	23	27	31	35	39	43	47	51	55	59	63	67
	—	**1**	**3**	**7**	**10**	**13**	**17**	**20**	**24**	**27**	**31**	**34**	**38**	**42**	**45**	**49**	**53**	**56**	**60**
14	—	0	2	6	10	13	17	22	26	30	34	38	43	47	51	56	60	65	69	73
	—	**1**	**4**	**7**	**11**	**15**	**18**	**22**	**26**	**30**	**34**	**38**	**42**	**46**	**50**	**54**	**58**	**63**	**67**
15	—	0	3	7	11	15	19	24	28	33	37	42	47	51	56	61	66	70	75	80
	—	**2**	**5**	**8**	**12**	**16**	**20**	**24**	**29**	**33**	**37**	**42**	**46**	**51**	**55**	**60**	**64**	**69**	**73**

Table B.7B *continued*

n_B \ n_A	1	2	3	4	5	6	7	8	9	10	11	12	13	14	15	16	17	18	19	20
16	—	0	3	7	12	16	21	26	31	36	41	46	51	56	61	66	71	76	82	87
	—	**2**	**5**	**9**	**13**	**18**	**22**	**27**	**31**	**36**	**41**	**45**	**50**	**55**	**60**	**65**	**70**	**74**	**79**	
17	—	0	4	8	13	18	23	28	33	38	44	49	55	60	66	71	77	82	88	93
	—	**2**	**6**	**10**	**15**	**19**	**24**	**29**	**34**	**39**	**44**	**49**	**54**	**60**	**65**	**70**	**75**	**81**	**86**	
18	—	0	4	9	14	19	24	30	36	41	47	53	59	65	70	76	82	88	94	100
	—	**2**	**6**	**11**	**16**	**21**	**26**	**31**	**37**	**42**	**47**	**53**	**58**	**64**	**70**	**75**	**81**	**87**	**92**	
19	—	1	4	9	15	20	26	32	38	44	50	56	63	69	75	82	88	94	101	107
		0	**3**	**7**	**12**	**17**	**22**	**28**	**33**	**39**	**45**	**51**	**56**	**63**	**69**	**74**	**81**	**87**	**93**	**99**
20	—	1	5	10	16	22	28	34	40	47	53	60	67	73	80	87	93	100	107	114
		0	**3**	**8**	**13**	**18**	**24**	**30**	**36**	**42**	**48**	**54**	**60**	**67**	**73**	**79**	**86**	**92**	**99**	**105**

Table B.8

Critical Values of *T* for the Wilcoxon Signed-Ranks Test*

*To be significant, the obtained *T* must be *equal to* or *less than* the critical value. Dashes (—) in the columns indicate that no decision is possible for the stated α and *n*.

	Level of Significance for One-Tailed Test						Level of Significance for One-Tailed Test			
	.05	.025	.01	.005			.05	.025	.01	.005
	Level of Significance for Two-Tailed Test						Level of Significance for Two-Tailed Test			
n	.10	.05	.02	.01		*n*	.10	.05	.02	.01
5	0	—	—	—		28	130	116	101	91
6	2	0	—	—		29	140	126	110	100
7	3	2	0	—		30	151	137	120	109
8	5	3	1	0		31	163	147	130	118
9	8	5	3	1		32	175	159	140	128
10	10	8	5	3		33	187	170	151	138
11	13	10	7	5		34	200	182	162	148
12	17	13	9	7		35	213	195	173	159
13	21	17	12	9		36	227	208	185	171
14	25	21	15	12		37	241	221	198	182
15	30	25	19	15		38	256	235	211	194
16	35	29	23	19		39	271	249	224	207
17	41	34	27	23		40	286	264	238	220
18	47	40	32	27		41	302	279	252	233
19	53	46	37	32		42	319	294	266	247
20	60	52	43	37		43	336	310	281	261
21	67	58	49	42		44	353	327	296	276
22	75	65	55	48		45	371	343	312	291
23	83	73	62	54		46	389	361	328	307
24	91	81	69	61		47	407	378	345	322
25	100	89	76	68		48	426	396	362	339
26	110	98	84	75		49	446	415	379	355
27	119	107	92	83		50	466	434	397	373

Acknowledgments

The statistical tables in Appendix B have been adapted or reprinted, with permission, from the following sources:

Table B.1   Appendix 2 of R. Clarke, A. Coladarci, and J. Caffrey, *Statistical Reasoning and Procedures.* Columbus, Ohio: Charles E. Merrill Publishing, 1965.

Table B.2   Table III of R. A. Fisher and F. Yates, *Statistical Tables for Biological, Agricultural and Medical Research*, 6th ed. London: Longman Group Ltd., 1974 (previously published by Oliver and Boyd Ltd., Edinburgh).

Table B.3   Table 31 of E. Pearson and H. O. Hartley, *Biometrika Tables for Statisticians*, 2nd ed. New York: Cambridge University Press, 1958. Adapted and reprinted by permission of the Biometrika trustees.

Table B.4   Table A14 of *Statistical Methods*, 7th ed. by George W. Snedecor and William G. Cochran, Copyright © 1980 by the Iowa State University Press, 2121 South State Avenue, Ames, Iowa 50010.

Table B.5   Table 29 of E. Pearson and H. Hartley, *Biometrika Tables for Statisticians*, 3rd ed. New York: Cambridge University Press, 1966. Adapted and reprinted with permission of the Biometrika trustees.

Table B.6   Table 8 of E. Pearson and H. Hartley, *Biometrika Tables for Statisticians*, 3rd ed. New York: Cambridge University Press, 1966. Adapted and reprinted with permission of the Biometrika trustees.

Table B.7   Table D.10 of *Introductory Statistics* by R. E. Kirk. Copyright © 1978 by Wadsworth, Inc. Reprinted by permission of Brooks/Cole Publishing Company, Monterey, California 93940.

Table B.8   Adapted from F. Wilcoxon, S. K. Katti, and R. A. Wilcox, *Critical Values and Probability Levels of the Wilcoxon Rank-Sum Test and the Wilcoxon Signed-Ranks Test.* Wayne, N.J.: American Cyanamid Company, 1963. Also adapted from R. P. Runyon and A. Haber, *Fundamentals of Behavioral Statistics.* Copyright © 1984 by Addison-Wesley, Reading, Mass., p. 435, Table J. Adapted and reprinted with permission of the American Cyanamid Company and Addison-Wesley.

Solutions to Selected Problems

Chapter 1: Introduction to Statistics

1. Scientific study is based on data collected from observation rather than hunches or feelings.

3. Correlations do not determine the cause-and-effect nature of a relationship.

5. An incorrect interpretation of an experiment can occur when a confounding variable is present or when the results have been affected by experimenter bias.

7. A nominal scale simply names the categories of measurement. An ordinal scale names and orders the categories. Order of finish is an ordinal measurement. Sex of jockeys is a nominal measurement.

9. A ratio scale has a zero point that represents "none" of the variable being measured. An interval scale does not have an absolute zero point.

11. a. $\Sigma X = 40$
    b. $\Sigma X + 5 = 45$
    c. $\Sigma(X + 5) = 65$
    d. $\Sigma(X - 3) = 25$
    e. $\Sigma X - 3 = 37$
    f. $N = 5$

13. a. $\Sigma X = 15$
    b. $\Sigma X^2 = 55$
    c. $(\Sigma X)^2 = 225$

15. a. $\Sigma X^2 = 192.68$
    b. $\Sigma Y = 40.90$
    c. $\Sigma Y^2 = 331.95$
    d. $\Sigma X \, \Sigma Y = 1406.96$
    e. $\Sigma XY = 179.26$
    f. $(\Sigma X)^2 = 1183.36$
    g. $(\Sigma Y)^2 = 1672.81$

17. a. $\Sigma X = 183.4$
    b. $\Sigma X^2 = 2486.56$

c. $(\Sigma X)^2 = 33{,}635.56$

d. $N = 15$

19. a. $\Sigma X = 5$

b. $\Sigma(X + 2) = 17$

c. $\Sigma X^2 = 95$

Chapter 2: Frequency Distributions

1.

X	f
6	2
5	4
4	3
3	2
2	1
1	1

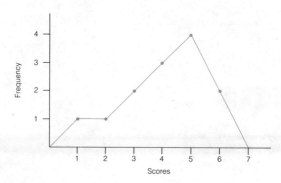

3. a.

X	f
10	1
9	0
8	1
7	3
6	2
5	3
4	6
3	7
2	4
1	1

c. 33%

d. $X = 10$

11. a. The independent variable is diet. The dependent variable is the number of errors on the discrimination task.

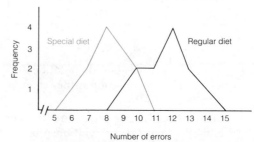

c. Yes, the diet appears to have an effect. Error scores with the regular diet are consistently higher than scores with the special diet.

5.

X	f		X	f
30–31	2		30–35	2
28–29	2		25–29	7
26–27	3		20–24	14
24–25	4		15–19	10
22–23	7		10–14	2
20–21	5			
18–19	5			
16–17	4			
14–15	2			
12–13	1			

7.

X	f	cf	c%
5	1	10	100%
4	2	9	90%
3	4	7	70%
2	1	3	30%
1	2	2	20%

9. a. 70%

b. $X = 20.5$

13.

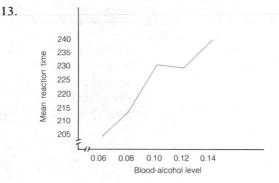

15.
```
      47013521273 │9│231
077926529365175 │8│2315690360503
      962774052 │7│03743650259869518
           2759 │6│30298765
              7 │5│8
```

17. a. In the regular table the 25th percentile is $X = 2.5$. In the grouped table, it is $X = 2.3$.

   b. In the regular table the rank is 61.25%. In the grouped table it is 56.875%. The value from the regular table should be more accurate.

19. a.

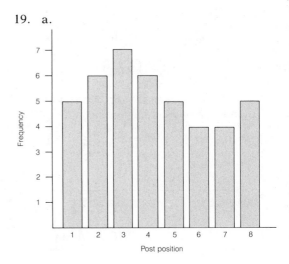

   b. The distribution is flat or rectangular.

   c. There is little evidence for any differences among the eight positions. However, post position 3 has produced more winners than any other.

Chapter 3: Central Tendency

1. Mean = $\frac{25}{8}$ = 3.125
   Median = 3.5
   Mode = 4

3. a. Mean = $\frac{53}{12}$ = 4.42
      Median = 4.0
      Mode = 3

   b. The distribution is positively skewed.

5. $\overline{X}$ = 330 seconds would be converted to $\overline{X}$ = 5.50 minutes.

7. a.

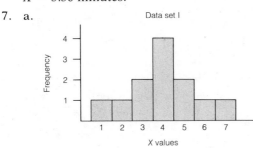

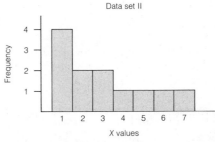

   b. For set I, the mean is approximately 4. For set II, the mean is approximately 3.

   c. For set I, mean = $\frac{48}{12}$ = 4. For set II, mean = $\frac{36}{12}$ = 3.

9. Use the median. The mean cannot be computed with undetermined scores.

11. For section I, $\Sigma X = 1890$. For section II, $\Sigma X = 5460$. For the combined group, $n = 100$, $\Sigma X = 7350$, and $\overline{X} = 73.50$.

13. a. $\overline{X}$ = 4.71.

b. After adding 20 points to each score, $\overline{X}$ = 24.71.

15. For the morning class, ΣX = 2690.1. For the afternoon class, ΣX = 1710.2. For the combined group, n = 95, ΣX = 4400.3, and $\overline{X}$ = 46.32.

16. a. Before $\overline{X}$ = 22.78 and after $\overline{X}$ = 17.67. The difference is 5.11.

b. The mean of the differences also is 5.11.

19. $\overline{X}$ = 0.973. Median = 0.967.

21. $\overline{X}$ = 7.18. This class is slightly above the national norm.

Chapter 4: Variability

3. ΣX = 20, ΣX^2 = 78, and the mean = 2. SS = 38 by either formula.

5. a.

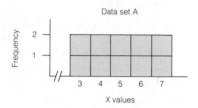

Data set A

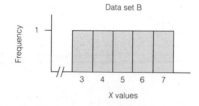

Data set B

b. The distributions are identical in shape. Data set A simply doubles the frequencies of data set B.

c. For A, SS = 20. For B, SS = 10.

d. σ^2 = 2 for both populations.

e. SS finds the total amount of variability, which is partially dependent on the number of scores. Variance finds the average squared deviation, which measures variability independently of the number of scores.

7. The standard deviation, σ = 20, provides a measure of the standard distance from the mean.

9. $\overline{X}$ = 433, SS = 24, s^2 = 4, and s = 2.

11. SS cannot be less than zero because it is computed by adding squared deviations. Squared values are always positive.

12. The total of the deviation scores must be zero, so the mystery person has a deviation of -6. Therefore, the score for this person is X = 14.

14. Range = 8. Semi-interquartile range = $(Q3 - Q1)/2$ = $(5.0 - 2.5)/2$ = 1.25. σ = 2.

16. a. μ = 3, SS = 8, σ^2 = 4, and σ = 2.

b. σ = 5.

c. σ = 0.5.

d. σ = 8.

18. a. College students $\overline{X}$ = 40.6, and businessmen $\overline{X}$ = 40.1. On average, both groups are very accurate.

b. College students s = 9.22, and businessmen s = 2.56. Age estimates for the businessmen are generally close to the correct value. The estimates for the college students are much more scattered.

21. a. For February, $\overline{X}$ = 25.64 and s = 4.63. For April, $\overline{X}$ = 55.40 and s = 17.09.

b. The standard deviations indicate that the daily temperatures are generally close to the mean in February but are widely scattered in April. The mean accurately describes a typical day in February but not in April.

23. a. General population $\overline{X}$ = 54.8 and s = 19.58. Salesmen $\overline{X}$ = 79.13 and s = 7.36.

b. On average, salesmen are more extroverted than the general population.

c. The salesmen are consistently extroverted (small variability), while personality type varies widely in the general population.

Chapter 5: z-Scores: Location of Scores and Standardized Distributions

1. a.

X	z	X	z
108	+0.50	104	+0.25
132	+2.00	92	−0.50
100	0	120	+1.25
124	+1.50	84	−1.00

b.

X	z	X	z
84	−1.00	108	+0.50
124	+1.50	80	−1.25
100	0	104	+0.25
132	+2.00	68	−2.00

2. A z-score specifies an exact location in a distribution. The sign of the z-score indicates whether the position is above (+) or below (−) the mean. The magnitude of the z-score indicates the number of standard deviations from the mean.

5.

X	z	X	z
65	+2.50	53	+0.50
56	+1.00	38	−2.00
32	−3.00	50	0
42	−1.33	47	−0.50
41	−1.50		

7. $\mu = 240$.

9. With $\sigma = 1$, $z = +1.00$, which is better.

11. Your z-score is +1.50, which is better than your friend's z-score of +1.10.

13.

X	z	Standardized Score
41	+1.00	13.00
32	−0.50	8.50
39	+0.67	12.00
44	+1.50	14.50
45	+1.67	15.00
24	−1.83	4.50
37	+0.33	11.00
27	−1.33	6.00

15. For the original population, $\mu = 76.14$ and $\sigma = 8.65$.

X	z	X	z	X	z
71	−0.59	61	−1.75	57	−2.21
72	−0.48	69	−0.83	80	+0.45
75	−0.13	88	+1.37	74	+0.25
79	+0.33	80	+0.45	64	−1.40
71	−0.59	79	+0.33	82	+0.68
78	+0.22	81	+0.56	86	+1.14
83	+0.79	92	+1.83	87	+1.26
84	+0.91	70	−0.71	81	+0.56
77	+0.10	67	−1.06	61	−1.75
76	−0.02	93	+1.95	76	−0.02
86	+1.14	62	−1.63	91	+1.72
80	+0.45	68	−0.94	73	−0.36
66	−1.17	71	−0.59	82	+0.68
78	+0.22	74	−0.25	73	−0.36

17. a For the original population, $\mu = 21.43$ and $\sigma = 5.75$.

b.

X	z	X	z	X	z
23	+0.27	24	+0.45	22	+0.10
22	+0.10	28	+1.14	10	−1.99
15	−1.12	23	+0.27	21	−0.07
16	−0.94	15	−1.12	31	+1.66
24	+0.45	19	−0.42	28	+1.14
11	−1.81	21	−0.07	11	−1.81
27	+0.97	22	+0.10	18	−0.60
26	+0.79	28	+1.14	33	+2.01
19	−0.42	22	+0.10	17	−0.77
15	−1.12	25	+0.62	23	+0.27
21	−0.07	21	−0.07	32	+1.84
23	+0.27	14	−1.29		

c. For the z-scores, $\mu = 0$ and $\sigma = 1.00$.

19. a. $\mu = 53.03$ and $\sigma = 19.83$.

b.

X	z	X	z	X	z	X	z
10	−2.17	27	−1.31	91	+1.91	55	+0.10
9	−2.22	63	+0.50	24	−1.46	26	−1.36
57	+0.20	74	+1.06	81	+1.41	73	+1.01
39	−0.71	60	+0.35	67	+0.70	66	+0.65
47	−0.30	42	−0.56	34	−0.96	90	+1.86
33	−1.01	52	−0.05	34	−0.96	40	−0.66
61	+0.40	56	+0.15	49	−0.20	49	−0.20
58	+0.25	83	+1.51	60	+0.35	51	−0.10
37	−0.81	77	+1.21	64	+0.55	38	−0.76
74	+1.06	71	+0.91	46	−0.35	53	−0.002

c. For the z-scores, $\mu = 0$.

21. Multiply each z-score by 10 and then add 100.

Original Score	Standardized Score	Original Score	Standardized Score
10	78.3	91	119.1
9	77.8	24	85.4
57	102.0	81	114.1
39	92.9	67	107.0
47	97.0	34	90.4
33	89.9	34	90.4
61	104.0	49	98.0
58	102.5	60	103.5
37	91.9	64	105.5
74	110.6	46	96.5
27	86.9	55	101.0
63	105.0	26	86.4
74	110.6	73	110.1
60	103.5	66	106.5
42	94.4	90	118.6
52	99.5	40	93.4
56	101.5	49	98.0
83	115.1	51	99.0
77	112.1	38	92.4
71	109.1	53	99.98

Chapter 6: Probability

1. a. $P = \frac{45}{60} = 0.75$

   b. $P = \frac{25}{60} = 0.42$

   c. $P = \frac{50}{60} = 0.83$

   d. $P = \frac{5}{60} = 0.08$

3. a. 0.3085

   b. 0.0401

   c. 0.0668

   d. 0.4013

5. a. $z = -1.28$

   b. $z = -0.67$

   c. $z = +0.25$

   d. $z = +0.84$

7. a. $z = +0.25, X = 125$.

   b. $z = +1.28, X = 145.6$ or greater.

   c. z between -0.84 and $+0.84, X$ between 103.2 and 136.8.

9. a. $P = 0.6915$

    b. $P = 0.0668$

    c. $P = 0.9772$

    d. $P = 0.8664$

11. Converted to z-scores, the correct order is

    John: $z = +0.75$,   highest
    Tom: $z = +0.50$,   middle
    Mary: $z = +0.25$,   lowest

13. You cannot find the probability. You cannot use the unit normal table because the distribution is not normal.

15. a. $P(A \text{ and } B) = 0.5(0.25) = 0.125$.

    b. $P(\text{not } A \text{ and not } B) = 0.5(0.75) = 0.375$.

    c. $P(A \text{ or } B) = 0.5 + 0.25 - 0.125 = 0.625$.

    d. $P(\text{not } A \text{ and not } B \text{ and not } C) = 0.5(0.75)(0.25) = 0.094$.

    e. The probability that at least one hits is one minus the probability that all will miss. $P = 1 - 0.094 = 0.906$.

17. a. Bill's z-score is $z = +0.92$, and his rank is 82.12%. If he were in the pre-engineering section, his z-score would be $z = +0.25$, and his rank would be 59.87%.

    b. A rank of 40% corresponds to $z = -0.25$ or $X = 70$. In the humanities section a score of $X = 70$ corresponds to $z = +0.58$ and a rank of 71.90%.

    c. Mary's score is $X = 66$. Jane's score is $X = 68$.

19. a. $z = +0.84$ or $X = 116.8$.

    b. $z = +0.40$, so $P = 0.3446$.

21. a. $z = -0.33$, so $P = 0.6293$.

    b. $z = -0.38$, so $P = 0.6480$.

    c. Students with scores between 450 and 470 were admitted last year but would have been rejected by this year's standard. These students account for 0.0855 of the total population last year, or $P = 0.0855/0.6293 = 0.1359$ of the students who were admitted last year.

    d. Students with scores between 450 and 470 were rejected this year but would have been admitted by last year's standard. These students account for 0.0877 of the total population this year, or $P = 0.0877/0.3520 = 0.2491$ of the students who were rejected this year.

Chapter 7: Probability and Samples: The Distribution of Sample Means

3. a. Standard error = $100/\sqrt{4} = 50$

    b. Standard error = $100/\sqrt{25} = 20$

    c. Standard error = $100/\sqrt{100} = 10$

5. a. $z = -0.50$, $P = 0.3085$.

    b. Standard error = 10, $z = -1.00$, $P = 0.1587$.

    c. Standard error = 4, $z = -2.50$, $P = 0.0062$.

7. a. Standard error = 5, $P = 0.8414$.

    b. Standard error = 1.5, $P = 0.5028$.

9. With $n = 4$, $\sigma_{\overline{x}} = 5$, $P(\overline{X} > 95) = 0.8413$.

11. a. Sample 1 standard error = 10, $z = +1.00$.

    Sample 2 standard error = 4, $z = +1.25$.
    Sample 3 standard error = 2, $z = +2.00$.

    b. Sample 3 is the most extreme and therefore the least likely of the three.

13. a. $\mu = 4.5$, $\sigma = 2.87$.

    b. With $n = 8$, $\sigma_{\overline{x}} = 1.01$, $z = 1.73$, and $P(\overline{X} > 6.25) = 0.0418$.

    c. With $n = 12$, $\sigma_{\overline{x}} = 0.83$, $z = -0.40$, and $P(\overline{X} > 4.17) = 0.6554$.

15. To total 600 screws, the mean must be at least 120. With $n = 5$, $\sigma_{\overline{x}} = 2.68$, $z = 1.86$, and $P(\overline{X} > 120) = 0.0314$.

17. a. $z = +0.31, P = 0.2434$.

b. $z = +0.70, P = 0.5160$.

c. $z = +0.99, P = 0.6778$.

19. a. The distribution is normal with $\mu = 85$ and $\sigma_{\bar{x}} = 4.74$.

b. z-Scores corresponding to -1.96 to $+1.96$ and sample means from 75.71 to 94.29.

c. z-Scores corresponding to -2.58 to $+2.58$ and sample means from 72.77 to 97.23.

Chapter 8: Introduction to Hypothesis Testing

1. a. The dependent variable is reaction time, and the independent variable is the position of the indicator light.

b. The position of the indicator light has no effect on reaction time.

c. $H_0: \mu = 200$
$H_1: \mu \neq 200$

where μ refers to the mean reaction time with the light at eye level.

d. The distribution of sample means is normal with $\mu = 200$ and $\sigma_{\bar{x}} = 4$. The critical region corresponds to z-score values greater than $+1.96$ or less than -1.96.

e. $\overline{X} = 195$ corresponds to $z = -1.25$. Fail to reject H_0.

f. With $n = 100$ $\sigma_{\bar{x}} = 2$ and $\overline{X} = 195$ corresponds to $z = -2.50$. Reject H_0. With the larger sample there is less error, so the five-point difference is sufficient to reject the null hypothesis.

3. a. $\overline{X} - \mu$ measures the difference between the sample data and the null hypothesis.

b. A sample mean is not expected to be identical to the population mean. The standard error indicates how much difference between $\overline{X}$ and μ is expected by chance.

5. With inferential reasoning it is easier to demonstrate that a hypothesis is false than to prove it is true. The null hypothesis states that there is no effect, and we try to show that this hypothesis is false.

7. a. $H_0: \mu = 98.6$ (no change during withdrawal)

$H_1: \mu \neq 98.6$ (there is a change)

b. The critical region consists of z-score values greater than $+2.58$ or less than $z = -2.58$.

c. $z = 6.06$.

d. The z-score is in the critical region, so we reject the null hypothesis.

9. a. $H_0: \mu = 100$ (oxygen deprivation has no effect on IQ)
$H_1: \mu \neq 100$ (oxygen deprivation does affect IQ)

b. With $\alpha = .05$ the critical region consists of z-score values greater than $+1.96$ or less than -1.96.

c. $z = 2.40$.

d. Reject the null hypothesis. Oxygen deprivation at birth does have a significant effect on IQ.

e. With $\alpha = .01$ the decision would be to fail to reject the null hypothesis.

11. a. $H_0: \mu = 55$
$H_1: \mu \neq 55$

b. The critical region consists of z-scores greater than $+2.58$ or less than -2.58.

c. $z = 8.25$.

d. Reject the null hypothesis. Scores for depressed patients are significantly different from scores for normal individuals on this test.

13. The null hypothesis states that scientists do not differ from the general public on the literary scale; that is, the mean for scientists is $\mu = 22$. For this sample, $\overline{X} = 23.50$, which corresponds to $z = +1.06$ if H_0 is true. Fail to reject H_0.

15. The null hypothesis states the new recovery program has no effect; that is, the mean with the new program is still

$\mu = 6.3$ days. For this sample mean, $z = 2.10$, which is in the critical region with $\alpha = .05$. Reject the null hypothesis.

17. The null hypothesis states that the mean IQ for children whose mothers had German measles is no different from the general population mean, $\mu = 100$. For this sample mean, $z = -0.81$ if the null hypothesis is true. Fail to reject the null hypothesis.

19. a. If there is no change and the population mean is still $\mu = 8.4$, this sample mean corresponds to $z = -5.65$. This is a very unlikely value, so reject the null hypothesis and conclude that there has been a change in homework time.

b. With $n = 20$ the standard error would be 0.74, and the z-score for this sample would be $z = -1.76$. In this case you would fail to reject the null hypothesis.

Chapter 9: Estimation, Directional Tests, and Power

1. a. Use $\overline{X} = 5.8$ for the point estimate of μ.

b. The amount of change is the difference between 6.3 hours and 5.8 hours. Children are watching TV 0.5 hour less now than in 1970.

c. Estimate μ between 5.544 and 6.056 hours per day.

3. a. Use $\overline{X} = 15.5$ as the point estimate of μ

b. With increased self-awareness the population mean is estimated to be between 13.54 and 17.46.

5. a. The critical region consists of sample means greater than $\overline{X} = 533$. If the training program increases scores by 40 points, then $P(\overline{X} > 533) = 0.6368$.

b. With $\alpha = .05$ the critical region (upper tail) consists of sample means greater than $\overline{X} = 539.2$. If there is a 40-point effect, then $P(\overline{X} > 539.2) = 0.5160$.

7. $H_0 : \mu \geq 55$. $z = -1.50$. This is not in the critical region, so you fail to reject the null hypothesis.

9. a. $H_0 : \mu \leq 24$. $z = +2.50$. Reject H_0.

b. Use $\overline{X} = 26.5$ miles per gallon as the point estimate of μ. Based on this estimate, the additive increases mileage by 2.5 miles per gallon.

11. $H_0 : \mu \leq 80$. $\overline{X} = 87.7$. $z = 2.03$. Reject H_0 and conclude that children from divorced families have higher scores on the depression questionnaire.

13. a. The critical region (lower tail) consists of sample means less than 47.81. If there is a five-point effect, then $P(\overline{X} < 47.81) = 0.9940$.

b. The critical region consists of sample means less than 48.15. If there is a five-point effect, then $P(\overline{X} < 48.15) = 0.9975$.

c. $\beta = 0.0060$ (see part a).

d. $\beta = 0.0025$ (see part b).

15. $H_0 : \mu \geq 16$. $\overline{X} = 15.91$. $z = -2.31$. Reject H_0 and conclude that the machine is averaging significantly below 16 ounces per can.

17. $H_0 : \mu \geq 100$. $z = -1.99$. Reject H_0 and conclude that individuals with a family history of personality disorder score significantly lower.

19. The critical boundary is below 120 by 1.96 standard errors ($z = -1.96$ in the null distribution). To have power of 75%, this same critical boundary must be above 115 by 0.67 standard error ($z = +0.67$) in the alternative distribution. Thus, the total distance between 115 and 120 is equal to 2.63 standard errors (2.63 $= 1.96 + 0.67$). Expressed as an equation, $2.63\sigma_{\overline{x}} = 5$ points. Therefore, $\sigma_{\overline{x}} = 1.90$. To have $\sigma_{\overline{x}} = 1.90$, n must be 27.67 or larger. Therefore, you must have a sample size of $n = 28$ or more.

Chapter 10: Introduction to the *t* Statistic

1. a. $H_0:$ $\mu = 20$
   $H_1:$ $\mu \neq 20$

   The null hypothesis states that watching other animals will have no effect on the number of trials needed to solve the problem.

   b. In the distribution of *t*-scores with $df = 3$, the critical region consists of values greater than 3.182 or less than -3.182.

   c. $t(3) = \frac{5}{5} = 1.00$.

   d. Fail to reject H_0. These data do not provide sufficient evidence to conclude that animals perform significantly differently after viewing others.

3. a. $s = 10$.

   b. Use $\overline{X} = 43$ to estimate μ.

   c. Estimate μ between 39.58 and 46.42.

5. The standard deviation (*s*) in the *t* formula is an estimated value and contributes to the variability.

7. The higher the percentage of confidence, the wider the interval. The larger the sample, the narrower the interval.

9. a. $H_0: \mu = 20$. $\overline{X} = 14.7$, and $s = 10.98$. $t(19) = -2.15$. Reject H_0.

   b. For $\alpha = .01$, we fail to reject H_0.

11. a. $H_0: \mu = 7.80$. $\overline{X} = 6.98$, and $s = 0.61$. $t(7) = -3.73$. Reject H_0.

    b. For a point estimate of μ, use $\overline{X} = 6.98$. The 95% confidence interval extends from 6.46 to 7.50.

13. a. $H_0: \mu = 166$. $\overline{X} = 188.86$, and $s = 20.54$. $t(20) = 5.10$. Reject H_0.

    b. Estimate the population mean weight between 176.11 and 201.61 pounds.

15. $H_0: \mu = 10$. $\overline{X} = 9.16$, and $s = 1.43$. $t(14) = -2.27$. Reject H_0 and conclude that the rats eat significantly less with high humidity.

17. $H_0: \mu = 5.0$. $\overline{X} = 6.3$, and $s = 2.03$. $t(326) = 11.82$. Reject H_0.

19. $H_0: \mu = 73.5$ for large classes. $\overline{X} = 71.2$, $s = 10.98$, $t(80) = -1.89$. Fail to reject H_0.

Chapter 11: Statistical Inference with Two Independent Samples

1. Pooled variance $= 20$, $t(18) = 4.00$. Reject H_0.

3. a. Pooled variance $= 40$, $t(8) = 3.50$, reject H_0 and conclude that the hormone produces a significant effect.

   b. For a point estimate, use $\overline{X}_1 - \overline{X}_2 = 14$. With 80% confidence, estimate the effect of the hormone between 8.412 and 19.588.

5. a. For experiment I, pooled variance $= 10$, and $t(8) = 2.50$. Reject H_0. For experiment II, pooled variance $= 40$, and $t(8) = 1.25$. Fail to reject H_0. For experiment III, pooled variance $= 10$, and $t(8) = 1.00$. Fail to reject H_0.

   b. Experiment II has greater variability, which produces a larger standard error. In this experiment the five-point mean difference is not sufficient to reject H_0.

   c. In experiment III there is only a two-point difference between the sample means. This difference is not sufficient to reject H_0.

7. a. Use the sample mean difference, $43 - 36 = 7$, to estimate the population mean difference.

   b. With 90% confidence, estimate the mean difference between 3.532 and 10.468.

9. Pooled variance = 30, and $t(13) = 3.67$. Reject H_0 and conclude that fatigue has a significant effect.

11. a. Pooled variance = 540, and $t(28) = 3.67$. Reject H_0 and conclude that pollution has a significant effect on life expectancy.

    b. Use the sample mean difference, 33 days, as a point estimate of the population mean difference.

    c. With 95% confidence, estimate the mean difference between 14.568 and 51.432.

12. a.

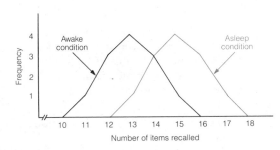

Number of items recalled

b. For the asleep group, $\overline{X} = 15$, and $SS = 14$. For the awake group, $\overline{X} = 13$, and $SS = 14$. $t(22) = 4.35$. Reject H_0.

14. For the regular course, $\overline{X} = 78.73$, and $SS = 1622.93$. For the programmed course, $\overline{X} = 76.33$, and $SS = 1465.33$. $t(28) = 0.63$. Fail to reject H_0.

17. For the first questionnaire, $\overline{X} = 56.8$, and $SS = 590.4$. For the second questionnaire, $\overline{X} = 49$, and $SS = 270$. $t(28) = 3.86$. Reject H_0.

19. a.

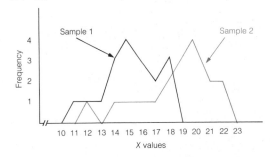

X values

b. The two sets of data appear to come from different populations.

c. For sample 1, $\overline{X} = 15.22$, and $SS = 69.11$. For sample 2, $\overline{X} = 18.5$, and $SS = 130.50$. $t(34) = -4.05$. Reject H_0.

Chapter 12: The Repeated Measures t Statistic

1. $s = 20$, $t(3) = 3.20$, reject H_0 and conclude that the beer has a significant effect on reaction time.

2. The 90% confidence interval extends from 8.47 to 55.53.

5. $s = 12$, $t(15) = 3.10$, reject H_0 and conclude that computerized instruction has a significant effect.

6. The 95% confidence interval extends from 2.907 to 15.693.

8. a. For experiment 1, $\overline{D} = 20$, $s = 5.29$, and $t(9) = 11.98$. Reject H_0.

   b. For experiment 2, $\overline{D} = 20$, $s = 37.68$, and $t(9) = 1.68$. Fail to reject H_0.

   c. For experiment 1 the effect of increased temperature is very consistent across subjects. In experiment 2,

there is no consistent effect which produces high variability and results in a conclusion that there is no significant effect.

11. For these data, $\overline{D} = 1.02$, $s = 0.85$, and $t(13) = 4.48$. Reject H_0 and conclude that the drug has a significant effect.

12. The 90% confidence interval extends from 0.62 to 1.42.

15. For these data, $\overline{D} = 7.33$, $s = 5.87$, and $t(11) = 4.33$. Reject H_0 and conclude that Ritalin significantly improves performance for hyperkinetic children.

16. The 95% confidence interval extends from 3.60 to 11.06.

18. For these data $\overline{D} = 2.63$ $s = 1.85$ and $t(7) = 4.02$. Reject the null hypothesis and

conclude that there is a significant increase in the number of dreams after one night of deprivation.

20. For these data $\overline{D} = 0.25$, $s = 0.75$, and $t(9) = 1.05$. Fail to reject H_0 and conclude that these data do not provide evidence that the additive has any effect.

Chapter 13: Introduction to Analysis of Variance

1.
Source	SS	df	MS
Between treatments	10	2	5.00
Within treatments	16	12	1.33
Total	26	14	

$$F(2, 12) = 3.75$$

3.
Source	SS	df	MS
Between treatments	14	2	7
Within treatments	9	9	1
Total	23	11	

$$F(2, 9) = 7.00$$

5.
Source	SS	df	MS
Between treatments	15	2	7.5
Within treatments	60	12	5
Total	75	14	

$$F(2, 12) = 1.50$$

7.
Source	SS	df	MS
Between treatments	24	2	12
Within treatments	54	27	2
Total	78	29	

$$F(2, 27) = 6.00$$

10. a.
Source	SS	df	MS
Between treatments	45	3	15
Within treatments	32	16	2
Total	77	19	

$$F(3, 16) = 7.50$$

b. Tukey's HSD = 2.56. The combination of the two drugs is significantly different from either drug alone and from the placebo.

12. a.
Source	SS	df	MS
Between treatments	30	2	15
Within treatments	12	12	1
Total	42	14	

$$F(2, 12) = 15.00$$

b. Of the three samples the largest variance is for the right-handed subjects ($s^2 = 1.50$), and the smallest is for the left-handed subjects ($s^2 = 0.50$). F-max = 3.00, which is not significant. The homogeneity assumption is satisfied.

14. a. The means and SS values for these data are

6 hours	12 hours	18 hours
$\overline{X} = 10.2$	$\overline{X} = 13.4$	$\overline{X} = 20.4$
SS = 22.8	SS = 75.2	SS = 45.2

24 hours	30 hours
$\overline{X} = 16.4$	$\overline{X} = 12.0$
SS = 45.2	SS = 60.0

The analysis of variance produces

Source	SS	df	MS
Between treatments	321.84	4	80.46
Within treatments	248.40	20	12.42
Total	570.24	24	

$$F(4, 20) = 6.48$$

b. Deprivation improves learning scores up to a point (around 18 hours) and then performance begins to fall off if deprivation is continued.

c. Tukey's HSD = 6.67. The scores in the 18-hour condition are significantly different from the 6-hour, the 12-hour, and the 30-hour conditions.

15. a. The means and SS values for these data are

Psychology	English
$\overline{X} = 17.17$	$\overline{X} = 19.25$
$SS = 85.67$	$SS = 80.25$

The analysis of variance produces

Source	SS	df	MS
Between treatments	26.04	1	26.04
Within treatments	165.92	22	7.54
Total	191.96	23	

$$F(1, 22) = 3.45$$

b. For the t test, pooled variance = 7.54, and $t(22) = -1.86$.

16. a. The means and SS values for these data are

Alphas	Betas	Gammas
$\overline{X} = 43.71$	$\overline{X} = 47.64$	$\overline{X} = 38.29$
$SS = 964.86$	$SS = 657.21$	$SS = 600.86$

The analysis of variance produces

Source	SS	df	MS
Between treatments	618.14	2	309.07
Within treatments	2222.93	39	57.00
Total	2841.07	41	

$$F(2, 39) = 5.42$$

b. Tukey's HSD = 6.94. The only significant difference is between the Betas and the Gammas. The Alphas are an intermediate group, not significantly different from either extreme.

18. a. The means and SS values for these data are

Attractive	Average	Unattractive
$\overline{X} = 4.50$	$\overline{X} = 5.92$	$\overline{X} = 2.33$
$SS = 23.00$	$SS = 24.92$	$SS = 12.67$

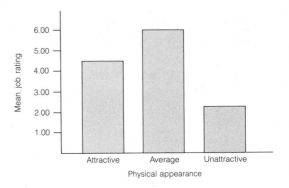

b.

Source	SS	df	MS
Between treatments	78.17	2	39.08
Within treatments	60.58	33	1.84
Total	138.75	35	

$$F(2, 33) = 21.24$$

c. Tukey's HSD = 1.37. All differences between groups are significant.

d. An average appearance produces the highest job rating. Individuals who are too attractive or too unattractive are rated lower, especially those who are very unattractive.

20. a.

Source	SS	df	MS
Between treatments	49.00	2	24.50
Within treatments	125.50	15	8.37
Total	174.50	17	

$$F(2, 15) = 2.93$$

b.

Source	SS	df	MS
Between treatments	48.00	1	48.00
Within treatments	84.00	10	8.40
Total	132.00	11	

$$F(1, 10) = 5.71$$

c. With all three treatments the mean differences between treatments are 1.5 (for 1 versus 2), 4.0 (for 1 versus 3), and 2.5 (for 2 versus 3). The average of these mean differences is 1.67. When only two treatments are considered, the mean difference is 4.0.

Chapter 14: Repeated Measures Analysis of Variance (ANOVA)

1. a. First $\overline{X}$ = 3, second $\overline{X}$ = 5, and third $\overline{X}$ = 1.

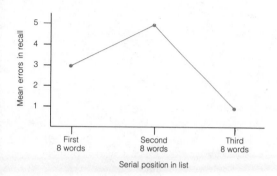

Mean errors in recall vs. Serial position in list
- First 8 words
- Second 8 words
- Third 8 words

b.

Source	SS	df	MS
Between treatments	32	2	16
Within treatments	24	9	
Between subjects	12	3	
Error	12	6	2
Total	56	11	

$F(2, 6) = 8.00$

3.

Source	SS	df	MS
Between treatments	200	4	50
Within treatments	500	45	
Between subjects	140	9	
Error	360	36	10
Total	700	49	

$F(4, 36) = 5.00$

6.

Source	SS	df	MS
Between treatments	18	3	6.00
Within treatments	12	8	
Between subjects	8	2	
Error	4	6	0.67
Total	30	11	

$F(3, 6) = 9.00$

7. a. The means are as follows: same $\overline{X}$ = 188.25, different $\overline{X}$ = 224.00, consonants $\overline{X}$ = 192.38.

b.

Source	SS	df	MS
Bet. treat.	6120.58	2	3060.29
Within treat.	2493.38	21	
Bet. subj.	2277.30	7	
Error	216.08	14	15.43
Total	8613.96	23	

$F(2, 14) = 198.33$

c. When the color word is different from the color ink, reaction time is slowed substantially. When the color ink and the color word are in agreement, reaction speed is increased.

9. The means for the five days are 85.29, 77.57, 73.14, 57.29, and 41.57.

Source	SS	df	MS
Bet. treat.	8573.83	4	2143.45
Within treat.	24981.14	30	
Bet. subj.	16612.97	6	
Error	8368.17	24	348.67
Total	33554.97	34	

$F(4, 24) = 6.15$

11. a. The means for the five test tones are 63.83, 137.33, 245.50, 147.83, and 65.50.

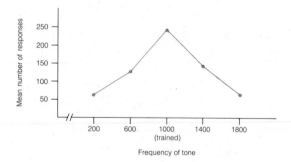

Mean number of responses vs. Frequency of tone
200, 600, 1000 (trained), 1400, 1800

b.

Source	SS	df	MS
Bet. treat.	133382.0	4	33345.5
Within treat.	65528.0	25	
Bet. subj.	15495.6	5	
Error	50032.4	20	2501.62
Total	198910.0	29	

$F(4, 20) = 13.33$

c. The pigeons respond most to the tone on which they were trained. The response level lowers as the stimulus becomes farther from the trained value.

13.

Source	SS	df	MS
Bet. treat.	111892.67	2	55946.33
Within treat.	155438.00	18	
Bet. subj.	68903.33	6	
Error	86534.67	12	7211.22
Total	267330.67	20	

$F(2, 12) = 7.76$

15. a. For an independent measures design the ANOVA produces

Source	SS	df	MS
Between treatments	40	2	20.00
Within treatments	74	12	6.17
Total	114	14	

$F(2, 12) = 3.24$

b. For a repeated measures design the ANOVA produces

Source	SS	df	MS
Between treatments	40	2	20.0
Within treatments	74	12	
Between subjects	54	4	
Error	20	8	2.5
Total	114	14	

$F(2, 8) = 8.00$

c. The independent measures design includes all the individual differ-

ences in the error term (MS_{within}). As a result the F-ratio, $F(2, 12) = 3.24$, is not significant. With a repeated measures design, the individual differences are removed, and the result is a significant F-ratio, $F(2, 8) = 8.00, p < .05$.

17. a. The means for the four conditions are 9.25, 8.125, 5.875, and 2.875.

Source	SS	df	MS
Bet. treat.	189.84	3	63.28
Within treat.	28.13	28	
Bet. subj.	8.72	7	
Error	19.41	21	0.92
Total	217.97	31	

$F(3, 21) = 68.48$

b. The results from problem 16 indicate that there was no change in the subjects' performance during the 48 hours they were awake. However, the results of problem 17 indicate that the subjects felt that their performance grew worse as they become more sleepy.

19.

Source	SS	df	MS
Bet. treat.	270	3	90
Within treat.	410	28	
Bet. subj.	200	7	
Error	210	21	10
Total	680	31	

$F(3, 21) = 9.00$

Chapter 15: Two-Factor Analysis of Variance (Independent Measures)

1.

Source	SS	df	MS	
Between treatments	50	3		
A	0	1	0	$F(1, 36) = 0$
B	40	1	40	$F(1, 36) = 5.00$
A × B	10	1	10	$F(1, 36) = 1.25$
Within treatments	288	36	8	
Total	338	39		

3. a.

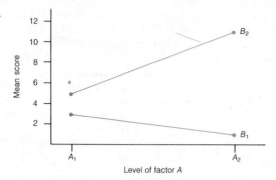

Level of factor A

b. Overall the scores in A_1 are slightly
lower than the scores in A_2. There
may be a small main effect for factor
A. There appears to be a large main
effect for factor B with scores in B_2
much larger than scores in B_1. The
lines are not parallel, so there
appears to be an interaction.

c.

Source	SS	df	MS	
Between treatments	280	3		
A	20	1	20	$F(1, 16) = 1.00$
B	180	1	180	$F(1, 16) = 9.00$
A × B	80	1	80	$F(1, 16) = 4.00$
Within treatments	320	16	20	
Total	600	19		

5.

Source	SS	df	MS	
Between treatments	30	3		
A (recall cues)	10	1	10	$F(1, 36) = 5.00$
B (learning cues)	10	1	10	$F(1, 36) = 5.00$
A × B	10	1	10	$F(1, 36) = 5.00$
Within treatments	72	36	2	
Total	102	39		

The significant interaction indicates that
the effectiveness of cues given at recall
(factor A) depends on whether or not the
cues were also given during learning
(factor B). Performance is best when cues
are given both at learning and at recall.
If cues are given only once, they are no
more effective than giving no cues at all.

7. a.

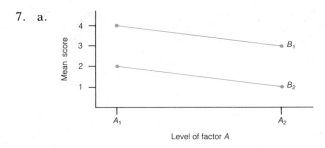

b. The lines are parallel, so there does not appear to be any interaction. There is a small difference between the lines for A_1 and A_2, so there may be a small main effect for factor A. The difference between B_1 and B_2 is larger, so there probably is a main effect for factor B.

c.

Source	SS	df	MS	
Between treatments	50	3		
A	10	1	10	$F(1, 36) = 2.00$
B	40	1	40	$F(1, 36) = 8.00$
A × B	0	1	0	$F(1, 36) = 0$
Within treatments	180	36	5	
Total	230	39		

9. a. The means for normal subjects are baseline $\overline{X} = 23.08$ and stress $\overline{X} = 18.25$. The means for antisocial subjectt are baseline $\overline{X} = 24.92$ and stress $\overline{X} = 24.17$.

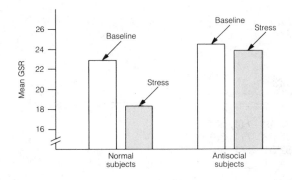

b.

Source	SS	df	MS	
Between treatments	323.73	3		
A (personality)	180.19	1	180.19	$F(1, 44) = 18.99$
B (arousal)	93.52	1	93.52	$F(1, 44) = 9.85$
A × B	50.02	1	50.02	$F(1, 44) = 5.27$
Within treatments	417.75	44	9.49	
Total	741.48	47		

c. The significant interaction indicates that stress affects normal and antisocial people differently. Stress appears to have an effect on normal people but no effect on antisocial individuals.

11. a.

Source	SS	df	MS	
Between treatments	947.4	3		
A (anxiety)	624.1	1	624.1	$F(1, 36) = 7.47$
B (counseling)	220.9	1	220.9	$F(1, 36) = 2.64$
A × B	102.4	1	102.4	$F(1, 36) = 1.23$
Within treatments	3006.6	36	83.52	
Total	3954.0	39		

13. a.

Source	SS	df	MS	
Between treatments	609.68	3		
A (class type)	112.23	1	112.23	$F(1, 36) = 1.94$
B (personality)	442.23	1	442.23	$F(1, 36) = 7.65$
A × B	55.22	1	55.22	$F(1, 36) = 0.96$
Within treatments	2081.30	36	57.81	
Total	2690.98	39		

b. Because the interaction is not significant, the psychologist must conclude that changing to a self-paced program would have the same effect on internals as on externals. Furthermore, it appears that this change would have no significant effect. The only significant result is that the internals have higher grades than externals.

15.

Source	SS	df	MS	
Between treatments	520.45	3		
A (self-esteem)	400.42	1	400.42	$F(1, 56) = 99.87$
B (audience)	58.02	1	58.02	$F(1, 56) = 14.47$
A × B	62.01	1	62.01	$F(1, 56) = 15.46$
Within treatments	224.53	56	4.01	
Total	744.98	59		

The significant interaction indicates that for high-self-esteem subjects the effect of the audience was different from that for low-self-esteem subjects. Specifically, the audience produced an increase in errors for the low-self-esteem subjects and had no effect on high-self-esteem subjects.

17. a.

Source	SS	df	MS	
Between treatments	200.48	3		
A (asleep/awake)	172.23	1	172.23	$F(1, 36) = 73.92$
B (delay time)	7.23	1	7.23	$F(1, 36) = 3.10$
A × B	21.02	1	21.02	$F(1, 36) = 9.02$
Within treatments	83.90	36	2.33	
Total	284.38	39		

The significant interaction indicates that the amount you forget over time (2 hours versus 8 hours) depends on whether you are asleep or awake. For the asleep group, there was no evidence for forgetting over time, and the scores were generally high. For the awake group, there was a substantial drop between 2 hours and 8 hours, and the scores were generally low.

19. a. The independent variables are violent/nonviolent and human/cartoon. The dependent variable is the number of aggressive responses.

b. The primary prediction is for an interaction. The main effects would depend on the interaction and are not particularly important.

c. The psychologist would expect a main effect for violence/nonviolence and no main effect for human/cartoon. Also, no interaction is predicted.

Chapter 16: Correlation

1. Set 1, $SP = 6$; set 2, $SP = -16$; set 3, $SP = -4$.

2. a.

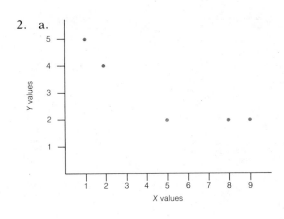

b. Estimate a strong negative correlation, probably $r = -0.8$ or -0.9.

c. $SS_x = 50$, $SS_y = 8$, $SP = -18$, and $r = -0.90$.

5. a.

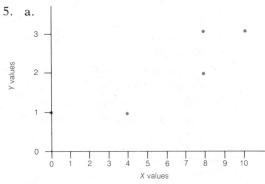

b. It appears to be a strong positive correlation, about $r = +0.8$ or $+0.9$.

c. $SS_x = 64$, $SS_y = 4$, $SP = 14$, and $r = +0.875$.

d. $SS_x = 64$, $SS_y = 14$, $SP = -16$, and $r = -0.535$.

7. First rank the number of art courses and then compute the Spearman correlation. $r_s = -0.986$.

9. With a sample of $n = 2$, the two data points always will fit perfectly on a straight line. Therefore, the correlation will be $+1.00$ or -1.00. With a sample of only $n = 2$, the correlation is meaningless.

11. a. $SS_x = 63.5$, $SS_y = 50.875$, $SP = -51.25$, and $r = -0.902$.

b. The correlation is still $r = -0.902$.

c. Adding a constant does not change SS or SP or the correlation.

d. The correlation is still $r = -0.902$.

e. Multiplying each score by 3 will cause all the SS and SP values to be multiplied by 9. However, this multiplication cancels out in the correlation formula, so the correlation is unchanged.

13. a. The Spearman correlation is $r_s = -0.793$.

b. The relatively strong negative correlation indicates that students who score high on the test tend to be ranked low (first, second, etc.) by the teacher. It appears that the test scores are in general agreement with the teacher's ranking.

15. a. $SS_x = 205,220.00$, $SS_y = 7.73$, $SP = 1078.86$, and $r = +0.857$.

b. Yes, there is a strong positive relation between SAT scores and grade point average. The coefficient of determination is $r^2 = 0.734$.

17. a. $r = -0.854$.

b. For the X-scores, $\mu = 8.33$ and $\sigma = 5.65$. For the Y-scores, $\mu = 15.00$ and $\sigma = 3.56$. The z-scores for each X and Y are

z_x	z_y
-0.24	0.84
0.65	-1.12
-1.30	1.40
1.71	-1.40
-0.94	0
0.12	0.28

18. $SS_x = 4194$, $SS_y = 1282.1$, $SP = 1829.6$, and $r = +0.789$.

20. $SS_x = 11,395.35$, $SS_y = 10,740.97$, $SP = -5215.61$, and $r = -0.471$.

Chapter 17: Regression

2. a. For company A, $Y = 6X + 10$. For company B, $Y = 5X + 20$.

b. For company A, $Y = \$70$, and for company B, $Y = \$70$.

c. Company A would charge $130, and company B would charge only $120.

4. a. $\hat{Y} = 3X - 3$.

b. For each X, the predicted Y value would be

X	$\hat{Y}$
1	0
4	9
3	6
2	3
5	12
3	6

c. $SS_{error} = 18$.

6. $H_0 : \rho = 0$, $F(1, 23) = 7.67$. Reject H_0 and conclude that these data provide evidence for a nonzero correlation in the population.

8. a. $\hat{Y} = 1.33X + 32.83$.

    b. For $X = 10$, $\hat{Y} = 46.13$ seconds.

    c. The standard error of estimate is 0.73 seconds.

9. $H_0 : \rho = 0$, $F(1, 16) = 0.67$. Fail to reject H_0. These data do not provide evidence for a significant correlation.

11. a. $\hat{Y} = -6.64X + 518.51$.

    b. For $X = 34$, $\hat{Y} = 292.75$.

    c. The standard error of estimate is 18.26.

13. a. $H_0 : \rho = 0$, $F(1, 20) = 2.13$. Fail to reject H_0. There is no evidence for a significant correlation.

b. The standard error of estimate is 15.36.

15. $\hat{Y} = 36.8X + 395$.

17. $H_0 : \rho = 0$, $r = +0.626$, $F(1, 12) = 7.74$. Reject H_0 and conclude that there is a significant relationship.

19. a. $H_0 : \rho = 0$, $r = 0.878$, $F(1, 8) = 26.93$. Reject H_0 and conclude that there is a significant relation between the time on TV news and the public opinion rating.

    b. $\hat{Y} = 0.80X + 22.28$.

    c. Correlation does not explain cause and effect. It would be just as reasonable to say that the time an item is on TV is determined by public opinion.

Chapter 18: The Binomial Distribution

1. Coin tosses are independent events. If the coin is balanced, $P(\text{heads}) = 0.50$ no matter what occurred on earlier tosses.

3. $H_0 : p = 0.8$ and $q = 0.2$; $z = -2.00$. Reject H_0 and conclude that there has been a significant change in opinion.

5. $H_0 : p = q = 0.5$ (no preference). By using the binomial formula, the probability of obtaining five or more red choices out of six is $P = 0.109$. Fail to reject H_0 because this probability is greater than .05. The data are not sufficient to decide that there is a significant preference.

7. Discard the 12 subjects who showed no change. The sign test with $n = 28$ gives $z = 2.26$. Reject H_0 and conclude that the teacher's sex has a significant influence.

9. $H_0 : p = q = 0.5$ (no preference). $z = 1.75$. Fail to reject H_0 and conclude that there is no significant preference.

11. a. $\mu = pn = 18$.

    b. With $p = q = 0.50$, $P(X > 24) = P(z > 2.00) = 0.0228$.

    c. A score of $X = 24$ is very unlikely to occur if the student is simply guessing. This should be a passing grade.

13. $H_0 : p = 0.04$ and $q = 0.96$. For $X = 40$, $z = 11.55$. Reject H_0 and conclude that executives are significantly more likely to get ulcers.

15. a. To have $z > 1.96$, you must have $X > 14.39$ out of 20.

    b. To have $z > 1.96$, you must have $X > 26.20$ out of 40.

    c. To have $z > 1.96$, you must have $X > 59.80$ out of 100.

17. a. Discarding 11 subjects, $n = 39$, $z = 3.04$. Reject H_0 and conclude that the biofeedback training works.

    b. Discarding only 1 subject and dividing the others equally, $n = 49$, $z = 2.71$. Reject H_0.

19. $H_0 : p = q = 0.50$ (no discrimination). For $X = 15$, $z = 1.00$. Fail to reject H_0. These data provide no evidence of discrimination based on taste.

21. $H_0 : p = 0.25$ and $q = 0.75$ (chance performance). $z = 3.43$. Reject H_0. The picture was hung correctly significantly more than would be expected by chance.

Chapter 19: The Chi Square Statistic: Tests for Goodness of Fit and Independence

1. H_0 : The four factors are equally important, $p = 0.25$ for each factor. The expected frequency is 25 for all four categories. Chi square $= 20$. Reject H_0 and conclude that the four factors are not equally important.

3. a. H_0 : The population proportions have not changed and are still 30% science, 50% social science or humanities, and 20% professional. The expected frequencies for these three categories are 30, 50, and 20, respectively. Chi square $= 4.08$. Fail to reject H_0 and conclude that there has been no significant change in freshman majors.

   b. With $n = 200$, chi square $= 8.16$. Reject H_0.

   c. A larger sample should be more representative of the population. If the sample continues to be different from the hypothesis as n increases, the difference eventually will be significant.

5. The null hypothesis states that the distribution of votes is independent of political party. The expected frequencies for Democrats are 25.2 yes and 19.8 no. For Republicans, the expected frequencies are 30.8 yes and 24.2 no. Using the Yates correction, chi square $= 5.32$. Reject H_0 and conclude that there is a significant relation between vote and party affiliation.

7. The null hypothesis states that there is no relation between extroversion and cigarette smoking. The expected frequencies for extroverts are 60 none, 12 less than a pack, and 18 more than a pack. For introverts the expected frequencies are 40 none, 8 less than a pack, and 12 more than a pack. Chi square $= 18.06$.

Reject H_0 and conclude that there is a significant relation between smoking behavior and personality.

9. The null hypothesis states that there is no relation between attitude and type of position. The expected frequencies for those who approve are 245.68 teachers, 32.21 administrators, and 34.10 counselors. For those against, the expected frequencies are 143.32 teachers, 18.79 administrators, and 19.90 counselors. Chi square $= 32.16$. Reject H_0 and conclude that attitude depends on position.

11. The null hypothesis states that career plans are independent of a student's year in college. The expected frequencies are

	Work	Grad School	Undecided
Freshman	40.34	26.11	23.55
Sophomore	41.23	26.69	24.07
Junior	46.61	30.18	27.21
Senior	44.82	29.02	26.17

For these data, chi square $= 60.19$. Reject H_0; there is a significant relation between career plans and college class.

13. The null hypothesis states that there is no preference among the three magazines ($P = \frac{1}{3}$ for each). Chi square $= 4.39$. Fail to reject H_0 and conclude that there is no significant preference.

15. The null hypothesis states that there is no relation between handedness and eye preference. The expected frequencies for left-handed subjects are 6.99 left eye and 25.01 right eye. For right-handed subjects the expected frequencies are 45.01 for left eye and 160.99 for right eye. Using the Yates correction, chi square $= 19.13$. There is a significant relation between hand and eye preference.

17. The null hypothesis states that opinions have not changed since 1970, so the distribution should still be 15% for, 79% against, and 6% no opinion. Chi square = 2.30. Fail to reject H_0. These data do not provide evidence for a change in opinion.

19. The null hypothesis states that the population distribution of scores is normal and has the proportions specified by the unit normal table The expected frequencies are:

z less than -1.50	z between -1.50 and -0.50
10.02	36.26

z between -0.50 and $+0.50$	z between $+0.50$ and $+1.50$
57.45	36.26

z greater than $+1.50$
10.02

For these data chi square equals 6.18. With $df = 4$ this value is not in the critical region. Fail to reject the null hypothesis.

Chapter 20: Nonparametric Tests for Ordinal Data: Mann-Whitney and Wilcoxon Tests

1. a.
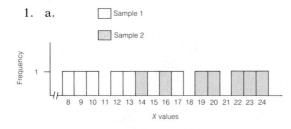

   b. The two samples appear to come from different populations.

   c. For sample 1, $\Sigma R = 31$, and for sample 2, $\Sigma R = 74$. $U = 3$. Reject H_0 and conclude that the two treatments are different.

3. The null hypothesis states that there is no difference between the two species. For species A, $\Sigma R = 73.5$, and for species B, $\Sigma R = 136.5$. $U = 18.5$. Reject H_0 and conclude that there is a significant difference in eating behavior.

5. The null hypothesis states that there is no difference in the time required to unscramble pronounceable versus unpronounceable anagrams. For increases, $\Sigma R = 1$, and for decreases, $\Sigma R = 35$. Wilcoxon $T = 1$. Reject H_0.

7. For the paint company, $\Sigma R = 28$, and for the competitor, $\Sigma R = 50$. Mann-Whitney $U = 7$. Fail to reject H_0. These data do not provide evidence for a significant difference between the two paints.

9. The null hypothesis states that the drug has no effect. For the increases, $\Sigma R = 39$, and for the decreases, $\Sigma R = 6$. Wilcoxon $T = 6$. Fail to reject H_0. These data do not provide sufficient evidence to conclude that the drug works.

11. a. For sample A, $\overline{X} = 2.43$ and $s^2 = 2.95$. For sample B, $\overline{X} = 14.86$ and $s^2 = 56.81$.

    b. The null hypothesis states that there is no difference between the two treatments. For sample A, $\Sigma R = 28$, and for sample B, $\Sigma R = 77$. $U = 0$. Reject H_0.

13. The null hypothesis states that the drug has no effect on maze learning. For the increases, $\Sigma R = 73$, and for the decreases, $\Sigma R = 5$. Wilcoxon $T = 5$. Reject H_0 and conclude that the drug does affect maze-learning performance.

15. The null hypothesis says that there is no difference between the two computer

systems. For system A, $\Sigma R = 755.5$, and for system B, $\Sigma R = 1074.5$. $U = 290.5$, and $z = -3.34$. Reject H_0.

17. The null hypothesis states that speaking will have no effect on balancing. For the increases, $\Sigma R = 4$, and for the decreases, $\Sigma R = 51$. Wilcoxon $T = 4$. Reject H_0.

19. The null hypothesis states that need for achievement has no effect on an individual's persistence. For the high nAch group, $\Sigma R = 163.5$, and for the low nAch group, $\Sigma R = 46.5$. $U = 10.5$. Reject H_0.

Statistics Organizer

The following pages summarize the statistical procedures presented in this book. For each procedure we have provided a brief description explaining when and why it is used, and we have presented the necessary formulas for calculation. In addition, there is a numerical example demonstrating the application of each statistical technique.

You will notice that the items in this section do not appear in the same order in which they were presented in the text. In this section we have grouped together statistical techniques that are used in similar situations. The five groups are the following:

   I. Descriptive statistics
  II. Single-sample techniques
 III. Independent measures techniques
 IV. Repeated measures techniques
  V. Techniques for evaluating relations between variables

I. Descriptive Statistics

A. Measures of Central Tendency. The goal of central tendency is to identify the single value that best represents an entire distribution of scores.

1. The Mean

For a population,

$$\mu = \frac{\Sigma X}{N}$$

For a sample,

$$\overline{X} = \frac{\Sigma X}{n}$$

X
14
12
10
19
17
72 = ΣX

$n = 5$

$$\overline{X} = \frac{\Sigma X}{n} = \frac{72}{5} = 14.4$$

2. The Median

Exactly 50% of the scores in a distribution have values less than or equal to the median. The median is the 50th percentile.

The median is found by using one of three procedures:

a. With an odd number of scores, list the scores in rank order, and the median is the middle value.

X
1
8
10
16
23

The median is $X = 10$.

b. With an even number of scores, list the values in rank order, and the median is the average of the middle two scores.

X
3
7
12
16
21
34

The median is $\dfrac{12 + 16}{2} = 14$

c. With several tied scores in the middle of the distribution, the median is found by interpolation.

X
1
2
3
3
3
3
4
4
5
6

The median is located within the interval 2.5 to 3.5. By using interpolation, the median is 3.25.

3. The Mode

The mode is the score with the greatest frequency.

X	f	
5	1	
4	3	
3	4	
2	6	The mode is $X = 2$.
1	3	

B. Measures of Variability. The goal of variability is to measure the degree to which a distribution of scores is spread out or clustered together.

---

1. The Range

Range = high − low + 1

A set of scores with a high of $X = 68$ and a low of $X = 36$ has a range of $68 - 36 + 1 = 33$ points.

---

2. SS, Variance and Standard Deviation

SS is the sum of squared deviations, variance is the average squared deviation, and standard deviation is the square root of the variance. Standard deviation provides a measure of the typical or standard distance from the mean.

For a population of scores,

$SS = \Sigma X^2 - \dfrac{(\Sigma X)^2}{N}$ (computational formula)

$SS = \Sigma(X - \mu)^2$ (definitional formula)

X	$X - \mu$	$(X - \mu)^2$
1	−5	25
8	2	4
10	4	16
4	−2	4
5	−1	1
8	2	4
		54 $= \Sigma(X - \mu)^2 = SS$

Variance $= \sigma^2 = \dfrac{SS}{N}$ $\sigma^2 = \dfrac{SS}{N} = \dfrac{54}{6} = 9$

Standard deviation $= \sigma = \sqrt{\dfrac{SS}{N}}$ $\sigma = \sqrt{\dfrac{SS}{N}} = \sqrt{\dfrac{54}{6}} = \sqrt{9} = 3$

STATISTICS ORGANIZER

For a sample of scores,

$$SS = \Sigma X^2 - \frac{(\Sigma X)^2}{n} \quad \text{(computational formula)}$$

$$SS = \Sigma(X - \overline{X})^2 \quad \text{(definitional formula)}$$

$$\text{Variance} = s^2 = \frac{SS}{n-1}$$

$$\text{Standard deviation} = s = \sqrt{\frac{SS}{n-1}}$$

X	X^2
8	64
4	16
3	9
4	16
7	49
4	16

$n = 6$

$\Sigma X = 30$

$\Sigma X^2 = 170$

$$SS = \Sigma X^2 - \frac{(\Sigma X)^2}{n} = 170 - \frac{30^2}{6} = 20$$

$$s^2 = \frac{SS}{n-1} = \frac{20}{5} = 4$$

$$s = \sqrt{\frac{SS}{n-1}} = \sqrt{\frac{20}{5}} = \sqrt{4} = 2$$

II. Using Data from a Single Sample to Draw Inferences About a Single Population

1. The z-Score Test

The z-score test uses sample data to test a hypothesis about the population mean. The null hypothesis states a specific value for the unknown population mean. The test statistic is a z-score.

$$z = \frac{\overline{X} - \mu}{\sigma_{\overline{x}}}$$

$$\sigma_{\overline{x}} = \frac{\sigma}{\sqrt{n}}$$

Note: The z-score test is used when the population standard deviation is known.

The original population forms a normal distribution with $\mu = 40$ and $\sigma = 6$. The question is whether or not a treatment has any effect on the population mean. A random sample of $n = 9$ is selected and given the treatment. The sample mean is $\overline{X} = 46$.

H_0: $\mu = 40$ (no change after treatment)

H_1: $\mu \neq 40$ (the mean has changed)

For these data, $\sigma_{\overline{x}} = \frac{6}{\sqrt{9}} = 2$

If H_0 is true,

$$z = \frac{\overline{X} - \mu}{\sigma_{\overline{x}}} = \frac{46 - 40}{2} = 3.00$$

Because this is a very unlikely value for a z-score ($p < .01$), the null hypothesis is rejected.

2. The Single-Sample *t* Test

The single-sample *t* test uses sample data to test a hypothesis about the population mean. The null hypothesis states a specific value for the unknown population mean. The test statistic is a *t* score with $df = n - 1$.

$$t = \frac{\overline{X} - \mu}{s_{\overline{x}}}$$

$$s_{\overline{x}} = \frac{s}{\sqrt{n}}$$

Note: The *t* test is used when the population standard deviation is unknown.

The original population forms a normal distribution with $\mu = 30$. The question is whether or not a treatment has any effect on the population mean. A random sample of $n = 9$ is selected and given the treatment. The sample mean is $\overline{X} = 28.5$ with $SS = 72$.

H_0: $\mu = 30$ (no change after treatment)
H_1: $\mu \neq 30$ (the mean has changed)

For these data, $s = \sqrt{\dfrac{SS}{n-1}} = \sqrt{\dfrac{72}{8}} = 3$

$s_{\overline{x}} = \dfrac{s}{\sqrt{n}} = \dfrac{3}{\sqrt{9}} = 1$

If H_0 is true,

$t = \dfrac{\overline{X} - \mu}{s_{\overline{x}}} = \dfrac{28.5 - 30}{1} = -1.50$

With $df = 8$, this t value is not in the critical region ($p > .05$), so we fail to reject the null hypothesis.

---

3. The Chi Square Test for Goodness of Fit

The chi square goodness-of-fit test uses frequency data to test a hypothesis about a population distribution. The null hypothesis specifies the proportion of the population for each category on the scale of measurement. The test statistic is χ^2 with degrees of freedom equal to the number of categories minus 1.

$$\chi^2 = \Sigma \dfrac{(f_o - f_e)^2}{f_e}$$

f_e is the expected frequency for each category if H_0 is true.
f_o is the observed frequency (data) for each category.

A researcher is testing whether or not there is any preference among four brands of cola (brands A, B, C, and D). A sample of $n = 80$ people is obtained, and each person is asked for his/her preference. The sample data (observed frequencies) are

	Brand			
	A	B	C	D
f_o	15	18	27	20

H_0: There are no preferences in the general population. One-fourth of the population prefers each brand.
H_1: There are preferences. The four brands are not equal.

If H_0 is true, the expected frequencies will be

	Brand			
	A	B	C	D
f_e	20	20	20	20

For these data the chi square statistic is

$$\chi^2 = \dfrac{(15 - 20)^2}{20} + \dfrac{(18 - 20)^2}{20} + \dfrac{(27 - 20)^2}{20} + \dfrac{(20 - 20)^2}{20}$$
$$= 3.90$$

With $df = 3$, this χ^2 value is not in the critical region ($p > .05$), so we fail to reject the null hypothesis.

4. The Binomial Test

When the individuals in a population can be classified into exactly two categories, the binomial test uses sample data to test a hypothesis about the proportion of the population in each category. The null hypothesis specifies the proportion of the population in each of the two categories. The two categories are identified as A and B, and the proportion in each category is identified as p for category A or q for category B. With relatively large samples, the binomial distribution is approximately normal, and the test statistic is a z-score:

$$z = \frac{X - \mu}{\sigma} = \frac{X - pn}{\sqrt{npq}}$$

where X is the number of individuals from the sample who are in category A.

In a sample of $n = 100$ people, 26 are classified as A and 74 are classified as B. Are these data consistent with the hypothesis that 20% (0.20) of the population is classified as A and 80% (0.80) is classified as B?

H_0: The population proportions are $p = 0.20$ and $q = 0.80$.

H_1: The population proportions are different from the values specified in H_0.

For these data, $\mu = pn = 0.20(100) = 20$ and $\sigma = \sqrt{npq} = \sqrt{100(0.2)(0.8)} = \sqrt{16} = 4$.

$$z = \frac{26 - 20}{4} = 1.50$$

Because the obtained z-score is not in the critical region ($p > .05$), we fail to reject the null hypothesis.

III. Using Data from Two or More Separate Samples to Draw Inferences About Two or More Populations

1. The Independent Measures *t* Test

The independent measures t test uses data from two separate samples to test a hypothesis about the difference between two population means. The null hypothesis states that there is no difference between the two population means. The test statistic is a t score with $df = n_1 + n_2 - 2$.

$$t = \frac{(\overline{X}_1 - \overline{X}_2) - (\mu_1 - \mu_2)}{s_{\overline{x} - \overline{x}}}$$

$$s_{\overline{x} - \overline{x}} = \sqrt{\frac{s_p^2}{n_1} + \frac{s_p^2}{n_2}}$$

$$s_p^2 = \frac{SS_1 + SS_2}{df_1 + df_2}$$

A researcher would like to determine whether or not there is a mean difference between two populations. A random sample of $n = 10$ is obtained from each population. For the first sample, $\overline{X}_1 = 32$ and $SS_1 = 190$. For the second sample, $\overline{X}_2 = 29$ and $SS_2 = 170$.

H_0: $\mu_1 - \mu_2 = 0$ (no mean difference)
H_1: $\mu_1 - \mu_2 \neq 0$

For these data,

$$s_p^2 = \frac{SS_1 + SS_2}{df_1 + df_2} + \frac{360}{18} = 20$$

$$s_{\overline{x} - \overline{x}} = \sqrt{\frac{20}{10} + \frac{20}{10}} = \sqrt{4} = 2$$

$$t = \frac{(32 - 29) - 0}{2} = 1.50$$

$$df = 18$$

Because this t score is not in the critical region ($p > .05$), the decision is to fail to reject H_0.

2. The Mann-Whitney *U* Test

The Mann-Whitney *U* test uses data from two separate samples to test a hypothesis about the difference between two populations. The null hypothesis states that there is no difference between the two populations. The *U* statistic is computed by combining both samples and rank-ordering the entire group of scores. The sum of the ranks is computed for each of the two samples (*A* and *B*), and a *U* value is found for each sample.

$$U_A = n_A n_B + \frac{n_A(n_A + 1)}{2} - \Sigma R_A$$

$$U_B = n_A n_B + \frac{n_B(n_B + 1)}{2} - \Sigma R_B$$

The Mann-Whitney *U* is the smaller of these two *U* values.
Note: The Mann-Whitney test requires that the scores be measured only on an ordinal scale.

A researcher would like to determine whether there is any difference between two treatments. A random sample of $n = 10$ is obtained. Half are assigned to treatment *A*, and half are assigned to treatment *B*. The scores for sample *A* are 1, 3, 4, 8, 12. The scores for sample *B* are 9, 15, 18, 24, 26.

H_0: There is no difference between the two treatments (the two samples come from the same population).
H_1: The two treatments are different.

When the two samples are combined and the scores are ranked, $\Sigma R_A = 16$, and $\Sigma R_B = 39$.

$U_A = 25 + 15 - 16 = 24$
$U_B = 25 + 15 - 39 = 1$

The Mann-Whitney *U* is 1. Because it is very unlikely that a value this small would be obtained by chance ($p < .05$), we reject the null hypothesis.

---

3. Analysis of Variance (Single-Factor, Independent Measures)

The single-factor independent measures ANOVA uses data from two or more separate samples to test a hypothesis about two or more population means. The null hypothesis states that there are no differences among the population means. Special notation for ANOVA includes

k = number of treatments
n = number of scores per sample
T = total for each sample
N = overall number of scores
G = grand total of all scores

The test statistic is an *F*-ratio with $df = k - 1, N - k$.

$$F = \frac{MS_{between}}{MS_{within}}$$

Each $MS = \dfrac{SS}{df}$

$$SS_{between} = \Sigma \frac{T^2}{n} - \frac{G^2}{N}$$

$df_{between} = k - 1$
$SS_{within} = \Sigma SS_{each\ treatment}$
$df_{within} = N - k$

The following data summarize the results of an experiment using three samples to compare three treatment conditions:

Sample 1	Sample 2	Sample 3
$n = 5$	$n = 5$	$n = 5$
$\overline{X} = 1$	$\overline{X} = 5$	$\overline{X} = 6$
$T = 5$	$T = 25$	$T = 30$
$SS = 26$	$SS = 18$	$SS = 16$

H_0: $\mu_1 = \mu_2 = \mu_3$ (no difference)
H_1: At least one treatment mean is different from the others.

$$SS_{between} = \frac{5^2}{5} + \frac{25^2}{5} + \frac{30^2}{5} - \frac{60^2}{15}$$
$$= 310 - 240$$
$$= 70$$

$df_{between} = 3 - 1 = 2$

$MS_{between} = \frac{70}{2} = 35$

$SS_{within} = \Sigma SS_{each\ treatment}$
$= 26 + 18 + 16$
$= 60$

$df_{within} = N - k = 15 - 3 = 12$

$MS_{within} = \frac{60}{12} = 5$

$F = \frac{35}{5} = 7.00$

With $df = 2, 12$, this is an extremely unlikely value for an F-ratio ($p < .01$). Therefore, the decision is to reject the null hypothesis.

IV. Using Data from Repeated Measurements of a Single Sample to Draw Inferences About Two or More Treatments

1. The Repeated Measures t Test

The repeated measures t test uses data from a single sample measured in two treatment conditions to test a hypothesis about the mean difference between the two treatments. The null hypothesis states that the population mean difference (μ_D) is zero. The difference (D) between the first treatment and the second treatment is recorded for each subject. The mean and SS for this sample of D values is used to compute a t statistic with $df = n - 1$.

$$t = \frac{\overline{D} - \mu_D}{s_{\overline{D}}}$$

$$s_{\overline{D}} = \frac{s}{\sqrt{n}}$$

$$s = \sqrt{\frac{SS}{n - 1}}$$

The following data are the results from a sample of $n = 9$ individuals tested in two treatment conditions:

Treatment

1	2	D	
18	12	−6	For the D-scores,
15	24	+9	
21	19	−2	$\overline{D} = +4$
12	23	+11	
15	27	+12	$SS = 288$
18	19	+1	
20	25	+5	$n = 9$
22	24	+2	
17	21	+4	

H_0: $\mu_D = 0$ (no mean difference)
H_1: $\mu_D \neq 0$ (there is a difference)

For these data,

$$s = \sqrt{\frac{SS}{n - 1}} = \sqrt{\frac{288}{8}} = \sqrt{36} = 6$$

$$s_{\overline{D}} = \frac{s}{\sqrt{n}} = \frac{6}{\sqrt{9}} = 2$$

$$t = \frac{4 - 0}{2} = 2.00$$

With $df = 8$, the obtained t value is not in the critical region ($p > .05$), so we fail to reject the null hypothesis.

2. The Wilcoxon T Test

The Wilcoxon T test uses data from a single sample measured in two treatment conditions to test a hypothesis about the difference between the two treatments. The null hypothesis states that there is no difference between the two treatments. For each subject, the difference between the first treatment and the second treatment is recorded. The absolute values of the difference scores are rank-ordered, and the sum of the ranks is computed for the positive differences (increases) and for the negative differences (decreases). The Wilcoxon T statistic is the smaller of these two sums.

The following data are the results from a sample of $n = 9$ individuals tested in two treatment conditions:

Treatment

1	2	Difference	Rank	
20	7	-13	8	$(-)$
28	22	-6	4	$(-)$
15	5	-10	6	$(-)$
31	32	$+1$	1	$(+)$
26	11	-15	9	$(-)$
19	11	-8	5	$(-)$
13	17	$+4$	3	$(+)$
23	20	-3	2	$(-)$
26	15	-11	7	$(-)$

H_0: In the general population there is no difference between the treatments.

H_1: The two treatments are different.

For these data, $\Sigma R_+ = 4$, and $\Sigma R_- = 41$. The Wilcoxon T is 4. With a sample of $n = 9$, we are very unlikely to obtain a T value this small ($p < .05$), so the decision is to reject the null hypothesis.

3. The Sign Test

The sign test uses data from a single sample measured in two treatment conditions to test a hypothesis about the difference between the two treatments. The null hypothesis states that there is no difference between the two treatments. For each subject the direction of the change from the first treatment to the second treatment is recorded (an increase is positive, and a decrease is negative). If the null hypothesis is true, then increases and decreases are equally probable; $P(+) = P(-) = \frac{1}{2}$. The sign test is a special case of the binomial test and uses the same z-score statistic.

$$z = \frac{X - \mu}{\sigma} = \frac{X - pn}{\sqrt{npq}}$$

where X is the number of individuals from the sample who show an increase (or the number showing a decrease).

In an experiment comparing two treatment conditions, a random sample of $n = 36$ individuals was tested in both conditions. Of these 36 subjects, 25 showed higher scores in the first treatment, and only 11 showed higher scores in the second treatment.

H_0: $P(+) = P(-) = \frac{1}{2}$. There is no consistent difference between the two treatments.

H_1: The two treatments are different.

For these data,

$$z = \frac{25 - \frac{1}{2}(36)}{\sqrt{36\left(\frac{1}{2}\right)\left(\frac{1}{2}\right)}} = \frac{7}{3} = 2.33$$

Because this is a very unlikely value for a z-score ($p < .05$), we reject the null hypothesis.

4. Analysis of Variance (Single-Factor, Repeated Measures)

The single-factor repeated measures ANOVA uses data from a single sample measured in two or more treatment conditions to test a hypothesis about the treatment means. The null hypothesis states that there are no differences among the treatment means. Repeated and independent measures ANOVAs use the same notation, but the repeated measures analysis adds P = the total for each subject. The test statistic is an F-ratio with $df = k - 1, N - k - (n - 1)$.

$$F = \frac{MS_{between}}{MS_{error}}$$

Each $MS = \dfrac{SS}{df}$

$$SS_{between} = \Sigma \frac{T^2}{n} - \frac{G^2}{N}$$

$df_{between} = k - 1$

$SS_{error} = SS_{within} - SS_{subjects}$

$$= \Sigma SS - (\Sigma \frac{P^2}{k} - \frac{G^2}{N})$$

$df_{error} = N - k - (n - 1)$

The following data summarize the results of an experiment using the same sample of $n = 3$ subjects in each of three treatment conditions:

	Treatment			
1	2	3		P
0	4	5		9
2	4	6		12
1	7	7		15
$T = 3$	$T = 15$	$T = 18$		
$SS = 2$	$SS = 6$	$SS = 2$		

$N = 9$

$G = 36$

H_0: $\mu_1 = \mu_2 = \mu_3$ (no mean differences)

H_1: At least one mean is different from the others.

$$SS_{between} = \frac{3^2}{3} + \frac{15^2}{3} + \frac{18^2}{3} - \frac{36^2}{9}$$
$$= 42$$

$df_{between} = 3 - 1 = 2$

$$MS_{between} = \frac{42}{2} = 21$$

$$SS_{error} = 10 - \left[\frac{9^2}{3} + \frac{12^2}{3} + \frac{15^3}{3} - \frac{36^3}{9} \right]$$
$$= 10 - 6 = 4$$

$df_{error} = 9 - 3 - (3 - 1) = 4$

$MS_{error} = \frac{4}{4} = 1$

$$F = \frac{21}{1} = 21.00$$

With $df = 2, 4$, this is a very unlikely value for an F-ratio ($p < .01$), so we reject the null hypothesis.

V. Statistical Techniques for Evaluating the Relationship Between Two Variables

1. Sum of Products

SP or the sum of products measures the sum of the products of the deviations for two variables. SP is a basic component of correlation and regression. There are two equivalent formulas for computing the sum of products:

$$SP = \Sigma XY - \frac{\Sigma X \, \Sigma Y}{n} \quad \text{(computational formula)}$$

$$SP = \Sigma(X - \overline{X})(Y - \overline{Y}) \, \text{(definitional formula)}$$

Using the computational formula, we obtain

X	Y	XY
1	7	7
3	5	15
6	1	6
3	4	12
2	3	6

$\Sigma X = 15$
$\Sigma Y = 20$
$\Sigma XY = 46$

$$SP = 46 - \frac{15(20)}{5}$$
$$= 46 - 60$$
$$= -14$$

Using the definitional formula, we obtain

X	Y	$X - \bar{X}$	$Y - \bar{Y}$	$(Y - \bar{Y})(X - \bar{X})$
1	7	-2	$+3$	-6
3	5	0	$+1$	0
6	1	$+3$	-3	-9
3	4	0	0	0
2	3	-1	-1	$+1$

$$-14 = SP$$

2. The Pearson Correlation

The Pearson correlation measures the degree of linear relation between two variables (X and Y). The sign of the correlation ($+$ or $-$) indicates the direction of the relationship. The magnitude of the correlation (from 0 to 1) indicates the degree to which the data points fit on a straight line. The formula for the Pearson correlation is

$$r = \frac{SP}{\sqrt{SS_x SS_y}}$$

X- and Y-scores are obtained for a sample of $n = 5$ individuals:

X	Y	X^2	Y^2	XY
1	1	1	1	1
4	10	16	100	40
2	3	4	9	6
4	7	16	49	28
4	4	16	16	16

For these data $\Sigma X = 15$, $\Sigma Y = 25$, $\Sigma X^2 = 53$, $\Sigma Y^2 = 175$, $\Sigma XY = 91$.

$$SS_x = \Sigma X^2 - \frac{(\Sigma X)^2}{n}$$
$$= 53 - 45$$
$$= 8$$
$$SS_y = \Sigma Y^2 - \frac{(\Sigma Y)^2}{n}$$
$$= 175 - 125$$
$$= 50$$
$$SP = \Sigma XY - \frac{\Sigma X \, \Sigma Y}{n}$$
$$= 91 - 75$$
$$= 16$$
$$r = \frac{16}{\sqrt{8(50)}} = \frac{16}{20} = 0.80$$

3. The Spearman Correlation

The Spearman correlation measures the degree to which the relation between two variables (X and Y) is one-directional or monotonic. The sign of the correlation ($+$

or $-$) indicates the direction of the relationship. The magnitude of the correlation (from 0 to 1) indicates the degree to which the relation is consistently one-directional. The Spearman correlation is computed with a two-step process:

1. Rank the X- and the Y-scores.
2. Compute the Pearson correlation using the ranks.

For the second step of this process, you may use either the Pearson formula or the special formula for the Spearman correlation,

$$r_s = 1 - \frac{6\Sigma D^2}{n(n^2 - 1)}$$

where D is the difference between the X rank and the Y rank for each individual. **Note:** When the original data consist of ranks (ordinal scale), you may go directly to step 2 to compute the Spearman correlation.

X- and Y-scores are obtained for a sample of $n = 4$ individuals, and the scores are ranked:

Original Scores		Ranks			
X	Y	X	Y	D	D^2
3	19	1	4	3	9
14	5	2	1	−1	1
15	12	3	3	0	0
26	7	4	2	−2	4

For these data, $\Sigma D^2 = 14$. The Spearman correlation is

$$r_s = 1 - \frac{6(14)}{4(16 - 1)}$$
$$= 1 - 1.40$$
$$= -0.40$$

4. Linear Regression

The purpose of linear regression is to find the best fitting linear equation for predicting Y-scores from X-scores. The solution is called the regression equation and minimizes the squared error between the predicted Y values ($\hat{Y}$) and the actual Y-scores. The general form of the regression equation is

$$\hat{Y} = bX + a$$

The values of a and b are found by

$$b = \frac{SP}{SS_x}$$
$$a = \overline{Y} - b\overline{X}$$

X- and Y-scores are obtained for a sample of $n = 5$ individuals:

X	Y	X^2	XY
0	4	0	0
1	2	1	2
2	5	4	10
3	8	9	24
4	16	16	64

For these data, $\Sigma X = 10$, $\Sigma X^2 = 30$, and $\Sigma XY = 100$.

$$SS_x = \Sigma X^2 - \frac{(\Sigma X)^2}{n}$$
$$= 30 - 20$$
$$= 10$$

$$SP = \Sigma XY - \frac{\Sigma X \, \Sigma Y}{n}$$
$$= 100 - 70$$
$$= 30$$

In the regression equation,

$$b = \frac{30}{10} = 3$$
$$a = 7 - 3(2) = 1$$

The regression equation is

$$\hat{Y} = 3X + 1$$

5. Chi Square Test for Independence

The chi square test for independence uses frequency data to test a hypothesis about the relationship between two variables. The null hypothesis states that the two variables are independent; that is, the frequency distribution for one variable does not depend on the classification for the second variable. With the number of categories for one variable identified by R and the number of categories for the second variable identified by C, the test statistic is χ^2 with $df = (R - 1)(C - 1)$.

$$\chi^2 = \Sigma \frac{(f_o - f_e)^2}{f_e}$$

f_o is the observed frequency for each category (the data), and f_e is the frequency that would be expected if H_0 were true. If the frequency data are displayed in a matrix, the f_e values can be obtained by

$$f_e = \frac{(\text{row total})(\text{column total})}{\text{grand total}} = \frac{f_r f_c}{n}$$

A researcher would like to know whether there is a relation between individuals' opinions on a political issue and their status as registered voters. A sample of $n = 300$ people is obtained, and each person's opinion and registration status are measured:

Registered Voter

	For	Against	No Opinion
Yes	110	70	20
No	40	20	40

H_0: The two variables are independent. The frequency distribution for opinions does not depend on registration status.

H_1: The two variables are related.

If H_0 is true, the expected frequencies are

Registered Voter

	For	Against	No Opinion
Yes	100	60	40
No	50	30	20

For these data,

$$\chi^2 = \frac{10^2}{100} + \frac{10^2}{60} + \frac{20^2}{40} + \frac{10^2}{50} + \frac{10^2}{30} + \frac{20^2}{20}$$
$$= 38.00$$

With $df = 2$, this is a very unlikely value for χ^2 ($p < .01$), so we reject H_0.

References

Betz, B. J., and Thomas, C. B. (1979). Individual temperament as a predictor of health or premature disease. *The Johns Hopkins Medical Journal, 144*, 81–89.

Blest, A. D. (1957). The functions of eyespot patterns in the Lepidoptera. *Behaviour, 11*, 209–255.

Boker, J. R. (1974). Immediate and delayed retention effects of interspersing questions in written instructional passages. *Journal of Educational Psychology, 66*, 96–98.

Brady, J. V., Porter, R. W., Conrad, D. G., and Mason, J. W. (1958). Avoidance behavior and the development of gastroduodenal ulcers. *Journal of the Experimental Analysis of Behavior, 1*, 69–72.

Camilli, G., and Hopkins, K. D. (1978). Applicability of chi-square to 2 × 2 contingency tables with small expected cell frequencies. *Psychological Bulletin, 85*, 163–167.

Cook, M. (1977). Gaze and mutual gaze in social encounters. *American Scientist, 65*, 328–333.

Craik, F. I. M., and Lockhart, R. S. (1972). Levels of processing: A framework for memory research. *Journal of Verbal Learning and Verbal Behavior, 11*, 671–684.

Darley, J. M., and Latané, B. (1968). Bystander intervention in emergencies: Diffusion of responsibility. *Journal of Personality and Social Psychology, 8*, 377–383.

Davison, G. C. (1968). Systematic desensitization as a counterconditioning process. *Journal of Abnormal Psychology, 73*, 91–99.

Festinger, L., and Carlsmith, J. M. (1959). Cognitive consequences of forced compliance. *Journal of Abnormal and Social Psychology, 58*, 203–210.

Friedman, M., and Rosenman, R. H. (1974). *Type A behavior and your heart.* New York: Knopf.

Gibson, E. J., and Walk, R. D. (1960). The "visual cliff." *Scientific American, 202*, 64–71.

Gintzler, A. R. (1980). Endorphin-mediated increases in pain threshold during pregnancy. *Science, 210*, 193–195.

Hays, W. L. (1981). *Statistics* (3rd ed.). New York: Holt, Rinehart and Winston.

Honzik, M. P., Macfarlane, J. W., and Allen, L. (1948). The stability of mental test performance between two and eighteen years. *Journal of Experimental Education, 17*, 309–324.

Hooke, R. (1983). *How to tell the liars from the statisticians*. New York: Dekker.

Katona, G. (1940). *Organizing and memorizing*. New York: Columbia University Press.

Keppel, G. (1973). *Design and analysis. A researcher's handbook*. Englewood Cliffs, N.J.: Prentice-Hall.

Levine, S. (1960). Stimulation in infancy. *Scientific American, 202*, 80–86.

McClelland, D. C. (1961). *The achieving society*. Princeton, N.J.: Van Nostrand.

Miller, N. E., and Dworkin, B. R. (1974). Visceral learning: Recent difficulties with curarized rats and significant problems for human research. In P. A. Obrist, A. H. Black, J. Brener, and L. V. DiCara (eds.), *Cardiovascular psychophysiology: Current issues in response mechanisms, biofeedback and methodology* (pp. 312–331). Chicago: Aldine.

Rogers, T. B., Kuiper, N. A., and Kirker, W. S. (1977). Self-reference and the encoding of personal information. *Journal of Personality and Social Psychology, 35*, 677–688.

Rosenthal, R. (1963). On the social psychology of the psychological experiment: The experimenter's hypothesis as unintended determinant of experimental results. *American Scientist, 51*, 268–283.

Rosenthal, R., and Fode, K. L. (1963). The effect of experimenter bias on the performance of the albino rat. *Behavioral Science, 8*, 183–189.

Sachs, J. (1967). Recognition memory for syntactic and semantic aspects of a connected discourse. *Perception and Psychophysics, 2*, 437–442.

Scaife, M. (1976). The response to eye-like shapes by birds. I. The effect of context: A predator and a strange bird. *Animal Behaviour, 24*, 195–199.

Schachter, S. (1968). Obesity and eating. *Science, 161*, 751–756.

Shrauger, J. S. (1972). Self-esteem and reactions to being observed by others. *Journal of Personality and Social Psychology, 23*, 192–200.

Snyder, S. H. (1977). Opiate receptors and internal opiates. *Scientific American, 236*, 44–56.

Sternberg, S. (1966). High-speed scanning in human memory. *Science, 153*, 652–654.

Tryon, R. C. (1940). Genetic differences in maze-learning ability in rats. *Yearbook of the National Society for the Study of Education, 39*, 111–119.

Tukey, J. W. (1977). *Exploratory data analysis*. Reading, Mass.: Addison-Wesley.

Tulving, E., and Osler, S. (1968). Effectiveness of retrieval cues in memory for words. *Journal of Experimental Psychology, 77*, 593–601.

Tversky, A., and Kahneman, D. (1973). Availability: A heuristic for judging frequency and probability. *Cognitive Psychology, 5*, 207–232.

Tversky, A., and Kahneman, D. (1974). Judgment under uncertainty: Heuristics and biases. *Science, 185,* 1124–1131.

Zigler, M. J. (1932). Pressure adaptation time: A function of intensity and extensity. *American Journal of Psychology, 44,* 709–720.

Index

Chapter 6
classical vs. empirical (free throws)
(coin tosses/cards)

$P(E) = \dfrac{\text{\# times E occurs}}{\text{total \# of trials}}$

$P(E) = \dfrac{\text{\# ways E could occur}}{\text{total \# of possible outcomes}}$

$\downarrow K \& C$

NON-Mut. exclu. events $P(K \text{ or } C) = P(K) + P(C) - P(K \& C) = 4/52 + 13/52 - 1/52$

at least one 3 = 11/36

$P(A \& B) = P(A) \cdot P(B)$ if A & B are indep. $P(A \& B) = P(A) \cdot P(B|A)$

w/out replacement (cond. prob)

$P(A \text{ or } B) = P(A) \& P(B) - P(A \& B)$

Sampling Distributions
C.L.T - no matter the shape of the original dist, for a pop w/
parameters $\mu \& \sigma$, r.s.d of Means, as n gets larger,
will tend to be normal $\mu_{\bar{x}} = \mu$, $\sigma_{\bar{x}} = \dfrac{\sigma}{\sqrt{n}}$

1shape 2central location 3 variability

$z = \dfrac{\bar{x} - \mu}{\sigma_{\bar{x}}}$ area beyond z or between & Mean for P

Chapter 8 Hypothesis Testing

def. - using sample data to evaluate the credibility of a particular hypothesis

1) Null Hypothesis $H_0: \mu = ?$
2) Alternative " $H_1: \mu \neq ?$
3) Choose an appropriate stat. test - z
4) Significance level $\alpha = .05$ or $\alpha = .01$
5) sampling distribution - normal curve
6) critical region $.05 \to z = \pm 1.96$ $\alpha = .01$ $z = \pm 2.58$
7) Make decision

reduce α & β by gathering more data

Actual

	H_0 true	H_0 false
Reject H_0	Type I error α	correct
fail to Reject H_0	correct	Type II error β

Chapter 9
Alternative to Answering Yes/No

Point Estimation
trying to pick out specific # from sample stat. to estimate pop. parameter

Confidence Intervals

$$\overline{X} \cong \mu \pm z\sigma_{\overline{X}}$$

Estimate μ w/ $\overline{X}$ / Estimate σ w/ $S = \sqrt{\frac{SS}{n-1}}$

95% between $\mu \pm 1.96\sigma_{\overline{X}}$

Factors influence width of CI $\sigma_{\overline{X}} = \frac{\sigma}{\sqrt{n}}$ 2 variability in scores
1 level of confidence desired $\overline{X} \pm z(\sigma_{\overline{X}})$
3 size of pop.

Relationship b/t CI and Hypothesis Testing
   -favors hyp testing now $\alpha = .01 \to CI\ 99\%$
       $\alpha = .05 \to 95\%\ CI$

Advantages of CI

'More info   ²helps explain contradictory results
3 tells if stat "sig" things are 'real world sig"

POWER $= 1 - \beta$
       prob. of rejecting a false H_0 a.k.a. sensitivity

   function of : larger effect, greater power, one tailed test
              $\downarrow \sigma, \uparrow \alpha \uparrow n$

   ∧

   1 tailed test
       reduce crit. value $z\ crit = 1.65$

Chapter 11
                                    $t = \dfrac{obs.\ value\ of\ stat - exp.\ value\ of\ stat\ under\ H_0}{standard\ error}$
$t = \dfrac{\bar{X} - \mu}{S_{\bar{X}}} = \dfrac{\bar{X} - \mu}{\sqrt{\dfrac{SS}{n-1}}/\sqrt{n}}$
                                                    $(S.D.\ of\ test\ stat)$

$df = n_1 + n_2 - 2$ → usually 0
                                         pooled
$t = \dfrac{(\bar{X}_1 - \bar{X}_2) - (\mu_1 - \mu_2)}{\sqrt{\left(\dfrac{SS_1 + SS_2}{n_1 + n_2 - 2}\right)\left(\dfrac{1}{n_1} + \dfrac{1}{n_2}\right)}}$ variance $S_p^2 = \dfrac{SS_1 + SS_2}{df_1 + df_2}$

                                                                    i.e written
homogeneity of variance $F = \dfrac{S^2\ larger}{S^2\ smaller}$ $\left| t_{.05, df = 79} \right| =$

   chapter 12 $S_D = \dfrac{\sqrt{\dfrac{SS\ for\ the\ Ds}{n-1}}}{\sqrt{n}}$ $n = \#$ of pairs of
$t = \dfrac{\bar{D} - \mu_{\bar{D}}}{S_{\bar{D}}}$ scores you have
                                                                             or # of Ds
                                         $\bar{D} = \dfrac{\Sigma D}{n}$ $X_1 - X_2 = D$

correlated design   - tuvks study (ideas)

repeated measures   matched pairs
same subjects   match variable on
would force   related indep. var.
                           then rand. assign
                           grp up dff : harder to show diff

corr des. a.k.a. w/in subjects design
indep. des. a.k.a. between   "   "

balance design - pain relievers & placebo

test - retest

(continued from front endpaper)

z-Score (for locating an X value)

$$z = \frac{X - \mu}{\sigma}$$

z-Score (for locating a sample mean)

$$z = \frac{\overline{X} - \mu}{\sigma_{\overline{x}}} \qquad \text{where } \sigma_{\overline{x}} = \frac{\sigma}{\sqrt{n}}$$

t Statistic (single sample)

$$t = \frac{\overline{X} - \mu}{s_{\overline{x}}} \qquad \text{where } s_{\overline{x}} = \frac{s}{\sqrt{n}}$$

t Statistic (independent measures)

$$t = \frac{(\overline{X}_1 - \overline{X}_2) - (\mu_1 - \mu_2)}{s_{\overline{x} - \overline{x}}} \qquad \text{where } s_{\overline{x} - \overline{x}} = \sqrt{\frac{s_p^2}{n_1} + \frac{s_p^2}{n_2}}$$

$$\text{and } s_p^2 = \frac{SS_1 + SS_2}{df_1 + df_2}$$

t Statistic (repeated measures)

$$t = \frac{\overline{D} - \mu_D}{s_{\overline{D}}} \qquad \text{where } s_{\overline{D}} = \frac{s}{\sqrt{n}}$$

Independent Measures ANOVA

$$SS_{total} = \Sigma X^2 - \frac{G^2}{N} \qquad df_{total} = N - 1$$

$$SS_{between} = \Sigma \frac{T^2}{n} - \frac{G^2}{N} \qquad df_{between} = k - 1$$

$$SS_{within} = \Sigma SS_{inside \ each \ treatment} \qquad df_{within} = N - k$$

$$F = \frac{MS_{between}}{MS_{within}} \qquad \text{where each } MS = \frac{SS}{df}$$

Repeated Measures ANOVA

$$SS_{between} = \Sigma \frac{T^2}{n} - \frac{G^2}{N} \qquad df_{between} = k - 1$$

$$SS_{error} = SS_{within} - SS_{subjects} \qquad df_{error} = (N - k) - (n - 1)$$

$$\text{where } SS_{within} = \Sigma SS_{inside \ each \ treatment}$$

$$\text{and } SS_{subjects} = \Sigma \frac{P^2}{k} - \frac{G^2}{N}$$

$$F = \frac{MS_{between}}{MS_{error}} \qquad \text{where each } MS = \frac{SS}{df}$$